MW01071076

WRITING AND REPORTING FOR THE MEDIA

JOHN R. BENDER
UNIVERSITY OF NEBRASKA-LINCOLN

LUCINDA D. DAVENPORT
MICHIGAN STATE UNIVERSITY

MICHAEL W. DRAGER
SHIPPENSBURG UNIVERSITY OF PENNSYLVANIA

FRED FEDLER
UNIVERSITY OF CENTRAL FLORIDA

THIRTEENTH EDITION

OXFORD
UNIVERSITY PRESS

OXFORD
UNIVERSITY PRESS

Oxford University Press is a department of the University of Oxford.
It furthers the University's objective of excellence in research, scholarship,
and education by publishing worldwide. Oxford is a registered trade mark
of Oxford University Press in the UK and in certain other countries.

Published in the United States of America by Oxford University Press
198 Madison Avenue, New York, NY 10016, United States of America.

© 2024, 2019, 2016, 2012, 2009, 2005 by Oxford University Press

Library of Congress Cataloging-in-Publication Data
Names: Bender, John R., author. | D. Davenport, Lucinda, author. |
  W. Drager, Michael, author. | Fedler, Fred, author.
Title: Writing and reporting for the media / John R. Bender, University of
  Nebraska-Lincoln, Lucinda D. Davenport, Michigan State University,
  Michael W. Drager, Shippensburg University of Pennsylvania, Fred Fedler,
  University of Central Florida.
Other titles: Writing & reporting for the media
Identifiers: LCCN 2023032521 (print) | LCCN 2023032522 (ebook) | ISBN
  9780197614853 (paperback) | ISBN 9780197614884 (ebook)
Subjects: LCSH: Reporters and reporting—Problems, exercises, etc.
Classification: LCC PN4781 .B385 2023 (print) | LCC PN4781 (ebook) | DDC
  070.4/3—dc23/eng/20230713
LC record available at https://lccn.loc.gov/2023032521
LC ebook record available at https://lccn.loc.gov/2023032522

Printed by Quad/Graphics, Inc., Mexico

CONTENTS

SECTION II   THE LAW AND ETHICS OF JOURNALISM   79

SECTION III   THE BASIC SKILLS OF JOURNALISM   141

CHAPTER 7   BASIC NEWS LEADS   143

CHAPTER 8   ALTERNATIVE LEADS   176

CHAPTER 9   THE BODY OF A NEWS STORY   196

CHAPTER 10   QUOTATIONS AND ATTRIBUTION   227

CHAPTER 11   INTERVIEWING   250

CHAPTER 12   FEATURE STORIES   276

CHAPTER 13   WRITING FOR BROADCAST NEWS   298

PREFACE

"Will I be able to get a job after I graduate with a journalism degree?" prospective students often ask. If the students do not ask about jobs, their parents do. The answer is yes.

In spite of—or perhaps because of—the many changes the news and information industry is experiencing, the prospects for employment are strong. The U.S. Department of Labor's Occupational Outlook Handbook projects 14 percent growth in media and communications jobs between 2020 and 2030, which exceeds the average growth expected for all occupations. The media and communications category includes jobs as DJs, announcers, technicians, editors, photographers, reporters and public relations professionals. And many of those jobs pay well. The median salary for jobs in those areas is $62,340, which is well above the median salary for all jobs of $45,760.

Why is the job outlook so bright? A major reason is the growth in digital news platforms and the continuing strength of the broadcasting industry. Although print circulation has been declining and traditional newspaper jobs along with it, digital circulation appears to be increasing sharply and creating new jobs. According to a 2021 Pew Research Center report, digital circulation increased 27 percent daily and 26 percent on Sundays. By some measures, daily digital circulation increased 38 percent. More recently, Gannett, the largest newspaper chain in the U.S., reported a 46 percent increase in digital subscriptions. Lee Enterprises, the fifth-largest chain, reported a 57 percent increase. Numbers for digital circulation vary from one source to another because it is difficult to gauge, and different organizations count it in different ways.

News organizations are drawing revenue from their digital operations in two ways: paywalls and advertising. In the past, most news organizations offered their digital content for free, seeing it as a way to attract subscribers to the print product. Now, many newspapers have set up paywalls, which require people to pay to access some or all content. This may annoy readers who liked the free content, but the revenue is essential to keep journalists on the job and the news organization in business. The increase in digital readership is bringing in advertising, too. Revenue from digital advertising in newspapers has been growing and should reach $5 billion by 2026. At that point, digital revenues will surpass revenues from print advertising.

Almost every traditional print news organization has a digital operation. Most television stations and all networks maintain online news sites where people can find text, video and audio reports. These websites allied with traditional news sources face competition from new digital-only news sites. Some digital news sites have a national focus, such as Vox, Axios, Salon and FiveThirtyEight. Others have a local or regional focus. One example is the Flatwater Free Press, a digital-only news organization that covers Nebraska. Other digital news sites offer specialized content, such as Indianz.com, a site that reports news about Native Americans. The74 is a news site that covers the U.S. educational system from elementary school through college. Jezebel offers a feminist slant on political and cultural news. And The Root covers Black culture, entertainment, fashion and other issues. These are just a few of the specialized news sites on the web.

On the broadcast side, both interest in TV news and advertising revenues for television networks and stations remain strong. During one week in mid-2022, the daily viewership of the three major network (ABC, CBS and NBC) evening news programs exceeded 17.7 million viewers. Among the cable news channels—Fox News, CNN and MSNBC—Fox has the largest viewership, about 2.3 million daily as of mid-2022. CNN and MSNBC have substantially smaller audiences. Total advertising revenues for the television industry rose from $198.1 billion in 2020 to $210.4 billion in 2021. Where that money went has been changing. Cable, satellite and telecom companies have lost revenue while video-on-demand companies have gained.

Clearly, the news business in all its forms is changing. The changes can be jarring to both the readers and viewers of news and to the people who work in the industry. But the need for news about the community, the nation and the world remains. A survey completed by the Associated Press and the American Press Institute found that 79 percent of young people—16 to 40 years old—read or watch news daily. They seek news from a variety of sources, including social media sites like TikTok, Snapchat and Twitter, but 45 percent also say they turn to traditional news sources, like newspapers and magazines and their websites. About a quarter of them pay for access to a news site.

While news organizations new and old try to adapt to a digital world, the news business is facing other challenges. A major one is the growing distrust and outright hostility some Americans feel toward the news and the people who report it. Distrust of news organizations has been increasing for decades. In 1976, the Gallup Organization found that more than 70 percent of Americans trusted the news media a great deal or a fair amount. By late 2021, that had dropped to 36 percent. It was even lower in 2016, when it hit 32 percent. Driving the decline in trusting mainstream media has been political polarization. Among Republicans, only 11 percent say they trust the news media. For Democrats, the number is 68 percent. The decline in trust in the news media has accompanied declines in public trust in other institutions such as government at all levels, education, business, law enforcement and the judicial system.

News organizations in other countries have not experienced the same decline in public trust. A study of public attitudes toward news media in 40 countries found that trust was lowest in the United States. In many developed countries, such as Finland, Denmark, the Netherlands, Belgium and Germany, 50 percent to 70 percent of the public expressed trust in the news media.

Public attitudes toward the news media have been shaped in part by complaints from political leaders. Donald Trump frequently has referred to journalists as "enemies of the people." Autocrats and dictators have used that phrase to describe ethnic, social or political groups they perceived as threats to their power. Soviet dictator Joseph Stalin used the phrase to describe monarchists, entrepreneurs, clerics, bourgeoisie and others who objected to his rule. Adolph

Hitler applied the term to Jews, millions of whom died in the Holocaust. Trump also described any news reports that were critical of him or that recounted shortcomings of his administration as "fake news."

Since Trump left the presidency, other politicians have adopted his tactic of attacking news reporters and their organizations in a highly emotional fashion. A Republican candidate for governor in Wisconsin criticized the Milwaukee Journal-Sentinel for publishing a story about his donations of money to anti-abortion groups, churches and other organizations. The candidate, Tim Michels, said after publication of the article: "I believe people should just, just be ready to get out on the streets with pitchforks and torches with how the liberal media has become. People need to decide 'Am I going to put up with this? Am I going to tolerate this, taking somebody that gives money to churches or cancer research and use that as a hit piece in the media?' I'm appalled. It's disgusting." The executive editor of the Journal-Sentinel, George Stanley, defended the report and said it ran the same day as a piece about how much the Democratic candidate for U.S. senator was spending on security.

The hostility of some public officials toward critical news stories makes the job of reporting harder and more dangerous. An investigative reporter for the Las Vegas (Nevada) Review-Journal, Jeff German, wrote articles critical of Clark County Public Administrator Robert Telles. German's stories said that workers in the office were experiencing bullying and intimidation and that Telles had had an inappropriate relationship with one of the employees of the office. After the stories were published, German was stabbed to death outside his home. A couple of days later, Telles was arrested on suspicion of having killed German.

Solving the problem of public trust may be more difficult than adjusting to the digital environment. The men and women who enter the business with journalism or related degrees from colleges and universities bring a strong sense of professionalism and ethical responsibility to their work. They do not fabricate stories or make up facts or sources. Nor do they intentionally distort, misrepresent or slant information they have obtained. They do make mistakes, as do all humans. But a segment of the public refuses to believe almost anything they see in mainstream news broadcasts and publications. Persuading these people that mainstream news organizations generally are reliable and unbiased will be a long-term project. Success will depend on the ability of the next generation of journalists to report information accurately and clearly and in a manner that will be meaningful to all citizens.

The news business has been changing, and journalism education has been changing along with it. This textbook has changed as well, adding material on new developments in news gathering and reporting. Nevertheless, the book remains committed to emphasizing the basic skills of journalism, skills that will be demanded of all reporters, no matter whether they are writing for a traditional newspaper, a television station, an online news organization, a blog or a public relations organization. Every journalist must be able to write clearly and correctly and make complicated issues understandable and interesting.

The function of journalism that sets it apart from other jobs and communication businesses is its role in providing citizens in a democracy with the information they need to govern their society. As James Madison said nearly 200 years ago: "Popular government without popular information, or the means of acquiring it, is but a prologue to a farce or a tragedy or perhaps both. Knowledge will forever govern ignorance. And a people who mean to be their own governors must arm themselves with the power that knowledge gives."

Self-government in the 21st century requires citizens to confront such issues as health care, global warming, criminal justice, economic stability, international trade, war and diplomacy. The catalogue of issues is long and daunting. To make sound judgments about these issues, people need reliable information. And most get it from journalists. The reporters who are best able to provide that information will be ones who have a broad understanding of how society works and the ability to explain the issues and how they affect citizens in an understandable and interesting manner. Fulfilling that role requires journalists to cultivate two traits:

1. Be engaged in the world around you.

2. Be articulate.

Being engaged in the world means reporters have a high degree of curiosity about their beats and life in general and they feel empathy for the subjects of their stories. Curiosity helps reporters see story ideas in almost everything around them and develop the stories assigned to them, as in these examples:

- Congress has passed a law providing money to states to rebuild or refurbish aging infrastructure, including bridges that have deteriorated to the point of being dangerous. How many bridges in your state need repair or replacement? How dangerous are they? How much traffic do those bridges carry? And does the state have a plan for spending the federal money to improve roads and bridges?
- Civil forfeiture laws allow states to confiscate money and property obtained illegally, as through the sale of illegal drugs, and use the money to finance law enforcement. What do state and local governments do with the money and property they confiscate? If the money goes to law enforcement agencies, on what do they spend it? Are the people whose property is confiscated always convicted of crimes?
- Some communities have experienced problems with their water systems leading to loss of water service or contamination of the water that the system provides. What is the status of the water system in your community? What is the quality of the water provided by the system? Is the water supply adequate for anticipated future needs? Does the community have plans for dealing with emergencies, such as floods or hurricanes?

These are just a few examples of the questions curious journalists ask, and each of those questions can lead to a news story that will attract readers or viewers. Reporters must constantly ask about the details of their beats, even when they have no expectation the answers will lead to stories. No reporter can predict what tidbit of information may help unravel a great story. Even the information that yields no specific story might help the journalist understand and explain events to an audience.

Being engaged also means having empathy for the sources and subjects of news stories. People in the news often confront highly emotional situations. They may be victims of crime or the relatives of a victim; they may have lost loved ones in a plane crash; they may be athletes who have just suffered a defeat; or they may be community residents worried about how a proposed development might affect their lives and their property. A story about a knife attack by a male employee on a female supervisor is not just an antiseptic crime story or an exercise in deductive logic. It is a story about anger, frustration, betrayal, terror and humiliation. A reporter who cannot empathize with the people involved cannot truly understand their experiences or tell their stories.

The ability to empathize does not require reporters to abandon objectivity and impartiality. Empathy differs from sympathy. Sympathy requires one to have the same feelings as another or to achieve a mutual understanding with another. Empathy involves projecting one's personality into that of another to understand the other person better. Journalists who have empathy for others can understand them without embracing or approving their emotions. Empathy is consistent with objectivity; it also is indispensable for producing a truly objective and thorough story. If reporters cannot understand the emotional states of the people they write about or assess the emotional changes events inflict on sources, they will fail to report the full story.

Curiosity and empathy enable reporters to get the who, what, when, where, why and how of a story. Putting those elements into a coherent, interesting and readable story requires that journalists be articulate, which combines at least two skills. One is the ability to use words effectively, to select the appropriate words and use them correctly and to arrange them in sentences that are grammatically correct and properly punctuated. The other skill is the ability to organize the elements of the story—the facts, the quotations and the anecdotes—in a manner that is captivating, informative and dramatic.

Reporters who understand grammar and diction can construct sentences that are clear and precise. The following sentences contain the same words but mean different things, simply because one word is in a different location:

> She only shopped for hats at Smith's Department Store.

> She shopped for hats only at Smith's Department Store.

A skillful writer understands that the first sentence says the only thing the woman would shop for at Smith's was hats; she might buy hats elsewhere, too. The second sentence says Smith's was the only place she would buy hats, but she might buy other things there, too.

A skillful writer also knows that one of these sentences accuses the subject of a crime:

> Wanda sent her husband Bob to the store.

> Wanda sent her husband, Bob, to the store.

The first sentence uses "Bob" as an essential modifier of "husband," meaning that Wanda has more than one husband and the one she sent to the store is Bob. The sentence implies Wanda has committed bigamy. The second sentence, because it uses commas before and after "Bob," makes it clear that Wanda has only one husband, and his name is Bob.

The ability to construct clear, correct sentences is fundamental. But a news story may contain nothing but clear, correct sentences and still be impossible to understand because the writer has failed to organize the material. Readers, listeners and viewers crave organization; if they do not find it, they give up. A story that jumps from one topic to another and back to the first without any sense of direction will confuse people and drive them elsewhere for information. Reporters need to know how to organize information so its significance and drama become clear.

All the skills one needs to become a great reporter—curiosity, empathy, knowledge of grammar and the ability to organize stories—are skills a student can learn. Some students may learn them more easily than others, or some may develop one set of skills more than the others. But anybody who can handle college-level coursework can cultivate the skills a professional reporter needs. The 13th edition of this textbook offers many features—some new to this edition—to help students master the skills of news reporting.

New Features in the 13th Edition

As with the previous editions of this textbook, the 13th edition contains several changes. It also adheres to the approach and practice Fred Fedler developed when he created this textbook nearly 45 years ago. That approach is to help students and beginning practitioners learn news judgment and become proficient through lots of practice exercises in the fundamentals of writing and reporting for news media. The coauthors, who have taken over the responsibility for this book, hope longtime users will be comfortable with it and new users will find it attractive.

Although the 13th edition contains many changes, some major ones are worth noting:

- Foremost, many of the exercises have been moved from a print workbook to an online website accompanying this text. The exercises are in addition to the ones in the textbook itself. Many of these exercises are automatically graded, and the scores students receive can be downloaded into the learning management system the instructor is using. By making many of the exercises automatically graded, instructors can assign them to students without increasing the burden of grading them. This can be helpful for drilling students in the basics of grammar, style, punctuation and usage.
- Chapter 1, Journalism Today, has been revised to include new information on current issues in journalism and new approaches to reporting news. For instance, the chapter includes a section on solutions journalism as an approach to making news more useful and helpful to citizens. It also includes new material on the media landscape and the impact of the COVID-19 pandemic on the business.
- Chapter 3, Newswriting Style, now includes material on curtailing cultural bias and the importance of diversity, equity and inclusion in the news.
- Chapter 6, Ethics, includes a discussion of the ethical importance of diversity in news reporting. It also has expanded on the need for compassion and ethical guidance in relations with victims of accidents and other tragedies and showing regard for the privacy of sources and people in the news. Along the same lines, Chapter 11, Interviewing, now has a section on ways of finding diverse sources to interview for news stories and guidelines on the appropriate and effective ways of interviewing people who are victims or relatives of victims of crimes or disasters.
- The online exercises accompanying Chapter 15, Speeches and Meetings, include videos of two short speeches and supporting information. These exercises could be used in the classroom so that instructors can evaluate and critique student stories on their completeness and accuracy.
- Chapter 17, Public Affairs Reporting, has been reorganized and expanded to include more about covering community activities other than "cops and courts." The chapter includes new sections on reporting about the

environment and public health, two areas of public affairs reporting that did not appear in previous editions. The section on reporting crimes and accidents includes a discussion of the shortcomings of relying on police sources for accurate information. In some cases, police have provided deceptively selective accounts of some encounters, such as the initial Minneapolis Police Department account of the death of George Floyd.

- This book is sold in both print and electronic formats. The content is the same, but if some students are using the electronic version and others the print version, assigning readings on the basis of page numbers may be confusing. With this edition every section and subsection of a chapter is numbered so that instructors can be sure students will be reading the same material no matter which version they use.

- The book contains many visual elements, including full-color photographs and colorful graphics. The chapters in the electronic version have short supplementary videos available online. New visuals and expanded captions reflect more recent events and correspond to and supplement the text.

- Many new examples appear in the 13th edition. These are examples drawn from events of the last three or four years, such as the Jan. 6, 2021, insurrection, the killing of George Floyd and the ensuing Black Lives Matter protests, the #MeToo movement, the COVID-19 pandemic, the war in Ukraine, celebrity news and natural disasters. These are events students are likely to remember and that can provide material for class discussion and reflection.

Other Features of Interest

Appendices

This book provides three appendices: a city directory to give students practice in verifying the names, addresses and backgrounds of people in the exercises, a summary of Associated Press style for quick reference, and rules for forming possessives as a ready source for mechanics.

Reporter's Guides

Nearly every chapter ends with a reporter's guide (e.g., "Reporter's Guide to Accuracy" in Chapter 2) that summarizes the major points covered in the chapter and helps students organize their writing assignments and make sure they are including all important information.

Flexibility

"Writing and Reporting for the Media" is flexible. Teachers can assign the chapters in almost any order. Moreover, the book and online supplement provide enough exercises that instructors can assign their favorites and then assign extra exercises for students who need more help. Some teachers use the book for two semesters: for basic and advanced reporting classes. There are enough exercises for both terms.

The book can be used in general media writing classes and those specific to newswriting and reporting. Still, those who prefer the book's traditional emphasis on the print media can assign the chapters on public relations and writing for broadcast media as optional readings.

Hundreds of Examples

The text contains hundreds of examples from the work of students and professionals. Each new topic or discussion of errors typically includes examples. Students are also shown how to avoid or correct errors.

Some examples have been written by prize-winning professionals, and students can use their stories as models. For instance, examples from the Associated Press, The New York Times, The Washington Post and several other U.S. newspapers, large and small, illustrate many of the concepts discussed in the text.

Realistic and Often Genuine Exercises

Many of the exercises in this book are from real events. Chapter 15 ("Speeches and Meetings") includes President Trump's speech announcing the decision to withdraw from the Paris climate change agreement. Chapter 17 includes exercises based on real traffic accidents, crimes and fires. Exercises in other chapters, although perhaps fictionalized, are drawn from real events.

To add to the realism, many of the exercises contain ethical problems: profanities, sexist comments, the names of sexual assault victims, bloody details and other material that many editors would be reluctant to publish. Students completing those exercises will have to grapple with these issues, and their decisions are likely to provoke class discussion.

An Instructor's Manual

The authors provide a detailed Instructor's Manual that includes ideas and recommendations and discusses accuracy, grades, suggested policies and assignments. These sections are followed by sample course outlines and lists of the exercises that contain ethical dilemmas and sexist remarks. Many exercises now online are automatically graded, but the prompts for writing exercises often have errors embedded in them that students are supposed to correct by using the stylebook or the city directory. The manual identifies in the prompts which exercises have errors and notes exercises that raise issues of ethics or sexism.

A Practical Approach

Like previous editions, the 13th edition is concrete, not abstract or theoretical. Its tone is practical and realistic. Its language is clear, concise, simple and direct. Because of the book's realism, students will encounter the types of problems and assignments they are likely to find after they graduate and begin entry-level jobs with the media.

Pro Challenge Exercises

A few exercises in the chapters about leads and the body of news stories have been completed by professional journalists. With these exercises, students can compare their work to that of the professionals. The leads and stories written by professionals are in the Instructor's Manual. The Pro Challenge exercises completed by professionals also include brief explanations of how and why the professionals approached the story as they did.

A Note of Thanks

Journalists are wonderful people: enthusiastic, interesting and helpful. While working on this book, we wrote to dozens of them. Reporters, photographers and editors from Portland to Philadelphia, from Miami to New York, answered our letters and provided advice and samples of their work for this and previous editions.

We would especially like to thank the many professionals who have given us permission to quote their work: Tom Rosenstiel, the executive director of the American Press Institute; Craig Silverman of the Toronto Star; Steve Buttry, the digital transformation editor of Digital First Media; Henry McNulty, the owner of Henry McNulty Communication Services and a former associate editor of the Hartford (Connecticut) Courant; David Cullier, an assistant professor of journalism at the University of Arizona; Matthew Stibbe, a freelance journalist and the CEO of Articulate and Turbine; Roy Peter Clark, a senior scholar and the vice president of The Poynter Institute for Media Studies; Don Fry, an affiliate of The Poynter Institute for Media Studies; Mary Grace Keller, a business reporter for the Frederick (Maryland) News-Post; Andrew J. Nelson, a freelance writer based in Omaha, Nebraska; Don Stacom, a reporter for the Hartford (Connecticut) Courant; Paula Lavigne, a reporter for ESPN's Enterprise and Investigative Unit; Libby Seline, a data journalist for the San Antonio (Texas) Express-News; Sue Hadden, a retired writer and an editor for The Record Herald of Waynesboro, Pennsylvania; Linda White, a former TV reporter and anchor who is working on a doctorate at Michigan State University; Adrian Whitsett, a morning anchor for WCPO-TV in Cincinnati; William Cote and Bonnie Bucqueroux, a former coordinator and an assistant coordinator, respectively, of the Victims and Media Program at Michigan State University; Kurt Krug, a freelance entertainment writer and PR professional at Henry Ford College; Jan Thornburg, the senior communications manager for the city of Sarasota; Brian O'Connor, the vice president of public relations for Princess Cruises; Tabitha Kube, a graduate student at the University of Nebraska-Lincoln; Kayla Nelsen, a reporter for GreatLakesEcho; Jack Hart, a former managing editor of The Oregonian in Portland; Scott Pohl, a radio news reporter for WKAR in East Lansing, Michigan; and Robert Gould, a television journalist and an instructor at Michigan State University.

Numerous organizations, publications and news services gave us permission to quote their stories or republish their photographs: AARP Mississippi, Alamy Stock Photo, Animal Wellness Action, Ann Arbor News, AP Photo, Arizona Daily Star, The Associated Press, Axios/HBO, BBC, Biloxi Sun Herald, Bizzaro Studios, Bloomberg News, The Booster Redux, The Bradenton Herald, Brian Crane, Brooklyn Daily/Brooklyn Courier, Cartoonstock, Chicago Tribune, CNBC, CNN, Cumberland Times-News, The Daily Mail, The Daily Pennsylvanian, The Dallas Morning News, Detroit Free Press, The Detroit News, ESPN, Federal Trade Commission, Getty Images, Goodwill, The Graphic News Service, Hagerstown Herald-Mail, Harrisburg Patriot-News, Hartford Courant, International Consortium of Investigative Journalists, iStockphoto, Jarrett Hill, Jennifer Bogo, John Atkinson, KTRK-TV, KUOW, LA Times, Lansing State Journal, LIFE, LogiGear Group, Lumiere Gallery, The Madison County Record, Madison State Journal, Mark Anderson, Mercury News, Miami Herald, Michigan Advance, Michigan Department of Health and Human Services, Mixte Communications, The Morning Call, MPR News, National Press Photographers Association, New American Economy, New York Post, The New York Times, The New Yorker,

NOLA.com, NPR, NY Daily News, Omaha World-Herald, The Orlando Sentinel, PBS, Pew Research Center, The Philadelphia Inquirer, Pittsburgh Post-Gazette, Pittsburgh Tribune-Review, Politifact, The Poynter Institute, ProPublica, Reporter's Committee for Freedom of the Press, Reuters, Robin Meadows, San Antonio Express-News, San Francisco Chronicle, Scott Adams, Shutterstock, Society of Professional Journalism, SOT News, SPOTLIGHT PA, Suffolk University, Tampa Bay Times, The Telegraph, The Texas Tribune, TopFoto, University of Washington, U.S. News & World Report, USA Today, The Wall Street Journal, The Washington Post, Waugoshance Lighthouse Preservation Society, WAVY, WTVF News Channel 5, Zach Morris, and ZUMA Press, Inc.

The following professionals completed the "Pro Challenge" exercises: Mary Grace Keller, business and non-profit reporter for the Frederick (Maryland) News-Post; Naomi Creason, managing editor of The Carlisle (Pennsylvania) Sentinel; and Caitlin West, reporter/copy editor at The Times-Tribune in Scranton, Pennsylvania.

Additional thanks for reviews and editing go to colleagues Geri Alumit Zeldes, Michigan State University and Patricia Mills, an independent writing professional and formerly of Ball State University; former students Duygu Kanver, Serena Carpenter Miller, Nicholas J. Robinson; Pyeongseon Oh and Julie Goldsmith at Michigan State University. Thanks also go to Jason Greene for reviews, Rachael Greene for pop culture examples and Jen Ware for contributing augmented content in a prior (11th) edition.

For their insightful comments and useful suggestions during the development process, thanks go to Israel Balderas, Palm Beach Atlantic University; Donna L. Halper, Lesley University; Gary R. Heller, Susquehanna University; Ellen Meacham, The University of Mississippi; Douglas L. Mendenhall, Abilene Christian University; Dante Mozie, South Carolina State University; Lucrezia Marie Paxson, Washington State University, Everett; Mildred F. Perreault, East Tennessee State University; Theodore Petersen, Florida Institute of Technology; Tony Rogers, Bucks County Community College; James Simon, Southern Connecticut State University; Daniel Sipocz, Berry College; Peter von Stackelberg, Alfred University; and all of those reviewers who have chosen to remain anonymous.

We would also like to thank the staff at Oxford University Press. They have worked wonders with making the text more visual, colorful, rigorous and intellectually challenging for instructors and their students. Our thanks go to Executive Editor Steve Helba, Portfolio Manager Jaime Burns, Content Development Editor Emma Guttman-Moy, Editorial Director Petra Recter, Senior Production Editor Ashli MacKenzie, Production Manager Theresa Stockton, and Art Director Michele Laseau.

About the Authors

JOHN R. BENDER is a William H. Kearns professor emeritus of the College of Journalism and Mass Communications at the University of Nebraska-Lincoln. Bender worked for six years for the Pittsburg (Kansas) Morning Sun, starting as a reporter covering local government and politics. He became the paper's assignment editor, news editor and then managing editor. During his term as managing editor, the Morning Sun won awards for farm coverage, photography and editorial writing. He has taught at the college or university level for 40 years. He was an assistant professor of journalism at Culver-Stockton College in Canton, Missouri, for five years, and he joined the faculty of the University of Nebraska in 1990. His teaching and research areas include news reporting and writing, communications law, media history and controls of information. In 2007, he won a College Award for Distinguished Teaching, and in 2011, he received UNL's James A. Lake Award for his work in promoting academic freedom. He is also a past executive director of the Nebraska High School Press Association. In 2019, he was named Kearns Professor of Journalism and selected by the Omaha Press Club as the journalism educator of distinction for that year. In 2022, he was elected to the Nebraska Press Association Hall of Fame. Bender held a number of faculty governance positions at UNL, including president of the Faculty Senate. His bachelor's degree is in sociology from Westminster College in Fulton, Missouri. He holds a master's degree in journalism from the University of Kansas and a doctorate in journalism from the University of Missouri at Columbia.

LUCINDA D. DAVENPORT is a university distinguished professor at Michigan State University, the former director of the School of Journalism at Michigan State University for 10 years, and a former dean of Graduate Education and Research for the College of Communication Arts and Sciences. She was awarded as the Outstanding Woman in Journalism and Mass Communication Education from the Association for Education in Journalism and Mass Communication (AEJMC), the MSU Robert F. Banks Award for Institutional Leadership and the John V. Field Award from the Michigan Interscholastic Press Association, among other recognitions. In 2023, she was inducted into the Michigan Journalism Hall of Fame. Teaching awards include the Michigan State University Excellence in Teaching Award and the College of Communication Arts and Sciences Faculty Impact Award. Additional recognitions include innovative teaching and diversity and community engagement. Davenport participates on numerous committees concerning journalism education and has been president of the board of directors for MSU's independent student newspaper. She has several Top Faculty AEJMC awards for her research and publications that focus on innovative technologies, journalism ethics, data analytics and media history. Davenport has worked as a reporter, broadcast journalist and announcer, public relations practitioner and online news editor. As an undergraduate at Baylor University, she earned a double major in journalism and radio/TV/film with a concentration in public relations. She earned a master's degree in journalism from the University of Iowa and a doctorate in mass media from Ohio University. Both her thesis and dissertation were global firsts about online news and information.

MICHAEL W. DRAGER is an associate professor in the Department of Communication, Journalism and Media at Shippensburg University of Pennsylvania. He graduated with a bachelor's degree in art from Millersville University in Pennsylvania. While working as a newspaper reporter, he earned a master's degree in communication at Shippensburg University. Drager received his doctorate in mass media from Michigan State University. As a journalist, Drager has worked as a reporter, copy editor, editorial writer, columnist and photographer. He has also worked in public relations as a writer and publications designer. As an educator, Drager has 35 years of experience in both public and higher education. He has taught courses in news writing and reporting, news editing and design, digital journalism, public relations writing, photography, photojournalism, magazine design, and media law and ethics. His research explores the pedagogical approaches to basic writing and editing instruction. In addition, he has conducted workshops and seminars on the relationship between journalism and public institutions. In 2011, Shippensburg University recognized his commitment to diversity by presenting to him the Dr. Martin Luther King Jr. Humanitarian Award.

FRED FEDLER taught journalism at the University of Central Florida for 38 years until his retirement in 2008. For 16 years he was the head of the UCF School of Communication's Journalism Division. Fedler received his bachelor's degree from the University of Wisconsin in Madison and then worked as a newspaper reporter in Dubuque and Davenport, Iowa, and as a copy editor in Sacramento, California. He received his master's degree from the University of Kentucky and doctorate from the University of Minnesota. He conducted research in the field of journalism but also wrote freelance for popular publications. Fedler's other books include "Introduction to the Mass Media," "Media Hoaxes" and "Lessons from the Past: Journalists' Lives and Work—1850–1950." In addition, Fedler served on numerous committees concerned with journalism education.

Many students and teachers have written us over the years telling us what they like and dislike about this book and suggesting new features. We have adopted many of those ideas, and we would like to hear from you. If you have a comment or suggestion, please write one of us:

John R. Bender
College of Journalism and Mass Communications
University of Nebraska-Lincoln
Lincoln, Nebraska 68588-0474
jbender1@unl.edu

Lucinda D. Davenport
School of Journalism
Michigan State University
East Lansing, Michigan 48824-1212
ludavenp@msu.edu

Michael W. Drager
Department of Communication/Journalism
Shippensburg University of Pennsylvania
1871 Old Main Drive
Shippensburg, Pennsylvania 17257
mwdrag@ship.edu

REFERENCE CHART FOR COPY-EDITING SYMBOLS

1. Abbreviate or use numerals — thirteen
2. Boldface — This line should be set in boldface type.
3. Capitalize — An american won the nobel prize.
4. Center —]Continued on Page 10[
5. Change letter — Their hoxe is expensive.
6. Change word — She received three gifts. (four)
7. Close up space between words — Their car was totally destroyed
8. Close up space within a word — Their children ran outside
9. Continues on next page — More
10. Delete letter — They receivedd the monkey.
11. Delete phrase — They did not use any unneeded or unnecessary words.
12. Delete punctuation — They asked, if he was safe. OR: They asked, if he was safe.
13. End of story — ### OR: -30- OR: -0-
14. Flush left — [The typesetter will begin this line at the left margin.
15. Flush right — The typesetter will begin this line at the right margin.]
16. Ignore correction (Correct as written) — Stet
17. Insert apostrophe — It's good you're going home.
18. Insert colon — He set three goals success, health and wealth.
19. Insert comma — The girl lives with her grandmother.
20. Insert dash — The score was 87 to 53 a disaster.
21. Insert exclamation point — "What I don't believe it" she exclaimed.
22. Insert hyphen — The 7 year old girl lives with her mother.
23. Insert letter — Their car filed to start.
24. Insert period — John C Kefalis received the scholarship
25. Insert quotation marks — This is easy, he said.
26. Insert semicolon — Don't go he needs your help.
27. Insert word — He writes poetry. (often) (clever)
28. Italic — Some publications set words in italics for emphasis.
29. Lowercase (Do not capitalize) — The Mayor failed to arrive.
30. No new paragraph — To generate more publicity, the candidate announced that he would work at different jobs. He spent the remainder of his campaign picking tomatoes, plucking chickens and driving trucks.
31. Separate words — Journalists are critical of political gimmickry.
32. Spell out numbers or words — She said 8 people will go to Ala.
33. Start new paragraph — ¶ Another man campaigned on roller skates. His wife explained: "We met at a roller skating rink, and we thought it would be a fun idea. He's going house to house, subdivision to subdivision on his skates, and people remember him."
34. Transpose letter — Typsits often transpsoe letters.
35. Transpose words — Happily, he accepted the award.

xxiv

THE TOOLS OF JOURNALISM

JOURNALISM TODAY

Pause for a minute to think about the events and issues happening across the world and in our hometowns. What are they?

Now imagine that you are not aware of these events because there are no journalists and there is no news coverage. How would you know about anything?

Without legitimate news outlets, you might have only social media, an echo chamber. Family or friends (who often think similarly) repost a friend of a friend's opinion or politicians announce what they want you to know or think. Nothing is fact-checked or reported from various viewpoints. This scenario is also reminiscent of the game called "telephone," where the original truth is replaced in the end by misinformation and disinformation.

Much of social media is hearsay and opinionated and has no professional oversight. Only one person in 10 thinks it has a positive influence on our lives while most others say it is responsible for misinformation, made-up news, hate, harassment and polarization. People are frustrated because they don't know what to believe on social media, and almost 65 percent of Americans believe it has contributed negatively to the way things are going in our country, according to Brooke Auxier of the Pew Research Center. Unfortunately, many people cannot tell the difference between postulation on social media and information on legitimate news outlets.

An example emerged shortly after Donald Trump won the 2016 presidential election. Protests against Trump were held in many U.S. cities, including Austin, Texas. Eric Tucker, an Austin businessman, spotted some buses parked near downtown the day of the protest. He photographed the buses, then checked Google to see if any conferences or conventions were scheduled. He found none, so he posted his assumption on Twitter.

Tucker assumed the buses had brought Trump protesters from out of town and out of state. He was wrong. The buses had been hired by a company called Tableau Software to transport some of the more than 13,000 people who were attending a conference the company was sponsoring. Tucker's tweet, however, went viral before it could be corrected. It was shared 16,000 times on Twitter and 350,000 times on Facebook alone. Other media organizations, mostly conservative ones,

erictucker @erictucker · Nov 9

Anti-Trump protestors in Austin today are not as organic as they seem. Here are the busses they came in. #fakeprotests #trump2016 #austin

picked it up as well. Tucker later told the New York Times: "I did think in the back of my mind there could be other explanations, but it just didn't seem plausible. I'm also a very busy businessman and I don't have time to fact-check everything that I put out there, especially when I don't think it's going out there for wide consumption."

Some like to say that because of cellphones and social media, everyone is a journalist. Eric Tucker's erroneous tweet shows that this is not true. Those who want to know about their communities and the world go to legitimate news outlets that employ professional journalists for comprehensive, ethical, inclusive and thoughtful news. Going to news professionals for accurate information is essentially the same as going to a licensed surgeon for a medical procedure instead of a person on social media offering an opinion on how they'd perform the operation.

As society, technology and economics have evolved, the news industry has had a long history of navigating change. The rest of this chapter offers highlights of current issues in the news business that are often debated.

1.1 Current Issues in Journalism

1.1.1 The Hutchins Commission on the Freedom of the Press: Social Responsibility, Diversity and Inclusion

Accusations of "fake news" and biased reporting are not new. Criticisms from the public and government officials through the years have targeted the motives and performance of media owners and those they employ.

Once upon a time, even small towns had multiple family-owned newspapers, offering varying viewpoints to the community. As large media organizations bought up and shut down these newspapers to eliminate competition, the number of voices contributing to public discussion decreased.

A response during World War II was to form the Hutchins Commission to determine the function of a free press in a democratic society. Margaret Blanchard's monograph on the Hutchins Commission quoted some of the original 1947 report, A Free and Responsible Press.

To equip the people for the complex world, . . . the press needed to provide a "truthful, comprehensive, and intelligent account of the day's events in a context which gives them meaning." And indeed the press must "provide a forum for the exchange of comment and criticism" becoming, if necessary, "common carriers of the public expression" in order to secure a hearing for a wide variety of viewpoints. Given the interdependency of the modern world, it was vital that the press project a "representative picture of constituent groups in society," avoiding stereotyping, and explaining group values and goals as completely as possible. Such portrayal would naturally lead to the presentation and clarification of "the goals and values of society" with the press serving as an educational instrument. Building further on this notion, it logically followed that the press would provide "full access to the day's intelligence" for the use of readers. With the implementation of these goals, the press, at least in the commission's view, would be on its way to meeting society's needs.

The commission responded that the media should embrace diversity in the coverage of their communities to fulfill obligations within a democratic society. Yet, news media today still fall short of providing comprehensive diversity in their stories and newsrooms, which would help us better understand one another and be good for business. People attend to news that includes them in the greater conversation.

Most media do not monitor source diversity and demographics in news stories to align with their community's census. Even analyzing demographics after the fact is guesswork, expensive and time-consuming. Yet, it is important. A freeware process, developed in part by a grant from the Online News Association, is now used by some media organizations and journalism programs to monitor the diversity of source demographics in real time, while covering a story. The Fair Chance Diversity Reporting Tool by Grimm, Davenport and Michigan State University students is explained at www.fairchancereporting.com. Source diversity within news stories builds trust that different groups are being represented, which adds to comprehensive and accurate reporting.

1.1.2 Solutions Journalism: Finding Answers and Helping Others

Journalism is a unique opportunity to help solve social issues and improve society while covering news objectively.

Solutions journalism is a global movement to focus on constructive responses to societal issues. Instead of simply reporting on a problem, journalists report on attempted solutions to the problem—if a response did or did not work, and why. Community members learn about other communities' success stories and implement them. Or they examine why a response did not work and try something new. Examples include how a community decreased pollution by planting trees, how registering females to vote in Libya led to empowering women, and how elevating conditions for health-care workers led to increased help for loved ones.

Some people avoid the news because it makes them feel hopeless as they read about problems in their community. However, solutions-journalism stories were found to energize community members, connect them more to their community and help community members realize that positive change can occur and that their individual efforts matter. They talk and collaborate with others about issues and hold politicians accountable.

Solutions journalism is good for the community and our global society. It is also good for business. About 83 percent of respondents to a survey said they trusted a solutions journalism story compared to 55 percent who trusted a problems-focused story on the same topic. News organizations adapting to constructive solutions journalism found their circulation increased, according to the Solutions Journalism website.

Solutions journalism is not the same as advocacy journalism, although both might have the best interests of the community in mind. Advocacy journalism advances a particular political or social agenda, whereas solutions journalism objectively reports on responses that worked and didn't work in an effort to improve society.

1.1.3 Story Tone: Good News/Bad News

The first line in this chapter asked you to think about what is happening in the world and your hometown. Some of those issues and events might have been the following: the Jan. 6 Committee hearings; Roe v. Wade abortion rights; the school shootings in Uvalde, Texas, and Nashville, Tennessee; the Ukraine-Russia war; Russian disinformation; COVID-19 and the pandemic; climate change; rising inflation; food shortages; #BlackLivesMatter; mass shootings; and the #MeToo movement, to name a few.

How do you feel after considering these topics? Happy? Depressed?

Journalism is providing people with the information they need to make good decisions to lead productive lives; to make good choices about their communities, state, country and world; and to govern themselves. News is not all bad, but it is often presented that way.

As noted in the section above on solutions journalism, many people avoid news because it leaves them depressed. Sadness is inherent in some situations, yet some upsetting facts are important to know. These stories are needed. However, journalists also shine a spotlight on potentially constructive or uplifting narratives hiding in the shadows.

Journalists (you) choose tone and story angles while offering facts. For example, under the shadow of the senseless tragedy of the Ukraine-Russia war, stories of human goodness were reported as people and countries helped one another. In the Nashville, Tennessee, massacre, heroism was evident.

In another example, U.S. vice-presidents have been elected since 1789, and only just now a woman occupies that office. That it took more than 230 years is depressing (the glass is half empty). However, it is encouraging that now someone in the White House represents more than half of the U.S. population (the glass is half full) and a story on Kamala Harris' background might inspire and encourage young women to pursue their dreams, whereas the path appeared blocked before.

1.1.4 Journalism Principles and Technology

The basic foundation and principles of journalism remain relatively constant while tools and technologies change: Journalists provide news to audiences accurately and ethically. Technology simply provides reporters with alternative ways to gather, organize, present and distribute information efficiently.

The journalism industry applies the strengths of developing technologies to its advantage. The printing press gave people greater access to information than handwritten transcriptions and provided it more quickly and broadly, making it cheaper and improving literacy. The telegraph sent information to distant places more rapidly than carrier pigeons could fly. Typewriters replaced handwritten copy. Trains distributed newspapers to communities faster than the Pony

Express or stagecoach did. Photography helped people see events more realistically than drawings; color photos appeared truer to life than black-and-white images; drones captured hard-to-reach images; and 360° cameras gave viewers control over what they saw. The telephone enabled the exchange of information more swiftly than letters or personal visits. Radio helped people hear events immediately instead of reading about them later. Cars helped reporters travel faster and cover events personally. Television allowed people to watch events as they unfolded; satellite brought global issues into our living rooms 24/7.

As time passed, the internet reduced the need for printer's ink and newsprint (paper), and news could be updated around the clock. Consumers became active seekers of news online instead of passively waiting for morning newspapers to be delivered on their doorstep or arranging their schedules for the timed broadcast of radio and TV news programs. Tweets helped journalists gather information and send updates, while reader comments and posts strengthened stories. Today, augmented content offers audiences additional information that is embedded in stories. Virtual reality (VR) and immersive journalism puts audiences inside the story, and live video sharing on social media carries breaking news as it happens. News is available to audiences in any form or platform convenient to them.

1.1.5 News Is a Business

News is a business that needs consumers to pay for stories. It takes income to pay journalists, buy supplies and maintain equipment to produce the news. Before the 1880s, readers supported newspapers and magazines through circulation (subscriptions and single copy sales). Then advertising became the major revenue source for printed media, TV and radio. Your grandparents and maybe your parents can remember when all radio and television were free. While certain news sources, such as many online newspapers, are still free today, the business model of consumers supporting the media is returning. News organizations no longer want to rely on unpredictable advertisers who can place ads with the competition or eliminate advertising when their budgets are tight.

A third of people are unaware of the economic challenges of the news business, according to the latest annual Reuters Digital News Report. News organizations have been slow to change their business model from depending on advertising revenue to subscriber-based income. And people are still slow to pay for news because they can get lot of it free online. Habits are hard to change, but consumers are now accustomed to paying for television and radio news programs. The hope is that consumers will pay for news if they want professional and ethical journalists investigating stories—not fake news possibly written by illegitimate sources. Paying for news and information may become a way of life, if news outlets are to thrive.

1.1.6 The News Media Landscape

News consumers go to a variety of sources and use various devices to access their news. Pew Research found 86 percent of news consumers use a digital device—a smartphone, tablet or computer—68 percent use television;

% of U.S. adults who get news____ from...

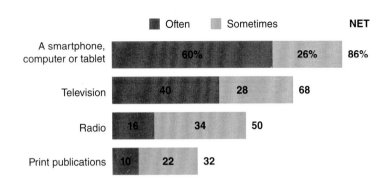

FIGURE 1.1 Large majority of Americans get news on digital devices.

% of U.S. adults who prefer____ for getting news

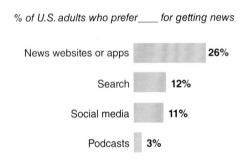

FIGURE 1.2 News websites most preferred way to get digital news.

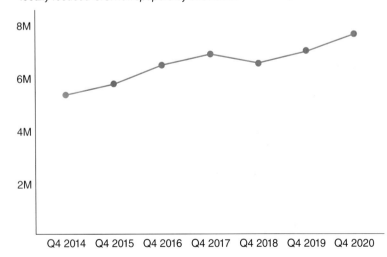

Average monthly unique visitors to newspaper websites among the top 46 locally focused U.S. newspapers by circulation

FIGURE 1.3 Traffic to locally focused newspaper sites continues to increase.

50 percent use radio; and 32 percent use print. That's the common line-up for people under 50.

Those who are 50 to 64 prefer digital devices and television almost equally. And people 65 and older mostly use television, then a digital device, then print and radio.

Consumers who use digital devices prefer to go to a news website or app (26 percent). A few like to search for news (12 percent) and still fewer prefer to get their news from social media (11 percent) or podcasts (3 percent).

Americans who rely on social media for their news are less knowledgeable and less engaged with current events—and are more likely to be misinformed, be exposed to made-up news and conspiracy theories and believe falsehoods—than those who rely on legitimate news websites, television, radio and print. An American News Pathways project published in Trust Magazine surveyed Americans' news habits and their news awareness over nine months and found that social media users, mostly young adults, answered fewer questions correctly than all other Americans about current events. Sometimes social media are used as a pathway to other news sources. But if not, then consumers are consistently exposed to misinformation on social media that is repetitive and often not attributed. The study's results add fodder to the debate that learning about media literacy is important for everyone.

1.1.7 Digital and Print Newspapers

The number of total subscribers and website traffic continues to climb for national newspapers, with digital increases compensating for print decreases: The New York Times Co. reached its target of 10 million subscriptions three years early and plans to add 5 million more subscribers by 2027. USA TODAY has more than seven million readers daily. The Wall Street Journal subscription number is 3.6 million and The Washington Post has more than 3 million.

Local newspaper daily circulation was 8.3 million for weekdays and 15.4 million for Sundays, according to Pew Research. Overall local newspapers remained steady in 2020 after a long decline. As this graph from Pew Research shows, digital circulation has increased by about 30 percent as print circulation has declined.

1.1.8 The COVID-19 Pandemic and the News Business

The coronavirus pandemic affected all industries, including the news business. Some hometown newsrooms temporarily closed their doors; some shut permanently, and others merged. Most news outlets still have a business model that depends on advertising, which was detrimental during the pandemic because businesses such as restaurants and stores halted or slashed advertising for walk-in customers when they were closed to the public. As companies experienced tight budgets, their advertising was often the first line item to be eliminated. Physical distribution of print newspapers was a concern as people worried about contamination. And in-person reporting decreased as pandemic shutdowns were announced. News media tried hard to cover events with remote reporting and Zoom and email interviewing to keep audiences informed. Nonetheless, the pandemic caused many local newspaper challenges.

A consequence of closures and mergers is a lack of stories about communities, and their people, events and issues. People feel less engaged with their community as they know less about their neighbors and town. Another consequence is decreased coverage of government groups and their decisions. Communities lose transparency and accountability, and taxes go up while voter participation goes down, according to the research of Penelope Abernathy of the University of North Carolina.

Trust in the media increased during the pandemic worldwide, but not in the United States, perhaps because of the tumultuous Trump years. Reuters Digital News Report said survey respondents noted that trust often meant adequate coverage of topics—not necessarily misinformation or disinformation. Put another way, people did not trust that the media were adequately covering important issues. This suggests that a decrease in the number of journalists or news outlets covering news comprehensively may reduce trust in the media. Yet another argument for media literacy education.

1.2 Journalism as a Profession

All news outlets need trained journalists with high standards. Reporters are professionals who cover topics with truth, passion and authority. It is a great responsibility to accurately, ethically and comprehensively report news to the public. People need journalists to sift through mountains of information to report news honestly and in context so they know what is happening and can make informed choices. In order to work together successfully in a democracy, people need to know the opinions of politicians and others, as well as the effects that issues have on all sectors of a diverse society.

The most essential tools for journalists are their minds and hearts. They are the very human qualities of curiosity, integrity and empathy, coupled with the storyteller's tools—scene, metaphor and imagery, said Poynter Institute's Chip Scanlon. Furthermore, managers of online websites told researcher Max Magee that the top requirements for story editing are news judgment and knowledge of grammar and style. Content creation abilities are reporting and writing original stories and editing visuals. Journalist attitudes and overall skills are attention to detail, communication skills, the ability to multitask and an awareness or ability to learn new technologies.

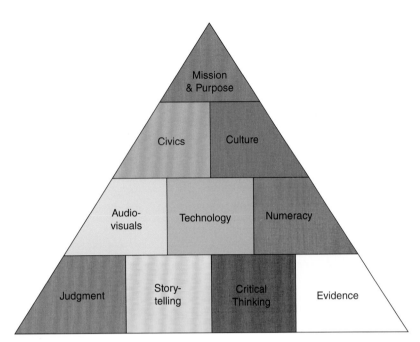

FIGURE 1.4 The Pyramid of Journalism Competence
This diagram encapsulates the various skills journalists need.

1.2.1 Journalism Competencies

A pyramid of journalism competencies that identifies the ideal attributes of a journalist was developed by The Poynter Institute (see Figure 1.4). Reporters do not need to be experts in all the areas included, but they should be versatile and conversant in them. The following list takes a closer look at each element.

- **Judgment:** Along with evidence, this competency is the cornerstone of the pyramid. Decisions on what to publish are generally based on two questions: Is it important? And, is it interesting? Some stories are important but not immediately interesting or vice versa, and other stories are both. Journalists become experts in recognizing the stories that matter and that are sometimes invisible to others. They make their stories relevant to audiences so consumers understand the impact of the information.

- **Evidence:** Reporters gather and verify information and present stories of public interest. They collect information through various methods, including examining documents, interviewing, observing and analyzing data. Journalists verify information through triangulation, which means using more than one source to determine whether something is true.

- **Storytelling:** The best storytellers are those who give audiences a unique experience. Journalists are versatile in telling stories in different genres and forms for different media and audiences. They know grammar and punctuation rules and use news elements to transform information into narratives. Stories are not simply reports.

- **Critical thinking:** Journalists look at patterns and trends as they interpret information for audiences. They give context to facts by asking such questions as, "Why is this person saying this?" and "Why now?"

- **Numeracy and data:** Numbers help us make sense of the world. Adjusting for inflation, breaking down tax increases and using spreadsheets enable reporters to perform their watchdog role. Many Pulitzer Prize winners have been recognized and corrupt politicians and corporations exposed through numbers.

- **Technology:** New devices provide different ways to gather, organize, present and disseminate information. Journalists use technology to do their jobs better. They also think about the ways that people use media.

- **Audios and visuals (multimedia journalism):** Journalists can shoot video, interview sources and write with just their mobile phones. Some reporters combine these elements in a story. Being versatile with audios and visuals enables journalists to improve storytelling. Photography, video, sound bites, data visualization and design are all elements to consider when gathering information in the field and presenting the story in different media.

- **Civics:** Knowledge about the foundations of democracy, government processes, politics, history and power within communities helps journalists to ask the right questions and put information into context for audiences.
- **Culture:** Society is made up of all types of people whose points of view should be represented in the news. Journalists are sensitive to including diversity and respectful of different points of view. Understanding others—different genders, ages, races, religions, ethnicities, abilities, sexual orientations and socioeconomic levels—is as important when reporting within a local community as it is when working as a foreign correspondent in another country.
- **Mission and purpose:** This element represents the pyramid's apex. A clear sense of the purpose of journalism determines its relevancy in society. Knowledge about ethics, standards, journalism history, the First Amendment, democracy, law and social contracts informs the role of journalism in local communities and in the global village.

1.2.2 Today's Journalist

While good writing is essential, the advent of digital media opened new avenues in storytelling. Stories can include text, audio, video, photo slideshows with music or narration, 3-D information graphics, animation, comics, augmented content and virtual reality. Each element makes the story more vivid.

For instance, a journalist covering a state senate race writes stories about the campaign and the candidates as they give speeches and meet voters. The story may run with a photograph or a bar chart of candidates' popularity among various communities. A web package can augment its story with audio and video podcast interviews with each candidate. It can link to the candidates' websites with their platforms, to a government site with voter registration information, to a nonpartisan site with the incumbent's voting record, to sites representing issues the candidates support or oppose and to their blogs. The package also may contain a 3-D map of communities that candidates visited, an animated timeline of the election race, a photo slideshow and more. A comment section allows readers to post their thoughts on the story or the candidates. Tweeting the story alerts followers about election coverage updates. In the not-too-far future, audiences will be able to scan the printed text with their smartphone for audio or video that demonstrates or supplements what the text describes. This is called augmented content.

Information is presented differently in various media, usually based on how people interact with a medium. For example, eyes become tired more quickly when reading from a monitor than on paper. Also, text will not appear sharp if the monitor's resolution is low, which also decreases readability and the time one spends reading news. Thus, text is formatted differently on news websites than on printed newspapers.

Stories printed on paper often have a serif typeface, such as Times New Roman or New Century Schoolbook. Paragraphs follow one another in sequence without any additional spacing, and the first line of each paragraph is indented. Stories published on the web usually are in a sans serif typeface, such as Arial or Helvetica, because they are less elaborate, sharper and easier to read on a computer monitor. Paragraphs are not indented but separated by extra space to give eyes a quick rest before starting the next section of information.

Journalists never lose sight that the story is the most important element in any news platform. Reporters write effectively for a standard story in print and broadcast, a digital news package, a blog or a tweet. Versatility is a key skill for today's journalists—this textbook examines the breadth and depth of news reporting and writing across storytelling forms and media platforms, giving a full picture of today's journalist.

1.3 Journalism Style

Journalism graduates should be able to walk into any newsroom and immediately write a story using standard guidelines that professionals follow. This textbook and your instructor will show you the standard Associated Press (AP)-style copy-editing symbols and format generally accepted by news organizations all over the world. Knowing the guidelines makes it possible for journalists to move seamlessly from one news organization to another.

1.3.1 AP Stylebook

The reason professional news stories from various outlets across the country can be read easily is because they are written in a consistent style. This consistency helps journalists in any news organization know, for example, how to refer to the coronavirus (COVID-19, Covid or covid-19) and how to correctly write and punctuate times (two o'clock, 2 o'clock, 2:00 p.m. or 2 p.m.) and dates (January 3, 2015, or Jan. 3, 2015), and to move seamlessly from one organization to another.

The Associated Press Stylebook and Briefing on Media Law is the style reference for journalists—writers, reporters, editors and students. Learning the guidelines becomes easy with practice. (The most frequently used rules are included in Appendix B.)

1.3.2 Journalism Terms

Journalists do not use jargon—terminology specific to a field—in their stories, but there is journalism jargon used within the profession. For example, if reporters talk about "the third graph," they are referring to a third paragraph of text and not a visual information graphic within the story. Here are some other common terms and their definitions:

Byline: Name of the journalist(s) who reported and wrote the story.

Copy: Written version or draft of the story. This term is a holdover from when reporters would keep an original of the story and give editors a copy to review.

Dateline: City or town, if outside the local area, where the story took place, followed by an em dash (e.g., "AUSTIN, Texas—").

Graph or graf: Abbreviation of "paragraph."

Headline: Title that summarizes the story, usually written by the editor before the story is published.

Lead or lede: News peg. This is the sentence(s) that encapsulates why the story is worthwhile. It is often the first sentence that summarizes the who, what, where, when, why and how. Students frequently confuse the lead with the headline.

Slug: Two or three words to describe the story uniquely, placed in the top left corner of the copy's first page. The second line is the journalist's name, and the third line is the date. The slug might be duplicated on each page of the story.

1.3.3 Copy-Editing

Almost all reporters write and revise their stories on computers before sending the final version to an editor. Sometimes, students, instructors and editors must print out the story (or "copy") to correct it by hand, using standard copy-editing symbols. This process of reviewing, revising and proofreading stories is called "editing." Copy-editing symbols and the editing process are used in almost all other writing professions, as well.

1.3.4 Copy Format

Journalists have developed a unique format for their stories that is relatively consistent from one newsroom to another. Instructors require students to follow the same format with minor variations. For example, some who review printed copy may require students to begin stories one-third of the way down the page; and they use the blank space for their comments. They might also ask students to type the word "more" at the end of the first page (to indicate that the story continues to another page), head the additional pages with the slug and a page number and

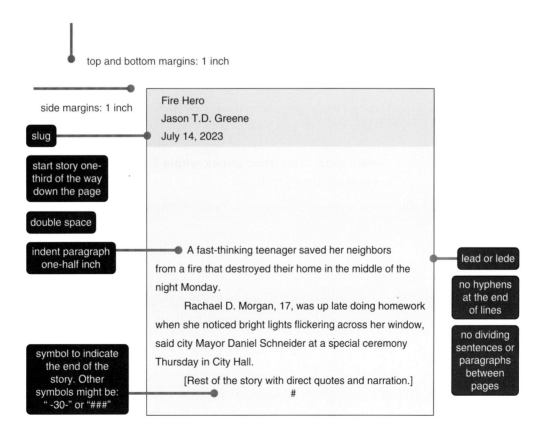

FIGURE 1.5 Journalists format their copy so that it can be edited and read easily.

type an end symbol at the bottom of the story (Figure 1.5). Other instructors who review stories on their computers might not impose these requirements.

Professional and ethical journalism skills are used in almost any industry, in addition to the news business. For example, most companies and nonprofit organizations need content creators for their websites and social media, communications with employees or promotion material. They produce information and stories in many different forms, such as text and multimedia. Most successful content creators and writers have journalism training to learn how to research information, analyze data, organize material and present stories in various formats to different audiences.

Thus, the objective of this textbook is to act as a springboard, training students in the fundamentals of news judgment, critical thinking and writing. Students who are thoroughly practiced in these fundamentals adapt their knowledge and expertise to all forms of news and media that they might experience as they move from one interesting job to another during their careers.

SELECTING AND REPORTING THE NEWS

Jan. 6, 2021, was a day that will forever be remembered. American citizens in disbelief watched video after video and read news updates as 2,000 rioters apparently incited by disappointed presidential candidate Donald Trump unlawfully stormed the U.S. Capitol in a futile effort to prevent Congress from certifying President-elect Joe Biden's victory. Scared lawmakers—Republican and Democrat—ran into hiding as the mob ransacked offices and took over the building for hours. Police used tear gas, smoke bombs and flash grenades to put down the insurrection. In the end, one person was killed and four others died in medical emergencies, including Capitol Police Officer Brian Sicknick. Trump was impeached a second time, most recently for inciting insurrection of the deadly Capitol riot. He was acquitted by the Senate, but nearly 850 rioters have been arrested and charged with crimes. Their trials continue today.

The insurrection touched the sensibilities of millions of people and captured top headlines all over the country and world. It still does. Almost 29 million people watched television news as events unfolded throughout that afternoon and about 33 million tuned in to major news stations during the evening prime time. Those viewers and millions more attended to journalists' updates on Twitter, Instagram and blogs, while others read texts from concerned friends or relatives. People shared stories from legacy news media websites and Facebook and discussed what they read or saw. The event continues to be in the news, with stories on the rioters and their charges. Movies and documentaries are planned.

"The basis of our governments being the opinion of the people, the very first object should be to keep that right; and were it left to me to decide whether we should have a government without newspapers or newspapers without a government, I should not hesitate a moment to prefer the latter."

—*Thomas Jefferson, the primary author of the Declaration of Independence and served as the third president of the United States*

Protesters enter the Senate Chamber on Jan. 6, 2021, attempting to disrupt the joint session to ratify Joe Biden's victory over President Donald Trump. When major events happen, such as insurgents attacking the democratic process in the U.S. Capitol, there is little doubt as to the importance of the story. The question becomes how to tell it.

Editors and news producers from all over the country had no difficulty determining what event to cover the day after the riots: There was only one news story. Even when the following days brought many compelling stories, editors emphasized similar stories in their respective news organizations because editors applied similar sets of news values—values they developed through years of experience communicating with their audiences. As the days went by, many perspectives surrounding the Capitol riots emerged. Using their news judgment, journalists filed thousands of stories with local and national angles, focusing on the significant and interesting details.

News judgment is a learned art. Journalists select stories from the many events and issues happening locally and globally. These stories inform, educate or entertain readers, viewers or listeners. Editors determine the angle or element of the story that is most important to their audiences.

2.1 News Characteristics and News Elements

Newsworthiness and cultural conventions vary from small towns to metropolitan areas. Although no single definition acknowledges all the factors affecting the selection process, journalists agree that news stories possess certain values.

Most journalists say that newsworthy stories possess the classic news values (or news elements) of timeliness, impact or magnitude, prominence, proximity, unusualness, and conflict.

Bottled water is delivered to a fire station in Flint, Michigan. Lawsuits regarding the state's and city's roles in the water crisis continue to be filed.

2.1.1 Timeliness

News is so named because it is new information about an issue or event that has just happened (a rioter was sentenced today to almost five years in jail for assaulting police) or that is new to audiences (the announcement of a festival). Reporters stress current information—stories occurring today or yesterday, not several days or weeks ago—and report it accurately. For example, residents of Flint, Michigan, wanted up-to-the-minute information on why the water in their homes was brown and what the health ramifications were for their families. They looked to journalists to tell them where to buy bottled water, how lead had poisoned the water, how long they would be without tap water and who was responsible for the crisis.

Radio, TV and the web are ideal media for publishing the latest information while newspapers and magazines offer new, in-depth information with more developed angles and added content. No matter the medium, reporters always look for fresh angles and new details to build their stories. They feature the newest information early in the story and keep older, background information to a minimum, weaving it throughout or adding it at the end.

Sometimes events from long ago can become newsworthy again because of some new development or discovery. King Richard III of England died in the Battle of Bosworth Field in 1485. He was buried in a friary in Leicester, but after the friary was dissolved, the location of his grave was lost for centuries. In 2012, archeologists launched a search for Richard's grave. They found a likely grave, and in 2013, DNA tests confirmed it was Richard's body. The discovery of the long-lost grave and Richard III's eventual reburial were worldwide news.

Journalism students often want to borrow ideas from existing stories. However, the original idea has lost its timeliness and is no longer new to the public. And "borrowing" is a slippery slope. In addition to borrowing other people's ideas, students may be tempted to use or paraphrase quotes from a published story or press release. This practice is unethical if it appears as though the student interviewed the source. It is plagiarism if they present the idea or work as their own and do not attribute it to the original reporter or news source.

The reburial of the remains of King Richard III drew a number of celebrities, including actor Benedict Cumberbatch accompanied by Canon Mike Harrison.

2.1.2 Impact or Magnitude

Journalists choose stories that affect (impact) large numbers of people (magnitude). The Russian invasion of Ukraine affects many countries and people around the world as the United States and NATO allies call up thousands of troops. The invasion is the largest military operation in Europe since the end of World War II. At stake are the safety of democracy in other countries around the world and the safety of the civilians and soldiers caught in the war. The importance of the Ukraine war is magnified by its impact on the U.S. economy and the world economy. The prices of oil and wheat—commodities that come from both Russia and Ukraine—soared in the wake of the invasion, pushing already high inflation rates even higher.

In another example, the forecast of the largest-ever snowstorm on the U.S. East Coast is more newsworthy than the story of a snowfall in Buford, Wyoming, with a population of one, because more families and friends are involved. Similarly, a new federal law releasing thousands of inmates across the country affects more people than a judge's ruling on a divorce.

2.1.3 Prominence

Unless that divorce involves the president of the United States. People want to know what is happening with their government representatives. Routine events can become newsworthy when they involve prominent individuals, such as state senators, business leaders or celebrities. The termination of Britney Spears' conservatorship made headline news; yet, other people have conservatorships that are not as public. And, for example, if a classmate appeared drunk at a party and stated that cocaine ought to be legalized, it would not be as newsworthy as it would if your governor did so. That's a double whammy.

Anniversaries are common, but when Queen Elizabeth II observed her 70th year as the British Sovereign, the event attracted worldwide attention. Here, the queen; Prince Louis of Cambridge; Catherine, Duchess of Cambridge; Princess Charlotte of Cambridge; Prince George of Cambridge; and Prince William, Duke of Cambridge watch a flyover from the balcony of Buckingham Palace in London as part of the celebration.

Ordinary people may become prominent when they are involved in a news event. When a crime is committed or an accident occurs, the media may name the adult suspects or victims. Once the story runs through a news cycle and is no longer considered newsworthy, the subject's status usually diminishes. The Elizabethan phrase "nine-days wonder" and Andy Warhol's reference to "15 minutes of fame" refer to short-lived publicity. The news story might be short-lived to audiences, but it might have a life-long effect on the people involved; therefore, journalists treat subjects with sensitivity.

2.1.4 Proximity

Proximity may be geographic or psychological. In terms of the former, an event becomes more newsworthy the more local it is. Readers, viewers and listeners are most interested in and affected by stories about their own communities and people they know. The sexual abuse allegations against the University of Michigan's former sports physician Robert Anderson and the resulting settlement of almost $500 million with more than 1,000 victims was covered more extensively—with more in-depth stories and for a longer period of time—in Michigan than in other parts of the United States and the world. Residents in other states were interested in the event, but not as likely to be personally affected as those in Michigan. Although other news organizations did not publicize up-to-the-minute events as they unfolded, they found local angles to connect their communities to the tragedy, such as a resident who had gone to the University of Michigan or the relative of a victim.

Psychological proximity refers to an emotional connection to an event. Individuals separated by thousands of miles but sharing a characteristic or an interest may want to know more about each other. For example, millions of parents and grandparents across the country felt a connection to the parents of the 19 children killed by a shooter at the Robb Elementary School in Uvalde, Texas. They empathize with the grief of the Uvalde parents, and they want to know what can be done to prevent such tragedies. Similarly, audiences throughout the world are riveted to news stories about the coronavirus and young children because they also have families and worry about their children's health. Christians all over the globe have similar beliefs and rituals. College students everywhere often have similar concerns.

2.1.5 Unusualness

Deviations from the norm—unexpected or unusual events, drama or change—are more newsworthy than the commonplace. A story of a robber who returned a victim's Apple 6 iPhone because it was too old is more newsworthy than one about a robber who simply stole a phone.

Journalists are alert for the unusual twists in otherwise mundane stories. For example, fires might receive only a brief mention if there is no significant damage and no one is harmed. However, the circumstances surrounding a house fire in rural Pennsylvania captured attention: A member of a conservative religious sect set the fire to punish three people from his church because he thought they were sinners. In an editor's mind, this story does not occur every day, and it was front-page news.

Some critics say that the emphasis on the unusual gives audiences a distorted view of the world. They say that the media fail to portray the lives of normal people on a typical day in a typical community. Editors respond that, because it is impossible to cover every piece of news, they report issues requiring the public's attention. Even so, journalists also report on more common events, such as first-line responders helping others in need, organizations striving to provide KN95 masks and restaurant openings during the pandemic.

2.1.6 Conflict

Conflict is apparent when people have different points of view. Their reasons for disagreeing about a social issue or government policy are more informative than the reasons of people who agree on everything. Conflict among government officials or agencies, private organizations or individuals often provides readers, viewers and listeners with different opinions about issues or resolutions that might affect them. Furthermore, it makes a story more interesting.

Conflict may also be internal to an individual. The student secretly living out of her car while working her way through college may face personal challenges and time and resource conflicts. A war amputee may struggle to live her life differently from before the war. In each of these stories, the conflict can be positive. Conflict can exist in any story.

2.1.7 Other Characteristics

Dozens of other factors affect journalists' selection of news and their efforts to inform, educate or entertain audiences. You probably recognize the following types of news stories.

- Reporters look for humorous stories—anything that will make the audience laugh.
- They report straightforward events—storms, forest fires, hostage situations—to help audiences learn more about what is happening in the community and elsewhere.
- They investigate complex issues that affect individuals and communities, such as the personal risks and social benefits of eating at restaurants during the pandemic. Journalists use their professional training to gather, sift through, organize and clearly explain complicated phenomena, such as the various types of coronavirus vaccines and each new coronavirus strain that appears. The internet and data journalism skills help them access and analyze information to present it concisely, and their ability to identify and interview people affected differently by an issue brings the data to life.

2.1.8 The Nature of the Medium and the Community

Other news characteristics are shaped by the type of medium. Printed daily newspapers emphasize local events occurring during the last 24 hours but provide updates on their website. Large metropolitan dailies cover their communities but may also include extensive national and international coverage. Weekly community newspapers focus on local news that has happened in the last seven days. Some weekly news magazines report events of national interest in more depth and explain an event's significance; others summarize interesting and important news events that happened in the past week. Television reports headline news—pertinent information about the day's major stories. Broadcasters also favor visual stories (ones with strong, dramatic pictures) over stories that are complicated and difficult to illustrate. Commercial radio reports the news in a few sentences. Public television and radio often give news more airtime to cover stories in greater depth, with documentary shows like "Frontline" or in-depth interview shows like "Fresh Air." All types of news organizations use social media to share quick updates on breaking news. Journalists tweet a new story in 280 characters, and they blog to add fresh perspectives on the beat they cover.

A news organization's size and the community it serves also influence news selection. A news organization in a small town may report several local traffic accidents; one in a medium-sized city may cover only those that cause serious injury; and one in a big city may report only those that involve the death of a prominent person. Community or weekly newspapers often publish news of all sports events, from elementary to high school competitions, and every wedding and engagement announcement. Metropolitan newspapers may report only professional and major college sports teams and may be more selective about what social announcements they publish, if any.

News organizations also develop tendencies and traditions to emphasize some types of news stories over others. The New York Post traditionally focuses on crime, sports and photographs and is more New York-centric. The New York Times, which appeals to a wealthier, and/or more educated audience than the Post, places a greater emphasis on political and business national and foreign news.

Many people subscribe to several news sources to get comprehensive news. Their community newspaper and local TV offer local news; the nearby metropolitan newspaper and website provide state and regional news; and national news organizations, such as the Wall Street Journal, USA Today or National Public Radio, cover events unfolding across the United States and in other countries.

High school sports may receive little coverage from metropolitan newspapers or television stations. For smaller news organizations, however, they are major events. An example is this match between two Berks County, Pennsylvania, high school volleyball teams. Berks Catholic High School's Michaela Rosenberger, left, and MacKenzie Givens block a shot by Wilson High School's Shana Hunter during the county's semifinals.

2.2 Types of News

Journalists recognize two major types of news: hard and soft. "Hard news" usually refers to serious and timely stories about important topics that inform or educate. These stories may describe an accident, major crime, fire, speech or press conference. Journalists sometimes call hard news "spot news" (reporting it on the spot), "straight news" (not fluff), or "breaking news" (events occurring or "breaking" now).

"Soft news" usually refers to feature or human-interest stories. Soft news entertains as well as informs; it may make readers laugh or cry, love or hate, envy or pity. Soft news might be a profile of a local person who has risen to prominence or a story about an unusual hobby (teaching dogs to "talk"), a "how to" (have a successful job interview), home decor (front-yard snow sculptures) or history (the first newspaper in the state was started in your town). Although still newsworthy, soft news often is less timely than breaking news. Consequently, editors can delay soft stories to make room for more timely items. See Table 2.1 for examples of

TABLE 2.1 APPLYING THE ELEMENTS OF NEWS

Element	Example
Timeliness	Rioters scaled the walls of the U.S. Capitol today in an attempt to stop Congress from counting electoral votes that confirmed Joe Biden as president-elect.
Impact or magnitude	A mob made up of 2,000 to 2,500 Trump supporters from different parts of the country hunted lawmakers and looted offices at the U.S. Capitol.
Prominence	President Joe Biden marked the one-year anniversary of the Jan. 6 insurrection on the U.S. Capitol by telling Americans that "Democracy was attacked."
	In a press conference aired on all major networks, Biden said, "You can't love your country only when you win," referring to Donald Trump's ungracious response to his defeat at the polls and subsequent rallying of protesters. "Democracy is not about our personal interests and winning at the polls, but our efforts at uniting people together as patriots in our great country."
Proximity	Fourteen men from [your state] were arrested and charged in the Jan. 6 riots at the U.S. Capitol.
Unusualness	A rioter known as QAnon Shaman carried a spear and wore face paint, a furry hat with horns and no shirt and he bellowed as rioters confronted police and forced their way into the Senate Chamber.
Conflict	It is ironic that 57 candidates running for public office were among the mob that tried to stop the electoral process and injure lawmakers, reporters and 138 police officers.
Hard news	A Florida man was sentenced to almost 5 years in jail for assaulting police officers and storming the Capitol building on Jan. 6.
	"It has to be made clear that trying to violently overthrow the government, trying to stop the peaceful transition of power, and assaulting law enforcement officers in that effort is going to be met with absolutely certain punishment," said U.S. District Judge Tanya S. Chutkan.
Soft news	The peaceful transition of power for the sake of the country has long been a hallmark of patriotism in our democratic society.

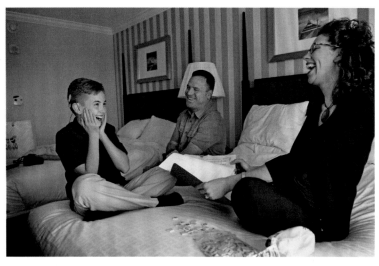

Neil Maes (left) prepares for the Scripps National Spelling Bee with the help of his parents, Peter and Christy. Eleven-year-old Maes, who is deaf, uses bilateral cochlear implants and other assistive devices in his spelling competitions. Stories on Maes' experience are examples of soft news pieces.

 HOT TIP

Public Journalism

In covering public affairs, or civic events and issues, reporters engage audiences in public debate by asking the following questions, sometimes called the five W's and H. The why and how of a story sometimes are not confirmed until later:

● **Who** is involved, cares, is affected, needs to be included, has a stake, is missing from this discussion?

● **What** happened, are the consequences, does it mean to citizens, would this accomplish, values are at work?

● **When** did this happen, were things different, can things be different, should talk lead to action?

● **Where** did it happen, are we headed, is the common ground, should debate take place, is the best entry point for citizens?

leads for hard and soft news stories, as well as the other characteristics discussed so far in this chapter.

2.3 The Concept of Objectivity

News stories are not opinion pieces nor editorials. News stories must be objective in the sense that they report actions, words or situations without commenting on them. Journalists gather information and report it as accurately as possible. If an issue is controversial, they interview representatives of all groups affected and include as many views as possible. Some sources may make mistakes, and some may lie. Journalists may point out inconsistencies or inaccuracies in sources' statements, but they should not call people liars.

Some criticize this approach as "both-sides-ism," a practice of including opposing or contrary points of view in stories where there is, in fact, little controversy. The leading example of this is reporting about climate change. Scientists who study the climate are nearly unanimous in agreeing that Earth is getting warmer and the cause of this is human activity, specifically burning fossil fuels like oil and coal. Lobbyists and public relations executives for industries that produce or rely on fossil fuels have tried to persuade the public and news organizations that climate change is controversial. It is not. Journalists do not need to give credence to opinions that are clearly contrary to the facts.

Biases, whether intentional or not, often appear in a story when a reporter covers only one side of an issue or gives one side more space or time than others. By going beyond one or two sources and treating all sides of an issue fairly, journalists provide their audiences with the facts they need to understand a story more fully. Total objectivity is an ideal; nonetheless, balance and fairness can be achieved through thorough reporting and clear writing.

There is a difference between being accurate and being truthful and journalists strive for both. Stories can be accurate with their facts but need context for better understanding about a situation or to be truthful.

Journalists also need to interview representatives of the community's diverse groups, such as race, ethnicity, gender, age and those with disabilities. Policies and issues affect various groups differently. Their stories need to be told so that the public has a more complete understanding of a situation or the ramifications of a proposed public program.

Routine newsroom practices encourage impartiality. For example, several reporters may contribute information to a story another reporter writes. Several editors may then evaluate and edit the story. Team members serve as checks on one another: If one expresses a subconscious bias in a story or omits important points of view, another has a chance to detect and eliminate the error.

Objectivity is important in public affairs, or civic, journalism. Public journalism is based on a fundamental concept of democracy espoused by former president James Madison: By participating in the governing of themselves, people preserve democracy. To achieve this kind of democracy, the press must inform the citizenry. This process allows the public to decide what is important. Professor Jay Rosen, a leading advocate of public journalism, has a philosophy about the field's

- **Why** did it happen, is this happening, do we need discussion, are things not happening, should we care?

- **How** did it happen, does it affect civic life, did the community cope, does my story encourage action or help the public decide?

proper task: Journalists should do what they can to support public life. The press should help citizens participate in public life and take them seriously when they do. It should create and nourish the sort of public talk some might call a deliberative dialogue. Most important, perhaps, journalists must see hope as an essential resource that they cannot deplete indefinitely without costs to the community.

To accomplish these goals, journalists must listen to all voices, not just the loudest, and listen particularly to those people whose views on issues fall near the center, not just those at the extremes. The routine five W and H questions (who, what, when, where, why and how) work well, but they may not be the only ones to ask (Refer to Hot Tip, p. 22).

Reporters explore the layers of civic life in their communities and are aware of the different

Citizens rely on journalists to inform them about the ideas and actions of public officials. Here, Senate Minority Leader Mitch McConnell, R-Ky., heads back to his office after talking to reporters.

neighborhoods because people in these areas may have various experiences and opinions regarding issues. Finally, reporters identify the community leaders who can be engaged as sources. Community leaders are not limited to elected officials: Private citizens can also be knowledgeable sources regarding issues facing a community.

2.4 What Is Not Newsworthy?

Reporters recognize what information is newsworthy as well as what is not. They rarely mention routine or expected procedures, such as that a city council met in a city hall and began its meeting with the Pledge of Allegiance or that a church group ended its meeting with a prayer. They also delete the obvious and the irrelevant, for example, that police officers rushed to the scene of a traffic accident or that an ambulance carried the injured to a hospital. In most of the following cases, journalists ask themselves if the information is central to the story.

2.4.1 Offensive Details

Editors generally omit material that is obscene, gruesome or in poor taste, usually on the grounds that their stories reach children as well as adults. There is no reason to show grisly photographs or video of a victim if the story's purpose is to bring attention to yet another car accident at a particular intersection with a broken traffic light, for example. Normally, news organizations avoid specifics about sexual assaults and omit most graphic or bloody details about accidents because they do not add to the point of the story.

2.4.2 Sensationalism

Most news organizations avoid sensationalism but not sensational stories. Historically, the word "sensationalism" has described an emphasis on or exaggeration of stories dealing with crime, sex and oddities. However, some events— presidential assassinations, wars and disasters—are inherently sensational and legitimate news.

Journalists evaluating a potentially sensational story, or potentially scandalous information to include within a story, ask themselves the following questions:

- Is the story newsworthy and important to the community? If so, how?
- Does each piece of information add to the reason for writing the story?
- Does the public need and have a right to this information?
- Whom will this story or piece of information help, and how many?
- Whom will this story or piece of information harm, and how many?
- How will people react to the information?

2.4.3 Rumors

Social media gaffes have reinforced the need for professional journalists. Anyone can tweet a comment or rumor—if it is repeated enough times, some people assume it must be true. Journalists do not assume; instead, they investigate the veracity of rumors. If they find no evidence that one is true, they usually conclude that there is no story. However, editors may decide that a story exposing a prevalent false rumor will be more helpful to the people involved (by clearing a person's reputation) or the community (by eliminating general anxiety) than if they remained silent. If a rumor is true and important to the public, editors may run it as a well-researched story.

Rumors or inaccuracies creep into news stories when reporters cover rapidly breaking stories. At one point during its coverage of the shooting at the Sandy Hook Elementary School in Newtown, Connecticut, The New York Times reported that the school principal had allowed the shooter to enter the school because she recognized him. That statement was attributed to an unnamed law enforcement official. In fact, the gunman shot his way into the school. The Times later said it should not have reported a statement from an unnamed law enforcement official.

2.4.4 Sexual Assault

Most news organizations refuse to identify victims of sexual assault, even when they have a legal right to do so. Some journalists believe that publishing the names of victims may discourage others from reporting assaults.

2.4.5 Names of Juveniles

The news media generally do not identify juveniles accused or convicted of a crime unless they are tried as adults for a serious offense, such as murder. In many cases, the names are withheld until authorities have filed charges and prosecutors have decided to try juvenile defendants as adults. However, high-profile mass shootings receive so much media attention that the victims and shooters often are quickly identified.

2.4.6 Trade Names

Some editors hesitate to mention trade names because they think it is unnecessary and provides free advertising for the products. Although specific names can add detail, which is important to a story, reporters should use generic names unless a trade name is pertinent or helps readers gain understanding. "Soft drink" is an acceptable generic term for Dr Pepper, "energy drink" for Red Bull or Monster. Similarly, a journalist should report that someone used a "tissue" rather than a Kleenex. Other trademarked names that are commonly used to describe all brands in their product category include Velcro, Breathalyzer, Seeing Eye Dog, Crock-Pot, Jacuzzi, Bubble Wrap, Jet Ski and Onesie.

Kyle Rittenhouse of Antioch, Illinois, was 17 when he shot three men, killing two of them, during civil unrest in Kenosha, Wisconsin. News organizations usually do not publish the names of juvenile suspects in crimes. In this case, Rittenhouse was tried as an adult because of the seriousness of the crimes. In this photo, Rittenhouse reacts to the jury's verdict finding him not guilty of all charges.

2.5 The Importance of Accuracy

Errors affect the public's perception of the media and ultimately the media's credibility with the public. Editors, instructors and the public do not tolerate sloppiness of any kind, and they are particularly critical of errors in spelling, names and facts because there is rarely any excuse for them. Reporters who repeatedly submit stories with errors may be suspended or fired and have a hard time finding another job.

2.5.1 Accuracy in Facts

Professional journalists do their best to report the news as fairly and accurately as possible. And they do a good job: The information appearing daily in the various media across the globe is overwhelmingly accurate. Imagine all the facts that are in all the stories on all the pages and websites of all news outlets. That's a lot of good reporting! Still, errors do get reported, and they can hurt the people involved in a story.

Carelessness, laziness and hurrying through a story cause the most factual errors. After finishing a news story, reporters must recheck their notes to be sure every detail is accurate. Journalists never guess or assume the facts. They should also check the veracity of their sources' quotes. If they lack some information, they consult their sources again. If the sources are unavailable or unable to provide the information, reporters may have to delete portions of the story or, in extreme cases, stop the entire story.

"Fake news" has become a catch-all phrase that frequently is used incorrectly. A candidate for presidency used the term in attempts to discredit news outlets and stories he did not like. Journalists do not participate in fake news or alternative facts, which is deliberate misinformation. They do not use quotes from sources in their stories without checking the information and the reliability of the source. Their job is to pursue accuracy; otherwise, mistakes can lead to incorrect labels of "fake news" or "alternative facts."

Journalists research and learn a topic in order to write about it. Too often when students are asked about a fuzzy sentence or paragraph, they respond, "I really didn't understand that myself." If the reporter does not understand something they have written, neither will the audience. Reporters who do not understand information return to their source and ask for a better explanation or find a source who can explain it.

Journalists also use words they know. Sometimes students incorrectly repeat words or phrases they do not understand but have obtained from a document, website or interview. For example, if a reporter uses the word "decibel," then they should know exactly how loud a decibel is in order to put the word into context for audiences.

Accurate writing requires specifics instead of generalities. Getting specifics requires more effort, but in the end the story will be clearer, more accurate and more interesting to readers, viewers and listeners. Journalists ask sources, "How do you know?" and they ask for examples. The response may provide additional sources for information.

Reporters are vulnerable to misinformation because many people want to publicize their views. Journalists might interview sources who have impressive titles or sound as if they know what they are talking about. But some sources may be ignorant of the facts, and others may lie. The reporter's job is to separate assertions from facts. A news organization's most important asset is its credibility, and journalists protect that asset.

2.5.2 Accuracy in Names

Many people—including the authors of this textbook and, perhaps, you—have something in common: Their names are frequently misspelled. Dozens of names have different spellings, such as Rachael/Rachel, Jason/Jayson and Fredrick/Fredric/Frederic/Frederick. Different cultures spell similar sounding names differently. Some parents employ onomastic creativeness. Reporters confirm the spelling of names and the use of nicknames, even if they need to contact sources again for clarification. Searching for a

Infowars.com, a site managed by Alex Jones, features fake news and conspiracy theories.

name on the internet is not good reporting and has resulted in similar names in similar occupations, but not the person interviewed. Some journalists ask sources to write their name and title, but they always confirm the spelling of both before ending an interview.

Most misspellings anger two sets of people—those who were intended to be named and those who are inadvertently named. Reporters verify the spelling of names of products and organizations, for example, by cross-referencing with a second or third source or calling the business or checking its website.

2.5.3 Accuracy Is a Priority

Some news organizations maintain a fact database composed of names, places, businesses, dates and numbers that have all been verified and reported in prior stories. Their journalists turn to these databases to check similar facts that appear in new stories.

In an effort to eliminate errors, a few editors may give the people named in news stories an opportunity to read and correct the item before publication. Although science writers and other journalists who deal with complex issues often follow this practice, most news organizations prohibit it because sources usually try to change statements they disagree with, not just factual errors. Other editors might ask sources to verify only their statements.

Another practice to prevent errors is to use a checklist such as the one in "The Reporter's Guide to Accuracy" box that follows. Craig Silverman, fake news expert and BuzzFeed's media editor, has led accuracy workshops at The Poynter Institute and encourages journalists to compose a best practices "to-do" list for their news writing. After all, airline pilots review a checklist before every takeoff and travelers often use a checklist for packing.

Guest Columnist

Why I Stayed at a Small-Town Newspaper

BY SUE HADDEN

I'm one of the lucky ones. After 35 years, I still actually enjoy coming to work.

That's because I work for a small-town newspaper (circulation 9,000) that cares about its community. Every single day, my fellow newsroom employees and I have a brand-new chance to inform, to inspire and to bring a smile to those who read The Record Herald.

I interview a lot of college graduates eager to land their first jobs. When I ask where they envision themselves in the next five years, most say they hope to land a spot on a big-city daily newspaper, move on to a public relations firm or go to work at a glossy magazine.

That's sad . . . not just for them, but also for small-town journalism.

I grew up in the town that is today such a vital part of my life. Like those fresh graduates, I had my eyes focused on big horizons when I set out to make my mark on the world. But a marriage, a daughter and lots of pleasure trips to far-off places big and small convinced me that the grass is pretty green in my own backyard.

My 17 years as a beat reporter gave me the opportunity to meet people and walk into environments I never knew existed, to ferret out violations of the open records law, to expose skullduggery in public office and to write about wrongs that needed to be righted.

It also gave me the opportunity to spotlight the small-town heroes who quietly meet the needs of those less fortunate, to bring a smile with just three paragraphs and to put everyday people on the front page.

When I learned about an asthmatic who lived in public housing and couldn't afford an air conditioner, I picked up the phone and talked with a human services worker with whom I was on a first-name basis. Now our town has a program that provides fans and air conditioners to the less fortunate.

A story about the poor attendance records of several members of the school board led to an overhaul at election time.

I got to write a feature story about the long-retired fourth-grade teacher who had inspired me to become a writer . . . returning the favor by telling her story using the words she taught me to love.

After an industry that had been in town for more than a century announced plans to build elsewhere, readers told me my commentary captured the emotions of losing an icon that had given employment to grandfathers, fathers, husbands and sons.

It concerns me that fewer and fewer young writers are interested in "paying their dues" at small-town papers like this one. It concerns me even more to see the brightest of them leave for higher-paying jobs in bigger places where they'll go from being hometown writers to just another cog in a very big wheel.

Who will write and edit local stories 20 years from now? I fear it will be fleeting journalists who will have very little connection to this community, its history, its places and its people.

The opportunities are huge for those who manage to "catch" small-town journalism fever. At a small paper, you can learn all there is to know about interviewing, writing, layout, photography and copy editing. You have a really good chance of seeing your byline on the front page each and every day.

Complete strangers will feel comfortable about picking up the phone and calling you to offer criticism, advice and tips, and perhaps set you straight on something you missed.

A publisher once told me a good newspaper is one that is in conversation with the community it serves.

I worry that conversation will one day turn to deafening silence.

Sue Hadden worked for 36 years as a staff writer and then editor for The Record Herald in her hometown of Waynesboro, Pennsylvania, until her retirement.

The Reporter's Guide to Accuracy

While Reporting

- Ask sources to spell or write down their names and titles; verify the spellings.
- Record or transcribe interviews.
- When someone cites numbers, ask for (and check) the source.
- Ask, "How do you know that?"
- Seek documentation.
- Verify claims with reliable sources.
- Save links and other research.
- Ask sources what other reports on the subject are wrong.

While Writing

- Note facts that need further verification (highlight, circle, etc.).

Before Submitting (Final Checks)

- Verify numbers and math (have someone else check your math).
- Check names with more than just your notes and one other source.

- Confirm titles (people, books, places, businesses).
- Validate locations.
- Verify quotes with your notes/recording/transcript.
- Confirm attributions.
- Check definitions.
- Confirm that URLs are correct and that the cited content is still there.
- Call phone numbers.
- Ensure that spelling and grammar are correct.
- Look for spell-checker errors.
- Verify or remove assumptions.
- Consult the original source if you have any doubts.
- Clarify by reading the final copy to someone who understands portions where your understanding is weak.

After Filing

- Correct any errors you found in your archives, databases or other resources you control (but be certain you verified the new information).

Adapted from http://stevebuttry.wordpress.com/2011/01/04/ MY-VERSION-OF-CRAIG-SILVERMANS-ACCURACY-CHECKLIST/. Steve Buttry was the former director of student media at Louisiana State.

 # Review Exercises

After you complete the following exercises, compare your answers with those of your classmates.

1. NEWS JUDGMENT

You are the editor of a news outlet in your city and have space for one more photo. For each of the following pairs, select the image you would use and explain your choice.

1. a. A college student who has gone missing over the weekend.

   or

   b. The first snowfall of the season.

2. a. Typical empty shelves in a grocery story during the pandemic.

   or

   b. The new manager of the largest insurance agency in town.

3. a. Kate Middleton visiting a local hospital.

   or

   b. College students protesting the local university's fourth tuition increase in five years.

4. a. Two students from one of your city's elementary schools participating in the semifinals of a national spelling bee.

 or

 b. Three high school seniors being led away in handcuffs after being charged with causing nearly $80,000 in damage to the school, allegedly by spraying fire extinguishers onto computers and into file cabinets and smashing computer monitors and other equipment.

5. a. A young child in Afghanistan handing a bunch of flowers to a U.S. soldier.

 or

 b. The bodies of an Afghan father and his four children killed in a suicide bombing near an American compound in Afghanistan.

2. NEWSWORTHINESS

Section I

Rank the following stories for your local news outlet as to newsworthy, somewhat newsworthy or not newsworthy. You can assume the stories are current. Be prepared to explain your choices.

1. Thunderstorms and high winds are about to wreak havoc in the community.

2. A large real estate agency in your community has hired two new vice-presidents.

3. The U.S. Department of Education released a report today that shows high school students in your city reached an all-time high in their SAT exam scores.

4. The state approved a plan to build a six-lane bypass around your city that will cost $584 million and destroy thousands of acres of prime agricultural and developable land.

5. A city man was charged in an arson fire that destroyed an apartment building and killed eight people, including five children.

6. FBI investigators have visited the public library in your city to check on the reading records of several local residents who might be linked to terrorism.

7. Three Israelis and 10 Palestinians were killed in a suicide bombing at a bus stop in a suburb of Tel Aviv.

8. The parents of quintuplets in your city saw their five children off to school for the first time, as the three boys and two girls were picked up by a bus that took them to kindergarten.

9. More than 100 people were killed and another 800 injured when a runaway passenger train collided with a freight train in Tanzania.

10. Los Angeles Dodgers star Mookie Betts announces his engagement to long-time love Brianna Hammonds.

11. A new prison facility is being proposed in your area.

Section II

Rank the following stories for your local news outlet as to newsworthy, somewhat newsworthy or not newsworthy. You can assume the stories are current. Be prepared to explain your choices.

1. One of the Jan. 6 rioters is from your city and will be tried for assaulting a police officer with a deadly weapon.

2. Melania Trump's hat auction attracted five bidders and fell $80,000 short of the estimated amount, "a portion" of which was to go to charity.

3. Another self-driving car experiment resulted in a crash. This time it ran off the road and killed a pedestrian in Tulsa, Oklahoma.

4. Police and prison officials in your city were conducting a mock prison escape when three inmates walked out of the prison and disappeared.

5. A new senior citizens' center opened on the east side of the city offering nearby residents a place to get a hot meal at lunchtime, participate in games and educational programs and pass time with friends.

6. Several long-time residents in the city are being deported, including Army veterans, as they are technically undocumented immigrants.

7. An Illinois couple have refused to get the coronavirus vaccination for their children.

8. Your state's Department of Labor and Industry announced today that the unemployment rate rose to 7.5 percent despite a rally that saw significant increases in the stock market.

9. A city police officer was arrested and charged with aggravated assault and using undue force after he broke the leg of a man who was attending a concert. The officer who was on duty patrolling the stadium parking lot mistook the man for a scalper, got into an argument with him and threw him to the ground.

10. A group of teenagers from a nondenominational church youth organization volunteered to help two elderly sisters maintain their home so that they would not be fined by the city for having a blighted property. The youths mowed grass, trimmed hedges and painted the sisters' house.

Section III

Danneisha Richards, a 52-year-old businessperson in your city, today announced that she is running for mayor. You know and can prove all the following facts, but you have never reported them because she was a private citizen. Which ones would you include in your announcement story?

1. Richards is a cancer survivor.

2. At the age of 17, Richards and two friends were charged with stealing a car. The charges were dropped because the car was recovered undamaged and the car's owner, a neighbor, declined to prosecute.

3. Richards established, owns and manages the city's largest chain of furniture stores.

4. Richards has diabetes.

5. Richards has been divorced three times and is now married to Nyasia Nassif.

6. Each year, she donates more than $1 million to local charities that help troubled young women, but always avoids publicity and insists that the charities never mention her donations.

7. Richards is a recovering alcoholic; she has not had a drink in 20 years.

8. Before going into business for herself, Richards was fired from two other jobs because of her drinking.

9. Richards' campaign literature says she attended the University of Dubai, yet you find that she never graduated.

10. Various tax and other public records reveal that her chain of furniture stores is valued at $20 million and, last year, earned a profit of $2.3 million.

Section IV

One of your state representatives, Manuel Sanchez, was involved in a car crash that resulted in the death of another driver and his passenger. Sanchez had minor injuries. Which of the following details would you use in a story on the incident and which would you discard?

1. Sanchez is married and has two children from different marriages.

2. As an attorney, Sanchez successfully defended two people who had been accused of vehicular manslaughter.

3. Sanchez was speeding and ran a red light.

4. A woman, who didn't want to be identified, called your newsroom and said the minivan she and her children were riding in was almost struck at an intersection one time by a car driven by Sanchez.

5. Friends of Sanchez said he often joked about having a "lead foot."

6. Police said alcohol was not a variable in this crash.

7. Sanchez has had five tickets in the past four years for speeding and reckless driving.

8. Sanchez was first elected to office nine years ago.

9. The driver of the other car often said he did not vote for Sanchez.

10. Two people called police in response to the incident to accuse Sanchez of sexual harassment.

NEWSWRITING STYLE

Journalism is nonfiction storytelling to a large audience with varied interests, education levels, ethnicities, ages, genders and other demographics.

With their good news judgment and audience in mind, journalists identify immediately the importance of a story and its supporting elements. They then communicate how the event is significant to the individual. They present complex information in a way that allows almost everyone to understand it easily. Furthermore, their writing makes audiences want to continue reading, watching or hearing the story.

Journalists achieve this goal by using a common newswriting style. This method lets them present factual information accurately, succinctly and clearly. It also ensures that they follow basic reporting principles to separate fact from opinion while being inclusive and seeking a diversity of voices affected by issues and events.

The following story is written in newswriting style from facts gathered by the reporter. It is clear about something that happened. Can you see why this event might be important to audiences?

A third robbery this month at University Apartments on Washington Street has tenants worried about their safety and building security.

Two thieves with nylon stocking face masks stole a cell phone, a computer, high-end gaming headsets and other items at about 11 p.m. Tuesday, according to Police Sgt. Katharine Jordan.

"This has never happened to me before, and it's frightening," said Marquis Williams, who was away from his apartment at the time of the break-in. "I thought a deadbolt would keep my stuff and me safe."

The thieves fled in a dark blue or black Charger. Police continue to investigate. Their tip line is 218-555-HELP.

CNN's Don Lemon reviews his story before going on air.

3.1 Simplify Words, Sentences and Paragraphs

A major part of newswriting style is simple and concrete language. George Orwell, in his classic "Politics and the English Language," complained that too often writers use abstract phrases. Abstractions obscure facts and confuse people. Having to guess or untangle the vague meaning of a word or phrase can frustrate readers and viewers. This confusion may cause them to miss important information or stop and turn away from a story.

Journalists also refrain from packing too many ideas into a single sentence. Too much information all at once can cause additional confusion or missed information. By the time readers get to the end of the sentence, they may have forgotten the information at the beginning or missed the point of the information altogether. Consider the following example:

> The mayor said she was happy that the city council had passed the long-awaited resolution to increase the town's public library tax to provide more economic funding to expand the library's book collection, to remodel its outdated website to make it more inclusively accessible and to add a new wing to house government documents, but that the amount of the increase was not enough to do everything that has to be done because repairs are needed to the roof of the public library building and facilities must be improved for patrons with disabilities.

Now read the revised, clearer version:

> The mayor said she was happy the city council passed the resolution increasing the public library tax, but that it was not enough to do everything needed.

> The increase will provide funds to expand the library's book collection, update the website for accessibility and add a new wing to house government documents, she said. Other needed work includes repairs to the library's roof and building access for patrons with disabilities.

Journalists use short sentences and short paragraphs. They focus on one idea within a sentence or even a paragraph. They rewrite long or awkward sentences and divide them into shorter ones that are easier to read and understand. Research consistently has found a strong correlation between readability and sentence length: The longer the sentence, the more difficult it is to understand. Put another way, more words mean more things to remember and connect.

A survey found that 75 percent of readers understood sentences containing an average of 20 words. Comprehension dropped rapidly as the sentences became longer. This statistic does not mean all stories should have only short sentences. Too many short sentences strung together makes the writing sound choppy. Long sentences, constructed well and used sparingly, can be effective tools for the writer. Moreover, sentences that vary in length make the writing more interesting. Kayla Nelsen, a reporter for GreatLakesEcho, wrote the following lead for a story on a recent U.S. immigration bill and its effect on international students enrolled at U.S. universities.

> 1-20 forms. I-94 forms. Tax filing forms. Visa fees.
>
> And more.
>
> For international students wanting to study in the United States, there is a lot more to the admission process than the common application, standardized testing or even financial aid forms that domestic students must do.

Notice the construction of these sentences, each of which is a paragraph. One is nine words, another is only two and the third is 35. The combination creates a vivid picture for the reader, as well as a rhythm that introduces drama. The following excerpt is another example from the same story. Its sentences are 26 words, 9 words and 29 words respectively. It continues with a direct quote.

> The bill also provides funds for educational institutions to implement programs that make it easier for international graduates to study in the United States.
>
> However, this might not be enough for some students.
>
> Emmanuel Kodua, a first-year student majoring in computer science who moved from Ghana, said he would like to see policies that address the financial struggles of international students.

Journalists write for the eye and also the ear, listening to the natural flow of the words and sentences they write. They test their stories by reading them aloud to themselves or to a friend. If the sentences sound awkward or unsuitable for a conversation, reporters rewrite them to eliminate complex phrases and long or awkward sentences. They also remove ambiguities and vague terms by being direct and factual.

One way to keep sentences short, clear and conversational is to use standard word order: subject, verb and direct object.

Another way to keep sentences short is to check that each sentence contains related ideas. If not, parts can be eliminated or go elsewhere in the story.

Notice how explicit and concise the following sentence becomes when the writer removes extraneous information and uses the standard word order of subject, verb and direct object.

in other words

cubic containment system

misapplication elimination device

follicle redistribution mechanism

vermin de-infestation apparatus

horizontal tranquility terminal

© John Atkinson, Wrong Hands • wronghands1.com

About 1,300 complaints were received by the FCC for the performance by Shakira and Jennifer Lopez, although it was the first to have two Latinas perform and to celebrate women and Latin music was the purpose, because the Super Bowl's 2021 halftime show was considered offensive by many.

Revised: The FCC received 1,300 complaints that Shakira and Jennifer Lopez's performance at Super Bowl 2021 was offensive.

Words that form sentences should flow smoothly, and the sentences that form paragraphs also should flow together, logically combining similar thoughts or ideas.

The common practice in journalism is to start a new paragraph with each shift in topic, no matter how slight. Paragraphs in news stories often are one sentence because nothing more is needed to get a point across. But ideas that are related or belong together should not be artificially separated just to create shorter paragraphs. Needlessly separating ideas can yield choppy writing.

Another reason to write in short paragraphs is that large, dense blocks of text discourage readers. That was true when people mainly read printed newspapers, but it is true for online text, too. Short paragraphs are best also when writing for audio or video. Journalists divide stories into bite-sized chunks that are easy to read, hear and understand.

3.2 Eliminate Unnecessary Words

Unnecessary words confuse audiences and make reading and listening more difficult. Journalists use brevity to help people grasp the main idea of a story and retain enough detail to make stories interesting and informative. Some words— "that," "then," "currently," "now" and "presently," for example—are almost always unnecessary. Writers who use two or more words when only one is needed waste time and space. For instance, eliminate redundant words referring to time, such as "*past* history," "is *now*" and "*future* plans."

Notice how easily unnecessary words can be deleted from the following sentences without changing their meaning:

- ~~Fatalities seem more common in that~~ one out of 100 Americans 65 and older ~~have perished~~ ∧ *die* from COVID-19.

- The architect ~~made an assessment of damages of~~ ∧ *assessed* $30 million ∧ *in damage* ~~or more~~ related to the attack on the U.S. Capitol.

🔥 HOT TIP

Simplify Language

To simplify stories, avoid long, unfamiliar words. Whenever possible, substitute common shorter and simpler ones (known as nickel-and-dime words) that convey the same meaning, such as the following examples:

"about" not "approximately"

"home" not "residence"

"bruises" not "contusions"

"cuts" not "lacerations"

And to eliminate confusion, keep together words that belong in one phrase:

- She threw ∧ *out* the baby ~~out~~ with the bathwater.

- He picked ∧ *up* the dog ~~up~~ from the kennel.

- Ten people ~~suffered to death from compression asphyxia~~ ^*suffocated* at Travis Scott's ~~tragic~~ concert at Astroworld.

- ~~An estimated 15 million to 26 million~~ ^*About 20 million* people have participated in ~~various~~ George Floyd and Black Lives Matter protests.

- ~~At the present time he is planning~~ ^*He plans* to leave for ~~the state of~~ New York at 3 p.m. ~~in the afternoon next~~ Thursday.

- ~~This is not the first elected office she has held in the city.~~ She ~~also~~ has been a city council member, a member of the library board and a tax collector.

Journalists also eliminate clichés so closely associated with newswriting that they are called "journalese." The term identifies phrases journalists use to dramatize the events they describe. Avoid the following clichés:

fires rage

temperatures soar

earthquakes rumble

floods rampage

developing countries are war-torn, much-troubled or oil-rich

Some words repeat the same idea. The following phrases contain only two or three words, yet at least one—marked in italics—is unnecessary:

true fact	*armed* gunman	*completely* demolished
exactly identical	split *apart*	*brand*-new
hurry *up*	*unexpected* surprise	more *and more*
mutual cooperation	*past* experiences	*fellow* colleague
reason *why*	free *of charge*	circle *around*

Although it is easy to overwrite, journalists try to avoid using too many words when just one or two will do. Here are examples of wordy phrases and their more concise replacements:

reached out to	called/asked
conduct an investigation into	investigate
appoint to the post of	appoint
rose to the defense of	defended
succeed in doing	do
came to a stop	stopped
devoured by flames	burned
shot to death	killed
have a need for	need
made contact with	contacted
proceeded to interrogate	interrogated/questioned
promoted to the rank of	promoted

 HOT TIP

Don't Write Like This

Here are some examples of bad writing from statements made on auto insurance forms. These drivers attempted to summarize the details of their crash in the fewest words possible. Note how the effort to avoid responsibility for their negligence leads the writers to use convoluted constructions.

- Coming home, I drove into the wrong house and collided with a tree I don't have.

- I thought my window was down, but I found out it was up when I put my head through it.

- I collided with a stationary truck coming the other way.

- The guy was all over the road. I had to swerve a number of times before I hit him.

- I pulled away from the side of the road, glanced at my mother-in-law and headed over the embankment.

- In my attempt to kill a fly, I drove into a telephone pole.

- I was on my way to the doctor with rear-end trouble when my universal joint gave way causing me to have engine trouble.

- My car was legally parked as it backed into another vehicle.

- The pedestrian had no idea which way to run, so I ran over him.

- A pedestrian hit me and went under my car.

- As I approached the intersection, a sign suddenly appeared in a place where no stop sign ever appeared before. I was unable to stop in time to avoid the crash.

- I was sure the old fellow would never make it to the other side of the road when I struck him.

- An invisible car came out of nowhere, struck my car and vanished.

- The indirect cause of the crash was a little guy in a small car with a big mouth.

- I was thrown from my car as it left the road. I was later found in a ditch by some stray cows.

- The telephone pole was approaching. I was attempting to swerve out of its way when it struck the front end.

3.3 Accuracy and Context Enhance Truthfulness and Curtail Bias

For most news stories journalists are observers who relate what happened. They are not advocates or participants, except in cases where they are the only ones to help someone in danger of being harmed. They strive to be as impartial as possible, reporting the facts and details of their stories, not their opinions about the issues and events. Journalists express their views only in editorials and commentaries, which are clearly labeled as such.

Reporters can inject bias into a story by the way they choose sources and people to interview. Audiences cannot be certain the story is complete if the sources fail to reflect all sides. This taints the story and the journalist who wrote it and lowers the public's esteem for the news organization and journalism generally. When audience members have all the information, even if it includes reporters' involvement, then they are informed and capable of reaching their own conclusions about issues in the news.

Journalists stick to the facts. They keep their bias out of stories by avoiding loaded words, for example, "extremist," "radical," "fanatic" and "zealot." Such words are often unnecessary and inaccurate. Furthermore, not everyone thinks the same way. A "cute kitty" to some people may be a "nasty-looking tom cat" to others. What is "big" to you might not be big to me. Many times, loaded words state the obvious: An argument was "heated" or a death "unfortunate." Reporters can eliminate the bias in some sentences by simply deleting a single adjective or adverb:

- ~~famous~~ celebrity

- ~~gala~~ reception

- ~~thoughtful~~ reply

Here are two more examples:

Tickets are $5
- ∧ ~~The price of tickets is inexpensive at $5~~.

- The ~~esteemed~~ author will discuss her ~~interesting~~ book at ~~a convenient time,~~ 6 p.m.

Entire sentences sometimes convey opinions, unsupported by facts. Editors (and instructors) will eliminate those statements. Notice how the second sentence in each of the following pairs contains a fact, not a personal view:

Opinion: Parents like the idea of gender-inclusive, or unisex, bathrooms.

Fact: Parents are permitted to accompany their children of the opposite sex to the bathroom.

"Don't editorialize."

CartoonStock.com

Opinion: Prince Andrew was ousted from the royal family because of bad behavior.

Fact: Queen Elizabeth removed Prince Andrew's honorary military appointments and royal patronages a day after a New York judge refused to dismiss a civil sexual assault case against the Duke of York.

Opinion: Biden was mad at Trump.

Fact: Biden said Trump was "cruel" to attempt to repeal the Affordable Care Act, leaving almost 14 million Americans without health insurance.

Journalists are truthful in their reporting. Reporting the facts alone sometimes does not help audiences understand a situation. Adding accurate context provides truthfulness about a situation or issue. For example, if a photographer were to shoot a close-up of a handful of protesters, then it represents the fact that people protested. But we don't know if anyone else cared about the rally. If, however, the photo were to show hundreds of protesters, then audiences have more information about the situation and that lots of people were concerned about a particular issue.

Journalists are careful about facts from someone else. News writers can report the opinions expressed by someone else—the sources for their stories—but must clearly attribute those opinions to the source. If journalists fail to provide the proper attribution, audiences may think the reporters are expressing their own opinions or agreeing with the source. Some reporters also may investigate the veracity or truthfulness of those statements. Consider the following example—the second statement correctly credits the speaker:

Opinion: Obamacare is great.

Fact: The Affordable Care Act, commonly known as Obamacare, lets children stay on their parents' health plans until they are 26, said Ali Hussain, the president of the University Student Senate.

3.4 DEI: Diversity, Equity and Inclusion

When journalists intentionally engage representatives of the diverse groups that comprise a community, audiences can build trust that all people are being represented and informed. A lack of diversity in news coverage weakens content and news judgment and undermines news media credibility.

Journalists practice inclusiveness to tell a complete story of how issues and events affect all community members. They interview representatives of different demographics—race, ethnicity, age, gender, socioeconomic levels and people with disabilities, for example—and choose stories that show varied experiences.

Diverse groups should see and hear themselves in news stories for others to know their experiences. News media that ignore inclusiveness will struggle for survival in an increasingly diverse population.

At the same time as journalists strive to be inclusive in their news coverage, they should avoid generalizing and stereotyping. They do not use offensive, condescending or patronizing terms or phrases in describing other individuals. Good writers are attuned to the "-isms"—racism, sexism, ageism—that can appear in a story even unintentionally. They understand the negative impact their words may have on audiences.

3.4.1 Racism

The Associated Press Stylebook guideline on race-related coverage notes that journalists mention a person's race, religion or ethnic background only when the fact is clearly relevant to a story. Employees at The New York Times are told, "The writer—or the [sources] quoted in the story—must demonstrate the relevance of ethnic background or religion. It isn't enough to assume that readers will find the fact interesting or evocative; experience shows that many will find it offensive and suspect us of relying on stereotypes."

A criminal's race is usually irrelevant to a story. Identifying a criminal by race, when that is the only characteristic known, is especially harmful because it casts suspicion on every member of the race. Henry McNulty, a former associate editor of The Hartford (Connecticut) Courant, explained his paper's policy on racial identification:

> A long-standing Courant policy states that race and sex alone do not constitute an adequate description. For instance, if the only thing a witness tells police is that a "white woman" or "Black man" committed the crime, the Courant will not use any description. Only when such things as height, weight, hair length, scars, clothing and so forth are given will the newspaper print the information.

By that policy, the following description makes appropriate use of a person's race to describe a specific individual whom some audiences might be able to identify:

> Witnesses said the thief was a white man, about 50 years old and 6 feet tall. He weighed about 250 pounds, had long white hair, wore a gray hoodie and blue jeans and escaped on a red Honda motorcycle.

3.4.2 Gender and Sexuality, Sexism

All genders should be treated equally in news stories. Most of the time, a person's gender is not central to a story and does not need to be pointed out. The Associated Press offers guidelines under its gender/sexuality entry and notes that language around gender is evolving.

Reference to male, female, lesbian, gay, bisexual, transgender and questioning or queer and nonbinary people (LGBTQIA+) is included only if it is central to the story. Not every person falls under the same categories when it comes to gender (social designation) and sex (biological determinant). "Transgender" is an umbrella term for people who have an identity different from that which was assigned at birth, while some transgender people have physically transitioned from one gender to another. Nonbinary people might identify as both male and female, or neither male nor female. For pronoun references, AP style recommends using either third-person or a plural pronoun.

Bill O'Reilly, formerly of the Fox News show The O'Reilly Factor, was admonished for comparing Rep. Maxine Waters' [D-Calif.] hair to a "James Brown wig." O'Reilly later apologized for the comment. He was forced out of Fox News a month later after he settled on five sexual harassment accusations.

Journalists use terms for occupations and roles that are gender neutral. They avoid terms such as "fireman," "policeman," "waitress" or "aviatrix." Instead, they use "firefighter," "police officer," "server" and "aviator." The Associated Press Stylebook recommends journalists use "council member," "spokesperson," "chair" or "chairperson," unless specified otherwise by the organization. When in doubt, refer to the AP Stylebook under "gender-neutral language."

People are treated as equals in news stories. Journalists who are writing about a woman ask themselves whether they would write the same words if the subject were a man (and vice versa). A headline that announces "Female Exec Fired" is inappropriate because no journalist would write "Male Exec Fired." Gender is irrelevant to this story, and the wording suggests that it is unusual for a woman to achieve a position of importance and sets a biased tone that perhaps she was fired because of being female. Sexism can go both ways, however. The headline "Male Nurse Runs for Secretary of State" implies that this man's occupation is unusual.

If it is not central to the story, journalists avoid writing about the attire of men or women. The clothing and hairstyles of all genders should be equally interesting or equally unimportant.

Journalists use "woman" or "man" when an adult's gender is important. The words "female" and "male" are too general because they include all ages. "Lady" is a specific class of woman, just as "gentleman" is for a man.

Journalists refer to all people by their first and last names on first reference. The last name is used in subsequent references. First names only are rarely used, except in stories in which multiple members of the same family are quoted as sources, and first names are necessary to clarify who is being quoted.

Too often news stories identify a partner only in relationship to the subject: "The farmer and his wife" does not offer the possibility that she is also a farmer. "Ellen DeGeneres's wife" or "Kanye West's girlfriend" indicates that one person is important and the other is not; it also connotes that the partner is only a possession. Spouses should be identified by first and last names ("Jill Biden," not "Mrs. Joe Biden.")

Journalists eschew using the pronoun "he" as a general reference to men and women. They reword sentences to avoid gender. Or, they use a plural pronoun. Plural pronouns are also used as a singular form to represent a gender-neutral person. The following strategies avoid this problem:

Substitute an article for gender-specific pronouns.

- An architect must always consult ∧ *the* ~~her~~ plans when designing a bridge.

Use no pronoun in place of "he" or "she."

- A nurse will always tell ~~his~~ patients to get some rest.

Substitute plural nouns and pronouns for gender-specific ones.

- ∧ *Journalists* ~~A journalist~~ must check ∧ *their* ~~his or her~~ notes for accuracy.

- Sam Smith's recent concert featured songs from their second album.

Mercury News
@mercnews

Olympics: Michael Phelps shares
historic night with African-American
bayareane.ws/2aQpPhv

8/11/16, 10:02 PM

See a problem with this headline?
Michael Phelps gets his name publicized while Simone Manuel (left)
is not named but is described by
her appearance/ethnicity. Penny
Oleksiak (right), who tied Manuel
for the gold medal in freestyle
swimming, is not mentioned. The
story tries to do too much and
should have been split into two
stories—one featuring Manuel
and "Oleksiak" and the other on
Phelps. The Cosmopolitan article
"The Most Sexist Moments from
the 2016 Olympics (So Far)" details
additional sexist faux pas in the
Olympics coverage.

3.4.3 Ageism

There is no magical line at which one becomes "old." For example, a 60-year-old may be considered a youngster when compared to a centenarian. Standard and Poor's 500 large U.S. companies have boards of directors whose ages average older than 60. Most of their new appointees were between 60 and 69. Many people are active and continue to work into their late 70s and beyond. When asked to describe their health, a majority of older Americans responded "good to excellent." Yet impractical stereotypes suggest they are all lonely, unproductive, unintelligent, poor, passive, weak and sick. They are portrayed as less adaptable and slow learners.

Neither is there a magical line for being "young." Reverse ageism can be if someone is seen as "too young" and not capable.

Journalists avoid using special terms for age. For example, using the word "spry" gives the impression that some older people are unusually active for their age. Using the phrases "fresh out of college" or "youngster" suggests someone lacks competence or good judgment.

Journalists may state someone's age, but they avoid a discussion of the age, unless it is relevant to the story. The fact that a 20-year-old father wins an election should not be treated any differently from the election of a 70-year-old grandmother. Neither one's age, gender nor family situation should appear in the headline nor in the lead of the story.

3.4.4 Avoid Stereotyping Other Groups

Many people with physical and mental disabilities lead active lives and contribute to society professionally and personally. The terms "disabled" and "challenged" have replaced "handicapped." More acceptable is "person with a disability," "person who is blind" and so forth. Such phrasing emphasizes the individual before the condition. As always, reference a disability only if it is relevant to the story.

Religious groups sometimes accuse the media of bias in the portrayal of members of their faiths. Journalists are careful to avoid stereotyping all followers of a faith because of the actions of a few members.

People are often too shy to ask questions about groups different from themselves. Faculty member and former Detroit Free Press journalist Joe Grimm and his students at Michigan State University have written more than 20 guides that start with the title, "100 Questions and Answers about [a different ethnicity, religion, age, occupation, etc.]" to combat stereotypes and help everyone understand more about others. For instance, they just completed a guide on "100 Questions and Answers about Black Churches."

Guest Columnist

Developing Diverse Sources

BY LINDA WHITE

As a reporter you'll be required to cover many different topics in diverse communities. But if you've moved to a new community, how do you develop diverse sources? Part of this means reaching out to diverse communities before the story happens. Here are a couple of recommendations.

You should search out formal organizations in the African American, Asian, Hispanic and Native American communities. These could be the National Association for the Advancement of Colored People, the Southern Christian Leadership Conference, churches, synagogues, temples and other organizations. When you need a diverse source, these organizations can help you find one. Contact them regularly or try to attend meetings to learn what and how issues are impacting them. This is what it means to build a relationship with them. When you gain their trust, they in turn will respect you as a reporter to tell their stories accurately. You may also be able to find and follow these groups on social media. However, going the extra mile means cultivating relationships and even friendships within these communities. Face-to-face conversations, outside of work, will help you as a reporter in the long run. Before you know it, they'll be calling you about issues, providing valuable story ideas.

On your daily assignments, when you're in need of sources, request a person of color first and a woman second. We know from scholarly research that Black, indigenous and people of color (BIPOC) and women have been framed in a stereotypical fashion: African Americans are seen as criminals; Hispanics as undocumented immigrants; Middle Eastern people as terrorists, and so forth. Your audience should learn that people of color are professionals, experts, and have impactful opinions. Their voices matter. When we omit them and how issues impact their communities from the conversation, we're symbolically annihilating them. Symbolic annihilation is a term for dismissing marginalized voices. Additionally framing people of color as angry, poor and unimportant reinforces stereotypes.

A term you should know is "intersectionality." American civil rights advocate Kimberlé Crenshaw coined this term in an article in the late 1980s to reference how Black women are doubly discriminated against in the legal system and in other institutions within our society (for example, medicine and health, news, education). Her article has been cited more than 25,600 times and it explains how a woman involved in a domestic violence situation (a possible news story) is afraid to leave her abuser because she's underemployed or can't find affordable and safe housing. This is how we as journalists develop a news story that describes how this type of situation impacts people of color.

Linda White has spent more than 25 years as a TV anchor and reporter in Ohio, Michigan, New York and Alabama, interviewing people from across the political and social spectrum. She is completing her doctorate from Michigan State University in journalism, specializing in racial diversity in TV news.

The Reporter's Guide to Newswriting Style

As you begin to write stories, make sure you follow these guidelines:

1. Identify the central point of the story to help your writing stay focused on the topic. It might help to complete this sentence with a few words: The objective of my story is

   _____.

2. Prepare a brief outline of the three or four major parts of the story.

3. Use short, familiar words.

4. Eliminate unnecessary words and opinions.

5. Replace ambiguous or biased words with fact.

6. Use short sentences. Separate a confusing sentence into two.

7. Use relatively simple sentences that follow normal word order: subject, verb, direct object.

8. Remove unrelated ideas within sentences.

9. Remove unrelated sentences with paragraphs.

10. Avoid generalizing and stereotyping.

Review Exercises

1. DISCUSSION QUESTIONS

1. Some people say journalists should use long or uncommon words to educate audiences and raise their reading level. Others say short, common words help audiences understand stories quickly and easily. What do you think? Give reasons to support your view.

2. You have just been named editor of your college news site. Formulate a policy that specifies when your staff can report that a person is "adopted," "biracial," "receiving welfare," "nonbinary" or an "ex-convict."

3. Kamala Harris' clothes are often the focus of news stories. As a journalist, what do you think about this?

4. Your city's new mayor, elected today, has never met her father and does not even know his identity. She was raised by her mother, who never married. Would you report those facts and discuss the circumstances while describing the new mayor? Why or why not? What is important to know about a new mayor?

5. A source you are interviewing uses an offensive stereotypical term about older people. Would you print the word? Why or why not?

6. A bank in your city has named a new president; she is the first woman and first Black person to hold the position. Should your story about her promotion emphasize these details? Why or why not?

7. For one week, examine news stories in any medium. Look for sentences or phrases that are not objective. Why is the sentence or phrase not objective? How would you rewrite it?

8. How do your favorite TV shows portray gender, age, people of color and people with disabilities? How do the portrayals foster or break stereotypical images?

9. For one week, examine every story published on the homepage of your campus or community newspaper. Identify or highlight words and phrases that you could replace with simpler ones. Do the simpler words and phrases change the meaning of the story? If so, how?

10. Authors of novels often use a woman's first name for characters and a man's last name for characters. They take more time describing a woman's physical appearance and detailing her clothing than a man's. (If they describe the man at all—for example, rarely are men's chests described.) Check the next five novels you read. How does the author introduce new characters and refer to them later? Is it fair and balanced? Why or why not? What should journalists do in news stories, and why?

2. BEING CONCISE

Section I: Using Simple Words

Substitute simpler and more common words for each of the following.

1. obliterate
2. objective
3. utilize
4. negligent
5. imbibe
6. duplicate
7. gargantuan
8. remainder
9. eccentric
10. abandon
11. deceased
12. cognizant
13. lacerations
14. presently
15. stated
16. manufacture
17. loathe
18. component

19. obtain

20. relocate

Section II: Avoiding Redundant Phrases

A. Cross out the unnecessary words in these phrases.

1. totally destroyed

2. really big

3. postponed until later

4. freak accident

5. seldom ever

6. major breakthrough

7. dead body

8. qualified expert

9. dangerous weapon

10. armed gunman

11. future plans

12. awkward predicament

13. fully engulfed

14. write down

15. free of charge

16. maximum possible

17. foreseeable future

18. lose out

B. Cross out the unnecessary words in these phrases.

1. necessary requirement

2. young girl

3. duplicate copy

4. shot to death

5. underground subway

6. both alike

7. underlying purpose

8. narrow down

9. broad daylight

10. calm down

11. divide up

12. front headlight

13. true fact

14. common accord

15. false pretense

16. radical transformation

17. blazing inferno

18. perfectly clear

19. entwined together

20. died suddenly

C. Cross out the unnecessary words in these phrases.

1. small in size

2. join together

3. general public

4. honest truth

5. acute crisis

6. fell down

7. lag behind

8. protrude out

9. resume again

10. usual custom

Section III: Avoiding Wordy Phrases

A. Use a single word to replace each of these phrases.

1. on the occasion of

2. despite the fact that

3. at an earlier date

4. is going to

5. tender resignation

6. united together in holy matrimony

7. give instruction to

8. on account of

9. was in possession of

10. register approval of

11. due to the fact that

12. exceeding the speed limit

13. made the acquaintance of

14. stated the point that

15. file a lawsuit against

16. be acquainted with

17. came to a stop

18. rose to the defense

19. draw to a close

20. arrived at a decision

B. Use a single word to replace each of these phrases.

1. raze to the ground

2. made contact with

3. bring to a conclusion

4. on a few occasions

5. for the reason that

6. made an escape

7. give encouragement to

8. file a lawsuit against

9. conducted an investigation of

10. summoned to the scene

Section IV: Eliminating Unnecessary Words

Eliminate the unnecessary words from the following sentences.

1. Duchess of Cambridge Kate Middleton talked to each and every child individually in the classroom.

2. The greatly anticipated stars performing at the Super Bowl halftime show are the fabulous Mary J. Blige, Dr. Dre, Eminem, Snoop Dogg and Kendrick Lamar.

3. The candidate running for the office of mayor will conduct a poll of the residents, appointing a gay couple to run it.

4. The North Korean president showed he was upset over the miserably failed missile launch that did not go as planned.

5. The birthday party was an unexpected surprise.

6. The police officer tried to calm down the accident victim, who was hurt.

7. The woman's old habit of sleepwalking in the middle of the night had a really unique pattern that would take a qualified sleep expert to explain, said one of her moms, a lesbian.

8. If past experience is any indication, the car club members will polish up the antique vehicles no matter whether or not they can predict rain in the foreseeable future.

9. The mayor asked the council members to make a definite decision about the ordinance even though those who support the measure are few in number and flatly reject any compromise.

10. Some people, like parents and siblings and other family members of military personnel, are worried about the bad feelings and tension that has been created with Russia's threat to invade Ukraine because they love their dads and brothers and sons.

11. The hockey player said she was acquainted with the author of the book about concussions on account of the fact they had made contact with each other years ago when she was experiencing post-traumatic concussion symptoms while he was doing research for the book.

12. The university's respected board of directors wanted to wait until later on a decision of how much money a settlement would be for the many, many, many survivors victimized by their disgusting sports doctor.

13. The mayor said the physical size of the new amphitheater was somewhat small, but it would have the maximum possible impact on the city's future plans.

14. Police have the belief that it was a freak accident that allowed the deadly poison to seep out of the tanker truck and cause the worst ever chemical spill in the country's history.

15. Firemen responding to the scene of the house fire were confronted with a blazing inferno and succeeded in doing their best to contain the flames.

16. Although he was in a really very quick hurry, he stopped to warn that, in the future, he will seek out textbooks that are sexist and demand that they be totally banned.

17. As it now stands, three separate and different members of the committee said they will try to prevent the city from closing down the park during the cold winter months.

18. Ben Affleck's nice convertible was totally destroyed and, in order to obtain the money

necessary to buy a new car, he now plans to ask J.Lo for a loan to help him along.

19. After police found the lifeless body, the medical doctor conducted an autopsy to determine the cause of death and concluded that the dead man had been strangled to death.

20. In the past, a mask was thought to help prevent and stop the COVID-19 virus from spreading out to people and it is still considered this way and will be in the future, too.

21. Citing her previous experience as an architect, she warned the committee members that constructing the new hospital facility will be pretty expensive and suggested that they step in and seek more donors.

22. Two people were hunting in a very wooded forest a total of 12 miles away from the nearest hospital in the region when both fell down in a very steep ravine and suffered really severe bodily injuries.

23. Based upon the results of several studies conducted in the past, she firmly believed that the newly prescribed medication will help people with bad liver problems and aid them in their progress toward improvement.

Section V: Rewriting Wordy Sentences

A. Remove all redundancies and unnecessary words from the following sentences, eliminating as many words as possible and correcting any other errors.

1. The #MeToo movement, using a social media hashtag as a symbol, is a social movement where victims can publicize sexual harassment or sexual abuse that they have experienced against theirselves.

2. It would appear that the new school mascot, which got a stamp of approval from alumni, will make an appearance at Saturday's game.

3. As a matter of fact, some of the tickets were free of charge to the contest winners while other tickets cost the sum of $50 for handling fees.

4. Police claimed the armed gunman was carrying a dangerous weapon when he entered the bank with the underlying purpose of robbing it.

5. Local residents said they planned to evacuate in the event that the floodwaters reached the banks of the river and completely destroyed the town.

B. Remove all redundancies and unnecessary words from the following sentences, eliminating as many words as possible and correcting any other errors.

1. When Marvel's Black Panther movie came to an end, audience members commented to the effect that they really liked the film.

2. The Russian figure skater at the Winter Olymoics in China was accused of doping with prohibited medications and drugs, which is unfortunate because she performed well.

3. The professor asked the student to make an approximation of how many people in the state would enter into bonds of matrimony this year and how many would postpone the decision until later.

4. The business owner said his inventory of things would depreciate in value due to the fact that there is now smoke damage when the warehouse in which it was stored went up in flames.

5. The motorist realized just now that she was all of a sudden exceeding the speed limit and then she came to a stop just before she saw the policeman on duty.

C. Remove all redundancies and unnecessary words from the following sentences, eliminating as many words as possible and correcting any other errors.

1. While they had not come to a final conclusion in regard to the plans for the new educational program, the members of the school board said that tentatively a total of about 800 to 900 students ultimately would be served.

2. According to the currently held belief on the part of the design engineer, Jonathan Emory, who is 56 years old and Hispanic, the important essentials for completing the construction project on time will require check points between the design phase and the actual construction.

3. A mobile emergency medical unit rushed the boy, who had been injured in the collision between two cars at the intersection of Main and King streets,

into the emergency ward where doctors later announced the boy was in critically serious condition at the time.

4. The policemen arrived at the scene of the accident, then chased the suspects vehicle down through town at a speed estimated to be in the vicinity of approximately 90 miles per hour after which the criminal's car managed to get away.

5. The attorney for the perpetrator said despite the fact that a dangerous weapon had been found at the scene of the crime it did not necessarily mean that the weapon happened to belong to her current client.

Section VI: Simplifying Overloaded Sentences

Shorten and simplify the following sentences and correct any other errors.

1. Two university students, Kyisha Johnson and Chaoxiang Li, both seniors and both majoring in business in the Department of Economic Sciences, were driving south on Addison Drive during a thunderstorm when a tree, which was blown down by strong winds, fell across the road in front of them and Li swerved to avoid the tree before hitting a utility pole and causing more than 10,000 people to lose electricity to their homes.

2. Policemen chased the gunmen, who had attempted to rob Justin Bieber and his wife, who live in a highrise building located at 1345 Grassland Avenue, of $35,000 in cash that was in a small safe in their home, into the park where he tried to climb through the window of a childrens playhouse and got stuck in the window because his belt buckle caught on a protruding nail and

officers had to cut the man's belt in order to get him out of the window and charge him with being a thief, burglary and resisting arrest.

3. Soo Shin, who is 51, and lives at 414 West Coast Boulevard, and who is an emergency room nurse at Mercy Hospital, and was on duty at 3 p.m. yesterday afternoon, was surprised when a woman who looked just like her was brought into the emergency room after a minor traffic accident at the intersection of Lakeview Drive and Darlington Avenue in which the woman's car was struck in the rear by a pickup truck while she was stopped at an intersection and Shin began asking the woman questions about her family and past history, discovering that the woman had been adopted, but had been told she had a twin sister who had been adopted by another family when the sisters were three years old, so Shin introduced herself to her long-lost twin sister.

4. The mayor said she was more than willing to support the ordinance the city council was proposing to begin the building of a new facility to house elderly city residents who needed to have a place they could go when they could no longer live independently in their own homes, but the cost of such a facility had to fall within the current fiscal realities of the revenue stream city taxes could generate to support such a building program without raising taxes for city residents, which the mayor knows will upset city residents who will hold her responsible for any proposal the city counsel approves in the long run.

5. The starlet and songstress Brittany Spears was ever-so-glad to be rid and free of the conservatorship by her father that has haunted her for many years.

3. -ISMS

Section I: Avoiding Sexual Stereotypes

Remove sexist language, excess words and comments from the following sentences. Correct any other errors.

1. The expert researchers, probably all knowledgeable men, compared all kinds and types of COVID-19 masks and declared that the expensive KN95 and N95 masks are much better than cheap cloth masks and one-layer masks covering the face.

2. The author, Oliver Brooks, was in an attractive open-necked, electric blue shirt that showed off his sweaty, heaving chest and tousled blond hair as he rushed in late to the book signing, around 3:20 p.m.

3. The salesman told the lady police officer that the accident occurred when the car swerved to avoid an old lady who tok forever stepping off the curb.

4. Needless to say, Congressman Janice Byron, a petite 38-year-old mother with a sunny disposition, voted in favor of the education bill, probably because her kids are of school age.

5. Harry and David and their girl friends were expecting the concert tickets to arrive an hour before the long-anticipated show started.

Section II: Avoiding Exclusively Gender-Specific Nouns and Pronouns

Replace the gender-specific language in these sentences with gender-neutral terms, reduce wordiness and correct any other errors.

1. A policeman has to inspect his weapons before going on patrol.

2. The secretary said she couldn't find the papers before the meeting that her boss incorrectly filed before that.

3. The councilman said it is a fact that the average man will not understand the ordinance.

4. The teacher wrote a letter to each individual student, welcoming him or her to her class.

5. Encounters with dogs can be frightening experiences for a mailman as he makes his rounds delivering mail to his customers each day.

Section III: Avoiding Stereotypes

Ensure that the following sentences contain no stereotypical language or comments. Correct any other errors.

1. Oldtimer Jackson Smith, a spry 86-year-old resident of Greeley Court, every day drives a 1936 Chevrolet coupe that he amazingly restored just last year.

2. The spunky newsboy dropped the paper on the porch just as the pretty housewife lazily opened the front door.

3. Margaret Adams, a pert woman dressed in a knee-length gray business suit and black high heels, became the first woman president and chief executive officer of the male-dominated Hudson Industries.

4. The spokesman for the club said she had reached a gentleman's agreement with the protesters which consisted of 20 gentlemen and 30 ladies.

5. Members of the American Indian Movement went on the warpath today when federal agents attempted to interrupt a powwow of tribal elders.

Section IV: Remaining Objective

Eliminate the words and phrases that reveal bias, opinions, stereotypes or -isms. Correct any other errors.

1. The surprisingly good student choral group from Central High won first place at the state conference.

2. Three soldiers training at a nearby army base died tragically in the helicopter accident despite heroic efforts to save them.

3. The female president of the board, who is a 68-year-old grandmother and the matriarch of the family-owned company, wanted to expand the business, but did not believe there were enough extra funds to do it at this time.

4. Tickets for a game at the new stadium will cost only $30 per person, which is really reasonable.

5. It was miraculous that only three people were injured in the 20-vehicle, chain-reaction collision on the fog-bound interstate.

6. The famous speaker, who truly will delight her audience, will discuss the relationship of economics and poverty at tonight's interesting presentation.

7. In a startling discovery, police claimed to have identified the despicable man who attacked the poor, defenseless 65-year-old man.

8. The tall master-of-ceremony towered over the buxom matron as he presented her with the prestigious award for her efforts on behalf of the animal shelter.

9. Theater-goers are urged to buy their tickets early, at a cost of only $20, for the sensational community theater production of "Frozen," which can look forward to a long run in the city.

10. The city council did a good thing when they voted to make it legal to manufacture medical marijuana in the zoned industrial parts of the city.

4. TESTING ALL YOUR SKILLS

Correct all errors in these sentences and eliminate wordiness. Check the appendices for the City Directory, AP Style and Forming Possessives.

1. It was an impetuous decision, but the 20-year-old surfer boy commented to the effect that he planned to purchase a new car when he graduated from college.

2. The students future plans for the recreation center would require university officials to reconstruct the entire facility at a cost of two million dollars, something the university president, a divorced father named Jim Smith, flatly rejected.

3. The church's layman committee, which was made up of four men and three girls, two of whom were Hispanic and one who was Asian, anticipated in advance that a reason for the construction of the new church would help more people be able to attend the services.

4. Adam Levine, the good lead singer for Maroon 5, stated the fact that the concert would be free and open to the public, and he had the belief that the number of attendees would be really a lot.

5. The incumbent senator, a man with a questionable past, planned to introduce legislation in the not-too-distant future on the grounds that poor people needed jobs.

6. Mike Deacosta, his wife and their two children, Mark and Amy, were invited to the congressmans reception along with several other local residents.

7. The police officer made it perfectly clear to the motorist that he had been exceeding the speed limit and would face the maximum possible fine if he did not locate his drivers license presently.

8. Before a young child can begin school, they must be able to read and write their name.

9. The informative information was presented at this point in time because all the members of the board, including Chairman Maggy Baille, were present and accounted for and would be able to vote on the newly introduced proposal.

10. An attractive young brunette, Donna Moronesi, seemes to be an unlikely candidate for the office, but she has surprisingly raised more than 1 million dollars before the campaign has even begun.

11. He sustained the loss of his right eye, had lacerations and contusions and broke his leg in the unfortunate accident.

12. As a matter of fact, the mayor claimed she had already considered the attorneys proposal, but the terms of the agreement to settle with the bitter old man who filed a lawsuit against the city over the death of his dog which had been taken to the city pound was not in accordance with the best interests of the city and its local residents.

13. The attorney was in possession of evidence that helped the jury to arrive at a decision.

14. It was the consensus of opinion of the board and chairman LaDonna Santini that the impetuous offer by the other company would be a hindrance to negotiating a fair and equitable contract with her employees.

15. He stated that the important essential thing to remember is that the deficit was then not nearly as large as it is today.

THE LANGUAGE OF THE NEWS

4

"The romance between Antonio and Luciana is truly magic," their friend said. Actually, the relationship was "magical." What's the difference? "Magic" is a noun meaning the "use of charms and spells to control events or the art of producing illusions by sleight of hand." "Magical" is an adjective meaning "producing extraordinary results as if by magic." But what about a similar pair of words, such as "tragic" and "tragical"? In this case, "tragical" is a noun meaning "the tragic element in art or life," whereas "tragic" is an adjective meaning "of or having to do with tragedy."

4.1 The Effectiveness of Words

All words have precise meanings. Two or more words may have similar meanings; however, one is never an exact substitute for another. Words are constructed into phrases and sentences to give context and meaning, which contributes to accuracy.

Writers sometimes misunderstand the words they use. Other times they fail to express their ideas clearly and precisely. In such cases, their sentences may state the obvious or impossible or carry unintended, often comical, meanings. Can you spot the flaws in these sentences?

The wine complimented the entrée.

The airport commission decided to hold a public hearing on the new runway.

The president worried about the influx of emigrates.

The police on duty are getting smaller.

Are taxpayers revolting?

Protesters stormed the U.S. Capital on Jan. 6.

A woman is better after she was thrown from her high-rise building.

"In the English language, it all comes down to this: Twenty-six letters, when combined correctly, can create magic. Twenty-six letters form the foundation of a free, informed society."

—*John Grogan, journalist/ writer*

51

People expect journalists to be experts in using the English language. When news organizations hire a reporter, they look for someone who understands and respects the language, knows spelling and grammar, possesses an extensive vocabulary and writes in a clear and interesting manner. Those who devote their lives to journalism strive to select the exact word needed to convey an idea, use the word properly and place it in a sentence that is grammatically correct. Of course, even careful writers make mistakes, sometimes hilarious ones. But if the errors become numerous, they can damage a news organization's credibility and require costly and embarrassing corrections. The journalists making the mistakes are often dismissed from their job.

When a major event occurs, such as the Indonesia earthquake that caused a tsunami, the election of President Joe Biden and Vice President Kamala Harris, the death of baseball player Hank Aaron, Prince Harry's split with the royal family, Russia's invasion of Ukraine, the killing of George Floyd or the midwinter Olympics in China, dozens and sometimes hundreds of journalists are at the scene, gathering information and then transmitting it to the public. They write about the same event, but some stories are much better than others. Why?

Some reporters are particularly adept at gathering the information needed to write exceptional stories. Others produce exceptional stories because of their command of the English language. Their language is forceful, and their stories are written clearly and simply so everyone can understand them. These reporters describe people, places and events involved in news stories and use quotations that enable the people involved to speak directly to the public. Skilled reporters can transform even routine events into front-page stories.

4.2 Mastering Grammar

Since the development of written languages, humans have created rules governing their usage. Basic understanding of English grammar begins with knowing the parts of speech and how they are used (see Table 4.1). All words are classified as one or more parts of speech. The rules and principles used to combine these parts into sentences are called syntax. Successful writers learn syntax and understand the importance of good sentence structure for conciseness and clarity.

Sentences can be either simple or complex. Simple sentences usually include a subject, a verb and a direct object. The subject is the person or thing doing the action; the verb describes the action; and the direct object is the person or thing acted on. Consider this sentence:

Elton John plays the piano.

"Elton John" is the actor (the subject of the sentence). "Plays" is the action (the verb), and "piano" is the thing acted on (the object).

TABLE 4.1 PARTS OF SPEECH

Nouns	Words that name any animate or inanimate thing: people, animals, places, qualities, acts or ideas.
Verbs	Words that describe action; they tell what things and people do.
Adjectives	Words that describe or modify nouns and pronouns.
Adverbs	Words that describe or modify verbs, adjectives and other adverbs.
Articles	The words "a," "an" or "the" and their equivalents used as adjectives.
Pronouns	Words that replace proper or common nouns to avoid needless and confusing repetition of a noun.
Prepositions	Words that show a relationship between a word or phrase that comes before a preposition, called an antecedent, and a word or phrase that follows, called an object or a subsequent.
Conjunctions	Words or phrases that connect other words, phrases, clauses or sentences.
Interjections	Words or short phrases that express strong, sudden emotions.

Sometimes sentences include indirect objects, which tell who received the action. To test for an indirect object, place "to" or "for" before the word. The following sentences have both direct and indirect objects:

Blake Shelton gave Gwen Stefani a ring.

Gwen Stefani showed her sister the ring.

Subject	Verb	Indirect object	Direct object
Blake	gave	Gwen	a ring
Gwen	showed	her sister	the ring

When a noun alone is used as an indirect object, it usually comes between the verb and the direct object, as in the preceding examples. But when the indirect object follows the direct object, it takes the form of a prepositional phrase.

Blake gave a ring to Gwen.

Gwen showed the ring to her sister.

4.2.1 Nouns

The subject of a sentence can be a noun, pronoun, gerund or infinitive. A gerund is formed by adding "-ing" to the base form of a verb. The infinitive is the basic dictionary form of the verb, appearing with or without the particle "to." Infinitives also can stand as a noun phrase (among numerous other uses).

© MARK ANDERSON, WWW.ANDERTOONS.COM

"Well, you have a subject and a predicate, so, content aside, nice job."

Noun subject: *The pope* blessed the crowd.

Pronoun subject: *He* blessed the crowd.

Gerund subject: *Blessing* the crowd is important.

Infinitive subject: *To bless* the crowd is an expectation.

4.2.2 Verbs

There are three types of verbs: transitive, intransitive and linking. The verbs are italicized in the examples below. Transitive verbs propel the action in the sentence from the subject to the object. They are always followed by a direct object.

People *believed* the mayor when she said the water was safe to drink.

"Mayor" is the object of "believed."

Intransitive verbs also show action, but they are not followed by a direct object. They can also describe an action or provide a sense of location and are often followed by prepositional phrases or adverbs.

People *believed* fervently in the mayor.

Or simply,

People *believed*.

In the first sentence, "fervently" is an adverb that describes "believed." The second example is a complete verb because it takes neither a direct object nor a predicate complement.

Some verbs may be either transitive or intransitive.

A U-Boat *sank* the Lusitania with a torpedo. (Transitive)

The Titanic *sank* after hitting an iceberg. (Intransitive)

Linking verbs express a state or condition and link a noun, pronoun or adjective that describes or identifies the subject. The most common linking verb is "to be."

The man with the snake tattoo on his arm *is* the only suspect in the case.

Other verbs may be used as linking verbs, as in these sentences:

The dog *looks* guilty.

The bridge *seems* sturdy.

In both examples the verb links the idea in the subject to the idea in the predicate (the part of the sentence containing the verb), stating that the subject possesses the condition described in the predicate.

4.2.3 Independent and Dependent Clauses

A clause is a group of words containing a subject and verb and is used as part of a sentence. An independent clause is a complete sentence; it can stand by itself. A dependent clause, on the other hand, is an incomplete thought. Consider the following two sentences:

The senior trip to the museum was very popular, but many parents complained about the cost.

We ordered pizza for the meeting, which everyone on the news staff likes.

Both sentences contain two clauses. However, one sentence contains two independent clauses and the other contains an independent clause and a dependent clause. How can you tell? Remove the conjunction (connecting word) and separate the two clauses to see if they make sense on their own.

The senior trip to the museum was very popular. Many parents complained about the cost.

We ordered pizza for the meeting. Everyone on the news staff likes.

If you picked the first sentence as the one that contains two independent clauses, you are correct. Both are complete sentences, joined by the conjunction "but." The first part of the second sentence is also an independent clause because it can stand alone. However, the second half, "which everyone on the news staff likes," makes no sense if it is disconnected from the other clause. Its clarity and meaning depend on the first part of the sentence.

Dependent clauses can come at the beginning, in the middle or at the end of a sentence. In the following examples, the dependent clauses are in italics:

When the sun came out, everyone felt more cheerful.

Typewriters, *which were once state-of-the-art word-processing machines*, disappeared when personal computers arrived.

You need to install an underground sprinkler system, *if you are planning to create a lawn in the desert.*

Writers can combine independent and dependent clauses in a number of ways. One way is to combine an independent clause with a dependent one (italicized below) to make a complex sentence.

I eat dinner *after my last class is over.*

Another is to combine two independent clauses to make a compound sentence.

Ice skating is her favorite sport, but she enjoys roller skating, too.

And yet another way is to string one or more dependent clauses (italicized) together with two or more independent clauses to create compound-complex sentences.

I visit my aunt *whenever I go home for the holidays*, but I call her almost every week.

Sentences can also contain phrases, which are related groups of words that lack a subject, verb or both. Prepositional phrases and verbal phrases are common types. They may be incorporated into the body of the sentence or introduce the main clause. The first of the following sentences ends with a prepositional phrase, and the second begins with a verbal phrase (both are italicized).

People spend more time outdoors *in the springtime.*

Tired from chasing the ball, the dog took a nap.

Sentence parts can be combined and arranged in endless ways. Writers vary sentence structure to keep their prose from becoming too predictable and simplistic, but simple sentences that stick to subject-verb-object order are the clearest and most easily understood.

4.2.4 Active and Passive Voice

Sentences that use the subject-verb-object order are active-voice sentences; the subject performs the action. A passive-voice sentence reverses the structure so that the direct object of the active-voice sentence becomes the subject; the subject becomes part of a prepositional phrase; and the verb is replaced with its past participle and a form of the verb "to be."

Passive-voice sentences are longer and less clear than active-voice ones. In this example, the passive-voice sentence is two words longer than the active-voice sentence, but it says the same thing.

> **Passive Voice:** The tsunami was caused by the earthquake.

> **Active Voice:** The earthquake caused the tsunami.

Changing a passive-voice sentence to an active one requires rearranging the parts of the sentence, but the result is a stronger sentence.

- ~~It was discovered by the company's~~ ∧ *Company* lawyers ~~that~~ ∧ *discovered* the financial records were incorrect.

- ∧ *A neighbor called the* Police ~~officers were summoned to the scene by a neighbor.~~

The actor or subject can disappear from a passive-voice sentence:

> **Active Voice:** The commanding general gave Lt. Jason Greene an Expert Soldier badge.

> **Passive Voice:** The Expert Soldier badge was given to Lt. Jason Greene.

Writers should avoid the passive voice not only because it is wordier than the active voice but also because it often camouflages responsibility. If a disaster strikes or a defective product harms someone, government or business officials may admit "mistakes were made," but the passive construction reveals nothing about who made the mistakes or why. The passive voice is the ally of all who seek to evade responsibility; it is the enemy of all who seek clarity.

4.2.5 Appositives

An appositive is a noun or noun phrase that renames, identifies, explains or in some way supplements the meaning of another noun or noun phrase. An appositive that is accompanied by modifiers is called an appositive phrase.

Appositives may be either essential or nonessential. An essential appositive defines the noun or noun phrase it accompanies. It is not set off with punctuation. A nonessential appositive adds supplemental information and is set off from the rest of the sentence with punctuation, usually commas or dashes. In the following examples, the appositive or appositive phrase is in italics.

Essential appositives:

The required class *Organic Chemistry 101* is one of the most difficult in the program.

Ben Affleck's film *"The Tender Bar"* has three Oscar nominations.

Team captain *Megan Rapinoe* called for a meeting of the players.

Nonessential appositives:

"Gone with the Wind," *a novel about the Civil War era*, is laden with subtle racism.

My car—*a real lemon*—is in the repair shop again.

That house is painted in the same tones as my university colors, *green and white*.

4.3 Common Grammatical Errors

4.3.1 Run-on Sentences

A run-on sentence contains two or more independent clauses with no punctuation separating them. The following are run-on sentences:

I love to read books I would read a new one every day if I could.

We did not know which restaurant we wanted to eat at and then we drove for miles until we found one we all agreed that we liked and stopped there.

To correct this type of error, add punctuation in the appropriate places, separate the clauses into separate sentences or rewrite the sentence:

I love to read books; I would read a new one every day if I could.

We did not know where we wanted to eat, so we drove for miles until we found a restaurant we liked.

Good writers carefully edit their stories to eliminate any run-on sentences.

4.3.2 Comma Splices

Some writers attempt to fix a run-on sentence by inserting a comma between the two independent clauses. Doing so creates another type of error known as the comma splice. Here is an example:

Picking out a special flower is hard, there are many beautiful ones available.

There are three ways to fix this sentence:

Picking out a special flower is hard. There are many beautiful ones available.

HOME » CULTURE » BOOKS » BOOK NEWS

How should Shakespeare really sound?

Audio: The British Library have released the first audio guide to how Shakespeare's plays would have sounded in the original pronunciation.

If The Telegraph were an American newspaper, this would violate subject-verb agreement. But British writers often use plural verbs for collective nouns.

Picking out a special flower is hard because there are many beautiful ones available.

Picking out a special flower is hard; there are many beautiful ones available.

4.3.3 Agreement Errors

A basic principle of grammar is that nouns and verbs should agree with each other, as should nouns and pronouns. The principle is simple, but the opportunities for error are numerous.

4.3.3.1 SUBJECTS AND VERBS

If the subject of a sentence is singular, use a singular verb; if the subject is plural, use a plural verb. Getting subjects and verbs to agree is easy when sentences are simple. But when prepositional phrases separate subjects and verbs or when the subject is a collective noun, agreement becomes trickier. In the next example, the singular noun "team" is the subject, and the prepositional phrase "of researchers" describes the subject. The verb should agree with the singular "team," not the plural "researchers." The subjects in these examples are in italics.

- A *team* of researchers ~~have~~ ∧ *has* gathered the information.

- *Examples*, such as this one, ~~is~~ ∧ *are* helpful to students.

Some nouns—such as "economics," "politics" and "physics"—may appear to be plural because they end in "s," but they are considered singular in certain senses.

- *Economics* ~~are~~ ∧ *is* a required course.

Nouns that refer to a group or a collection of individuals as a whole are called collective nouns. Examples include "committee," "club," "jury," "regiment" and "team." Proper nouns that identify organizations—"Congress" and "Microsoft," for instance—also are collective nouns. In American English, collective nouns are considered singular and require singular verbs and pronouns:

- The *jury* ~~announce their~~ ∧ verdict.

  announces its

Note the change in pronoun, from "their" to "its."

- The *American Society of Newspaper Editors* ~~have~~ ∧ begun a program to help journalists with their writing.

  has

4.3.3.2 NOUNS AND PRONOUNS

Not only must pronouns agree with nouns, but they also must have the same number and gender as their antecedents. A singular feminine noun requires a singular feminine pronoun, and a plural neuter noun requires a plural neuter pronoun. In the following examples, the pronouns are underlined and their antecedents are in italics.

Rachael took <u>her</u> work with <u>her</u> when <u>she</u> visited New York.

The carpenter replaced the *nails* in <u>their</u> container.

Collective nouns cause the most problems with noun–pronoun agreement. When beginning writers are unsure whether a collective noun is singular or plural, they often try to have it both ways. They use singular verbs with collective nouns but plural pronouns to take their place:

- *General Motors* is expanding ~~their~~ ∧ product line.

  its

- The *faculty* gave ~~their~~ ∧ vote to the director.

  its

However, if the subject is a plural collective noun, a plural pronoun is needed:

- The *committees* reviewed ~~its~~ ∧ policy on requiring masks and social distancing.

  their

4.3.4 "That"/"Which" Confusion

"That" and "which" are relative pronouns that introduce clauses referring to ideas, inanimate objects or animals without names. They are little words, but they can make a big difference in the meaning of a sentence. The following sentences illustrate this point:

Jaycia used the lawn mower that is in the garage.

Jaycia used the lawn mower, which is in the garage.

In the first sentence, "that" implies many lawn mowers exist on the property—in the yard, the garage and the barn—but Jaycia took the one from the garage. In the second sentence, the clause introduced by "which" is not essential. There is only one lawn mower on the property, so it is the only one Jaycia could use. It helps to know where the lawn mower is, but the information is not necessary to understand the sentence.

Here's a rule that can help decide between "that" and "which": If the sentence is read without the subordinate clause and the meaning does not change, "which" should introduce the clause. Otherwise, use "that."

4.3.5 "Who"/"Whom" Confusion

"Who" and "whom" are also relative pronouns, but they begin clauses that refer to people and animals with names.

- It was *Morgan* ~~that~~ ∧ came by the house yesterday.
  [who]

- It was a stray *cat* ~~who~~ ∧ ate the bird.
  [that]

The distinction between "who" and "whom" torments some writers. "Who" is the subject of a clause; "whom" is the object of a verb or a preposition ("Who tweeted whom?"). Whether a word is a subject or an object might not always be clear in relative clauses or questions, both of which may depart from normal word order.

Either "who" or "whom" may appear as the first word in a question, depending on its grammatical relationship to the rest of the sentence. These two sentences illustrate the difference:

Who gave you the Apple Watch?

Whom should you thank for the Apple Watch?

In the first example, "who" is the subject of the clause, the initiator of the action "gave." In the second, "whom" is the direct object of the verb "thank." Here are two more examples:

- ~~Who~~ ∧ did you speak ~~to~~?
  [To whom]

- The report names the person ~~who~~ ∧ the police suspect of the crime.
  [whom]

In the first sentence, the relative pronoun is the object of the preposition "to." In the second, it is the direct object; it refers to the person the police suspect. Both should be "whom."

One way to avoid or reduce confusion over these words is to replace them with a personal pronoun. Isolate the "who" or "whom" phrase. If "he," "she" or "they" sounds right, use "who." If "him," "her" or "them" would be more natural, use "whom." Do that in the following sentence and it is easy to see that "whom" is wrong:

- The candidates argued about ~~whom~~ ∧ was responsible for the tax increase.
  [who]

At first, the relative pronoun "whom" appears to be the object of the preposition "about," but it doesn't sound right when replaced with "him" or "her." That's because the relative pronoun is the subject of the clause "was responsible for the tax increase." No one would say "her was responsible," but "she was responsible" makes sense. Therefore, the relative pronoun to use here is "who."

4.3.6 Misplaced Modifiers

Modifiers are words or phrases that limit, restrict or qualify some other word or phrase. Modifiers should appear as close as possible to the word or phrase they modify. Misplaced modifiers can make sentences ambiguous, confusing or nonsensical:

> She retold the ordeal of being held hostage with tears running down her cheeks.

Readers might think the phrase "with tears running down her cheeks" modifies "hostage"—that she was crying while she was a hostage. But the phrase really tells how the woman behaved as she talked about her ordeal. The following version is clearer:

> With tears running down her cheeks, she retold the ordeal of being held hostage.

In the next example, the revision clarifies that the victim is left lying on the back seat, not just his hands and feet:

- The gunmen tied the victim ∧ *, taped his hands and feet* and left him ~~with his hands and feet taped and~~ lying on the back seat.

4.3.7 Dangling Modifiers

Modifiers dangle when the word or phrase they are supposed to modify does not appear in the sentence. This error may happen when a thoughtless or hurried writer starts a sentence intending to state an idea one way and then switches in midsentence to express it in another way:

- Pleased with everyone's papers, ~~the class received congratulations~~ ∧ *the teacher congratulated the class*.

- ~~Angered by the unannounced closure of the plant,~~ security guards hurriedly cleared the area ∧ *of employees who were angered by the unannounced closure of the plant*.

Readers understand that introductory words and phrases modify the subject of the sentence. If that is not the case, the modifiers are either misplaced or dangling.

4.3.8 Personification

Avoid treating inanimate objects or abstractions as if they were human. Objects such as buildings, cars, stores and trees cannot hear, think, feel or talk. Yet some writers see—and repeat—the error so often they fail to recognize it and continue to personify such things as vehicles, corporations, countries and machines:

> Memorial Hospital treated her for shock and a broken arm.

> She was driving west on Hullett Avenue when two cars in front of her slammed on their brakes.

> The ambulance rushed her to the hospital.

Can a hospital treat patients, or is that the job of a hospital's staff? Can an ambulance steer itself or did its drivers put the pedal to the metal? Can a car slam on its own brakes (without AI)? Of course not.

Luckily, personifications are easy to correct:

- The ∧ store said it̶ ∧ will not reopen ∧.
  owner of the   *she*   *it*

- T̶h̶e̶ ̶i̶n̶t̶e̶n̶t̶i̶o̶n̶ ̶o̶f̶ ̶t̶h̶e̶ ̶r̶o̶a̶d̶ ̶w̶a̶s̶ ∧ to help farmers transport their crops to market.
  Highway planners intended the road

Personification also contributes to two other problems. First, audiences cannot determine a story's credibility if reporters fail to identify their sources. The public can assess the credibility of a statement attributed to a mayor or governor, but not the credibility of a statement attributed to a city or state. Second, personification allows people to escape responsibility for their actions. Officials cannot be held accountable if reporters attribute their activities to a business or government.

4.3.9 Parallelism

When writers connect similar ideas, they do so with parallel structures. Grammatically parallel structures create harmony and balance in writing, and they help readers compare and contrast the ideas that are linked within the sentence.

The principle of parallelism requires that items in a series take the same grammatical form: for example, all are nouns, all are verbs or all are prepositional phrases. If the first verb in a series uses the past tense, every verb in the series uses the past tense. If the first verb ends in "-ing," all must end in "-ing."

If reporters fail to express like ideas in the same grammatical form, their sentences become convoluted and confusing:

- Police said the plastic handcuffs are less bulky, n̶o̶t̶ ̶a̶s̶ ∧ expensive and
  less
  n̶o̶ ̶k̶e̶y̶ ̶i̶s̶ ̶n̶e̶e̶d̶e̶d̶ ∧ to remove t̶h̶e̶m̶ from a suspect's wrists than metal handcuffs.
  less difficult

- The Ellis family has three children: 4̶-̶y̶e̶a̶r̶-̶o̶l̶d̶ Gordon, ∧ Andrea, w̶h̶o̶ ̶i̶s̶ 3̶;̶ ∧
  4;   *;*
  and l̶i̶t̶t̶l̶e̶ Fielding i̶s̶ ̶n̶o̶t̶ ̶q̶u̶i̶t̶e̶ ̶2̶5̶ ̶m̶o̶n̶t̶h̶s̶ ∧.
  , 2

4.3.10 Syntax

As mentioned earlier, syntax refers to the arrangement and relationships of the words and phrases in a sentence. If parts of the sentence are disjointed or improperly arranged, the sentence will confuse readers.

Sometimes, the syntax error is simply the misplacement or omission of words:

- President Biden said people cannot afford to be partisan but, instead,
  should   with
  w̶i̶l̶l̶ ∧ work ∧ each other to help fix the world.

Other times, the syntax errors are more extensive, requiring a rewrite:

> **Wrong:** Le Roux said she was certain that her many years of attempts at being a creative writer, would be her calling, but found it was not.

> **Better:** Le Roux said she spent years trying to become a creative writer but discovered it was not her calling.

Three practices can help writers avoid syntax errors: (1) Keep sentences as simple as possible. Sentences that follow the subject-verb-object order are least likely to have syntax problems. (2) Think about what you want to say before writing the sentence. Planning the sentence forces you to think about the selection and arrangement of the words and phrases. (3) Reread and edit what you have written. Reading your writing aloud is especially helpful. Often the ears can detect syntax problems the eyes overlook.

4.4 Spelling

When readers complain about inaccuracies in news stories, they are often referring to spelling errors. Misspellings reflect laziness on the part of the writer, and they sometimes cause readers to doubt the facts in the story.

Correct spelling is as important for writers in broadcast journalism as it is for those in print. News announcers often lack time to review the reporter's copy for misspelled words, and misspellings may cause them to make mistakes on air.

Common phrases such as "a lot" and "all right" are frequently misspelled. Confusing words that look or sound alike but have different meanings, such as "accept/except" and "capital/capitol," are another common source of spelling errors. (See the vocabulary exercise at the end of this chapter.) Reporters usually follow formal rules for spelling. For example, they normally use "until" rather than "till" and "although" rather than "though."

A final point about spelling: Spell-check programs for computers help many writers. However, a computer program can look only at the spelling of a word, not how it is used. If you were to write, "There cat's name is Savannah," the spell-checker would not catch that "there" should be "their." No one should depend solely on a spell-check program.

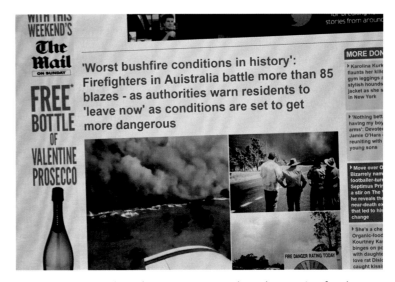

Spelling errors such as this one are not only embarrassing for the journalist and news organization but also make people distrust the story's content.

4.5 Punctuation

Punctuation marks (see Table 4.2) help make the meaning of a sentence clear to a reader. Some punctuation marks indicate the pauses and stops that the voice makes when speaking. They specify not only where the pause goes, but the length of the pause as well. Other marks indicate inflections in the voice, such as questions

TABLE 4.2 **PUNCTUATION MARKS**

Period (.)	A period ends a sentence—period. Without a period, thoughts and ideas in sentences would collide and confuse the reader.
Comma (,)	A comma creates a short pause within a sentence.
Semicolon (;)	The semicolon is often used to connect two independent clauses without using a conjunction. It also separates phrases that contain commas.
Colon (:)	The colon lets the reader know that a list, a sentence fragment, a sentence or a quotation follows.
Hyphen (-)	The hyphen is a connector without spaces and often is used to join words to form compound modifiers.
Dash (– or —)	An en dash (–) is primarily used to show a range between dates or numbers. The em dash (—) is used to create an abrupt and longer pause than a comma. It often is used to highlight an aside or brief change in thought that accompanies a sentence. Neither dashes have spaces before or after them.
Parentheses ( )	Like an em dash, parentheses are used to set off additional information.
Quotation marks (" . . .") **Quotation marks** (" ' ' ")	Double quotation marks enclose the exact words spoken or written by someone else. Single quotation marks indicate a quote within a quote.
Apostrophe (')	The apostrophe is used to form possessives and contractions.
Question mark (?)	The question mark ends any sentence that is a question.
Exclamation point (!)	The exclamation point ends sentences uttered with great emotion or emphasis.

or exclamatory remarks. Taken together, a sentence is only as clear as effective punctuation can make it. A misplaced punctuation mark can completely change the meaning of a sentence. Therefore, mastering punctuation is essential for anyone who aspires to write clearly.

4.6 Writing Like a Pro

4.6.1 Diction

Writing like a professional is hard work. It requires practice and an understanding of the effectiveness of the words selected to convey a thought or idea. A writer's choice of words and style of expressing them is called diction.

Diction in writing can be either formal or informal. By choosing one type, a writer establishes a tone for the story and the characterization of the subjects. A light, breezy feature story may use informal language and contractions, setting a conversational tone. A news story about the president may use more formal language and set a more serious tone.

When in doubt, stick with formal diction. As William Safire notes in his book "How Not to Write: The Essential Rules of Grammar," contractions are not as powerful. The word "not" is strong. Safire says, "'I won't' sounds stubborn, but 'I will not' sounds determined and slightly more emphatic."

4.6.2 Precision

To communicate effectively, reporters must be precise, particularly in their selection of words. Mark Twain wrote, "The difference between the right word and the almost right word is the difference between lightning and the lightning bug." The perfect choice makes a sentence crackle; imprecision creates mush.

Some errors occur because the reporter is unaware of a word's exact meaning. Few journalists would report that a car "collided" with a tree, a "funeral service" was held or a child "was drowned" in a lake. Why? Two objects collide only if both are moving; thus, a car can strike a tree, but never collide with one. A funeral is a service; therefore, "funeral service" is redundant. A report that a child "was drowned" would imply that someone was responsible for drowning the child.

Such considerations are not trivial. Journalists who fail to use words correctly can undermine their credibility and the accuracy of their stories and confuse or irritate their audience. Thus, instructors will object when students use language that is sloppy and inaccurate.

When reporters fail to express ideas clearly and precisely, audiences can derive meanings different from the ones intended. The unintended meanings may be difficult for the writer to detect. Double meanings in the following headlines, all of which appeared in news oulets, illustrate the problem:

> Police Begin Campaign to Run Down Jaywalkers
>
> Farmer Bill Dies in House
>
> American Sentenced to Life in Scotland
>
> Prison Parolee Indicted for Killing Flees
>
> Iraqi Head Seeks Arms
>
> Aging Expert Joins Faculty

Confusion sometimes arises because words look or sound alike. College students often confuse words such as "buses" and "busses," "naval" and "navel," and "reckless" and "wreckless." The word "busses" refers to kisses, not the vehicles people ride in. A "navel" is a belly button, and some motorists drive "wrecks" but are convicted of "reckless" driving.

Some words are simply inappropriate in news stories. Few editors or news directors permit slang such as "cop" or "kid" (they prefer the more formal and proper "police officer" and "child") or derogatory terms about a person's race or religion.

Editors and news directors also ban the use of contractions except in direct quotations. Professional journalists object to using nouns as verbs. They would not write that someone "authored" or "penned" a book, a city "headquartered" a company or an event "impacted" a community.

4.7 Use Strong Verbs

Verbs can transform a drab sentence into an interesting and powerfully descriptive one. They help readers visualize the action. Notice the impact of the underlined words in the sentence below.

> Original: She scored a goal.

> Revised: Soccer Team Captain Maddie Duncan <u>seized</u> control of the ball from the opposing players, <u>maneuvered</u> it down the field and <u>booted</u> it into the goal keeper's net.

By comparison, the following original sentences are weak and bland, yet it is easy to improve them. Simply add a strong verb and change them from passive to active voice.

- ~~The bodies were located by~~ rescue workers ∧ shortly after 6:00 p.m.
  unearthed the bodies

- ∧ A historic railroad bridge that was once the tallest and largest in the world ~~was downed by strong thunderstorms that crossed the state Monday afternoon.~~
  Blustery thunderstorms sweeping across the state Monday afternoon toppled

Strong verbs describe one specific action. Weak verbs cover a number of different actions. The first sentence in the following example is ambiguous because it uses a weak verb. The last four use specific, descriptive verbs and are more informative:

> My mother got an Apple iPhone 14.

> My mother bought an Apple iPhone 14.

> My mother won an Apple iPhone 14.

> My mother stole an Apple iPhone 14.

> My mother received an Apple iPhone 14 for her birthday.

Avoid the repeated use of forms of the verb "to be," such as "is," "are," "was" and "were." These verbs are overused, weak and dull.

4.8 Problems to Avoid

4.8.1 Overuse of Adjectives and Adverbs

News writers avoid adverbs and adjectives because they lack the force and specificity of nouns and verbs. William Strunk Jr. and E. B. White, authors of the influential book "The Elements of Style," wrote, "The adjective hasn't been built that can pull a weak or inaccurate noun out of a tight place." Along the same lines, Mark Twain warned, "When you catch an adjective, kill it."

Most adverbs and adjectives waste space by stating the obvious. They may also unintentionally inject a reporter's opinion into the story. If you write about a child's funeral, you do not have to comment that the mourners were "sad-faced," the scene "grim" and the parents "grief-stricken." Nor is there reason to report that an author is "famous," a witness "alert" or an accident "tragic."

Editorial comments can often be removed by eliminating adverbs and adjectives:

- ~~It was not until Friday that~~ university officials ~~finally~~ released the
  Friday
  report ∧.

- Upon hearing about the ~~frivolous~~ lawsuit, the mayor ~~made it quite clear~~
  promised to fight it
  ~~that she plans to fight the outrageous complaint~~ ∧.

The word "finally" in the first sentence implies that university officials were negligent and should have released the report sooner. Similarly, reporting the facts in the second story clearly and concisely eliminates the need for words like "frivolous" or "outrageous." And saying the mayor made something "clear" implies she is stating a fact, not an opinion.

4.8.2 Clichés

Clichés are words or phrases that writers have heard and copied over and over. Many are so old and overused that they have lost their original impact and meaning. Clichés do not startle, amuse or interest the public.

The news media can overuse a fresh phrase so much that it quickly becomes a cliché. Within one day news stories used "jaw-dropping" to describe Rihanna's pregnancy clothes, Blake Lively's Instagram selfies, Elon Musk's ignorance about Social Security, travel facts, a Porsche 911 and more.

Journalists employ clichés when they lack the time or talent to find words more specific, descriptive or original. A reporter under deadline pressure may say that a fire "swept through" a building, an explosion "rocked" a city, police officers gave a suspect a "spirited chase" or protesters were an "angry mob."

Other clichés exaggerate. Few people are really as "blind as a bat," "cool as a cucumber," "light as a feather," "neat as a pin," "straight as an arrow," "thin as a rail" or "white as a sheet."

Political reporting is especially susceptible to clichés. A push to pass a bill becomes a "last-ditch effort." Opponents of the bill will say it is "chock full" of "pork." Legislators will hold meetings "shrouded in secrecy" to reach a "face-saving" compromise. If negotiations drag on, "pundits" will say it "begs the question" of whether "the much ballyhooed" plan will become law "at the end of the day."

4.8.3 Slang

Journalists avoid slang, which tends to be more faddish than clichés. Some words that started out as slang, such as "googled," have won acceptance as standard English. Most do not.

Feature stories and personality profiles sometimes employ slang effectively, but it is inappropriate in straight news stories because it is too informal and annoying. Moreover, slang may baffle readers who are not of the age or ethnic group to understand it. The result is that confused audiences will stop reading the story.

Slang is often specific to each generation and rapidly becomes dated so that a term used in a story may already be obsolete. During the 1990s, young people developed a set of "slammin'" slang terms and "dissed" anyone still using the slang of the 1980s. In the early 2000s, someone may have given "props" to friends who knew the "off the hook" films showing at the "grind-house" and gotten "stoked" about "poppin' tags" and looking for "lollipops" at the mall. Slang used to describe something that is awesome was "cool" and then "hot," and then "dope" or "sick." Some slang terms, such as GOAT or OMG, have evolved from abbreviations used in texts. If you are confused about these terms, try not to get "salty."

4.8.4 Technical Language and Jargon

People in trades and professions develop their own technical language or jargon. When professionals use jargon to impress or mislead the public, critics call it gobbledygook, bafflegab, doublespeak or bureaucratese. Most jargon is abstract, wordy, repetitious and confusing. For example, a government agency warned, "There exists at the intersection a traffic condition which constitutes an intolerable, dangerous hazard to the health and safety of property and persons utilizing such intersection for pedestrian and vehicular movement." That sentence contains 31 words. A good journalist could summarize it in four: "The intersection is dangerous."

Many of the sources reporters routinely use—doctors, lawyers, business people, press releases, technical reports, and police and court records—speak in or contain jargon. Journalists must translate such language into plain English. Consider this quote:

> Dr. Priya McKay said, "Ethnic groups that subsist on a vegetarian diet and practically no meat products seem to have a much lower level of serum cholesterol and a very low incidence of ischemic diseases arising from atherosclerotic disease."

The statement can be clarified by removing the jargon:

> Dr. Priya McKay said ethnic groups that eat little meat have low rates of coronary heart disease and related illnesses.

Technical language may be appropriate in some specialized publications or broadcasts intended for experts in a particular field, such as medicine, business or engineering. It is not appropriate in pieces aimed at a mass audience.

4.8.5 Euphemisms

Euphemisms are vague expressions used in place of harsher, more offensive terms. They often are used by journalists, public relations professionals, industrial and corporate leaders—as well as ordinary people—to soften blunt language, but they sometimes can lead to unintended consequences.

Howard Schultz, the chief executive officer of Starbucks, objected to being called a billionaire. Schultz, whose net worth is estimated at $3.6 billion, prefers the term "people of means" to describe him and others with similar wealth. Schultz was ridiculed for his idea, and super-rich people are still called billionaires. Other euphemisms have proved more enduring.

Some etiquette experts say that good manners require the use of euphemisms. Americans often say that a woman is "expecting" rather than "pregnant," and that they have to go to the "restroom" rather than the "toilet." Although etiquette may call for euphemisms, they can detract from good news writing, in which clarity and precision are the most important goals. And sometimes news events force reporters to use descriptive words in place of awkward euphemisms. A classic example is the story of Lorena Bobbitt, a Virginia woman who used a kitchen knife to cut off her husband's penis after he allegedly raped her. The word "penis" rarely had appeared in news stories, and some organizations were squeamish about using it, especially in headlines. Euphemisms like "member," "organ" or "offending organ" appeared instead. The widespread coverage the Bobbitt case received apparently diminished journalistic sensitivity to the word. A computer search found more than 1,000 news stories that used the word "penis" in the six months after the Bobbitt story broke, compared to only 20 mentions in the previous six months.

As with sex, Americans often employ euphemisms when talking about death. They say that a friend or relative "passed on" or is "no longer with us," not that he or she has died and been buried or cremated. Killing deer to control a population is "wildlife management" to "thin the herd" or "harvest" the deer. War spawns grotesque euphemisms, perhaps to hide the human pain and suffering every war causes. Airplanes no longer bomb enemy soldiers;

they "visit a site." Civilians who are killed during attacks are called "collateral damage."

During a recession, major companies lay off thousands of employees without admitting it. Instead, corporate executives say they are "restructuring," "downsizing" or "rightsizing" to get rid of "excess workers."

4.8.6 Profanity

Most newsrooms' ethics policies prohibit profanities in stories except when they are essential to a story's meaning; even then, they refuse to publish the most offensive terms. A leaked audio conversation between Victoria Nuland, former U.S. assistant secretary of state for European and Eurasian affairs, and Geoffrey Pyatt, the former U.S. ambassador to Ukraine, included profanity. The two were discussing using the United Nations to resolve a political crisis in Ukraine in 2014. Nuland said, "So that would be great, I think, to help glue this thing, and have the UN help glue it, and you know . . . fuck the EU." In an opinion piece in The New York Times, Jesse Sheidlower noted that most major news organizations, including The Washington Post, The Associated Press, The Wall Street Journal and CNN began the offensive word with "f" and completed it with dashes or asterisks. The Los Angeles Times said that Nuland used "a blunt expletive when expressing frustration." The New York Times noted that she had "profanely dismissed" European efforts in Ukraine. However, Reuters used the profanity in a direct quote.

To understand why news writers and editors avoid profanity, one has to look only at their audience. They provide information to a wide general public—one that encompasses many age, cultural and social groups—unlike the magazine industry, which often targets a specific audience. "Rolling Stone" readers can expect profanity in a story, but readers of The New York Times do not.

4.8.7 Stating the Obvious

Dull, trite, obvious remarks are called "platitudes," and journalists learn to avoid them.

When people stop reading, watching or listening to a story, they rarely think about why it bored them. Perhaps it is just a series of platitudes, which say nothing new. People quit reading the story because it is no longer interesting or newsworthy.

To avoid repeating platitudes, reporters must recognize them when they conduct interviews. Winners are always happy about winning an award. Couples get engaged because they are in love. If a bartender is robbed at gunpoint, there is no reason to quote him saying he was scared. Most people confronted by guns are scared, and they often say so. If journalists want to quote the bartender—or any other source—they should ask more penetrating questions until they receive more specific, interesting or unusual details.

4.8.8 First-Person References

Except in extraordinary circumstances, journalists should remain neutral observers. They should not mention themselves in news stories. Journalists avoid the words "I," "me," "we," "our" or "us," except when they are directly quoting some other person.

Beginning reporters sometimes use these words when referring to the community in which they work or the United States. Use of first-person pronouns implies the writer and the news organization endorse what is said. When the story involves political situations or actions, that implication undermines the objectivity of the news organization. Consider this example:

- The governor said ~~our~~ ∧ state ~~demands that we take action to~~∧ curb∧ ~~our government~~ spending. *(the)* *(must its)*

The pronouns "our" and "we" in the first version suggest the writer agrees with the governor, but others may think the amount the state spends is just right or too low.

4.8.9 Negative Constructions

For clarity, avoid negative constructions. Sentences should be cast in positive form, as in the following examples:

- The student ~~did not often come~~ ∧ to class. *(rarely came)*

- The defense attorney tried to ~~disprove her client's sanity~~ ∧. *(prove her client was insane)*

Sentences containing two or three negatives are wordy and even more difficult to decipher. These negative constructions force the reader to pause to determine their meaning:

- The women said they ~~are not against~~ ∧ the change. *(favor)*

- The senator said she would ~~not~~ accept ~~any~~ campaign contributions ∧ from people ~~who do not live~~ ∧ in her district. *(only)* *(living)*

- ~~Do not~~ turn in story assignments ~~after~~ ∧ deadline. *(on)*

4.8.10 Gush

Reporters avoid quoting sources who "gush" with exaggerated enthusiasm. They write news stories to inform members of a community, not to please their sources. News stories should report useful information. They should not praise or advocate.

One way to avoid gush is to use more than one source for a story. Another is to demand that sources provide specific details to support their generalizations. Using multiple sources who are independent of one another prevents reporters from being misled or manipulated by sources seeking favorable publicity about themselves. By insisting that sources provide data and precise examples to support their claims, reporters can minimize sources' tendency to engage in the kind of self-praise found in these sentences:

> "We feel we are providing quality recreational programs for both adults and children," Lavinia Holden, the director of the community center, said.

> Police Chief Barry Kopperud said the city's mounted horse patrol, which he began one year ago, has become a great success.

When a journalist finishes an article, it should sound like a news story, not a press release. Yet one travel story gushed that a new hotel has "state-of-the-art architectural appointments and beautiful landscaping." Gush cannot be rewritten because there is nothing of substance to rewrite. It should simply be deleted. News releases, as noted in Chapter 19, Journalism and Public Relations, are filled with gush in the form of laudatory adjectives ("informative lecture"), puffery ("well-known speaker") and empty quotes ("Our new HR director is an exciting addition to our team.")

4.8.11 Specific Time References

Unless your instructor tells you otherwise, use the day of the week to refer to events that occur on the day of publication or within seven days before or after publication. For events that are more than seven days in the past or future, use a specific date, such as July 23 or March 4.

Using the date or day of the week eliminates the confusion that might arise with the use of "today," "tomorrow" or "yesterday" in news stories. For example, if a fire destroyed a home at 5 p.m. Tuesday, a reporter would write the story later that evening for publication in the Wednesday newspaper. If the reporter wrote that the fire happened "today," readers would think the fire occurred on Wednesday.

"Yesterday," "today" and "tomorrow" may be used in direct quotations or to refer to the past, present or future in general and not to specific days. Journalists also avoid the word "recently" because it is too vague.

4.8.12 Use of the Present Tense

Print reporters avoid the present tense and terms such as "at the present time" in stories for the printed newspaper because many of the events they report end before readers receive the paper. A reporter working on deadline should not say, "A fire at the Grand Hotel threatens to destroy the entire block." Firefighters almost certainly would have extinguished the blaze before readers receive the paper hours later. For the same reason, a reporter covering a fatal accident should not say, "The victim's identity is not known." Police might learn the victim's identity in a few hours, and local radio and television stations might broadcast the person's name before subscribers receive their papers. Consequently, print journalists must use the past tense:

> A fire at the Grand Hotel was threatening to destroy the entire block at 11:30 p.m.

> Police were unable to learn the victim's identity immediately.

Stories written for broadcast or for immediate publication on a website or social media are more likely to use the present tense. When the story is likely to reach readers or viewers as the events are unfolding, the present tense may be more accurate and more compelling than the past tense.

4.8.13 Excessive Punctuation

Journalists avoid excessive punctuation, particularly exclamation points, dashes and parentheses! Exclamation points are rarely necessary and should never be used after every sentence in a story, regardless of that story's importance! Parentheses interrupt the flow of ideas and force people to pause and assimilate some additional, often jarring, bit of information:

> She (the governor) said the elderly population (people 65 and older) had grown twice as fast as any other segment of the state's population during the last 20 years.

Removing the parentheses makes the sentence easier to read:

> The governor said the percentage of people 65 and older had grown twice as fast as any other segment of the state's population during the last 20 years.

If a source says something that is vague or convoluted, the writer should paraphrase or use a partial quotation rather than insert explanations in parentheses. Here is an example, followed by the revision:

> "I wish they (school administrators) would quit fooling around," she said. "They say they don't have enough money (to hire more teachers), but I don't believe that. I know they have it (the money); it's just a matter of priorities—of using their money more wisely."

> The school administrators should "quit fooling around," she said. They say they do not have enough money to hire more teachers, but she does not believe that. "It's just a matter of priorities—of using their money more wisely."

The Reporter's Guide to the Language of News

Practice Using . . .

1. Subject-verb-object order for sentences.

2. Singular subjects with singular verbs, and plural subjects with plural verbs.

3. Pronouns that agree with their antecedents.

4. Active verbs and vivid nouns.

5. "That," "which," "who" and "whom" correctly.

6. Modifiers placed immediately before or after the noun they describe.

7. Precise words to convey fuller meaning.

8. Detail and explanation to answer all the questions one logically might ask about the topic.

9. Sentences in a positive rather than negative form.

10. Parallel sentence construction.

Avoid Using . . .

1. Adjectives and adverbs in your sentences.

2. Clichés, slang and euphemisms.

3. Loaded words and opinionated or artificial labels.

4. Gush, exaggeration, contrived labels and excessive punctuation.

5. First-person (I, we, our, etc.).

6. Personification.

7. Platitudes and stating the obvious.

8. "Yesterday," "today" or "tomorrow." (Use the day or the week or a date.)

9. Present tense when writing for print media; most events you write about already will have occurred. But for web or broadcast news stories, the present tense may be appropriate.

10. Spell-check programs to find all misspelled words.

 # Review Exercises

1. VOCABULARY

Choose the correct words in the following sentences and fix any errors in style and possessives. Consult The Associated Press Stylebook for preferred usage and Appendix B for the rules for forming possessives.

1. Social media are a (phenomena/phenomenon) of modern technology that (has/have) (altered/altared) the communication landscape.

2. The (envelop/envelope) the treasurer misplaced contained (about/around) $1,000 in contributions.

3. A large (bloc/block) of voters (alluded/eluded) to pollsters that the candidates were (elusive/illusive) when discussing (their/there/they're) views on foreign affairs.

4. She said rather (than/then) trying to (convince/persuade) the board of (trusties/trustees) to vote on the measure, she would work with the president and his (aids/aides).

5. They (hanged/hung) the new banner from a (pole/poll) and invited (more than/over) 200 (people/persons) to the ceremony.

6. Students are (liable/libel/likely) (to/too/two) demand (less/fewer) regulations (regardless/irregardless) what rules the committee might (adapt/adept/adopt).

7. The defendants (consul/council/counsel) (waived/waved) her right to a jury trial, saying he (adviced/advised) the defendant not to (chose/choose) that option.

8. The fire commissioner said the (forth/fourth) option to (reign/rein) in the cost of the firehouse expansion would be to (altar/alter) the (alley/ally) that is located behind the existing firehouse.

9. The woman, an (alumna/alumnae/alumni/alumnus) of the university, (implied/inferred)

that the restrictions she placed on her donation may seem (bizarre/bazaar), but eventually they would be (cited/sited/sighted) as revolutionary.

10. The teacher was (discreet/discrete) when he (complemented/complimented) the group (composed/comprised/constituted) of six students for their paper (entitled/titled) "News and Social Media in the Modern World."

2. ACTIVE AND PASSIVE VOICE

Rewrite the following sentences, changing passive to active voice and correcting other errors.

1. Some healthy choices can be made by cafeteria diners.

2. Most shoplifting by teenagers is done on impulse.

3. The robber was described by witnesses as a 20 year old male.

4. The car was destroyed by the flood waters.

5. The money was contributed to the foundation by a wealthy benefactor.

3. AGREEMENT

Correct all agreement errors in the following sentences. Rewrite the sentence if necessary.

1. The judge ruled that the committee acted within their rights when they voted to close the factory.

2. Each of the students were glad to be out of school for the summer.

3. The jury said they could not reach a decision, leading to a mistrial.

4. The performance of the first three musical acts were very good.

5. Every one of the students want the exam postponed a week.

4. PLURALS AND POSSESSIVES

Edit the following sentences, correcting for plurals, possessives and any other errors. Check Appendix B for the AP Style guide and Appendix C for Forming Possessives.

1. The womens car was parked nearby, and sheriffs deputies asked to see the owners drivers license.

2. The juror said she opposes assisted suicide because its a doctors job is to save peoples lives, not end them.

3. The principle insisted that parents unsafe complaints about the schools playground are unfounded.

4. Manvel Jones parents said there younger childrens teacher earned her bachelors degree in journalism and her masters degree in education.

5. Everyones money was stolen, and the neighborhood associations president said the policemen might not get it back.

5. WHO AND WHOM

Choose the correct relative pronoun in the following sentences.

1. You went with (who/whom) to cover the George Floyd protests?

2. (Who/whom) covered the George Floyd protests?

3. With (who/whom) did you go to the movies yesterday?

4. (Who/Whom) ate at the Waffle House with (who/whom) last week?

5. (Who/Whom) told (who/whom) to call if there were an emergency?

6. THAT AND WHICH

Choose the correct relative pronoun in the following sentences. Observe when a comma is needed.

1. She told us to get up early in the morning, (that/which) we already knew.

2. The snowblower (that/which) is in the garage is one of many he owns.

3. The church choir sings the service's only anthem, (that/which) always follows the sermon.

4. The lead, (that/which) is the first paragraph of the story, should catch the reader's attention.

5. The Camaro (that/which) was crumpled against a tree raced the other Charger (that/which) was overturned in the ditch.

7. MODIFIERS

Edit the following sentences, correcting for misplaced or dangling modifiers.

1. Touched and emotional, the letters to the soldiers were appreciated.

2. The child opened the box with the toy truck he received from his mother painted red.

3. Coming in soaking wet from the rain, the clothes were thrown in the dryer.

4. Having begged for bicycles for months, the father was thanked by his children.

5. While eating the hotdog, the ketchup and mustard tasted great to the boy.

8. PERSONIFICATION

Rewrite the following sentences, eliminating personification and any other errors.

1. The medicine bottle warns that its adverse effects include slowed heart beat, decreased respiratory function, sweating and nausea.

2. The accident occurred when the car driving east in the 100-block of Main St. collided with a dump truck that was driving west.

3. The meeting will decide whether the students have a right to protest the tuition increase.

4. Several vehicles pulled off the highway to assist police during the incident.

5. Witnesses told the jury they saw the tree collide with the car.

9. PARALLELISM

Rewrite these sentences in parallel form and correct all errors.

1. She said after paying their rent, tuition and shopping for food, students have little money left.

2. To be admitted to the program, students must submit a written application, a portfolio and complete a 500-word essay.

3. The accident victim sustained a broken right arm, a fractured pelvis and his right lung was punctured.

4. The waitress said the robber is in their mid 20s, was medium build, with dark blonde hair, wearing blue jeans, a green t-shirt and a blue cap.

5. The veterinarian said when the poor pooch was brought to the emergency room it was whimpering, obviously hurt and had been limping.

10. STRONG VERBS AND SENTENCE STRUCTURE

Rewrite the following sentences, using stronger verbs and normal word order (subject, verb, direct object) and correcting any other errors.

1. The decision to postpone construction of the building by university officials will come soon.

2. With no sugar or cream, the customer wanted a coffee from the waitress.

3. The accident had 5 cars.

4. Patients in dire need of treatment for serious injuries are required to be taken to the nearest hospital by paramedics.

5. The three-vehicle accident that closed Main Street for two hours so authorities could investigate was witnessed by a bystander who called police to the scene.

11. COMPLETE THE CLICHÉ

Fill in the missing word to recognize clichés.

1. a close brush with _____

2. a step in the right _____

3. could not believe her _____

4. evidence of foul _____

5. fell into the wrong _____

6. has a nose for _____

7. last but not _____

8. left holding the _____

9. lived to a ripe old _____

10. full of hot _____

12. CLICHÉS AND SLANG

Rewrite the following sentences, eliminating any clichés and slang.

1. The president of the company asked employees to give the benefit of the doubt to his restructuring plan, but his plea fell on deaf ears.

2. The crowd erupted in violence when the doors to the club were closed, leaving them outside.

3. The Democrat said the election had tipped the scales in favor of that party.

4. The students believed the program was doomed to failure because few supported it.

5. That movie made the character as dumb as an ox.

13. JARGON

Rewrite the following sentences, eliminating jargon. Correct any other errors.

1. Police said the perpetrators of the burglary would be arraigned later in the week.

2. Teresea Phillips, a/k/a Marie Phillips, testified that she entered the store and helped the defendant steal an unknown quantity of jewelry from the premises on or about the 9th day of last month.

3. The company said it would maximize efforts and utilize every department it had available to overcome the budget crisis.

4. The journalist said the lead, bridge and third graph needed to be reearranged.

5. Brown's lawsuit charges that he experienced the accused's threat of *bodily harm* in a convincing way which was followed by unlawful and unwelcome physical contact.

14. PLACEMENT

Rewrite the following sentences, moving the related words and ideas as close together as possible. Correct any other errors.

1. A 45-year-old man was sentenced to five years in prison after being convicted of embezzling $250,000 in Circuit Court Monday.

2. On streets around campus, the city counsel raised the parking fees from 75 cents to $1.50 an hour.

3. The police outside the bank arrested the man.

4. Born in Los Angeles, she moved with her family to Philadelphia where they opened a real estate business.

5. The principle suspended the student for possessing alcohol for one week.

6. The 16-year-old girl was driving home after school when her car struck the bridge traveling an estimated 50 mph.

7. He called owners of the dirt lots in the neighborhood to ask if he can plant them next summer.

8. The policeman said the suspect from an empty house stole electronics.

9. The new university president met to discuss student concerns with the board.

10. Over $5 million was needed in order to begin construction of the new arts center by the city.

15. MULTIPLE ERRORS

Rewrite the following sentences, correcting all errors. Most sentences contain more than one error. Check Appendix B for the AP Style guide and Appendix C for Forming Possessives.

1. A sheriffs deputy said she saw the teenagers Charger pull out of the alley, driving recklessly without its headlines on, and arrested it's driver.

2. The city said that they cannot silence Zheng Chen, the woman whom keeps harping that sure as shooting pollution is likely to effect the neighborhoods 321 residents.

3. Seeking more money, publicity, and to help the poor, the churchs members said it wants the city to help it by providing food and offer housing for the homeless.

4. The Public Works Department said they could pave the developments road themselves for less than $1.2 million, the Roess Company submitted a bid of $2.74 million.

5. A jury awarded almost $10.5 million to the operators of an abortion clinic (that praised the jury's verdict as a precedent) that charged that picketers tormented them and there clients.

6. The committee feels the program is a beneficial one (because a student can get class credit for all he does at the internship).

7. Pretty as a picture, she laid on the beach from 8 a.m. in the morning until 3 p.m. in the afternoon.

8. The policeman addressed the jury to say that they needed to understand how the robbery occurred during the trial.

9. The consensus of opinion among hospital administrators is that a pay raise of 15 to twenty percent should be received by nurses, first responders.

10. The woman said her son (who she considered to be a budding genius) was champing at the bit to get to college next year.

THE LAW AND ETHICS OF JOURNALISM

LIBEL, PRIVACY AND NEWS-GATHERING ISSUES

Shkelzen Berisha, an Albanian, sued the Simon & Schuster publishing company and Guy Lawson, an investigative journalist, in U.S. district court in 2017 for libel. Berisha said they had defamed him by publishing a book that suggested he was involved in the Albanian "mafia" and illegal arms sales. The focus of the book was how three Americans had become international arms dealers and had run afoul of U.S. law. Berisha was mentioned only a few times in the book.

A federal district court in Florida dismissed Berisha's lawsuit on the grounds that he lacked evidence to prove Lawson and Simon & Schuster published the book with actual malice. "Actual malice" means the publisher of a defamatory statement either knew it was false or had a high degree of awareness of its probable falsity at the time of publication. Berisha appealed to the U.S. Court of Appeals for the 11th Circuit, which affirmed the trial court's decision.

Berisha then asked the U.S. Supreme Court to review his case. It refused. With that, Berisha's case might have faded from public view. It has not, however, because two justices, Clarence Thomas and Neil Gorsuch, dissented from the decision to refuse to review the case. Both said the Supreme Court should reconsider the 1964 New York Times v. Sullivan decision that established the requirement that public officials and public figures must prove actual malice when they sue for defamation.

The dissents by Thomas and Gorsuch chilled many in the news business and many legal scholars. For nearly 60 years, the Sullivan decision has stood as the main pillar of First Amendment protection for the press and the public to report on, debate and criticize the actions, ideas and characters of public figures. It has protected vigorous investigative reporting, the kind that has revealed wrongdoing on the part of government agencies and officials, private businesses and others. It also protects the kind of commentary and criticism that is common in

> "The newspaper industry . . . serves one of the most vital of all general interests: the dissemination of news from as many different sources, and with as many different facets and colors as is possible. That interest is closely akin to, if indeed it is not the same as, the interest protected by the First Amendment; it presupposes that right conclusions are more likely to be gathered out of a multitude of tongues, than through any kind of authoritative selection. To many this is, and always will be, folly; but we have staked upon it our all."
>
> —*Learned Hand, U.S. judge*

publications such as right-wing talk radio, cable television news, partisan news sites on the web and magazines specializing in political opinions.

So far, only Thomas and Gorsuch have expressed an interest in reconsidering the Sullivan decision. At least four justices must vote to hear a case before it is put on the docket. No one knows whether any of the other seven justices want to reject or modify one of the most important protections for free expression in American law. The opinions of Thomas and Gorsuch, however, come at a time when a flurry of libel cases raises questions about how libel law should be applied.

- Alex Jones, who runs the Infowars website and purveys right-wing conspiracy theories, was facing three libel suits brought by parents of children who had died in the mass shooting at the Sandy Hook Elementary School in Newtown, Connecticut, in 2012. Jones had proclaimed the shootings never occurred, the children had not died, the parents were crisis actors, and the whole thing was a fraud perpetrated to push draconian gun-control laws. Because of Jones' statements, the parents suffered threats and harassment from Infowars followers who believed the allegations. All three lawsuits resulted in default judgments against Jones because he refused to disclose to the plaintiffs information they needed to demonstrate actual malice on his part. A Texas jury awarded plaintiffs nearly $50 million in damages, and a Connecticut jury awarded plaintiffs more than $1.4 billion. Jones is appealing both verdicts.
- Fox News, Newsmax, the Trump presidential campaign and several other organizations and individuals have been sued for libel in connection with allegations they have made about vote fraud in the 2020 presidential election. Closely watched was the lawsuit Dominion Voting Systems had brought against Fox News. Dominion, a manufacturer of machines and software for tabulating votes, claimed Fox News had disseminated defamatory allegations that its systems, used in several states, had erroneously switched votes for Donald Trump to Joe Biden. No evidence supported the claims, which were coming from Rudolph Guliani, Sidney Powell and others associated with Trump's campaign. During the weeks leading up to the trial, Dominion's lawyers filed briefs that described in detail some of the internal emails and messages sent by Fox officials and news personnel, such as Tucker Carlson and Laura Ingraham. Those emails indicated Fox news personnel and leaders knew the allegations of voter fraud were false. As the trial was about to begin, Fox reached a settlement with Dominion in which it agreed to pay Dominion $787.5 million in damages, the largest libel award ever. Dominion has other libel suits pending against other defendants. Smartmatic Inc., another maker of machinery and software for tabulating votes, also is suing Fox, the Trump campaign and others over allegations that their systems were used to switch

Alex Jones, seen here using a megaphone to speak to demonstrators at the Texas State Capitol in Austin, was sued by several families whose children died in the 2012 Sandy Hook massacre in Newtown, Connecticut. For years, Jones falsely said the massacre never happened and that the families were 'crisis actors.' Two juries have awarded the families nearly $1.5 billion in damages.

votes. Several private individuals, including Eric Coomer, the former director of product strategy and security for Dominion, and two election workers in Georgia are suing some of the same individuals and organizations. Those suits are still pending.

- Devin Nunes, a former member of Congress from California, sued Esquire magazine and journalist Ryan Lizza over a 2018 article titled "Devin Nunes's Family Farm Is Hiding a Politically Explosive Secret." The article said the family had quietly moved its dairy operations from California to Iowa and was employing undocumented workers. Nunes was not involved in running the farm—a fact Lizza reported—but the congressman did make reference to it when campaigning in California. Initially, Nunes' suit was dismissed for lack of evidence of actual malice, but the 8th U.S. Circuit Court of Appeals reinstated the suit, saying a tweet by Lizza after the suit had been filed might be evidence of actual malice. More recently, a federal district court again dismissed the suit, saying the defamatory allegations were essentially true.

- Johnny Depp, the star of the "Pirates of the Caribbean" movies, sued his ex-wife, Amber Heard, for libel over a column she wrote for The Washington Post. Heard said she was writing as a domestic abuse victim who had felt "culture's wrath for women who speak out." Depp was not named in the column, but he said it was tantamount to accusing him of having abused Heard. After a widely watched trial, a Virginia jury awarded Depp more than $10 million in actual damages and $5 million in punitive damages. The punitive damages were reduced to $350,000, the maximum allowed under state law. The jury also awarded Heard $2 million in damages for defamatory statements made by Depp's attorney. Initially, both Depp and Heard appealed parts of the verdict, but they later reached a settlement in which Heard agreed to pay Depp $1 million.

The Sullivan decision made it much more difficult for plaintiffs who are public officials, like Devin Nunes, or public figures, like Johnny Depp, to win libel suits. But it is not impossible. Several plaintiffs in similar situations have done so.

Journalism students usually investigate legal restraints on the media in specialized media law courses. This chapter introduces three areas that affect reporters almost daily: libel, privacy and access to news. The first two are covered more extensively because the danger of a lawsuit is high and the cost of losing—or even defending—one can be great.

5.1 Libel

Libel is defamation by written words or by communication in some other tangible form, whereas slander is defamation by spoken words or gestures. Traditionally, the law has treated

Amber Heard and Johnny Depp attend the 72nd Venice Film Festival in 2015.

libel more harshly because the written word was more permanent and could reach more people than the spoken word. Broadcasting blurred that line long ago because it can reach millions of people instantly. Many states now consider broadcast defamation libel rather than slander. The internet further erodes the distinction: Words, moving images and sounds can reach millions through the web, where they can remain almost indefinitely.

Libel is a major concern for the mass media. Juries sometimes award millions of dollars to successful plaintiffs. Damage awards in the hundreds of thousands of dollars are not uncommon. In 2019, an Ohio jury awarded $44 million in damages to the owners of a bakery who sued Oberlin College. Students had accused the bakery of racial profiling and discrimination. A judge later lowered the award to $31.5 million, which included attorneys' fees and expenses. Even when media organizations win libel suits, they still might spend millions on court costs and attorneys' fees.

Libel suits jeopardize not only a news organization's pocketbook but also its reputation. News organizations build their reputations on fairness and accuracy. A libel judgment blemishes that status, sometimes irreparably. Individual journalists involved in libel suits may also lose their reputations or their jobs. Therefore, journalists must know what constitutes libel and what defenses can protect them if they are sued.

5.1.1 The Elements of a Libel Suit

A person who files a libel suit involving a statement published in the mass media must prove certain elements. Different authorities have different requirements, but here are six generally recognized parts of a libel suit:

1. Defamation: A communication is defamatory if it is likely to injure the plaintiff's reputation among upstanding members of the community.

2. Identification: The defamatory communication is either explicitly or implicitly about the plaintiff.

3. Publication: The defamatory communication has been distributed to at least one person other than the plaintiff.

4. Falsity: Plaintiffs must present credible evidence that the defamatory communication is false.

5. Injury: Plaintiffs must present evidence that they have suffered some actual injury, which may be emotional or reputational as well as physical or economic. Plaintiffs who can prove the defendant published the statement with actual malice do not have to prove actual injury.

6. Fault: Plaintiffs must prove defendants either were negligent (failed to act reasonably in the circumstances) in publishing the defamatory communication or published it with actual malice. In most states, private individuals who sue for libel must prove only negligence to recover actual damages. Public officials and public figures must prove actual malice to recover any damages. Private individuals also must prove actual malice to recover punitive damages.

5.1.1.1 DEFAMATION

Proving that a statement is defamatory involves two steps. The first requires a judge to determine that the statement is legally capable of a defamatory meaning; in the second, a jury decides whether a substantial segment of the respectable public understood the statement as defaming the plaintiff.

Some statements obviously have the power to injure reputations—for example, statements that a person has committed a crime, has a terrible disease, has been incompetent in business or has engaged in serious sexual misconduct. A woman identified in court documents as Jane Doe sued singer and songwriter Sammy Hagar for libel over a passage in his autobiography, "Red: My Uncensored Life in Rock." The passage described an encounter Hagar had with Doe, who was working as a Playboy bunny. Hagar said Doe came to his hotel room while he was on tour with a band and engaged in sex with him, even though they were barely acquainted. The woman later claimed to be pregnant by him and wanted him to pay for the child. Hagar said a friend persuaded him to pay Doe some money, but he insisted, "I knew it was not my baby. It was extortion." Doe initially filed suit in Iowa state court, but the case was removed to a federal district court, which granted Hagar's motions to dismiss the case. The 8th U.S. Circuit Court, however, reversed in part. The appeals court said a jury should be allowed to decide whether the allegations of extortion and of engaging in promiscuous sex were defamatory per se.

But not every unflattering or even offensive statement is legally capable of a defamatory meaning. A statement must seem factual and believable. Calling a person a "scumbag," for instance, is too vague and imprecise to be defamatory. The context in which the statement appears may determine how recipients are likely to understand it. Before he died, the former Beatle George Harrison and the Honolulu Advertiser were sued by two of Harrison's neighbors. The newspaper had reported on Harrison's objections to a court order allowing his neighbors to cross parts of his property. "Have you ever been raped?" Harrison asked the Advertiser. "I'm being raped by all these people. . . . My privacy is being violated. The whole issue is my privacy." The neighbors claimed Harrison's remarks accused them of the crime of rape, but the Hawaii Supreme Court concluded "rape" was being used in a metaphorical rather than a literal sense and reasonable readers would understand it as such.

Sometimes, a statement conveys no obviously defamatory meaning. Instead, readers, viewers or listeners must combine the statement with known facts to find the defamation. Max Braun sued Armour & Co. over an advertisement that said his meat market carried Armour bacon. There's nothing obviously defamatory about selling bacon, but Braun ran a kosher store catering largely to Orthodox Jews. Many of Braun's customers who saw the ad stopped coming to the store. The New York Court of Appeals agreed that he had a case for libel.

Even when a publication is not explicitly defamatory, it may create defamatory implications by omitting key facts or by using certain combinations of words and pictures. When James Humphreys, a criminal defense lawyer, ran as a Democrat for a West Virginia congressional seat, he asked his former neighbors Harry Bell and his wife to endorse him and appear in a photograph with him. The photo ran in a Humphreys campaign brochure and on his website; it also appeared in an attack pamphlet prepared by the National

Republican Congressional Committee, with the headline "Humphreys Defended Sex Offenders as a Criminal Defense Lawyer." Next to the heading was the photo of Humphreys and Harry Bell, with Bell's wife cropped from the picture. Bell claimed the brochure defamed him because the juxtaposition of the headline and the photograph implied he was a sex offender. A federal district judge agreed.

5.1.1.2 IDENTIFICATION

Libel plaintiffs have no trouble establishing identification in cases involving the news media. News stories usually identify sources or subjects clearly by name. In fact, detailed identification protects reporters against libel suits.

Many suits arise from situations in which similar names create confusion. If a Sam Johnson is arrested for selling cocaine, the commonness of the name creates the possibility of misunderstanding. By identifying the person arrested as Samuel H. Johnson Jr. of 3517 N. Forest St., Apt. 303, the reporter eliminates the possibility of inadvertently defaming other Sam Johnsons in town.

A publication can identify a plaintiff without using a name. In response to a lawsuit, a New York hospital issued a press release that referred to "misconduct carried out by former executives." Joseph A. Pisani, a former vice president of the hospital, sued for libel. The press release never used Pisani's name, but a federal district court held that the hospital's statement did identify him. The press release contained a hyperlink to the complaint in the original lawsuit, which mentioned him in connection with the misconduct, and he was fired on the day the hospital issued the press release.

5.1.1.3 PUBLICATION

Obviously, when a statement has appeared in a newspaper or on a television broadcast, it has been published. However, a statement does not have to be so widely disseminated for a person to sue for libel. The law requires only that the defendant made the statement to someone other than the person defamed. For example, Greenmoss Builders sued business services company Dun & Bradstreet for releasing a credit report with erroneous and damaging information about the contractor. Greenmoss won, even though only five clients received the report.

Writing a blistering email that accused someone of stealing money would not constitute publication if the only person to receive it were the one accused. Posting the same accusation on Facebook, Twitter, Instagram or some other internet platform where it could be seen by other people—even just a few—would satisfy the publication requirement.

Once a defamatory statement is published, the plaintiff must sue within the time specified by the state's statute of limitations. In most states, the statute of limitations is one or two years. A few allow as many as three years. In all states, the statute of limitations runs from the most recent publication; republishing a defamatory statement extends the time during which the plaintiff may sue. Courts have held that the statute of limitations for online publications begins when the content is posted, while updates to the page and hyperlinks to an older page are not considered new publications that restart the clock.

Another issue connected with the internet is the liability of interactive service providers. Ordinarily a publisher is responsible for any material it publishes, but a federal law, Section 230 of the Communications Decency Act, says interactive service providers shall not be treated as publishers of information others provide to them. East Coast Test Prep LLC, a company that provides test preparation services for nursing students and others, sued Allnurses.com, Inc., the operator of an online discussion board for nurses. One of the threads on the discussion board dealt with Test Prep's services and its advantages and disadvantages. A couple of the posts said Test Prep was under investigation and another said people commenting in other forums accused the service of having deceived them. Test Prep contended the comments were libelous, but a federal district court dismissed the case, partly because of Section 230. That decision was affirmed by the 8th Circuit Court of Appeals. The court said Test Prep had presented no evidence Allnurses was in any way responsible for the creation of development of the content.

5.1.1.4 FALSITY

Some students confuse falsity and defamation. A statement may be false but not defamatory. Falsely saying someone is a war hero, for instance, does not defame that person. Conversely, a true statement may be defamatory. Saying someone was arrested for selling cocaine would defame that person, but he or she must be able to present evidence of falsity to sue for libel. The U.S. Supreme Court imposed this burden on all plaintiffs when the allegedly defamatory statements involve a matter of public concern. Making plaintiffs prove falsity means some defamed persons might not recover damages, but making defendants prove truth means some truthful publications will be punished. The court decided that, when the mass media publish statements about matters of public concern, the First Amendment requires tipping the balance in favor of freedom of the press.

So, what is a matter of public concern? The Supreme Court did not define that when it ruled that libel plaintiffs would have to prove falsity. Years later, in a case that did not involve defamation, the Supreme Court defined "public concern" as speech that related "to any matter of political, social, or other concern to the community. . . or . . . is a subject of legitimate news interest; that is, a subject of general interest and of value and concern to the public." That definition is not fully satisfying; indeed, it is circular. Nevertheless, it suggests that if professional journalists find something to be interesting and valuable to the public, it probably will be a matter of public concern, and if it becomes the subject of a libel suit, the plaintiff will carry the burden of proving it false.

5.1.1.5 INJURY

Under traditional libel law, courts presumed obviously defamatory statements had injured plaintiffs. They did not have to produce any evidence of injury to reputation, monetary loss or emotional suffering unless the defamatory nature of the statement was not readily apparent. In 1974, the U.S. Supreme Court said the presumption of injury was incompatible with the First Amendment. Since then, libel plaintiffs usually have had to prove "actual injury," meaning damage to reputation, humiliation and mental anguish to recover damages. There are two exceptions to this requirement: if the plaintiff can prove the defendant made the defamatory statements with actual malice or if the defamatory statements do not involve a matter of public concern.

A case requiring proof of injury involved former Chicago Bulls player Scottie Pippen, who lost much of his fortune because he received bad financial advice. When news organizations learned of his financial problems, some falsely reported he had filed for bankruptcy. Pippen sued for libel. A federal appeals court held that saying Pippen had filed for bankruptcy was not defamatory on its face. Many people go bankrupt through no fault of their own, and his work as a sports commentator and product endorser did not depend on his financial management skills. Pippen contended he had lost business opportunities after the publication, but a federal appeals court said Pippen would have difficulty showing the false news stories were the cause. The business opportunities for retired athletes decline after they have been out of the game for several years. In any event, the court said, he would lose his lawsuit because he could not prove actual malice.

5.1.1.6 FAULT

The most crucial issue in modern libel cases is fault, which refers to the state of mind of the person who uttered the allegedly defamatory statement. In other words, did the publisher knowingly, recklessly or negligently say something false and defamatory? Before 1964, many states said publishers of defamatory statements would have to pay damages even if they had taken every reasonable step to ensure the accuracy of the story. The Supreme Court changed that rule in 1964 for public officials who sue for libel and changed it for public figures in cases decided in 1967 and 1974.

Public officials and public figures must prove that a defamatory statement was published with actual malice. The word "malice" causes confusion because many people think it means ill will or an intent to harm, but whether the defendant disliked or wanted to harm the plaintiff is not an issue. All that matters is whether the defendant knew the statement was false or had a high degree of awareness of the statement's probable falsity when it was published. Proving actual malice can be difficult, as the plaintiff must produce evidence about the defendant's state of mind.

Sarah Palin, the former governor of Alaska and Republican vice-presidential candidate, sued the New York Times in 2017 over an editorial that falsely suggested an advertisement published by her political action committee had helped inspire the gunman who killed six people and wounded 14, including U.S. Rep. Gabrielle Giffords, in Phoenix in 2011. The editorial was written on the day of another shooting, an attack on Republican members of Congress who were practicing for a softball game. The Times corrected the error the next day, but Palin was not satisfied. Her suit was initially dismissed by the

This March 1960 advertisement initiated the lawsuit that led to the Supreme Court's ruling that public officials must prove actual malice to recover damages for libel.

federal district court in New York, but it was reinstated by the 2nd U.S. Circuit Court of Appeals. After a trial in 2022, a jury found in favor of the Times. The judge who presided over the trial, Jed Rakoff, said he would have dismissed the case regardless of the jury's verdict because Palin had failed to produce evidence of actual malice on the part of the Times staff member who wrote the editorial. Palin asked Rakoff for a new trial, but he refused. She is appealing the verdict with the hope the U.S. Supreme Court will use her case to overturn the Times v. Sullivan decision.

Since 1964, courts have handed down hundreds of decisions elaborating on what is and is not evidence of actual malice. The following list is not exhaustive but indicates the factors the courts consider.

It may be evidence of actual malice if the news organization:

- Simply made up a story or the parts of it that are defamatory, such as fabricating quotations that make the source look immoral, incompetent or criminal.
- Published without investigating allegations from a source known to be unreliable or biased against the person defamed.
- Published an unverified story that is so inherently improbable that only a reckless person would believe it.
- Failed to check known sources that could conclusively confirm or deny a defamatory allegation.
- Published an allegation based on nothing but speculation or a guess on the part of the reporters.
- Published information from a source who, prior to the publication, had retracted the statement and the reporter was aware of the retraction.

It generally is not evidence of actual malice if a news organization:

- Displayed ill will toward or an intent to harm the subject. A news organization's editorials against a political candidate, for instance, are not evidence by themselves that it published a defamatory news story with awareness of its falsity.
- Failed to investigate a story when the journalists responsible had no reason to doubt its truthfulness.
- Failed to investigate all the facts in a breaking news story—a story that had to be published quickly—and had no reason to doubt the truthfulness of what it was publishing.
- Made negligent errors in reporting a story, such as confusing or misspelling names or reporting complicated statistics incorrectly.
- Selected a reasonable, but mistaken, interpretation of a complicated or ambiguous document.
- Adopted an adversarial or investigative stance in reporting a topic.
- Published allegations even though the subject of the story denied them but failed to offer any evidence that they were false.

Private individuals have less difficulty winning libel suits. In most states, they must prove only that the defendant acted with negligence to recover actual damages. "Negligence" essentially means acting unreasonably under the circumstances. Whether a news organization acted unreasonably is a decision the jury will make. Jurors might think reporters acted unreasonably if they made errors by failing to check public records, misspelling or confusing names or accidentally transposing dates or figures.

5.1.2 Who Is a Public Official? Who Is a Public Figure?

Because public officials and public figures must prove actual malice to win a libel suit, determining whether a plaintiff fits either category often decides the outcome of a case. The Supreme Court has provided only hazy guidelines for distinguishing public officials and public figures from private individuals, leaving states with plenty of room to expand or contract the categories.

The more clearly defined category is that of public official. The Supreme Court has said public officials must hold some government position. The category includes not only elected officials, such as U.S. senators, state legislators and city council members, but also appointed officials and government employees. Even unpaid government officials can be public officials for purposes of libel law. But being on the government payroll is not enough. While upper echelon officials such as governors and school superintendents are clearly public officials, a low-ranking worker in the city sanitation department or a secretary in the city attorney's office probably would not be one. A gray area exists between the top and the bottom levels, with the state courts deciding who belongs where. Most courts have found law enforcement officers and others who make decisions that affect the rights, liberty, health and safety of the public to be public officials.

Identifying public figures is even more difficult than identifying public officials. The Supreme Court tried to define "public figure" in a way that would keep the category small. It recognized three types: involuntary, general-purpose and limited-purpose. The court said the essence of public-figure status is that a person has voluntarily assumed some special prominence or role in society; therefore, the involuntary public figures must necessarily be rare, almost to the point of being nonexistent. The other two groups are somewhat larger.

The general-purpose public figure has such persuasive power and influence as to be a public figure for all occasions. Celebrities from entertainment and sports, such as Ansel Elgort, Taylor Swift, Denzel Washington, Lady Gaga, LeBron James and Patrick Mahomes, would probably fit this definition. So would people from other walks of life who have become unusually prominent—people like Elon Musk, Ann Coulter and Neil deGrasse Tyson. The Supreme Court said this group also must be small because few people attain such widespread notoriety. Someone would not have to be nationally famous to be a general-purpose public figure, however. Local celebrities could be general-purpose public figures in their communities.

U.S. Sen. Ted Cruz, R-Texas, at the 2022 Conservative Political Action Conference in Texas. Cruz is an example of a public official for purposes of libel law.

The largest category of public figures consists of those who hold that status for the limited purpose of commenting on some particular topic or issue. These public figures have taken the lead in trying to influence the public on some controversial issue. People who organize an abortion-rights march, lead an effort to persuade a school board to change the curriculum in history classes, or argue publicly for laws allowing people to carry concealed weapons are limited-purpose public figures. They must prove actual malice only if the defamatory statements are germane to the public controversy in which they are involved.

Journalists need to remember that just being involved in a newsworthy event does not make a person a public figure. The Supreme Court has said that people involved in civil court cases, criminal suspects and defendants, individuals and businesses that receive money from the government, and lawyers representing people in court are not automatically public figures. Such people have not necessarily stepped forward to influence the resolution of a public controversy.

Beyoncé and Jay-Z, seen here at the Metropolitan Museum of Art Costume Institute Gala, are public figures for the purposes of libel law.

5.1.3 Major Defenses to Libel Suits

The difficulty of proving actual malice has become media organizations' major defense in libel cases. Other defenses are available, and they can be important in some cases. The main ones are truth, fair-report privilege and fair comment and criticism.

5.1.3.1 TRUTH

The use of truth as a defense arose when courts presumed defamatory statements were false. Although plaintiffs must now prove falsity, proving a statement true can still defeat a libel claim.

Proving truth does not mean proving a news report accurate in every detail. Most courts require defendants to prove only the sting or the gist of the charge is true. For example, a television news report about four Florida teenagers being arrested for bullying and defaming other teens on Facebook said "dozens" had been victimized, implying there were at least 24 victims. One girl who had been arrested and her parents sued for libel, arguing that this number was wrong, and the police had never said how many teens were defamed. But a Florida court said the sting of the news report was that the girl had been arrested for cyberbullying, which was true. The precise number of victims did not affect the truth of that report.

The defense of truth does not protect the accurate republication of defamatory charges made by other people. A news organization that reports a defamatory statement a bank president makes about a competitor cannot escape liability by demonstrating that it accurately quoted the speaker—it is also responsible for proving that the underlying statement is true. There are some exceptions to this rule; the main one is the fair-report privilege, which allows news organizations to report on official proceedings and documents.

5.1.3.2 FAIR-REPORT PRIVILEGE

The law recognizes certain occasions when people need absolute protection from libel suits. Public officials such as legislators or prosecuting attorneys cannot be sued for defamation because of what they say in carrying out their official duties. People who testify in court cannot be sued over what they say. News organizations enjoy a similar privilege to report on what happens in courtrooms and legislative chambers and on what official documents say. As a result, a reporter covering a trial cannot be sued for reporting false and defamatory statements made by a witness so long as the story accurately summarizes the testimony.

This defense is powerful, but it can lead to injustices. New Jersey resident Janice Lee, a sales account manager for a distributor of hair products, was arrested by New York police during their bust of an alleged sex-and-prostitution ring. The New York attorney general's office announced at a press conference and in a press release that Lee had been arrested along with several other suspects. News of the arrest was disseminated by media in both states. Lee was innocent of all charges filed against her. Nevertheless, she spent nearly a week in jail and several more days getting the charges dropped. She later sued several news organizations for libel for having publicized her arrest. The federal district court that heard her case ruled that the fair-report privilege protected the news stories because they were "full, fair and accurate" reports of statements issued by the New York attorney general.

Journalists have the fair-report privilege when describing such governmental proceedings as court hearings, administrative agency meetings and legislative sessions at all levels of government, from town council to Congress. In most states, the privilege extends to official documents, such as police reports, health inspection reports, official government correspondence and court records. In some states, the privilege also applies to reports of nongovernmental meetings open to the public for discussion of matters of public concern.

Justin Bieber's arrest report in Miami on January 23, 2014, for suspicion of drunk driving. News reports based on official documents like this one are protected from libel suits so long as they fairly and accurately describe the documents, even if those documents contain defamatory falsehoods.

A news organization loses the protection of the fair-report privilege if its report of the official proceedings or documents is distorted in ways that would injure the plaintiff's reputation. Also, the privilege does not apply to information obtained from sources other than official documents or proceedings.

5.1.3.3 FAIR COMMENT AND CRITICISM

Everyone has the right to an opinion. The fair comment and criticism defense protects from libel suits people who express their opinions about matters of legitimate public interest. Usually, the defense applies only if the opinions are based on true facts, are the sincere opinions of the speakers and are not motivated solely by ill will.

Courts have struggled with how to separate statements of fact from statements of opinion. Much of what newspapers, magazines, TV news broadcasts and blogs publish blends fact and opinion. Editorials may state opinions, but they also contain facts. News stories may report facts, but they also report the opinions of the journalist's sources. Courts must carefully parse language to separate the two. A persistent issue is how much emphasis courts should give to the context in which a defamatory statement appears.

A case involving a book review published in The New York Times illustrates the difficulties courts have with the fair-comment defense. In his review of "Interference," a book on organized crime's influence on professional football, Gerald Eskenazi concluded that the work contained "too much sloppy journalism." The book's author, investigative reporter Dan Moldea, thought the remark libeled him and sued. After a federal district court granted The Times' motion to dismiss the case, Moldea appealed to the U.S. Court of Appeals for the District of Columbia Circuit. At first, the appeals court ruled that the statement was sufficiently factual that a jury could decide whether it was true. Furthermore, the appellate court said U.S. Supreme Court precedents prevented it from attaching much weight to the fact that the statement appeared in a book review.

A short time later, however, the court reconsidered its decision and concluded that the Supreme Court's rulings did not prevent courts from considering context in libel cases. When context is relevant, it helps indicate whether people will understand a statement as factual. The court said that, in the context of a book review, the accusation of sloppy journalism was exactly the kind of thing a reader would interpret as opinion and not as something that could be proved true or false.

5.1.4 Steps for Avoiding Libel Suits

No checklist or set of steps can guarantee that a news organization will never face a libel suit. Some have been sued even after they have checked stories and found evidence for every potentially defamatory statement. Usually, the conscientious news organization will win, but the cost of defending against the suit can be daunting.

Here are some things journalists can do to limit their risk:

a. Make sure everything in the story, especially any potentially defamatory statement, is newsworthy. Nothing is gained by risking a lawsuit over a statement that has no news value.

b. Identify everyone mentioned in the story as fully as possible.

c. Ask people who are attacked or criticized in news stories to respond, and include the response, even if it is just a flat denial. If a person refuses to respond, say so in the story.

d. If a person who has been attacked or criticized offers evidence to support his or her denials, check out that evidence.

e. Interview every relevant source and read every relevant document; do not ignore sources or information that might contradict any potentially defamatory statements.

f. Find out what basis a source has for making a defamatory charge and what the source's motives might be.

g. If a source for a story has credibility problems, explain them in the story.

h. Avoid confidential or anonymous sources. Reporters might be asked to reveal their sources at a libel trial. If they refuse to do so, judges may tell jurors to assume the reporters made up the information.

i. Never use confidential or anonymous sources for making attacks on a subject. Use them only for facts that can be verified by other sources or documents.

j. If a story uses documentary sources, make sure the documents are understood and quoted accurately. Double-check the information in any documents; even official records may have errors.

k. If a story is not breaking news, take additional time to make sure the investigation is thorough and the story is accurate.

l. Adhere to organizational policies regarding keeping notes, tapes and other materials. If the policy is to keep all such materials, be sure everything is kept. If the policy is to destroy materials, make sure all are destroyed. Do not destroy some and keep others.

5.2 Privacy

At just over 130 years old, the right to sue for invasion of privacy is relatively new in terms of legal history. Yet lawsuits over various forms of this type of offense have become a major concern to media organizations because people worry about their privacy.

The law recognizes four kinds of invasion of privacy: intruding on a person's seclusion or solitude, giving publicity to private facts, placing a person in a false light and appropriating a person's name or likeness for one's own benefit (see Table 5.1). The last is primarily a concern for advertisers, although news and advertising messages could be the basis for a lawsuit over any of the four forms. The status of these four ways of invading privacy varies from state to state. Some states have recognized them in statutes; in others, rights to sue for invasion of privacy have been recognized in court decisions. Some states do not recognize all four forms. Nebraska, for example, does not recognize a right to sue for giving publicity to private facts, and Texas does not recognize false-light actions.

TABLE 5.1 **TYPES OF PRIVACY INVASION**

Type	Legal Requirement
Intrusion	To establish a case for invasion of privacy by intrusion, the plaintiff must show that a. the defendant intentionally intruded, physically or otherwise, on the plaintiff's solitude or seclusion, and b. the intrusion would be highly offensive to a reasonable person in the plaintiff's situation.
Publicity to private facts	A plaintiff suing over publicity given to private facts must prove a. the defendant gave publicity to b. private facts about the plaintiff, c. the disclosure of which would be highly offensive to a reasonable person in the plaintiff's situation, and d. the facts disclosed are not a matter of public concern.
False light	The plaintiff in a false-light lawsuit must prove a. the defendant portrayed the plaintiff in a false light b. that would be highly offensive to a reasonable person in the plaintiff's situation. In some states, all false-light plaintiffs must prove the defendant portrayed the plaintiff in a false light with the knowledge of its falsity or reckless disregard for whether it was false (actual malice). Some states say only public officials and public figures who sue for false light must prove actual malice. Private individuals can win by proving the defendant was negligent.
Appropriation	A person suing for appropriation (sometimes called misappropriation) must prove that a. the defendant used the plaintiff's name or likeness b. without consent c. for the defendant's benefit (usually meaning some kind of commercial benefit). A similar type of lawsuit, usually brought by a celebrity, is over infringement on one's right of publicity. This requires the plaintiff to show that the defendant a. used some distinctive element of the plaintiff's identity b. without consent and c. caused injury to the plaintiff (which may simply be the loss of an opportunity to capitalize on one's fame).

5.2.1 Intrusion

Intrusion represents what most people think of as invasion of privacy. Barging into a person's home without permission or rummaging through someone's private desk is intrusion. But one does not have to enter another's space physically to commit intrusion. One could intrude by technological means, such as using a powerful telephoto lens to see someone in a private location or using highly sensitive microphones to pick up a private conversation.

Plaintiffs in an intrusion case must be able to show they had a reasonable expectation of privacy in the place into which the defendant intruded. Some places obviously are private: a person's home, a hotel room, a hospital room, a handbag or a briefcase. Even if a newsworthy event is happening on private property, a journalist may not enter without the owner's or legal occupant's permission.

The California Supreme Court has also found that the reasonable expectation of privacy extends to at least some workplace situations. An ABC reporter, Stacy Lescht, worked undercover at a company that offered psychic readings by telephone. While on the job, Lescht wore a hidden microphone and camera. She recorded conversations she had with some of her co-workers, among them Mark Sanders. After ABC aired a story about the telepsychic business, Sanders sued for invasion of privacy. A jury awarded him $1.2 million in damages. An appeals court reversed the award, but the California Supreme Court reinstated it. ABC contended Sanders had no expectation of privacy because the telepsychics worked in open cubicles and could hear one another's conversations. However, the Supreme Court noted the office was not open to the general public; therefore, Sanders had a reasonable expectation that his conversations with colleagues would not be recorded or photographed surreptitiously and broadcast. Patrons and employees of businesses that are open to the public, such as restaurants and stores, may also have some reasonable privacy expectations.

As this case shows, the surreptitious recording of conversations is an issue closely related to intrusion. Reporters should always ask sources for permission to record conversations with them, even though under federal law—18 U.S.C. §2511(2)(d)—and the law of most states, reporters may record conversations to which they are a party without asking permission from others. However, 12 states—California, Delaware, Florida, Hawaii, Illinois, Maryland, Massachusetts, Montana, Nevada, New Hampshire, Pennsylvania and Washington—currently require the consent of all parties, at least in situations where there is an expectation of privacy.

Surreptitiously photographing people also presents legal problems. At least 24 states outlaw using hidden cameras in private places. The laws vary widely: Some apply only to unattended cameras; others prohibit only attempts to use hidden cameras to photograph people in the nude. Dani Mathers, a former Playboy Playmate of the Year, was charged with a misdemeanor after she took a photo of a nude 71-year-old woman in a Los Angeles fitness club locker room. Mathers posted the photo on Snapchat, along with the comment, "If I can't unsee this then you can't either." After changing her initial not-guilty plea to no contest, she was sentenced to 30 days' community service and three years' probation; the fitness club also banned her from all 800 of its U.S. facilities.

A case that applies intrusion law to the internet arose from a dispute between a woman seeking to sell a business property and a real estate agent in Montana. The seller was Sherry Spencer, the mother of Richard Spencer, a prominent neo-Nazi. The real estate agent was Tanya Gersh, who is Jewish. Spencer and Gersh discussed the sale of the business property, but a dispute arose. Andrew Anglin, the publisher of Daily Stormer, a neo-Nazi publication and a friend of Spencer's, learned of the dispute and began publishing articles about Gersh's dealings with Spencer. The articles culminated in one that asked Daily Stormer readers, "Are y'all ready for an old fashioned Troll Storm?" It gave readers Gersh's phone numbers, email addresses and social media profiles and similar information about her husband and 12-year-old son. Anglin asked readers, "Tell them you are sickened by their Jew agenda to attack and harm the mother of someone whom they disagree with." Gersh and her family received more than 700 messages filled with ethnic slurs, Holocaust references and threats of violence. She sued Anglin in federal district court for intrusion, intentional infliction of emotional distress and violation of Montana's Anti-Intimidation Law.

Anglin asked the court to dismiss the case, but the district judge refused. He said that Anglin may be liable for wrongful intrusion under Montana law. That law imposes liability for intruding on another's private activities in a way that causes mental suffering, shame or humiliation. If the facts Gersh alleged in her complaint were proven in court, it could satisfy the legal test for wrongful intrusion.

While someone on a public street or in a public park has no expectation of privacy, there are limits to what reporters can do even in public places. Photographers or reporters who become so aggressive that they place their subjects in danger may be committing intrusion or other torts. Courts do not consider ordinary news-gathering techniques—examining public records; interviewing someone's friends, relatives, enemies and associates; and interviewing or attempting to interview a person—intrusive.

5.2.2 Giving Publicity to Private Facts

Everybody has secrets, and most people would be upset if theirs became public. Lawsuits for publicizing private facts allow people to receive compensation for injuries when their secrets are revealed. This form of privacy lawsuit, however, presents a potential for conflict with the First Amendment because an unfavorable judgment may punish someone who published the truth.

For such a case to be successful, the information disclosed must be truly private. Publicizing—meaning disseminating widely—facts that appear in public records, even if they are not generally known, cannot be the basis for a lawsuit. For example, property tax information is public record in most states. If a news organization publishes a list of the most valuable homes in the community, who owns them and how much the owners pay in property taxes, the people named cannot sue for invasion of privacy. Even if the information is not in a public record but is merely known to a large number of people, publicizing it does not invade that person's privacy.

The information publicized must also be highly offensive to a reasonable person. Disclosure of information that is merely embarrassing cannot be the basis for a lawsuit. The "reasonable person" standard is imprecise, but it asks juries to decide not by what would be offensive to the most sensitive or insensitive individual but by what a reasonable person in the plaintiff's situation would find highly offensive. Not surprisingly, many of the cases involve sex or nudity. Publicizing private medical information, relationships with spouses or children and personal financial information might also be highly offensive.

Even if the matter publicized is highly offensive to a reasonable person, the plaintiff still must prove there is no legitimate public interest in the information. Courts generally have held that news organizations may publish private facts about people so long as they bear some logical connection to a matter of public concern, such as information about people who are victims of accidents or crimes.

Terry Bollea (aka Hulk Hogan) testifies against Gawker at the Pinellas County Courthouse in St. Petersburg, Florida.

Gawker Media pushed the limit of what is newsworthy when it posted portions of a video of Terry Bollea, better known as former wrestling star Hulk Hogan, having sex with Heather Clem. Bollea sued Gawker for invasion of privacy. Lawyers for the website argued that, as Hulk Hogan, the plaintiff had bragged about his sexual prowess and penis size; thus, he could not claim that his sexual activities were private. Bollea said that Hulk Hogan was a public character, but the video showed a private moment. A Florida jury concluded the video was not newsworthy and awarded Bollea $115 million in actual damages and $25 million in punitive damages. Gawker later agreed to pay Bollea $31 million, but the settlement drove Gawker Media and its founder, Nick Denton, into bankruptcy.

Courts generally have interpreted the phrase "matter of public concern" to include not only political and governmental information but also news of sports, entertainment, fashion and other matters likely to engage popular attention. The public interest is broader in people who are public figures—movie stars, sports heroes and important political figures—but the public may also have a legitimate interest in private individuals who have been caught up in newsworthy events. Moreover, this interest extends beyond the specific event or situation and includes other aspects of the subject's life and information about his or her relatives, so long as those facts bear on the matter of public concern.

5.2.3 False Light

A false-light invasion of privacy lawsuit resembles a libel suit in many respects. In fact, a person often may sue for either or both on the same evidence. The major difference between them is that a libel suit redresses injury to a person's reputation, whereas a false-light suit protects a person's interest in being left alone.

Actor José Solano Jr., who played Manny Gutierrez on the TV show "Baywatch," sued Playgirl magazine after it used his picture, without permission, on its cover. Solano said the picture and accompanying headlines gave the false impression he had posed nude for the magazine. The headlines said things like "12 Sizzling Centerfolds Ready to Score With You," "TV Guys: Prime Time's Sexy Young Stars Exposed" and "'Baywatch's' Best Body: José Solano." A federal appeals court said the juxtaposition of the photo and the headlines could convey the false and highly offensive impression that Solano had posed nude for the magazine. Furthermore, there was evidence the editors knew they were conveying a false impression. The magazine's senior vice president had ordered the editors to "sex up" the magazine. And subordinate editors were aware the headline about the centerfolds was positioned where headlines about the person pictured on the cover normally run.

5.2.4 Appropriation

People who use the name or likeness of another for their own use or benefit may be sued for invasion of privacy by appropriation. This was the first form of invasion of privacy to win recognition in a statute. The most common form of appropriation is the use of a person's name or likeness in an advertisement.

Retired basketball star Michael Jordan received substantial payouts from two supermarket chains when their advertisements featuring his name and jersey number appeared in a commemorative issue of Sports Illustrated recognizing his induction into the Naismith Memorial Basketball Hall of Fame. Jewel-Osco argued that its ad was not a commercial advertisement, but a federal appeals court said such image advertisements advanced the company's commercial interests. Dominick's Finer Foods admitted liability but contested the amount of damages the plaintiff wanted. After a jury awarded Jordan $8.9 million, Jewel-Osco reached an out-of-court settlement with him.

In recent cases, the tort of infringement on a person's right of publicity has replaced the older concept of appropriation. Right of publicity is a concept that emerged in lawsuits involving celebrities and the use of some aspect of their personas other than name or likeness. A classic case is a lawsuit brought by Vanna White, co-star of the "Wheel of Fortune" game show, against Samsung Electronics. Samsung had run a print advertisement promoting the durability of its VCRs that showed a robot turning letters on a set like that for "Wheel of Fortune." The robot had a blond wig, large jewelry and a long dress, all characteristic of White's appearance on the show. She sued saying Samsung had infringed on her right of publicity, and federal courts agreed. The 9th U.S. Circuit Court of Appeals said infringement on a celebrity's right of publicity could be by using a name, likeness or some other attributes of the celebrity's persona that would make the public associate the celebrity with the advertiser's product or services.

The use of a person's name or likeness in a news story is not considered appropriation or infringement on a person's right of publicity, even though it might benefit the newspaper, magazine or broadcast by attracting readers, viewers, listeners and advertisers. The use must have some reasonably direct connection to a matter of public interest. Courts have considered the public interest to include a broad range of topics and have been reluctant to second-guess journalists as to what is newsworthy and relevant.

The exemption from appropriation or right of publicity lawsuits for news publications and broadcasts extends to advertisements promoting them. An advertisement for a news interview program can include the name and likeness of a future guest. The advertisement, however, must not suggest that the person is endorsing that

Vanna White on the set of "Wheel of Fortune."

program, network or station. Nor can a broadcast or publication encroach on a performer's right to make money from his or her act. The U.S. Supreme Court upheld a judgment against an Ohio television station that broadcast a human cannonball's act in its entirety, ruling that the station had infringed on this right.

5.3 News-Gathering Issues

The First Amendment expressly protects the right to speak and to publish, but it says nothing about the right to gather information. The Supreme Court has recognized that freedom of the press means very little without this right, but the rights reporters have to information are largely defined by a hodgepodge of state and federal statutes and court opinions. This section covers three news-gathering issues: access to nonjudicial events and records, access to judicial proceedings and confidentiality for sources and information.

Reporters should always remember that the First Amendment does not protect them from prosecution if they engage in illegal conduct to gather news. Posing as a police officer, buying drugs or stealing documents are all illegal activities, and reporters who are prosecuted for crimes cannot plead that they were doing so to gather information for a news story.

5.3.1 Access to Nonjudicial Events and Records
5.3.1.1 NEWS SCENES

When a river floods a city, police discover a murder or a fire destroys a building, police, rescue workers and firefighters try to control the area to save lives and protect property. Reporters have a right to cover such events, but their conduct can be controlled by emergency workers to assure public safety. Some officials, however, worry as much about their images and how they will appear in news accounts as they do about citizens and their property. They may try to control what reporters and photographers see and how they report what they see.

The killing of George Floyd, a Black man, by four white police officers in Minneapolis in May 2020 ignited outrage. Protesters appeared on streets across the United States and around the world. Many of the protests were peaceful, but some turned violent, with protesters setting fire to buildings and cars and looting businesses. Police needed to restore order to their communities, but reporters also needed to record what was happening and explain it to their readers and viewers. Some of those reporters were struck by rubber bullets or subjected to tear gas or other crowd-control agents. And some of them were arrested.

Perhaps the most dramatic arrest was that of CNN's Omar Jimenez. Working with his producer and cameraman, Jimenez was reporting from a street south of downtown Minneapolis around 5 a.m. after a night of protests and riots. He was near a police precinct building that had been set on fire. The building was still smoldering when 100 state police in body armor and some firefighters arrived. A line of police officers approached Jimenez and his crew, who were on the air and reporting for CNN's "New Day" show. Viewers could hear Jimenez tell the police officers, "We can move back to where you like. We are live on the air here. Put us back where you want us." Nevertheless, the police arrested Jimenez and his crew. The police issued a statement later saying Jimenez and his crew had been arrested but were released after they were confirmed to be news reporters. The police rationale was puzzling because Jimenez and his colleagues were wearing press IDs and had identified themselves as a CNN news crew.

Another CNN reporter on the scene that morning had a different experience. Josh Campbell was reporting for CNN from the same area at the same time as Jimenez. He was not with the on-air crew, but he was approached by police. The police allowed Campbell to remain even as they arrested Jimenez. Campbell is white, and Jimenez is Black.

A burning building silhouettes a protester during a demonstration in Minneapolis following the death of George Floyd.

After Jimenez and his crew were released from custody, Minnesota Gov. Tim Walz apologized to the network and called the arrests unnecessary. "We have got to ensure that there is a safe spot for journalism to tell the story," Walz told reporters.

Many journalists believed some police were intentionally targeting them. A Wall Street Journal reporter, Tyler Blint-Welsh, was hit multiple times by police officers as he covered a protest in New York City. "I was backing away as requested, with my hands up" and his NYPD press badge was clearly visible, Blint-Welsh said on Twitter. A police officer in Minneapolis drew his weapon and pointed it at Maggie Koerth of the website FiveThirtyEight and another journalist as they were covering a protest. Koerth told The New York Times they identified themselves as journalists and held up their press credentials, but the officer kept pointing his weapon at them. Ellen Shearer, a professor at the Medill School of Journalism at Northwestern University, blamed the police treatment of reporters at least in part on President Donald Trump's labeing journalists "the enemy of the people." Trump, however, blamed the protest and violence on the "Lamestream Media" and journalists, whom he called "truly bad people with a sick agenda."

According to statistics compiled by the U.S. Press Freedom Tracker website, 139 reporters were arrested between May 1 and Dec. 31, 2020. By comparison, the website showed only nine arrests of reporters for all of 2019 and only four between May 1 and Dec. 31, 2019. For the same time frame in 2021, the Press Freedom Tracker shows only 13 arrests. Arrests in 2020 were reported from 26 states, and all but a handful of them were in connection with the Black Lives Matter protests that were a reaction to the killing of George Floyd. Most of the reporters were released quickly from custody, as were Jimenez and his CNN crew. Most of them were either never charged with a crime or the charges were later dropped by prosecutors. One case, however, resulted in a reporter's going to trial.

Andrea Sahouri, a reporter for the Des Moines, Iowa, Register, was arrested as she was covering a Black Lives Matter protest at a mall in Des Moines. Some

HOT TIP

Covering News Scenes

The Reporters Committee for Freedom of the Press recommends reporters and photographers do the following to minimize the risk of being harassed by police when covering protests, crimes or disasters:

- Always carry press credentials.

- Don't trespass on private property or cross clearly marked police lines.

- Don't take anything from a crime scene.

- Obey all orders from police officers, even if doing so interferes with getting the story or the photo. (The alternative might be going to jail.)

- Don't argue with arresting officers.

- Have $50 to $100 on hand to purchase bail bond.

- Have a government-issued photo ID.

Scott Olson, a photographer with Getty Images, offered some additional tips for reporters covering protests:

- Know your limitations. If you lack experience in covering protests, go with a reporter or photographer who has such experience.

- Wear the proper protective equipment. Have goggles to protect your eyes from rubber bullets. Wear a helmet to protect your head and have a gas mask in case the police use tear gas. Gloves, sturdy boots or shoes and pads for knees and elbows are also helpful.

protesters had vandalized a Target store, broken windows, blocked an intersection and thrown bottles and rocks at police in riot gear. Police charged into the protesters and used tear gas to dispel them. Sahouri, who was accompanied by her then-boyfriend, Spenser Robnett, tried to flee the gas. As Sahouri rounded a store, she encountered an officer who sprayed her with pepper spray and cuffed her with zip ties. Although she repeatedly told the officer she was a reporter, she was put in a police van and arrested. She and Robnett were charged with failure to disperse and interfering with official acts, both misdemeanors punishable by fines and up to 30 days in jail.

The Iowa prosecutors were criticized by media organizations and civil rights groups for refusing to drop the charges and insisting on bringing Sahouri to trial. Sahouri refused an offer from the prosecutor to drop the interference charge if she pleaded guilty to failure to disperse. "This will continue," Sahouri said. "We've seen an upward trend of journalists' being arrested just in the past year, in 2020, and it's really important to stand by your convictions." After a three-day trial, the six members of the jury needed only two hours to acquit both Sahouri and Robnett of all charges.

The arrests of reporters and other incidents of harassment and intimidation prompted journalism organizations to complain. The Reporters Committee for Freedom of the Press wrote to officials in Minnesota to demand a halt to attacks on reporters who are clearly identifiable and carrying credentials. The letter was co-signed by 115 media and press freedom organizations.

In Portland, Oregon, where protests against the police were among the most intense and long-lasting of any city in the United States, news organizations asked a federal judge to intervene and protect journalists doing their job. The judge, Michael Simon, issued a temporary restraining order on July 23, just a day after the mayor of Portland had been among those subjected to tear gas by federal agents. Judge Simon ordered federal agents not to arrest, threaten to arrest or use physical force against journalists or legal observers from organizations such as the American Civil Liberties Union and the National Lawyers' Guild. He also prohibited federal agents from seizing photographic or audio recording equipment from journalists or ordering journalists to stop photographing or recording events at protests. The judge limited the order to journalists carrying press passes or wearing or carrying other identification of their being journalists.

5.3.1.2 RECORDS AND MEETINGS

All states and the federal government have laws that help citizens and reporters access government records and meetings. The main federal law is the Freedom of Information Act (FOIA, which can be pronounced as FOY-ah and is used as both a noun and a verb). Washington Post reporters David Farenthold, Josh Dawsey and Joshua Partlow used the FOIA to obtain spending records showing that federal agencies had paid businesses owned by Donald Trump more than $900,000. When President Trump traveled to resorts he owned, something he did more than 270 times during his presidency, Secret Service agents had to accompany him. The Trump-owned businesses charged the agency for the agents' accommodations. Ralph Blumenthal of The New York Times and Leslie Kean used the law to get eight formerly classified safety reports of Navy jet fighters having dangerously close encounters with unidentified flying objects between June 2013 and February 2019. One Navy pilot reported passing within 1,000 feet of an object he said he was unable to identify.

Sometimes the inevitability that documents will have to be disclosed encourages federal agencies to release them without a legal fight. The Small Business Administration supervised the $669 billion Paycheck Protection Program, which was designed to help small businesses survive and keep employees on their payrolls during the economic shutdown caused by the COVID-19 pandemic. The SBA had promised to disclose who received the money, but Treasury Secretary Steven Mnuchin said the amounts awarded and the names of recipients should be withheld as proprietary information. The criticism Mnuchin and the Treasury Department received caused them to change course and release the documents. They showed that large amounts of money had gone to elite law firms, hate groups that opposed immigration and anti-government activists. One of the recipients was the Americans for Tax Reform Foundation. ATRF adamantly opposes tax increases of any kind and government bailouts. The organization received between $150,000 and $350,000, saying it needed the money to avoid laying off employees.

Basically, the FOIA opens to public inspection all records held by agencies of the federal executive branch, unless the records fall into one of nine exempt categories (see Table 5.2). If a record is exempt, the agency may still release it but is not required to do so. Much litigation under the FOIA concerns whether records are exempt.

Since passing the FOIA in 1966, Congress has amended it several times. It has excluded information about foreign intelligence, counterintelligence and terrorism. It has also made it easier for law enforcement agencies to withhold information about their investigative procedures and techniques. When Congress created the Department of Homeland Security, it exempted from disclosure information that the department receives from private businesses about weaknesses in the country's critical infrastructure.

- Write down useful phone numbers. You may need to call your supervisor or lawyers. Olson recommends writing the numbers on your leg with permanent marker. Protesters write them on their arms, so putting them on your legs differentiates you.
- Have multiple forms of identification. Some people keep all of their identification on their cell phones, but if you are arrested, your cell phone is the first thing police will seize. Have paper copies of your IDs and any phone numbers, too.

TABLE 5.2 FOIA RECORD EXEMPTIONS

1. Classified information.
2. Information related solely to internal personnel rules and practices.
3. Information exempted by other statutes.
4. Trade secrets and confidential commercial information.
5. Interagency and intra-agency memoranda that would reveal decision-making processes.
6. Information that would be a clearly unwarranted invasion of personal privacy.
7. Law enforcement investigative files, the disclosure of which would or could cause certain harms.
8. Information about financial institutions.
9. Geological and geophysical information such as maps showing the locations of oil and mineral deposits.

The Pentagon houses the headquarters for the U.S. military. Many of the millions of records created by officials in the Pentagon must be disclosed to the public under the Freedom of Information Act.

The FOIA says federal agencies should release nonexempt information in response to any written request that reasonably identifies the records. The relevant agency is supposed to respond within 20 working days, but it may have 10 additional days if a request involves unusual circumstances. Actually getting the information, however, can take much longer. The National Security Archive, a private organization that frequently uses the FOIA, discovered that some requests had been pending for more than 20 years. Most agencies have backlogs of requests—Congress has encouraged them to reduce this problem by making more information available online. The change has dramatically reduced backlogs at some agencies like the National Aeronautics and Space Administration, but the impact at others, such as the Department of Justice, has been minimal.

State and District of Columbia laws about opening government records and meetings to the public and the press vary considerably. Some are very broad and have few exemptions. Others exempt dozens of kinds of records or meetings or have other qualifications that limit access.

Some public officials flout or ignore the laws because they dislike having their records opened to public inspection. News organizations in most states have conducted statewide surveys of official compliance with public records laws and have found many instances of withheld records. New Jersey reporters discovered that, although they had no trouble getting local budgets, they received only 22 percent of their requests for police logs and 31 percent of school superintendents' contracts. In spite of such noncompliance, reporters rely on state open records laws almost daily because they apply to local governments, like cities, counties and school boards, as well as to state agencies.

When embarrassing information gets out, states sometimes amend their laws to limit disclosure. During a court hearing on the way Missouri administered lethal injections to execute prisoners, the doctor who supervised executions admitted he was dyslexic, sometimes confused the dosages of the drugs used to kill the prisoners, and had been sued for malpractice so often that two hospitals had revoked his privileges to practice. If the drugs used in the lethal injection procedure are not administered properly and in the right dosages,

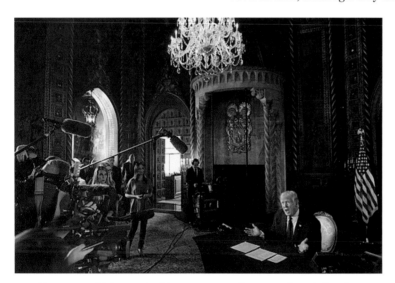

President Donald Trump holds a press conference after delivering a Thanksgiving Day address to military personnel by teleconference. Media access to official governmental events should be granted without regard to whether a new organization's coverage has been favorable or unfavorable.

the prisoner can suffer excruciating pain. The doctor was identified as "John Doe" during the hearing, but the St. Louis Post-Dispatch later identified him as Dr. Alan R. Doerhoff. The response of the Missouri General Assembly was not to require more training or competence on the part of its executioners. Instead, it passed a law making it illegal to disclose the identities of those who assist in the execution process. It also prohibited medical licensing boards from taking disciplinary action against any members who participate in executions.

5.3.2 Access to Judicial Proceedings

Freedom of the press is just one of many rights the Constitution guarantees to people in the United States. The Sixth Amendment to the Constitution says a person accused of a crime has the right to a trial by an impartial jury. These two rights appear to conflict when news organizations publish information that might sway potential jurors. Some authorities have labeled this problem "free press vs. fair trial," suggesting one right must be sacrificed to the other. Most judges, including those on the U.S. Supreme Court, reject that view. Instead, a judge presiding over a trial must protect both the right of a defendant to a fair trial and the freedom of the press.

In the 1960s, the Supreme Court said trial judges must protect judicial proceedings when there is a reasonable likelihood that news coverage could prejudice the trial. The court did not say how a judge should curb prejudicial publicity but focused on steps he or she could take to protect the trial without interfering with the news media. For example, a judge can sequester jurors, move trials to new locations if publicity becomes too intense, delay a trial or limit the kinds of statements prosecutors and defense attorneys make to the press about a pending trial.

Although the Supreme Court said nothing about restraining what journalists say about court proceedings, judges in the 1970s started issuing "gag" orders prohibiting reporters from publishing certain information even when they learned it in open court. The court declared this kind of limitation on the press a prior restraint. It is unconstitutional unless the nature and extent of the news coverage threatens the fairness of a trial, no alternative to a prior restraint would protect the trial and a prior restraint would be effective in preventing prejudice.

After the Supreme Court sharply limited judges' ability to impose gag orders, trial courts started denying journalists access to information by closing the courtroom door. Again, the court stepped in to restrict what judges can do. The high court declared in 1980 that the press and the public have a First Amendment right to attend criminal trials and other court proceedings that historically have been open to the public and where public observation benefits the proceeding. That right is not absolute, however, and may be curtailed when necessary to protect a fair trial. Judges may close a proceeding if they find a substantial likelihood of prejudice that closure would prevent and alternatives to closure would not work. This is a very difficult standard to meet because it requires the court to find facts establishing both conditions.

Access to a particular court proceeding—jury selection—has become contentious. Jury selection is considered part of the trial; some attorneys consider it the most important step. But concerns for juror privacy and safety have persuaded some judges to close access to the selection process or prohibit release of jurors' names. Ronell Wilson, who had the nickname "Rated R," was accused of killing two undercover police officers. Prosecutors persuaded the federal trial judge that Wilson presented such a threat that the jurors should be selected in sequestered sessions and their identities, addresses and occupations should be kept confidential.

Occasionally, courts have closed jury selection even in cases where their safety was not threatened. The court that tried Martha Stewart on charges she had lied about insider stock trading barred news organizations from the jury selection process. News organizations objected, and a federal appeals court said the trial court had failed to show that closure of jury selection was necessary to protect Stewart's right to a fair trial.

Some states close or limit access to proceedings in juvenile, family or divorce courts. Other states allow public access to such courts. The U.S. Supreme Court has not specifically ruled on the matter.

The problems with gag orders and court closures became so severe in the 1970s that some state press and bar groups collaborated to write guidelines for dealing with each other during trials. These voluntary guidelines, which are also supposed to protect the interests of news organizations and criminal defendants, generally say the media should be free to report the following:

- Basic information about a suspect, such as name, age, address and marital status.
- The charges against the suspect.
- The circumstances under which the suspect was arrested, including whether any weapons were used.
- The names of those who have filed complaints against the suspect.
- If the crime involved a death, who died and how.
- The identities of the investigating agencies and officers.

The following information should not be published under most bar-press guidelines:

- The existence and nature of any statement or confession the suspect made to authorities.
- The results of any tests.
- Opinions on the credibility of the suspect, witnesses or evidence.
- Opinions about the outcome of the trial.
- Any other statements made outside the presence of the jury that might be highly prejudicial.

Furthermore, the guidelines strongly discourage publishing a suspect's criminal record because such information is considered highly prejudicial. However, preventing its disclosure might be impossible, given that it is a matter of open record in many states and could be in a news organization's files of old stories.

Although bar-press guidelines are voluntary, reporters should pay attention to them and think carefully about the risks that publishing certain information may pose to criminal defendants. Many people think a person who has been charged with a crime is guilty, even before a trial. The National Registry of Exonerations, a joint project between the University of Michigan and Northwestern University law schools, lists more than 3,000 cases since 1989 in which a person who was convicted of a crime was later found to have been innocent, often because of DNA evidence that was tested years later.

In many of these cases, the people who were later exonerated seemed clearly guilty at the time of their trials. A well-known example is the 1990 trials of the Central Park Five, which drew national attention. Teenagers Yusef Salaam, Kevin Richardson, Antron McCray, Raymond Santana and Korey Wise were arrested for the brutal rape and beating of a 28-year-old woman in New York's Central Park. Under intense and possibly coercive interrogations, all confessed to the crime. Although they recanted their statements, the fact they had confessed convinced the jury—and most of the press and public—of their guilt. Even before their trials began, many presumed the youths were guilty. All five served time in prison. Nearly 13 years after the crime, Matias Reyes said he alone was responsible; DNA evidence confirmed his confession.

5.3.3 Confidentiality for Sources and Information

For almost as long as reporters have written news, they have used confidential sources. Reporters depend on such people for some of their best stories. Because many sources will provide valuable information only if they know they are safe, reporters may promise to protect their identities.

If the confidential information reporters receive discloses illegal activities, law enforcement agencies may start investigations. Sometimes police, prosecutors, grand juries, courts, legislative bodies or administrative agencies demand the names of confidential sources or other information the reporter wants to protect. Reporters may receive subpoenas ordering them to testify before an official body. The subpoena may also direct them to bring their notes, photographs, tapes and other materials they collected. If reporters comply and identify confidential sources, they lose credibility, and no sources will trust them. But if reporters fail to comply, they can be cited for contempt of court and sent to jail, fined or both. Faced with the dilemma of losing their sources or going to jail, reporters have argued they should have a privilege to withhold confidential sources and information based on the First Amendment.

The U.S. Supreme Court dealt with this issue in a 1972 decision named Branzburg v. Hayes. The decision combined four separate cases, all involving the question of whether reporters have a First Amendment privilege to withhold confidential information and sources from grand juries. The Supreme Court decided the First Amendment requires no such privilege. Grand juries historically have been entitled to every person's testimony, with only a few narrow exceptions. The court, in an opinion written by Justice Byron White, said the important work of grand juries in identifying crimes and criminals and bringing them to justice overrode the interests of journalists in protecting sources. The court also noted the difficulty of deciding who is a journalist and under what circumstances any privilege should apply. Those questions, the court said, are best left to state legislatures and Congress, which could pass laws recognizing some privilege for journalists.

Several major cases have underscored the dilemma reporters sometimes face. Judith Miller, a former reporter at The New York Times, spent 85 days in jail for contempt of court when she refused to disclose whether a confidential source told her about the identity of covert CIA agent Valerie Plame Wilson. Although Miller never published a story naming Wilson (it had been published in a story by a different journalist), the agent's name had been revealed to her in conversations with White House officials. Eventually, Miller's source, I. Lewis ("Scooter") Libby, released her from her pledge to keep his name secret, and she testified to the grand jury. Libby eventually was convicted of perjury.

More recently, Bryan Carmody, a freelance journalist who creates news packages for local television stations in the San Francisco area, was the target in 2019 of subpoenas and search warrants seeking the identity of the person who leaked a police report. The report involved the death of Jeff Adachi, the elected public defender in San Francisco. Police initially considered his death suspicious. The report Carmody obtained said Adachi had died in the apartment of a woman who was not his wife and his death was caused by a combination of cocaine, alcohol and a weakened heart. Carmody prepared a package based on the report and sold it to several stations. The San Francisco Police Department initially asked Carmody to cooperate in identifying his confidential source, but he refused to do so. Weeks later, the police returned with search warrants. They searched both his home and office and kept him in handcuffs for six hours while conducting the searches. Carmody challenged the search warrants in court. Five different judges heard the challenges to the search warrants, and all five agreed they had been illegally issued in violation of California's legal protections for journalists. One judge, who had issued one of the search warrants, said police had failed to tell her Carmody was a journalist. Carmody later received a $369,000 settlement from the city of San Francisco.

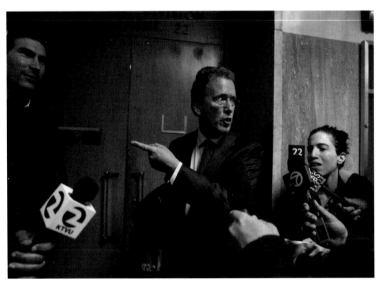

Thomas R. Burke, center, represented freelance videographer Bryan Carmody in his efforts to quash warrants allowing San Francisco police to search his home and office. Police wanted information that would lead to the identity of one of Carmody's confidential sources. California courts eventually held the search warrants had violated statutory protections for journalists.

Telephone and email records are another way law enforcement agencies, particularly federal ones, can identify a reporter's confidential sources. The Trump Justice Department used a secret order issued by a federal magistrate judge requiring that CNN turn over 25,000 to 30,000 emails to or from reporter Barbara Starr. David Vigilante, CNN's executive vice president and general counsel, worked with outside attorneys to handle the order, but he was forbidden from telling anyone—even Starr herself—about the order. And the Department of Justice refused to explain to CNN what its investigation was about, who was the target, or what kinds of information were relevant to the investigation. CNN went to court to have the order quashed or at least narrowed, but the federal government fought those requests, often in hearings from which CNN was excluded and with briefs and legal arguments CNN was prohibited from seeing. Only after Joe Biden became president was CNN able to reach an agreement narrowing the scope of the government's request and allowing Starr to be informed of the government's request. The Justice Department, however, already had obtained information about Starr's communications through other companies holding some of Starr's communications. Starr, who covers the Pentagon for CNN, said she was glad Biden's Justice Department would no longer seize reporter's records, but Congress needed to write that policy into law to prevent other presidents from trying to get reporters' communications.

Subpoenas are a common problem for news reporters. Generally, broadcast news organizations receive more subpoenas than print news outlets. Most of the orders to broadcast stations ask for video or audio recordings, both outtakes and portions aired. Newspapers are more likely to receive subpoenas demanding that reporters reveal confidential information or sources.

Reporters have had mixed success resisting subpoenas. Some state and federal courts have recognized a reporters' privilege to protect confidential sources and information. The extent of this protection varies greatly, but usually it allows reporters to shield confidential sources and information except when the information is essential to a case, can be obtained in no other way and would serve a compelling governmental interest. Courts generally have held that this privilege does not apply to nonconfidential information and sources or to actions a reporter or photographer might have witnessed firsthand. Even in states that recognize a privilege, news organizations sued for libel must disclose confidential sources or information that the plaintiffs might need to make their case.

In addition to the privilege recognized by some state and federal courts, 40 states and the District of Columbia have shield laws that specifically guarantee a journalist's right to protect confidential sources or information. Again, the laws vary. Some let journalists protect confidential sources and unpublished information; others limit the protection to confidential sources. State laws also differ in who is protected. Some shield laws apply to anyone engaged in gathering and disseminating information to the public. Others cover only professional journalists, often meaning people associated with traditional media. Such laws may leave bloggers and other nontraditional journalists unprotected. Furthermore, some states grant reporters a nearly absolute privilege to refuse to testify, whereas others qualify the privilege. Yet even in states that recognize an absolute privilege, journalists may have to reveal confidential sources or information in three situations:

1. The news organization is the defendant in a libel suit and the identity of sources is necessary for determining whether the defamatory statements were made with actual malice.

2. Reporters are asked to testify about events they personally witnessed.

3. The information is essential for a defendant's receiving a fair trial.

Although 40 states have shield laws, Congress has refused so far to pass a federal shield law. This means that in any case where federal law enforcement agencies are investigating, reporters may be compelled to testify about confidential sources and information. Even in a state with a strong shield law, such as California, reporters with information relevant to federal investigations can face jail time for contempt of court if they refuse to reveal confidential sources or information to federal authorities.

The Reporter's Guide to Libel, Privacy and News-Gathering Issues

Defamation

1. "Libel" is defamation by written words or communication in another tangible form; "slander" is defamation by spoken words or gestures.

2. Libel plaintiffs often must prove six elements: defamation, identification, publication, falsity, injury and fault.

3. Fault is often the most important issue in a libel case. Public officials and public figures who sue for libel must prove actual malice (knowledge that the information is false or reckless disregard for its probable falsity). Private individuals must prove only negligence.

4. "Negligence" means the publisher failed to do what a reasonable and prudent person would have done in the same circumstances.

5. Public officials are people in government who hold positions high enough that they have or appear to have influence over public affairs.

6. Public figures are people who are widely known and influential or who have taken a leadership role in trying to influence decisions about issues of public concern.

7. The major common-law defenses to libel suits are truth, fair-report privilege and fair-comment privilege.

Privacy

1. Invasion of privacy comprises four types of lawsuits: intrusion, publicity to private facts, false light and appropriation.

2. Intrusion is one person intentionally intruding on the privacy of another, by physical or other means, in a manner that would be highly offensive to a reasonable person. To sue for intrusion, the plaintiff must show that the defendant intruded on an area where the plaintiff had a reasonable expectation of privacy.

3. In most states, reporters may record surreptitiously conversations with a source without his or her consent. Twelve states require the consent of all parties, at least where there is an expectation of privacy.

4. Publicity to private facts involves publicizing private information about another person, the disclosure of which would be highly offensive to a reasonable person and which is not of legitimate public concern.

5. False light involves portraying another person in a way that is false and highly offensive (but not necessarily defamatory) to a reasonable person.

6. Appropriation is the use of another person's name or likeness for one's own benefit, usually meaning some kind of commercial use. Using a person's name or likeness in a news story is not considered appropriation if it bears some connection to a matter of public interest. The commercial use of characteristics that might evoke another person, usually a celebrity, without using that person's name or likeness, may constitute a violation of that person's right of publicity.

News-Gathering Issues

1. Journalists gather information at scenes of crimes, fires and natural disasters.

2. Reporters should never interfere with the work of police, firefighters, medical personnel or other officials. Police or other authorities sometimes object to the presence of news gatherers.

3. Access to meetings and records is governed by state and federal laws.

4. The U.S. Freedom of Information Act opens the records of the federal executive branch to public inspection, but nine categories of records are exempt from disclosure.

5. The Sunshine Act opens meetings of some federal agencies, such as the Federal Communications Commission and the Federal Trade Commission, to the public.

6. State open records laws require disclosure of the records of most state and local

governmental bodies. The agencies and governmental units governed by open-records laws and the records that are exempt vary from state to state.

7. State open meetings laws require that the meetings and associated records of various governmental units be open to the public. Some meetings may be exempt, and most state laws allow for executive sessions under some circumstances.

8. Court proceedings are generally open to the public. Limited closures to prevent news coverage that might prejudice potential jurors against a defendant are permissible, especially during pretrial hearings.

9. Judges may not impose prior restraints on what news organizations may report about criminal

proceedings unless the news coverage has been extensive and highly prejudicial, alternatives to a prior restraint would be ineffective or a prior restraint would be effective.

10. Journalists need confidential sources to report some stories, but if a grand jury or a trial court wants to know the identity of a confidential source, the reporter must either reveal the source or face the possibility of going to jail for contempt of court.

11. Forty states and the District of Columbia have shield laws, which allow journalists to withhold the names of confidential sources and other confidential information. The laws vary greatly in what is protected and how strongly. The federal government has no shield law.

 # Review Exercises

1. LIBEL

Decide which of the following sentences and paragraphs are potentially libelous. Label each statement that is dangerous for the media with a D and each statement that is safe with an S.

1. Police officers said they shot and wounded Ira Andrews, a 41-year-old auto mechanic, because he was rushing toward them with a knife.

2. Testifying during the second day of the trial, Mrs. Andrea Cross said her husband, Lee, never intended to embezzle the $70,000, but that a secretary, Allison O'Hara, persuaded him that their actions were legal. Her husband thought they were borrowing the money, she said, and that they would double it by investing in real estate.

3. A 72-year-old woman, Kelli Kasandra of 9847 Eastbrook Lane, has been charged with attempting to pass a counterfeit $20 bill. A convenience store clerk called the police shortly after 8 a.m. today and said that she had received "a

suspicious-looking bill." The clerk added that she had written down the license number of a car leaving the store. The police confirmed the fact that the $20 bill was counterfeit and arrested Mrs. Kasandra at her home about an hour later.

4. Margaret Dwyer said a thief, a boy about 14, grabbed her purse as she was walking to her car in a parking lot behind Memorial Hospital. The boy punched her in the face, apparently because she began to scream and refused to let go of her purse. She said he was blond, wore glasses, weighed about 120 pounds and was about 5 feet 6 inches tall.

5. "I've never lived in a city where the officials are so corrupt," Joyce Andrews, a Cleveland developer, complained. "If you don't contribute to their campaigns, they won't do anything for you or even talk to you. You have to buy their support."

6. The political scientist said that Americans seem unable to elect a competent president. "Look at whom they've elected," she said. "I'm convinced that Carter was incompetent, Reagan was too lazy and senile to be even a mediocre president, the first George Bush cared nothing about the people, Clinton was a scoundrel and the second George Bush—the worst of the bunch—was a liar and a buffoon."

7. Police Chief Barry Kopperud said: "We've been after Guiterman for years. He's the biggest drug dealer in the city, but it took months to gather the evidence and infiltrate his operations. His arrest last night was the result of good police work, and we've got the evidence to send him away for 20 or 30 years."

8. Officer George Ruiz filed a $100,000 personal injury suit against Albert Tifton, charging that Tifton punched him in the nose last month while the police were responding to a call about a domestic dispute at Tifton's home. "It's the third time I've been hit this year," Ruiz said. "I'm tired of being used as a punching bag by these criminals, and I'm doing what I can to stop it."

9. Ruth Howland of 1808 Gladsen Blvd. is running for president of the local coin collectors society. Her opponent is Thomas C. Paddock of 1736 Hinkley Road. Howland has sent a letter to all members of the local society saying Paddock is a communist and an anarchist.

10. A prosecuting attorney, who asked not to be identified, said charges would be filed within the week against Mayor Sabrina Datolli, accusing her of having accepted bribes.

11. The firefighters union held a no-confidence vote on Fire Chief Tony Sullivan. The president of the union said Sullivan had been arbitrary and capricious in his decisions about layoffs resulting from budget cuts.

12. An activist for a local animal-rights organization, Julie Allyn, said she had investigated a fire at Weston's Pet Hotel that had killed 19 dogs and had smelled fire accelerant on the bodies.

13. Suzanne Kopp, whose husband died of lung cancer, is the president of a local group advocating tougher regulation of tobacco products. In a speech to high school students, Kopp said, "Tobacco company executives are nothing but murderers. Morally, they stand no better than the paid assassin."

14. Officer Daniel G. Silverbach is investigating a convenience store robbery. Silverbach said of the store clerk, Wayne Brayton, 410 University Ave., Apt. 279, "He's acting suspiciously and is not able to give a coherent account of the robbery. I think he's doing drugs of some kind."

15. Professor Ahmad Aneesa, a microbiologist, said of a paper published by Professor William Baxter, a microbiologist at another university, "These results run contrary to everything we know about microorganisms. I know Baxter has a great reputation, but only a fool would accept his findings without more investigation."

2. PRIVACY

For each of the following passages, choose the form of invasion of privacy that fits best. Write I for intrusion, P for publicity to private facts, A for appropriation and F for false light.

1. A story describes a man as a veteran of combat in Iraq who has received a Purple Heart and medals for valor. In fact, the man served in the military during the Iraq War but was never in Iraq or in combat.

2. A local car dealer wants to run an advertisement that promotes the low prices for his vehicles with the headline "Bargains That Outshine the Stars." To illustrate the advertisement, he wants to use photos of famous Hollywood stars such as Jennifer Aniston and Matt Damon.

3. A news story reports that a member of the city council is having a romantic affair with a local business executive. Both the council member and the business executive are married to others.

4. A newspaper reporter follows up on the story of the affair between the council member and the business executive. The reporter follows the business executive to a motel. When she sees the

council member arrive, she takes photographs of him getting out of his car in the motel parking lot. Although the reporter is some distance away, she is using a powerful telephoto lens that allows her to photograph the executive and the council member in their room.

5. An in-depth news story reports on a local family whose members have been involved in a number of crimes over the years. The story describes each family member and the crimes they have committed. The story also mentions in passing a member of the family who has never committed a crime.

6. A reporter is investigating a local judge who is reported to have accepted bribes from people accused of crimes in return for lenient sentencing. The reporter tries to interview the judge as he is getting out of his car to go to work, but the judge refuses to talk. However, the reporter sees the judge put an envelope in the glove compartment of his car, which he leaves unlocked. After the judge

has left, the reporter opens the car and the glove box to find the envelope, which holds $1,000 in cash and a thank-you note from a defendant in a recent criminal case.

7. A television station reports that police are concerned about the rash of accidents, injuries and even deaths involving children playing in the streets. The station illustrates its story with some video footage of children playing in streets, some of whom are identifiable, and titles its story "They Beg to Be Killed."

8. A private college in the community recently hired a new dean of students, the first woman to hold the position at that college. A reporter, while preparing a profile of the new dean, discovers that she was born a male and underwent gender reassignment surgery 15 years ago. She told the college officials of her gender reassignment when she interviewed for the job, but she has not made that information public. The profile the reporter writes includes the gender change.

6 ETHICS

News includes stories that might be upsetting yet crucial for the public to know. Other stories can be uplifting and important for audiences to learn. All stories require sensitive, ethical reporting. The Uvalde, Texas, school shootings; the $6 million GoFundMe donations to the victims' families; the Ukraine-Russia war; worldwide support for Ukraine; COVID-19 and the pandemic; first responders and inoculations against the virus; climate change; windmill farms, electric cars and ride shares; #BlackLivesMatter; and the first Black woman nominated to the Supreme Court are just a few topics that have filled our world. These national stories are also localized to community levels so that audiences know what is happening in their towns and neighborhoods.

The public depends on journalists to report and write about events ethically and comprehensively. When journalists investigate multi-sided stories, they make many decisions with ethical implications. This chapter spotlights the types of situations that are harder to cover and require special sensitivity and ethical decision making. Although most of these situations are not regular occurrences for most journalists, they should follow ethical standards.

6.1 Ethical Decisions Every Day

Journalists in local communities and across the globe make good, ethical decisions every day. Consider the many choices that reporters and editors make for each story: Which issues and events to cover? What angles to take? Whom to interview? What questions to ask? What quotes to use? How to organize facts? What length of story? What visuals and multimedia? What blog posts and other social media? Where to place a story among other stories? Other questions may lurk in stories. Even thinking about where and when to interview someone and to offer or accept a meal can have ethical ramifications.

Multiply all the good decisions for each story with the many stories published daily in thousands of news outlets. For example, journalist Robinson Meyer found that The Washington Post published online an average of 1,200 stories, graphics and videos a day. The New York Times, The Wall Street Journal and BuzzFeed publish online about 230 stories and videos daily, in addition to social media posts, graphics and multimedia content. The Post's count is higher because it includes wire stories and other content produced elsewhere. Each story, graphic, video and post requires critical thinking, hard work and good ethical decisions to inform the public accurately and comprehensively.

Every choice a journalist makes requires value judgments. These choices have consequences that are direct and indirect, intended and unintended, short-term and long-term. They also affect others. A story about how far someone walks to work might influence others to donate a bicycle or even a car to that person. Another story about how a nearby town cleaned up their community parks might persuade local townspersons to do the same. A political story may influence thousands of people's opinions about an issue. After being featured in a sensitive sexual harassment story, a person may decide to move or remain in their community.

Reporters examine their decisions and actions based on professional and personal standards. They abide by the ethical codes of their organization, industry, community and society. If they are unsure of a decision, they always take the high road, the morally superior way to deal with something. Most decisions become second nature, based on experience.

Above all other principles, journalists must:

● act and think morally;
● distinguish between right and wrong;
● stay within the bounds of fairness, good taste and common decency.

6.2 Codes of Ethics

Professional news outlets have established individual ethics codes to reflect community standards because what is permissible in a metropolitan area might not be acceptable in a rural town. Journalists adhere to their news organization's customized guidelines. Some news outlets, however, adopt one of the codes of ethics issued by a professional journalism organization, such as the Society of Professional Journalists, the News Leader's Association or the National Press Photographers Association.

Codes of ethics may be specific enough to discourage the most obvious abuses, especially freebies, junkets and conflicts of interest (discussed later in this chapter). Other standards may also be stated generally to guide thinking when exceptional cases arise. Thus, decision making will vary from one news organization to another, which might be one of journalism's great strengths. After considering their news organization's code of ethics, journalists decide the proper (i.e., ethical) course of action. But any effort to force every reporter in their different situations and communities to conform to an identical national predetermined standard would limit the media's diversity and freedom, as well as the public's access to information.

The American Society of Newspaper Editors (ASNE) adopted one of the industry's first codes, the Canons of Journalism, in 1923. Among other things, the ASNE declared that newspapers should act responsibly by being truthful, sincere, impartial, decent and fair. (The organization modified its name to The American Society of News Editors in 2009 and merged with The Associated Press Media Editors to become the News Leaders Association in 2019.)

The oldest journalism organization, formed in 1909 originally as Sigma Delta Chi, is the Society of Professional Journalists (SPJ). It has a well-known code with headings such as seek truth and report it, minimize harm, act independently and be accountable and transparent.

Some professional journalism organizations help journalists in different areas of news media. The National Press Photographers Association (NPPA) provides ethical guidelines for visual journalists who produce video and still images. The Radio, Television, Digital News Association (RTDNA) has a code for broadcast journalists and the Online News Association (ONA) code focuses on the use of information gathered from members of the public.

Other professional organizations reflect ethnicities and have codes of ethics. The National Association of Black Journalists (NABJ), the National Association of Hispanic Journalists (NAHJ), the Native American Journalists Association (NAJA), and the Asian American Journalists Association (AAJA) are a few. A goal of the Association of LGBTQIA+ Journalists is to enhance the professionalism, skills and career opportunities for LGBTQIA+ journalists.

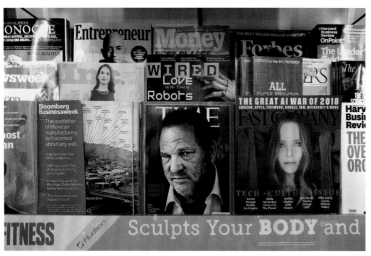

Legitimate news publications, such as these magazines, must include only articles that adhere to the organization's and the industry's ethics.

Society of Professional Journalists
C⊙DE of ETHICS

PREAMBLE
Members of the Society of Professional Journalists believe that public enlightenment is the forerunner of justice and the foundation of democracy. Ethical journalism strives to ensure the free exchange of information that is accurate, fair and thorough. An ethical journalist acts with integrity. The Society declares these four principles as the foundation of ethical journalism and encourages their use in its practice by all people in all media.

SEEK TRUTH AND REPORT IT
Ethical journalism should be accurate and fair. Journalists should be honest and courageous in gathering, reporting and interpreting information.

Journalists should:

- Take responsibility for the accuracy of their work. Verify information before releasing it. Use original sources whenever possible.
- Remember that neither speed nor format excuses inaccuracy.
- Provide context. Take special care not to misrepresent or oversimplify in promoting, previewing or summarizing a story.
- Gather, update and correct information throughout the life of a news story.
- Be cautious when making promises, but keep the promises they make.
- Identify sources clearly. The public is entitled to as much information as possible to judge the reliability and motivations of sources.
- Consider sources' motives before promising anonymity. Reserve anonymity for sources who may face danger, retribution or other harm, and have information that cannot be obtained elsewhere. Explain why anonymity was granted.
- Diligently seek subjects of news coverage to allow them to respond to criticism or allegations of wrongdoing.
- Avoid undercover or other surreptitious methods of gathering information unless traditional, open methods will not yield information vital to the public.
- Be vigilant and courageous about holding those with power accountable. Give voice to the voiceless.
- Support the open and civil exchange of views, even views they find repugnant.
- Recognize a special obligation to serve as watchdogs over public affairs and government. Seek to ensure that the public's business is conducted in the open, and that public records are open to all.
- Provide access to source material when it is relevant and appropriate.
- Boldly tell the story of the diversity and magnitude of the human experience. Seek sources whose voices we seldom hear.
- Avoid stereotyping. Journalists should examine the ways their values and experiences may shape their reporting.
- Label advocacy and commentary.
- Never deliberately distort facts or context, including visual information. Clearly label illustrations and re-enactments.
- Never plagiarize. Always attribute.

MINIMIZE HARM
Ethical journalism treats sources, subjects, colleagues and members of the public as human beings deserving of respect.

Journalists should:

- Balance the public's need for information against potential harm or discomfort. Pursuit of the news is not a license for arrogance or undue intrusiveness.

- Show compassion for those who may be affected by news coverage. Use heightened sensitivity when dealing with juveniles, victims of sex crimes, and sources or subjects who are inexperienced or unable to give consent. Consider cultural differences in approach and treatment.
- Recognize that legal access to information differs from an ethical justification to publish or broadcast.
- Realize that private people have a greater right to control information about themselves than public figures and others who seek power, influence or attention. Weigh the consequences of publishing or broadcasting personal information.
- Avoid pandering to lurid curiosity, even if others do.
- Balance a suspect's right to a fair trial with the public's right to know. Consider the implications of identifying criminal suspects before they face legal charges.
- Consider the long-term implications of the extended reach and permanence of publication. Provide updated and more complete information as appropriate.

ACT INDEPENDENTLY
The highest and primary obligation of ethical journalism is to serve the public.

Journalists should:

- Avoid conflicts of interest, real or perceived. Disclose unavoidable conflicts.
- Refuse gifts, favors, fees, free travel and special treatment, and avoid political and other outside activities that may compromise integrity or impartiality, or may damage credibility.
- Be wary of sources offering information for favors or money; do not pay for access to news. Identify content provided by outside sources, whether paid or not.
- Deny favored treatment to advertisers, donors or any other special interests, and resist internal and external pressure to influence coverage.
- Distinguish news from advertising and shun hybrids that blur the lines between the two. Prominently label sponsored content.

BE ACCOUNTABLE AND TRANSPARENT
Ethical journalism means taking responsibility for one's work and explaining one's decisions to the public.

Journalists should:

- Explain ethical choices and processes to audiences. Encourage a civil dialogue with the public about journalistic practices, coverage and news content.
- Respond quickly to questions about accuracy, clarity and fairness.
- Acknowledge mistakes and correct them promptly and prominently. Explain corrections and clarifications carefully and clearly.
- Expose unethical conduct in journalism, including within their organizations.
- Abide by the same high standards they expect of others.

The SPJ Code of Ethics is a statement of abiding principles supported by additional explanations and position papers (at spj.org) that address changing journalistic practices. It is not a set of rules, rather a guide that encourages all who engage in journalism to take responsibility for the information they provide, regardless of medium. The code should be read as a whole; individual principles should not be taken out of context. It is not, nor can it be under the First Amendment, legally enforceable.

The Society of Professional Journalists (SPJ) adopted its current code of ethics in 1996 and revised it in 2014.

6.3 Ethical Decision Making

In addition to following the standards of their news outlet and professional organizations, reporters learn a set of decision-making questions to help them make good, ethical choices. A few decision-making processes are offered in the following sections.

6.3.1 Who and How Many? (Two Questions)

Two fundamental questions that a journalist should ask when facing an ethical dilemma are:

- Who will be hurt, and how many?
- Who will be helped, and how many?

News stories sometimes discomfort someone or some group. If the story upsets or embarrasses a few people and helps several hundred, then publishing it is most likely justified. Perhaps court records show a local doctor has been held liable for misdiagnosing symptoms, which has led to unnecessary surgeries and uncured ailments. The story would most likely hurt the doctor and his family, but it would help many people when choosing a physician.

6.3.2 What Is the Purpose of the Story? (Two Follow-Up Questions)

While writing a story, journalists sometimes get too entangled with a lot of facts and lose sight of the objective for reporting on an event or issue. The story starts to wander or digress from its purpose as the journalist tries to fit in all the information that was learned. When considering what content or visuals to include, journalists ask a second set of questions:

- What is the objective of the story?
- Will my decision contribute to the reason for writing the story?

The answers will help a reporter decide, for example, not to include how a teenager committed suicide because that would not be the purpose of the story. The objective most likely would be to either celebrate the teenager's life or to reference the incident while educating the community about the increase of teenage suicides and the signs of teenage depression.

Here is another example. Prostitution, crack houses and violence are directly correlated in some cities. In neighborhoods confronting these problems, families, business owners and government officials try to combat the illegal and unsafe activities by encouraging the police to make more arrests and encourage news organizations to cover the busts. Editors realize that such publicity could ruin reputations, marriages and careers. Both clients and prostitutes often have families and colleagues who know nothing of their outside activities or criminal actions. In a big bust of 20 accused, one "john" was a scout leader and another was the diversity, equity and inclusion administrator at the local community college. One of the prostitutes attended law school and another was trying to make ends meet for his family.

As the editors discussed the story, they initially focused on several micro issues: placement—a story placed on a jump page is less damaging to the accused than a story on the home page; space—a short story is not as noticeable as a longer one; and graphics and visuals—the type and number of illustrations, if any, can set the tone. They then revisited the macro issue—ridding their community of an unsavory business that attracted drugs, violence and disease and other threats to family neighborhoods. Once they clarified their reasons for running the story, they were able to resolve the micro issues more easily. They put the story on the home page with a list of the names and mug shots of both the accused customers and prostitutes.

6.3.3 Can I Explain My Decision? (Six Questions)

Former journalist and professor H. Eugene Goodwin advised journalists and students to ask themselves six guiding questions while making an ethical decision. These are in addition to the four already discussed.

1. What do we usually do in cases like this? (What is the news organization's policy on this type of situation, and is it a good policy?)

2. Is there a better alternative? (Harmful results often can be avoided or eased by trying something different.)

3. Can I look myself in the mirror tomorrow? (You must think about how you feel and whether you can live with your decision. How do you want to remember this decision for the rest of your life?)

4. Can I justify this to family, friends and the public? (A faceless audience of people we do not know personally is one thing. But, if we know we have to explain our decisions to our family—such as, "What would Mom think of my actions?"—or to the public in an editor's column, we might be more careful about our decisions.) Try listening as you talk to yourself out loud.

5. What principles or values can I apply? (Some overarching principles, such as truth, justice or fairness, will take priority over others.)

6. Does this decision fit the kind of journalism I believe in and the way people should treat one another? (Our judgments should correspond with the way we believe the media ought to be and the way people in a civilized society ought to behave. How would I want someone to treat me? Take the high road.)

6.3.4 The Potter Box

The Potter Box, shown in Table 6.1, is a moral reasoning framework to guide decision making. It is based on the four categories that its creator, social ethicist and theologian Ralph Potter, believed were universal to ethical dilemmas. A reporter might use the Potter Box when experiencing inner turmoil on running a story about a personal friend and beloved community member who embezzled from the local elementary school. This process is shown in Table 6.2.

TABLE 6.1 **THE POTTER BOX**

Facts, without judgments	Values, such as personal, moral, professional and societal
Principles or classic ethical philosophies	Loyalties, such as whom you care most about

TABLE 6.2 **USING A POTTER BOX**

Facts, without judgments:	Values, such as personal, moral, professional and societal:
A school staff member embezzled thousands of dollars. The school does not have any extra money in its budget. The loss will affect the business of running the school.	The story would help parents understand why the school cannot provide as many supplies and services for children as it had in the past.
Principles or classic ethical philosophies:	Loyalties, such as whom you care most about:
Rawls' Veil of Ignorance states that we should remove our personal interests and treat everyone the same way. (Thus, we cover an embezzler who is a family friend the same way we cover an embezzler we do not know.)	The public and the overriding principle for the greater good. (And maybe my reputation, if I don't cover the story.)

6.3.5 News Media Credibility Considerations

Professional journalists are trained to think ethically and act responsibly. However, when a story is wrong or the journalist is unethical, the news outlet suffers a blow to its reputation, and sometimes the whole industry suffers because the infraction adds to the stereotype of "fake news." If it is a large or repeated error, the organization may dismiss the reporter or editor responsible. This alone gives journalists a powerful reason to think through ethical issues.

Ethical and accurate credibility is important to news organizations for two main reasons:

1. People depend on news media for their information. Unlike social media and bloggers who write opinions, professional journalists are trained in news judgment, vet their sources and report news accurately. News stories influence audiences, helping them form opinions ("It is important to get a COVID vaccination and here's why.") and decide on activities that can have a great impact on their quality of life ("I think I'll wait to buy my first house because of housing shortages and rising interest rates.").

2. News media must be credible to succeed as businesses. They need audiences for financial support. If people doubt the credibility of a particular news outlet, they will change websites, channels or newspapers. When audiences turn away, advertising and subscription revenues decline, news budgets shrink and comprehensive coverage diminishes, which drives away more audiences. The downward spiral usually continues until the outlet ceases business.

6.4 Diversity, Equity and Inclusion (DEI)

One reason audiences avoid news is a lack of diversity. If people don't see themselves or their situations represented in the news, then they will not pay attention to it. However, audiences will support news outlets if they see all members of a community treated equally and are included in the news. Respecting differences invites inclusion.

Journalists should constantly consider and monitor diversity, equity and inclusion in their reporting and writing. Issues affect different groups differently, and audiences should know how others in their community are faring. Accurate and comprehensive reporting means covering events important to various groups and hearing diverse voices within a community.

6.5 Ethics Issues Regarding Conduct

Some ethics issues arise from a journalist's conduct—decisions, behaviors and practices. Journalists are aware that their personal actions affect other people and influence how the public sees the news media.

6.5.1 Plagiarizing and Fabricating Information: Never Acceptable

"Plagiarism" is copying somebody else's work or taking somebody else's ideas and passing them off as one's own. Copying and pasting quotes and other passages from the internet have made plagiarizing easy, but it is also illegal. Journalists who are caught plagiarizing or fabricating information often are dismissed. Some complain that deadlines and competition forced them to act unethically. However, legions of other reporters work under the same deadlines and uphold high principles. They understand that the reason doesn't matter—if journalists plagiarize or make up information, they are lying to the public. The Boston Globe argued in an editorial that journalists who fabricate or plagiarize stories are stealing something more valuable than money: They are stealing the public's trust and the news organization's credibility.

NBC News fired political reporter Teaganne Finn in 2022. The network said she had used passages from other news organizations in 11 of her stories. Although the passages were for context and not primary to the story, Finn stole someone else's work. A New York Post article by Thomas Barrabi noted that NBC Senior Vice President of Global Digital News Catherine Kim told staffers: "It is a bright line we can't cross. Our trust with each other . . . with the public, the reputation of NBC News, the reputation for the journalism we produce, is core to what we do."

6.5.2 Finding Sources

Journalists search for and interview people who can be good sources for their stories. For example, sources for a story about government student loan forgiveness programs include former and current students with different demographics who can talk about the impact of borrowing, repayment and debt, a financial aid administrator and perhaps a government official. Journalists seek people with different opinions so that various angles of an issue are presented. Some instructors require at least three different types of sources instead of similar ones, such as all current students.

6.5.2.1 FRIENDS AND RELATIVES

Journalism students often want to use friends and relatives as sources in their stories. This is a bad idea because it lessens the story's credibility. Sources should be varied and come from backgrounds different from the reporter. The practice also compromises a journalist's integrity because a relative or friend usually will not mind if the reporter makes up or changes a quote to fit the story. Furthermore, when a journalist uses friends as sources, they expect to be presented in a positive manner, or the journalist tries to make them look good in exchange for being in the story.

6.5.2.2 SCRATCHING BACKS AND BECOMING TOO CHUMMY

Journalists need to know where to draw the line between being friendly and being friends with sources. Once that line is crossed, it becomes harder for them to remain objective. Also, sources who become friends expect preferential treatment. They may assume journalists will clean up their bad language or omit quotes that would reflect badly on them.

The adage "You scratch my back and I'll scratch yours" applies here. Sources give credibility to stories, offer ideas, add a different perspective and help with leads for more information. However, they do not consistently offer their time and information freely or out of the goodness of their hearts. They usually expect something in return, such as having only their point of view published or receiving publicity in another story to further their own interests.

The job of reporters is to be honest and objective. They should not fear or ignore stories that cast sources, particularly political or governmental ones, in a negative light. Informants might freeze out journalists for a while but not forever. If reporters cultivate a variety of sources representing different opinions, they can continue to do their job. Reputation is important: Journalists gain respect for writing balanced, fair stories. To avoid problems, they might request that a particularly negative story about an important source be assigned to another reporter or ask their editor for a change in beats if they become too chummy with a contact.

Many audiences want comprehensive information and were turned off by Fox News' obviously biased support of Donald Trump. For example, CNN obtained more than 2,300 text messages of Mark Meadows, former President Trump's chief of staff, that reflected activity surrounding the Jan. 6, 2021, insurrection. They showed more than 80 texts in which Fox News television and radio hosts,

MEDIA *EXCLUSIVE DETAILS*

NBC News says 11 articles written by politics reporter contained plagiarism

By Thomas Barrabi   May 2, 2022 | 6:27pm | Updated

NBC News fired political reporter Teaganne Finn after discovering 11 of her stories that contained passages lifted from other publications without attribution.

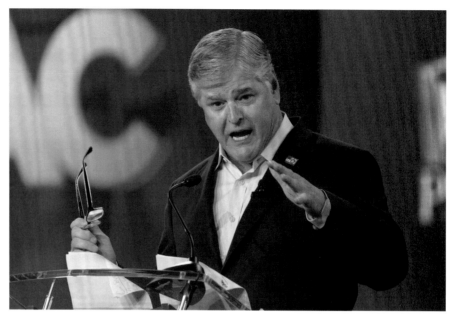

CNN fired Chris Cuomo, one of its program hosts, after the disclosure that he had been offering political advice to his brother, Andrew Cuomo, the former governor of New York. Sean Hannity, the host of a program on Fox News, suffered no consequences, however, after the disclosure that he and other Fox personalities had been offering advice to President Donald Trump.

including Sean Hannity, took orders from Meadows as to what they should say on their programs. In one thread before the elections, Meadows told Hannity to "Stress every vote matters. Get out and vote. On radio." To which Hannity responded, "Yes, sir. On it." He then asked, "Any place in particular we need a push?" Meadows affirmed, "Pennsylvania. North Carolina, Arizona, Nevada." Hannity answered, "Got it. Everywhere." And his afternoon radio program followed through on Meadows' instruction.

6.5.2.3 CURBING ANONYMOUS SOURCES

Reporters make clear at the beginning of an interview that everything is on the record and attributable. The public doubts sources who do not want to be named or held accountable for what they say. The credibility of the story and the journalist diminishes when no one is named to back up assertions. If a source for an important story supplies initial information but does not want to be attributed, the journalist finds someone willing to talk on the record. For some beats, such as national security, reporters must deal with anonymous sources, but these are rare (see Chapter 10). Most newsrooms have a two-source rule to confirm reports—and more is better, especially when the source is anonymous.

6.5.3 Recording Interviews: Audio Recorders and Video Cameras

Many reporters interviewed sources over Zoom during the pandemic. Before beginning the interview, journalists tell the sources if they are recording the interview and why.

Journalists record interviews so they can refer to the audio when their notes are confusing. They also use recorders to prove their stories are accurate and to protect themselves: Sources might claim the reporter misquoted them or even fabricated the entire interview. Some sources honestly forget what they said.

Transparency is a form of trust between the reporter and the source.

Journalists avoid secretly recording interviews because that tactic is devious and unfair (but see Chapters 5 and 11). The use of hidden video cameras raises additional issues. While audio recordings capture a person's voice only, videos—which often end up on television or the internet—also include people's faces, clothing and actions. Hidden cameras are a greater intrusion than hidden audio recorders.

'Isn't That the Trump Lawyer?': A Reporter's Accidental Scoop

By KENNETH P. VOGEL SEPT. 19, 2017

Reporter Kenneth Vogel got a scoop when, at a Washington restaurant, he overheard Trump's lawyers discussing the investigation of Russian election meddling. Vogel took notes on his phone and also shot this photo of the men.

Lawsuits for invasion of privacy can arise when journalists hide recording devices in places where people reasonably expect their words and actions to be private. The threat of lawsuits discourages reporters from using hidden cameras or audio recorders. If the story is extraordinarily important and they have exhausted all other means of getting the information they need, then they need to discuss alternatives with their editor.

6.5.4 Eliminating Conflicts of Interest

A conflict of interest exists when journalists, their friends and relatives, or news organizations are in a position to benefit directly from a story or when they or their family or friends have participated in the story. Reporters want to avoid even the appearance of such conflicts, which compromise their objectivity. In an effort to be transparent, they disclose any conflicts of interest in their stories. Audiences will decide if an issue exists and if it caused any bias.

6.5.4.1 ACCEPTING GIFTS: "FREEBIES"

Journalists refuse to accept money or anything else of value from the people they write about—before or after the story is published. Businesses do not give gifts without expecting something in return, whether it is currying favor for a current story or greasing the wheels for any potential stories. Gifts could subconsciously bias a journalist's story, and the appearance of giving/receiving such items may cause the public to suspect they have influenced the coverage. An editor at The Washington Post has said, "On some newspapers (this one included), the acceptance of a bribe—for that is what it is—is a firing offense."

Unless it is worth only a few dollars—a cup of coffee, for example—journalists refuse gifts. They tell the giver that the item cannot be accepted because of their organization's policies. Other newsroom guidelines require journalists to return the gift or send it to a charity. For example, reporters at the Detroit Free Press auction the amassed gifts annually and give the proceeds to charity.

Journalists also avoid the perception of accepting a gift. The public may misunderstand the action. For example, the Sierra Leone Association of Journalists

(SLAJ) was recently criticized for compromising its integrity and independence when it accepted food (rice, onions, cooking oil, etc.) as a Ramadan gift from the country's president to members who were fasting. SLAJ's president explained in an open letter that SLAJ members do not own media outlets, the donation was not secret and was covered in the news so that it was transparent. SLAJ's members had also given gifts during Ramadan. He noted:

> Now, there are two things about gifts or donations given to organizations like SLAJ. One is how we receive it and, two is what we do with it after receiving it. We are aware that accepting gifts goes a long way to undermine our principles of independence, credibility, and objectivity, and there is also the issue of conflict of interest. All these actually do [not] need to happen, they only need to be perceived, and that is exactly what has happened in this particular instance.

6.5.4.2 ACCEPTING TRIPS: "JUNKETS"

Free trips, called "junkets," were once common. Fashion writers were invited to New York and television critics to Hollywood, with all their expenses paid. Sports writers might accompany their local teams to games in distant cities, with the teams paying all the writers' expenses.

Many travel writers insist they could not afford to travel if hotels, airlines or other sponsors did not pay for them. Their stories are often compromised and unrealistic, however, because most people do not get complimentary trips with first-class transportation and managers' red-carpet treatment. Thus, the writer's experience neither resembles that of most travelers nor helps them decide how to spend their vacations.

6.5.4.3 PARTICIPATING IN THE NEWS

Journalists have lives outside of the newsroom, and those activities sometimes turn them into newsmakers. When that happens, editors worry that their journalists' involvement in events might undermine public confidence in the news organization's objectivity. Editors insist journalists' first obligation is to their primary employer. Reporters continue to represent their employers as objective news gatherers even after they leave work for the day; therefore, as stated in the SPJ's Code of Ethics, they should "remain free of associations and activities that may compromise integrity or damage credibility."

News executives generally agree that reporters should not hold public office (either elected or appointed), serve as party officials or help with anyone's election campaign. When in doubt about a possible conflict, journalists talk with their supervisors. Journalists are perceived as having a conflict when their spouses or family members are public officials or candidates for public office. In these cases, editors often move reporters to another beat or they take a leave of absence until the election or term ends.

6.5.4.4 FREELANCING

At most news organizations, full-time journalists are free to accept outside jobs, provided these roles do not conflict with their regular work. Typically, reporters can work as freelancers, but they cannot sell their work to their employers' competitors, such as other media in the same market.

Many journalists prefer to freelance full-time. It gives them the option to work remotely and choose their hours. Using freelancers also gives news organizations the opportunity for more reporter diversity and 24-hour news coverage.

6.5.5 Maintaining Objectivity

One component of objectivity, as discussed in the earlier chapters, is absence of bias. Objectivity also means integrating balance, fairness and accuracy within stories. And, presenting just facts without context can create inaccurate impressions.

Objectivity is important to discuss with colleagues and classmates because everyone has biases and opinions that make up who they are as individuals. Most people do not realize they have preconceived opinions about certain subjects. They are also unfounded assumptions that people do not think to question. Subconscious biases can be a product of family, upbringing, society, environment and even experienced isolated incidents. It is important to be aware of one's biases and to expose oneself to other points of view. It is the job of journalists to report all points of view when they cover an issue or story or else to be transparent within the story and tell audiences about a bias or conflict of interest.

Journalists' biases can greatly affect a story. Biases may influence a selection of story topics, sources, questions asked, story angle, organization and presentation. For instance, reporters who are politically active or who have an opinion about gun rights might have had difficulty writing objectively about the Uvalde, Texas, school shootings that killed 19 children and two adults. When covering the massacre, they might disregard that Texas Gov. Greg Abbott signed a bill the prior year allowing the purchase of a handgun without a permit.

Journalists who are passionate about the topic of sexual harassment could have had a hard time covering both sides of the Johnny Depp-Amber Heard defamation trial. Or, if journalists are fans of either actor Depp or Heard, then they might have trouble giving balanced reports during the trial.

Those aware of their prejudices might overcompensate in the opposite direction to present an impartial story. Journalists let their supervisors know when they cannot cover a subject objectively, and the editor or news director will assign the story to another reporter.

6.5.6 Interviewing Victims

Journalists are sensitive to victims and the public's sense of decency as they interview victims and grieving family members. They avoid having victims and their families relive a horrific event.

Few journalists are psychologists. They may not realize many disaster victims and family members are in shock, which can affect people in different ways, for several days or even months after an event. People in shock sometimes inadvertently twist or forget facts. They may later recant their stories or accuse journalists of making up the interview because they were still in a state of confusion. Many reporters obtain more accurate and complete stories if they wait several days to speak to victims. Although hard news stories can be written immediately after an event without these interviews, stories with more context and facts from the victim's family can follow later. Sometimes journalists can only know the who, what, where and when to an incident. The why and how might be known much later and appear in a follow-up story.

Victims or their family members sometimes choose to speak to only one journalist during their time of grief. And, families may have a representative, who might be a relative or close friend. In this case, journalists give their names and contact information to the representative, asking them to let the journalist know if, and when, victims feel ready to talk. Compassionate, respectful journalists who do not pressure victims and their families receive more in-depth information.

Journalists' zeal for getting out the news quickly can sometimes backfire if they are not sensitive to both the victim's family and their audience. For example, audiences rebuked NFL reporter Adam Schefter for his insensitive tweet announcing the death of Dwayne Haskins, a former quarterback at Ohio State: "Dwayne Haskins, a standout at Ohio State before struggling to catch on with Washington and Pittsburgh in the NFL, died this morning . . ." (For more information on interviewing victims and their families, see Chapter 11.)

6.5.7 Respecting Privacy of Sources

The media sometimes intrude on the privacy of individuals. Although journalists are often within their legal rights, they are not necessarily proceeding ethically. Some people who become involved in major lawsuits, crimes and accidents may expect to be mentioned in news stories about them, but others might be surprised or confused about being in the media spotlight. Reporters are sensitive to individuals who have been thrust into the news and consider potential consequences of naming names. Journalists also do not include the names of relatives or friends, if they are not central to the story. The coverage of private citizens is often different from that of celebrities and politicians, who seek publicity.

6.5.8 Avoiding Deceit: Posing and Misrepresentation

Journalists strive to be trusted. Deceit is a form of lying and lying is unethical.

On one hand, journalists, after careful consideration with their editors, may think deceit is the only way to get an interview or a story. On the other hand, most experts say the press should not criticize deceitfulness by public officials or businesses if reporters are also being devious while pursuing a story. An investigative story with many in-depth interviews and extensive background research provides a better story than one in which journalists use deception.

Passive posing, where reporters might appear to a business owner or government official as simply another member of the public, presents few ethical problems. They may experience a situation as an average citizen and gather information available to any person. Restaurant reviewers would be ineffective if everyone knew their identities. Restaurant owners, eager to obtain favorable

"Actually I'm not the queen - I'm undercover for the Daily Mirror..."

publicity, would offer reviewers special meals and service, making them unable to describe what the average customer receives. Another example is a journalist who wants to cover a protest rally: If protesters realize a reporter is present, they might either act more cautiously or perform for the reporter in hopes that they get into the news.

More serious ethical—and legal—problems arise when journalists actively misrepresent themselves to gain access to places and information closed to the public. For instance, student reports might want to investigate how their university handles sexual assault claims by posing as a victim or an accused person. Although it might be exciting and easier to write a story in the first-person, it is not a good idea. Journalists should not misrepresent themselves; it is a form of lying. In this case, the reporters should review the reason for the story. If the macro issue is to inform students about the university's system, researching campus sexual assault policies and interviewing students who experienced the process, university officials, parents and lawyers would be helpful. Finding data on universities nationally would put the individual school into context.

In the past, journalists have posed as patients to gather information about a mental hospital or as laborers to write about migrant workers' exposure to pesticides. Although reporters could be exposing a social ill, the public disapproves of their conduct. They may even face legal penalties because of their dubious methods of gathering information.

Journalists talk to their supervisors before they use any form of deceit if there is no other safe way to obtain an important story. In this case, journalists state their use of deception in their stories and explain why it was necessary; they also call all people criticized in their stories and give them an opportunity to respond. Shane Bauer, a writer for Mother Jones magazine, followed these guidelines for reporting on the Winn Correctional Center in Louisiana. Bauer used his real name and real work history, including the fact he worked for the foundation that publishes Mother Jones, when he applied for a job as a guard at Winn. He worked in the prison, which is operated by the Corrections Corporation of America, for several months before quitting to write an exposé of conditions in the prison. Bauer's article and a subsequent book, "American Prison," won multiple awards.

6.5.9 Witnessing Crimes and Disasters

Many consider journalists to be first responders. They are often among the first at a scene, along with medics, firefighters and police officers. They are sent into emergency situations to report the events so that others within their communities can learn what happened.

Journalists and photographers might be on the front lines and witness terrible tragedies, such as wars, terrorist attacks or car crashes. They react in the same way they would if a member of their family was in physical danger—they help people, particularly if they are the only ones on the scene. But when a victim is already receiving help from trained first responders, journalists stay out of the rescuers' way and concentrate on reporting the event.

Journalists often are among the first to arrive at accident, crime or disaster scenes and witness the effects of the events.

Reporters occasionally learn about a crime or hostage situation while it is in progress and are tempted to interview the suspect, who often has a weapon. Journalists are not hostage negotiators. The potential risk to the hostage outweighs the value of the information gleaned. Audiences will be informed just as well, if not more comprehensively, if the reporter learns information later from police. Furthermore, if journalists interrupt rescuers trying to do their jobs, they may be unable to stop the suspect from harming someone or from escaping.

Sometimes journalists are repeatedly assigned to cover tragic events because they are good reporters in these situations. It is important for journalists to take a break from this type of coverage and to also talk with a professional counselor to unpack their experience. For instance, ITV News Correspondent Dan Rivers reported on the Ukraine-Russia war and said that many events he witnessed will stay with him forever.

6.6 Ethics Issues Regarding Content

News executives consider the best ways to inform, educate or entertain their audiences. As the fourth estate, news media are respectful and considerate to sources, subjects and audiences while balancing society's need to know. Audiences might ignore or criticize an important story if the reporter obtained or presented the content in a controversial or unethical manner.

6.6.1 Avoiding Speculation: Get the Facts and Provide Accurate Context

When reporters do not know why things happen, they sometimes want to speculate about it to audiences. Their conjectures, however, mislead the public. Journalists refrain from guessing the "why" or "how" until the information is known for a follow-up story. They steer clear of sensationalism, respect an individual's privacy and focus on the objective of the story.

When journalists omit important facts or context, they can inadvertently transform heroes and victims into bad guys and vice versa. When a teenage boy was killed while a friend and he tried to stop a burglar from getting into a neighbor's home, one newspaper stated that he was out at 4 a.m., smoking, had a gun and was a high school dropout. An anonymous source said the boy "liked to party." Very little information was presented about the burglar. A different newspaper called the boy a hero and quoted the positive things his family and friends had to say. This story noted that, at the time of the incident, the teenagers were sitting on the porch of one of the boys' homes because they were minding the rule that smoking was not allowed in the house. The victim was enrolled at an alternative school for dropouts because he was determined to get a GED and he had a job. The gun belonged to the other boy, whom the victim was defending when the burglar stabbed him. The burglar had been arrested several times for burglary and aggravated assault with a deadly weapon.

6.6.2 Using Visuals: Newsworthy or Sensational?

Editors and producers run photographs and videos because they tell a story. But the visual coverage of disasters, including civil wars, bombings, hate crimes, mass shootings and natural disasters challenge many news executives. They seek the proper balance between giving the public what it needs to see without presenting unnecessarily gory images, descending into sensationalism or being accused of running the visual for shock value. Too much repetition of the same graphic can distract people from the purpose of the story and, as researchers explain, numb viewers' reaction to the horrific events.

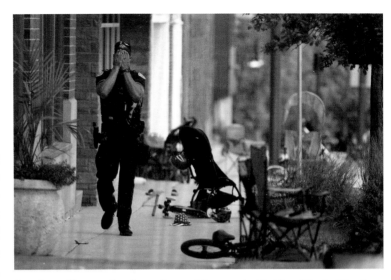

A police officer walks down Central Avenue in Highland Park, Illinois, on July 4, 2022, after a shooting at the suburb's Fourth of July parade. The gunman killed seven people and injured dozens more. Editors and producers want to inform the public about such events without sensationalizing them or publishing needlessly gory images.

Sometimes, however, words alone cannot convey the situation as well as a photograph or video can. All journalists make decisions about whether to shield the public from unpleasantness or to educate them on a case-by-case basis. The Nieman Reports website offers examples of how newsrooms have handled graphic images when debating if some images are too distressing to publish or too important to ignore, especially when covering gun violence, such as the 19 elementary children and two teachers in Uvalde, Texas; the 10 people in the Tops grocery store in Buffalo, New York; and the victims at the Presbyterian Church in Laguna Woods, California; and more—all within May 2022.

Journalists use their ethical decision-making processes to discuss publishing an image or finding a middle ground by cropping it or giving a long view instead of a close-up. But reporters who cover a lot of murders and accidental deaths might not be able over time to objectively judge what an audience will find appropriate. Thus, news organizations keep in touch with the attitudes of their local readers or viewers. What is acceptable to city dwellers in the East might not be acceptable to rural folks in the Midwest.

6.6.3 Altering Images

It is dishonest and unethical to change news images. Just as writers do not lie about the content of their stories, photographers do not lie about the content of their captured images. Still, they have always been able to alter their photos. In the days of 35 mm prints, photos could be cropped, enlarged or burned to provide more contrast. With today's computers and photo-editing programs, photojournalists must be careful to avoid crossing a line between clarifying an image and changing the essence or meaning of the scene.

Media outlets are particularly careful to verify the authenticity of images that originate from bystanders—untrained "citizen journalists"—to avoid publishing photos that were altered, staged or faked, according to Salim Amin in the International Journalists' Network (IJNet), a website for international correspondents.

Magazines are often criticized for altering images on their covers. Jamaican Rapper Shenseea rebuked Numero magazine recently for giving her a thinner body and sculpting the outline of her face and nose to appear more European. (For more on photojournalism and manipulating images, see Chapter 14.)

6.6.4 Deciding When to Name Names

News organizations have policies requiring journalists to fully identify everyone mentioned in their stories. However, some participants might make forceful claims for anonymity.

6.6.4.1 NAMING JUVENILES

Journalists usually do not name children who are connected to a crime. Children are not capable of dealing with the associated infamy, which might affect them for the rest of their lives. Traditionally, the criminal justice system has also shielded children under 18 who are accused or convicted of a crime. This protection has been explained on the grounds that juveniles understand neither what they did nor the consequences of their actions.

The main exception occurs when juveniles are tried in adult court because the charge is a serious crime or the suspects have already been punished for earlier serious offenses. If several teenagers are charged with committing crimes that terrorized a neighborhood, news executives might feel a need to identify them and perhaps their parents as well. Journalists might decide their obligation to calm people's fears by informing the community about the arrests outweighs their normal obligation to protect the accused and their families.

6.6.4.2 WRITING ABOUT VICTIMS OF SEXUAL ASSAULT

Journalists are careful to avoid re-exploiting victims. A national study of news executives showed that most news organizations withhold the names of rape victims. The nature of the crime and the subsequent attention traumatizes and stigmatizes victims in unique ways. Sexual assault is an under-reported crime, and news coverage discourages some from going to the police. A study on rape victims showed that most were angry about being identified, and a few said they would not have reported the crime if they had known news media would name them. As a result of being named, most victims reported emotional trauma as well as embarrassment, shame and difficulties in their relationships. Thus, identifying a victim has little benefit for audiences but may have negative effects on the individual.

Although the media do not usually name people who report a sexual assault, they do for those charged. Another study showed that audiences wanted to know the accused's name but felt that news organizations should not identify victims. Sexual assault suspects, like those in other crimes, are always identified so the public has full knowledge about the situation. Moreover, bystanders might come forward with information about the accused, and his or her neighbors can take steps to protect themselves.

6.6.5 Covering Killers

People remember events based on how the media covered them. When the news focuses on killers—their backgrounds and their families—and not the victims, some critics say the media glorify killers and imply that they are important and victims are not. For example, many people who saw news coverage of a man ramming his vehicle into anti-racist protesters in Charlottesville, Virginia, say they remember the perpetrator better than they do the person killed and the 19 others injured. Were repeated stories about the driver's background verging on sensationalism? Was his story more important than those of the victims? Who should be remembered?

Serial killers and terrorists often crave publicity and notoriety. Two examples are the Zodiac Killer in 1969–70 in the San Francisco area and the Unabomber, Ted Kaczynski, who operated from 1979 to 1995. Both sent communications to newspapers and demanded they be published or they would continue killing. Zodiac was never caught, but the publication of Kaczynski's 35,000-word manifesto led to his identification and capture. Serial killers often plan their horrific attacks to ensure they become famous. They welcome being featured in news stories during their trials and sentencing. It is a balancing act for journalists to report the news, yet not help killers achieve their publicity goals.

6.6.6 Reporting on Public Figures and Celebrities

The public's right to know usually outweighs a government official's or public figure's right to privacy. Journalists should expose government officials who abuse their power, such as those who steer lucrative contracts to cronies, or who have personal problems, such as alcoholism, that affect their work.

But does the public have a right to know about a public figure's private affairs, such as adultery? Proponents argue that if politicians break a solemn promise, such as a wedding vow, then pledges to their constituency might also be meaningless. The public has a right to know about the character of the person who represents them. Another variable is whether the affair is with a member of the government, which could lead to abuse of power or favoritism.

Public figures and celebrities want to be the center of attention when promoting their causes, such as a new policy or an upcoming movie. Yet, they do not want the public to know personal things that might be damaging to their image or causes. Critics say those in the public eye cannot have it both ways.

Melania Trump, Prince Andrew, Gwendolyn Beck and Jeffrey Epstein at a party at the Mar-a-Lago club, Palm Beach, Florida, in February 2000. Prince Andrew was accused of raping a minor who was trafficked by Epstein and Ghislaine Maxwell, both of whom were convicted of sex offenses.

Journalists identify the purpose of a story and what audiences need to know, such as in the case of England's Prince Andrew, who was accused of raping a minor trafficked by Jeffrey Epstein and Ghislaine Maxwell, convicted sex offenders. Coverage of his sex scandal and trial were important, especially to the British, because he was removed from his royal duties and was responsible for his own legal bills. Rapper Snoop Dogg and his associate Don Juan were recently accused of sexual assault and battery by one of Dogg's backup singers, which could affect performances and other public appearances.

6.6.7 Reporting Rumors and Speculation

Audiences usually come across rumors through their social media and then use legitimate news sources to check them out. Unfortunately, many people do not know how to verify if something is fake news or disinformation nor can they tell the difference between researched news stories and opinion pieces.

Journalists publish established and investigated facts, but the temptation to run unsubstantiated stories grows with the oft-repeated rumors that quickly fly across Instagram, Twitter, Facebook and other social media. Nonetheless, news organizations risk their reputations by publishing false information. All information should be checked out.

When an event occurs, some news elements—such as the who, what, where and when—are readily available. However, it might take days or weeks to find out the why or how. Journalists do not provide the why through speculation and interpretation, which could mislead audiences. Theories and conjectures are not news.

6.6.8 Reporting on Terrorism

Terrorists want publicity for violent acts. They want to scare people. Media coverage makes them feel important, and they think it legitimizes their cause. To attract even more publicity, terrorists conduct press conferences. Some want journalists to photograph and interview their captives. Others make videos that show hostages pleading for their lives, reading the terrorists' demands and warning that they will be killed if the conditions are not met.

Terrorists are responsible for bombings, hijackings and mass murders—events that news organizations cannot ignore. Yet some critics insist the media coverage encourages terrorists. They believe that if the media ignored terrorists, they would become discouraged and abandon their acts of violence. The late Margaret Thatcher, who was the British prime minister from 1979 to 1990, encouraged journalists to stop the coverage, to starve terrorists of "the oxygen of publicity." Other critics think the public has a right to know what is happening in the world, and a news blackout might result in rumors about the terrorists' activities that are more frightening than the truth. They also fear terrorists would escalate their violence to force publicity if journalists tried to ignore them.

6.6.9 Advertising

News organizations sell advertising space for revenue. They are under no obligation to publish any advertisements. Many outlets refuse to publish ads for products and services—tobacco products, alcoholic beverages, happy hours, movies rated

NC-17 (adults only), sexual aids, abortion services, handguns, massage parlors and escort services—that are considered harmful according to community standards.

Some advertisers, especially in magazines and on websites and social media, want to dictate story content within the publication and placement of their ads to be close to certain articles. News outlets usually refuse to comply.

"Native Advertising" is another advertising tactic used to fool the public. Editors consider it unethical and dishonest to present paid-advertising material as story content because ads are one-sided and biased. Social media and many non-news stories on the internet regularly accept native advertising without telling their audiences that the content is not objective nor reported by a trained journalist. The Federal Trade Commission, an agency that regulates advertising, has been issuing rules and guidelines to make it easier for citizens to distinguish advertising from news, opinions and features.

Companies may threaten to pull their advertising if news stories reflect negatively on their company's image or products or they do not agree with a publication's stance on an issue. Although not a news outlet, social media giant Facebook was blasted for its nonaction toward former President Trump's hate speech and misinformation tactics. The NAACP, Anti-Defamation League and Color of Change called for companies to boycott advertising on Facebook. Several companies joined the boycott, including Microsoft ($116 million), Starbucks ($95 million), Ford ($70 million), Best Buy ($29 million), Chipotle ($6 million) and many others (Table 6.3). (On a different note, about 30 years ago these companies advertised only in traditional media, before the internet and social media became popular.)

TABLE 6.3 TOP 10 BRANDS BOYCOTTING FACEBOOK, BY $ AMOUNT OF ADVERTISING IN PREVIOUS YEAR (US)

Microsoft	$115.9 million
Starbucks	$94.9 million
Pfizer	$54.5 million
Target	$46.4 million
Unilever	$42.4 million
Hershey's	$36.5 million
CVS Health	$34.5 million
Best Buy	$29 million
HP	$24.7 million
Diageo	$22.9 million
Verizon	$22.9 million

Data from Tiffany Hsu and Gillian Friedman, 2020, "CVS, Dunkin', Lego: The Brands Pulling Ads From Facebook Over Hate Speech," The New York Times, June 26, https://www.nytimes.com/2020/06/26/business/media/Facebook-advertising-boycott.html.

The Reporter's Guide to Ethics

1. The major principles guiding a journalist's decisions are to act and think morally; distinguish between right and wrong; stay within the bounds of fairness, good taste and common decency; and be honest with your audience.

2. Many professional journalism organizations—such as the American Society of Newspaper Editors, the Society of Professional Journalists, and the Radio, Television, Digital News Association—have codes of ethics.

3. When considering a story, reporters ask themselves who and how many will be hurt by the publication and who and how many will be helped.

4. Plagiarizing another person's work is never permissible and often results in a journalist's firing.

5. Reporters avoid using friends or relatives as sources and avoid becoming too friendly with sources.

6. Electronically recording an interview without the interviewee's consent may be legal in most jurisdictions, but it is unethical.

7. Reporters do not accept gifts or junkets from the people or organizations they cover because they usually expect favorable content in return.

8. Journalists, like everyone, have biases, but they should be aware of them and select sources with different views. When reporters cannot set aside their biases on a story, they ask their editors for reassignment.

9. Journalists are especially sensitive and follow a set of guidelines when interviewing victims and survivors of crimes or disasters.

10. Reporters do not misrepresent themselves to their sources; they always reveal they are working on a news story. And nothing is "off the record."

11. News stories should be free from speculation and should present facts accurately and in context.

12. Photographs and videos provide audiences with helpful information and avoid gore and sensationalism. They should never be manipulated.

13. People in news stories should be fully identified; however, news organizations usually avoid identifying juveniles who are accused of crimes or the victims of sexual assaults.

14. The public may have an interest in knowing what celebrities and public officials are doing, but public figures still have some expectation of privacy. That expectation is even greater for private individuals who become entangled in news events. Ethical reporters and entertainment journalists are not paparazzi.

15. Crimes and acts of terrorism are of public concern, but news organizations avoid giving the perpetrators excessive publicity.

 # Review Exercises

1. ETHICAL DECISION-MAKING PROCESSES

1. Many journalists memorize a set of ethical decision-making questions that they use regularly. Which ones would you use most often? Why?

2. Choose a local issue that presents an ethical dilemma. Use the **Potter Box** to help you determine a solution.

3. An alum who is a frequent visitor, guest speaker and donor of an accumulated $500,000 to your journalism program referred to your state's governor as a white supremacist in a tweet. Is this a story? What is the process you would use to find an ethical course of action?

2. DISCUSSION QUESTIONS

After completing the following questions, discuss your decisions with the class.

1. Which of these actions is plagiarism or unethical? Add a few words to explain your answer.

   A. Selling the notes you took in class.

   B. Turning in a paper that you purchased online.

   C. Using, without attribution, a five-word phrase from a tweet.

   D. Using, without attribution, a 20-word paragraph from a magazine story.

   E. Using YouTube copyrighted content for your news story.

   F. Duplicating a copyrighted image or GIF.

   G. Posting an image of someone, even if it originated in a public place.

   H. While recording an audio podcast, borrowing a quote from an interview in another reporter's podcast, while attributing the source, but not the reporter.

   I. Using the responses that you crowdsourced, if you were transparent about the reason you were gathering the information.

   J. Telling sources how their information will be used and distributed to other platforms.

   K. Including a portion of your recorded Zoom interview in a multimedia story without asking recording permission from the source.

   L. While writing about a celebrity, copying a quote you found online.

   M. Using your own words, but another writer's ideas, that appeared in a TV newscast.

   N. Using, but totally rewriting without attribution, a story from another newspaper.

   O. Using, but totally rewriting with attribution, a story from the internet.

   P. Publishing a press release without changing a word.

   Q. For background while working under deadline pressure, reprinting verbatim several paragraphs from an old story written by another reporter at your news organization.

   R. While working for a radio or television station, reading your city's daily newspaper to find out what's happening in your community and what stories you should cover.

   S. While working for a radio or television station, broadcasting stories found in a citizen journalism site without rewriting or attributing.

   T. While working for a radio or television station, rewriting stories from your local news website and attributing the website.

   U. Duplicating the background or organization of a story, but not copying the words, verbatim, from another source, such as Wikipedia.

   V. While working for a television station, reusing footage shot by another reporter in a previous story.

2. Aside from the scenarios in the previous questions, what other examples of plagiarism have you experienced, especially online or with social media?

3. As editor of your student news organization (radio, TV, print, online), you receive an anonymous letter that accuses a faculty member of repeatedly making sexist remarks. With the prevalence of the #MeToo movement, would you publish the letter? If your answer is "no," at which point would you change your mind? (You can choose more than one response.)

   A. The student who wrote the letter identifies herself but, because she fears retaliation, insists that you keep her name a secret.

   B. Two more women come in and corroborate the letter's content but also insist that you keep their names a secret.

   C. All three students agree to let you quote them and publish their names.

   D. The three students play a recording they secretly made in class, one that clearly documents their complaints.

   E. The students complain that the faculty member also touched them.

F. You submit a public-records request to the university's Office of Inclusion and Equity and use that information and students' names.

4. As editor of your student news organization, which of the following gifts would you allow members of your staff to accept? Explain your decision.

A. Free tickets to local plays, movies and concerts for your entertainment editor.

B. Free meals at local restaurants for your food critic.

C. Free trips to out-of-town games with your college team for your sports editor.

D. Free loan of a sophisticated computer that a manufacturer offers to your technology editor for the school year so she can test new games and software.

E. Free one-week trip to Daytona Beach, Florida, for your entertainment writer and a friend to write about the popular spring break destination.

F. An alcoholic drink at the local hangout. The source is buying!

G. Free donuts from the new bakery that was reviewed favorably in a prior story.

5. As editor of your student news organization, indicate the products and services you would be willing to advertise. Explain your reasoning.

A. Hate letters

B. Medical marijuana or cannabis clinics

C. Guns

D. E-cigarettes or cigarettes

E. An essay claiming the Holocaust is a hoax

F. Fortune tellers

G. Alcohol, such as bourbon, vodka and gin

H. Abortion clinics

I. Couples who want to adopt newborns of only a certain race

J. Escort services, massage parlors, nude dancers

K. Happy hour at a local bar

L. Websites with pornography

6. As editor of your student news organization, which of the following cases of deception would you permit? Discuss your reasoning.

A. After hearing complaints that the university is going overboard on the number and type of penalties regarding Title IX, allow a reporter to pose as a student with a complaint and another reporter to pose as the accused.

B. Allow a reporter using a fake identity to join a rebellious group that often marches and holds rallies in the region.

C. After hearing that some people may be cheating local charities by collecting food and money from several simultaneously, allow a reporter to pose as a destitute parent to see how much food and money they can collect in one day. The reporter promises to return everything after the story's publication.

D. Let a reporter pay a source for sensitive information.

E. Allow two journalists to pose as a same-sex couple wanting to rent an apartment. Friends have told members of your staff about instances of discrimination.

F. A reporter informs you that his brother is opening a bar, and that city inspectors seem to be asking for bribes to approve the building's plumbing, electrical and health inspections. The reporter suggests that you notify the district attorney, install hidden cameras in the bar and begin to pay the bribes to see if there is a story.

G. Let a journalist apply and get a job in a grocery chain butcher shop, using their own name but without identifying their intent, to verify rumors that old meat is mixed with fresh cuts and repackaged.

7. As editor of your student news organization, choose the practices you would permit. Justify your decisions.

A. Allowing the sports editor to host a daily program on a local radio station.

B. Allowing the sports editor to appear in television advertisements for a chain of sports stores in the city.

C. Allowing the business editor to own stock in local companies.

D. Allowing a popular columnist, a local celebrity, to charge $1,000 for each one-hour speech they give.

E. Allowing a local freelance cartoonist, whose cartoons your newspaper has agreed to publish regularly on the editorial page, to donate money to local politicians.

3. DISCUSSION QUESTIONS

Read the following situations and decide what actions you would take. Discuss your choices with the class.

1. Without your knowledge, a talented young reporter on your staff hacks into the computer system at a competing news organization. The reporter gives you a list of all the stories the rival's staff is working on. Would you:

   A. Compliment the reporter on their initiative and quickly assign your own staff to cover the stories so you are not scooped?

   B. Destroy the list and tell the reporter to never again enter the rival's computer system?

   C. Reprimand the reporter, suspending them for a week?

   D. Notify your rival and apologize for the reporter's actions?

   E. Notify the police that the reporter may have unknowingly violated a state law?

2. One of your journalists is writing about a local country club that apparently excludes certain cultures and religions. The reporter also learns that your publisher and other influential members of your community are members of the club. Would you:

   A. Abandon the story?

   B. Inform your publisher about the story?

   C. Inform your publisher about the story and suggest that they resign from the club?

   D. Tell your reporter to interview the publisher, giving them an opportunity to explain their membership in the club?

   E. Publish the story but never identify any of the club's members?

   F. Publish the story, listing your publisher and other prominent citizens who belong to the club without offering them a chance to respond?

   G. List all 1,200 of the club's members?

3. As editor of your local daily, you learn that the next day's installment of Doonesbury, a popular comic strip, shows a political bias that might offend many readers. Would you:

   A. Publish the strip without change or comment?

   B. Kill that day's strip?

   C. Stop publishing the strip forever?

   D. Change any wording to something less offensive?

   E. Kill that day's strip but, in its place, publish a brief explanation?

   F. Move the strip to your newspaper's editorial page and publish an editorial explaining that you believe in freedom of speech?

4. Each year, the SPJ in your state sponsors an awards competition. Minutes ago, you learned that a reporter on your staff won first place in feature writing and that your chief photographer won second place in sports. However, another news website in the city won five awards and a local television station won four. How would you handle the story? Are there any ethical ramifications?

   A. Ignore the story.

   B. Report all the awards.

   C. Report only the awards won by your staff.

5. You run the evening news, and a sports reporter mistakenly credited the wrong football player with scoring two game-winning touchdowns. Would you:

   A. Broadcast a correction the next evening?

   B. Broadcast a correction and identify the reporter responsible for the error?

   C. Broadcast a correction and punish the reporter, placing them on probation?

   D.   Broadcast a correction that identifies the reporter and reports the punishment?

   E.   Order the reporter to write a letter to the school, apologizing for the error?

   F.   Privately punish the reporter, placing him on probation, but publish nothing, treating the incident as a private personnel matter?

   G.   Do nothing, hoping nobody noticed? (Good luck with that one.)

6. Decide how you would respond in each of the following situations. Are any unethical? Discuss your reasoning.

   A.   As news director of a local television station, you think an emphasis on crime and violence is bad journalism but don't know if it affects your newscasts' ratings. Would you continue to emphasize crime and violence? Are there alternatives ways to cover stories?

   B.   A reporter on your staff has terrible vision, undergoes a new laser procedure to correct nearsightedness and wants to write a series about the operation and the doctor who successfully performed it. The story is likely to interest thousands of readers, but you learn that the reporter's operation was performed for free. Would you let them write the series?

   C.   After serving three terms, your city's mayor—a popular and successful politician—decides to step down. They then apply for a job as a political columnist for your editorial page and are obviously a good writer. Would you hire them?

   D.   A manufacturer for popular candy-flavored e-cigarettes wants to advertise only if you publish positive stories on vaping. How do you respond?

   E.   A member of your state legislature proposes applying your state sales tax to advertisements, a policy that would cost the news site, of which you are publisher, millions of dollars a year. When asked, would you contribute $50,000 to a campaign your state press association is waging against the tax? Would you report your decision and the size of any contribution?

   F.   An extortionist says they have poisoned groceries in your town's largest chain of supermarkets. Customers continue to shop in the stores. Police say the threat is almost certainly a hoax, and that it will be easier for them to catch the extortionist in a day or two if you delay publishing the story. Would you immediately run the story?

4. ETHICAL DILEMMAS

Read the following ethical dilemmas and answer the related questions, giving support for your answers. Discuss your responses with the class.

1. A student at a local high school brought their father's gun to school and shot another student. The school security guard killed the shooter. In an interview, the principal tells you that the student with the gun was "a troubled child"; they immediately ask you to please not run this statement, that it shouldn't have been said. Does this quote contribute to the purpose of the story? Would you run it? Why or why not? Does it matter that the shooter died?

2. After a deadly car crash, you interview the mother of a deceased driver. She tells you that he would have lived if the hospital had not acted so slowly. In describing the hospital, she uses several expletives. For your small-town news outlet, would you use the expletives? What about in a bigger outlet like The New York Times? Are the expletives necessary? Does including them support the objective of the story?

3. While listening to a police scanner, you hear that a man has been arrested for raping a 16-year-old girl. You go to the police station and talk to the arresting officer. While discussing the case, he says he believes that "this man should fry." Is it ethical to publish this, or is it editorializing? Is the quote necessary? Does it support the objective of the story?

4. You want to do a story on #BlackLivesMatter and interview a local Black business owner who has just donated a large amount of money to a fund helping the urban Black community. While

discussing it, he drops a racial slur. Should you use it in your story? Are there reasons you would or would not use it?

5. Your regular beat includes stopping by the mayor's office most days of the week, and you regularly talk with the mayor's secretary. One day she says that she will treat you to lunch and the two of you can discuss what goes on "behind the scenes." Should you accept the offer of the free lunch, even though she says that it is the only way you will get the information? Would it make a difference if you paid for the lunches? Are there alternatives to this situation?

6. A local soldier was killed in Ukraine and brought home. During the woman's graveside service, your videographer captured the deceased's 5-year-old son wiping away a tear and holding a stuffed bear dressed like Uncle Sam. Should you use the video in your story? Does the decision change, depending on the medium, such as TV or internet or as a photo in print? Should a journalist be at the graveside service, or is that invading the family's privacy? A graveyard might be public, but a service might be considered private.

5. STORIES THAT RAISE ETHICAL CONCERNS

Each of the following stories involves several ethical dilemmas. Write a news story based on each set of facts, thoughtfully deciding which ones to use and which ones do not support the story's objective. Check spellings, AP style, bias and any other errors. Use the City Directory to verify names. Be careful not to cut and paste phrases and quotes because their errors are often missed.

1. Nursing Home Employees

It's a shocking tale and an exclusive for your newspaper, revealed by a diligent and exhaustive month-long investigation by a team of 5 journalists and one editor on your staff. While visiting a nursing home where her mother is living, your police reporter recognized three aides, all ex-cons. The following investigation revealed that felons have daily contact with the most frail and defenseless of your city's elderly residents. No one can say how many nursing home employees have been convicted of theft, prostitution, domestic violence, or other crimes because people in those jobs don't have to undergo a criminal background check. Using city directories and a multitude of other sources, the team learned the names of 412 employees in the town's nursing homes and found that 1 in 5 was arrested or convicted for a felony. Esther Onn, president of the state Coalition to Protect Elders, told one of the reporters that she wants and is fighting for all nursing home employees to be screened: "Our parents deserve the best care society can give them. They shouldn't have to worry about being robbed or beaten. In some nursing homes in the city we've found evidence of real

brutality, of residents being terrorized by these thugs. These people work in nursing homes because they can get jobs there. The operators of the places know if they hire ex-cons, they don't have to pay them much. Giving them jobs at low wages increases the owners profits, and they're already exorbitant." Yet, Beatrice Rosolowski, Spokesman for the State Federation of Nursing Homes, says checking on everyone goes too far and they themselves are pushing other reforms to the system they agree is flawed. "The cracks are their and they are big enough for people to be slipping through," Rosolowsky admits. Theft is the most common crime against nursing home patients, and they are vulnerable because many residents are incapable of even reporting crimes against them, whether theft, brutality, intimidation or neglect. At least some of those crimes are committed by nursing home staffers, which is why people residing in nursing homes everywhere are told to keep their valuables hidden and drawers and doors locked. Even if a background investigation of nursing home employees are conducted, the team learned they could be far from adequate since people convicted in other states would likely not be detected and background checks often are not run on people until after they have begun to work. And employees arrested or convicted after their initial check may not be detected until they apply for a job at another nursing home. Blanket screening would be expensive and not likely to make homes much safer, she said. Another source, Atty. Harold Murray, represents 150 clients currently suing nursing homes in and around the state. Some have been abused, he said, while others have had their possessions stolen by nursing home workers. "You've got housekeepers, custodians, dieticians, physical therapists and a host of other employees who go into these rooms every day and who have contact with residents. Who are these people?" Murry asks. While pursuing the lawsuits Murry obtained records of nursing home workers and did his own background check. Of 378 employee names he submitted, 76 had been arrested for or convicted of felonies. The convictions included prostitution, assault, and spousal abuse. Two former prostitutes work at Elder Haven, 3110 East River Parkway, and so does a bank robber released after 14 years in prison. A convicted child molester, Grady Smith, was found by Murray working at Sunnyview Nursing Home, 1012 Peters Dr. Smith was in prison from 1981 to 1993, when he got his current job as a janitor at Sunnyview and, according to police, has been in no trouble since then. The reporters also heard—but have been unable to document—allegations that some nursing home employees strap some residents difficult to handle to their chairs or beds, leaving them in such condition for prolonged periods of time every day on a daily basis. Unhappy residents families allege but have no proof that some residents are kept heavily sedated even when there is no clear medical or physical reason to do so simply because it makes residents easier to handle.

2. Teen Gang

Beginning at the start of last year the police in your city noticed an abrupt increase in crime, especially car thefts and residential burglaries, in the Oakwood Subdivision. As dawn broke early today police went to the homes of 4 teenagers, all students currently at Oakwood high school. The teens were arrested by police, who now say they were part of a ring suspected of involvement in a total of approximately 100 to 150 or more car and home burglaries. Police are looking for two other teens but did not identify them. All are white. All are male. All are medium height. Two of the 6 are on the schools honor roll, which requires a 3.5 gpa or higher. All are between the ages of 16 to 18 yrs of age. In a press conference today your citys police chief said the students apparently took orders from fellow students. His officers recovered property valued at $15,000, including computers, televisions, guns, cameras, stamp and coin collections, video consoles and games. "Some of these kids were making a lot of bucks," the chief said. The youngest students, one age 16

and one age 17, were immediately taken to the county juvenile detention centre for incarceration and were subsequently released to their parents. The other two, both 18, were charged with multiple counts of burglary, possession of stolen goods, and contributing to the delinquency of a minor, and are being held in the county jail with their bail set at $50,000. Because of the seriousness of their crimes, police charged all 4 as adults and identified them as:

Claude Nunziata, 16, son of Carmen Nunziata

Burt Dolomovich, 17, son of Sandra M. Dolmovich

Michael Gandolf, 18, son of Sandra Gandolf

Giles Grauman, 18, son of Alyce and Samuel Graumann

The police chief, who personally released the youths names to the press today, said "The information our investigation is uncovering is that they've done a lot more than what we know. One of these punks told my men he'd been involved in at least 80 burglaries himself. What's worse, what's really depressing here, is that we think dozens of students at the school knew what they were doing and, because it was cheap, were buying things from them, things they knew were stolen". Police Detective Sargent Barry Kopperud was happy that the parents of three of the boys voluntarily cooperated by allowing police to search their homes for stolen property taken in the crimes. Carman Nunzieta, the mother of Claude, refused to let the police into her home and refused to talk to the press when you called her today. Police subsequently obtained a search warrant, then proceeded to search the premises. She is divorced and on welfare, with a total of four children to support and is not currently working, having been on welfare for 11 years according to public records maintained by the city that you were able to see. The whereabouts of Nunziatas father is unknown at this point in time. "Some parents were aware their sons were wheeling and dealing with property, but they figured they were just swapping with one another" Kopperudd said "I don't know, maybe some knew their kids were crooks." Some of the recovered property has been returned to its owners. For people who may be wondering whether or not some of the property could be theirs, Kopperud expressed that most of that which was recovered was stolen in the past 30 days and a lot of the rest was sold to other students and at flea markets, so its mostly now all gone.

THE BASIC SKILLS OF JOURNALISM

BASIC NEWS LEADS

A story—whether fiction or nonfiction—has to begin somewhere. The opening of a story needs to grab people's attention and hold it. The rest has to flow logically to its conclusion. The easiest thing for anyone to do is stop reading, watching or listening, and if the story fails to attract the audience's attention at the beginning, they may ignore it. Just as a story needs a beginning, the process of writing must have one. Few writers can sit at a keyboard and tap out a story without first planning it.

> "In addition to curiosity and a passion for innovation, the most successful journalists are also knowledgeable, creative, flexible and open-minded."
>
> —*Germany Kent, print and broadcast journalist*

7.1 Prewriting

7.1.1 Identifying the Central Point

Writing requires preparation and organization. The preparation begins before gathering information, when the story is just an idea in the mind of the reporter, editor or producer. Earlier chapters of this textbook explained the changing nature of journalism and the concepts of digital journalism, which require much more planning and organization to deliver content across multiple platforms. The story tree is a helpful tool for organizing and gathering information for a story (see Figure 7.1).

When reporters have gathered all the information they need for a story, they still must organize it. The best way to start is to find the central point, a one- or two-sentence summary of what the story is about and why it is newsworthy. It is a statement of the topic and more. Several stories may have the same subject, but the central point of each should be unique.

A number of devastating weather catastrophes struck throughout the U.S. in 2021. The Caldor and Dixie fires in California, as well as fires in other Western and Southwestern states destroyed homes and businesses and scorched millions

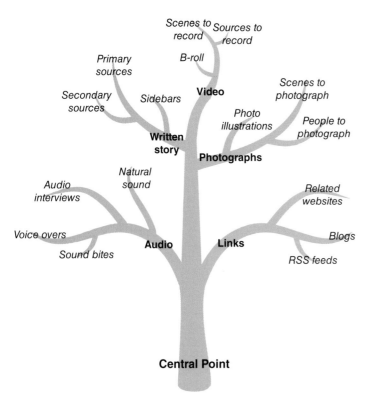

FIGURE 7.1 The Story Tree

of acres. Deadly cold swept down from the Arctic into Texas during the winter, crashing the electric grid, leaving more than 4 million people without power and causing more than 200 deaths. In the early summer, a deadly heat wave enveloped the Pacific Northwest with Salem, Oregon, hitting 117 degrees, matching the highest temperature ever recorded in Las Vegas. Deadly tornadoes hit the South, and Hurricane Ida came ashore in Louisiana and spread destruction from that state all the way to New England. People turned to newspapers, television, news websites and social media to find out as much as they could about the devastating weather. Audiences wanted to know what areas were affected and how many people had died or were injured. They wanted to know the status of local, state and federal government relief and recovery efforts, as well as whether the violent weather was tied to climate change. All these weather-related catastrophes made headlines, but every story about the many disasters— whether from the view of the rescue and recovery agencies, government officials, witnesses or victims and their families—had its particular central point that distinguished it from all other stories on the same subject.

Reporters usually have a good idea what the central point of their stories will be even as they begin gathering information. However, unexpected details may emerge and force them to rethink this element. Therefore, journalists always review their notes and other materials before they start writing. Doing so ensures that they have identified the most newsworthy central point and have the information they need to develop it. It also helps them decide what the major sections of their stories will be. Reporters who fail to identify a central point or who lose sight of it risk writing incoherent and incomplete stories.

Every well-written news story contains a clear statement of its central point. It may be in the first paragraph, called the "lead," or in a later paragraph, called a "nut graph," that follows an anecdote, describes a scene or uses some other storytelling device to entice the audience into the story. By including the central point, writers clearly tell people what they will learn from the entire story.

7.1.2 Story Outlines

The next step in organizing a news story is to create an outline. A reporter covering a shooting and robbery at a local convenience store might draft this central-point statement: "A convenience store clerk was shot by a robber who escaped with only $15." The outline might have these major sections:

Victim and injuries

Police identify suspect

Witnesses' descriptions of robber

With this skeleton, the reporter needs only to develop each section.

Once reporters select a central point and write a brief outline, they go through their notes again to decide what information belongs where. Some number passages; others use colored pens, markers or highlighters to indicate where to put particular facts, quotes or anecdotes. They omit information that does not fit in any of the sections.

Donald L. Barlett and James B. Steele, investigative reporters who have written for several periodicals and published eight books, say one of the keys to their success is organizing information. They spend months gathering documents and conducting interviews, all of which are filed by topic or name of individual, agency or corporation. Then they read the material several times because important issues and ideas often become clear only after time. Once they have an outline of the story's major parts, they start drafting it section by section. Finally, they polish sections and spend most of their time working on leads and transitions between parts. Barlett and Steele's description of their process confirms what most writers say: No one sits down and writes great stories. Writers must plan their work.

Collaborators for over 30 years, Donald L. Barlett (right) and James B. Steele have won two Pulitzer Prizes, two National Magazine Awards, and five George Polk Awards together.

7.1.3 Planning the Digital Story

Even when developing a story for distribution across multiple digital platforms, reporters first establish a central point. If the story is about training police on better ways to deal with citizens of differing ethnic backgrounds, the central point might be the effect the change will have on trust in local police. Using the story tree, reporters would begin by developing a list of sources to interview— government officials, police officers, members of minority communities, business owners and others who might be affected. They would also develop a list of government databases to scan for information on such things as crime rates and complaints against police. They would also make decisions about what photos, videos and audio would be most helpful in developing the central point.

7.1.3.1 THE VIDEO STORY

Digital journalists need to consider how best to use video with their story. Will it be a highlight segment with quotes from someone who is a source or subject of the story? Will it be a several-minute analysis with comments by several people involved in the story, with voice-over narration and b-roll? (Supporting video that provides context for a story is called "b-roll.") Or will it be a mini-documentary with multiple long interviews, interspersed with environmental shots to give viewers a sense of place and voice-over narration and music? It often depends on the type of story and the amount of time the reporter has to write the story and to edit and prepare the video. Video is often used when something can be explained better visually or to emphasize and dramatize something in the story, but it also can be used to tell the entire story.

In planning video for a story on multicultural training for police, reporters would first determine whom they want to record. From government officials, they would learn why the training is needed and how much it will cost. They then might record interviews with police officers and local residents for reactions to the proposal. They also would determine what b-roll sequences they would have to record to add context to the story. If reporters plan to attend a training session, they would want to capture video of the session in progress and any reaction from the police officers. If it is not possible to observe a session, they might shoot video of a meeting at which the training program is discussed or described. (See Chapter 13 for more on video journalism.)

7.1.3.2 THE AUDIO ELEMENT

Journalists have been recording their interviews since the invention of small compact tape recorders and microcassette recorders. With small digital audio recorders and smartphones, the process is easier than ever before. And the digitally recorded interviews can be uploaded to a computer to be edited and added to the digital news package (see Chapter 13).

In planning the story package, reporters have to decide how to use audio clips. As with video, the package could use brief statements from someone being interviewed to explain, emphasize or dramatize a point, or it could use a long interview that tells the entire story. It is important to determine how audio will be used in order to know how much has to be recorded.

Audio may also accompany photographic slideshows. This audio may be a narrator explaining what the images represent or music or natural sounds in the background as the viewer reads the captions, or cutlines, beneath each photo.

Planning for audio requires reporters to determine whom they want to record; where they want to record; what natural, or environmental, sound they need; and what music, if any, is appropriate. If reporters use any words, images or music others have created, aside from sources' quotes, they must get permission to use them in their stories. Failure to do so could violate copyright law.

7.1.3.3 PHOTOGRAPHS AND PHOTO SLIDESHOWS

Reporters also need to think about still photographs. For example, a newspaper story might appear both in print and online. While the former version may publish one or two photographs, the latter can accommodate as many photos as the editor wants to use. Slideshows often range from six to 15 photographs and may be accompanied by music and/or voice-over narration.

Many news organizations have staff photographers who are assigned to stories and take the shots that reporters need. At smaller news organizations, reporters often carry digital cameras to take their own photographs. And most news organizations have their reporters carry digital video recorders because staff photographers are often too busy to hang around for an entire interview.

Much like planning for the video story, reporters must take time to think about the photographs they will need. Using the example of the multicultural training for police, photos may include close-up, or mug, shots of the police chief, the mayor of the community and other government officials; people who advocated for or opposed the training; or leaders from various ethnic groups in the city. The reporter also may want to include crowd or background shots if covering a meeting is involved.

7.2 The Summary News Lead

The first paragraph or two of a news story is called the "lead" (also spelled "lede"). It is the most important part of a story—and the hardest part to write. Like the opening paragraphs of a short story or novel, the lead attracts the audience and, if well written, arouses interest. It should reveal the story's central point, not hide the subject with unnecessary or ambiguous words and phrases.

Every news story must answer six questions: Who? What? When? Where? Why? How? The lead, however, should answer only the one or two that are most important, interesting, newsworthy and unusual. For example, few urban residents know the ordinary citizens involved in news stories, so the names of those people—the "who"—rarely appear in leads. The exact time and place at which a story occurred may also be unimportant.

When writers try to answer all six questions in one paragraph, they create complicated and confusing leads. Here's an example of an overloaded lead and a possible revision:

Today's digital audiences expect reporters to provide visual content that will explain and enhance news stories.

> Charles E. Vickers, 47, of 1521 Yarmouth Drive, died and John Aston Walters, 39, of 1867 Colonial Ave., was severely injured Sunday afternoon when the bicycles they were riding were struck near the intersection of Weston and Falmouth roads by a car driven by a man police said had a blood alcohol count of nearly .23 percent and was driving without a license because it had been revoked last year after his fourth conviction for driving under the influence of alcohol.

> One Mechanicsburg man is dead and another severely injured after the bicycles they were riding were struck by a drunken driver Sunday afternoon near the intersection of Weston and Falmouth roads.

Because people and what they do are central to many news stories, some journalists recognize two variations on the summary news lead: the immediate-identification lead and the delayed-identification lead. Reporters use the first type when the identities of the story's major subjects are important or are well known:

> President Joe Biden on Monday pledged to support governors struggling with the omicron variant of COVID-19, but acknowledged the states will need to take the lead in controlling the pandemic.
>
> *(CNBC web story)*

FROM THE NEWS

Leads and the Basic Questions

Each of the following leads answers the basic question that seems most important for the story.

Who	Ukrainian President Volodymyr Zelenskyy said early Sunday the siege of the port city of Mariupol would go down in history for what he said were war crimes committed by Russian troops. *(The Associated Press)*
What	Ten people were killed during a mass shooting Saturday afternoon at a Buffalo grocery store in what law enforcement officials described as a racially motivated hate crime. *(The Washington Post)*
When	A day after Hurricane Ida blew through Louisiana as a Category 4 hurricane, Louisianans are starting to assess the damage of the powerful storm. *(NOLA.com)*
Where	Texas has added 36 more deaths to the official death toll from the February snow and ice storm, bringing the total to 246 in what was one of the worst natural disasters in the state's history. *(The Texas Tribune)*
Why	In deciding to take the highly unusual step of issuing subpoenas to five Republican members of Congress, the House committee investigating the Jan. 6 attack concluded that trying to compel their testimony was important enough to justify an escalatory step involving their colleagues. *(The New York Times)*
How	Northern California may get a respite from wildfire season when rain and snow fall on tinder-dry trees and brush in the coming days. *(Bloomberg.com)*

In many stories, the names of the main subjects are not as important as what occurred. For those stories, reporters use delayed-identification leads, which withhold complete identification of the people involved until the second or third paragraph. Here are two examples:

A California man is in custody after he called authorities to inform them that he was near the home of Supreme Court Justice Brett Kavanaugh and planned to kill him over impending decisions by the court.

A 58-year-old woman from Queens nearly drowned Wednesday when she became trapped in her flooding basement apartment as torrential rain from the remnants of Hurricane Ida drenched New York and New Jersey.

Leads that hold back details so the reporter can get to the central point of the article more quickly are called "blind leads." Beginners should not misinterpret the terminology. A blind lead does not hide the central point of the story, only information that the audience does not need immediately. Blind leads let the journalist tell people what the story is about, to pique their interest and get them into the story.

A "catchall graph" usually follows the blind lead to identify sources and answer questions created by the lead. Missing details can be placed in subsequent paragraphs. Here's an example of a blind lead:

> It was an Altoona company that lost its appeal to Commonwealth Court, but it's the state agency charged with overseeing construction matters that's feeling the pain.
>
> *(The [Harrisburg, Pennsylvania] Patriot-News)*

In its second paragraph, the article identified the company and what the case involved. In the third paragraph, the article identified the state agency involved and what it had done wrong.

Before reporters can write effective leads, however, they must learn to recognize what is news. After selecting the most newsworthy facts, journalists must summarize those facts in sharp, clear sentences, giving a simple, straightforward account of what happened. Examine these leads, which provide clear, concise summaries of momentous events in the nation's history:

> Washington—Congress confirmed President-elect Joseph R. Biden Jr.'s victory early Thursday morning, overwhelmingly repudiating a drive by President Trump to overturn his defeat after it culminated in a mob of loyalists storming and occupying the Capitol in a shocking display of violence that shook the core of American democracy.
>
> *(The New York Times)*

> Denver—Timothy McVeigh, the decorated soldier who turned his killing skills against the people of Oklahoma City, was condemned Friday to die.
>
> *(The Dallas Morning News)*

> Dallas, Nov. 22—A sniper armed with a high-powered rifle assassinated President Kennedy today. Barely two hours after Mr. Kennedy's death, Vice President Johnson took the oath of office as the thirty-sixth President of the United States.
>
> *(The Associated Press)*

Leads that fail to emphasize the news—the most interesting and important details—are sometimes described as burying the lead. Here's an example of an unsuccessful lead:

> Wentworth County is required to give inmates the same level of medical treatment the general public receives, Corrections Director Maria Sanchez said.

The news in the story, however, was not the level of medical care the county provides inmates. It was the financial problems the county was facing because of the requirement. This rewritten lead makes the significance of the story clearer:

> Wentworth County's costs for medical care for jail inmates doubled— from $50,000 to $100,000—last year because of a new state regulation. Friday morning, county and state officials gathered to find a way to pay the bill.

7.3 Sentence Structure in Leads

Most leads are a single sentence. They must be complete sentences and follow all the normal rules for punctuation, grammar, word usage and verb tense. For example, if an event occurred in the past, the lead must use the past tense, not the present. Leads should also include all the necessary articles, nouns, verbs, prepositions and punctuation for a standard English sentence.

Some problems with sentence structure arise because beginners confuse a story's lead with its headline. The lead is the first paragraph of a news story; the headline is a brief summary that appears in larger type above the story. To save space, editors use only a few key words in each headline. However, that style of writing is not appropriate for leads.

Headline: Impeached Once Again

Lead: WASHINGTON—President Trump was impeached by the U.S. House for a historic second time Wednesday, charged with "incitement of insurrection" over the deadly mob siege of the Capitol in a swift and stunning collapse of his final days in office.

(The San Francisco Chronicle)

Most leads begin with the subject, which is closely followed by an active verb and then by the object of the verb (i.e., subject-verb-object order; see Chapter 4). Reporters deviate from that style only in the rare case that a different sentence structure better tells the news. Leads that begin with long qualifying clauses and phrases lack the clarity of simpler, more direct sentences. Long introductory clauses also clutter leads, burying the news amid a jumble of less significant details. Author and writing coach Paula LaRocque calls these "backed-into leads." She describes them as "one of the most pervasive and uninviting habits a writer can fall into." Consider the following example:

- Washington—~~In the most significant court case dealing with money and~~

  ~~politics since 1976,~~ a special three-judge panel today upheld ~~several~~
  major ~~provisions~~ ∧ of a sweeping new ∧ law limiting political ∧ ~~dona-~~
  ~~tions~~ but ∧ found ~~that~~ some ∧ ~~of its measures were~~ unconstitutional.

  portions   *federal*   *campaign contributions,*
  it also   *parts of the law*

(The New York Times)

The original lead delayed the news—information about the court's decision—until after a 13-word introductory phrase containing information that probably could have gone in the story's second or third paragraph.

7.4 Guidelines for Writing Effective Leads

7.4.1 Be Concise

The concise style of writing found in journalism makes it easy for the public to understand leads but difficult for reporters to write them. Two- or three-sentence leads often become wordy, repetitive and choppy, particularly when all the sentences are very short. Like most multi-sentence leads, the following example can be made more concise as a single sentence:

- Two women ∧ ~~robbed~~ a shopper in a local supermarket Tuesday. ~~One woman distracted the shopper, and the second woman grabbed her purse, which contained about $50.~~

    stole a purse containing $50 from

The original lead was redundant. It reported two women robbed a shopper, and then described the robbery. Reporters use two-sentence leads only when there is a compelling need to do so. Often, the second sentence emphasizes an interesting or unusual fact of lesser importance. Other times, the second sentence is necessary because it is impossible to summarize all the necessary information about a complex topic in a single sentence.

The lead in the accompanying story about the Jan. 6, 2021, assault on the U.S. Capitol uses a second sentence to emphasize the drama of the first. Many readers would find this 56-word lead difficult to read—a better average would be 18 to 20 words. However, sometimes a story is so dramatic that reporters try to not only provide information but also set the tone and atmosphere of the story. Reporters should examine their leads critically to determine whether they are wordy or repetitious or contain facts that could be shifted to later paragraphs.

Journalists shorten leads by eliminating unnecessary background information—dates, names, locations—or the description of routine procedures. Leads should omit many names, particularly those whom the public is unlikely to recognize or who played minor or routine roles in a story. Including the names of people may also require identifying them, which uses more words. Descriptive phrases can substitute for names. Similarly, a story's precise time and location could be reported in a later paragraph.

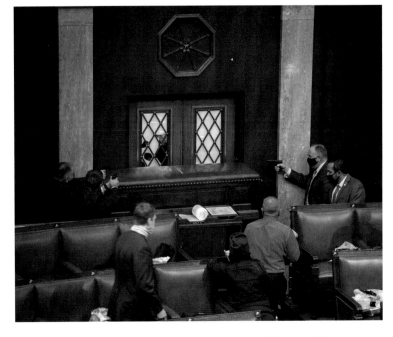

As President Trump told a sprawling crowd outside the White House that they should never accept defeat, hundreds of his supporters stormed the U.S. Capitol in what amounted to an attempted coup that they hoped would overturn the election he lost. In the chaos, law enforcement officials said, one woman was shot and killed by Capitol Police.

The second sentence in this lead makes it rather long, but adds a compelling detail about the consequences of the actions taken by the mob that attacked the Capitol, and helps to set the tone of the story.

A lead should report a story's highlights, not all its minor details, as concisely as possible:

- *The FBI on Wednesday arrested*
  ∧ ~~A~~ Å former Roxbury woman~~,~~ who has eluded ~~federal law enforcement~~
  1983, when was accused of hijacking an airplane
  authorities since ∧ she ∧ ~~allegedly hijacked a flight from San Juan to Cuba using a plastic flare gun in 1983, was arrested Wednesday as she stood alone on Union Street in Boston, according to the Federal Bureau of Investigation~~.

Although leads can be too long, they cannot be too short. An effective lead may contain only four to six words: "The president is dead," "Americans landed on the moon" or "There's new hope for couch potatoes."

7.4.2 Be Specific

Good leads contain interesting details and are so specific that the audience can visualize the events they describe. As you read the following lead from The Bradenton (Florida) Herald, you should be able to imagine the dramatic scenes it describes:

> Women's voices were heard in Sarasota on Saturday — as they were around the world.
>
> *(The Bradenton [Florida] Herald)*

Even longer leads, such as this one that appeared in the Madison, Wisconsin, State Journal about the youth marches in 2018 protesting gun violence, need to be specific to entice readers to continue reading. The lead emphasizes the raw emotion the teenager felt about the topic she was addressing.

> Sixteen-year-old Stephanie Trask stood before the massive crowd gathered at the steps of the state Capitol Saturday and spoke about leaving for school each morning with the fear that she might not make it home again.
>
> *(The Madison [Wisconsin] State Journal)*

Reporters can easily transform vague, dull leads into interesting ones by adding more specific details. The second of the following leads is more successful:

> The City Council passed an ordinance that will affect all parents and teenagers living within city limits.
>
> **Revised:** The City Council ignored the objections of the mayor and numerous parents and voted 6–1 Monday to enact a dusk-to-dawn curfew to keep youngsters off city streets.

Some leads use worn-out clichés—a lazy way of summarizing a story. Avoid saying that "a step has been taken" or that someone has moved "one step closer" to a goal. Present specific details:

- *The university's Board of Governors voted Tuesday to increase*
  ∧~~University officials moved one step closer to increasing~~ tuition and
  10 percent next year to offset cuts in state funding
  fees ∧~~for the upcoming school year, leaving students up in the air~~.

Avoid "iffy" leads that say one thing may happen if another happens. In addition to being too vague, "iffy" leads are too abstract, tentative and qualified. Report the story's more immediate and concrete details.

7.4.3 Use Strong, Active Verbs

A single descriptive verb can transform a routine lead into a dramatic one. As you read the following lead, you may be able to picture what happened:

> Deland—After rushing her 7-year-old daughter to safety, Ann Murray raced back to the docks and pounded on her friends' boats while flames and explosions tore through Boat Show Marina early Friday morning.
>
> *(The Orlando [Florida] Sentinel)*

Strong, active verbs, such as "rushing," "raced," "pounded" and "tore," paint a vivid picture of the scene. They capture the drama and emotion of a news event and help the reader understand the impact of the story. The following lead uses several colorful verbs to describe the capture of a wayward Angus steer that escaped his handlers:

> The suspect tore through a homeowner's fence, ripped the wires from a satellite dish with his teeth, slammed head-on into a travel trailer, then bolted down the street on his way to a weird encounter with a canoe.
>
> *(The Orlando [Florida] Sentinel)*

Avoid passive-voice constructions, which combine the past participle of a verb with some form of the verb "to be," such as "is," "are," "was" and "were" (see Chapter 4). Compare the italicized verbs in these two leads:

> **Passive Verbs:** One person *was killed* and four others *were injured* Sunday morning when their car, which *was traveling* west on Interstate 80, hit a concrete bridge pillar and *was engulfed* in flames.

> **Active Verbs:** A car traveling west on Interstate 80 *swerved* across two eastbound lanes, *slammed* into a concrete bridge pillar and *burst* into flames, killing one person and injuring four others Sunday morning.

Writers can easily convert passive voice to the active voice. Simply rearrange the words so the sentence reports who did what to whom. Instead of reporting "Rocks and bottles were thrown at firefighters," report "Rioters threw rocks and bottles at firefighters."

7.4.4 Emphasize the Magnitude of the Story

If a story is important, reporters emphasize its magnitude in the lead. Most good leads focus on the impact stories have on people. When describing natural disasters or human-made catastrophes, such as airplane crashes, tornadoes or major fires, journalists emphasize the number of people killed, injured and left homeless, as well as the financial cost of the damage to buildings or other objects. When describing a storm, reporters may highlight the amount of rain or snow that fell. If the story is about a new business coming to town, it may emphasize the number of employees it will have and the amount of money it will contribute to the local economy. The following lead shows how magnitude can be emphasized in a story:

> With more than 580,000 cases, the United States shattered its own record for new daily coronavirus cases — beating a milestone it already broke just the day before.
>
> *(The New York Times)*

Also notice the use of the strong verbs "shattered" and "beating" in the lead to help emphasize the magnitude of the statistics noted. Strong verbs such as those propel readers into the story.

7.4.5 Stress the Unusual

Leads also emphasize the unusual. By definition, news involves deviations from the norm. Consider this lead:

> Officers say Jeremiah James Taylor was joy riding in a stolen sheriff's patrol vehicle early Monday when a domestic violence call from a neighboring county came over the radio system. Taylor, 33, decided to go to the scene, officials say—and he was the first to arrive.
>
> *(The Washington Post)*

A lead about a board of education meeting or other governmental agency should not report "The board met at 8 p.m. at a local school and began its meeting with roll call." Those facts are routine and not newsworthy. Most school boards meet every couple of weeks, usually at the same time and place, and many begin their meetings with a roll call. Leads should stress the unique—the action that follows those routine formalities.

Bank robberies are so common in big cities that newspapers normally devote only a few paragraphs to them. Yet a robbery at the Burlington National Bank in Columbus, Ohio, became a front-page story, published by newspapers throughout the United States. A story transmitted by The Associated Press explained:

> A 61-year-old man says he robbed an Ohio bank with a toy gun—he even told the FBI ahead of time when and where—because he wants to spend his golden years in federal prison.
>
> After his arrest, the bank robber insisted he did not want a lawyer. Instead, he wanted to immediately "plead guilty to anything." The man explained he recently was divorced, had no family ties and was disabled with arthritis. He had spent time in at least three federal prisons and wanted to return to one of them. "I knew what I was doing," he insisted. "I wanted to get arrested, and I proceeded about it the best way I knew how."

Reporters must learn to recognize and emphasize a story's unusual details.

7.4.6 Localize and Update

Reporters localize their leads whenever possible by highlighting their communities' involvement in stories. Audiences are most interested in stories affecting their own lives and the lives of people they know.

Reporters also try to localize stories from other parts of the U.S., as well as the world. When a gunman went on a shooting rampage in Las Vegas in 2017, killing 59 people and injuring more than 500, news organizations around the country and the world ran the story of the attack. Many of the concertgoers were not from Las Vegas—some had come hundreds or thousands of miles for the country music festival where the shooting took place. News organizations around the U.S. checked the identities of the victims and ran stories about victims from their areas. News organizations in south-central Pennsylvania, for example, ran stories of a well-known man who was attending the concert with his wife when he died in the fusillade of bullets.

Similarly, when the FBI reports on the number of violent crimes committed in the United States, reporters stress the statistics for their communities:

> The number of violent crimes committed in the city last year rose 5.4 percent, compared to a national average of 8.3 percent, the FBI reported Tuesday.

Reporters update a lead by highlighting the latest developments in the story. The adoption of digital media platforms—both web and social media—have allowed news organizations to become 24/7 operations, capable of updating information throughout the day. By posting a story online, journalists can retain much of the original story but update the lead with new information as often as necessary.

Before the digital revolution, if a breaking story appeared in an early edition of a newspaper, a writer would gather new information and rewrite the story for publication the next day. Instead of saying a fire destroyed a store the previous day, reporters may stress that authorities have since learned the fire's cause, identified the victims, arrested an arsonist or estimated the monetary loss. In today's digital media environment, stories may be updated within minutes or a few hours after first appearing on social media or the web. Stories are updated so they offer the public something new—facts not already reported by other news outlets. Major stories about such topics as economic trends, natural disasters, wars and political upheavals often remain in the news for months and must be updated regularly.

Not every lead can be updated or localized. If a story has no new or local angles, report it in a

How Federal Dollars Fund Local Police

June 9, 2020 · 5:10 AM ET

BRIAN NAYLOR

This web story by NPR about demands to defund police after the death of George Floyd and subsequent Black Lives Matter demonstrations explored the impact of federal funding of local police departments, helping local residents understand how difficult defunding law enforcement might actually be.

simple, straightforward manner. Do not distort the story in any way or fabricate any information.

7.4.7 Be Objective and Attribute Opinions

The lead of a news story, like the rest of the piece, must be objective. Reporters are expected to gather and convey facts, not commentary, interpretation or advocacy. They may anger or offend an audience when they insert their opinions in stories.

Calling the people involved in news stories "alert," "heroic" or "quick-thinking" or describing facts as "interesting" or "startling" is never justified. When accurate, these comments usually state the obvious. Leads that include opinion or interpretation must be rewritten to provide more factual accounts of the news:

- ~~Speaking to the Downtown Rotary Club last night,~~ Emil Plambeck, su- *wants developers to set aside 5 percent of the land in new subdivisions for parks* perintendent of the City Park Commission, ∧ ~~discussed a topic of concern to all of us—the city's park system~~.

The original lead is weak because it refers to "a topic of concern to all of us." The reporter does not identify "us" and is wrong to assume any topic concerns everyone.

Here are other examples of leads that state an opinion or conclusion:

> Adult entertainment establishments have fallen victim to another attempt at censorship.

> Recycling does not pay, at least not economically. However, the environmental benefits make the city's new recycling program worthwhile at any cost.

To demonstrate that both leads are statements of opinion, ask your friends and classmates about them. Do they all agree that the regulation of adult entertainment establishments is "censorship"? Do they all think that recycling programs are "worthwhile at any cost"?

Although journalists cannot express their own opinions in stories, they often include the opinions of people involved in the news. A lead containing a statement of opinion must be attributed so that the audience clearly understands the opinion is not the reporter's.

A lead containing an obvious fact or a fact the reporter has witnessed or verified by other means generally does not require attribution. An editor at The New York Times, instructing reporters to keep leads brief and clear noted, "One thing that obstructs that aim is the inclusion of an unnecessary source of attribution. . . . If the lead is controversial, an attribution is imperative. But if the lead is innocuous, forget it." Thus, if a lead states undisputed facts, the attribution can be placed in a later paragraph:

> Washington—Cars and motorcycles crash into deer more than 4,000 times a day, and it's taking an increasingly deadly toll—on people.
> *(The Associated Press)*

7.4.8 Strive for Simplicity

Every lead should be clear, simple and to the point. Here is an example:

> A Gilpin man died in a house fire early Friday morning when he was unable to escape the burning structure, the Armstrong County coroner said.
>
> *(Tribune-Review/TribLive)*

The next lead suffers from far too much detail:

> Officials of the city and the Gladstone School District are breathing sighs of relief following the Clackamas County Housing Authority's decision to pull out of a plan to build an apartment complex for moderate-income people on 11 acres of land between Southeast Oatfield and Webster roads.

The lead could be rewritten any number of ways. The reporter must decide what the important point is. Here are two versions of a simple blind lead for the same story:

> Several city and school district officials applauded the county's decision to scrap plans for a subsidized housing complex.

> A new subsidized housing complex will not be built, and city and school district officials are relieved.

7.5 Some Common Errors

7.5.1 Beginning with the Attribution

Names and titles, the essentials of attribution, are dull and seldom belong in the lead. Moreover, if all leads started with attribution, they would sound too much alike. Place an attribution at the beginning of a lead only when it is unusual, significant or deserving of that emphasis:

- ~~At a press conference in Washington, D.C., today, Neil A. Schuster, spokesperson for the U.S. Bureau of Labor Statistics, announced that~~

  last month

  ~~last month~~ the cost of living rose 2.83 percent ∧, a record

  , U.S. Bureau of Labor Statistics officials said Friday

  high ∧.

Originally, the lead devoted more space to the attribution than to the news. As revised, it emphasizes the news—the information the Bureau of Labor Statistics released. The attribution can be condensed and reported more fully in a later paragraph.

7.5.2 Minimizing the News

Chronological order rarely works in a news story. By definition, news is what just happened. The first events in a sequence rarely are the most newsworthy. Decide which facts are most interesting and important, and then write a lead that emphasizes them regardless of whether they occurred first, last or in the middle of a sequence of events.

Here are two leads. The first begins with actions taken at the start of a city council meeting. The second begins with an action likely to affect a large number of city residents. Which would attract a larger audience?

> The City Council approved the minutes from its last meeting, approved paying omnibus budget bills and examined a list of proposed ordinances.

> **Revised:** The City Council voted 6-1 Monday night to increase the city's police department budget by 15 percent to hire more officers and buy new weapons.

Look for a story's action or consequences. That's what the lead should emphasize. The second version of the following example stresses the effects of the accident:

> A 15-year-old boy learning to drive his family's new car struck a gasoline pump in a service station on Hall Road late Tuesday afternoon.

> **Revised:** A 15-year-old boy learning to drive created a fireball Tuesday. The family car he was driving struck a gasoline pump at a Hall Road service station, blocking traffic for three hours while firefighters extinguished the blaze.

7.5.3 Using Agenda Leads

An opening paragraph that places too much emphasis on the time and place at which a story occurred is called an "agenda lead." Although these leads are used to announce an upcoming event—public relations news releases use them to promote an organization's product or event—they should never appear in a news story about something that occurred the previous day. A lead should focus on the news, as the following revised lead does:

> ● ∧ ~~James Matthews,~~ president of ~~International Biotech Inc.,~~ a company
>
> *There's gold in the garbage society discards, the*
>
> *said, staking his claim on the future of recycling*
>
> that manufactures recycling and composting machinery ∧ ~~was the keynote speaker at Monday night's opening ceremony of the Earth Preservation Society's annual conference at the Lyceum Center.~~

The revised lead focuses on what the speaker said, something the original lead failed to do.

Here is a lead that focuses on the time of a story:

> ● ~~Last weekend~~ the women's volleyball team ∧ ~~participated~~ in the re-
>
> *won five of its seven games and placed second*
>
> *last weekend*
>
> gional playoffs ∧.

7.5.4 Using Label Leads

"Label leads" mention a topic but fail to reveal what was said or done about it. Leads should report the substance of a story, not just its topic. A good lead does more than report that a group met, held a press conference or issued a report. It reveals what the group did at the meeting, what was said at the press conference or what was written in the report.

Label leads are easy to recognize and avoid because they use similar words and phrases, such as "was the subject of," "the main topic of discussion," "spoke about," "delivered a speech about" or "interviewed about." Here are two examples and how they might be improved:

- *An additional fee for business licenses is one way is considering*
  ∧ The City Council ~~Tuesday night discussed ways of~~ ∧ regulating a new topless club ~~in the city~~.

- *College   said*
  ∧ Faculty and staff ~~members and other experts~~ ∧ Thursday
  they favor a new scholarship program as a way of recruiting
  ∧ ~~proposed strategies to recruit~~ more minority students.

7.5.5 Listing Details

Most lists are dull. If one must be used in a lead, place an explanation before it, never after it. The audience can more quickly grasp a list's meaning if an explanation precedes it. The following lead is improved by reversing the order:

> The company that made it, the store that sold it and the friend who lent it to him are being sued by a 24-year-old man whose spine was severed when a motorcycle overturned.

> **Revised:** A 24-year-old man whose spine was severed when a motorcycle overturned is suing the company that made the motorcycle, the store that sold it and the friend who lent it to him.

7.5.6 Stating the Obvious

Avoid stating the obvious or emphasizing routine procedures in leads. For a story about a crime, do not begin by reporting police "were called to the scene" or ambulances "rushed" the victims to a hospital "for treatment of their injuries." This problem is particularly common in sports news, where many leads have become clichés. For example, stories that say most coaches and players express optimism at the beginning of a season report the obvious: Both want to win most of their games.

The following lead is ineffective for the same reason:

> The Colonial Park school board has decided to spend the additional funds it will receive from the state.

Including the specifics of the decision improves the lead:

> The Colonial Park school board voted Monday night to rescind the
> 5 percent spending cut it approved last month after learning the
> district will receive more money from the state.

7.5.7 Reporting the Negative

When writing a lead, report what happened, not what failed to happen or what
does not exist:

their greatest fears are poor health and poverty

●   Americans over the age of 65 say ∧ ~~that crime is not their greatest fear~~,
two sociologists reported Friday.

7.5.8 Exaggerating

Never exaggerate in a lead. If a story is weak, exaggeration will make it weaker,
not stronger. A simple summary of the facts can be more interesting (and shocking) than anything that might be contrived:

> A 78-year-old woman left $3.2 million to the Salvation Army and 2 cents
> to her son.

> A restaurant did not serve a dead rat in a loaf of bread to an out-of-
> town couple, a jury decided Tuesday.

**Straight from the horse's mouth? I don't think so:
This article has been heavily edited...**

7.5.9 Distorting the Story

Every lead must be truthful. Never sensationalize, belittle or misrepresent. A lead must also set
a story's tone—accurately revealing, for example, whether the story that follows will be serious
or whimsical:

The party went to the dogs early—as it
should have.

Parents who host parties for their children
can understand the chill going up Susan
Ulroy's spine. She was determined guests
wouldn't be racing over her clean carpeting
with their wet feet. "This could be a real free-
for-all," she said.

Even though only seven guests were invited,
eight counting the host, that made 32 feet to
worry about.

This was a birthday party for Sandi, the
Ulroys' dog.

(The Ann Arbor [Michigan] News)

7.5.10 Following All the Rules

Reporters who use their imagination and try something different sometimes can report the facts more cleverly than the competition.

Edna Buchanan, who reported on police and crime for the Miami Herald, consistently made routine stories interesting. Here's a lead she wrote with some imagination. Notice the active verbs and description she uses:

> Gary Robinson died hungry.
>
> He wanted fried chicken, the three-piece box for $2.19. Drunk, loud and obnoxious, he pushed ahead of seven customers in line at a fast-food chicken outlet. The counter girl told him that his behavior was impolite. She calmed him down with sweet talk, and he agreed to step to the end of the line. His turn came just before closing time, just after the fried chicken ran out.
>
> He punched the counter girl so hard her ears rang, and a security guard shot him—three times.

7.5.11 Forgetting Your Audience

While writing every lead, remember the audience. Leads must be clear and interesting to attract and keep people's attention. The following lead, until revised, fails both tests:

● Two ∧ ~~policy resolutions will come~~ before the Student Senate this week ∧.

proposals *would raise student parking and athletic fees by more than $100 a year*

Is the original lead interesting? Why not? It emphasized the number of resolutions the student senate was scheduled to consider. Yet almost no one would care about the number of resolutions or, from the lead, would understand their significance: the fact that they would affect every student at the school.

7.5.12 Using the First Draft

Critically examine all leads and rewrite them as often as necessary. First drafts are rarely so well written that they cannot be improved. Even experienced professionals often rewrite their leads three or more times.

Guest Columnist

News Business Exciting, Changing Rapidly

BY ADRIAN WHITSETT

Get ready for a wild ride.

Over the course of nearly 15 years in broadcast news, I've covered the highest highs and the lowest lows. I've shared the stories of parents with bright smiles, crying the happiest of tears as their loved one made it safely home from the battlefields of Afghanistan and Iraq.

I've also shared the stories of parents and loved ones of mass shooting victims of malls, schools, and Orlando's Pulse nightclub, finding out in that moment, their loved ones would never come home.

I can tell you a couple things I've learned through it all.

1. The stories you tell will stay with you long after your live shot. There will be days where the pendulum of emotion swings sharply back from adrenaline to sorrow. Don't be afraid to feel and don't be afraid to share it with the characters in your story.

2. Your opinion matters, just not in the way you think. Your job (if you so choose to accept the responsibility) is to be an arbiter of information and other people's opinions, not your own. Highlight yours in your editorial meetings, figuring out what stories are worth your viewers' time and attention and with your colleagues and compatriots, who I promise you in your first TV job will be people you stay in touch with forever.

Today's media environment is vastly different from that of your parents' generation. In the 1970s and '80s daily newspapers and a few networks were the norm. By 2020 there were a multitude of ways to consume news, via the daily paper and its website, a plethora of cable and TV networks, Facebook, Twitter. You have even more. Thousands of different websites, blogs and apps are now available to find a niche or be a subject-matter expert.

In one sense, this makes it easier to begin a career in news. But "broadcasting," in its purest form, has changed.

Gone are the days of the single anchor sitting at a desk, lording over the news as a gatekeeper for a viewership who wouldn't get their information otherwise. Instead, reporters and anchors are doing more and showing more of how they got the story. You'll hear it described as "process reporting." Maintaining trust in local news is a struggle, but it's still the spot people turn to first to find out what's happening in their neighborhood. Surveys from 2021[1] showed local news is more trusted than national news and more people turn on the TV as their prime source of local news. That's a good sign, but other surveys[2] show trust in mass media altogether down since the late 1990s.

I am grateful that you budding journalists are reading this, at this moment. You'll have big decisions to come, but you've already started down a path of storytelling, in whatever form that may take.

I won't presume to know what TV markets will look like by the time you graduate. In a relatively short time, I've watched as phones became the primary way to consume video despite starting at a time when running tapes through a building was still a preferred method to ensure video made it to air.

It will change in drastic ways, likely before you even hit the ground running, but the important piece will remain.

This is a profession and can be a career that illuminates the best and worst in people. It's what YOU bring to the stories each day that can make a difference.

Each day is an adventure in patience, grace, loss, life and learning.

Buckle up!

Adrian Whitsett is the anchor for the Good Morning Tri-States news show on WCPO-TV in Cincinnati.

1 https://knightfoundation.org/articles/local-news-most-trusted-in-keeping-americans-informed-about-their-communities/
2 https://news.gallup.com/poll/355526/americans-trust-media-dips-second-lowest-record.aspx

The Reporter's Guide to Writing Leads

1. Be specific rather than vague and abstract.

2. Avoid stating the obvious or the negative.

3. Emphasize the story's most unusual or unexpected developments.

4. Emphasize the story's most interesting and important developments.

5. Emphasize the story's magnitude and its impact on its participants and the public.

6. Use complete sentences, the proper tense and all the necessary articles—"a," "an" and "the"—and other parts of speech.

7. Be concise. If a lead exceeds three typed lines, examine it for wordiness, repetition or unnecessary details and rewrite it to eliminate the problems.

8. Avoid writing a label lead that reports the story's topic but not what was said or done about it.

9. Begin leads with the news—the main point of the story—not the attribution or the time and place the events occurred.

10. Use relatively simple sentences and avoid beginning leads with a long phrase or clause.

11. Use strong, active and descriptive verbs rather than passive ones.

12. Avoid using unfamiliar names. Any names that require lengthy identification should be reported in a later paragraph.

13. Attribute any quotation or statement of opinion appearing in the lead.

14. Localize the lead, and emphasize the latest developments, preferably what happened today or yesterday.

15. Eliminate statements of opinion, including one-word labels such as "interesting" and "alert."

16. Remember the audience. Write a lead that is clear and concise and that emphasizes the details most likely to affect and interest people.

17. Read the lead aloud to be certain that it is clear, concise and easy to understand.

 ## Review Exercises

1. EVALUATING GOOD AND BAD LEADS

Critically evaluate the following leads. Select the best ones and explain why they are effective; point out the flaws in the remaining leads. Finally, look for lessons—"dos and don'ts"—that you can apply to your own work.

1. A 24-year-old Greeley man was charged with multiple counts of first-degree murder and arson in the deaths of his wife and three children who died in an early morning fire in their home.

2. City Council has to return a grant it received last year to fix deteriorating road conditions on Main Street.

3. People are jumping into swimming pools and switching buttons to high on air conditioners as temperatures in the Midwest soared to record numbers over the past three days.

4. University administrators say they are considering imposing the largest tuition and fee increases in a decade because of state budget cuts.

5. A petition filed by Councilman William Bellmonte to force the City Council into a special session to reduce local property taxes was thrown out in court Monday after it was discovered that half the names listed on the petition were dead people.

6. A local woman docked her 45-foot sailboat in Portsmouth, England, on Wednesday. She became the oldest woman to sail from New York to England singlehandedly. She was 81.

7. Ray's Mini-Mart at 2357 S. Alderman St. was the location of a burglary sometime Friday night.

8. Police Chief Barry Kopperud is concerned that crime is rising in the city.

9. This weekend will offer the best chance yet to see a brilliant performance of "My Fair Lady" at the Fairwood Community Theater, so reserve your tickets now.

10. Loans become a popular way to cut college costs.

11. The tree-lined campus is home to many wild and stray animals.

12. Two men suspected of burglarizing five churches, two homes and a pet store all in one night were captured Wednesday during another burglary attempt.

13. The union representing university secretaries and maintenance workers reached a tentative agreement Friday that will give members a 6.5 percent raise over three years.

14. Fingerprints on a butane lighter led the FBI to a man accused of setting a fire that destroyed his failing business and injuring four of his 30 employees.

15. A teenage driver lost control of his car Wednesday night killing himself and a female passenger, while a 14-year-old friend who was riding in the back seat walked away with only scratches and bruises.

2. WRITING LEADS

Section I: Condensing Lengthy Leads

Condense each of these leads to no more than two typed lines, or about 20 words. Correct all errors.

1. Christina Shattuck, 43, and Dennis Shattuck, 45, and their three children, ages 7, 3 and 9 months, all of 532 3rd St., returned home from a shopping trip Saturday night and found their two-story frame house on fire and called firefighters, who responded to the scene within five minutes, but were unable to save the house and its contents, which were totally destroyed.

2. The local school board held a special meeting Tuesday night so Superintendent of Schools Greg Hubbard could address a group of angry parents who were demanding to know why they were never informed that a middle school student had brought a gun to school and may have been targeting their children during an incident on school grounds last Friday.

Section II: Using Proper Sentence Structure

Rewrite the following leads, using the normal word order: subject, verb, direct object. Avoid starting the leads with a long clause or phrase. You may want to divide some of the leads into several sentences or paragraphs. Correct all errors.

1. In an effort to curb what city officials are calling an epidemic of obesity among young people in the city, which mirrors national data on overall obesity of the population, your local city council voted 7-0 to offer free memberships at its meeting Monday night to local youth centers and health clubs in the city for children ages 8 to 15 whose parents do not have the financial wherewithal to purchase the memberships.

2. Despite the efforts of Karen Dees, 19, a student at your university who lives at 410 University Avenue, Apartment 52, and performed cardiopulmonary resuscitation for more than 20 minutes, she was not able to help sheriffs deputy William McGowen, 47, of 4224 N. 21st St., who died while directing traffic after being struck by lightning during an electrical storm.

Section III: Emphasizing the News

Rewrite the following leads, emphasizing the news, not the attribution. Limit the attributions to a few words and place them at the end of the leads. Correct all errors.

1. The National Institutes of Health in Washington, D.C., released a report today indicating that more than 90 percent of all heart attack victims have

one or more classic risk factors: smoking, diabetes, high cholesterol and high blood pressure.

2. According to a police report issued Monday, accident investigators concluded that Stephanie Sessions, 16, daughter of Jeffrey D. and Michelle A. Sessions, of 9303 Vale Drive, had just gotten her drivers license two days before she was involved in an accident in which she rolled the Jeep Wrangler she was driving, injuring herself and two other passengers.

Section IV: Combining Multi-sentence Leads

Rewrite each of the following leads in a single sentence, correcting all errors.

1. Gary Hubard, superintendent of schools, announced a new program for your local school district. It is called the "Tattle-Tale Program." The program involves paying students to tell on classmates who bring guns or drugs to school or violate other school rules. The program is in response to an incident last month in which a high school student was caught carrying a loaded handgun on school property.

2. The Bureau of Justice Statistics of the U.S. Department of Justice released a report Monday on the number of people in the United States who have spent time in prison. Last year, about one in every 37 adult Americans was imprisoned or had been in prison at one time. The 5.6 million people who were either serving or had served time in prison represented 2.7 percent of the adult population of 210 million people, according to the report. The figures represent people who served time in federal, state and county prisons after being sentenced for a crime, not those temporarily held in jail.

Section V: Stressing the Unusual

Write only the lead for each of the following stories, correcting all errors.

1. The city is sweltering under a heat wave. Temperatures have hit 100 degrees-plus for the past week and humidity levels have hovered between 75 and 90 percent each day. Authorities have been cautioning people, especially the very young and the elderly to stay inside in air conditioning and avoid exerting themselves outside in the sun. City Health Department officials held a press conference this morning to announce that three people had died over the past two days because of the heat. All three were elderly people who lived in the downtown area. Two of the three were a married couple. The one victim was identified as Betsy Aaron, 86, of 410 Hillcrest Street, Apartment 302. Aaron was a retired teacher who had taught elementary school for more than 30 years. The other two victims were Jeffrey Ahsonn, 84, and his wife, Teresa Ahson, 79, both of 49 Groveland Avenue. Ahsonn was a retired mechanical engineer who had worked for the city for many years. Police and health department officials were alerted to the deaths in each case by relatives who discovered the bodies. When they entered the dwellings, police told officials that they found a pair of fans and an air conditioner in each dwelling. The fans and air conditioners had been delivered by city workers to disabled elderly people to help them cope with the heat wave. But authorities found the fans and air conditioners still in their boxes. They had never been installed.

2. Destiny Schfini is a vice president with SunBank. Schifini is divorced and the mother of two children—a 10-year-old girl and an eight-year-old boy. The children visit her once a month. Schifinis son, Ronald, was visiting this weekend. Schfini is 36 years old and lives at 3260 Timber Ter. Ronald was injured in an accident Saturday afternoon around 2 p.m. The boy was struck by a train. Police said Schifini and her son were riding bikes along Fremont Avenue when the mother decided to take a shortcut across the railroad tracks that run along Fremont Avenue. The boy is on life support in Mercy Hospital and listed in critical condition. He was struck by a train. Witnesses said the mother saw the train coming and crossed anyway and encouraged her son to cross. The boys bike got caught on the tracks and as he tried to free it, the train struck him. Ronald was thrown through the air and sustained broken ribs, a broken pelvis and a bruised heart. Police charged Destiny Schifini with aggravated assault, reckless endangerment,

endangering the welfare of a child and failure to obey a train signal. Police said they charged Schfini after they learned from witnesses that Schifini did not help the boy, but taunted him as the train approached.

3. Julius Povacz is a paramedic in your community who serves with the rescue squad in the fire department. The 34-year-old Povaz lives at 210 East King Avenue, Apartment 4. Eight years ago he was tested for human immunodeficiency virus, or HIV, the virus that causes AIDS, and told that the test was positive. Povacz never told his superiors that he had tested positive. A routine check of his medical records last month by fire department officials found the notation that the test was positive. Povacz was relieved of his duties. Povacz said at the time he may have been infected with the virus accidentally by coming in contact with an infected patient at the scene of an emergency. When he learned that he lost his job, Povaz said it was worse than learning that he had tested positive for HIV. Being a paramedic was all he ever wanted to do. He said for eight years he has feared that his medical condition would be discovered or that he would develop AIDS and die. The state Department of Health computer system tracks HIV patients and periodically reviews cases. An official at the state Health Department informed Povacz and his superiors yesterday that Povacz is not and never was HIV positive. A second test that was performed eight years ago to confirm the first test indicated no presence of HIV, but the information was never placed in Povaczs medical records by his physician, Dr. Nadine Caspinwall, and Caspinwall never informed Povacz. Povacz is now fighting to get his job back.

4. The police department in your community are investigating a two-vehicle crash. The crash occurred at 5:38 p.m. Thursday during rush hour. The collision occurred at the busy intersection of Huron Avenue and Timber Trail Road. Police said a blue Toyota Camry driven by Cheryl Nicholls, 25, of 1287 Belgard Avenue, ran into the rear of a pickup truck driven by Ronald Dawkins, 44, of 1005 Stratmore Drive. Dawkins is a bricklayer. Nichols Toyota suffered severe damage, but she sustained only bruises and a laceration on her leg. Police said the car was a total loss. Police charged Nicholls with inattentive driving and operating a cell phone while driving. The cell phone law was passed last year by the state legislature and banned the operation of a cell phone while driving. Nicholls was talking to her car insurance company about an error on a car insurance bill when she struck the rear of Dawkins pickup truck.

5. A home at 2481 Santana Avenue was burglarized between the hours of 1 p.m. and 4 p.m. yesterday afternoon. The owner of the home is Dorothy R. Elam, a sixth-grade teacher at Madison Elementary School. She said no one was home at the time. Neighbors said they saw a truck parked in the driveway but thought some repairmen were working at the home. The total loss is estimated at in excess of $8,000. The items stolen from the home include a color television, a videocassette recorder, stereo, sewing machine, computer, 2 pistols and many small kitchen appliances. Also, a stamp collection valued at about $1,000, some clothes, silverware and lawn tools were taken. Roger A. Elam, Mrs. Elams husband, died 2 days ago. The robbery occurred while she was attending his funeral at 2:30 p.m. yesterday at the Powell Funeral Chapel, 620 North Park Avenue. Elam died of cancer after a long illness.

Section VI: Localizing Your Lead

Write only the lead for each of the following stories, correcting errors if necessary. Emphasize the information that would have the greatest local interest.

1. The U.S. Department of Justice is calling identity theft the crime of the 21st century. Identity theft is the illegal appropriation of another persons personal information—Social Security card number, driver's license number, credit card numbers, etc.—and using them to drain bank accounts or go on a buying spree. Justice Department officials say it is the fastest-growing crime in the United States. Criminals can get access to peoples personal information by going through their trash or stealing their mail. The Federal Trade Commission estimated the dollar loss to businesses and individuals last year was in the billions. The number of victims nationally

is running as high as 750,000 a year. The rate of identity theft complaints nationally is averaging 22 victims per 100,000 people. Justice Department officials say that is too high. But the rate of identity theft complaints in your city is 77 victims per 100,000 people. State Representative Constance P. Wei is sponsoring a bill that would establish a web site that would allow credit card holders to check to see if their numbers have been stolen. The bill also would increase the penalties for identity theft and raise the crime from a misdemeanor to a felony.

2. Your state's department of education announced that it is awarding more than 30 million dollars in federal grant money to 53 school districts throughout the state. The money is to be used to offset recent cutbacks in state funds given to school districts for educational programs and materials. Among the programs eligible for grant money are innovative programs to help identify and support at-risk youth who are not receiving the help they need. At-risk youth are more prone to failing in school and dropping out, becoming involved with drugs, becoming involved in crime or gang-related activity, and ending up in prison. The states Commission on Crime and Delinquency identified your local school district as a leader in the effort to help at-risk youth with its Community Helping Hands program. The program identifies at-risk youth at an early age and then engages teachers, community members and other students to help at-risk youth through academic tutoring, social activities and counseling. The state Commission on Crime and Delinquency through the state department of education is providing $1.2 million to your school districts at-risk program. The funds will help support the programs operation for at least three years.

Section VII: Updating Your Lead

Write only the lead for each of the following stories, emphasizing the most recent information. Correct all errors.

1. Dorothy Heslin is the manager of the Mr. Grocer convenience store at 2015 North 11th Avenue. Heslinn is a 48-year-old single mother with three children. She is seen as a hero by some and a villain by others. Yesterday, two masked men carrying guns barged into the Mr. Grocer and demanded money. As she reached for the cash drawer, Heslinn pulled a.357-caliber Magnum pistol from beneath the counter and fired four shots, killing one robber and seriously wounding the second. Some in the community say it was justified because her life was in danger, but others say she used excessive force. Police today charged Heslinn with aggravated assault with a handgun, attempted murder, second-degree murder and failure to properly register a handgun.

2. There was a grinding head-on collision on Cheney Road yesterday. Two persons were killed: Rosemary Brennan, 27, and her infant daughter, Kelley, age 2, both of 1775 Nairn Dr. The driver of the second car involved in the accident, Anthony Murray, 17, of 1748 North 3 Street, was seriously injured, with multiple fractures. Police today announced that laboratory tests have confirmed the fact that Brennan was legally drunk at the time of the accident.

3. The Steak & Ale restaurant is a popular restaurant and lounge in your community. It is especially popular with college students. The restaurant is located at 1284 University Boulevard. Last year, a group of students was celebrating at the restaurant after a football game. The five students became rowdy and were asked to leave by Sarah Kindstrom, a waitress at the Steak & Ale. The students left the restaurant, but one of them, James Ball, who was 20 at the time, of 1012 Cortez Avenue, Apartment 870, became separated from the group, wandered into the street and was struck by a car. He died at the scene. His parents sued the Steak & Ale for serving underage students alcohol and causing the death of their son. Monday the restaurants owners settled the suit for one million dollars.

3. WRITING BASIC NEWS LEADS

Write only a lead for each of the following stories. Correct all errors.

1. It was nearly a tragedy on Monday. Police said it is amazing no one was killed. A train struck a sport utility vehicle at a crossing on Michigan Avenue near the intersection with Wayne Boulevard in your city. Police said the accident occurred at 5:48 p.m. in the evening. Abraham and Estelle Cohen were the passengers in the 2010 Ford Explorer that was struck by the eastbound train. Abraham is 35 years old, and he was driving the vehicle. Estelle is 33 years old and is five months pregnant. The couple's daughter Emily, who is three years old, was a passenger in the back seat. No one was seriously injured. Abraham works for the city school system. He is assistant director of computer services. Estelle is a public relations representative for Evans Public Relations Group. Abraham, Estelle and their daughter live at 1903 Conway Rd. All three were taken to the local hospital for observation. Abraham suffered contusions on his ribs. Estelle received a small laceration on her forehead that required six stitches. Their daughter, Emily, suffered minor bruises to her right arm and face. Two ambulances were called to the scene to take the family to the hospital. Police said Mr. Cohen was driving west on Michigan Avenue when he came to the train crossing. The crossing does not have warning lights or an automated barrier gate. There are warning signs and a stop sign that require motorists to stop and look for trains before crossing the tracks. Police say Mr. Cohen failed to stop at the stop sign and drove into the path of the train. The train was traveling at approximately 15 to 20 miles per hour when it struck the car. Emily was riding in a child safety seat, which police said saved her life. Police said the vehicle suffered extensive damage and had to be towed from the scene.

2. For the past five years, researchers at the National Institutes of Health in Bethesda, Maryland, have been studying a sample of 4,000 adult males. The men range in age from 45 to 75. The research cost $1,500,000 and was paid for through the U.S. Department of Health and Human Services. The researchers announced the results today. The researchers have been studying the effects of meditation on men suffering with heart disease. Many of the men involved in the study either had suffered one or more heart attacks and/or had heart valve or heart bypass surgery. The study attempted to determine what effects meditation had on the heart for those suffering from heart disease. Researchers found that the men who were involved in a regular program of meditation lowered their stress and had fewer occurrences of repeat heart attacks or other problems associated with coronary heart disease. Dr. William Smithson, one of the researchers at the NIH who participated in the study, said: "Not only did we find that 75 percent of the men who meditated for an hour to an hour and a half at least three times a week lowered their blood pressure significantly during the period of the study, but we also found that their cholesterol and triglyceride levels dropped significantly. And even the numbers for the other 25% of the men in the study who participated in the meditation group showed some improvement. On the other hand, nearly 80 percent of those who did not participate in the meditation program saw an increase in their episodes of heart attacks, angina or chest pain, shortness of breath and other coronary symptoms. The link between the effects of stress on the heart and coronary heart disease are well known, but this study attempted to find a link between reducing stress levels and the effect on the heart." Researchers plan to release more information as they analyze the data. Researchers said that meditation alone would not help all heart disease patients, but could be used in conjunction with a good diet and exercise.

3. People in the United States are concerned about the environment. Many are concerned about the waste that is generated by Americans each day and buried in landfills. The Environmental Policy Group, a non-partisan environmental research and lobbying organization based in Washington, D.C., released a report recently. According to the report, only about one-quarter of the country's paper, plastic, glass, aluminum and steel is

recycled. That amount is only a slight increase from what it was 20 years ago. "This rate needs to be doubled or tripled in the next decade to have a positive impact on the environment. Steps must be taken to increase collection of recycled materials, increase public awareness, increase public partic- ipation, increase the development of new markets for recycled products and increase government support for recycling programs. Without these efforts, the planet's resources will be exhausted," the report said. Mayor Sabrina Datoli announced a new program at Tuesday nights city council meeting and council voted 6-1 to implement the new program. The new program will provide blue recycling bins throughout the city. Residents will be able to drop their recyclable items in any of the designated bins. In addition, the city will provide smaller blue recycling bins to keep in their homes for recyclable items. Residents will place the smaller household bins by the curb with their normal trash cans. The city will have special trucks that will pick up recyclable items on trash collection days. Datolli said residents will be able to use the larger recycling bins if they have a large quantity of items to recycle. Businesses also will be able to use the bins. Even if someone has only one item to place in a recycling container, it will be worth it, according to Datolli. "Too many times while I have been walking or driving around the city, I have seen someone finish drinking a bottle of water or soda and throw the plastic container in the trash because there is no convenient place to put the recyclable material. These public, recycling bins, placed in strategic places around the city, will address that problem," Datolli said. The pro- gram will cost around $280,000 initially to pur- chase and distribute the recycling containers and another $120,000 a year to gather and haul away the recycled items. City Council Member Roger Lo is opposed to the program because of the cost. He is in favor of turning the program over to a private contractor who would collect and sell recycled ma- terials for a profit as a way to pay for the program.

4. It's another statistical study, one that surprised many sociologists around the country. The re- search was conducted by sociologists at the University of Florida. The $1.5 million study was funded through grants provided by the National Institute of Mental Health and the National Science Foundation. For years, sociologists thought that advanced education translated into greater marriage stability. Now, with new data from the study released Monday, researchers have discovered that marital disruption is greater among more highly educated women than any other group, except those who have not graduated from high school. The study found that many young women who do not graduate from high school cohabitate rather than get married. The sociologists who conducted the new study found some of the reasons why women with graduate degrees are more likely to divorce. The key factor seems to be timing. Women who married early, before they began graduate school, are more likely to have established traditional family roles which they find difficult to change. When the wife goes back to school and no longer wants to handle most of the housework, it causes resentment on the part of husbands. If the husband refuses to pitch in and do his share, it creates tension. Such unhappiness on both sides often leads to divorce. The study found that more than one-third of the women who began graduate school after they were married ended up separated or divorced. By comparison, only 15.6 percent of those who married after they had finished an advanced degree ended up di- vorced or separated. This group of women seemed more likely to find husbands supportive of their educational goals, according to the study.

5. It was a sad tragedy. There was a fire Saturday evening in your city. Firefighters said the fire broke out around 9:15 p.m. Ann Capiello, a nine- teen year old student at the local university, called 9-1-1 to report the fire. Firefighters arrived on the scene around 9:25. The fire occurred at the residence of Johnnie and Jacquelin Lewis, 1840 Maldren Avenue. Jonnie, is 29 years old and works as an inspector for Vallrath Industries. Jacquelin is 28 and is a stay-at-home mother who cares for their two children, Krista, age 5, and Jeremy, age 3. Jacquelin and Jonnie had gone out for the eve- ning to go to dinner and a movie. They were cele- brating their 10th wedding anniversary. Capiello was babysitting their two children. Capiello was

watching television in the living room while the children were playing in Krista's bedroom. According to Tony Sullivan, the city's fire chief, the children apparently were playing with matches and attempting to light a candle. Capiello told Sullivan she smelled smoke and ran to the bedroom. She did not hear the smoke detectors go off. She heard the children crying and screaming for help, but she could not reach them because of the smoke and heat from the flames. She called 9-1-1 before returning to the bedroom to try to rescue the children. She suffered first-and second-degree burns on her hands, arms and face as she tried to get back into the bedroom. Firefighters were able to extinguish the blaze quickly, but not in time to save the children. They were found dead in a corner of the bedroom. Sullivan said the children most likely succumbed to the heat and smoke from the fire. Firefighters determined that the batteries in the smoke detectors were dead and were not working at the time of the fire. The fire caused an estimated $39,000 in fire, water and smoke damage to the house. Mr. and Mrs. Lewis discovered the tragedy when they arrived home around 10:30 p.m. to find firefighters and ambulances at their house.

6. Vernon Sindelair is the treasurer for your county. He has served as county treasurer for 31 years. He is responsible for overseeing the economic and financial business of the county. He is responsible for generating revenue through tax collection and paying the bills for the county. He appeared in the county's Court of Common Pleas Wednesday morning to plead guilty to charges of embezzlement. State police investigators and County Attorney Ronald McNally had been investigating Sindelair for more than a year before charging him three months ago with embezzling more than $1.7 million in tax receipts. Sindelair is 63 years old. He told investigators he embezzled the money to pay medical bills for his wife who died of cancer last year. MacNally said Sindelair faces up to 30 years in prison and fines of more than 1.5 million dollars. Judge Edward Kocembra delayed Sindelair's sentencing for two weeks until a sentencing report is completed. Sindelair resigned as county treasurer two weeks after he was charged with embezzlement by state and county officials.

4. WRITING BASIC NEWS LEADS—PRO CHALLENGE

Write only a lead for each of the following stories. You can compare your leads to ones written by professional journalists, which are available to your instructor. Correct all errors.

1. A random survey of Americans was recently conducted by the United States Congressional Research Service. CRS staff members analyze current policies and present the impact of proposed policy alternatives to members of Congress. Pollsters asked a random cross-section of more than 2,000 American adults about their attitudes toward the nation's federal income tax, and the results are contained in a 12-page report. The survey was conducted because members of the House of Representatives are about to sponsor a bill to abolish the federal income tax and the Internal Revenue Service. More than 56 percent of those surveyed said the federal income tax is unfair and the system needs to be changed. A similar survey conducted 10 years ago found that most Americans expressed more dissatisfaction with their property taxes than with their federal income taxes. However, that trend seems to be reversed because the new survey revealed that only 38 percent of those surveyed were dissatisfied with their current property taxes. The survey, which did not reveal the identity of those surveyed, also found that nearly 30 percent of respondents admitted to cheating on their taxes at some point during the past five years. The characteristic most respondents used to describe their feelings toward the income tax was "unfair." Many said they favored a simplified flat tax rate or a national sales tax.

2. Workers from your state's Department Environmental Resources and rescue personnel from your city's fire department responded to an emergency around 1 p.m. Thursday. The emergency was at the office of Vallrath Plastics, 1620 Industrial Boulevard. A large thermometer used

on a display of the company's products broke loose from the display board and crashed to the floor. The thermometer contained mercury, which spread around the office. Fire Chief Tony Sullivan said the thermometer contained about two pounds of mercury. A special hazardous materials unit from the city's fire department responded to the scene to clean up the mercury. Workers from the Department of Environmental Resources responded with special monitors to make sure all the mercury was cleaned up and that no one in the office was contaminated with the substance. Exposure to mercury can cause birth defects and poisoning, Sullivan said. Wanda Albertson, 39, of 529 Adirondack Avenue, is the personnel director at Vallrath Plastics. She was in the office when the incident occurred. She told emergency workers that it sounded like a bomb going off when the thermometer crashed to the floor and that she saw what looked like little silver balls of metal rolling around on the floor.

3. Don Brame is an inmate in the state correctional facility in your state. Braem is a former city employee whose former address was 3402 Virginia Avenue. He is 32 years old. He was an inspector for your city's housing authority. He is serving an 8-year sentence for burglary. He was found guilty last year of breaking into people's homes and stealing jewelry, money and electronic devices such as cell phones and iPods. Two months ago he was charged with swindling dozens of women of thousands of dollars from his prison cell. Wednesday he pleaded guilty to the new charges against him and was sentenced to an additional 10 years in prison. Police officials said Barlow mailed letters to men who recently died. The letters were received by the men's widows. Brame told police he got the names of the men from the obituaries in the local newspaper. The letters were written as bills seeking payment for "services rendered." The amounts of the "bills" were usually less than 100 dollars. Most of the women who received the bogus bills paid them because they thought their dead husbands had incurred the debt before their deaths. Or the women may have been too upset at the time to give the bills much thought, said Detective Larry Chevez of the

city's police department. The scam was discovered when Chevez's mother received one of the letters and asked him about paying the bill shortly after Chevez's father died.

4. Teachers in your local school district are facing a dilemma. The local school board voted to ban the teaching of critical race theory in any K–12 classes. Milan Scott teaches 10th-grade history classes at Kennedy High School. Some of the teaching materials he used last year were drawn from the New York Times "The 1619 Project," an exploration of the history of slavery in America. Critics, including some parents, attended last Monday's school board meeting at 7 p.m. in the cafeteria of Kennedy High School and said that critical race theory should not be taught because it would just inflame racial tensions and make white students feel bad. Some parents said CRT should be banned from all schools in the city because it is racist. School board member Jane Tribitt agreed with the critics and proposed a resolution asking the local school board to ban the teaching of CRT along with reclassifying terminology around the study of slavery. She submitted that instead of using the term "slavery," teachers should use the term "involutary servitude." The board voted 5-4 to ban the teaching of CRT, but voted against Tribitts suggestion to reclassify the term "slavery." Many students and parents who attended the meeting were against the ban. Gary Hubbard is the superintendent of schools. Hubbard said students can access "The 1619 Project" in the local public library. Teachers just will not be permitted to use the project in class or for reading assignments. Scott announced that he intends to ignore the ban and continue to use the material in his classes. He said "The 1619 Project" is a valuable resource in teaching the history of America. Hubard says Scott will face disciplinary action if he defies the ban.

5. A Kennedy High School soccer player died early Monday morning. Thomas Alvarez was 18 years of age. He is the son of Harold and Tina Alverez of 854 Maury Drive Apartment 11B. Police said he was speeding because he was late for school and lost control of his 2016 Ford Fusion and collided with a tree in the 5000 block of Cypress

Avenue. He was rushed to Memorial Hospital with severe head injuries and later pronounced dead by County Coroner Devin White. The crash occurred around 7:15 a.m. He was pronounced dead at 8:30 a.m. Two friends who were riding in the car with Alvarez, James Foucault, 17, of 1452 Penham Avenue, and Margaret Hamill, 16, of 811 North Cortez Avenue, walked away from the incident with minor lacerations and contusions, police said. Fire Chief Tony Sullivan said emergency personnel had to cut Alvarez out of the car. He said Alvarez was not wearing a seatbelt. Maureen Verdugo, principal of Kennedy High School, said the school's crisis intervention team would be available to talk to students, teachers and staff who are mourning Alvarez's death.

6. Marc Johnson, a construction worker who lives at 2643 Pioneer Rd., was arrested last week and charged with speeding, drunken driving and vehicular manslaughter after the pickup truck he was driving struck and killed a 13-year-old boy and severely injured the boy's 41-year-old father while they were riding their bicycles in the 4000 block of Holbrook Drive. Johnson is 23 years of age. Johnson was pronounced dead at Memorial Hospital at 2:30 a.m. today. He was rushed to the hospital from the county jail. A corrections officer at the jail checks each cell in the jail every 30 minutes. At about 1:30 a.m. an officer saw Johnson lying in his bed. When the officer came by Johnson's cell at 2 a.m., he found Johnson hanging from a bar in his cell. He had torn strips of cloth from his shirt and fashioned a noose around his neck that he then attached to the bar. Corrections officers attempted to revive him before emergency personnel arrived, but were unsuccessful.

5. CITY, STATE AND NATIONAL LEADS

Write only a lead for each of the following stories. The first set of stories involves events in your city; the second involves events in your state; and the third involves events in the nation. As you write the leads, correct the stories' spelling, style and vocabulary errors. Discuss your leads with your classmates.

City Beat

1. There was a shooting in your city last week. The incident occurred early Wednesday morning. Barry Koperud, the chief of police for your city, said the shooting was senseless and was an execution-style killing of one of the citys police officers. Killed in the incident last week was Officer Allison Biagi, 26 years old, who lived at 2634 6th Street Apartment 906B. Biagi was a 4 year veteran of the police department. According to police reports, Biagi was sitting in her patrol car when a twenty-two year old white male approached her vehicle and fired eight shots through the driver side window. Bullets struck Biagi in the arm, neck and head, according to reports. She died at the scene. Police, with help of witnesses and video from a nearby bank's surveillance camera, later identified the shooting suspect as Ronald Collins, 20 years of age, of 2814 Ambassador Dr. Apartment 47D, a constuction worker for Wagnor Development Corporation. Police gave no motive for the shooting. Chief Kopperud announced this morning that Collin had surrendered to police. The Police Chief said that Collin walked into the newly remodeled and modern police headquarters at 9:03 a.m. this morning and calmly said, "I am the one you are looking for. I'm the one who shot the police officer." Collins did not resist officers as they arrested him and officers handcuffed him without incident.

2. Your city has a planetarium that was built in 1970, the year after American astronaut Neil Armstrong walked on the moon. The facility is located at 625 Park Place adjacent to Memorial Park, which has soccer fields, baseball and softball diamonds, a running track and public swimming pool. The land for the planetarium was donated by Jonathan Herwarthe, a local real estate developer, who also donated some of the money for its construction. The planetarium is supported through a trust fund established by Herwarthe in his will. However, the planetarium, which is enjoyed by many people in the city, is in need of repair. It needs a new projector, new seats, repairs to the roof, better handicapped access, as well as many other repairs and improvements. Jonathan Hurwarthes son, Gregory Hurwarthe, 56 years of

age, and his wife, Ruth, of 410 Baltimore Avenue, told city council members that the repairs will cost $500 thousand. Mayor Sabrina Datolli told council members at Tuesday nights meeting that the city did not have the money to fix the planetarium and would shut it down at the end of the year if repairs could not be made to bring the building in compliance with city building codes. Jonathan Herwarthe told council members at the meeting that he had been able to raise only $250,000 of the half million dollars needed. Thursday morning, the mayor announced that two local attorneys, James R. and Margaret Ungarient, of 7314 Byron Avenue, had pledged $100 thousand dollars to help repair the building and started a crowd-funding campaign to raise the other $150,000 needed. The planetarium is named The Jonathan Herwarthe Memorial Planetarium. "I always thought the planetarium was an asset to our young people," Datolli said. "It's there to help children study and learn about the universe. But the city just does not have the funds to make all these major repairs."

3. Mayor Sabrina Datoli and City Council members William Belmonte and Sandra Gandolf want the city to launch an investigation into a construction accident that killed a local man and injured another man last month. James Randolph, 39 years old, who lived at 654 Harrison Street, was the construction worker who was killed in the accident. The injured construction worker was Lynn R. Pryor, 28 years of age, who lived at 2634 Sixth Street Apartment 45. Both men were employed by Rittmann Engineering Company. According to a report by the police who investigated the accident, the two men were working on a stormwater drain project when the trench they were working in collapsed. Randolph was completely buried in the collapse and Pryor was buried up to his chest in dirt and rock. Passersby heard Pryor screaming for help and were able to dig him out. However, by the time rescuers reached Randolph and were able to dig him out, he had already expired. City Medical Examiner Dr. Marlene Stoudnaur pronounced Randolph dead at the scene. Stoudnour later conducted an autopsy and reported that the cause of death was suffocation. Datolli and

Belmonte claim that Rittmann Engineering Company violated city, state and national safety standards, which led to the tragedy. Director of the Code Enforcement Board Todd Drolshagen told city officials he inspected the construction site 2 weeks before the accident happened and ordered engineers at Rittmann to halt work on the drain project until the trench could be reinforced to make it safer. Drolshagen said the work never stopped and the safety measures were never implemented. The citys district attorney Ramon Hernandez filed papers in county court charging Rittmanns president Anthony Rittmann, 61 years of age, who lives at 9600 Holbrook Drive, with manslaughter and willful negligence in the death of Randolph. A Rittmann spokesman declined to comment on the charges.

State Beat

1. Last week, officials in your state announced the name of the winners of the state's weekly lottery. It was the largest lottery prize ever won in the state. The value of the winning ticket was 330 million dollars with a cash payout option of 208 million dollars. One of the winners is Ethel Shearer, 28 years of age, who lives at 408 Kasper Avenue Apartment 718. Shearer is a waitress at the Melody Lounge, which is located at 2790 Bolling Drive. Shearer bought her winning ticket at the Jiffy Foods convenience store when she was driving home from work early one morning. It was the first time she had ever won any money playing the states lottery. Shearer contacted officials at the state lottery office the day after the winning number was drawn and she checked her ticket to identify herself as one of the winners. The other winner was identified as Joel Fowler, who lives at 2006 Hillcrest Street. Fowler is a student at your school. He is an out of state student who transferred to your school last year. Fowler came forward with his winning ticket two days after Shearer identified herself as one of the winners of the top prize. It was the first time in the history of the state lottery that two winning tickets of the top prize have been sold in the same city. Fowler, however, will not be able to claim his winnings. State officials claim that Fowler purchased his

ticket illegally. State law requires that players must be twenty-one years of age to purchase lottery tickets in the state. Fowler is only 19 years of age. Fowler is eligible to purchase lottery tickets in his home state because the eligible age to purchase tickets is 18. He told lottery officials he thought the eligible age to buy tickets was the same for all states. Fowler bought his ticket at a Safeway Supermarket in the city and state lottery officials are investigating to determine if Safeway employees are checking identifications of ticket purchasers to see if they are of age to legally buy tickets.

2. A 13 year old girl wanted to know what happened to money that was earmarked for arts programs in public schools around the state. The girls name is Alyssa Allen. She is the daughter of Christopher and Julie Allen, who live at 1504 Lincoln Drive. Christopher is the director of the Center for the Arts in your city and Julie is a university professor. Julie teaches in the universitys art department. Alyssa filed a Right-To-Know request at the state capital to get information about the grant program that was approved by the state legislature three years ago but schools have never received any grant money. State officials are saying that Alyssa has no legal right to file the request because she is too young. State officials also said Alyssa will have to pay attorneys fees for placing a burden on the state and wasting officials time. Mr. and Mrs. Allyn are threatening to sue the state over the rejection of Alyssa's request.

3. James Rueben is a state center from the district that represents your city. Mr. Rueben, 54 years of age, who lives at 12494 Hillcrest Rd., received a letter from one of his constituents, Shirley Dawson, 59 years of age, who lives at 492 Melrose Avenue. Mrs. Dawson is a teacher at Colonial Elementary School. She is also a widow. Her husband, Steven, was killed in a car crash involving a drunk driver. Mrs. Dawson filed a negligence lawsuit against the driver of the vehicle that killed her husband. Mrs. Dawson was struggling financially after the death of her husband and after seeing an advertisement for a lawsuit loan program, in which a finance company would loan her money in advance of her settling the lawsuit against the driver involved in her husbands

death. She borrowed $25,000 dollars, pledging to repay the sum when the suit was settled. The company she borrowed the money from was Sunset Legal Finance. When her lawsuit was settled for $500,000, Mrs. Dawson received a bill from Sunset Legal Finance for $265,000, which company officials said represented interest and processing fees. Mr. Rueben claims that the loan program is abusive because it is not regulated by the state and takes advantage of people who are in financial trouble. Mr. Rueben wants to introduce a bill that would require lawsuit loan companies to be licensed and establish disclosure requirements, as well as cap the amount of interest and processing fees the companies can charge.

National Beat

1. Cellphones are outlawed in prisons across the United States. However, a recent government study found that in your state alone, prison officials confiscated more than nine thousand smartphones from inmates in federal and state prisons located in the state. The study estimated that the nine thousand devices were used to place 1,643,500 calls and text messages over a year. Congress recently passed a law making possession of a cellphone or a wireless device in a federal prison a felony, punishable by up to a year of extra sentencing. But the phones are still getting into the hands of prisoners who use the phones to connect to Facebook and play games. Some inmates, however, use the phones to stay in touch with gang members outside the prison walls and continue to conduct unlawful business, such as drug trafficking, according to the government study that was released Monday. The study stated that cellphones have been smuggled into prisons by guards, visitors and new prisoners entering the prison system. However, the study also stated that cellphones have been concealed inside footballs, tossed over prison walls, or launched from a device called a potato cannon, which shoots a projectile through a pipe. Federal legislators say that they are proposing a bill that would authorize federal and state prison officials to jam cellphone signals in federal and state prisons. Opponents of the proposal say

the technology used to jam the signals in prison is not precise enough and could also jam the signals of residents living near the prisons.

2. According to government statistics, more than 300,000 American service members who served in Iraq and Afghanistan are suffering from Post Traumatic Stress Disorder or major depression. Officials at the Veterans Administration say that fewer than 800 service members attempted suicide last year. Members of Congress are saying that the figures released by the Veterans Administration are wrong and amount to outright lies. A federal investigation into the Veterans Administration uncovered a string of emails that indicated that more than 1,000 veterans that the VA is caring for attempt suicide each month. That is more than 12,000 attempts last year. Federal investigators are saying that Veterans Administration officials are misleading Congress in regard to the number of suicide attempts to hide the strain the conflicts in Iraq and Afghanistan are having on the United States Department of Defense and the Veterans Administration. Members of Congress claim that the Veterans Administrations mental health programs are being overwhelmed and are seeking remedies. Some legislators are proposing providing funds so veterans can seek help through private mental health services in order to get the help they need to deal with their depression and Post Traumatic Stress Disorder. Congress is looking at providing as much as 50 million dollars to launch the program to pay for private mental health care.

3. Its another national study, this one of married men and women. It found that many married Americans admit keeping a major secret from their spouses, but most secrets have nothing to due with an affair or fantasy. Of those married men and women with a secret:

- 48 percent said they had not told their spouse the real price of something they bought.
- About 40 percent of the wives and 30 percent of the husbands said they wish they could persuade their spouses to be less messy.
- About a quarter of each sex said they cannot get their partners to lose weight.
- About 20 percent of the nations marrieds have dreams or aspirations they haven't mentioned to a spouse, ranging from living somewhere else (50 percent) to getting a dog (8 percent).
- 16 percent of both men and women admitted that, at least once during their marriage, they wished they could wake up and not be married any more.
- About 15 percent had not told their spouse about a failure at work.
- About 15 percent had not told their spouse about a childs misbehavior.
- 14 percent kept quiet about being attracted to another person.
- Only 9 percent of the respondents, equally split among men and women, said they had an extramarital affair that remains a secret.

The poll was conducted last month by the Centers for Disease Control, which interviewed by phone 700 husbands and 700 wives.

8 ALTERNATIVE LEADS

"Journalism is what maintains democracy. It's the force for progressive social change."

—*Andrew Vachss, American attorney and author of crime fiction*

Two reporters from competing news organizations attend a city council meeting where the mayor, Sabrina Datolli, announces that the city faces a $6.7 million deficit. Datolli tells council members that a tax increase will be needed unless the city has a little luck. Specifically, tax revenues must exceed expectations, expenditures must stay within estimates, and health care costs and other employee benefits must remain reasonable.

Both journalists listen carefully and take copious notes, intent on capturing the sometimes-contentious tone as city officials debate this fiscal dilemma. When the meeting ends, the reporters write their stories. But one piece will be more widely read than the other. One begins with the following lead:

> City officials Wednesday night debated the possibility of a tax increase to erase the city's $6.7 million deficit.

The other starts this way:

> City officials are going to need a pretty big rabbit's foot to keep the city's budget in the black.
>
> Mayor Sabrina Datolli told the council during a budget meeting Wednesday night it will take a lot of luck to keep the city out of a financial hole next year.
>
> "If we're lucky, health care costs and our other insurances won't have a big increase. If we're lucky, our tax revenues will come in higher than expected," Datolli said. "If we're unlucky . . ."
>
> If the city is unlucky, it will be looking at a deficit of more than $6.7 million.

The first reporter began the story with a standard summary lead, covering the who, what, when, where, why and how (see Chapter 7). Such leads are acceptable, but sometimes a story begs for a more creative approach. The second writer began with an alternative, or "soft," lead—in this case, a multi-paragraph lead. Journalists employ at least a dozen variations of soft leads, but most begin with a story's most interesting details, often an anecdote, description or question. These leads, which may run four or five paragraphs, are usually followed by a nut graph that states the story's central point and serves some of the same functions as the summary news lead.

Situations like this, showing Elvis Presley impersonator Brendan Paul with a couple getting married at a wedding chapel in Las Vegas, can provide reporters the opportunity to be more creative in developing leads for their stories. They can choose from a variety of alternative leads that focus on the unusual or humorous nature of a story, an ironic twist or dramatic suspense that can grab and hold the attention of an audience.

8.1 Summary and Alternative Leads

Basic summary news leads are more common—and probably easier to write—than alternative leads. The former concisely state the central point of the story, but the latter may linger over one aspect. Writing an alternative lead requires thought and imagination: the ability to recognize and convey an interesting idea uniquely. The reporter must paint a picture with words, with an attention to details that the summary lead cannot include because of its conciseness.

Alternative leads do not require an unusual story. In the following example, the first lead appears as a routine report about how using Zoom and other digital meeting platforms for government meetings may continue after the COVID-19 pandemic subsides. The alternative lead, which is the one that appeared in this story, is better at capturing the audience's attention:

> **Summary Lead:** Local government officials see the continued use of virtual meetings, which skyrocketed during the COVID-19 pandemic, as a way of increasing civic engagement.

> **Alternative Lead:** When Washington, D.C., reenfranchised people serving time for felonies in 2020, Joel Castón, then at the D.C. Central Detention Facility, realized that not only could he now vote, he could also run for commissioner of his local Advisory Neighborhood Commission, one of about 40 of the hyperlocal governing bodies in the district. And if he could find a way to participate in ANC meetings from jail, he could serve out his term in office.

> *(Bloomberg)*

The story told how Castón was elected to and served in his position from jail until his release on parole by using virtual meeting apps such as Zoom. The reporter interviewed government officials and digital experts, explaining how civic engagement blossomed with the ability of people to access meetings from a computer, a tablet or smartphone.

Good reporters can write many kinds of leads, choosing an appropriate one for each story. This versatility allows them to avoid the trap of blindly following a particular formula in news writing. Although summary leads are effective for many stories, alternative leads allow journalists to stretch the boundaries of their creativity. However, appropriateness is important. The use of alternative leads depends on the publication and the self-imposed stylistic restraints of the writer.

When reporters finish a story, their editors expect it to be well written: clear, concise, accurate and interesting. If a story meets these criteria, editors are unlikely to object if its lead uses an alternative form. Nor are they likely to object to a summary lead that creatively and freshly captures the essence of a story.

Consider this example. When members of a Bronx street gang crashed a christening party, a fight broke out, someone fired shots and a 10-year-old girl was killed. The New York Post, the Daily News and The New York Times all covered the incident. The first two papers used summary leads; the third used an alternative lead that linked the killing to the shooting of another girl in Brooklyn:

> A 10-year-old altar girl was killed by stray bullets outside her Bronx church yesterday after a gang of armed street thugs crashed a christening party and began arguing with guests.
>
> *(New York Post)*

> Little Malenny Mendez went to church to celebrate a new life, but instead she lost her own.
>
> *(New York Daily News)*

> Malenny Mendez, a 10-year-old girl from the Bronx, loved to strap on her in-line skates and smile at anyone who sauntered past her parents' grocery store. Katherine Crisantos, a 4-year-old girl from Brooklyn, loved the connotation of the word Friday, because it meant a trip with her big sister to Burger King for fries and soda.
>
> Early yesterday morning, both girls, children of Mexican immigrants, were shot in the head less than an hour apart at parties given by friends and relatives.
>
> *(The New York Times)*

8.2 Criticisms

During the 1940s, The Wall Street Journal became one of the first daily newspapers to use soft leads. Many others, including the Los Angeles Times, The Miami Herald and The Boston Globe, have since given their reporters more freedom to experiment with their writing, leading the dailies to become known as "writers' newspapers." Proponents of soft leads say whether the lead works is what matters, not the type. They disparage the traditional summaries as "suitcase leads," meaning that newspapers try to jam too many details into leads, like a traveler trying to fit too many clothes into a suitcase. They also say summary leads are unnatural, deter reporters from writing good stories and eliminate the possibility of surprise, thus making all stories sound alike.

FROM THE NEWS

Summary and Alternative Leads

Here are more examples of standard summary leads and the alternative leads that lend freshness to the story:

Summary Lead	Alternative Lead
The company that licenses the use of Elvis Presley's name and image is demanding that wedding chapels in Las Vegas stop using "The King" in their themed ceremonies.	Las Vegas chapels of love that use Elvis Presley's likeness could find themselves becoming Heartbreak Hotels. *(Associated Press)*
Police are investigating the theft of more than $17,000 in cash and checks from a Sunday night religious service in Franklin County.	The Lord giveth and the Lord taketh away, but He is not a suspect in the theft of $17,000 in checks and an undetermined amount of cash Sunday from the collection taken at the Cumberland Valley Steve Wingfield Encounter. *(Hagerstown [Maryland] Herald-Mail)*
Parents in Tampa Bay are confused and frustrated as they struggle to find COVID-19 vaccines for their infant children after Florida officials declined to preorder doses.	It's been almost two weeks since federal regulators authorized COVID-19 vaccines for infants and preschoolers, but Katie Old Crow still hasn't been able to get her 14-month-old son vaccinated. The Town 'N Country mother is waiting for her family's pediatrician to vaccinate her son, Rollin, because most pharmacies only offer shots to kids ages 3 and older. Her pediatrician's office on June 21 told her and other parents that they expected the child-sized doses to become available "within the next few weeks" and would email parents once the shots arrived. But Old Crow said she hasn't heard anything since last week. She wonders if the long wait is the result of Florida's decision against preordering vaccines for children under age 5. "It's disappointing because we've been waiting for two years," she said. Florida was the only state in the nation that did not preorder the newly authorized vaccine for children ages 4 and younger. That's because the Florida Surgeon General recommended that healthy children need not be vaccinated against COVID-19, contrary to guidelines from the Centers for Disease Control and Prevention. It has left the state with a confusing patchwork of vaccine providers that some parents are struggling to navigate. *(Tampa Bay [Florida] Times)*

The more literary style of soft leads may help traditional print versions of newspapers compete for readers in an ever-changing media landscape. By using soft leads, newspapers can make their stories more interesting. Even as newspapers have moved into web-based news delivery, thereby increasing the immediacy of their content, alternative leads are still being employed to entice readers.

But not everyone embraces alternative leads. Critics call their use "Jell-O journalism." They complain that soft leads are inappropriate for most news stories: too arty, literary and pretentious. Furthermore, they are too long and fail to emphasize the news. If a story begins with several paragraphs of description or quotations, for example, its most important details may be buried in a later paragraph. Critics also complain that some reporters strain to write fine literature, and many lack the necessary ability.

The following example illustrates how poorly constructed alternative leads can confuse readers and make them impatient. You have to read more than 145 words before getting to the story's main point:

Eleanor Lago considers herself an intelligent, educated woman.

She's read the information provided her by the Grand Rapids Township Board. She's talked to friends and neighbors. And she intends to vote Tuesday in a special election that could determine the township's future.

"I just want to do what's best," says Lago.

Like many residents, though, she's not sure what that is.

An unusual battle is being fought in this smallest of Kent County townships, a raggedy-shaped 16 square miles set cheek to jowl against the cities of Grand Rapids, East Grand Rapids and Kentwood. The battle is not about zoning, the more typical flash point of local politics. Nor is it about leaf burning ordinances or other grass-roots laws in this suburb of nearly 11,000 people.

This battle is about what the community can do to keep from being nibbled to pieces by annexation.

The writer's intention was good: describing an intelligent voter who is confused about an important issue. But the introduction would have been more effective if

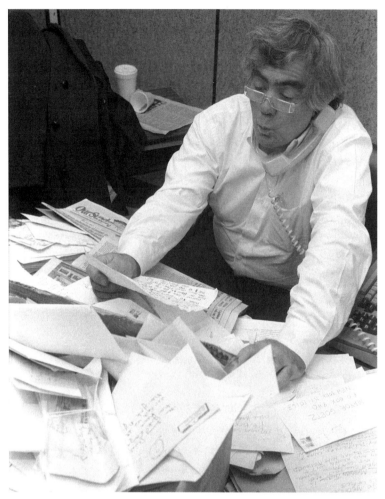

Jimmy Breslin was an iconic journalist who worked for several New York newspapers including The New York Times. Breslin was renowned for finding stories that many other journalists overlooked. When President John F. Kennedy was assassinated in 1963, Breslin wrote about the Black man who had dug his grave. In covering the Civil Rights Movement in the South in the 1960s, Breslin wrote about an unheated school for Black children that had been "a wooden building that was a church when people in Lowndes County wore Confederate uniforms."

cut in half. The reporter could have eliminated some description, cut the clichés and avoided saying what the election was not about.

The remaining sections of this chapter describe and offer examples of the various alternative leads.

8.3 Types of Alternative Leads

8.3.1 "Buried" or "Delayed" Leads

A "buried," or "delayed," lead is the most common type of alternative lead. Typically, it begins with an interesting example or anecdote that sets a story's theme. Then a nut graph—perhaps the third or fourth paragraph—states the central point and provides a transition to the body, moving the story to the general issue or problem. Like a traditional lead, it summarizes the topic; it may also explain why the topic is important.

Here are two examples of buried leads. The first is by Jaclyn Diaz of NPR, who takes a different approach to writing about the connections between two mass shootings. The second is by Jeremy Roebuck of The Philadelphia Inquirer, who wrote about the sale of a dilapidated landmark wooden bridge.

> In the span of less than two weeks, an elementary school and a grocery store more than 1,700 miles apart were shattered by gun violence. Uvalde, Texas, and Buffalo, N.Y., now both share the tragic loss of friends and family.

> These two tragedies happened on separate ends of the country and yet, both share similarities: how the violence was carried out, certain aspects of the suspects, and the ease in which the weapons were accessed.

> Philadelphia—While his childhood friends spent their days on the sports fields, Mike Hart spent his digging through dumps.

> Trolling the detritus for old bottles and kerosene lamps, he found fascination in objects other people cast aside.

> Now 49 and head of his own historic building preservation firm, Hart, of Harleysville, plans to take home one of his greatest finds yet.

> He's getting the bridge no one wanted.

After giving more details about the bridge's history, the story reaches the central point in the ninth paragraph, which is the nut graph:

> But four years after the Pennsylvania Department of Transportation closed it to pedestrian and motorist traffic, citing concerns about its structural integrity, the township decided the bridge had to go.

PAINT OUT
Students: Pratt booting beloved recycled art store for dull chain

BY ALLEGRA HOBBS

Call it a brush off.

Pratt Institute is short-changing its students by booting a beloved store that sells recycled art materials off its Clinton Hill campus because it already has a contract with a national art-store chain, claim cash-strapped scholars of the art and architecture school.

"I'm paying for school on my own

campus by Nov. 1 — and Turn Up Art can't stay on as a regular business because the school already has a contract with Blick Art Material, giving it exclusive rights to sell art supplies on its grounds.

Pratt claims the store always had a set expiration date — participants in the incubator have to clear out by an agreed upon time in order to make

This alternative lead, from an article in the Brooklyn Courier, connects with the subject of the story.

The rest of the story addresses the struggles of government officials to come up with the money to remove the bridge, the attempt to sell it on an internet auction site, the agreement with Hart to remove the bridge and what he will eventually do with it.

A delayed lead can introduce a complex or abstract problem by showing how the problem affects a single individual—someone the audience may know or identify with. Or an anecdote can illustrate a problem and arouse interest in the topic.

Some buried leads surprise their public with an unusual twist. If a story is only three or four paragraphs long, journalists may save the twist for the last line. If a story is longer, they use the twist to lure readers to the nut graph, which then provides a transition to the following paragraphs.

8.3.2 Multi-paragraph Leads

Other news writers think of a lead as a unit of thought. Their summary leads consist of two or three paragraphs that flow into each other as if they were one:

> Librarian Suzette Baker said she faced a hard choice last year when her boss asked her to hide a book on critical race theory behind the counter.
>
> "OK, I'll look into it," Baker recalled telling her boss at the time.
>
> But eventually, Baker—a librarian at the Llano County Public Library's Kingsland Branch—decided to ignore the request. And she continued to vocally protest other decisions, like the ban on ordering new books. She spoke up, telling her supervisors that the library was facing a censorship attack.
>
> By February, the pressure to keep new or donated books from the shelves increased, she said. After waiting weeks for a local library board to approve the books Baker wanted to add to her library, Baker's boss would tell her that even donated books could not reach the shelves.
>
> On March 9, Baker was fired for insubordination, creating a disturbance and failure to follow instructions.
>
> "This change is inevitable and you are allowing your personal biases, opinions and preferences to unduly influence your actions and judgment," her dismissal documents stated.
>
> Baker's experience represents one of many new conflicts facing Texas librarians as book challenges continue to multiply. Many feel left out of decisions on banning books while also facing increased scrutiny from politicians, parents, and county and school district staff. Some have already quit, and others are considering it.
>
> *(The Texas Tribune)*

> Carlisle—It didn't take Mark Toigo and Jay Shettel long to realize they had bought an aerodynamic pile of junk.

They had paid $75,000 to a West Coast aircraft broker who'd advertised the early 1950s Grumman Albatross amphibious plane on the Internet auction site eBay.

It was a sight-unseen deal.

Toigo of Shippensburg and Shettel of Carlisle didn't get a good look at the Albatross until they ventured to a Brazilian air force base outside Sao Paolo, where the venerable old bird was roosting. The Albatross was grimy, beaten-up, partially scavenged and anything but airworthy.

"Right away, we named her 'Dirty Girl,'" Toigo said.

Four years and about $500,000 worth of work later, Dirty Girl still needs a final face-lift, but she flies.

(The [Harrisburg, Pennsylvania] Patriot-News)

8.3.3 Quotation Leads

Reporters usually avoid using quotations in leads. Sources generally do not provide quotes that meet three criteria for leads: summarize the entire story (not just part of it), be brief and be self-explanatory. Some editors prohibit the use of quotation leads because they lack clarity and often are too long and complicated.

As with the use of any quotation in a story, the source's statement should be so effective the reporter cannot improve it. When used in the first line of a story, a quotation also must reveal the central point, as these two examples do:

"When I saw my father lying alone in that hospital bed hooked up to a ventilator and not being able to comfort him, there was just a sense of helplessness and hopelessness," Carol Jacobs said after her father died last month of COVID-19.

Jacobs, whose father was hospitalized for nearly four months, is only one of hundreds of thousands of people struggling with the loss of a loved one as the number of victims of the pandemic in the U.S. nears 1 million.

"The western U.S. is running out of water. Think of that the next time you turn on the tap to get a drink or take a shower," the head of the Bureau of Reclamation said Thursday during a scientific conference on the effects of climate change in the West.

If a quotation is only sensational, it fails to satisfy the criteria for a lead. It may be suitable elsewhere in the story, however. Reporters have other ways to startle an audience or grab its attention. Remember that the lead provides the organization for the rest of the story. If the quotation fails to bring people into and set the stage for the story, it will confuse and discourage them. A long, complicated quotation, even within the body of a story, will raise unnecessary questions.

Quotations that begin with words needing identification or explanation—such as "he," "she," "we," "they," "it," "that" and "this"—should not be leads. The audience has no way of knowing to whom or what the words refer and, when the subject's identity is revealed, may have to reread the quotation to understand its meaning.

Consider the following example:

"The water was rising so fast and the bank was so muddy and slippery I just didn't think I could get away from that torrent of water." That's how a Bremerton man described his ordeal just before rescue workers used a utility truck to pluck him out of a tree he had climbed to escape a flash flood during Monday night's thunderstorms.

Such leads can be rewritten with a brief introduction to enhance clarity:

A Bremerton man who was rescued from a tree he had climbed to escape a flash flood Monday night said, "The water was so fast and the bank was so muddy and slippery I just didn't think I could get away from that torrent of water."

8.3.4 Question Leads

Questions can make effective leads. Some editors, though, prohibit this type because they believe news stories should answer questions, not ask them. Question leads also often run the risk of being clichés.

To be effective, question leads must be brief, simple, specific and provocative. The question should contain no more than a dozen words. Moreover, the audience should feel absolutely compelled to answer it. Avoid questions if people's responses may discourage them from continuing with the story, as in this example:

Do you have a dog?

Some readers may answer "yes" to that question, but many more may not. Even if the story provides important information about how to care for a dog's health, the lead does not attract readers' attention. However, if the writer had a more intriguing question lead, it may attract readers who might not have a dog but become interested in the story enough to read it and pass the information to those who do. The question lead above fails simply because someone can answer "yes" or "no" and still ignore the story.

A question should concern a controversial yet familiar issue that interests and affects an audience. Avoid abstract or complicated questions requiring a great deal of explanation. The following question is ineffective because it is too abstract, long and complicated. Furthermore, it fails to ask about issues that everyone is certain to care about:

When you're at the grocery store and pick up a head of lettuce, or you go shopping for clothes and pick out a cotton shirt, do you think about the person who harvested the produce or hung the shirt on the sale rack?

"I said I would take questions - I didn't say I would answer them."

The following questions also fail, but for different reasons. The first asks about an issue unlikely to concern most people. The second is unanswerable and flippant, treating a serious topic as a trivial one:

> Have you thought lately about going to prison?

> Someone was swindled today. Who'll be swindled tomorrow?

Here are two effective question leads. Notice that each reporter immediately answers the questions.

> Is omicron leading us closer to herd immunity against COVID-19?

> Experts say it's not likely that the highly transmissible variant — or any other variant—will lead to herd immunity.

> *(The Associated Press)*

> Fill out college application? Check.

> Take the SATs? Check.

> Have three or four college courses already under your belt?

> For students hoping to get accepted at higher-end colleges, taking a few Advanced Placement courses—accelerated high school classes that count for college credit depending on how students score on a standardized test—is no longer a nice add-on to college résumés. It's the norm.

> *(The [Harrisburg, Pennsylvania] Patriot-News)*

8.3.5 Suspenseful Leads

Some reporters write leads to create suspense, arouse people's curiosity or raise a question in their minds. By hinting at some mysterious development explained in a later paragraph, this type of lead compels the audience to finish a story:

> NASHVILLE, Tenn.—Marianne Sung lives in a small brick house in a sleepy town outside Nashville. It's quiet and quaint, surrounded by rolling hills, and she likes that cell phone coverage is spotty.

> Marianne lives with her partner, two dogs, and two sons—Eli, age 11, and toddler Charlie. She says she feels at peace with her life, but admits she sometimes wonders about how it might have turned out differently—if she'd made a different decision, more than a decade ago.

> *(NPR.com)*

> It is difficult to run a successful business when you keep losing half of your work force year after year.

> Just ask James Griffe—or any other beekeeper.

> *(The [Harrisburg, Pennsylvania] Patriot News)*

The first story focuses on two sisters who took different paths on abortion; the second reports on the economic devastation an insect parasite was causing for beekeepers.

8.3.6 Descriptive Leads

Other leads begin with descriptive details that paint a picture before moving gradually into the action. The description should be colorful and interesting so that it arouses the public's interest. It should also help summarize the story.

The following examples show the effectiveness of descriptive leads. Notice the use of concrete images in the first one: "arid and affluent hills," "red and white rose bushes" and "lush green grass." The second sets the scene and provides background details for a feature story about a couple with Parkinson's disease. The focus of the story is the doctor who treats them and the relationship his father had with Maurer's family as their doctor in Illinois many years ago.

> AGOURA HILLS, Calif. — From behind the wheel of his work van, Fernando Gonzalez took in the immaculate front yard amid the arid and affluent hills north of Los Angeles. The red and white rosebushes. The loquat and pear trees. The expanse of lush green grass and the two peacocks lounging beneath the portico.
>
> The stately residence had been consuming about 40,000 gallons of water a month, and had already received a warning and a fine for overuse. Amid the historic drought now entering its third painful summer, Gonzalez's employer, the Las Virgenes Municipal Water District, has demanded this home and millions of others cut irrigation by 35 percent as of June 1. If things don't improve by September, authorities say, outdoor water use could be banned entirely.
>
> *(The Washington Post)*

> Parkinson's disease worked on Goldie Maurer like a slow-moving robber, taking away things one at a time.
>
> Baling hay. Birthing calves. Working the controls of a John Deere tractor.
>
> Each lost activity seemed to pull Maurer further from what she was—a Midwestern-born farm girl, raised in the 1920s on a farm near tiny Lena, Ill.
>
> The tremors and faulty sense of balance started 25 years ago, long after Maurer moved from Illinois to a farm in northern Dauphin County.
>
> First, she surrendered garden chores, such as tending strawberry and potato plants. Then, she had to give up handling equipment, such as riding a snowmobile to far-flung parts of her farm in Washington Township.
>
> It was the tremors, she said.
>
> *(The [Harrisburg, Pennsylvania] Patriot-News)*

This story from The New York Times by Jon Mooallem about the wildfire that destroyed Paradise, California, and its aftermath employs a descriptive lead to pull the reader into the story.

Burned-out cars and leveled homes are all that remain of Paradise, California, following a massive 2018 fire.

> The fire was already growing at a rate of one football field per second when Tamra Fisher woke up on the edge of Paradise, Calif., feeling that her life was no longer insurmountably strenuous or unpleasant and that she might be up to the challenge of living it again.
>
> She was 49 and had spent almost all of those years on the Ridge — the sweeping incline, in the foothills of California's Sierra Nevada, on which Paradise and several tinier, unincorporated communities sit. Fisher moved to the Ridge as a child, married at 16, then raised four children of her own, working 70-hour-plus weeks caring for disabled adults and the elderly. Paradise had attracted working-class retirees from around California since the 1970s and was beginning to draw in younger families for the same reasons. The town was quiet and affordable, free of the big-box stores and traffic that addled the city of Chico in the valley below. It still brimmed with the towering pine trees that first made the community viable more than a century ago. The initial settlement was poor and minuscule — "Poverty Ridge," some called it — until a new logging railroad was built through the town in 1904 by a company felling timber farther uphill. This was the Diamond Match Company. The trees of Paradise made for perfect matchsticks.

8.3.7 Shockers: Leads with a Twist

Reporters like "shockers": startling leads that immediately capture the public's attention. The following examples have an unusual twist that adds to their effectiveness:

> On the deadliest day of a horrific week in April 2020, COVID took the lives of 816 people in New York City alone. Lost in the blizzard of pandemic data that's been swirling ever since is the fact that 43-year-old Fernando Morales was one of them.
>
> *(The Associated Press)*
>
> Managua, Nicaragua—She had been raped. She was pregnant. And she was poor. And Rosa was 9. That gave her one more reason to want an abortion.
>
> *(Los Angeles Times)*

8.3.8 Ironic Leads

Closely related to shockers are leads that present a startling or ironic contrast. The use of striking details is likely to arouse curiosity:

> A high-profile pro-gun activist was shot in the back by her four-year-old son after he found her pistol lying on the back seat of her truck just 24 hours after she boasted about his shooting skills online.
>
> *(The Daily Mail)*

> It's just a strange coincidence, West Virginia pols say.
>
> State lawmakers passed a bill allowing people to drink raw milk — then became sick after consuming some.
>
> *(New York Daily News)*

8.3.9 Direct-Address Leads

Reporters occasionally use a form of direct address, speaking directly to their audience:

> SAN FRANCISCO (AP) — Google wants to know where you go so badly that it records your movements even when you explicitly tell it not to.
>
> *(The Associated Press)*

> Say you've had COVID-19. After your quarantine has finished and you're no longer deemed infectious, it's time to return to work.
>
> *(The Washington Post)*

8.3.10 Words Used in Unusual Ways

Journalists who are clever and have a good imagination (or a good grasp of literature) might use a common word or phrase in an uncommon way:

> Sufferin' succotash—Sylvester had better stay home. A statewide vote in Wisconsin could pave the way for legally shooting stray cats there.
>
> *(USA Today)*

> Perhaps it was God's joke on a newly ordained priest when the Rev. Jim Farnan, former class clown and no stranger to the detention room, was asked to speak with the occasional clone of his former self at Our Lady of Fatima School.
>
> *(The Pittsburgh Post-Gazette)*

This style is difficult, because what seems funny or clever to one person may seem corny or silly to another. Also, the subjects may be too serious for such a light touch:

> Oakland County Prosecutor Richard Thompson wants to be known by the criminals he keeps.
>
> *(The Detroit Free Press)*

The story was about the high costs a prosecutor was creating for the county by refusing to plea bargain with criminals.

8.3.11 Other Unusual Leads

The following leads are effective but difficult to categorize. Notice their simplicity, brevity and clarity, as well as their emphasis on the interesting and unusual. The first lead introduces a story describing the effects of uncommonly cold weather on the economy. The second reports the death of actress Audrey Hepburn, who starred in the movie "My Fair Lady." The third introduces the man in charge of demolishing Three Rivers Stadium in Pittsburgh, Pennsylvania.

Washington—Jack Frost is nipping at our growth.

(The Wall Street Journal)

Audrey Hepburn was the fairest lady of them all.

(The Detroit News)

Circuses have ringmasters. Military boot camps have drill sergeants. The Three Rivers Stadium implosion has Greg Yesko, who's a bit of both.

(The Pittsburgh Post-Gazette)

Guest Columnist

No Story Is Too Small

BY MARY GRACE KELLER

I've spent hours reporting on chickens.

Sitting in a borough hall in rural south central Pennsylvania years ago, I watched one resident after another stand up to address the members of the borough council.

The topic at hand was whether the council should allow residents to keep up to six chickens outside certain types of homes.

One resident said they'd like to be able to raise chickens for eggs to feed their family.[1] Another person expressed concern over the potential hazards to public health chickens could bring.

When the discussion continued at a second meeting, a resident threatened to sue[2] his neighbor for having chickens. People were fired up about this.

I'd just graduated with my journalism degree from Shippensburg University a few months prior.

Chicken reporting wasn't the beat I had in mind when I got hired at my first daily newspaper. I wanted to change the world with journalism, cover big stories and undercover wrongdoing.

I remember filing my chicken stories, incredulous at how much locals cared about the topic.

These were chickens, for cluck's sake.

But it didn't matter what I thought of backyard chickens.

The duty of small-town reporters—frankly, any reporter—is to cover the issues that affect the community they serve.

The local reporter is the one that will tell residents if their taxes are going up, when the old road will get fixed, if the pool has enough lifeguards to open this summer or whether elected officials are carrying out their promises to voters.

Small-town reporters write about your 100-year-old neighbor's birthday or the crowning of the next dairy princess. These stories may seem inconsequential, but they matter.

When that elderly neighbor dies, the stories they told will become part of history and the article chronicling that person's life will be a cherished family keepsake. The dairy princess may go on to study agriculture and find new ways to better grow crops that feed the community.

Reporting has a ripple effect.

While covering municipal government, there were times when I was the only person in the audience at a meeting. Then at the next meeting, I'd see a group of citizens come to share their concerns after reading the paper. Elected officials were held to task and forced to listen.

Research shows local news has a direct impact on government and civic engagement.

A working paper[3]—published in 2018 and written by professors at the University of Notre Dame and University of Illinois at Chicago—found that when newspapers close, municipal borrowing costs increase by hundreds of thousands of dollars on average.

Local news can provide a place for voters to obtain unbiased, fact-checked information about those in power. Studies show citizens are less likely to vote, be politically informed and run for office when local news disappears, according to a 2019 PEN America report.[4] The same report cites the work of The Flint Journal, which first reported residents experiencing water issues in the Michigan city in 2014.

But whether you're on the cusp of breaking the story that will make national headlines or listening to locals squabble about chickens, know that your words have an impact.

No story is too small. No community is undeserving of news coverage.

Mary Grace Keller is an award-winning journalist who has worked at local newspapers in Pennsylvania and Maryland covering crime, local government, education and business. She is a 2016 graduate of Shippensburg University of Pennsylvania.

[1] https://www.gettysburgtimes.com/local_updates/article_f85b8a51-1b8c-52fd-ab72-485c013991bc.html

[2] https://www.gettysburgtimes.com/news/local/article_e6457bcf-00e3-5a33-b912-98e4d54e50da.html

[3] https://www.brookings.edu/research/financing-dies-in-darkness-the-impact-of-newspaper-closures-on-public-finance/

[4] https://pen.org/wp-content/uploads/2019/12/Losing-the-News-The-Decimation-of-Local-Journalism-and-the-Search-for-Solutions-Report.pdf

The Reporter's Guide to Writing Alternative Leads

1. Be curious. Be observant. Be creative.

2. Make sure the alternative lead is appropriate for the story.

3. Understand that the "news" is still the most important aspect of the story—don't focus on writing a brilliant lead and then not apply the same rigor to the rest of the story.

4. Use alternative leads with the proper story structure.

5. Vary your use of alternative leads. Don't rely on just one or two types because your story leads will become predictable and your writing stilted.

6. Know that some alternative leads—quotation, question and direct-address leads—should be used sparingly. Don't overuse them or they lose their power.

7. Look for a play on words—using words in an unusual way—to catch the audience's attention.

8. Make sure that the alternative lead fits the story in tone and content. Do not use an ironic lead if there is no irony present in the story or a suspenseful lead if the story is merely about a routine government meeting in which there is nothing controversial or suspenseful. Do not try to oversell the story with an alternative lead.

9. When writing question leads, be sure to answer the question in the story, preferably near the question itself.

10. Paint a picture with words when using a descriptive lead to set the scene of the story. Use descriptive nouns and powerful, active verbs.

 ## Review Exercises

1. EVALUATING ALTERNATIVE LEADS

Critically evaluate the following leads, each of which uses one of the alternative forms discussed in this chapter. Select the best ones and explain why they succeed. Point out the flaws in the remaining leads. As you evaluate, look for lessons—"dos and don'ts"— that you can apply to your own work.

1. Are you ready for a big change?

2. "I saw the train coming at us and I knew it would never get stopped."

3. No shirt! No shoes! No service!

   Unfortunately, the 350-pound black bear that wandered into the city limits and pried open a window to break into the Oakhill Restaurant couldn't read. The bear was captured by state game commission officers after it had ransacked the restaurant's kitchen and helped itself to a variety of treats.

4. Amy Clauch sat beside the rough-hewn pine fence, her fingers rubbing the worn knuckles of the knots in the rope she held in her hand.

   The sweet scent of clover hay wafted on the light breeze that blew through the barn. She sucked in a deep breath and held it. The scent lingered. She wished it always would.

   The sun hung in the early morning cobalt blue sky like a spotlight in a theater, illuminating her, the actor on this stage. This is where she wanted to be—free from the confines of the four pale beige walls that surrounded her in clinical sterility for months.

   She tugged at her jeans. Her lips pursed. "You can do this," she whispered in prayer to herself. Clauch rocked the wheelchair to the left and reached for the stirrup hanging limply from the saddle. Pulling herself upright, she grimaced as she felt the braces tighten on her legs. The muscles in her arms clenched as she pulled herself into the saddle. The chestnut mare flinched at the load and Clauch grabbed the worn leather saddle horn to steady herself. Her smile stretched her cheeks to their limit. She was back where she belonged.

It had been eight months since a riding accident left Clauch temporarily paralyzed from the waist down.

5. Too much work. Too many demands. Too many responsibilities. Not enough time.

Stress is killing Americans, the American Medical Association said in a report released Monday.

6. Should high school students have to take a competency test before receiving their diplomas?

7. The state's motorcycle riders won the right today to have the wind in their hair and bugs in their teeth. The state Legislature passed a bill eliminating the state's helmet requirements for riders 18 and older.

8. How much would you pay for, say, a triple heart bypass? Or gallbladder surgery?

As government officials struggle to rein in health care costs without sacrificing the quality of care, they find themselves confronted with the question of who should pay how much.

9. "If we can't solve the state budget crisis today, the students of tomorrow will suffer the consequences," school Superintendent Gary Hubbard said about the state's failure to pass a budget before the start of the school year.

10. The Freedonia County Fair begins today and if you want to catch all the action this week, you better get to the fairgrounds.

11. Billy Lee Anderson pushes the blond hair away from his blue eyes, exposing the dusting of freckles on his forehead.

The 12-year-old sits in a chair that is a bit too adult for his small frame, his feet, clad in gleaming white athletic shoes, dangling several inches above the floor.

There is an air of innocence surrounding the boy that will make it hard for any jury to believe that he could have set the fire that killed his parents and baby sister. But that is what prosecutors will attempt to do as Anderson's murder trial gets underway today.

12. You're driving down a tree-shaded city street when a child runs out from between two parked cars. Could you stop in time?

13. Thompsontown hit a grand slam over the weekend as all four of its Little League teams won their championship games.

14. When Jim and Suzanne Baker left the mall, they were loaded down with Christmas presents and laughing about the surprises they had in store for their children.

Half an hour later, they were dead.

15. It actually was a dark and stormy night when Sharon Murphy sat down in front of her typewriter to start writing her first novel.

2. WRITING ALTERNATIVE LEADS—PRO CHALLENGE

Using techniques you studied in this chapter, write an alternative lead for each of the following stories. Your instructor has leads written by professionals to which you can compare your leads. Correct any errors you find.

1. A group of ecologists and biologists at your university and other schools have come up with a unique idea. They want to transplant African wildlife to the Great Plains of North America. Julie Allen, 1504 Lincoln Drive, is an associate professor of biology at your university. She had this to say about the idea, "I think it would be wonderful to drive across the Great Plains and see lions and elephants and giraffes roaming the prairie." The idea was developed by more than 30 scientists as a way to perpetuate species that are slowly facing extinction because of declining habitat in Africa. The scientists say there is plenty of room left in the American West for these types of animals. Relocating the animals could help them increase their numbers. The plan is being criticized by ranchers, developers and other scientists, who say that it would be difficult to introduce animals to a

place they had never lived. Ranchers, such as Jim Smithson, who lives in North Dakota and is vice president of the Western Stockman's Association, claims such a move would devastate the regions cattle industry. "How many steers or dairy cows can a pride of lions eat in a week?" Smithson said. Supporters of the idea say the animals they want to relocate would be held in large game parks or private reserves. They would not be allowed to roam free. Other critics say the transplanting of alien creatures could have devastating effects on native creatures. The animals being brought to places they have never lived could introduce new diseases or could destroy native wildlife. In addition, taking wildlife from Africa could hurt the tourist trade on that continent.

2. State police trooper Lucas Frank was on routine patrol on Interstate 10 westbound just after 12 p.m. on Wednesday. Traffic was not heavy and the weather was clear. As he was passing the exit for Mount Vernon Street, he noticed a silver late model Ford Explorer coming down the entrance ramp. Corporal Frank moved over into the passing lane to let the SUV merge onto the highway. The driver of the Explorer activated the vehicle's turn signal and pulled onto the interstate. The speed limit on that section of interstate is 55 miles per hour because it runs through a congested area of the city. As the SUV came onto the interstate, Frank noticed that the vehicle was only travelling about 35 to 40 miles per hour. He saw it cross over the line into the passing lane and then swerve back into the right lane. He saw the vehicle travel like this for more than a mile, crossing the line several times and never reaching highway speed. Frank thought he might have an impaired driver. The windows of the vehicle were tinted and he could not see the driver through the rear window. Frank activated his siren and warning lights to pull the car over. The right turn signal of the Explorer started blinking and the vehicle rolled slowly to a stop on the berm of the highway. Frank got out of his patrol car and approached the SUV, wary of what he might find. As he approached the driver's side window, he could still not see the operator of the vehicle and thought perhaps the driver was slumped over in the driver's seat. When he got

closer, he was surprised at the reason he could not see the operator of the vehicle. The driver was less than four feet tall and probably weighed about 40 pounds. Frank motioned to the driver to lower the window and he complied. Frank observed that the boy behind the wheel was sitting as far forward on the seat as he could so he could reach the gas and brake pedals. He had his seat belt on and his hands at the 10 and two position on the steering wheel. The boy had managed to put the vehicle in park when he was stopped by Frank. Frank asked the boy if he had a driver's license and the boy started to cry, saying that he did not. Frank asked how old he was and where he was going. The boy told Frank he was six and that he was going across town to visit a friend of his who had recently moved to another part of the city and they were going to have lunch at McDonald's. His friend really likes the chicken nuggets, the boy told Frank. Both parents were at work at the time. The boy had called his mother to ask her to take him to his friends for lunch but his mother refused, telling him that she could not take off work. She told him that she would take him later. He told Frank that he did not want to go later, he wanted to go now because he missed his friend. The boy said he has an older sister who is ten years old and an older brother who is 16. They were home at the time because school was out for the summer. He wanted his older brother to take him, but his mother told him his brother only has a learner's permit, not a driver's license and cannot drive without having an adult driver in the vehicle. Frank said in his report that the boy got a spare set of keys for the Explorer out a draw in the kitchen. His parents are Franklyn and Rene Peters of 484 Sugar Ridge Court. Police are reviewing the circumstances to determine what, if any, charges to file against the Peterses and the boy. Frank waited at the scene until a tow truck came to get the Peters' vehicle off the road. He put the boy in his patrol car so that he could take him home.

3. It was just one of those days for Representative Constance P. Wei. Wei is the representative for the 86th District. Wei, who lives at 206 North Wabash Avenue, is a proponent of limited government. State representatives have been trying to

pass a ban on using cell phones while driving. Wei thinks it is an infringement on individual rights. "All this is is Big Brother telling you what to do," she said. Advocates of the ban say it is an issue of safety. They point to a recent incident in which five people were killed in a two-car collision. The driver who caused the crash was a 48-year-old man who was talking on his cell phone while trying to pass another car on a two-lane stretch of road. Witnesses said the man swerved into the path of the other car and the two vehicles collided head-on. Two of the five people killed were children. The state legislature has never backed a ban on cell phone use, but other states have instituted successful bans. Opponents of the ban, including Wei, claim the ban will not affect safety because forcing people to pull off the road and get out of their cars to talk on the phone could be more hazardous. In addition, opponents say that the state cannot ban all distractions drivers create, such as eating, reading or applying makeup while driving. Proponents of the ban want it to take affect in January of next year. Wei was on her cell phone Wednesday as she was driving home. She was talking to State representative Peter Mackey, 89th District, about postponing a vote on the bill banning cell phone use while driving when her Cadillac Sedan de Ville struck the rear of a car driven by Michael Jeffreys, 41, of 2781 Collins Ave. Jeffreys suffered minor injuries and was taken to Mercy Hospital. He was treated and released. Police said the crash occurred at 5:37 p.m. at the intersection of 29th Street and Melrose Avenue. Jeffreys was stopped at a traffic light. Wei did not see the red light or the cars stopped in front of her and rammed the rear of Jeffreys Toyota Camry. Police said the Camry suffered severe damage. Weis Cadillac sustained an estimated $8,000 in damage.

4. It's a unique idea. The National Association of School Boards said it had no record of any other district doing it or considering it. School board members and school administrators in your local school district are considering changing the school week to cut costs. The state announced that it does not have enough money to fund schools because of the slow economy and schools will have to cut their budgets. Superintendent of schools Gary Hubbard told school board members at Monday night's meeting that the district has cut all the fat out of the budget that it can. "We've cut out after-school programs and eliminated all but the essential teacher's aides positions," Hubbard said. "We've even raised the price of school lunches, but we are still coming up short." Hubbard and school board members are proposing to go to a four-day school week to help the district save money. The school day, which now runs from 8 a.m. to 2:30 p.m. would be lengthened by two hours, running from 8 a.m. to 4:30 p.m. to make up for the loss of one day during the week. Hubbard and the board say the district could save more then one million dollars in transportation, food service and janitorial costs. The board voted 7-0 in favor of the proposal.

5. Your city officials received a gift on Tuesday. Attorney Richard Cycler handed a check for over $2 million to Mayor Sabrina Datolli. The money will be used to build the Willie Hattaway Center in an annex of City Hall. Plans to develop the annex into a community center, senior citizens center, a historical exhibit hall and meeting and conference rooms had been postponed for several years because of a lack of funds to complete the project. The city had built the annex with money from a federal grant but could not raise enough money to complete the project. The building has been an empty shell for more than seven years. City officials were using the space to store boxes of old water bills and other papers. Willie Hattaway gave the money to the city in his will. Hattaway died last year. He was 98. He was a widower. His wife, Estelle, died 10 years ago. Everyone, including his neighbors, was surprised that Willie had that much money in the bank. Willie lived in a modest two-story, white clapboard house on Virginia Avenue for more than 60 years. Flowers surrounded the house. Hattaway loved to work in his garden and flower beds. He was particularly fond of roses and grew several assorted varieties. He had entered Sunnyview Retirement Home on Wisconsin Avenue last year, shortly after his 97th birthday. Neighbors said he could no longer take care of himself after he fell and broke his

hip. Neighbors said Hattaway drove a car that was 40 years old and never traveled very far from home. The car, a green Chevrolet Impala, is still parked in the garage. Hattaway did not want to sell the car even though he had not been driving since he was 90. He enjoyed sitting on his porch and talking to neighbors or giving neighborhood children treats of candy or fruit. He did not live extravagantly. "It just goes to show that you never really know your neighbors. Willie was such a wonderful, friendly gentleman. He was so generous with his time helping neighbors and playing with the neighborhood children. It doesn't surprise me that he would be so generous with his money, too," said a former neighbor Marilyn Boudinot, 41, of 4340 Virginia Ave. Hattaway and his wife had no children. He was a retired construction worker who had invested his money in the stock market for many years.

6. It was an unusually harsh sentence, according to some people. Sarah Zerwinn, 27, of 2021 Dyan Way, was sentenced yesterday by Circuit Court Judge JoAnn Keappler. Zerwinn was sentenced to 60 days in jail for failing to take her daughter to kindergarten. Or Zerwinn could go back to school. Public education is compulsory in the state, and school officials have been asking the courts for years to provide stiffer penalties for the parents of chronically truant children. School officials say that children who fall behind early because they do not attend school regularly have a harder time succeeding in the higher grades. Zerwins daughter, Jennifer, who is six years old, missed 111 out of 180 days of school last year and was late an additional 21 times. All of the absences were unexcused.

Jennifer told school officials that her mother often slept late and was not able to help Jennifer get ready for school. Several months ago, school officials declared Jennifer a habitual truant, and Zerwinn was ordered to appear in court. A judge ordered Zerwinn to make sure Jennifer attended school, but the absences continued. Zerwinn was taken back to court by school officials and Kaeppler found her in contempt of a court order to ensure she took her daughter to school. After pronouncing the sentence, Zerwinn was led away in handcuffs. Zerwinns attorney, Miguel Aceveda, asked the judge not to sentence his client to jail, but give her probation instead. Kaeppler said during the sentencing that Zerwinn could avoid jail time if she agreed to attend kindergarten with her daughter to make certain that she attended and got there on time. Zerwinn would have to attend the classes her daughter attends and participate in the activities here daughter does. "Perhaps you will learn something about the importance of your daughters education," Kaeppler said. Acevede told the court that Zerwinn works nights and is unable to wake up in time to get her daughter ready for and off to school. However, Kaeppler said that is no excuse for Zerwinns failure to provide an education for her daughter. Acevde told the judge he felt the judges sentence was too harsh because it would place an unreasonable burden on the defendant. Karen Bulnes, attorney for the school board who brought the case against Zerwinn, said, "I certainly think this sends a message that the courts are willing to take a strong stance against parents of chronically truant children. We are doing this for the good of the children."

9

THE BODY OF A NEWS STORY

The portion of a news story that follows the lead, called the "body," contains the information a reporter believes the public needs to know. This information can be presented in several styles: inverted pyramid, hourglass, focus or narrative. While no single technique works best for all stories, each requires thorough reporting, organization and effective presentation. Whatever story style writers choose, they must determine how best to convey information to the audience.

Think of writing a news story as driving a train along a track. The rails are the story's central point and give the story direction. The railroad ties—who, what, when, where, why and how—provide a foundation. The train's engine is the lead; it must be strong enough to pull the rest of the story, and its whistle must capture the public's attention. Each car that follows represents a paragraph containing information and providing structure; these "cars" can be arranged in whatever sequence—for example, from most important to least or chronologically—seems most effective. Cars filled with research, verification, multiple sources, quotes, anecdotes and descriptions strengthen the train. The amount of information needed to complete the story determines the number of cars. Holding the train cars together are couplings, which represent the transitions between paragraphs. Without strong transitions, the paragraphs disconnect from one another and the story does not flow smooothly.

This chapter discusses the writing styles and techniques reporters often use to write effective bodies for their news stories.

9.1 The Inverted-Pyramid Style

Inverted-pyramid stories arrange the information in descending order of importance or newsworthiness. The lead states the most newsworthy, important or striking information and establishes the central point for the rest of the story. The lead for an inverted-pyramid story is most often a summary lead, like those described in Chapter 7. The second paragraph (and sometimes the third and fourth) provides details that amplify the lead. Subsequent paragraphs add less important details or introduce subordinate topics. Each paragraph presents additional information: names, descriptions, quotations, conflicting viewpoints, explanations and background data. Beginning reporters must learn this style because it helps them decide what is most important and what is least important. It also helps discover holes in their information—details that have not been collected and need to be found.

Audiences skim pages whether they are reading in print or online. Headlines attract their attention, and the lead pulls them into the story. The inverted-pyramid story structure can give the audience important information about events quickly.

The primary advantage of the inverted pyramid is that it allows someone to leave a story after only one or two paragraphs yet still learn the newest, most newsworthy and most important facts. Another benefit is that it helps the reporter to organize the story's information. The inverted pyramid also ensures that the main facts of the story are immediately understandable. Moreover, if a story is longer than the space or time available, editors can easily shorten it by deleting paragraphs from the end.

The inverted-pyramid style also has several disadvantages:

- Because the lead summarizes facts that later paragraphs discuss in greater detail, some may be repeated in the body.
- A story that follows the inverted pyramid rarely contains any surprises; the lead immediately reveals the major facts.
- The inverted-pyramid style evolved when newspapers were the public's first source for breaking news; now radio, television, social media and the internet fill that role.
- Readers with less than a high school education cannot easily understand stories written in this style.
- The inverted pyramid locks reporters into a formula and discourages them from trying new styles.

Many writing coaches discourage using the inverted pyramid, saying it is overused, confusing and often irrelevant. Nevertheless, the style remains a common format for organizing news stories, partly because of its inherent advantages and partly because using it is a difficult habit to break. It also is effective for writing quick briefs of information to upload to the internet and social media. The daily—or sometimes hourly—deadline pressures in the age of the internet and social

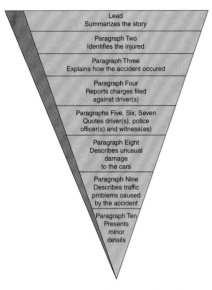

FIGURE 9.1 Inverted-Pyramid Style

media make it difficult to develop new styles or use more complex story structures because they require more time, critical thinking and, perhaps, more rewriting to be effective.

9.1.1 Organizing the Information

An inverted-pyramid story about a two-car collision that injured several people might contain a sequence of paragraphs similar to those outlined in Figure 9.1. Normally, reporters emphasize people: what they do and what happens to them. Consequently, the injuries to the people would be described early in the story. Damage to the cars is less important and would be reported later; it might also be left out, unless it was unusual. Paragraph three would describe the accident itself—the recent action and main point of the story. Quotations add detail and color as well as a pleasing change of pace. The remaining paragraphs add less essential information and might be deleted if space or time was limited.

The exact organization varies depending on the story's unique facts and most newsworthy points. The second, third and, maybe, fourth paragraphs should provide details that develop and support the lead. The following inverted-pyramid stories are cohesive because the leads summarize their topics and the second and third paragraphs present their most important details. Neither story ends with a summary or conclusion; instead, the final paragraphs present the least important details.

LAVALE — A Lonaconing man who allegedly robbed M&T Bank's LaVale branch late Thursday morning was apprehended minutes later by Maryland State Police troopers at the nearby Arby's restaurant.

Police said Leonard Kaschenbach, 62, was armed with a handgun when he entered the bank just after 10:30 a.m. and handed the teller a note demanding money. The bank is located at 1201 National Highway, adjacent to the state police barracks.

Kaschenbach was given an undisclosed amount of cash and fled on foot, reportedly crossing National Highway and heading south on Campground Road.

Police said a witness helped them locate Kaschenbach in the restaurant. Kaschenbach was arrested without incident.

Investigators from the Allegany County Combined Criminal Investigative Unit responded to the scene and are assisting in the investigation. Personnel from the Allegany County Sheriff's Office and Maryland State Fire Marshal's Office also assisted.

Anyone with information is asked to call the Allegany & Mineral County Crime Solvers at 301-722-4300.

(The Cumberland [Maryland] Times-News)

HARRISBURG, Pa. (AP)—Lawmakers overwhelmingly passed the main Pennsylvania state budget bill Friday, more than a week after it was due—a plan fattened by federal stimulus cash and unusually robust state tax collections.

Big winners were public schools, environmental programs and long-term care facilities, but the budget also will leave some $5 billion in the state's rainy-day fund, create a multibillion-dollar cushion for next year and cut the tax on corporate net income.

The Senate approved the bill 47-3 after the House passed it by a similar margin the prior evening. A spokesperson for Democratic Gov. Tom Wolf said he will sign it.

"This is government, this is progress," said Appropriations Chairperson Pat Browne, R-Lehigh, shortly before the vote.

The $42.8 billion general fund spending plan includes hundreds of millions to clean streams and renovate or repair parks and forest land, and new money for home repairs, flood control, sewer and water infrastructure, child care, additional state troopers, anti-gun violence efforts and mental health support. Along with $2.4 billion in federal American Rescue Plan Act and federal Medicaid match money, the total spending is $45.2 billion.

(Associated Press)

In the first example, the last two paragraphs provide additional, but not necessarily essential, information. The second example contained a total of 14 paragraphs; the last nine provided more detailed information about where the money was being spent and comments from legislators about the budget negotiations. An editor could easily cut the final paragraphs of either story and still retain the essential facts at the beginning without affecting significant information the reader needs.

Many of the facts reported in longer news stories are of approximately equal importance. These stories are more likely to resemble Figure 9.1. However, other stories are organized in the manner shown in Figure 9.2.

Immediately after the diagram's summary lead, Section 1 presents several paragraphs that contain information of roughly equivalent importance. Those paragraphs may present some additional information about a single topic or several different but related subtopics. Section 2 may describe a somewhat less important aspect of the story. Section 3 presents more facts of about equal importance to one another but of less importance than those in Section 2. Section 4 contains the least important details, perhaps routine procedures, background information or a reminder of related or similar incidents that occurred in the past.

9.1.2 Writing the Second Paragraph

The second paragraph in a news story is almost as important as the lead—and almost as difficult to write. Like the lead, the second paragraph should emphasize the news. In addition, it should provide a smooth, logical transition from the lead to the following paragraphs. When using the delayed-identification style of summary lead (discussed in Chapter 7), it is important to identify the story's source or subject in the second paragraph. Journalists must also use an effective transitional word or phrase to ensure that the audience understands the connection of

FIGURE 9.2 An Alternative Inverted-Pyramid Style

the source or subject identified in the opening paragraph. Here is an example of a lead and second paragraph:

> An Indiana woman died early Monday morning in a fiery three-vehicle accident on the Pennsylvania Turnpike that closed the highway for more than six hours.
>
> The victim, Mary A. Burnett, 56, of Bloomington, lost control of her SUV, crossed the median and collided with an oncoming westbound tractor-trailer, according to Pennsylvania State Police.

Note that the words "The victim" are used as a transitional device to identify "Mary A. Burnett" as the "Indiana woman" used in the lead to avoid confusion.

Sometimes reporters fail to emphasize the news in a story's second paragraph. Other times they fail to provide smooth transitions. As a result, their stories seem dull or disorganized. The following sections discuss both of these problems and present some solutions.

9.1.2.1 AVOID LEAPFROGGING

Journalists often introduce an individual in their lead and begin their second paragraph with a name. However, many fail to say clearly that both refer to the same person. The audience is forced to guess. Most people usually guess right— but not always.

This problem is so common that it has a name: "leapfrogging." To avoid it, provide a one- or two-word transition from the lead to the name in the second paragraph:

- ALLENTOWN (AP)—A man rammed his car into his wife's car, then shot her in the arm and leg before bystanders tackled him, police said.

    the man suspected of the attack,
    Police expressed gratitude to the bystanders who helped bring ∧ Felipe M. Santos, 53, of Allentown ∧ into custody Monday.

9.1.2.2 CONTINUE WITH THE NEWS

After providing a smooth transition between the lead and the second paragraph, continue with information about the topic summarized in your lead. Some reporters shift to a different topic, a mistake certain to cause confusion:

> The mayor and City Council agreed Monday night to freeze wages and make city workers pay more for benefits in an effort to close a budget deficit that is now larger than officials expected.
>
> Mayor Sabrina Datolli, who has been a lifelong resident of the city, is in her fourth term as mayor. She has seen many ups and downs over her years as mayor, but hopes the city can overcome its problems.

This story seems to discuss two different topics. The lead summarizes a problem that confronts city officials everywhere: balancing budgets. The second paragraph shifts to the mayor's career and hopes. It fails even to mention the problem of balancing the budget. The following revision corrects the error:

The mayor and City Council agreed Monday night to freeze wages and make city workers pay more for benefits in an effort to close a budget deficit that is now larger than officials expected.

Mayor Sabrina Datolli said the wage freeze and other measures are needed to prevent layoffs of city employees, cuts in programs and more drastic fiscal surgery to balance the city's budget.

9.1.2.3 NAMES, NAMES: DULL, DULL

Reporters sometimes place too much emphasis on their sources' identities. As a result, their second paragraphs fail to convey any information of interest. Consider the following example:

A highway engineer was killed Wednesday at an Interstate 95 construction site when a tractor-trailer owned by Shearson Trucking Inc. plowed through a concrete barrier and struck him.

A materials engineer, Riley Patterson of Independent Testing Laboratory Inc., was killed in the mishap. Jonathan Martin, a site manager for Baldini Construction Co., saw the accident happen.

The paragraph can be rewritten to emphasize the news—what the source said, saw or did, not who he is:

A tractor-trailer plowed through a concrete barrier at an Interstate 95 construction site Monday, killing a highway engineer.

The force of the crash pushed the concrete barrier into a piece of road equipment, crushing the engineer, Riley Patterson. Patterson had been using a core-drilling machine to bore a sample hole in the concrete roadbed when the accident occurred. He was pronounced dead at the scene.

Jonathan Martin, a worker at the site, said he saw the truck crash through the barrier but could not warn Patterson because of the noise of the drilling machine.

9.1.2.4 BACKGROUND: TOO MUCH, TOO SOON

Avoid devoting the entire second paragraph to background information. The second paragraph in the following story is dull because it emphasizes routine, insignificant details:

Local Red Cross officials expressed alarm Wednesday that blood supplies are dangerously low prior to the beginning of the long holiday weekend.

Nancy Cross, executive director of the Broward County Chapter of the American Red Cross, said the Red Cross strives to maintain an adequate blood supply for emergency situations. "The role of the Red Cross since it was founded is to help people during times of need," she said.

The story shifts from the news—the lack of adequate blood supplies—to the organization's purpose. Yet that purpose has not changed since the Red Cross was established. Thus, the second paragraph says nothing new, nothing likely to retain interest in the story. Fortunately, the problem is easy to correct:

> Local Red Cross officials expressed alarm Wednesday that blood supplies are dangerously low heading into the long holiday weekend.
>
> Restocking those supplies will require a 50 percent increase in blood donations over the next three days, said Nancy Cross, executive director of the Broward County Chapter of the American Red Cross.
>
> "Holiday periods are often a problem because people are traveling or have other plans and don't think about the need for blood," Cross said. "But the holiday period is also a busy time for emergency rooms and trauma centers, which increases the demand for blood."

The revised second and third paragraphs describe the solution to the blood supply problem and explain the reasons for the issue—details central to the story, not minor or unnecessary ones.

9.1.3 Ending the Story

The term "kicker" can have two meanings: It can refer to an additional line set above the main head of a story that helps draw attention or to the ending of the story. Ending the story well is important because it helps to nail down the central point and can leave a lasting impression in people's minds. Sometimes the kicker, in the latter sense of the word, is just as important as the lead.

By default, many writers will use a dramatic quote to end the story. While this can be an effective kicker, there are other ways to end a story that rely on the reporter's skills of observation and creativity to tell the audience the story is over. Waiting until the end to use a dramatic quote can often diminish its power. It may be better to use an anecdote that ties into the story's lead, describe a scene as a wrap-up, or focus on a detail, such as a statistic, that is tied to the central point.

Here are the first several paragraphs from a story in The Washington Post about how the highest rate of inflation in 40 years was affecting the economy and ordinary people as well as how government officials are tackling it:

> Inflation soared in June, continuing to climb at the fastest pace in 40 years across many sectors of the economy, driven in large part by higher energy prices.
>
> The blistering consumer price index was 9.1 percent higher in June than it was compared to a year ago, and 1.3 percent higher than it was in May, according to a report released Wednesday by the Bureau of Labor Statistics, revealing scant signs of progress in the fight against inflation. The last time inflation reached over 9 percent was November 1981.
>
> The June data showed broad increases in the prices of food, energy and housing, confirming that inflation is now the nation's most challenging economic problem, while raising new fears that other sources

of strength in the economy — like the labor market and consumer spending — won't be enough to fend off another recession.

The story continues, providing statistical information and facts provided by government officials and economic experts. Other subsequent paragraphs describe how the jump in inflation is affecting ordinary citizens and businesses, with quotes from several sources. The last three paragraphs form the kicker, tying the story to the central point:

> The Fed hiked interest rates by three-quarters of a percentage point in June, marking its sharpest increase since 2000. In the past few weeks, several Fed leaders have suggested that another hike of three-quarters of a percentage point may be necessary at their next policy meeting later this month. It's unclear whether the June data will push the Fed in an even stronger direction. Asked about the possibility of a full-percentage-point hike, Atlanta Fed President Raphael Bostic told reporters Wednesday that "everything is in play." (Bostic does not have a vote on the Fed's policy committee this year.)

> The Fed's argument is that the economy, though burdened by high inflation, is still solid enough to withstand higher interest rates.

> "The U.S. economy for now is strong. Spending is strong. Consumers are in good shape. Businesses are in good shape," Fed Chair Jerome H. Powell told the Senate Banking Committee on June 22. "Monetary policy is famously a blunt tool. And there's risk that weaker outcomes are certainly possible. But they're not our intent."

Notice that the second paragraph at the beginning of the story builds on the lead and adds detail to the central point it introduced. The last three paragraphs of the 34-paragraph story mention details about the efforts government officials are taking to tame inflation and their outlook for the economy. The story ends with a quote kicker from Federal Reserve Chair Jerome H. Powell.

This story from the Michigan Advance reports on government efforts to identify and preserve old-growth forests:

> President Joe Biden signed an executive order Friday to establish a federal strategy to protect old-growth forests, a move the administration says will help curb destructive wildfires and fight climate change.

> The Earth Day order tasks the Interior and Agriculture departments with creating a federal definition of old-growth and mature forests. Such forests are generally considered to be areas where trees are at least 60 years old and have not been meaningfully affected by humans.

> The agencies would build a database of forests on federal lands within a year, then create "climate-smart management" strategies to protect the forests. The order also directs the departments to establish 2030 targets for reforestation.

The second paragraph explains what the executive order entails, adding details to the central point for the rest of the story—the government's efforts to save and protect the nation's dwindling old-growth forests. In the story, the writer provides facts on the importance of old-growth forests as a natural way to combat climate change and offers statements from government officials and environmental experts who support the initiative. The story ends with a kicker that explains the significance of the executive order to the president's agenda:

> The executive order comes at the end of a week in which the White House has sought to spotlight its climate efforts after a rocky period for Biden's climate agenda.
>
> Though he secured some climate provisions in the infrastructure law, court orders, opposition from members of Congress and the administration's attention on other crises have stalled other priorities.

The following story from The New York Times about scientific research on Australian magpies begins with an explanation of the species' innate intelligence. The last paragraph, the kicker, asks a question that ties back to the beginning.

> The Australian magpie is one of the cleverest birds on earth. It has a beautiful song of extraordinary complexity. It can recognize and remember up to 30 different human faces.
>
> But Australians know magpies best for their penchant for mischief. An enduring rite of passage of an Australian childhood is dodging the birds every spring as they swoop down to attack those they view as a threat.
>
> Magpies' latest mischief has been to outwit the scientists who would study them. Scientists showed in a study published last month in the journal Australian Field Ornithology just how clever magpies really are and, in the process, revealed a highly unusual example in nature of birds helping one another without any apparent tangible benefit to themselves.

The kicker of the 21-paragraph story ties into the central point and leaves the reader to ponder future research:

> Dr. Jones calls the magpies' "gorgeous, glorious caroling song" another example of their intelligence.
>
> With more than 300 separate elements, he said, "it's unbelievably complex. In order to remember and repeat a song of that complexity every single morning without error, you have to have a big brain."
>
> Dr. Potvin and her team have shelved their original study. But they can't help but ponder a bigger question: "What else are magpies capable of?"

9.1.4 Complex Stories

Stories that contain several major subtopics may be too complex to summarize in a brief lead. Government organizations at all levels hold meetings that may cover many topics of concern and may make multiple decisions or take action on several of those topics. Some topics and actions by governmental agencies or organizations may be more important than others. Two or three may be important, but most news outlets report them all in a single story to save space and time. Because reporters can mention only the one or two most significant actions in their leads, they often summarize the remaining ones in the second, and sometimes the third, paragraphs of their stories.

After summarizing all the major actions, reporters discuss each in more detail, starting with the most important. By mentioning the important actions taken in their stories' opening paragraphs, journalists alert the audience to their entire contents. People interested in the second or third action immediately learn that it will be discussed later in the story. If the lead and following paragraphs mention only the most important action, people might mistakenly assume that the entire story concerns that one decision by government officials. Many might stop reading before reaching the story's account of other actions that might be of greater interest to them.

The following story begins with the Supreme Court's most important, compelling or interesting decision and, in subsequent paragraphs, lists other decisions handed down the same day:

> WASHINGTON—The Supreme Court Monday refused to overturn a ban on the private possession of machine guns. A National Rifle Association lawyer called it "the first ban on firearms possession by law-abiding citizens in American history."
>
> In a defeat for the NRA, the justices refused to hear a Georgia gun manufacturer's argument that the Second Amendment "right of the people to keep and bear arms" allows him to make or possess a fully automatic weapon.
>
> The Court also decided cases involving anti-abortion protests, the sanctuary movement, libel and local regulation.
>
> NRA lobbyist Jack Lenzi said his organization was "disappointed but not surprised." He said the federal ban is "an infringement on the rights" of about 100,000 Americans who collect automatic weapons.
>
> Gun control and law enforcement groups told the high court that the NRA's argument would permit private persons to have "bazookas, hand grenades, Stinger missiles and any other weapon of mass destruction. . . . The public safety implications of such a position are truly staggering."
>
> In other matters, the court:
>
> ● Refused to lift limits on demonstrations by opponents of abortions at a Dayton, Ohio, abortion clinic and a ban on protests by the opponents at the homes of the clinic's staff and patients.
>
> ● Left intact the criminal convictions of eight sanctuary movement members who helped Central American aliens smuggled into this country.

- Heard arguments in a libel case in which a psychologist says a New Yorker magazine staff writer made up quotes attributed to him.

- Agreed to decide whether communities may regulate the use of pesticides or whether such local regulations are pre-empted by federal law.

Journalists often use lists in news stories that involve several ideas, subtopics or examples. If all the ideas or examples are important, reporters may begin a news story by summarizing one or two main points, adding a brief transition and presenting the other ideas or examples in a simple, orderly list. They can discuss each point in greater detail later in the story. The initial summary may contain all the essential information about a topic; in that case, it need not be mentioned again.

Each item in a list must be in parallel form. If one item is an incomplete sentence that begins with a verb, the rest must have the same structure, as in the following example:

The governor said he wants to raise the state's sales tax and to increase state spending on education.

He told the National Education Association he would use the money to:

- Raise teachers' salaries.

- Test new teachers to assess their competence.

- Place more emphasis on English, science and math.

- Reduce the number of students in each class.

- Give schools more money to educate gifted students.

Reporters also use lists to summarize less important details placed at the end of news stories. Lists are particularly useful when the details are minor and concern several diverse topics that would be difficult to organize in any other manner. Some newspapers number each item in a list; others mark each item with a dash, bullet, asterisk, check mark or some other typographical symbol.

9.2 The Hourglass Style

Roy Peter Clark, former senior scholar at The Poynter Institute, found that the inverted pyramid often forced writers to tell their stories in unnatural ways. It also homogenized the news, making stories about bank robberies and congressional debates sound similar. At the same time, writers who experimented with narrative structures for their stories often lost sight of the news. The most important and newsworthy information might be buried so far down that frustrated audiences never found it. Clark offered the hourglass style (Figure 9.3) as one that combines the strengths of the inverted pyramid and the narrative format (discussed later in the chapter).

The hourglass story has three parts: an inverted pyramid top that summarizes the most newsworthy information, a turn (or pivot) paragraph and a narrative. The inverted pyramid top, which may be only three to five paragraphs, gives the

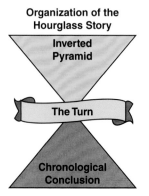

Organization of the Hourglass Story

Inverted Pyramid

The Turn

Chronological Conclusion

FIGURE 9.3 The Hourglass Style

audience the most newsworthy information quickly. The narrative allows the writer to develop the story in depth, using the storytelling power of chronology. The key, Clark says, is the turn, which makes the transition between the two formats.

In an Associated Press story about the investigation into the police response to the shooting at the Robb Elementary School in Uvalde, Texas, reporters Acacia Coronado and Jay Reeves begin with a summary lead followed by seven paragraphs that provide facts supporting the central point of the story:

> UVALDE, Texas (AP) — The state agency investigating the mass shooting at an elementary school in Uvalde has determined that the commander facing criticism for the slow police response was not carrying a radio as the massacre unfolded, a Texas state senator said Friday.
>
> Sen. Roland Gutierrez told the Associated Press in a brief telephone interview that a Texas Department of Public Safety official told him school district police Chief Pete Arredondo was without a radio during the May 24 attack by a lone gunman at Robb Elementary School that left 19 students and two teachers dead. Seventeen more people were injured.

The story then pivots into a chronology of events with the turn:

> The news emerged amid tensions between state and local authorities over how police handled the shooting and communicated what happened to the public.

Following the turn are several paragraphs that provide the chronology. The chronology is then followed by several paragraphs of additional information to complete the story:

> The gunman in Uvalde, 18-year-old Salvador Ramos, spent roughly 80 minutes inside the school, and more than an hour passed from when the first officers followed him into the building and when he was killed by law enforcement, according to an official timeline.
>
> Ramos slipped through an unlocked door into adjoining fourth-grade classrooms at 11:33, authorities said. He rapidly fired off more than 100 rounds.
>
> Officers entered minutes later, exchanging fire with Ramos, and by 12:03 there were as many as 19 officers in the hallway outside the classroom, McCraw said. Authorities have not said where Arredondo was during this period.
>
> Officers from other agencies urged the school police chief to let them move in because children were in danger, according to two law enforcement officials who spoke on condition of anonymity because they had not been authorized to discuss the investigation publicly.
>
> A U.S. Border Patrol tactical team used a school employee's key to unlock the classroom door and kill the gunman around 12:50 p.m., McCraw said.

While the hourglass story structure doesn't work for every story, some news beats will employ the style more than others. Journalists on the sports beat often use the hourglass style for their stories. In a 16-paragraph story, The New York Times describes how the U.S. women's national soccer team clinched a spot in the 2023 Women's World Cup.

The story opened with a lead stating the women's team had accomplished one of its objectives by defeating Jamaica at the CONCACAF (Confederation of North, Central American and Caribbean Association Football) women's championship match. Subsequent paragraphs added some of the most important facts about the match and its meaning for the team's progress toward the finals. The ninth paragraph is the turn: It tells the reader what the next goal of the team is.

> The next goal for the United States, meanwhile, will be securing a place in the Paris Olympics. Only the winner of the CONCACAF tournament will earn a direct place in that tournament, though there will be a lifeline for the runner-up and third-place nations through a CONCACAF Olympic playoff in September 2023.

The remainder of the story adds quotations and anecdotes and concludes with a chronology of the scoring and some final details.

The hourglass style will not work for all stories, as Clark admits. For stories that have no meaningful chronology, such as an account of a city council meeting in which topics are discussed in no particular order, the hourglass style is useless. But for stories about many newsworthy events—sports contests, criminal investigations, natural disasters and political campaigns—the hourglass can be an effective way of organizing information.

9.3 The Focus Style

The Wall Street Journal's front-page feature stories usually employ the focus style, which the newspaper has used for years. Many other newspapers and their reporters have adopted the focus style as well. Like the hourglass style, this method tries to incorporate storytelling techniques in news writing. But unlike the hourglass, the focus story begins with a lead that focuses on a specific individual, situation or anecdote and uses it to illustrate a larger problem.

The focus story has four parts. The first is the lead; unlike the lead for an inverted pyramid story, it may run three or more paragraphs. Also, unlike the hard news lead, the focus lead describes a person, place, situation or event that may not be newsworthy by itself but exemplifies a larger problem that is newsworthy. Such leads are described in Chapter 8.

The second part of the focus story is a nut graph—which can actually be two or three paragraphs—stating the central point of the story and how the lead illustrates that point. The nut graph in a focus story accomplishes the same thing the summary lead does for an inverted-pyramid story. The third part is the body, which develops the central point in detail. The final part is a one-, two- or three-paragraph close kicker that concludes the story. The kicker usually relates to the person, place or situation described in the lead.

The following excerpts from a story in U.S. News and World Report about tobacco use in Kentucky demonstrates some elements of a focus story:

> Having returned to work as a hospital administrator in Russell Springs, Kentucky, not long after her final chemotherapy treatment, Teresa Spaw learned the hold cigarette smoking had on her co-workers.

The focus style begins with a focus lead, an anecdote of one to several paragraphs that highlights someone involved in the story. That person's experiences are used to introduce the story.

> "I was trying to help them roll out a tobacco-free initiative where the grounds will be free from tobacco, and we had a difficult time," says Spaw, then the director of administrative services at Russell County Hospital and a former smoker who'd just lost a lung to cancer. "It was 2011. I was sitting in a conference room, still bald from chemo, with a scarf on my head, listening to people say, 'I have a right to smoke. I'm not hurting anyone but me.'"

The beginning of the story is often very descriptive in order to give a general impression of what the story is about and dramatically highlights the experiences of the person in the focus lead.

> Spaw, 58, knew that wasn't true. She lost her father, 40 years old and a longtime smoker, to lung cancer. Her toddler son hated Spaw's secondhand smoke, and she was "bad with money," yet still bought cigarettes. When doctors diagnosed her with cancer years later, Spaw's son, then in high school, was depressed and worried.
>
> "He said, 'Mom, I knew it was bad, because no one can look at you without crying,'" Spaw says.
>
> So when her co-workers argued smoking only hurts the smoker, "I just wanted to scream," Spaw says. No one is in it alone, she says, because "everyone who knew and loved me got a front-row seat to the terrifying world of cancer."
>
> While the hospital did become a smoke-free workplace, experts say Spaw's experience is typical in many Kentucky localities. Nearly six decades after a landmark government report identified the dangers of smoking — and with data showing the percentage of smokers has plunged nationally — the adult cigarette smoking rate in Kentucky is far above the national rate. Experts say the Bluegrass State's agricultural history, along with deeply entrenched economic interests and the state's identity as a tobacconist to the world, combine to keep smoking rates stubbornly high.

The nut graph of the story is used to create a transition from the focus lead into the body. The latter then adds details about the subject of the story.

The first paragraphs of the story describe the focus, the sometimes-difficult struggle to convince others of the dangers of smoking. The writer introduces Teresa Spaw and describes her battle with cancer and how it influenced her to push to ban smoking in her workplace. Several paragraphs into the story the writer then provides the nut graph—explaining in detail the story's central point, how difficult it is to enact such bans in a state that relies heavily on tobacco farming for its economy. Following paragraphs expand on the nut graph, providing much more detail.

The body of the story continues for another 29 paragraphs, weaving Spaw briefly into the story in some parts but mainly focusing on the statistics about the tobacco industry and smoking in Kentucky and the difficulty in raising awareness of health issues related to smoking. In those paragraphs, the reporter cites sources including government officials, tobacco industry spokespeople and public health officials to provide context to the story and add balance so that all sides of the issue are explored.

The last three paragraphs of the story provide the kicker—tying the end of the story back to the beginning and providing a sense of conclusion to the story:

> *The kicker is used to conclude the story. It ties the body of the story back into the beginning and sometimes the person who was the subject of the focus lead.*

Still, Spaw knows firsthand that getting committed smokers to quit, as she did — and convincing teens to put down the nicotine-filled vape pen — is a tough sell in a state addicted to smoking, the pride of growing tobacco and the money that comes with it.

Growing up, she says, tobacco fields stretched across the countryside, and farmers talked of bumper crops making for a merry Christmas. Her high school had a smoking area for students, and the principal kept an ashtray on his desk. Even Spaw confesses: "I liked smoking."

But the price for her pleasure — a lung — was far too high. She wants tobacco smokers and e-cigarette users to know that when they are ready to quit, she and others are ready to help.

"If I could talk to anyone that has an issue with tobacco, I would say, 'If you think you don't have the resources, look, you can find them,'" Spaw says. Big tobacco companies, she says, "have millions of dollars that they can spend on marketing their product and everything. But at the end of the day, your health is more important."

Courtesy US News

The success of the focus story depends on the selection of the lead. Some beginners start their stories with interesting anecdotes or descriptions that have little or no connection to the central point. Without this connection, the audience is likely to be confused and frustrated.

The focus style also has flexibility. The body of the story can be developed in any number of ways. If the story has several subtopics, they can be arranged in descending order of importance. Or if the material lends itself to a narrative structure, the information can be arranged chronologically.

9.4 The Narrative Style

A narrative has two components: a story and a storyteller. A storyteller writes as a playwright or novelist would, depicting people interacting with other people and within their surroundings. To write in the narrative style, a reporter must find people who are crucial to the story and record their actions. This technique requires more than just interviewing sources, recording quotes and reporting numbers. It requires observation.

Observation does not mean reporters are free to inject their opinions into a story. Instead, journalists observe people, places and events important to a story and describe them in vivid detail. Through those particulars, the audience gets a better sense of what is occurring. But to paint a picture with words, reporters must be specific. Notice the difference between the following sentences:

> Students are angry about the board of trustees' decision.

> Students gathered in the administration building lobby waving signs denouncing the board of trustees' decision as a betrayal of academic freedom.

The first sentence presents an opinion. Without using attribution, it says the students are angry at the board's decision. The reader does not know whether the writer is reporting a fact or his or her opinion. The second sentence, however, reports the manner of and reason for the protest.

The narrative approach allows reporters to be more creative. Reporters can describe the drama—even if it is not high drama—at a school board meeting, for example. What happened? What did they see? Were people shouting? Were people laughing? Did the participants exchange views? Journalists cannot answer these questions and others unless they take extensive notes.

Longtime writing coach Don Fry describes the style this way:

> Narrative writing requires narrative thinking, narrative reporting and narrative forms.

> Narrative thinking means seeing the world in terms of people doing things, not as piles of disparate facts. Actions connect to one another to create meaning, mostly based on human motives. The best journalistic storytellers let their curiosity lead them into stories, because they want to find out why real people do things.

A story written in narrative style can still lead with the news—the most important part of the story—but then quickly switch to using chronology, flashbacks, dialogue and other storytelling techniques. Or it can employ a strictly chronological organization, ending with the most recent (and perhaps most newsworthy) information. Generally, such stories have a beginning, middle and end, each of relatively equal importance. It is more difficult to cut the final paragraphs of narrative stories than those of stories written in the inverted-pyramid style.

A story in The New York Times by Christopher Flavelle about the environmental crisis facing Salt Lake City as the Great Salt Lake dries up illustrates the narrative style:

> SALT LAKE CITY — If the Great Salt Lake, which has already shrunk by two-thirds, continues to dry up, here's what's in store:

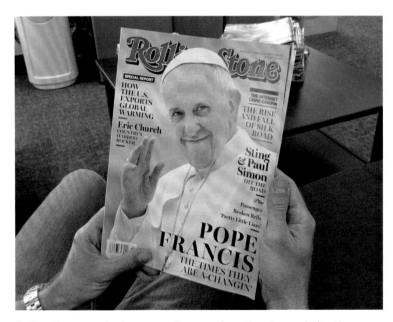

Rolling Stone and other magazines, such as Esquire and The New Yorker, are well known for the narrative style of their articles.

The lake's flies and brine shrimp would die off — scientists warn it could start as soon as this summer — threatening the 10 million migratory birds that stop at the lake annually to feed on the tiny creatures. Ski conditions at the resorts above Salt Lake City, a vital source of revenue, would deteriorate. The lucrative extraction of magnesium and other minerals from the lake could stop.

Most alarming, the air surrounding Salt Lake City would occasionally turn poisonous. The lake bed contains high levels of arsenic and as more of it becomes exposed, wind storms carry that arsenic into the lungs of nearby residents, who make up three-quarters of Utah's population.

"We have this potential environmental nuclear bomb that's going to go off if we don't take some pretty dramatic action," said Joel Ferry, a Republican state lawmaker and rancher who lives on the north side of the lake.

The lead sets up the tone and central point of the story for the reader. Note that the reporter includes a powerful quote from a source that uses very descriptive language, such as "environmental nuclear bomb," to highlight the importance of the story.

The story continues with a description of the region and an explanation of how the Great Salt Lake created an oasis in largely desert area, making possible the development and growth of the Salt Lake City area, where 2.5 million people live.

Narrative stories are often much longer than stories written in the inverted-pyramid structure. This story about the Great Salt Lake is 47 paragraphs long. Often editors will break up the stories by using subheads. Subheads indicate to a reader that the story is shifting focus. The Times story included sections that described how the growing salt concentrations in the lake threaten the survival of all life in it, the efforts to balance the growth of population in the Salt Lake area and the need to preserve water in the lake, and likely scenarios for what may happen in the future.

Descriptive passages are sprinkled throughout the story and often use simile or metaphor to describe things in a way readers can understand and picture in their minds. The difference between simile and and metaphor depends on how the writer describes the scene or object. A simile is a figure of speech that compares two otherwise dissimilar things, often introduced by the words "like" or "as." A metaphor is when a word is used in place of another to suggest a likeness. "The ocean breeze on that hot day was like a drink of cold water" is a simile. "The ocean breeze on that hot day was a drink of cold water" is a metaphor.

The long-term risks are even worse. One morning in March, Kevin Perry, a professor of atmospheric sciences at the University of Utah, walked out onto land that used to be underwater. He picked at the earth, the color of dried mud, like a beach whose tide went out and never came back.

The soil contains arsenic, antimony, copper, zirconium and other dangerous heavy metals, much of it residue from mining activity in the region. Most of the exposed soil is still protected by a hard crust. But as wind erodes the crust over time, those contaminants become airborne.

As will be discussed in Chapter 14, visual media is an important part of communicating news to an audience. These three photographs were among several used in the story about the environmental crisis affecting the Great Salt Lake in Utah. The images help to dramatize and emphasize key points of the story.

> Clouds of dust also make it difficult for people to breathe, particularly those with asthma or other respiratory ailments. Dr. Perry pointed to shards of crust that had come apart, lying on the sand like broken china.

The ending of a narrative story may tie back to the beginning of the story, much like the focus style, or it may not. However, the ending still may cover several paragraphs as the writer concludes the story for the reader.

The Times story about the Great Salt Lake ended with a long anecdote about what happened in the early 20th century when Los Angeles was able to divert the Owens River to provide water for its growing population. That diversion caused Owens Lake to dry up and largely killed the nearby town of Keeler, California.

Throughout the story, the reporter used quotations, dialogue and descriptions to give readers a sense of what is happening environmentally to the Great Salt Lake and its potential impact on Salt Lake City. The details easily bring images to the reader's mind. One can imagine traveling through the vast reaches of the American West and seeing what the writer is describing. Passages such as "the earth, the color of dried mud, like a beach whose tide went out and never came back" paint a dramatic picture for readers. Although narrative stories tend to be longer, the rich detail and concrete imagery make them easier to read than many shorter, straight news stories.

Narrative style can be a refreshing change from the inverted pyramid, but it is not appropriate for all stories. Stories about breaking news events, speeches or most government meetings, for instance, often make more sense to readers when told in traditional inverted-pyramid fashion. Narrative touches, such as dialogue and colorful descriptions, can make any story more readable, however. Regardless of the occasion, the success of a narrative story depends on the depth of the reporting. A writer who has not attentively gathered details and quotations will have difficulty constructing a narrative story.

9.5 Using Transitions

Transitions help stories move from one fact to the next in a smooth, logical order. Recall from the train analogy we used at the beginning of the chapter that the transitions are the couplings that hold the cars together. Reporters introduce ideas by relating them to others reported earlier in a story. Often, the natural progression of thought, or sequence of facts and action, is adequate. Alternatively, journalists may repeat a key name or pronoun:

> Richard Nolles, editor of the Weekly Outlook, said the newspaper tries to report the truth even when its readers do not want to hear it.
>
> "A newspaper that reports only what its readers want to hear is dodging its moral obligations," Nolles said.
>
> In a speech Wednesday, Nolles added that many readers want to avoid unpleasant news, and threaten to cancel their subscriptions when he reports it.
>
> "But if a problem exists, they need to know about it so they can correct it," he said. "Ignorant citizens can't make wise decisions."

In the example, the repetition of the words "Nolles," "newspaper" and "readers" and the use of the pronouns "they" and "their" make it easier for readers to follow the progression of thought.

Other transitional devices include words that can indicate time, addition, causation, comparison or contrast. Word phrases, sentences and questions also can serve as transitional devices.

9.6 Explain the Unfamiliar

Reporters should avoid words that are not used in everyday conversation. When an unfamiliar word is necessary, journalists must immediately define it. Stories that fail to explain unfamiliar terms may annoy as well as puzzle the audience. A story about a 19-year-old Olympic skater who collapsed and died before a practice session at the University of Texas reported that she died of clinical terminal cardiac arrhythmia. The journalist placed the term in quotation marks but failed to define it. Many people would be interested in the death of an Olympic skater and would wonder why an apparently healthy young athlete had died, but the story failed to satisfy their curiosity because it failed to explain the medical term.

Instead of using an unfamiliar term and then defining it, journalists may use only the definition instead:

● She said the school will ∧ ~~have K-6 facilities~~. *accept children from kindergarten through the sixth grade*

Journalists can make even the most complicated stories understandable. For example, former (Tucson) Arizona Daily Star environmental reporter Jane Kay wrote about several wells in Arizona contaminated by trichloroethylene. The topic was complex, yet the stories were clear and dramatic. Kay explained that the chemical, also called "TCE," is an industrial degreaser that may cause cancer in humans:

> TCE is a tasteless, odorless, colorless—and very toxic—chemical. It is volatile, meaning that it evaporates quickly, much like common household cleaning fluids.
>
> Only a teaspoon of it poured into 250,000 gallons of water—about the amount used by five people in an entire year—would create a taint slightly beyond the 5 parts per billion suggested as a guideline for safety by the state Department of Health Services.

The wells contaminated by TCE were closed, and government officials assured people their drinking water was safe. But after hundreds of interviews, Kay discovered, "For 10 to 30 years, many South Side Tucson residents unknowingly got minute quantities of TCE almost every time they turned on the tap water." As many as 20,000 people "drank TCE at home, inhaled it in the shower and absorbed it through their skin when they washed the dishes." Apparently as a result of the TCE contamination, residents of Tucson's South Side suffered from an unusual number of serious illnesses, including cancer.

Large numbers also need explaining. For example, few people who read, watch or listen to stories about a city's or the country's budget and deficits would really comprehend the numbers. Reporters can help audiences understand large numbers by converting them into something related to everyday life.

For example, The Washington Post reported that an investment bank offered to pay $20.6 billion to take over RJR Nabisco Inc., a conglomerate that made Oreos, LifeSavers and Camel cigarettes. (The company later split into R.J. Reynolds Tobacco Co. and Nabisco, and since then they have been purchased by or merged with other corporations.) RJR Nabisco rejected the offer, saying it was not big enough. If $20.6 billion cannot buy a cookie company, what is it good for? A Post writer calculated it could, among other things, provide shoes for every American for a year, house two million criminals in prisons for a year, sponsor 80 million destitute children around the world for one year and cover the cost of every movie ticket bought in the United States in the previous four years.

When a sentence must explain several items in a list, the explanation should precede the list, not follow it. If the explanation follows the list, people might fail to grasp the relationship between the items or the significance of the list:

- *The senator said he voted for the bill to*
  ~~To~~ ∧ provide children with better nutrition, better health care and better educational opportunities ~~were the reasons the senator voted for the bill~~.

9.7 The Importance of Examples

Examples make stories more interesting, personalize them and help audience members understand them more easily. A story about a teenager who became an alcoholic and flunked out of college might include examples of the problems she experienced:

> She said school became unimportant, adding: "I can remember staying up all night before my public health final. When I took the test, I was smashed. And if that wasn't bad enough, then I ran the entire 10 blocks back to my apartment so I could drink some more. Of course, I flunked public health."

Examples are especially important in stories about abstract issues. Sometimes numbers help put those issues into perspective. A story about the lives of people who drop out of college might include the percentage of students who drop out of college nationally, their reasons for dropping out and what they do afterward: join the military, get married, find a job. In addition to reporting the general

 HOT TIP

Three Ways to Explain the Unfamiliar

Here are three techniques journalists can use to define or explain unfamiliar terms:

1. Place a brief explanation in parentheses:

   The law would ban accessory structures (sheds, pool houses and unattached garages) in new subdivisions.

2. Place the explanation immediately after the unfamiliar name or term, setting it off with a colon, comma or dash:

   Amy and Ralph Hargis of Carlton Drive filed for bankruptcy under Chapter 13, which allows them to repay their creditors in monthly installments over a three-year period.

   About 800 foreign students at the university are on F-1 student visas—which means that they are allowed to stay in the United States only until they complete their degrees.

3. Place the explanation in the next sentence:

   The major banks raised their prime rate to 12.5 percent. The prime rate is the interest rate banks charge their best customers.

trends, a good writer would illustrate the story by describing the lives of two or three dropouts—specific examples of the trend.

Reporters can clarify unfamiliar concepts by comparing them to familiar things. Many people struggle to understand business and finance, and stories of financial fraud can be extraordinarily complex. Paul Krugman, a columnist for The New York Times and Nobel-Prize-winning economist, used the following analogy to help readers understand how mutual fund managers and major investors were cheating ordinary investors:

> You're selling your house, and your real estate agent claims that he's representing your interests. But he sells the property at less than fair value to a friend, who resells it at a substantial profit, on which the agent receives a kickback. You complain to the county attorney. But he gets big campaign contributions from the agent, so he pays no attention. That, in essence, is the story of the growing mutual fund scandal.

9.8 The Use of Description

Descriptions, like quotations, make stories more interesting and help people visualize scenes. But many journalists are reluctant to use descriptive phrases; they summarize whatever they hear but are less likely to describe what they see, feel, taste and smell. For instance, a student who attended a speech by an expert in communications technology handed her instructor a story that said:

> The speaker, John Mollwitz, showed some examples of electronic newspapers and talked about how they fit into the newspaper industry.

The student failed to describe what the electronic newspapers looked like and how they "fit into the newspaper industry." She also neglected to mention that the crowd intermittently applauded Mollwitz, who has developed some profitable electronic newspapers.

When asked to write descriptions, most students rely too heavily on adverbs and adjectives. Nouns and verbs are more effective. They are also less redundant and less opinionated than adverbs and adjectives.

Beginning reporters sometimes resort to vague generalities when they try to write descriptions:

> She spoke with authority.

> She seemed to enjoy talking about her work.

Neither sentence is an actual description. The first fails to explain why the writer concluded that the woman spoke authoritatively. Moreover, what one observer interprets as speaking with authority might seem as overbearing arrogance to another. The second does not specifically describe either the speaker or what she said.

Reporters train themselves to observe and describe specific details, such as descriptions of people's voices, mannerisms, facial expressions, posture, gestures and surroundings. They may also include details about the height, weight, age, clothing, hair, glasses, jewelry and family of the people they write about. For example, a journalist might describe a man's hands by mentioning their size, calluses, nails, smoothness, wrinkles or veins. Avoid generalities and conclusions. In the following examples, the first sentence is vague, but the second is descriptive:

He is a large man.

He is 6 feet tall and weighs 210 pounds.

Butler looked as though he had dressed in a hurry.

Butler's shirt was buttoned halfway, his socks were mismatched, his shoelaces were untied and his hair was not brushed.

Descriptions help the audience see the situation or person through the eyes of the reporter. When describing people, however, journalists should not write

FROM THE NEWS

Describing the Search for the Ring in the Ashes

The following excerpt from a Washington Post story by Hannah Dreier and Andrew Ba Tran follows Michael Goetze and his son, Jeremy, as they search for the titanium wedding ring Michael had worn for 40 years. His wife had died after an illness. The ring was lost when he had to abandon his home in Grass Valley, California, during the River Fire of 2021. The two are accompanied by members of their church. Here is how Dreier and Tran described what Goetze and his companions saw and did:

They had put it off for weeks, but now the ground had stopped smoldering and the weather had cooled, so Michael Goetze set out with his son to see the home that a wildfire had turned to rubble and ash.

They had one goal: Find the wedding band Michael had worn for 40 years of marriage.

They drove through the foothills of the Sierra Nevada, past the dense pine trees that looked suddenly ominous and overgrown. "This whole place is just turning into a tinderbox," Michael said.

Their street, Mount Olive Road, was lined with charred remnants of cars and houses, all destroyed in August by what came to be known as the River Fire. When they parked and got out, smoke from a wildfire miles away caught

in their throats. Pieces of ash were drifting down in clumps.

"It's bad today with the ash," Jeremy said. "Kind of claustrophobic."

This was the road where Michael had lived for most of his life, where Jeremy, 40, had grown up, and where both men had worked every day making granite countertops. It had always felt safe to them. But a map filed away in a county office told a different story: The local emergency management department had traced Mount Olive in brown highlighter, singling it out as a place highly likely to burn in a wildfire.

Since the fire, Michael had been ruminating over all the things he left behind when he evacuated. He hadn't wanted to come back, but Jeremy hoped the wedding band might bring him some peace.

Before they walked up to what was left of Michael's home, the group stood in a circle and prayed. "We know that you are a God of comfort, and we hope that we find comfort today," a man read. "Amen," Michael said. Someone had brought disposable hazmat suits and he tried to put one on, but it was too small for his 6-foot-7 frame. He put on a cloth mask instead and said he was ready.

anything about a woman that they would not write about a man in the same situation and vice versa. Do not note, "The woman had long slender legs" if you would not write in the same situation, "The man had long slender legs."

9.9 The Need to Be Fair

Regardless of how a story is organized, it must be balanced, fair and accurate. Reporters who write about a controversy should present every significant viewpoint fully and fairly. They must exercise particular care when their stories might harm another person's reputation. A reckless or irresponsible charge can destroy an innocent person's reputation, marriage or career.

If a story contains information critical of an individual, that person must have an opportunity to respond. It is not enough to get the person's response after a story has been published and report it in a later story because not everyone who read, watched or heard the original criticism will catch the second story. The New York Times has an unbreakable policy requiring that a person criticized in a news story have an immediate chance to respond. If the person cannot be reached, editors and reporters should consider holding the story. If the story cannot be held, it must describe the efforts made to reach the person and explain that those efforts will be renewed the next day.

When the subject of a negative story is unavailable or refuses to respond, that fact should be mentioned. A brief sentence such as one of the following three options might explain:

> Repeated attempts to reach a company employee were unsuccessful.

> A vice president at the company declined to comment about the charges.

> Company officials did not return phone calls made by reporters.

9.10 The Final Step: Edit Your Story

After finishing a story, edit it ruthlessly. Novelist Kurt Vonnegut said, "If a sentence, no matter how excellent, does not illuminate your subject in some new and useful way, scratch it out." Vonnegut also urged writers to have mercy on their readers: "Our audience requires us to be sympathetic and patient teachers, ever willing to simplify and clarify—whereas we would rather soar high above the crowd singing like nightingales."

Good reporters will reread and edit their stories. Lazy ones immediately submit their stories to an editor, thinking their work needs no editing or expecting the editor to correct any mistakes. That attitude ignores the realities of today's newsrooms. Many news organizations have reduced staff, including copy editors. Increasingly, journalists are expected to edit their own copy, particularly if the story is one that will appear online almost immediately. Copy editors have less time nowadays to edit more stories, which increases the possibility that errors will be missed. In such cases, the reporters are the ones who suffer the embarrassment and bear the responsibility. If a poorly written story receives careful editing, the editor may decide it needs extensive changes, perhaps even total rewriting. When that happens, reporters often complain about the changes. Reporters who correct their own errors will develop reputations as good writers and earn better assignments, raises and promotions.

Guest Columnist

How to Interview Data

BY LIBBY SELINE

It took me two months to apply for a Texas driver's license. In my opinion, that was ridiculous.

I knew I must have been one of thousands of people establishing residency in the growing state, but the two-month waiting period to give paperwork to the Department of Motor Vehicles heightened my already existing question: Exactly how many people were moving to Texas?

Multiple journalists had already attempted to answer this question, most relying on mail-forwarding data from the United States Postal Service. But the data had caveats. Did everyone who moved provide a forwarding address? Did it account for everybody in a household?

So, given my recent struggle, I decided to answer the question by learning how many people had surrendered a driver's license to a Texas DMV. Granted, this avenue also had disadvantages. It also didn't account for everyone who moved—especially those younger than 16. But it was a different perspective on the number of people who established residency in Texas, and this method was worth a shot.

In my job as a data journalist, I take a question I have about the real world—whether that be about a new annoyance or a topic my peers consistently mention—then I find the data to answer it and write about my findings. This is usually my first step in an unruly, chaotic, frustrating yet rewarding process of producing a data story.

I also produce stories after stumbling across new or interesting datasets. I subscribe to emails from the U.S. Census to learn about new data releases, and I examine datasets stored on the city's data portal. My colleagues have gathered datasets on dog names in a city and scraped data from websites to answer questions about how many times a keyword appears in a song. Thousands of datasets exist on the internet, just waiting to be analyzed.

Regardless of how you generated a story idea and located the data, it's important to treat it as if it were a human source.

Before you interview a person, you look at their qualifications or experiences to learn if they can teach you about a subject area or event. With data, you look at its cleanliness. Does the data have duplicates? Are people's names misspelled? If the data was entered by hand, it's likely to have errors that need to be cleaned.

A data journalist should also learn how the data was kept—and avoid jumping to conclusions in that process. For instance, I once received five different datasets about births in Texas—one for different years. I assumed the column labeled "county" in each dataset was the county the child was born in. But I was wrong. Some of the datasets had a county column that stood for the mother's residential county. If I had failed to realize that, the story I published about births in each Texas county would have been inaccurate.

The data cleaning process is not always straightforward, but if you find the people who manage the data, you can ask them what you need to know before you begin analyzing. At the very least, learn if the agency offers a data dictionary or a methodology that informs you about the dataset.

Once you understand the data and its caveats, create a list of questions to ask. Are you looking for a specific trend? Do you have a hypothesis you are looking to prove?

Of course, asking the data is not as easy as talking to a person. Data journalists often utilize Microsoft Excel or Google Spreadsheets to create queries and form pivot tables, which summarizes the data. Some data journalists also use programming languages such as SQL, Python or R. While learning these skills isn't required, the programming languages are better equipped for examining large datasets and performing a more complicated analysis.

Generating questions for the story means relying on your curiosity. Let's look again at the driver's license story. That data gave me the state of the surrendered license, the county where the drivers surrendered their licenses and the date they surrendered them. I knew I could answer three main questions: What states did the new Texans come from? What county did they move to? And when did people surrender their driver's licenses?

Using R, I manipulated the data to answer these questions. In that process, I took notes of my findings to help myself check my work and ensure I was drawing correct conclusions from the data. I also created more specific queries, learning how many people from a specific state moved to a specific county. I then uploaded my clean spreadsheets to Datawrapper and Flourish—both are excellent data-visualization tools—to generate maps and graphs that display the data.

The visualizations helped me better identify trends and outliers in the data. My final product was an exploratory guide to help readers learn who is moving to the state, but the story didn't need to stop there.

Perhaps people from a specific state flocked to a small county in Texas. Why did that happen? Maybe one of the most populous counties in Texas barely received any new residents. What's that about? I could've dug deeper and learned about why people moved during the pandemic and what they miss the most about home. Data is so powerful, but nothing replaces the human voice.

So, the final part of a data story is to add voices when you're able. Find a person who is a data point in your spreadsheet and ask them about their experiences. Talking to people both strengthens the findings and humanizes a data-heavy story.

Following all these steps, a reporter can produce a data-centric story that interests readers. The process of cleaning the data can be grueling, but using data can bring problems to light or unearth fascinating trends about a variety of subjects. Thousands of questions can be answered with data; all you have to do is ask.

Libby Seline is a data journalist at the San Antonio Express-News in Texas.

The Reporter's Guide to Writing News Stories

Use the following checklist to evaluate all your stories.

1. Place the most important details in your lead.

2. Throughout the story, emphasize the details most likely to interest and affect your audience.

3. Include details from your observations to create a picture your readers can visualize.

4. In the story's second paragraph, continue to discuss the topic initiated in your lead.

5. Do not leapfrog. If your lead mentions an individual, and your second paragraph begins with a name, provide a transition that makes it clear you mean the same person.

6. Make your sentences clear, concise and to the point. (Avoid passive verbs. Also, use the normal word order of subject-verb-direct object.)

7. Vary your sentence structure.

8. Avoid overloading your sentences.

9. If your story discusses several major subtopics, mention all the major subtopics in your story's opening paragraphs so your audience knows what to expect.

10. If you use a list, make sure each item is in parallel form.

11. Provide transitions to lead your readers from one sentence or paragraph to another smoothly and logically.

12. Make your transitional sentences specific; say something intriguing to sustain interest in the topic.

13. If you use a question as a transition, make it clear, short and simple.

14. Avoid generalities that have to be explained in a later sentence or paragraph. Be specific.

15. Resist the temptation to end your story with a summary, conclusion or opinion.

16. After finishing your story, critically edit and rewrite it.

Review Exercises

1. THE BODY OF A NEWS STORY

Section I: Second Paragraphs

Second paragraphs are almost as important as leads. Like leads, second paragraphs must help arouse the public's interest in a topic. Critically evaluate the second paragraphs in the following stories. Judge which of the second paragraphs are most successful in providing a smooth transition from the lead; continuing to discuss the topic summarized in the lead; and emphasizing the news—details that are new, important and interesting. Give each second paragraph a grade from A to F.

1. A Pinkerton courier was robbed at gunpoint and fatally wounded on Tuesday while leaving Merchants Bank with the day's daily transaction records.

   Edwin James, 59, of 826 Bell Drive, was following standard bank procedures and carrying no money.

2. A 41-year-old teacher who fell and broke an ankle while stopping for a cup of coffee on her way to work sued a convenience store Monday.

   The teacher, Tina Alvarez, has worked at Washington Elementary School for 21 years.

3. Two young men are presumed dead after falling off a 30-foot rock formation into the Pacific Ocean at a California park Saturday.

   The men remain unidentified, and their bodies have not been recovered.

4. Police responding to a 911 call about a shooting at 10 p.m. Sunday discovered Ralph Beasley on Bennett Road with a gunshot wound to his head.

   County sheriff's deputies arrived at about the same time in response to a radio request for assistance. An ambulance was already at the scene, as were Fire Department paramedics.

5. A 32-year-old woman who said she smoked marijuana to ease the pain of a rare intestinal disease was charged Tuesday morning with possessing illegal drugs.

   Ruth Howland was stopped at the Municipal Airport after a K-9 dog singled out her suitcase. She and her husband, Terry, were returning from Mexico.

6. Three gunmen who entered a restaurant on Wilson Avenue at 10:30 p.m. Tuesday held four employees and 12 customers at gunpoint while taking more than $3,000 from several cash registers.

   Peggy Deacosti, the restaurant's hostess, was on duty when the robbery occurred.

7. Eileen Guion, 38, a food and beverage coordinator at Walt Disney World for 18 years, died at her home Tuesday of unknown causes.

   Although she was offered many other jobs at restaurants, she never accepted them. She once said, "I've loved working at Disney because I get to work with people from all over the world, and I think that is very neat."

8. Police are searching for a man who attacked a woman outside the Bayside Bar & Grill Thursday night.

   Terry Smythe, a bartender at the restaurant, said he heard a woman screaming outside the entrance at 9 p.m. Smythe darted to the foyer, where he saw the woman trapped in the entryway. Smythe said it was "kind of like a tug of war," with the assailant trying to pull the woman outside while waitresses tried to pull her inside.

Section II: Transitions

Critically evaluate the following transitions. Which would be most likely to entice you to continue reading the stories? Which provide a smooth, specific, informative and interesting introduction to the next idea? Give each transition a grade from A to F.

1. Other students said they would tell their teachers about cheaters because cheating is not fair to those who take the time to study.

2. But what should happen when a husband and wife disagree about having a baby?

3. A concerned citizen then addressed the commission about the fence.

4. Next, the Task Force presented its plan for preservation and renovation of the downtown.

5. In a flat, emotionless voice, Howard responded that he and Jackson stole a red Mustang convertible on the night of June 3, picked up the two 14-year-old girls and took them to the motel.

6. Gary Hubbard, superintendent of schools, then addressed his concerns about security in the city's schools.

7. Police Chief Barry Kopperud said his department is trying to combat juvenile crime by changing the way officers interact with children.

8. He then discussed prejudice as a problem that plagues society.

9. She also spoke about the different religious celebrations and rituals.

10. Parents who love, care for and respect their children don't raise delinquents, she said.

2. PRO CHALLENGE: WRITING COMPLETE NEWS STORIES

Write complete news stories based on the following information. Select the story structure that best fits the information in the scenario. Where more than one story structure could be used, write a story using each and compare the results. Be thorough; use most of the information provided. Because much of the material is wordy, awkward and poorly organized, you will have to rewrite it extensively. Correct all errors in your rewrite.

When you finish, you can compare your work to a professional's. Experienced reporters have been asked to write stories for each set of facts, and their work appears in a manual available to your instructor.

1. Your county officials are running out of money. The need for services in the county has increased with the growing population. According to 2010 census data released by the United States Census Bureau, the county population increased more than 18 percent. Revenue for the county declined by more than 31 percent. The county is growing faster than its ability to generate revenue, county officials said. The county needs a new, larger jail, which could cost 30 million dollars to build. The county also needs to modernize and expand its courthouse, which could cost between $20,000,000 and $30,000,000 as well. The county also needs to expand and modernize its nursing home facilities and roads and bridges in the county are in need of repair. The county library system needs more money as well, according to officials. "The county has been growing so rapidly that it will be unable to supply these services without more revenue. The county needs more income to deal with the unprecedented growth it is experiencing," said Harold Alvarez, who is the county administrator. County commissioners want to increase revenue two ways. They want to institute an impact fee on all new construction—residential, commercial and industrial—in the county. They want to reassess all existing properties—residential, commercial and industrial—that are subject to property taxes. County officials say they want new residents, businesses and industry moving into the county to pay for some of the impact the growth is having on the county, but that current residents should share in the burden as well because they are getting benefits from the growth as well. Six months ago the county hired a consulting firm to investigate the situation. The consultants presented their report last week and county commissioners intend to vote on the recommendations at their meeting next Tuesday at 7 p.m. According to the recommendations, the impact fee to construct a single-family home in the county would be $3,500. Construction of a multi-unit dwelling consisting of three or more units, such as an apartment complex, would have an impact fee of one thousand dollars per unit. Current residential, business and industrial properties that are subject to county property taxes would be reassessed according to their market value. Many residential properties have not been reassessed for more than 20 years. The reassessment could raise property taxes more than 10 to 15 percent for some residents and five to 10 percent for some businesses. Developers object to the idea, saying the proposed fees would raise the price of a new home above the level that many new and current residents could afford. In addition, developers say the increased cost to do business in the county would cause business and industry to look to other counties in the state to locate their facilities. County commissioners

plan to issue $500 million in bonds to finance the needed improvements for the county. The impact fee and the reassessment of existing property are expected to generate approximately $38,000,000 a year, which will be used to repay the bonds. County commissioners say their goal is to keep pace with and perhaps get ahead of the unprecedented growth the county is experiencing. County officials say that without new revenue services that residents have come to expect will have to be curtailed. Roads and bridges will deteriorate. The library system will have to be shut down. The county nursing home facility would have to close because it will not meet state regulations.

2. Accidents occur in your city nearly everyday. One of the crashes listed in the police reports Tuesday morning was a hit-and-run incident. A pedestrian who was walking along the roadway in the 700 block of Meadow Creek Drive was killed. Police said the incident occurred around 11:20 p.m. Monday. The victim was identified as Vivian Hoffmann, who is 67 years of age and lives at 711 Meadow Creek Drive. Hoffman was a clerk at the Quik Shoppe convenience store located four blocks from her home on the corner of Meadow Creek Drive and Gladsen Boulevard. Hoffman was a widow whose husband Gary died five years ago. There were no witnesses to the incidentbut this morning, three days later, police announced the arrest of a suspect in the case. The suspect is Todd Burnes, 27, of 1502 Matador Drive, Apartment 203. Police Chief Barry Kopperud made the announcement at a press conference this morning. "No one—not one of our officers, not even me—is above the law. Sadly, today, I have to take one of our own into custody because he failed to live up to our motto of to protect and to serve," Kopperude said. Burnes is a police patrol officer with your city's police department and has been with the police department for four years. Police charged Burnes with vehicular manslaughter, fleeing the scene of an accident, failure to report an accident, failure to render assistance and filing a false police report. Burnes was driving a tan unmarked police car when he hit Hoffmann occurred. Kopperud said the investigation is continuing and charges are pending against police detective Marlene Griffin, a 10-year veteran of the police department. Griffin is 32 years of age and

lives at 3130 Joyce Drive. Griffin is facing charges of conspiracy, aiding and abetting a crime and filing a false police report. Griffin was the detective who was investigating the hit-and-run crash that killed Hoffmann. According to the police report, Burnes was responding to a reported car accident and was driving west on Meadow Creek Drive when his police vehicle apparently struck Hoffmann as she walked along the road. There are no sidewalks or streetlights and the road is narrow along the wooded section of Meadow Creek Drive where the incident occurred. Burnes told investigators that he did not see the victim but heard a loud thump. He said he thought he hit a dog or deer or something but did not stop to check because he was hurrying to respond to the accident call. The morning after the incident news organizations reported the death of Hoffmann, Burnes noticed that the front right fender of his patrol car was damaged. He is dating Griffin and told her about the incident. Griffin told Burnes not to say anything until he heard from her. The two later took the patrol car to a secluded, abandoned building lot and drove toward a utility pole, sideswiping the passenger-side fender to hide the damage. She told Burnes to report that the damage occurred as he was responding to the accident, but that he did not think the car was damaged that badly until he checked it the following morning. Burnes filed a false report stating that he had lost control of his vehicle on the way to the accident scene and damaged the car. Police said a resident of the apartment complex where Burnes lives saw the detective and the officer the morning after the hit-and-run incident looking at the fender. The witness said she saw the officers leave and later Burnes returned, but there was more damage to the fender than she noticed before. The witness' report was handed over to the Internal Affairs Division of your city's police department and detectives began to question Burnes about the incident and his report. They found gray wool fibers stuck to the fender of the car. Hoffmann was wearing a gray wool coat at the time of her death. Griffin had reported to her superiors earlier that there were no suspects in the hit-and-run case.

3. The demand for energy products is growing. Your state has seen a growth in the number of gas wells being drilled. Many of the wells being drilled use

a process called hydraulic fracturing or fracking. The process involves injecting millions of gallons of water, chemicals and sand deep into shale rock beds to fracture, or shatter, the rock and release methane gas that is trapped there. The problem is what to do with the wastewater byproduct of the drilling. The wastewater contains salts and heavy metals that are harmful to humans. Your state's Department of the Environment recently announced that it will conduct a study in an effort to determine the most effective way to dispose of the wastewater. Currently, gas drilling companies treat the wastewater to remove the most harmful byproducts in the wastewater and then dump the treated water into rivers and streams that are the source of drinking water for many residents of your state. State regulators and state legislators are trying to deal with the boom in gas drilling and tighten environmental regulations because of health concerns regarding the wastewater. State environmental officials say the brine that gushes from the wells as wastewater contains carcinogenic chemicals used by the gas drillers in the fracking process, as well as barium, radium and strontium. The wastewater brine is 10 times saltier than seawater and often contains bromides. Bromides can mix with the chlorine used to disinfect public drinking water to form trihalomethanes. High levels of trihalomethanes can cause an increased risk of cancer. State researchers want to determine whether it is better to treat the wastewater and discharge it into streams as is currently done or if the drilling companies should be forced to drill wells thousands of feet deep to dispose of the wastewater. In the past year, drilling companies have released more than 4.5 million gallons of treated wastewater into the state's rivers and streams. Jim Abbott is the director of public information for CleanEnergy Oil and Gas Company, a major driller. He said: "The wastewater from fracking has not caused any serious harm anywhere in the state. The water that is dumped into the state's rivers and streams is treated to remove many of the harmful chemicals and minerals, and it is safely diluted by the streams and rivers we dump it into. We wouldn't do anything that is harmful to the environment because we live in that environment and our employees live in that environment, too. Treating the wastewater and dumping it into streams is the most cost

effective and efficient way to dispose of it. If the state requires CleanEnergy and other gas drillers to dig wells that are thousands of feet deep to dispose of the wastewater, it is going to increase the cost of energy and cost jobs." CleanEnergy Oil and Gas Company is a subsidiary of APEC Corporation, which is a holding company that also is a major stockholder of News Media Company, the media organization that owns your newspaper, as well as the local television station. State Representative Constance P. Wei is spearheading the effort to create stronger regulation of the drilling process. Wei said: "We want to determine the best way to dispose of the wastewater in a safe and cost effective way. No one wants to drive the drilling companies out of business. But we want regulations, sensible regulations, that will set guidelines on how the wastewater should be disposed of and how dirty that wastewater can be when it is disposed of." The study by your state's Department of Energy is expected to cost $3.3 million and take 18 months to complete. Currently the Department of Energy is requiring daily testing of drinking water in cities and towns that get their drinking water from streams that are downstream from drilling wastewater treatment sites. According to Department of Environment records obtained by you, several communities in the state have reported rising levels of salts and heavy metals in their drinking water.

4. Yesterday happened to be "Take Our Daughters to Work Day," a special occasion observed by people all over the United States, including people in your local community as well as people nationwide. No one knows how many people participated nationally or locally, but from accounts you received at least several hundred local parents took the opportunity on this special day to take their daughters to work with them. The purpose of the occasion local sponsors and promoters say was to expose young girls to a variety of career opportunities, some traditionally not pursued by women. One of the persons locally who participated with his 14 year old daughter was Joseph Murphy, who is 40 years old and lives at 114 Conway Road. Murphy is the director of research at Collins Industries, which specializes in making and selling health care products and medical equipment. Murphy and his daughter, Jennifer, arrived for work at 8 a.m., Murphy's normal starting time.

Jennifer observed her dad at work much of the morning, talked to some co-workers, and ate lunch with her dad in the company cafeteria. "Its better than school lunches," Jennifer said. At 2 p.m., Joseph was called in to talk to the director of personnel, who told him he was being fired. Marilyn Quentin, the personnel director, told him that, because of financial problems, the company was eliminating a number of middle managers in the company and his position was one that was being eliminated, that the company no longer needed his services. A total of 8 mid-level managers were being let go effective immediately as a necessary cost cutting measure. Murphy was then escorted back to his office by security officers, given an hour to pack his office, then escorted from the building with his daughter, then in tears. Murphy had worked for the company since graduating from college 18 years ago. He started as a research assistant. He got two promotions during that period of time and eventually was appointed director of research, managing a staff of fourteen researchers and their assistants. The President of the company was called five times by you but has not yet returned your call. "It's not me I worry about," Murphy told you. "It's my daughter. It's not right. They shouldn't have fired me yesterday when I had my daughter there. I can't believe they couldn't have waited one damn day. It was too traumatic for Jennifer, seeing me treated like that, and I think we'll have to get help for her, professional help. It was just so unbelievable, so cruel, that they would do that with my daughter there." All company employees had been sent by the company's Office of Human Resources an email reminder that they were free and encouraged to bring their daughters to work with them for the day. The company will give Murphy three months severance pay and help finding a new job. "The timing of the dismissal of Mr. Murphy was regrettable," said Quentin. The company has been laying off employees and restructuring itself after disclosing unexpected and mounting financial losses last Summer in the wake of the economic downturn that hit the nation. Murphy's wife, Kathleen, told you that she thinks the family should sue the company for the way the dismissal was handled.

5. Marilyn Picott is a judge in your city. She has served as a judge for eight years after a distinguished career as one of the areas most successful defense attorneys. As a judge, she has a reputation as being a tough, no-nonsense presider over trials. Attorneys who appear late are chastised. Her sentences are tough. She attended a party one night several weeks ago at a daughters home, celebrating the daughters engagement. On the way home, her BMW sport sedan rammed into the back of a Chevrolet Traverse stopped at a stop sign at the intersection of Hanson Road and Wendover Avenue. Police called to the scene cited Picot for failure to have her vehicle under control. Officers at the scene testified today that she appeared unhurt but belligerent and wobbly with the odor of alcohol they smelled emanating from her. They therefore proceeded to administer a roadside sobriety test, which she failed. Today she appeared in court for her trial, since she pleaded not guilty, on a charge of drunken driving, which lasted five hours. She was convicted after the officers testified, and Circuit Court Judge Edward Johnson sentenced her to serve one year on probation, pay $750 in fines and court costs and drive only on business for the duration of her probation. The jury in her case deliberated less than an hour. Prosecutors were hampered because Judge Johnson prohibited them from telling jurors that her blood alcohol content had been measured at 0.21 percent. He made that ruling after the defendant's attorney pointed out to the court that the machine used to measure such blood alcohol levels had not been properly maintained according to its manufacturer's specifications, or at least there were no records showing that it had been properly maintained although such records are supposed to be meticulously kept. Her defense attorney also throughout the trial attacked the credibility of the prosecution witnesses. After her conviction her defense attorney said an appeal is very likely. As part of her sentence, Picot must attend a victim awareness program. Counselors determined she has no alcohol problem. Picot refused to take all but one field sobriety test, claiming that blindness in one eye would affect her ability to perform successfully. Prosecutors, however, showed a video of Picot during her arrest and called some of her answers slurred and argued that she seemed unable to walk straight or steadily and that she was loud and belligerent, telling her arresting officers that they were "making a big

mistake" that they would soon regret. Her defense attorney tried to discredit the accident victims, Samuel and Lucinda Jones of 4851 Edmee Circle, who were in the Chevrolet Traverse when it was struck and who were both injured so they required hospitalization for treatment of their injuries, and who both testified that judge Picot seemed drunk in their opinion from what they saw, smelled, and observed, pointing out that a verdict against the judge would help the Joneses in their civil lawsuit against her, as they are suing her for thousands of dollars as compensation for their pain, suffering, loss of work, and damage to their vehicle in a separate civil suit. Her defense attorney also argued that people at the party said the judge drank only two drinks, both vodka, and that she seemed sober to them as she left.

6. It is a bizarre story. It is a sad story. It involves a wealthy couple in your city. Both were sick, very sick. Police notified by neighbors found their dead bodies this morning. They were in their car, a Cadillac Sedan de Ville, parked in the garage attached to their home at 976 Grand Avenue. The motor was still running and the couple apparently died from asphyxiation brought about by carbon monoxide poisoning. A friend, Sonia Meir, who lives two blocks away at 811 Moor Street who attends church with the couple, found them. Meyer told police that when she got up this morning to get her newspaper off the front porch, she found an envelope containing a letter taped to her front door. The letter was from the couple and asked her to notify the authorities. The note was apparently taped to the door sometime after Meyer went to bed around 11:30 p.m. last night after watching the 11 p.m. local news cast on television. Also enclosed was a lengthy letter explaining the couple's actions. Samuel and Terest Pinckney had no family, no children, no known relatives still alive. Mrs. Pinkney had an older sister, but she died eight years ago. Their estate is estimated by their attorney to be worth about a total of $10 million, and their will states that they want to leave the entire amount to local charities. The attorney said that $1 million each goes to the Salvation Army, Boy Scouts, Girl Scouts and United Way, $5 million goes to their church, the Faith Assembly of

God, and smaller amounts go to other charities in the city. The couple had been married 52 years. Samuel was 78 and his wife, Teresa, was age 79. Both were well educated with college bachelor's degrees, his in business and hers in home economics. In recent months, Samuel had been confined to a wheelchair after suffering a third stroke, which partially paralyzed the left side of his body and made it impossible for him to walk or even go to the bathroom by himself. His wife, Terese, suffered from rheumatoid arthritis and diabetes and was losing her vision so she could no longer read a book or newspaper or magazine. Meyer told you that Mrs. Pinckney was afraid that the state was going to take her driver's license away because of her health problems and she would no longer be able to get around. The Pinkneys needed 24-hour care and, after Samuel's third stroke, hired nurses to help care for them. "We have the means to afford the best doctors, hospitals and around-the-clock home care to the end of our lives, which could be years away, but neither of us wants that kind of life, confined to our house in constant pain," the Pickneys said in the note to Meyer. Identical notes were found in the car with their dead bodies and also on a kitchen table. "It would consume a substantial part of our money, which through our will and through the mission work of our church and other charities is destined to help many young people throughout the world who may one day be able to help many more. We have no immediate family or heirs. In a sense, this legacy represents the final purpose of our lives. It would be a poor use of money to spend it on care for our deteriorating bodies." The Pinckneys made their money through hard work. As a young couple, newly married, they established a bakery, Pinckney's Bakery, worked 12 to 14 hours a day 6 days a week, never on Sundays, gradually over a period of years expanded, eventually employing a total of 74 employees, selling their goods to restaurants and supermarkets throughout the city as well as to individuals who came to their shop at 1012 2nd Avenue where they continued to work, although only about 10 hours a day in their later years, until they retired at the age of 70 at which time they sold the bakery to their employees.

QUOTATIONS AND ATTRIBUTION

The Constitution says the president shall nominate federal judges, including those who sit on the U.S. Supreme Court, and the Senate shall decide whether to confirm them. For most of the country's history, judicial nominees have been confirmed with little fanfare. Now, every nomination to the Supreme Court is a battle both in the Senate and in public opinion.

President Joe Biden's nomination of Ketanji Brown Jackson to the Supreme Court was just such a battle and, in some ways, one of the nastiest. Brown, who is the first Black woman to serve on the court, had already compiled a record of high accomplishments as a lawyer and as a judge in federal trial and appellate courts. But she was the first justice to have served as a public defender. She had also worked to defend some of the suspected terrorists detained at Guantanamo Bay on the island of Cuba. And for some senators, that record of defending people accused of crimes was grounds to oppose her.

One senator in particular, Tom Cotton, a Republican from Arkansas, expressed his opposition to Jackson in dramatic terms. Explaining his position on the Senate floor, Cotton said: "The last Judge Jackson left the Supreme Court to go to Nuremberg and prosecute the case against the Nazis. This Judge Jackson might have gone there to defend them."

By the "last Judge Jackson," Cotton was referring to Justice Robert H. Jackson, who was an associate justice of the Supreme Court from 1941 until his death in 1954. In 1945–46, he took a leave of absence from the court to serve as chief prosecutor of World War II Nazis for various war crimes.

Cotton's remark captured the attention of many news organizations and was widely reported. Politico, a website and publication devoted to national politics, reported Cotton's remark in a story that included responses from Democrats on the Senate Judiciary Committee condemning his remarks as contrary to the constitutional requirement that every accused person is entitled to legal representation and a presumption of innocence. Esquire magazine said Cotton's

> "A customer at a breakfast spot in Appalachia, or a worker in a union office in Columbus, is able to repeat the latest dubious campaign sound bites within days, if not hours. Everyone hates the media, and everyone sounds like a talking head."
>
> —*George Packer, U.S. journalist, novelist and playwright*

ADL ✓ @ADL · Apr 5
Absolutely shameful conduct from @SenTomCotton. To use a Nazi analogy as some sort of twisted way to attack Judge Ketanji Brown Jackson is reprehensible. We've said it a thousand times and we'll say it again: stop trivializing the Holocaust for political gain.

The Recount ✓ @therecount · Apr 5
Sen. Tom Cotton (R-AR) literally says Ketanji Brown Jackson might have defended Nazis at Nuremberg:

"The last Judge Jackson left the Supreme Court to go to Nuremberg and prosecute the case against the Nazis. This Judge Jackson might have gone there to defend them."

Show this thread

RECOUNT   LIVE

SUPREME COURT NOMINATION
U.S. SEN. TOM COTTON   left, the Supreme Court to go to Nuremberg   C·SPAN2
       R-ARKANSAS
0:08 1.5M views

○ 319   ⇅ 1,168   ♡ 3,327   ⬆

remark "would gag a maggot." Indy100.com reported that the Anti-Defamation League said in a tweet, "Absolutely shameful conduct from @ SenTomCotton. To use a Nazi analogy as some sort of twisted way to attack Judge Ketanji Brown Jackson is reprehensible. We've said it a thousand times and we'll say it again: stop trivializing the Holocaust for political gain." The Michigan Chronicle said Cotton's words were "racial and absurd." And the National Review, a conservative opinion magazine that generally supports Republicans, called Cotton's remark a cheap shot and added: "You know what? If she had done that, it would have been fine." Assuring a fair trial even to the most unpopular suspects is essential to the rule of law, the National Review said.

A day later, after much of the criticism of his remark had aired, Cotton was interviewed by John Roberts on Fox News. Roberts asked, "So, you don't think it was a bridge too far to make the link with Nuremberg and Nazis?" Unabashed, Cotton said no and added, "Again, in three separate cases she was representing not American citizens charged with a crime entitled to due process in our Constitution, [but] foreign terrorists who had committed acts of violence against Americans."

Cotton's words clearly struck a nerve with many Americans, even those who might agree with him on many policy issues. Quotations do not have to be as inflammatory as Cotton's to be noteworthy. A quotation can illuminate issues, reveal emotions and heighten the public's understanding of events and the people involved in them. That is why reporters attach so much importance to getting and effectively using quotations.

10.1 Quotations

Reporters can incorporate quotations into their stories in one of three ways: direct, indirect or partial. Direct quotations present a source's exact words and, consequently, are placed entirely in quotation marks. Indirect quotations lack quotation marks because reporters use their own words to summarize, or paraphrase, the source's remarks. Partial quotations directly quote key phrases and paraphrase the rest. See Table 10.1 for examples.

10.1.1 When to Use Direct Quotations

Reporters use direct quotations when their sources say something important or controversial or state their ideas in a colorful manner. The best quotations are often short and full of emotion. A story about a herpetologist included this

TABLE 10.1 TYPES OF QUOTATIONS

Direct quotation	Ambrose said, "Journalism students should be dealing with ideas of a social, economic and political nature. There's too much of a trade-school atmosphere in journalism schools today. One spends too much time on minor technical and mechanical things, like learning how to write headlines."
Indirect quotation	Ambrose said journalism students should deal with ideas, not mechanical techniques.
Partial quotation	Ambrose criticized the "trade-school atmosphere" in journalism schools and said students should study ideas, not mechanical techniques.

quotation: "I've caught over 1,000 rattlesnakes in Nebraska, and I've liked every one. I can't say the same for the people I've met." In 22 words, the writer captured and conveyed to the audience why this man enjoys his work and some insight into his personality.

Direct quotations are so much a part of news stories that reporters and editors may think a story is incomplete without them. But journalists who merely decorate stories with quotations are not using them effectively. Jack Hart, a former managing editor for staff training and development at Portland's The Oregonian, identified several reasons for using direct quotations:

- To let the sources talk directly to the reader.
- To give the speaker's exact words when you cannot improve on them or match the speaker's wit, rhythm, color or emotion.
- To tie a controversial opinion to the source.
- To provide evidence for a statement.
- To reveal the speaker's character.

If a quotation is not serving at least one of those functions, it is not being used effectively.

The late Archbishop Desmond Tutu, in a speech recalling the days when he and others worked to end apartheid in South Africa, told of meeting a nun in California who said she prayed every day for him and for all opponents of segregation. "We're being prayed for in the woods in California at 2 in the morning. What chance does the apartheid government stand?" Tutu asked. His remark satisfies many of Hart's criteria.

The best stories combine quotations and paraphrases for a pleasing effect. Good reporters can summarize facts and major ideas more succinctly than their sources, but a story that has only a reporter's voice can be dull. In the following passage, the journalist's description and summary effectively sets up a direct quotation from the source:

The most important thing women's basketball coach Vance Coleman carries in his briefcase is not a sketch of a new defensive scheme, a game plan for the upcoming opponent or even the phone number of a basketball colleague.

It's a crumpled, yellowed piece of paper with a list full of scratches and redos. It's his list of five life goals. Coleman lists living a long and healthy life, playing the role of a good father and husband and earning a million dollars as his top three goals. The other two, he said, constantly change as he ages.

But the point, Coleman said, is to always have them.

"There is an equation I use that works on the basketball court, on the playing field, in business and in life," Coleman said, "and that is performance equals ability times motivation. You may have all the ability in the world, but with no motivation, you won't accomplish anything. Zero times anything is nothing.

"No matter what you do in life, you have to have goals. And you have to stick to those goals."

Reporters often summarize a major point before offering a direct quotation. The quotation augments the summary with emotion, details or controversy, but it must provide new information. The following excerpt, from a story about a corporate executive's speech to college students, is an example of how a quotation can effectively support a point:

Gather five people in your life who helped to shape your views, Johnson said. Whether it's a mentor, a parent, a preacher or a friend, he said, advisory board people can provide support and confidence.

"My mom is part of my advisory board. As a person of color, it really wasn't popular to be nonwhite in my elementary school," he said. "My mom had to come to school every day because I was picked on. She'd say: 'Art, you are the best. Always remember that.' She instilled a sense of self-confidence in me that I still have today."

A quotation should not repeat, or echo, facts reported earlier in a story:

Company officials said they are not worried about the upcoming audit.

"We're not expecting anything to worry about," treasurer Peter VanNeffe said.

Quotations can emphasize a story's dramatic moments, which, because of their importance, should be described in detail and placed near the beginning of a story. Myeshia Johnson, the widow of La David Johnson, a U.S. soldier killed in an ambush while combating terrorists in Niger, said the way President Donald Trump spoke to her in a phone call angered her. "He (Trump) couldn't remember my husband's name. The only way he remembered my husband's name is because he told me he had my husband's report in front of him," she told reporters. That quotation appeared high in many of the news stories reporting on the incident and even in some of the headlines.

10.1.2 When to Use Indirect Quotations

Some sources are more quotable than others, but even colorful sources sometimes say dull things. Reporters may be tempted to use whatever quotations happen to be available, but a weak quotation is worse than none. If a quotation bores or confuses people, many will immediately stop reading, listening or watching. Compare Myeshia Johnson's quotation with these:

> "It's something that's pretty unique here," she said.

> "The positive response was tremendous," Wesely said.

Neither of these quotations is interesting; each should be paraphrased or omitted entirely.

Reporters use indirect quotations when sources fail to state their ideas effectively. Indirect quotations allow reporters to rephrase sources' remarks and state them more clearly and concisely. Journalists can also emphasize the source's most significant comments and revise or eliminate ones that are unclear, irrelevant, libelous, pretentious or otherwise unprintable.

Here's a quotation from an FBI statement about a shoot-out in which an agent was killed. The quotation is wordy and dull; the paraphrase that follows it states the essential point more clearly:

> "Preliminarily, information suggests the agent may have been fatally wounded as a result of the accidental discharge of another agent's weapon during a dynamic arrest situation."

> An FBI statement said the agent might have been killed by a round fired by another agent during the shoot-out.

Reporters can never justify a weak quotation by responding, "But that's what my source said." They should use their interviewing skill and judgment to elicit and report quotations that are clear, concise, dramatic and interesting. Asking questions that encourage the source to elaborate on her or his ideas or reactions or provide examples or anecdotes often produces good quotations.

Avoid quotations—direct or indirect—that state the obvious or let sources praise themselves:

> "We really want to win this game," coach Riley said. (Does any coach want to lose?)

> Lyons called her program a success. "We had a terrific crowd and a particularly good turnout," she said. (Would she be likely to say her program flopped?)

Extracting material for an indirect quotation can be difficult, especially when the source is unclear or simply incoherent. President Trump's stream-of-consciousness style of speaking produces "word salad," or passages that jump from topic to topic with little logical connection. In one campaign address, Trump covered several topics in 90 seconds:

> Look, having nuclear—my uncle was a great professor and scientist and engineer, Dr. John Trump at MIT; good genes, very good genes, OK,

very smart, the Wharton School of Finance, very good, very smart—you know, if you're a conservative Republican, if I were a liberal, if, like, OK, if I ran as a liberal Democrat, they would say I'm one of the smartest people anywhere in the world—it's true!—but when you're a conservative Republican they try—oh, do they do a number—that's why I always start off: Went to Wharton, was a good student, went there, went there, did this, built a fortune—you know I have to give my like credentials all the time, because we're a little disadvantaged—but you look at the nuclear deal, the thing that really bothers me—it would have been so easy, and it's not as important as these lives are (nuclear is powerful; my uncle explained that to me many, many years ago, the power and that was 35 years ago; he would explain the power of what's going to happen and he was right—who would have thought?), but when you look at what's going on with the four prisoners—now it used to be three, now it's four—but when it was three and even now, I would have said it's all in the messenger; fellas, and it is fellas because, you know, they don't, they haven't figured that the women are smarter right now than the men, so, you know, it's gonna take them about another 150 years—but the Persians are great negotiators, the Iranians are great negotiators, so, and they, they just killed, they just killed us.

Not only is this passage difficult to read, it is difficult to paraphrase what Trump was trying to communicate. This example is an extreme one, and any person who speaks extemporaneously is likely to utter jumbled sentences. The reporter's job is to clarify such sentences by asking speakers to explain or rephrase their ideas.

10.1.3 When to Use Partial Quotations

Sometimes reporters try to get around the problem of weak or confusing quotations by directly quoting only a few words from a sentence. Most partial quotations, however, are awkward, wordy or unnecessary. Sentences that contain several partial quotations are particularly distracting. Usually, the quoted phrases can be turned into indirect constructions and the quotation marks eliminated:

● He said the press barons "such as William Randolph Hearst" created

   "~~an amazingly~~ ∧ rich variety" of newspapers.

Journalists also should avoid using orphan quotes, which put quotation marks around an isolated word or two used in an ordinary way. The quotation marks imply the word or phrase is being used in an unusual, sarcastic or ironic way. Such implications are inappropriate for news stories. Similarly, there is no reason to place quotation marks around profanities, slang, clichés or grammatical errors:

● He complained that no one "understands" his problem.

● She said that having to watch her child die was worse than "hell" could possibly be.

FROM THE NEWS

Defamatory Quotation Marks

Can sloppy use of punctuation make a sentence defamatory? A New York judge said yes.

New York police were investigating the murder of a business executive named Brenhouse. A story about the investigation in the New York Post contained these paragraphs:

> As police delved into his tangled business affairs, several women described as "associated" with Brenhouse were questioned at Hastings Police Headquarters.
>
> Among those questioned were Mrs. W.B. Wildstein who, with her husband, shared the second half of the two-family house in which Brenhouse lived.

Walter and Arlene Wildstein sued the Post, saying the quotation marks around "associated" implied she was having an extramarital affair with Brenhouse. The judge agreed, saying, "The use of quotation marks around the word 'associated' might be found by a jury to indicate that an inverted meaning was intended by the writer and so understood by the average reader of that newspaper in the community, and not its normal or customary meaning."

Reporters may use partial quotations to attribute more clearly controversial, important or interesting phrases to a source:

> Phil Donahue accused the television critic of "typing with razor blades."

> The petition urged the City Council to ban the sale of Penthouse and Playboy magazines "for the sake of our wives and children."

10.1.4 When Sources Seek Quote Approval

Sources often ask that information be kept off the record or on background (the information can be used, but the source cannot be named or quoted in the story). Lately, they have been making a new demand: the opportunity to approve specific quotations that appear in the stories.

Officials in a range of federal agencies have made this demand, as have politicians. When Barack Obama ran for re-election, leaders of his campaign and that of Republican Mitt Romney routinely demanded the right to approve quotations as a condition for any interview. The campaign workers were not objecting to the accuracy of the quotations; they wanted to prevent the publication of statements their opponents might use against them.

News organizations pushed back. The New York Times, the National Journal, the Washington Examiner and other publications prohibit their writers from allowing sources to approve quotations. Others urge their writers to resist such requests. Reporters confronting such a demand should know their organization's policy. Even if the organization does not forbid such agreements, they should carefully weigh the value of the information they expect to learn from the interview before agreeing. They should also remember that allowing sources to approve or edit quotations drains interview stories of their spontaneity and humanity. The result is a story that portrays the sources and the issues less accurately and completely.

10.2 Blending Quotations and Narrative

Every news story must have a central point, and everything in the story must relate to that point. The sources may speak about a number of topics, but only some of what they said may bear on the story's central point. Reporters must blend relevant quotations with the narrative to create a coherent, well-focused news story. This blending presents several problems and dilemmas for journalists.

10.2.1 Explaining Quotations

Sometimes reporters use a quotation and then realize the audience needs background information to understand it. In print journalism, they might insert explanatory material in parentheses or tack on the explanation after the attribution. Others might put a large block of background information high in the story, hoping it will give readers the information they need to understand the quotations and new facts reported elsewhere. Neither of these approaches works well.

Lazy writers insert explanatory material in parentheses within the quotation. When reporters pepper their sentences with inserted explanations, the stories become difficult to read. Each bit of parenthetical matter forces readers to pause and absorb additional information before moving on with the rest of the sentence. The occasional use of parentheses to insert brief clarifications may be acceptable, but reporters should paraphrase quotations that need several explanations. If reporters find themselves using parentheses repeatedly, they should consider reorganizing their stories. The following sentence can be rewritten to remove the parentheses:

> "When (head coach Tom) Whitman decides on his starter (at quarterback), the rest of them (the players) will quit squabbling," the athletic director said.

> The football players will quit squabbling when head coach Tom Whitman selects a starting quarterback, the athletic director said.

The next example includes an acceptable use of parentheses:

> Dr. Harold Termid, who performed the operation, said, "The technique dates back before the 20th century, when it was first used by the French to study ruminants (cud-chewing animals)."

Adding the explanatory information after the quotation or attribution is little better than using parentheses. Such backward constructions force readers to complete the sentence before they can figure out what the topic is. Here's an example:

> "We're mobilizing for an economic war with other cities and states," the mayor said of his plan for attracting new businesses to the city.

Instead of using this "said-of" construction, turn the sentence around and quote the speaker indirectly:

> The mayor said his plan for attracting new business amounted to mobilization for an economic war with other cities and states.

Beginning journalists sometimes think they must report their questions so that the audience can understand the source's answers. The news is in the answers, however, not in the questions. Using both is repetitive and dull:

> The president was asked whether he plans to seek a second term, and he responded that he would not announce his decision until winter.

Reporters usually omit the question. If the question provides important context, they incorporate it in the answer:

> The president said he would not announce his decision regarding a second term until winter.

Or

> In response to a question, the president said he would not announce his decision regarding a second term until winter.

10.2.2 To Change or Not to Change Quotations

A source may use words inappropriate for a news story; reporters may be tempted to alter these words to make the quotation usable. Whether writers should ever change a quotation is a matter of debate among journalists. Some accept minor changes to correct grammatical errors or delete profanity. Most, however, say reporters should never change quotations.

The Associated Press Stylebook says, "Never alter quotations even to correct minor grammatical errors or word usage. Casual minor tongue slips may be removed by using ellipses but even that should be done with extreme caution." The guide also states that if a speaker's words are unclear, seek a clarification or don't use them. The New York Times follows a similar policy: "Readers should be able to assume that every word between quotation marks is what the speaker or writer said. . . . The Times does not 'clean up' quotations."

Some sources are well known for the way they misuse words or create confusing sentences. Cleaning up their quotations would rob stories about them of their color. For example, President George W. Bush is famous for his malapropisms, mispronunciations and fractured syntax. When during his first presidential campaign he mispronounced "subliminal" as "subliminable," many news reports noted the slip. Bush later joked about it by intentionally mispronouncing the word.

Using a source's exact words also eliminates questions about accuracy. Reporters who are uncertain about the source's exact words or who think a statement needs rewriting should use indirect rather than direct quotations. Doctoring a quotation could lead to a mistake that would injure the source's reputation and the journalist's career.

Even those who oppose altering quotations recognize a few instances where changes are necessary. A reporter should paraphrase a quotation if it is so ungrammatical that it becomes difficult to understand:

> "The council and the mayor is giving them corporations too much tax breaks so the load's not fair no more," Andrews said.

Paraphrasing makes the sentence much clearer:

> The council and the mayor have given so many tax breaks to corporations that the tax burden is no longer shared fairly, Andrews said.

Other situations involve the deletion of unnecessary words and profanities (discussed in the next section):

- He said, "~~Look, you know I think~~ nuclear power is safe, absolutely safe."

Reporters may use an ellipsis—three periods—to show where they deleted a word or phrase. An ellipsis that appears at the end of a complete sentence should have four periods. Policies vary from news organization to news organization, and some journalists do not use ellipses in reporting ordinary interviews. Reporters are more likely to use them when quoting formal statements or documents.

Reporters are obliged to present a source's views as faithfully as possible; therefore, they must be certain that they are not removing important context when quoting a source. During his campaign for the Republican presidential nomination, U.S. Sen. Ted Cruz argued against Obama's plan to allow 10,000 refugees from Syria to enter the United States. Cruz said ISIS terrorists were likely to be among the refugees and, to support his view, said Obama's director of national intelligence, James Clapper, agreed with him:

> *There is a reason the director of national intelligence said among those refugees are no doubt a significant number of ISIS terrorists. It would be the height of foolishness to bring in tens of thousands of people including jihadists that are coming here to murder innocent Americans.*

In fact, Clapper said no such thing. He had described the situation in Syria as a major humanitarian crisis that western nations had to address. Then he added,

> *I don't, obviously, put it past the likes of ISIL to infiltrate operatives among these refugees. So that is a huge concern of ours. We do have a pretty aggressive program for those coming to this country, for screening their backgrounds. I'm not as uniformly confident about each European country that is going to be faced with welcoming or allowing refugees into their countries. So this is a*

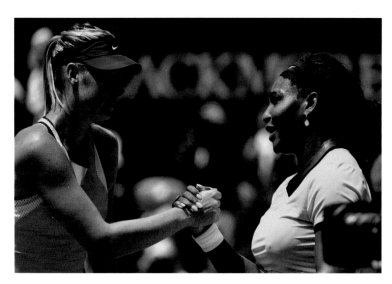

Tennis star Serena Williams (right) told Vogue some people may see her game face and think she's mean, whereas they are likely to think of Maria Sharapova as nicer. A British newspaper distorted the quotation and made it appear there was a feud between the two players.

huge issue for all kinds of reasons. The security implications are just one small part of it. The economic, the social impacts, are huge.

While Clapper admitted there were security concerns, he stopped far short of saying a significant number of the refugees admitted into the U.S. would be ISIS terrorists.

10.2.3 Deleting Profanities

Reporters usually omit profanities from quotations. Children read, view and listen to news, and many adults find four-letter words offensive. News organizations are becoming more candid, however, and some publish mild profanities that are essential to a story. Casual profanities—those used habitually and unnecessarily by many people—remain forbidden in most newsrooms:

- "~~Shit,~~ I wasn't going to try to stop that ~~damned~~ idiot," the witness testified. "He had a knife."

Print and broadcast journalists face a dilemma when a prominent official uses profanity in a public statement. What government officials say is important to voters, but reporting quotations with profanity verbatim may offend many people. Donald Trump, both as a candidate and as president, said things that forced news organizations to ponder whether to use the offensive words. On one occasion, he said companies that do not like his tax plan can "go fuck themselves." Most news organizations omitted or disguised the profanity. In a video released late in the 2016 campaign, Trump talked about grabbing women "by the pussy." Many broadcast news organizations bleeped the last word and many publications avoided using it as well. Later, as president, Trump was meeting with Republican and Democratic legislators to work out a change in immigration law to allow undocumented aliens who arrived in the United States as children to remain in the country. Trump reportedly balked at extending this to immigrants from Central and South America, the Caribbean and Africa. Officials at the conference said Trump called countries in those areas "shithole countries." The New York Times and other news organizations included the full term in their stories. Even network news shows included the word. Their willingness to use the vulgarity stemmed from the national and international ramifications of the president's holding such views.

10.2.4 Editorialization

Avoid unintentional editorials. If worded carelessly, partial quotations, and even the form of attribution used, can express an opinion:

- The mayor ~~made it clear that~~ ^*said* the city cannot afford to give its employees a raise.

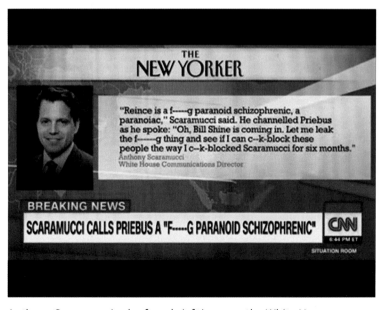

Anthony Scaramucci, who for a brief time was the White House communications director, gave a profanity-laced interview to Ryan Lizza of The New Yorker. The interview made big news, and news organizations had to decide whether to use any of the profanity and how much.

Defense Secretary Lloyd Austin and Gen. Mark Milley, chairman of the Joints Chiefs of Staff, take questions from reporters about the withdrawal of U.S. troops from Afghanistan. Readers, viewers and listeners have more confidence in news stories when they know the source of the information.

The phrase "made it clear" implies that the mayor stated a fact in a convincing manner. Others might regard the statement that the city cannot afford pay raises for employees as an opinion or political posturing.

10.3 Attribution

10.3.1 The Purpose of Attribution

Reporters are not economists or ecologists, detectives or diplomats. Nevertheless, they must write effectively about such things as unemployment, the effects of oil spills on the environment, the search for serial killers and the prospects for peace in the Middle East. To write these stories, reporters rely on experts and insiders for information and ideas. Attribution lets the readers know who the reporter's sources are. Ideally, all direct quotations, opinions, evaluations and secondhand statements of fact should be attributed to specific individuals. This information lets readers draw their own conclusions about the credibility of the story.

Reporters can attribute information to people, documents or publications but not to places or institutions. For example, reporters can quote a hospital official, but not a hospital:

- ~~The~~ A hospital spokesperson said the epidemic had ended.

- The mayor of Atlanta announced that all city offices would be closed Monday.

10.3.2 Statements That Require Attribution

Reporters need not attribute undisputed facts, such as that World War II ended in 1945, that Boston is in Massachusetts or that three people died in a given accident. Nor must they attribute things they witness. However, they must attribute facts that are not common knowledge, statements about controversial issues, statements of opinion and all direct and indirect quotations. An audience will interpret statements lacking attribution as the reporter's opinions instead of those of the sources. Just a few words of attribution are usually adequate:

- Director Sally Malone said The Birthing Center is an alternative for pregnant women who prefer more personalized care.

Reporters must attribute statements that praise or condemn any person or organization. The audience should immediately recognize that a story reports what someone else said, not the journalist's or news organization's opinions:

- The House Republican leader said Congress has wasted time while the problem of unemployment has worsened.

- ∧*A̶cting* in self-defense ∧*;̶ t̶h̶e̶ d̶e̶p̶u̶t̶y̶* shot the teen three times in the chest.

  The deputy said she was a *when she*

Statements that imply carelessness, recklessness or culpable conduct can provoke lawsuits. Careful attribution, particularly if the statements come from official sources, reduces the risk of being sued.

10.3.3 Guidelines for the Placement and Frequency of Attribution

Attribution may be placed at the beginning or end of a sentence or at a natural break within it. However, it should never interrupt a thought:

- *"̶I̶ s̶h̶a̶l̶l̶,̶"* Gen. MacArthur said, " ∧ return."

  I shall

This form of attribution is acceptable:

- "Some men are killed in a war and some men are wounded," President Kennedy said, "and some men never leave the country. Life is unfair."

Attribution should appear as early as conveniently possible; readers, viewers and listeners should never have to guess who is speaking. Stories written for broadcast usually put the attribution at the beginning of the sentence. In print stories, the attribution should appear near the beginning of quotations of one long sentence or of two or more sentences. It should not be delayed until the end of the second or third sentence:

- "However close we sometimes seem to that dark and final abyss, ∧let no man of peace and freedom despair. For he does not stand alone. If we all can persevere, if we can in every land and office look beyond our shores and ambitions, then surely the age will dawn in which the strong are just and the weak secure and the peace preserved;̶ ∧" t̶h̶e̶ p̶r̶e̶s̶i̶d̶e̶n̶t̶ s̶a̶i̶d̶.̶

  " the president said, "

For print stories, the attribution should come at the beginning of any quotation—even a short one—when there is a change of speakers. If reporters fail to provide transitions from one speaker to another, readers may not understand who is speaking, particularly when the statements are contradictory:

> The newspaper's editor said he no longer will accept advertisements for movies rated NC-17. He explained: "These movies are worthless. They contribute nothing to society and offend our readers. They're depressing and pornographic."

> "Newspapers have no right to pass judgment on matters of taste. If they do, they should also ban the advertisements for other products considered harmful: cigarettes, liquor and pollutants like automobiles," a theater owner responded.

These two paragraphs are confusing. Readers beginning the second paragraph might think the editor is contradicting himself. The writer can avoid the confusion by placing a brief transition at the beginning of the second paragraph, such as the following:

> However, a local theater owner responded, "Newspapers have no right. . . . "

10.3.4 Direct Quotations

A direct quotation should be attributed only once, regardless of the number of sentences it contains:

● "I'm opposed to any laws that prohibit the sale of pornography," the attorney said. "The restriction of pornography infringes on Americans' First Amendment rights," he said. "I like to picture myself as a good guy defending a sleazy thing," he concluded.

Even a direct quotation that continues for several paragraphs needs attribution only once.

Reporters must avoid "floating" quotations, direct quotations that lack clear attribution to a speaker. Careless writers sometimes name a source in one sentence and then deliver an unattributed quotation in the following sentence or paragraph. The reader must guess whether the quotation comes from the person just named or someone who will be identified later. The uncertainty halts the reader, and several such delays can cause him or her to put down the newspaper or magazine. Clear attribution makes the reader's work easier:

● Wendy Mitchell, a sociologist, said there is a trend toward vocationalism on college campuses.

    "Many students now demand from college not a chance to think," she said, "but a chance to become qualified for some job."

10.3.5 Partial Quotations

On the rare occasions when writers quote part of a sentence, they should separate it from complete sentences that also are being quoted. Combining partial and complete quotations sometimes causes confusing pronoun shifts, which can be avoided by either placing attribution between the partial quotation and the full-sentence quotation or paraphrasing the partial quotation:

● Ross said he expects to find a job "within a few weeks." He added, "And when I do get a job, the first thing I'm going to buy is a new car."

    Or

● Ross said he expects to find a job "within a few weeks. "And when I do get a job, the first thing I'm going to buy is a new car," he added.

The original passage is confusing because of a shift in pronouns. The first sentence uses the third person, referring to Ross as "he." But in the second sentence, which is the full quotation, Ross refers to himself in the first person. Rewriting the partial quotation eliminates the confusion.

10.3.6 Indirect Quotations

Indirect quotations need more frequent attribution than do direct quotations. Every opinion or unverified fact in an indirect quotation must be attributed. In the following example, the first version is missing attributions; the revised version corrects the problem:

> The police chief insisted that the death penalty must be retained. The death penalty, harsh as it may seem, is designed to protect the lives and rights of law-abiding citizens. Without it, criminals' rights are overly protected. Because of the almost endless mechanisms of the appeal system, it is unlikely that an innocent person would be put to death.

> The police chief insisted that the death penalty must be retained. The death penalty might seem harsh, he said, but it is designed to protect the lives and rights of law-abiding citizens. Without it, criminals' rights are overly protected, he said. Because of the almost endless mechanisms of the appeal system, he said, it is unlikely that an innocent person would be put to death.

Often, every sentence of indirect quotation should have attribution, but writers should avoid inserting phrases that attribute a quotation twice, as in this example:

- In making the announcement, the fire chief said arsonists caused 20 percent of the blazes reported in the city last year.

Here are more examples of double attribution, each of which can be replaced by either "said" or "added":

made it clear that	said that he thinks that
further stated that	brought out the idea that
went on to say that	went on to say that in his opinion

With both direct and indirect quotations, writers strive to vary the location of the attribution. Writing becomes dull if every sentence begins "She said" or some variation. Moving the attribution keeps stories interesting. Often the most effective location for attribution is after the first natural pause in the sentence.

10.3.7 Word Choice in Attributing Statements

The verbs used to attribute statements must be accurate and impartial. For straight news stories, they also should be in the past tense. For feature stories, writers may use present tense attribution. Present tense is acceptable in broadcast news copy, too.

Some form of the verb "to say" best describes how sources speak. For variety, reporters sometimes use such verbs as "comment," "reply," "declare," "assert," "explain," "state," "continue," "point out," "note," "urge," "suggest" and "warn." Each has a more specific meaning than "say" and can be used only when that meaning accurately reflects how the source spoke. "Explain," for instance, means to make something comprehensible or less obscure. Unless the source was discussing a complicated or unclear topic, "explain" would not be an appropriate verb for attribution:

> The city council meeting will begin at 8 p.m., he explained.

This sentence states a fact that needs no explaining. The next sentence clarifies a point of law that may be confusing; therefore, "explained" is acceptable:

> She explained that tort law requires that the injurious consequences of a person's actions be foreseeable before that person can be held liable for damages.

Even worse than using an inappropriate verb for attribution is using no verb at all, as with "according to." Beginning reporters find it tempting to use this phrase, but they should remember that verbs always strengthen sentences.

10.3.8 Identifying Sources

Ideally, every source quoted should be fully identified so that what he or she says is on the record and can be quoted directly and attributed properly. The amount and nature of the identification depends on the type of story and the source's contribution.

For many basic news stories—crimes, fires, business actions or rallies by interest groups—the major sources are public officials, business executives or owners and officers of interest groups. The best way to identify these sources is by name, title and organization:

> The robbers left the store in a dark red 2011 Chevrolet Malibu, police Sgt. Maureen Fonoti said.

> "The purpose of this protest is to demand that the legislature repeal or revise the state's voter identification law," said Robert Watson, the executive director of Voters Unbound.

People being quoted because they witnessed newsworthy events or because their opinions have been sought through an informal poll should be identified by name, age (if the person is willing to reveal it) and address, if they live in the same city where the news is published, or hometown, if they live in another town. A person's occupation may also be relevant:

> Patricia Mulrooney, 39, of 1748 N. Third St. said she first saw the smoke about 3 p.m. and called the fire department.

> Wendell Morgan of Altoona, Kansas, said he had opposed the Affordable Care Act when it was before Congress. But Morgan, a 56-year-old hardware store owner, said he had changed his mind now that he can find an insurance policy that fits his budget.

People increasingly are concerned about their privacy. They may prefer that news organizations not use their home address in a story. In such cases, the reporter can identify people by their neighborhoods.

Names alone fail to provide enough information about the sources for a story. Audiences want to know enough about the people quoted to form at least a general picture of who they are. This is especially important with people who are quoted in or are the subjects of feature stories or are the subjects of anecdotal leads.

Here are the first few paragraphs from a story about December as a popular time of the year for couples to get engaged:

> Carmen Nunziata loves this time of year.
>
> Every Thanksgiving, she puts up holiday decorations and listens to nothing but Christmas music until the beginning of January. Each room in her house has Christmas flair, even the bathroom, which has a Santa hat hanging from a towel rack.
>
> Grady Smith, her live-in boyfriend, knows how special the holidays are to Nunziata. He also loves the holiday season and thought it would be the perfect time to propose.
>
> Nunziata and Smith are certainly not the only couple to become engaged during this holiday season. In fact, a trendy new label describes this time of year as "Engagement Season."

"In Washington, today, an unidentified source made an unattributable statement which under the agreed ground rules is not to be quoted."

Who are Nunziata and Smith? What do they do? How old are they? Where do they live? The story provides none of these details. One might have a different reaction to it if Nunziata and Smith were retirees living in a center for senior citizens than if they were university students getting ready to graduate. A story that fails to identify sources fully is incomplete.

Occasionally, reporters use sources who want their identities concealed. They will speak only on background—sometimes called not-for-attribution—meaning the reporter can quote the sources directly but cannot use their names. In this case, the journalist must describe the sources using phrases such as "a law enforcement officer familiar with the investigation," "a source close to the president" or "a legislator who is participating in the negotiations."

Editors and producers dislike the use of unnamed sources because it diminishes the credibility of the news. Readers, viewers and listeners are skeptical of stories with unnamed sources, in part because of some well-known incidents in which reporters simply made up sources and quotations. Editors at The New York Times, which was the victim of a journalist who manufactured sources, tell their staff that anonymity for sources is a last resort.

If reporters want sources on the record, why do so many stories use anonymous sources? Sometimes sources want to remain anonymous for legitimate reasons. Corporate or government officials who want to blow the whistle on waste, fraud or other illegal or unethical conduct at their workplace may fear retaliation. Many have lost jobs or been demoted because they disclosed truths that made their supervisors uncomfortable.

Reporters on some beats have to rely on anonymous sources. Bill Hamilton, The New York Times' Washington editor, says people with knowledge about

HOT TIP

Guidelines for Using Anonymous Sources

On the rare occasions when justification exists for using anonymous sources, news executives tell their reporters to follow guidelines like these:

- Do not use anonymous sources without the approval of your supervising editor or news director.

- Be prepared to disclose the identities of anonymous sources to your editors or news directors and, possibly, to your news organization's lawyer.

- Use anonymous sources only if they provide facts that are essential to the story, not just interesting quotations or opinions. Be sure the sources are appropriate for the story and are in a position to give authoritative information. Even then, information from anonymous sources should be verified.

- Be sure you understand the motives of anonymous sources, such as whether they are carrying a grudge or trying to puff a program or an agency. The motives help you evaluate the reliability of the information.

- Identify sources as specifically as possible without revealing their identities so that the audience can judge their importance and reliability. For example, instead of attributing information to "an informed source" or "a key official," you might attribute it to "an elected city official." This tells readers, viewers or listeners the level of government in which the official works and alerts them to the fact that he or she may have political interests. Never include any misleading information about the identity of sources, even if your motive is to protect them.

- Explain in the story why the sources do not want to be identified.

- Never allow anonymous sources to attack other individuals or groups. Anonymous attacks risk involving you and your employer in a libel suit and are inherently unfair to the people attacked.

security issues almost never talk on the record. Obtaining information about the National Security Agency or the Central Intelligence Agency has become increasingly difficult as federal officials have tried to stop leaks. Some people who have spoken to reporters have been criminally prosecuted or threatened with prosecution under the Espionage Act. And reporters who cover national security issues have been subpoenaed to reveal their sources' identities. If they refuse to do so, they may be jailed for contempt of court.

The Reporter's Guide to Quotations and Attribution

QUOTATIONS

1. Use quotations sparingly to emphasize a point or change pace, not to tell the story or state facts.

2. Place only the exact words of the source within quotation marks.

3. Use quotations to serve a purpose, such as to reveal the source's character, describe or emphasize a point or present an opinion.

4. Include direct quotations that are clear, concise, relevant and effective.

5. Avoid awkward combinations of partial and direct quotations.

6. Report only the source's answers, not the questions you asked.

7. Eliminate orphan quotations and floating quotations.

8. Make sure the quotations do not repeat facts reported elsewhere in the story.

9. For a one-paragraph quotation that includes two or more sentences, place the quotation marks only at the beginning and end of the entire quotation, not at the beginning and end of each sentence.

10. Capitalize the first letter of all quotations that are full sentences but not of partial quotations.

11. Divide long quotations into shorter paragraphs; place open quotation marks at the beginning of each paragraph, but place closed quotation marks at the end of only the final paragraph.

12. Use single quotation marks for quotations that appear within other quotations.

ATTRIBUTION

1. Attribute all secondhand information, criticisms, statements about controversial issues, opinions and all direct and indirect quotations. (Do not attribute undisputed facts.)

2. Punctuate the attribution properly. Put a comma after an attribution that introduces a one-sentence direct quotation and a colon after an attribution that introduces two or more sentences of direct quotation.

3. Put the attribution at or near the beginning of a long quotation.

4. When including an attribution in the middle of a sentence, place it at a natural break rather than interrupt a thought.

5. Vary sentences and paragraphs so that all do not begin with attribution.

6. Place the attribution outside the quotation marks.

7. Attribute each direct quotation only once.

8. Attribute each separate statement of opinion in indirect quotations.

9. Attribute statements only to people, documents or publications, never to places or institutions.

10. Provide transitions between statements from different sources, particularly when a quotation from one source immediately follows a quotation from a different source.

11. Select the verb of attribution that most accurately describes the source's actual meaning and behavior.

12. Do not use such verbs as "hope," "feel," "believe," "think," "laugh," "cough" and "cry" for attribution.

13. Make the attribution as concise as possible.

Review Exercises

1. IMPROVING QUOTATIONS AND ATTRIBUTION

Section I: Avoiding Double Attribution

Rewrite the following sentences, attributing them only once. Correct any other errors.

1. In a report issued Tuesday, the state Department of Environmental Quality said fertilizer runoff from farms was endangering fish populations in 12 percent of the state's rivers and streams.

2. In her speech to the members of the Home Builders Association, Carson added that the demand for new homes and apartments was expected to pick up in 18 months, she said.

3. Professor Heather Wong said the companies that benefitted the most from U.S. defense spending were concentrated in six states, according to her data.

Section II: Correcting Placement Errors

Correct the attribution placement in the following sentences. Correct any other errors.

1. No matter how famous a person has, she said, been, no one can win an election on fame alone.

2. The team should win, the coach said, every game this season.

3. Kopperud said, "Crime is down in this city for two reasons. First, the department has added 30 new patrol officers who have concentrated on high-crime areas. Second, unemployment is down, and the crime rate always declines when more people are working."

Section III: Condensing Wordy Attributions

The attributions in the following sentences are too wordy. How many words can you eliminate? Rewrite the attribution if necessary. Correct any other errors.

1. *Mayor Datoli announced to the council members at the start of her speech that* she will interview 10 candidates for the city comptroller job.

2. School board member Judy Lu *pointed out that in her opinion* the district was spending 20 percent too much on salaries.

3. *Judge Hall added that her experience shaped her belief that* short sentences for nonviolent offenders were more effective than long ones.

4. *Grauman went on to point out how surveys by several local professors demonstrated that* few people were willing to pay more taxes to have more paved roads.

5. Modern corporations waste too much of their investors' money on public relations, *Carson said as he began offering his analysis of the stock market in a speech to the Chamber of Commerce.*

6. Politicians must pay more attention to climate change, *he continued by insisting that listeners realize the need for immediate action*, or the country will face droughts and famine in the near future.

Section IV: Multiple Errors

Correct all the problems and errors in the following sentences.

1. Hendricks said, 'winning this case was the most satisfying of my career. It's saved the county's tax-payers $5 million.

2. Saul Bellow once said "a novel is balanced between a few true impressions and the multitude of false ones that make up most of what we call life."

3. When Datolli was asked why she had rejected the Fire Department's request for three new fire trucks, she replied "because we don't want to raise taxes this year."

4. The bank president said the "dollar" and the "euro" were the two currencies that were most likely to suffer because of the "economic policies" of China.

5. "All immigrant groups in the United States, said the FBI director, deserve the same level of respect and legal protection as citizens of this county." he explained

6. The president spoke to the students telling them that. "The challenge of the next half century is whether we have the wisdom to use our wealth to enrich and elevate our national life.

7. "The basic tenet of black consciousness" said Steve Biko "is that the black man must reject all value systems that seek to make him a foreigner in the country of his birth".

8. "For several years, winter has been bringing less and less snow." "Meanwhile, summers have been longer and hotter." Said Bonita Nichols, the director of the state Office of Agriculture.

9. "The enemy of the market." argued economist John Kenneth Galbraith. 'is not ideology but the engineer.

10. The $1 million shortfall in revenues for the city should be "easy to replace," Mayor Sharon Datolli said. "Although no one wants to pay more in taxes." She said. "The city should be able to cover the deficit with a small additional tax on cable television".

11. The veteran of fighting in Iraq and Afghanistan praised the commanders and comrades of her military police battalion. "I've never worked with a more determined group of people". "The conditions were horrible and the enemy implacable". "If we hadn't held together, we all might have died".

12. Sure, I swipe credit card numbers sometimes." said the waiter who asked not to be named. "Its easy to just write down the numbers and then use them to order stuff over the Internet." "I've done that several times and haven't been caught so far. "I think these people must not look at their credit-card statements." The waiter added.

13. "Too many pupils think school is dull or doesn't matter." 'They must be getting these ideas from their parents or siblings. And their coming to school with these attitudes at younger and younger ages, as young as 7 or 8, said the principal.

14. Chester Johnson, a teller, described what happened during the bank robbery. I was in my teller's cage when these three guys came in. They were all wearing raincoats, which was strange on a sunny day. But then they pulled out their guns. One had a shotgun I think and the others had pistols.

2. USING QUOTES IN NEWS STORIES

Write complete news stories based on the following information. Use some quotations in each story to emphasize its highlights, but do not use them to tell the entire story. Use the most interesting, important and revealing quotations, not just those that happen to appear first. Correct errors of fact, style, spelling and grammar.

1. Carlos Vacante is a police officer who has worked 3 years for your city's police department. Last night he had an unusual experience. This is his story, as he told it to you in an interview today: "I remember his eyes. They were cold, the eyes of a killer. He was pointing a gun at me, and it fired. I smelled the gunpowder and waited for the pain. I thought I was dead. The whole thing had started at about 11 p.m. This man was suspected of stealing from parked cars, and I'd gotten his description by radio. Then I spotted him in a parking lot. This morning we learned he's wanted in the robbery and murder of a service station attendant in Tennessee. There's no doubt in my mind he wanted to kill me last night just because I stopped him. I was an object in his way. I'd gotten out of my car and called to him. He started turning around and I spotted a handgun in his waistband. As he drew the gun and fired, I leaned to the right and dropped to one knee. It was just a reflex that saved my life. When I heard the shot, I thought he hit me. I couldn't believe it was actually happening to me. I thought I was going to cash everything in. Then I was running—zig-Zagging—behind some cars. He fired another shot, but my backup arrived, and he fled. Maybe 60 seconds had passed from the time I spotted him. Five minutes later, we found him at the back door to a house, trying to break in and hide. I ordered him to stop, and he put his hands up and said, 'You got me.' I still smell the gunpowder this morning. I thought I was dead."

2. The city's Ministerial Alliance spoke out today against the death penalty. A copy of a resolution it adopted will be sent to the governor and to every member of the state legislature. As its spokesman, the Rev. Stuart Adler declared: "None of us is soft on crime. There must be just punishment for those who commit violent crimes, but what we are saying is we stop short of taking another person's life. We object because several independent studies have concluded that the death penalty is no deterrent to crime, rather the violence of the death penalty only breeds more violence. Also, the method of sentencing people

is inconsistent. There is a great disparity between the victim being black or white. Defendants accused of killing black victims often are not sentenced to death, but when the victim is white, the death penalty is often imposed. People are frightened by the amount of violence in our society, and they've been sold a bill of goods. They've been told that the death penalty is a deterrent, and yet every major study disproves that reality. We're not getting at the deeper causes. We're a violent society, and getting more violent. Half the households in this city have guns, and it's inevitable some are going to use them. If we're really serious about stopping crime and violence, we have to recognize and correct its root causes: poverty, racial and sexual discrimination, broken homes and unloved children. Also drugs and alcohol. That's what's responsible for most crimes. And television. Studies show the average child in America witnesses, on television, 200,000 acts of violence by age 16. So we're against the death penalty. It's not going to solve our problems, and it's not fair, not fairly applied. It'll take time, but we intend to abolish it, and we'll persist. We're already beginning to stimulate discussion, and we expect that discussion to spread."

3. A rise in insurance rates is being blamed for a rise in hit-and-run motor vehicle accidents within the state. Richard Byrum, state insurance commissioner, discussed the problem during a press conference in his office today. He said, "The problem is serious. At first, we thought it was a police problem, but police in the state have asked my office to look into it. There has been a dramatic increase in hit-and-run accidents in the state, particularly in big cities where you find the higher insurance rates. I'm told that last year we had nearly 28,000 motor vehicle accidents in the state, and 4,500 were hit-and-run. People are taking chances driving without proper insurance coverage, or they're afraid of a premium increase if they have insurance and stop and report an accident. They seem to think, 'What the heck, no one saw it, and I won't get caught,' and they just bug out of there. If you look at the insurance rates in the state, it's practically impossible for some people to pay them, and as insurance rates go up, the rate of leaving the scene of an accident increases. Drivers with the worst records—those with several accidents and traffic citations—pay as much as $3,600 a year in insurance premiums, and they may pay even more

than that if they are young or have a high-powered car. Even good drivers found at fault in an accident may find their rates going up several hundred dollars for the next three to five years. So leaving the scene of an accident is definitely tied to the economic situation, yet the insurance company people I've talked to say they can't do anything about it. It's just not realistic to expect them to lower their rates; they aren't making that much money. Right now, I'm not sure what we'll do about the situation. In the meantime, we can expect more hit-and-run accidents and more drivers going without any insurance coverage because of its high cost."

4. Michael Ernest Layoux, 22, is a clerk at a convenience store at 1284 East Forest Boulevard. He was robbed late yesterday. Here is his account of the incident: "First, you have to understand where the store is. It's located in a remote area in the northeast corner of town. There's nothing around that's open at night, so I'm all alone in the store. I started carrying a gun to work last year after I read where two clerks at another convenience store in the city were robbed and killed. Carrying a gun is against company policy, but I figured I had to protect myself. We're open 24 hours, and the store has a history of holdups, particularly at night when there aren't any customers in the store. But it never happened to me personally before. Just after 11, when the store was empty except for me last night, this guy walks in and asks for a pack of Winston cigarettes. I handed him a pack, and then he pulled a gun and says, 'You see what I got?' He had a pistol, and he held it low, level with his hip, so no one outside the store could look in and see it. Then he asked me for the money, and I gave it to him. We never have more than $30 in cash in the register. It's company policy. We put all the big bills we get into a floor safe we can't open. So he didn't get much, maybe $20. Then he motioned for me to move toward the cooler. We have a big cooler in the back for beer and soda and other stuff we have to keep cold. When he started shoving me toward the cooler I really got scared. There's no lock on the cooler, so he couldn't lock me in while he was getting away. There's no reason for him to put me in the cooler; I could walk right out. The only thing I could figure was that he wanted to shoot me, and he wanted to do

it in some place where no one could see what was happening. That's where the two other clerks were shot last year, in a cooler in their store. Since they were killed, I've kept a .25-caliber pistol under the counter, and when he motioned for me to get into the cooler I shot him. He'd started turning toward the cooler, and then he must have heard me cocking the pistol because he started jerking his head back around toward me. I shot him 3 times in the chest and side, but I didn't know right away that I hit him. He just ran out through the front door. He didn't even open it. He ran right through the glass. I called the police, and they found his body in a field about 200 yards away. He was dead, and now I've lost my job. But I wouldn't do it any different. The police talked to me for almost two hours, and they said it was OK, that I acted in self-defense. Then this morning, just after 8, I got a call at home from my district manager, and he said I'm fired because it's against company policy to have a gun in the store. It's a real shame, because I'm still a college student, and I need the job. I can attend classes during the day and then work at night at the store. I've been doing it for 4 years now, and I want to graduate in a couple more months. But I can understand the company's rules. Most people don't know how to handle guns. I do. I've been around them and using them all my life." Company officials refused to comment about the robbery or the firing. Ramone Hernandez, the district attorney, confirmed that his office considered the shooting self-defense and would not prosecute Layoux. Officer Alan Nega, who investigated the incident, said the body found in the field near the store was that of Robert A. Wiess, 2032 Turf Way, Apt. 388.

5. Lillian Shisenaunt is a pharmacist. She was elected president of your County Pharmacists Association at a meeting held last night. During an interview with you today, she talked about an issue of concern to pharmacists, one that the group talked about at the meeting, along with possible solutions. She said: "We find that we've got an awful lot of older people taking three or four or five different drugs all at once. If they think that's going to do them any good, they're fooling themselves. We find that, in many cases, the medicine—the dosage and the way it's taken—are all wrong. Patients, especially the elderly, sometimes get all their different drugs confused, and then they take two of one and none of the others. Even when the elderly take all the right pills, sometimes the different drugs nullify each other. Different doctors these people see give them prescriptions without knowing what else a patient is taking for some other problem. So some of these oldsters become real junkies, and they don't even know it. As they get older and have more problems, they take more and more medication. After a few years, their children think their minds are going because they're so heavily sedated all the time. But if they get a good doctor, or a good druggist, they probably can stop taking some of the medicines, and then they don't actually have all the problems people think they have. A lot of these older people aren't senile; they just take too many different drugs, and then it hits them like senility. Drug companies don't help. If you look at most drug companies, they test their products on healthy young adults, a 25-year-old, 180-pound male. Then the companies set a normal adult dosage based on the clinical tests with these young adults. But the things that determine how drugs affect you change with age, so what the drug companies set as a normal daily dosage doesn't always fit an older person with a number of conditions. If you look at studies of hospital emergency rooms, you'll find that people over 60 are admitted twice as often for adverse drug reactions as the young. Most people don't know that. They think about all the problems of the young, not the old. But most of the problems can be solved, and without too much effort. People should talk to a good pharmacist or physician. Unfortunately, we find that most people are scared of their doctors and don't ask them enough questions and don't understand what their pharmacists have to offer. Patients also should make a list of all their different medicines and dosages each time they go to a doctor and tell him what they're taking. Then when they get a new prescription, they should write down the doctor's instructions, and they should get all their prescriptions from just one pharmacist so the pharmacist knows everything they're taking and can watch for any problems. If they ask, the pharmacist can color code their pill bottles so they can't be confused. But patients also have a responsibility for their own health care. Each morning, they should sort out all that day's pills ahead of time, and then they'd be less likely to make a mistake."

INTERVIEWING

Presidents often sit for interviews with reporters, especially when they are in the midst of a re-election campaign. Donald Trump was facing a tough campaign against Joe Biden in August 2020 when Jonathan Swan of Axios conducted an interview with him that appeared on HBO. The COVID-19 pandemic was surging, and no vaccine was yet available. At the time of the interview, COVID deaths in the United States had gone from one on March 1 to more than 150,000. Swan questioned Trump on his response to the virus and at one point asked the president how he could consider it under control when more than 1,000 people a day were dying. Trump responded: "They are dying. That's true. And it is what it is. But that doesn't mean we aren't doing everything we can. It's under control as much as you can control it. This is a horrible plague that beset us."

President Joe Biden had just concluded an event at the White House celebrating the reauthorization of the Violence Against Women Act when he was asked by Fox News reporter Jacqui Heinrich if he was ready to brand Vladimir Putin a war criminal for the way he was conducting war against Ukraine. Biden responded "no" and turned and walked away. After a couple of minutes, however, he came back to Heinrich and asked her to repeat the question, which she did. This time, Biden responded, "I think he is a war criminal." A day later, Biden expanded on that saying Putin is "a pure thug who is waging an immoral war against the people of Ukraine."

The comments Trump and Biden made in response to reporters' questions made headlines. Anything a president says can be newsworthy simply because of the importance of the person saying it. These remarks, however, had broader impact. Trump's comment on his handling of the COVID-19 outbreak suggested he had adopted a fatalistic attitude toward the many deaths and illnesses Americans were experiencing. Biden's remarks attracted broad attention because heads of state rarely call each other "war criminals" or "thugs," and doing so threatened to escalate the tension between the United States and Russia.

Interviewing—asking questions, getting answers and asking more questions—is a basic tool of the journalist. For the experienced investigative reporter as well as the fresh-from-college police reporter, interviewing provides much of the fact, background and color for any news story. Interviewing, properly used, can be an effective method of gathering information.

President Donald Trump answers a question from CBS 60 Minutes correspondent Lesley Stahl during an interview conducted less than two weeks before the 2020 elections.

11.1 Preparing for the Interview

No matter what kind of story a reporter writes, it usually will require at least one interview. Successful interviews do not just happen; they are the product of thought and planning. An interview's purpose determines the length and required preparation. Often interviews are short and focused on gathering a few specific pieces of information. A journalist may ask a legislator a few questions about a bill's objective or provisions. Another may question a police officer to get details about a recent crime. On other occasions, reporters may ask one or two specific questions of many people to gather an unscientific sampling of public opinion. Some reporters specialize in writing profiles of famous or interesting people. They usually conduct long interviews—sometimes stretching over several days—with the subjects of their stories.

Reporters preparing to interview a source should ask themselves, "Why am I conducting this interview? What kind of story will I write from this information?" The answers to these questions will determine what they ask, the sources they seek and their conduct during the interview. The reasons for interviewing are as varied as the resulting stories, but most often journalists are seeking information for one of three story types: the news story, the feature story or the investigative story (see Table 11.1).

Reporters who cover a news story, such as a crime or a city council action, usually interview several individuals to gather all the relevant information. They may seek just a few facts or a brief reaction from each individual. Collectively, however, the material allows them to construct a complete narrative of a newsworthy event or explanation of an important issue.

Reporters writing feature stories, such as personality profiles, must gather additional information that will provide the color and detail the audience needs to better understand a person or a situation (see Chapter 12). Investigative reporters must dig deeper still to uncover actions and motives that their subjects may prefer to keep hidden (see Chapter 18).

TABLE 11.1 INFORMATION REPORTERS SEEK, BY STORY TYPE

Information Reporters Seek	Stories in Which the Information Is Used		
	News	Feature	Investigative
Facts and details, including dates, names, locations and costs	✓	✓	✓
Chronology showing the unfolding of events	✓	✓	✓
Relationships among the people, organizations or issues involved	✓	✓	✓
Context and perspective, including the significance of events or issues and their relationships to other issues	✓	✓	✓
Anecdotes that illuminate events or issues and make them more dramatic and understandable for readers or viewers	✓	✓	✓
Quotations that allow readers, viewers or listeners to hear other voices	✓	✓	✓
The environment in which the subject lives or works		✓	✓
How the subject appears and dresses		✓	✓
The subject's mannerisms		✓	✓
Smells, sounds and textures associated with the subject's home or work		✓	✓
The subject's version of events and how it differs from that of other sources and records			✓
Explanations of contradictions between the subject's version of events and that of other sources or of contradictions within a subject's version			✓
The subject's replies to all charges and allegations the reporter may have heard from other sources during an investigation			✓

Many experienced interviewers think of an interview as a conversation, but it is a conversation with a specific purpose: gathering information for an unseen audience of readers, viewers or listeners. To accomplish that purpose, interviewers must control the conversation, and they can do that only if they have properly prepared. In the case of in-depth personality interviews or investigative interviews, the planning process might be long and complicated, but even with simpler interviews, it can involve several steps.

11.1.1 Selecting Interview Sources

Once reporters know an interview's purpose, they decide whom to interview. For a personality profile, they will interview the subject and his or her friends, enemies and co-workers. But when the story is about an issue or event, they may have to determine who has the necessary information.

Reporters working on stories that will be published days or weeks later can try to interview everyone who might have relevant information. They can ask each subject for the names of people who might contribute information and repeat the process until the list of potential sources has been exhausted. Journalists working on deadline must find the best possible sources quickly. They want sources who possess knowledge, expertise or insight relevant to the story. The subjects should be able to explain complicated matters in a clear and interesting manner. Sometimes the best available source is a document or record rather than a person. Reporters can save themselves and their interviewees time and trouble if they begin by searching for documents or public records that provide the factual background for a story.

When choosing interview subjects, reporters should never let any organization, governmental or private, make its public relations person the scapegoat. Tony Kovaleski, an investigative reporter for KMGH-Channel 7 in Denver, said the job of the reporter is to hold accountable the real decision maker, not the PR person.

Col. Steven C. McCraw, director of the Texas Department of Public Safety, addresses reporters about the mass shooting at the Robb Elementary School in Uvalde, Texas, that killed 19 children and two adults. Reporters look for sources who are knowledgeable and can speak with authority.

11.1.1.1 HOW MANY SOURCES ARE ENOUGH?

Beginning reporters sometimes wonder how many sources they need for a story. The answer depends on at least four factors: deadline pressure, the expertise of the sources, the degree of controversy raised by a topic and the complexity of a topic.

When stories involve breaking news, which readers, viewers and listeners need as soon as possible, reporters lack the time to search widely for sources and information. They must construct a story from the materials readily available. Still, they should get as complete an account of the event and include as many points of view as possible. If journalists could not interview key sources before the deadline, their stories should say so clearly.

If sources possess broad expertise in a topic, three or four might be enough. If interviewees have more limited experience, reporters might need to speak to dozens. Academic and government economists, for instance, may have extensive knowledge about the economy of a city or region, while individual business owners may know what is happening only in their particular business.

The degree of controversy also affects the number of sources. If a topic is not controversial—the cause of polio, for example—one source may be sufficient. If the topic is the likelihood of developing cures for diabetes or Alzheimer's disease from fetal stem cells, about which experts disagree, a reporter must include all reasonable points of view in the story.

Finally, the more complex the story, the more sources the reporter will need. A story about a particular homicide may need only a few sources. A story about why homicide rates soared during the COVID pandemic would require talking to dozens of sources from such fields as law enforcement, criminology, psychology and social work.

However many sources reporters talk to, they must evaluate each one by asking, "What is the basis of the source's knowledge?" "How credible or reliable is the source?" When sources make an assertion, ask them, "How do you know that?" Determining the credibility and reliability of sources requires asking about their credentials and cross-checking information from one source with that from others. The process is not simple or easy, but it is essential for producing sound, accurate news stories.

11.1.1.2 FINDING DIVERSE SOURCES

A long-standing problem in journalism is a lack of diversity in the newsroom and in the sources used in news stories. The news is supposed to reflect the entire community, and to do so, reporters must draw upon sources that reflect the racial, ethnic, religious and gender diversity of the community. A story about business conditions in a city would not reflect the entire community if it included only the views of white bankers and businessmen. The experiences of Black, Latino, Muslim and other business women and men are equally relevant. As The Associated Press says in its guide on inclusive reporting, "We strive for storytelling that both represents all people and shines a brighter light on those who have been underrepresented in traditional narratives." (Chapter 1 also discusses the issue of diversity of sources.)

To find diverse sources, The Associated Press recommends two things: cast a wide net and focus on individuals. Casting a wide net means looking beyond some of the traditional places for finding sources. For instance, reporters working on stories about elementary education might automatically turn to experts at state universities. They might overlook sources at historically Black colleges and universities who also have extensive expertise on elementary education. Focusing on individual stories means looking for people in situations that are often overlooked. A story about the effects of inflation on a community should include the experiences and views of people who work in factories or retail stores, not just business owners. It should also include single parents and people living on fixed incomes, all of whom might be affected in ways different from those of middle-class, two-parent families.

Experienced reporters develop their own databases of sources for stories on their beats, but some resources exist for young reporters seeking new sources. One is a database called Diverse Sources (diversesources.org). The database lists people willing to be sources for news stories. A user can search the database by a topic, such as sexual assault, and find sources who have expertise on that area. The database provides the nature of their expertise, where they work and how to contact them.

Another resource is Help a Reporter Out (helpareporter.com). HARO is a website that matches reporters and sources. It has about 800,000 sources registered with it, and about 55,000 journalists and bloggers use it. Reporters register by providing HARO their names, emails (which are kept private) and outlets. Reporters can find sources by submitting a request that includes a summary of the story and the qualifications for the sources sought. HARO then matches that with the qualifications of the sources in its database and emails pitches from the sources to the reporters, who then select whom to interview.

Yet another tool for finding diverse sources is a website called Diverse Databases (editorsofcolor.com/diverse-databases). The site, which is a database of databases, is run by Editors of Color. Reporters working on stories on such issues as science, politics, technology, food and more can go to Diverse Databases and find databases that list experts who are women or members of underrepresented groups.

11.1.2 Researching Sources and Topics

Lawrence Grobel, a journalist who has interviewed scores of famous and important people and has written about interviewing, says the successful interviewer must be well informed. That means reading books and articles by or about the person the reporter will interview, researching a company's annual reports and reviewing public documents. When Grobel prepared for an interview with mystery and western novelist Elmore Leonard, he read 14 of the author's books. Sportscaster Jeanne Zelasko was once assigned to cover the Daytona 500, but she knew nothing about NASCAR—in the two weeks she had to prepare for the assignment, she read every book she could find about the sport in a local bookstore. Pat Stith, a former investigative reporter for The Raleigh (North Carolina) News & Observer, says the goal is to know more about the small portion of the subject's job the reporter is interested in than the subject knows.

Journalists who have thoroughly researched a person or topic before an interview will

- Have fresher, more interesting questions for the interview subject.
- Not waste time asking about already established facts.
- Not embarrass themselves by appearing ignorant.
- Be prepared to recognize newsworthy statements the subject makes and ask intelligent follow-up questions.
- Be prepared to spot inconsistencies and evasions in a source's responses.
- Discover additional sources.
- Encourage sources to speak more freely, because they are more likely to trust knowledgeable reporters.

11.1.3 Preparing Questions for the Interview

Good questions elicit interesting quotations and details. Constructing good questions begins when reporters select a unifying central point for their story. With this point in mind, interviewers can decide whom they should interview and what questions they should ask. Say a journalist is planning a profile of a local bank executive who has won several marathons. The central point for the story may be that long-distance running enhances the bank executive's personal and professional life. That idea suggests certain questions to ask the executive and that person's friends and family. If the purpose of the story is to investigate the bank's treatment of minorities, however, the reporter may still want to interview the same executive, but the central point will be different. It may be how the bank's lending practices affect minorities who want to buy homes or start businesses.

HOT TIP

Steps in Preparing for an Interview

1. Define the purpose. Is this a news, feature or investigative interview? What information is necessary for the story?

2. Decide whom to interview. Sometimes the choices are obvious; other times the reporter may have to research who the best sources are.

3. Assess the character of the interviewee. This may be crucial for feature and investigative interviews where the reporter will have to shape the interview strategy to the interviewee's character.

4. Identify the areas of inquiry. What topics will the interview focus on? What questions will yield the information necessary to write about those topics?

5. Anticipate possible answers to questions. Reporters often can predict an interviewee's answers from their advance research. On the basis of those predictions, they can plan the interview and prepare possible follow-up questions.

FROM THE NEWS

Preparation Helped FBI Interrogate Al-Qaida Suspects

Ali Soufan—a former FBI agent, native of Lebanon and Arabic speaker—was one of the lead interrogators of al-Qaida suspects following the 9/11 attacks. Al-Qaida operatives had been coached to appear to cooperate with investigators by answering questions without offering any new information. Nevertheless, Soufan was able to get valuable information from the suspects he questioned, without using torture—or enhanced interrogation techniques, as it was euphemistically called by some U.S. officials.

The key to a successful interrogation, Soufan explained in his book "The Black Banners," is thorough preparation. He and other FBI interrogators studied al-Qaida extensively and learned as much as they could about the background of each person they questioned. "You have

to convince the detainee that you know all about him, and that any lie will be easily uncovered," Soufan wrote. "To do this, you plan the interrogation around what you know."

Journalists rarely will encounter interview subjects as reluctant to cooperate or as well trained in techniques for deflecting questions as al-Qaida operatives. But the principle of thorough preparation still applies. The reporter who has prepared thoroughly for an interview will know when interviewees are being deceptive, trying to spin a topic to make themselves look good or providing newsworthy information.

Sometimes, a journalist may find it helpful in an interview to feign ignorance. While this tactic may be useful in certain cases, being ignorant never helps the journalist.

Once reporters have selected a central point and have researched the topic, they write their questions in advance. They need not write out full questions. Often it is enough to jot down a word or phrase to remind themselves what to ask.

Reporters craft questions to elicit as much information as possible. This means asking open-ended rather than closed-ended questions. The latter can be answered with a yes or no: "Will the state's new tax lid hurt schools?" If journalists want more information, they have to ask follow-up questions. An open-ended question would be, "What will be the effect of the state's new tax lid on schools?" The question requires the source to provide an analysis of the problem.

John Sawatsky, an investigative reporter renowned for his interviewing skill, advises journalists to ask short, neutral questions that begin with "what," "how" and "why" and to a lesser extent "who," "when" and "where." Questions structured as Sawatsky suggests encourage interviewees to tell their stories and reveal their feelings. Questions like "Are you angry?" or "Were you scared?" are not only closed-ended but also imply that the interviewer has a preconceived notion about how the subject should have acted or felt. The source might not want to tell his or her story to a reporter who appears to have already decided what happened.

When interviewees have a story to tell, such as how they survived a plane crash or what happened during a bank robbery, reporters should simply let them talk. Something like "Tell me what happened to you" might be enough to encourage people to tell their story as they remember it. As interviewees talk, journalists should listen carefully. They might think of questions as the subject tells the story, but they should not interrupt. They should wait until the interviewee has finished and then ask any specific follow-up questions.

For feature interviews or personality profiles, some reporters have questions they often use to gain insight into the subject. Here are some examples:

- What do you read?
- Who are your heroes?
- What goals do you have?
- What is a typical day like for you?
- What are your weaknesses or drawbacks?
- How do you compensate for your weaknesses?
- What caused the most significant change in your life?
- How did you cope with that change?

When news sources generalize or give vague answers, reporters ask for anecdotes and examples that support the generalizations or clarify ambiguous responses. Reporters can use the anecdotes, examples and quotations to make their stories more colorful, interesting and understandable. Here are examples of questions crafted to elicit anecdotes and quotations:

- What crime was the most difficult for you to solve in your career as a detective?
- How has the state's new social science curriculum changed the way you teach?
- What do you fear the most when you perform before a live audience?
- What steps will you take to prepare your business for the state's increase in the minimum wage?
- How did you overcome your fears following your accident?

Reporters should ask for clarification when they do not understand things sources say. Sometimes that means asking questions that might appear naive or silly, but journalists should not fear asking them. Those who assume they understand what a source said or who fail to ask a critical question out of fear of appearing ignorant could make serious and embarrassing mistakes when they write their stories.

11.2 Conducting the Interview

11.2.1 Selecting a Location

The prospect of being interviewed creates anxiety for some people, making it harder for them to answer questions. Reporters can reduce the unease by conducting interviews in sources' homes or offices, where they feel more comfortable. Additionally, reporters can learn more about a subject by being in his or her environment. Eric Nalder, an investigative journalist who is now retired, advises reporters to survey the person's office or home, looking for clues and details. The photos people display on their walls, the clutter on their desks or the items on their refrigerator doors all give insights about their lives or suggest questions to ask them.

No matter where reporters interview people, they always look for details that will reveal information about the subject. They look for body language, facial expressions, manner of dress, tone of voice and anything else that reveals the source's character. Louisa Thomas' profile of Australian tennis star Nick Kyrgios for The New Yorker included a brief conversation between the two after he had lost a match in a French tournament. Notice how Thomas incorporates description of Kyrgios' dress and appearance:

> Half an hour after the match, I was waiting for the elevator in the lobby of my hotel, when I heard Kyrgios request a new room key. He was still in his kit: black shorts, a magenta Nike top, shoes smeared with ochre clay. His beard was trimmed tight along his jawline, his dark hair shaved on the sides of his head and sculpted on top like a flame.
>
> He stared at his phone as he shuffled to the elevator. As he stepped inside, he looked up. We had met the previous day, and he sounded surprisingly cheerful as he greeted me. "Sorry about the match," I said.
>
> He gave a quick, harsh laugh, and then his voice lightened. "It's all right. It's not a big deal," he said.
>
> He stepped out of the elevator, and I watched the doors close behind his slumped shoulders. There are message-board threads dedicated to Kyrgios's posture, with dozens of comments debating whether the curvature of his upper back requires surgery, interferes with his hormone circulation, or is a faker's lazy pose.

Some places are poor locations for interviews. For example, people unfamiliar with newsrooms may find their noise and chaotic pace intimidating. Lunch appointments also have drawbacks. The idea of a leisurely interview over a meal sounds pleasant, but crowd noise and interruptions from servers interfere with the conversation. Also, reporters or their news organizations should pay for lunch to avoid any appearance that they can be influenced by a generous source. Thus, the practice of interviewing people at a restaurant can become expensive. Whatever the location, a journalist should always arrive early, keep the interview within the agreed-on time and dress appropriately, usually in business clothes.

As shown in the documentary "Citizenfour," Glenn Greenwald (right) interviews Edward Snowden about the NSA documents he leaked to the public. The interview took place in a Hong Kong hotel room, not for Snowden's comfort but to protect him from extradition to the United States.

11.2.2 Organizing the Questions

Reporters should start an interview with a clear statement of its purpose, if that's not already understood. For brief news interviews, they usually try to get right to the main questions. Longer interviews often begin with a few minutes of small talk to put a source at ease.

Once the serious questioning begins, reporters should take charge of the conversation, decide what questions to ask, keep the interview on track and make sure the source answers every question fully. If a subject wanders or tries to evade questions, journalists bring the conversation back to the central topic and politely but firmly ask him or her to respond to the questions.

Questions should be grouped by topic. A reporter who is planning to profile a candidate for mayor, for example, may want to cover the person's education, work history, family life, community service, political experience and campaign platform. For each of these topics, the reporter might have four or five questions. Journalists try to organize the topics, making it easy for the interviewee to move from one to the next. Chronological organization and reverse chronological order are two methods used. For a reporter interviewing a scientist about the effects of global warming, chronology is meaningless; it would make more sense to use a different organization, such as moving from effects on oceans and ocean life to effects on land animals and finally to effects on humans. In still other situations, the reporter might let the topics come up on their own and simply make sure that the interviewee covers all essential points.

Reporters organize the questions they ask as well as the topics they want to cover. One approach—sometimes called the funnel—starts with a general question and moves to progressively more specific ones (see Figure 11.1). The reverse funnel starts with questions about specifics and moves to more general matters.

Some journalists like to rehearse their interviews, particularly when they are confronting the target of an investigative story. Martha Mendoza, a reporter for The Associated Press, likes to role-play her interviews with an editor. This allows her to test questions and anticipate possible answers she will receive from the source. Robert Cribb of the Toronto Star uses a flow chart to plan his questions and anticipate possible answers. The chart helps him plan the possible routes the interview may take.

Journalists start interviews with some noncontroversial comments or soft questions that will break the ice. Even a polite question about the weather can start the conversation. Once the interviewee becomes comfortable talking, the reporter asks more difficult questions. The most embarrassing or difficult questions are held for the end. By then, the subject should be more at ease. Moreover, if a source refuses to answer embarrassing questions and abruptly ends the interview, the reporter will have already obtained most of the information needed for the story.

Experienced interviewers prepare so thoroughly before an interview that they encounter few surprises, but occasionally an interview yields unexpected information. If the information is newsworthy, reporters abandon their original plans and pursue the new angles. "Morning Joe" hosts Joe Scarborough and Mika Brzezinski were wrapping up an interview with Michael Avenatti, attorney for Stephanie Clifford (better known as Stormy Daniels) who claimed to have had a sexual encounter with President Donald Trump, when Brzezinski asked Avenatti if Clifford had been threatened to keep silent about the incident. Avenatti's

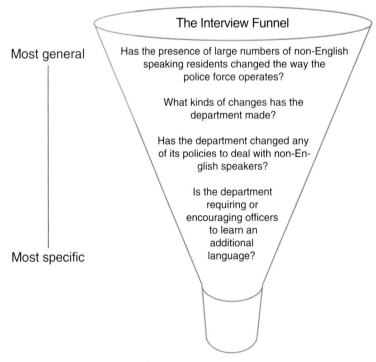

The Interview Funnel

Most general

Has the presence of large numbers of non-English speaking residents changed the way the police force operates?

What kinds of changes has the department made?

Has the department changed any of its policies to deal with non-English speakers?

Is the department requiring or encouraging officers to learn an additional language?

Most specific

FIGURE 11.1 The Interview Funnel
The funnel style of organization places the broadest—or most general—questions at the top and the most specific at the bottom. The reverse funnel approach moves from most specific to the most general. The approach a reporter uses depends on the situation, topic and source.

HOT TIP

Interview Traps to Avoid

Reporters have an infinite number of approaches they can take to conducting an interview, but they should avoid some traps:

- Don't make statements; just ask questions: Questions will elicit the subject's opinions and ideas, but statements might lead the subject to suspect the journalist is biased and will not report the interview fairly.

- Don't ask double-barreled questions, which might have more than one correct answer: An interviewer asked Bill Clinton, when he first ran for president, "Was Gennifer Flowers your lover for 12 years?" Clinton answered, "That allegation is false." But which part was false? Splitting the question into two might have yielded a better answer.

- Don't use loaded words in questions: "Mayor Datolli, will your budget scheme save the city from bankruptcy?" A "scheme" may seem disreputable or risky. A more neutral term would be "plan."

- Don't ask questions that suggest what you think the answer should be: Asking "Was the robber carrying a shotgun?" implies that you think the robber did so. An uncertain interviewee might be tempted to confirm that suspicion, even if it is wrong.

statement that she had been threatened surprised them and became the most newsworthy disclosure of the interview.

At the end of an interview, reporters should always ask sources if they have anything to add. Sometimes the most newsworthy information emerges in their response. Journalists should ask for the names of other people to interview or for documents that might provide additional information or verification. They also should determine the best time to call sources if they have follow-up questions. Finally, they should thank subjects for granting the interview.

11.2.3 Dealing with Reluctant Sources and Asking Tough Questions

Most sources cooperate with reporters because they welcome the opportunity to tell their side of a story. Some, however, may be reluctant to talk or even hostile toward journalists. Some may wish to avoid the public attention that might accompany being on television or radio or in a news story. Others may fear their words or actions will be misunderstood or sensationalized. Still others may be trying to hide actions or situations that are embarrassing or illegal. In recent years, Donald Trump's description of journalists as "enemies of the people" and purveyors of fake news has compounded the problem. Trump supporters often want nothing to do with reporters from mainstream news organizations.

Reporters ask sources why they are hesitant to speak. Reporters can overcome sources' objections once they know what they are. For instance, if sources fear the interview will turn into an interrogation, reporters can ease this anxiety by showing empathy. Lawrence Grobel has said, "To be a good interviewer, you have to become a chameleon, changing the colors of your personality to fit the mood of the person you are interviewing." Good interviewers convey the feeling they are more interested in sources than in themselves.

When sources fear their words will be distorted or misunderstood, reporters can demonstrate their knowledge of the topic and background by asking intelligent questions or pointing to other stories they have written on the topic. The interviewees may then be willing to fill in the gaps. Explaining the purpose of the interview and the story also can help convince sources that reporters are knowledgeable and trustworthy.

Some sources worry the story will cause them to lose their jobs or money or even to face criminal prosecution. Reporters can soothe these fears by explaining that the interview is an opportunity for subjects to put their side of a story before the public and that failure to do so will make them look worse.

Interviewers have a variety of tactics for getting reluctant sources to talk. If an interviewee is unresponsive, reporters may switch topics, trying to find something that will get him or her to talk. In some instances, journalists can build rapport with sources by expressing admiration (if it is genuine) for something the person did or said. Or they might draw on their background to establish a connection with a reluctant source. If the interviewee is a college president, the reporter might mention that his or her father was a college professor (if that is true).

Many interviews—whether done for feature or investigative stories—require reporters to ask tough questions that the source might find embarrassing or potentially harmful. Failure to ask the questions, however, means an interview will be incomplete and lack news value. Asking difficult questions is easier when reporters maintain their neutrality. If interviewees believe reporters are just asking questions and not expressing opinions, they answer tough questions more willingly.

Reporters can enhance their appearance of neutrality by asking questions in ways that distance them from the opinions the questions may imply. They can, for example,

- Attribute the question or point of view implied in the question to a third party or to public opinion generally. For example, "Chancellor Smith, some faculty members have said you attach more importance to intercollegiate athletics than to academics. What is your response?"
- Sugarcoat questions. Asking a person, "Is there anything about your marriage that you now regret?" is easier than asking, "Did you abuse your spouse?"
- Ask interviewees to explain their previous statements or actions or give their versions of controversial events.
- Show the interviewees what you know. Martha Mendoza brings a dossier to interviews. The dossier contains the documents and information she has gathered. She lets the interviewee review the material. If the interviewees, particularly ones who are the subject of an investigation, know the reporter already has most of the facts, they will be more likely to want to explain their side of the story.
- Ask interviewees to talk about others. Once they begin, it often is easier to shift the interview to their own ideas and actions.
- Ask interviewees for the names of people who support or criticize them. Then ask them to guess what their critics are most likely to say about them. Eric Nalder says this tactic often elicits information and tips for additional interviews.

Sometimes the best approach is to simply ask the question, no matter how blunt or embarrassing it may be. Stephanie Lee, who reported on science for BuzzFeed, says when she has to ask a question about allegations of wrongdoing or impropriety, she writes the question out verbatim. Formulating an accusatory question on the spur of the moment can be difficult.

No matter what approach reporters use, they must be persistent. If sources refuse to talk, hang up the phone or slam the door, reporters should go back the next day or next week and try again.

Sources pressed to talk about sensitive topics sometimes try to evade the question or even lie. When subjects avoid an issue or give fuzzy answers, reporters can restate the question, forcing them to be more forthcoming. Reporters can also simply remain silent, which tells sources their answers are insufficient and pushes them to elaborate. In some cases, journalists might want to confront sources directly about evasive answers, saying they will note evasions in the story.

Reporters who have done their homework will often know when a source is lying. Nalder lets interviewees he suspects are lying spin out their tales. He interrupts them only to ask for elaboration or more detail. Once he has the source's

Award-winning journalist Eric Nalder, former chief investigative reporter for the Seattle Post-Intelligencer who is now retired, offers various tips for interviewing reluctant sources in his article "Loosening Lips: The Art of the Interview."

entire story, he can begin to use the facts he has already gathered to pick the story apart and get that person to tell the truth.

Although he probably was not aware of it, Soufan's interrogation method, described earlier in this chapter, follows Nalder's techniques for dealing with sources who lie. In his book mentioned earlier, Soufan says the questioning never began with big or intimidating questions like "Did you meet Osama bin Laden?" Instead, the FBI agents focused on getting details with questions like these:

- Why did you go to Afghanistan?
- How did you travel there?
- How was the trip funded?
- Who picked you up at the airport?
- Where did you stay in Afghanistan?
- Whom did you meet?

By focusing on the small details, the FBI investigators made it hard for the al-Qaida operatives to maintain a cover story. Inconsistencies in the details exposed lies and revealed areas where the interrogators could focus their efforts.

Reporters should never try to bully hostile sources or try to deceive them about the purpose of an interview. Information obtained from a source who has been intimidated may be unreliable. People who have been led to believe an interview will be about one topic when the reporters want information about something else will feel unprepared to respond fully and accurately.

11.2.4 Interviewing Victims or Witnesses of Tragedy

Many breaking news events involve crimes, accidents or natural disasters. The people who have survived those events may have been injured or may have lost loved ones, and they may be experiencing extreme emotional distress. The families of victims and witnesses may be similarly traumatized by such events. The Dart Center for Journalism and Trauma (www.dart.com) offers a number of resources for reporters to help them deal wth sources who have experienced some tragedy. Among the Dart Center's major recommendations are these:

- Treat victims with dignity and respect.
- Identify yourself clearly and immediately and state why you want to talk to them.
- Do not condescend to victims. Avoid patronizing comments like "I know how you feel" or "I understand."

Preparation is important, even when covering a breaking news story. Reporters should know as much as possible about the situation they are entering. They should also talk with their producers or editors before going to the scene to

FROM THE NEWS

An Interview with Bill Cosby

Sometimes a source will simply refuse to answer the hard question, as happened when National Public Radio's Scott Simon interviewed Bill and Camille Cosby for Weekend Edition. Simon was interviewing the Cosbys because they had contributed to an art exhibit. But shortly before the interview, The Washington Post published a column by Barbara Bowman, who said Cosby had sexually assaulted her several times in 1985. Simon felt obliged to ask Cosby about it. Here is their exchange:

> SCOTT SIMON: This question gives me no pleasure, Mr. Cosby, but there have been serious allegations raised about you in recent days.

> BILL COSBY: [SILENCE]

> SIMON: You're shaking your head no. I'm in the news business. I have to ask the question. Do you have any response to those charges?

> COSBY: [SILENCE]

> SIMON: Shaking your head no. There are people who love you who might like to hear from you about this. I want to give you the chance.

> COSBY: [SILENCE]

> SIMON: All right. Camille and Bill Cosby. They have lent 62 pieces from their collection of African and African-American art to create an exhibit called *Conversations: African and African American Artworks in Dialogue*. It's now on display at the Smithsonian National Museum of African Art through early 2016. Thank you both.

formulate a plan for conducting interviews and what specific information they hope to gather.

When reporters are interviewing people at the scene of a disaster or crime, they need to consider the security and safety of all involved. Reporters should find a safe place to conduct any interview, both for the protection of the sources and for their own safety. If possible, interviews should be conducted in a quiet place where the reporter and source can hear each other and will not be interrupted.

Reporters usually like to control interviews, but when the sources have experienced trauma, the reporter should let them control the interview. Most importantly, sources should know that they can end the interview, take a break or refuse to answer questions that make them feel uncomfortable. Reporters should also ask sources for permission to take notes or record interviews. All questions should be open-ended so that the sources are encouraged to provide as much information as possible.

The way questions are formulated can have a major effect on how helpful traumatized sources will be. Questions should never imply that the source behaved improperly or criminally. If the person being interviewed was the victim of a crime, a question like "Why did you go to such a dangerous neighborhood?" might suggest the victim was somehow to blame for the incident.

Showing empathy toward victims can ease the interview process. People who have endured some kind of tragedy will be more likely to respond to reporters who exhibit understanding, patience and attentiveness. Some victims may show strong emotions, such as crying or anger. Reporters should be patient with them and remain calm. Sometimes the source is able to continue the interview, although if the emotions are too strong, reporters should look for a way to end the interview and find other sources.

People who have just experienced a crime or disaster may have trouble recalling events in chronological order. Some details they may not remember at all. The emotions they experienced during the events may affect how they remember them. Reporters should try to verify the information they get from sources. People who have survived a hurricane or tornado or have been the victims of a criminal attack have valuable perspectives to share about the events. But witnesses, police or others at the scene can verify or amplify the accounts of the survivors.

Interviewing children who have been victims of crimes, accidents or disasters presents special problems. Most obviously, reporters should get permission from parents or guardians before interviewing a child. While some exceptions to this are possible with breaking news stories or situations where the parents cannot be located, reporters should discuss them with their producers or editors. Reporters should also make sure children and their parents understand the purpose of the interview, what reporters want to learn, how the information will be used and when it will be published. Children under 13 often cannot provide detailed, factual information. For that, reporters should turn to police or documents. And reporters should remember that children, particularly younger ones, may lose patience with being interviewed after 30 minutes or so.

11.2.5 Special Situations

11.2.5.1 TELEPHONE INTERVIEWS

Telephone calls save reporters enormous amounts of time. Some sources are more comfortable talking without someone watching them; others consider it a welcome break in the day. But telephone interviews have disadvantages, too. They must be brief and superficial. Sources usually have other work, and long telephone conversations may bore or annoy them. Particularly frustrating for reporters is playing phone tag with sources while on deadline.

Telephone calls are an unsatisfactory means of conducting in-depth interviews about controversial or complex issues and personalities. Cultivating sources is difficult if they are known only by telephone. Getting a source to discuss embarrassing or personal matters requires a rapport best established face to face.

11.2.5.2 EMAIL INTERVIEWS

Email offers another way of interviewing sources. Reporters use this method to contact hard-to-reach or reluctant sources. Even people who travel a lot check their email. Sources who dodge phone calls or hesitate to return voice mails may answer a journalist's email. Reporters trying to contact several sources for similar information can use email to send the same message to each of them.

Email interviews have some advantages over telephone interviews. Besides being more convenient for some sources, the format also affords them an opportunity to develop their thoughts in detail, which means reporters get more thorough answers to their questions. Email also provides a written record of the interviews, lessening the chance for misquotation.

However, journalists relying on email interviews are deprived of their sources' facial expressions, vocal inflections and body language, all of which can help reporters understand their sources better. Also, the email response is less spontaneous. The offhand comments sources make in person or telephone interviews give reporters additional insights that they can follow up on quickly. Finally, reporters conducting email interviews recognize the possibility that the person responding is not the one they want to contact. For example, a business executive might have a PR person draft an answer to a journalist's email.

11.2.5.3 ONLINE INTERVIEWS

Reporters can use their computers to interview subjects, using programs like Skype or Zoom. Because the programs use the computer's video capabilities, reporters and subjects can see as well as hear each other. And the responses the journalist gets are more spontaneous than those obtained through an email interview. Some of the programs for online video allow one or both parties to record the conversation, creating a permanent record of what was said.

Online interviews, however, are essentially high-tech telephone interviews, so subjects are just as likely to get bored. If the subject is at work or at home, he or she may have to deal with distractions. And if one party or the other has a poor internet connection, the interview may become difficult or impossible to carry out.

11.2.5.4 INTERVIEWING FOR BROADCAST

Reporters interviewing sources for radio or television experience problems print reporters don't face. Terry Gross, host of the NPR program "Fresh Air" and one of the best interviewers in the business, told American Journalism Review, "For most print journalists the interview is the raw material for the piece, along with everything else the reporter has seen and heard in researching the story. For me the interview is the piece." Gross arranges her questions so that the answers produce a narrative, not just a series of disconnected answers.

Television reporters need to plan their interviews in advance with the technicians who will be operating the cameras and sound equipment, especially if the interview needs to be shot quickly for broadcast that day or if the source does not want to appear on camera. They also should show the interview subject doing more than talking. Where possible, television journalists ask the subject to demonstrate an activity or respond to a video or another source.

11.2.6 Taking Notes

Skilled interviewers take copious notes, writing down much more information than they can possibly use. Unless reporters take detailed notes, they will forget much of what is said. They might not recognize the importance of a piece of information until well after the interview—or several interviews—when they are writing their stories. Recording as much as possible decreases the chances for errors or omissions. Reporters can easily ignore notes that later prove to be unimportant or irrelevant, but filling gaps left by poor note-taking is more difficult.

 HOT TIP

Telephone and Email Etiquette

For telephone interviews, reporters should

● Identify themselves and their news organizations clearly at the start of the conversation.

● Never pose as someone other than a reporter.

● Ask permission to record the interview digitally or on tape.

For email interviews, reporters should

● Use a salutation (such as "Dear Ms. Ramirez,").

● Identify themselves and the news organization they represent.

● Usually review the background of an event or issue before they ask their questions.

● Tell sources their deadline and thank them for their time and expertise.

● Never write in all capital letters, which some regard as the equivalent of shouting.

● Never use acronyms, such as "BTW" ("by the way"), because not everyone understands them.

Terry Gross interviews musician Questlove for a live "Fresh Air" recording at the Penn Museum in 2016.

Most reporters develop their own shortcuts for taking notes. They leave out some words, abbreviate others, or jot down names, numbers, good quotations and key ideas. When sources speak too rapidly, interviewers can ask them to slow down or repeat important statements. Note-taking makes some sources nervous. Journalists should explain that the notes will help them write more accurate and thorough stories.

After completing interviews, reporters review their notes immediately, while everything is fresh in their minds. They may want to fill gaps in their information or be certain they understand everything a source said. Journalists often write their stories as soon as possible after their interviews. The longer they wait, the more likely they are to forget some facts or distort others.

11.2.7 Recording Interviews

Using a digital or a tape recorder frees reporters to concentrate on the questions they want to ask and sources' responses. Recorders also provide verbatim and permanent records, so interviewers make fewer factual errors. When reporters play the recording, they often find important statements they failed to notice during the interviews.

Recorders also have drawbacks. After recording a one-hour interview, reporters may have to replay it at least once before writing the story. They may also have difficulty locating important facts or quotations. By comparison, they may need a minute or less to find a fact or a quotation in their handwritten notes.

Even reporters who record major interviews usually augment recordings with written notes. They can consult their notes to write the stories and use the recordings to verify important facts and quotations. If a recorder has a counter, reporters can use it to note the location of important or interesting quotations.

Although recorders are commonplace, some sources refuse to be recorded. Recorders are small enough that reporters can easily hide them in their pockets or handbags, but taping a conversation without the other party's consent is sometimes illegal. As noted in Chapter 5, in most states, one may record a conversation with the consent of only one party. In the case of an interview, the consenting party would be the person doing the taping. Twelve states require the consent of all parties in most or all circumstances. Even where it is legal, taping a conversation without the other party's consent raises ethical

Reporter Vanessa Schledier Bild interviews Major Aryeh Shaliker, a spokesman for the Israeli army, near Ashkelon, Israel.

questions. Undisclosed recording seems manipulative and invasive. Audiences may consider any information reporters obtain in this manner tainted.

11.2.8 Final Thoughts

Interviewing is an art form that requires practice. Journalists who are most successful at interviewing have done it for years and have developed insights into their sources and into their own strengths and weaknesses in relating to other people. Terry Gross says: "My theory of interviewing is that whatever you have, use it. If you are confused, use that. If you have raw curiosity, use that. If you have experience, use that. If you have a lot of research, use that. But figure out what it is you have and make it work for you." Student journalists often lack the experience and the maturity to know what they have and how to make it work for them. Their initial attempts at interviewing may disappoint them. Young reporters should not become discouraged, however. With time and persistence, they can become excellent interviewers.

11.3 Writing the Interview Story

Writing a story based on an in-depth interview, such as a personality profile, is little different from writing any other news story. Most interview stories begin with a summary lead that presents the story's central point. The following paragraphs include the highlights. Reporters may use an alternative lead, such as an anecdote or description that introduces a nut graph containing the central point.

The body of the story usually is organized by topic, with facts and quotations presented in the order of their importance, not the order in which the source provided them. Reporters must be sure that they keep every direct and indirect quotation in its proper context. A well-written interview story will not string together quotations from the sources but use them for emphasis and impact. Journalists also usually limit background information to a minimum and incorporate it where it is most necessary and helpful for explaining a source's remarks.

An alternative form for writing an interview story is the question-and-answer format. Few reporters use it, however, because it requires too much space and makes it difficult for the audience to grasp a story's highlights quickly. The Q-and-A structure works best with celebrity interviews, self-help stories and sidebars for main stories. Q-and-A stories are never verbatim transcripts of interviews, even though the format creates that impression. The interviews are usually heavily edited to eliminate boring and irrelevant passages.

Guest Columnists

Tips on Interviewing Victims

BY WILLIAM COTE AND BONNIE BUCQUEROUX

Here are basic tips and techniques that the Michigan State University School of Journalism suggests journalists follow when covering victims of violence:

Grant the victim a sense of power and control. Remember that victims of violence and their family and friends are suffering from horrific stress that has robbed them of their sense of mastery. Also remember that they are not experts in journalistic conventions. One small thing to address both concerns: Tell people they can take a break from interviews whenever they need to. Instead of discussing the theory of "off the record," empower victims by giving them permission to turn off the tape recorder whenever they want to say something that they do not want used. Tell them to tell you to put down your notebook. Take advantage of opportunities to include them in the decision-making. Ask them: "Are you ready to go on?" "Is it all right for me to ask a tough question?" An excellent way to even the playing field is to give the subjects your business card—tell them that they can call you to discuss the story or just to talk.

Take care with first impressions. How you initially approach the victim can set the tone for all succeeding interactions. Body language in particular can be important, and the goal is to exude confidence, poise and caring. Reporters who seem pushy turn victims off. Nothing turns them off faster than feeling that they are being ambushed or railroaded. If you have any doubts about how you are perceived by others, ask for criticism from colleagues and former interviewees.

Discuss ground rules up front. Some experts have suggested, only half-jokingly, that reporters should be forced to read a version of the Miranda warning: You have the right to remain silent. Ambush tactics have no place in a victim interview, and experience confirms that discussing issues of privacy and confidentiality at the beginning can prevent misunderstandings and problems later. Discussion of the rules of engagement also can help establish trust. This is the time for you to explain what you need, when the article will appear, whom you want to talk with and for how long. Encourage the victim to ask questions.

Prepare for the possibility you will be the first to deliver the bad news. Time and again, reporters have telephoned or appeared on a family's porch looking for quotations about someone who has been killed or maimed, only to find that no one had yet been informed. The time to decide what you would do and say is before you make the call or ring the doorbell. The military always sends two people to deliver a death notice, one of whom is a chaplain, and both receive extensive training in how to deliver the news and provide comfort. The role of the reporter is different, and you do not always have the luxury of a companion, but at least you should organize your thoughts before you act.

Ask permission. This is particularly important whenever you approach the victim's physical "zone of intimacy." Even caring gestures can be misinterpreted as threatening or out of bounds. It is best to approach without your notebook in hand. Ask if you can take notes. Ask if you can use a tape recorder. It is better to say "Would you like a tissue?" than to thrust the box at them.

Watch what you say. Devotees of the TV show "NYPD Blue" know that the detectives always say "Sorry for your loss." To our ears, the phrase may begin to sound trite and artificial, but it is far better to use a canned phrase that strikes the right note than wrong words that wound. Martin Symonds, a former New York Police Department deputy police commissioner who went on to become a therapist, suggests that at least one of the three following sentiments will always be appropriate:

- I'm sorry this happened to you.
- I'm glad you weren't killed.
- It's not your fault.

Avoid the banal. Never say, "I know how you feel." You don't (even if you think you may have suffered a similar victimization). In an egregious case a reporter approached a man who had just learned that his daughter had been savagely raped and murdered. "I know how you feel, I remember when my dog died," the reporter said. If you find yourself at a loss for words, John Brady, author of "The Craft of Interviewing," suggests asking a "when" question: "When did you hear the news?" "When did the police arrive?" Not only are such queries less threatening for reporter and interviewee alike, but they also tend to elicit detailed responses.

Be accurate above all. Accuracy is the overarching goal in all reporting, but the stakes are much higher in cases of violence. Keep in mind that errors that make ordinary people angry can become monumental issues for traumatized people looking for a target for their frustration.

Be especially sensitive to imputations of blame. Fortunately, we have come a long way since the days that rape reports regularly included mention of what the victim was wearing—but only if it was "scanty." Yet victims often question why certain details are used or how they are handled. If you mention that the victim had been drinking, does it imply that he or she was drunk? Editors should always fix their antennae to spot any inadvertent suggestion that the victim was at fault.

Be alert to the special impact of photos, graphics and overall presentation. A picture can also cut a thousand times deeper than words. How much blood do readers need to see? Time and again, a sensitive and respectful story on a difficult issue like domestic violence is undercut by an illustration of a fearful woman, portrayed as cowering and pitiful. Or there is the headline that obliterates all of the nuances crafted into the story.

William Cote was coordinator and Bonnie Bucqueroux was assistant coordinator of the Victims and the Media Program at Michigan State University.

William Cote and Bonnie Bucqueroux. 1996. "Tips on interviewing victims," Nieman Reports L, 3: 27. Available at https://niemanreports.org/wp-content/uploads/2014/04/Fall-1996_150.pdf. Courtesy Nieman Reports.

Guest Columnist

Interviewing Three People About a Deadly Crash

BY DON STACOM

Celebrating one of the last summer nights of school vacation in Connecticut, four teenagers hung out at a friend's pool party and then sped home on a dark, two-lane road in a Subaru WRX.

Police estimate the driver was doing 100 to 140 when he lost control on a curve. The WRX slid sideways, demolished a Taurus in the other lane and then slammed roof first into a utility pole. Everyone in the WRX was killed.

For news reporters across the state, this was another "reckless teenage drivers" story. They happen a lot.

Covering them can be as depressing as a funeral, and every bit as predictable: It starts with a splashy story, follows with profiles of the dead teens, and then shifts to the memorial services, the weeping friends, the grieving relatives.

And that's about it. The news moves on.

Every so often, though, there's a chance to report something much deeper. At these times, the reporter's work becomes as challenging, emotionally draining—and as rewarding—as any job that exists. You get to do something that genuinely makes a difference.

With the WRX case, it began with thinking about all the people who were hurt: Literally hundreds of teenagers showed up at the crash scene to stare and cry. And there were, of course, the four devastated families.

Beyond that were the overlooked victims: the innocent people in the Taurus who sustained crippling injuries, and the emergency crews who saw carnage that battered their psyches.

They all suffered in very different ways, but they also shared an agonizing frustration at how needless this tragedy was. They desperately wanted to put some meaning to their pain.

All of that provided the structure for a story showing how one bad decision could crumple many, many lives. The plan was simple, though not easy: Months after the crash, three people would tell exactly how they experienced that night of horror. The father of one of the dead girls, the first cop on the scene and the front-seat passenger in the Taurus would relive what they went through.

That was the theory. But how do you make that actually happen? Step one is the research; a reporter who already knows the fundamental facts will have much more credibility when approaching these people to talk. To do that, reporters for the Hartford Courant reviewed the police reports, read obituaries and Facebook memorials and revisited the scene.

Next came building rapport with the dad, the cop and the woman from the Taurus. This story hinged on their cooperation; a reporter must develop their trust that the story won't be tawdry or exploitative. At the same time, the reporter gently talked them through what the interviews will be like—letting them know ahead of time that these conversations would bring up the worst of the painful stuff. This was the time to invite them to decline; if they're committed, they'll persevere.

Pre-interview preparations are crucial here. To build intelligent questions, first imagine a bit of what they saw and felt. Imagine being the first police officer at such devastation; this brings the interview questions "Whom do you go to first?" and "How does your mind even process all of this?" For the woman from the Taurus, you ask about her memory of the moments before the impact—and those right afterward, too. Has she made peace with being the entirely innocent victim of such a horrific crash?

Through the interview, the reporter had to stay alert for what's fresh and what's powerful, for the sights and sounds and feelings that these people recall. And most importantly, the end of the talk was time to softly, genuinely thank each person for putting themselves through that again. After that came the job of organizing and writing a story that would make it worthwhile.

Don Stacom is a reporter for The Hartford Courant in Connecticut.

The Reporter's Guide to Interviewing

1. Determine whether the story will be a news story, a feature or an investigative story.

2. For all types of stories, interview to get facts, details, chronologies, context and anecdotes.

3. For feature stories, capture the source's environment, appearance and mannerisms.

4. For investigative stories, get the source's version of events, explanations of contradictions and replies to charges.

5. Identify the best available sources who can provide the necessary information for the story.

6. In deciding how many sources to interview, keep in mind deadlines, the expertise of the sources, the degree of controversy regarding the issue and the complexity of the issue.

7. Research people and issues as thoroughly as possible before conducting any interviews.

8. Select questions that will address the central point of the planned story.

9. Use questions that will encourage interviewees to talk—then let them talk with as few interruptions as possible.

10. Interview sources in places where they will be comfortable, not newsrooms or restaurants.

11. Organize questions by topic and raise topics in an order that will make it easy for sources to move from one to the next.

12. If a source is reluctant to talk or is hostile, find out why and try to address the concern.

13. Maintain neutrality when asking tough questions. Sources are more likely to answer tough questions from neutral interviewers than from those who seem to be advocates for a point of view.

14. Treat sources who are victims of crimes, accidents or disasters with dignity and compassion; let them control the interview.

15. Telephone interviews save time, but they are unsatisfactory for long, in-depth interviews.

16. Email is an effective way of interviewing some sources, but the interviewer is deprived of information about the source's demeanor and personality.

17. Remember that a broadcast interview is the story and not just raw material for a story.

18. Take thorough notes during the interview, making sure to write down names, dates, numbers and good quotations.

19. Recorders provide a verbatim permanent record, but they are sometimes clumsy to use.

 # Review Exercises

1. CLASS PROJECTS

1. List 10 interviewing tips provided by other sources.

2. Interview an expert on interviewing, body language or nonverbal communication, perhaps someone in your school's psychology or speech department, and report on the information's usefulness to journalists. You might also invite the expert to speak to your class.

3. Interview government officials who frequently deal with reporters. Ask what they like and

dislike about the interviews and how they handle the questions (to avoid echo) and the reporters conducting the interviews.

4. Ask several government officials which local reporters are the best interviewers, and then someone in your school's psychology or speech department, and report on the information's

usefulness to journalists. Or you could talk to the reporters about their interviewing techniques.

5. Ask every student in your class to write one paragraph about the three most newsworthy experiences in his or her life. Select the students with the most interesting events and have your entire class interview them, one by one, and write news stories about their experiences.

2. INTERVIEW WITH A RETIRED FBI AGENT

Write a news story based on the following interview with Edward Vargas. He was born in your city 62 years ago, and graduated from your university 40 years ago with a degree in sociology. For the last 35 years, he has been an FBI agent, much of it working undercover. He retired from the bureau earlier this year after being recognized as one of its top agents. He lives in the Cleveland area, but he is on campus to receive an award as a distinguished alumnus. Vargas has agreed to be interviewed for a story you're writing for the school newspaper. Here are your handwritten notes of the interview. Statements in quotation marks are the words of Vargas; all other material is a paraphrase.

Came to the university when he was recruited by Coach Bill Sandman to play football. Was recruited by several other major universities, but chose this university because of Sandman.

"When I came here to visit, I talked with Sandman. He took me to lunch and then to a basketball game that night. And we hit it off pretty well. Recruiting wasn't the big deal it is nowadays. It was all pretty informal. I really loved the school spirit here, so it just seemed natural to come here."

Was lineman. Weighed 250 pounds, height 6'2".

"At 250, I was big for that day. It wasn't like today where you have linemen who are 300, 320 or even 340. I don't see how any one that big can move, but they do, and they're faster than I was when I played."

Majored in sociology because it didn't require too many hours, could take lots of other courses. Also, really loved professor Ed Mitchell's criminology class. "That's where I got my first taste of law enforcement. I didn't think about it as a career until several years later, but Mitchell's class really set my imagination on fire."

Jobs were scarce when he graduated. Tried to find some entry-level job in a business or corporation. But everyone wanted either business administration grads or people with experience.

"I even took the test for a federal government job, but I didn't do well enough to get ahead of those guys who had been in the military. They kind of went to the head of the line, so to speak."

Only job available was working in a meat packing plant. His ability to speak Spanish was key. Many meat workers were Spanish speakers even then. Helped him move up to foreman after about a year.

Also played for a semi-pro football team for three years.

"Man, that was tough. I thought college ball was physical, but some of those semi-pro guys were suicidal. And you were playing with second-rate equipment. Hell, you even had to buy your own helmet. Actually, they took it out of your pay, so the first half of my first season I was paying off the helmet."

After a little more than 3 yrs at the meat packing plant, got a call from a local FBI agent asking if there were any Spanish-speaking college grads at the plant. FBI needed Spanish-speaking agents. Vargas couldn't think of any other than himself. Wasn't sure he was interested.

"But then I got another call from the agent and he said, 'Why don't you give it a try?' So I figured, what the hell, I'll take a shot at it and I bombed completely."

After that he got a job at the university supervising maintenance crews, but the agent called again. That was about the time he married Ellen, his sweetheart from college.

"I wasn't sure it was worth trying to take the test again, but this guy was persuasive. I flew back to Washington to take this test I was sure I would fail, so I really didn't care. That attitude must have worked because I aced the thing."

Less than a month later, he was sent to the FBI training center at Quantico, Va. Split his time for next 17 weeks between Quantico and Washington.

After training sent with Ellen to El Paso, Texas. First job was trailing a KGB agent from Soviet Union who was getting information from someone on the Ft. Bliss Army base. Had to trail agent w/o being seen and get enough photos and information on his travels through Texas, Mexico and Cuba that he would be worthless to KGB as an agent. The plan worked. KGB realized its agent was known. Stopped using him or gathering information from Ft. Bliss. "I don't know who on the base was giving out information or whether it was intentional or simply carelessness. That end was handled by someone else, but I think they did get that leak plugged."

While Vargas working on this assignment, Ellen gave birth to their first child, a son named Edgar.

He next went to Denver where he was assigned to help with the investigation of a group of militant Chicanos.

"I was only one of 45 Mexican Americans employed by the FBI at this time. So we received a lot of assignments dealing with Mexican gangs and drug dealing."

First assignment over quickly. The gang was suspected of making bombs. Were being tailed while delivering bombs to others in gang.

"These guys were real amateurs, though. They didn't know how to handle the explosives, and they blew themselves up, all except one guy who had left the car to buy some beer from a liquor store. He was pretty shaken when he came out and saw what happened. But we picked him up and he spilled all the details when we questioned him."

Next assignment was undercover doing sting operation on robbers and burglars in the Denver area. This was first of several undercover assignments.

Vargas and team set up a sting operation in Denver. He posed as a fence for stolen goods. Guys with stolen property came to him to unload it. "They didn't know they were selling their booty to a federal agent. Nor did they know they were being photographed, videotaped and audio taped throughout the whole process. So it was easy to go back and arrest all of them."

Worked that for more than 2 1/2 years. Made many arrests. Still holds the record for sting arrests in the state of Colorado.

From Denver he was sent to Miami. Family had grown to two children with birth of daughter, Daniella.

In Miami, his first target was gangs of Haitian revolutionaries. Jean-Claude Duvalier was the ruthless dictator of Haiti. Had the nickname Baby Doc. But U.S. State Dept. saw Duvalier as a bulwark against spread of Communism in Caribbean and Central America.

"Knowing what I knew about conditions in Haiti, I kind of hated to bring some of these guys in. If I'd been a Haitian, I probably would have been trying to get rid of Baby Doc Duvalier myself. But I don't set policy."

Helped round up most of the revolutionaries, about 20; rest fled U.S.

Much of rest of career was focused on drugs. "95 percent of all cocaine that comes into the United States moves through Miami. That was true then and it's still true now."

His assignment was working on air transport of illegal drugs. He used impounded planes to make contact with dealers, to buy and sell drugs and build cases for arrest of dealers.

"Some of the deals I worked on involved 150 to 300 kilos of cocaine. When you consider that one key of cocaine at that time sold for $2,500 on the streets, well, you can see a lot of money was involved."

Most of the information FBI used came from former dealers or couriers who were in trouble with one or another of the South American drug cartels.

"Once you got crossways with one of the drug cartels, you needed to find some protection, and the FBI could offer that. It was from sources like these that we learned that most of the drugs coming into the U.S. were being smuggled in small, single-engine planes that could carry about 150 keys."

Vargas offered tips for students interested in career in FBI.

"You should never do drugs, not even once. The FBI will find out and most likely you won't get the job. Also, you should learn a foreign language, and today, it would be best to learn Russian or Chinese as these are the new drug traffickers and violent gangs entering the world market."

Vargas now retired. Living in Cleveland area with wife. Children grown and in college, one at Ohio State and one at Penn State.

3. INTERVIEWS WITH SPELLING CHAMPIONS

Next week the State Spelling Bee will be held in your community. The winner of the competition will go to the National Spelling Bee, which is held in Washington, D.C. You have found the names of five people who won your state's spelling bee in past years and you want to write a story about them, their recollections of the event, how it affected their lives and what word they misspelled. Your notes from the five interviews follow. The material in quotation marks is the subject's exact words and may be quoted directly. All other material is paraphrased. Use this information to write your story.

Wendy L. Shavers of Cotter Creek

Born Wendy Langston. Won state Spelling Bee 35 years ago. Was 14 at the time. Went to school in the same town where she lives now.

Misspelled "turnstile." Had excuse. At the time there was a chain of department stores in the area called Turn Style. Remembered seeing the name on the store and in newspaper advertisements for the store. So when she was given that word to spell, she spelled it the same as the department store chain. Now she thinks about it all the time.

"Every time I walk through a turnstile, I think about that. I had gotten so many harder words right, and I go out on 'turnstile.'"

Finished 20th at the national bee. Came home and was a successful student at Cotter Creek H.S. Graduated 3rd in her class and won a scholarship to a state university. Scholarship didn't pay for everything she needed. And she met Cole Shavers. Fell in love and married him. He was two years older and had graduated. Wendy dropped out to help him start a business, but Cole died 7 years later in a car crash. The business—a hardware store—failed. Had a 4 yr. old son to raise, so she took a job as a truck driver.

"There were damn few women driving over-the-road trucks when I started. And the other guys were not friendly to me. And the long stretches away from home were hard. But the money was so good, I was determined to stick it out. I'm lucky my mom and sister lived in town so they could keep an eye on Jimmy as he was growing up."

Never remarried.

Still loves words.

"I'm addicted to crossword puzzles. I'll do them in almost any newspaper, except the New York Times. I only do that when I'm brave."

Todd Drolshagen, 2604 Alabama Av

Competed in the bee 22 years ago at 13 yrs old. In 8th grade at North Middle Sch.

Prepping for bee taught good study habits. Helped later in H.S. and college. Graduated at top of class from North H.S. and went to Stanford University.

"It shaped the study habits for the rest of my life. It helped me develop a tolerance for really diligent, repetitive study that I used in high school and college."

Bee also helped him bond with his mom, Daniella Drolshagen—died 3 yrs ago. Spent 2 evenings every week with his mother studying for the bee.

"It really brought us closer together. A teenage boy doesn't have a lot in common with his mother, but those memories are something I'll never forget."

Was nervous from start at nationals. Didn't recognize the first word he was asked to spell—paronymous.

"I swear, the guy who read that word mispronounced it or I didn't hear it or something. I thought almost every vowel in the word was an a. So I spelled it p-a-r-a-n-a-m-o-u-s. And that's how I ended my spelling career."

Studied public affairs at Stanford and returned to work in city government. Is now director of the City Code Enforcement Board. Has held the job for 8 yrs.

Paronymous—derived from the same root; a cognate.

Tonya Livermore, Chicago

Won the state spelling bee 18 years ago. Was in 8th grade at Kennedy Middle Sch.

"I loved the atmosphere at the nationals. Everywhere we went we were treated like royalty. We got attention from the media, from politicians, from almost everyone. That's what sparked my interest in performing, that's what made me want to be on stage."

After H.S., went to Northwestern University to study music. She specializes in religious music and broadway show tunes. Did some acting in Chicago and New York. Eight yrs ago returned to Chicago, got teaching certificate.

Now teaches music to middle and elementary school children in Chicago. Also performs occasionally in community theater productions, esp in the summers.

"The spelling bee was a great experience. It gave me a lot of confidence and opened up a lot of different people and opportunities."

The word she misspelled was "pelisse."

"I had no idea what it meant. The judge said it was a long cloak or outer robe. I certainly didn't know how to spell it. I don't remember what spelling I gave it, but I know I was way off."

Clara Warneky, 428 N. Wilkes Rd.
Won the state bee 28 years ago. Was 13 yrs old and in 7th grade at Colonial Middle.

Of the 108 in the national bee, she finished roughly in the middle of the pack. The word she missed was "acetone." Knew what it was because father was a painter and had used it as a solvent. Had seen containers of it. But botched the spelling of it.

"I was deeply disappointed by that. I knew how to spell that word. But I guess I just got nervous or overconfident or whatever. Anyway, that's how I was eliminated."

"The trip to D.C. did reinforce my love of words, though. I wasn't so disappointed that I didn't continue reading and studying. I still love to read. I read almost everything I can get my hands on. My big love is biographies. I finished a biography of F.D.R. last week, and I'm working on a book on Rachel Carson now."

"I'd love to be a writer. That's always been and still is my dream. With work and family, I don't have time for it now. Maybe in a few years I'll be able to sit down and try to write something of my own."

Thinks she inherited her passion. Mother, grandmother and brother were all ace spellers and all voracious readers.

Works as a manager for Hertz car rental. Has held job for 15 years.

Her oldest daughter, Karen, 15, seems to share interest in words and writing. But she may not be interested in competing in spelling bees.

"I told my husband I had to see if she has the gift. My other two children are younger, so I don't know if they're going to have it too. I'll have to see later if they have the gift and the desire."

Colin Castilango, Eureka, Calif.
Placed 18th in the National Spelling Bee 48 years ago. Was a 7th grader at North Middle—then called North Jr. High.

Won $50 because of 18th place finish. Disappointed because his grandmother had promised him $100 if he won. "That was a lot of money then. Now, you can spend $100 in the time it takes to sneeze."

After H.S. went to the state university and graduated cum laude with a degree in teaching. Took a job teaching English to H.S. students in San Jose, Calif. Taught for about 35 years and spent last few years as district coordinator for teaching literature in H.S. Retired 3 yrs ago.

Still loves words and considers them magical.

"I dream about words. I dream about pronouncing them, spelling them and teaching them. I just love words."

Continues to teach, but now teaching English to refugees in Eureka area. Taught a woman from Guatemala how to read. After reading her first book the woman "thrust her hands into the air to thank God and then gave me a big hug."

"Getting gifts like those makes it easy to go to work."

Tries to keep his income below the level at which he must pay federal income tax. "I don't want a penny of my money going for these wars in Iraq and Afghanistan. They're stupid and wasteful. When I saw on TV one of my last students had been killed in Iraq, I just broke down in tears. Why do we have to do this?"

Misspelled "plebiscite" to lose the national contest.

"I spelled it p-l-e-b-e-s-c-i-t-e. Too many e's and not enough i's. I didn't even know what it meant. Now, I know what it means and why it's important."

12 FEATURE STORIES

People love stories. And stories are everywhere—in movies, books, magazines, newspapers, radio, TV and online. They can evoke emotions: a craving for adventure after learning about a found shipwreck, inspiration after reading about a child's fight with cancer or encouragement when discovering how a family opened a restaurant while many others closed during the pandemic.

Feature stories are nonfiction. They are fact-based storytelling. They are called "human-interest" stories because they say something about life. Features are soft news because they exclude the news element of immediacy found in hard news stories.

Journalists borrow techniques from short stories, often using descriptions, sensory details, quotations, anecdotes and even personification. They might use characterization, scene setting, plot structure and other novelistic elements to dramatize a story's theme and to add more details. Yet feature stories are journalism, not creative fiction writing. Everything is factual; nothing is made up. After all, fact can be stranger than fiction! Features are fair and balanced, based on verifiable information. They also are objective—they are not essays nor editorials.

12.1 Finding Story Ideas

Everything has a story behind it! Journalists just open their eyes and ears to find an interesting theme. Writers find ideas by being curious and observant about life. They ask questions and listen to the topics that people are debating. They go to different places to experience diverse groups of people and their discussions.

Journalists also find stories that spin off news topics. A story on the number of dog adoptions in the area may prompt a sidebar on the journey of a particular pet finding a forever home. A report on the nation's receding coastline may generate stories about the plight of families whose homesteads are now covered in water. A news story about a tornado may spark human-interest stories about the reactions of survivors, heroism in crises and other "people" angles that bring natural disasters into sharper focus.

It takes practice to see story ideas everywhere and in everything. Sometimes beginning journalists have trouble with finding ideas. The concept of universal needs might help. It is a method that journalists sometimes use to find stories to attract large audiences, which is a major news value. Universal needs are those that all human beings have in common: food, clothing, shelter, love, health, approval, belonging, self-esteem, job satisfaction, entertainment and more. Exercise 1 presents a universal needs grid; completing such a chart can help reporters think of ideas for stories.

The concept of a grid can be applied to almost any topic to elicit ideas. COVID-19 and the pandemic has touched everyone's lives in recent years. Table 12.1 shows that journalists might write elements of daily life across the top of the grid and list ages of people down the side. Intersections may produce story ideas, such as parents and home life. For example, parents who newly experienced working remotely might consider including office space in their next home. Another intersection is college students and education. After learning remotely, some students might feel intimidated by in-class discussions. In-person dynamics and expectations are different from remotely typing responses in Zoom's chat or clicking on a raised-hand symbol. Since March 2020, when the World Health Organization declared the coronavirus outbreak as a pandemic, journalists have been writing feature stories such as "How the Coronavirus Has Changed Campaign Season" and "Can Small Movie Theaters Survive?" and "Rethinking Family Get-Togethers" and historical feature stories retold of past pandemics and survival rates.

A grid can be expanded or narrowed to almost any topic, such as the pandemic's effect on different industries (across the top) and their products, services, consumer and employees (along the side).

12.2 Gathering Information

After selecting an interesting topic, journalists narrow it to a central point that emphasizes, perhaps, a single person, several people, a situation or an episode. If they fail to identify a central point, their stories become long and disorganized. This leaves audiences confused, and they will quit the story because the point is lost.

12.2.1 Firsthand Observations—Seeing, Listening, Smelling, Touching, Tasting

Journalists use observation to illustrate character and personality. Instead of saying a student was timid, they describe how the person acted or what they did, such as "sat quietly in the back corner of the room"; "listened, but never talked in class"; or "blushed and stammered" when answering questions.

Journalists personally visit and observe the places they write about, and they interview people in their customary surroundings. Audiences experience places and people through the writer. And, the reporter's experiences will be interesting and unique from what can be seen online. Journalists research a story's background to ask good questions when interviewing sources and to provide context when writing. Reporters use all their senses; record how people move, speak and dress; and use concrete nouns and descriptive verbs instead of adjectives and adverbs. They give audience members a reason to care about the subject. They remember that audiences like stories that feature people.

TABLE 12.1 LIFE DURING THE PANDEMIC

	Family	Home	Education	Work	Food	Health/Hygiene	Sports	Self-Esteem	Habits	Social
Elderly					Learn to order deliveries remotely	Highly susceptible				
Grandparents	Taking care of grandchildren		Homeschooling grandchildren	Quit work						
Adults				First responders		What mask is best	Paused so nothing on TV		Drinking more alcohol	
Parents	Juggling work and home-schooling	Cramped more than before, but together								
Young Adults				Few jobs after graduation	Ordering online is expensive			Hoodies every day		
College Students		Pay for apartment on campus while learning remotely?	Repercussions of satisfactory/not satisfactory grades	No work so now need loans		Flu or COVID-19? Stay home or go to class?			Eating on-camera while in class	
K-12 Students	Silver lining of having family around all day		Bounced from in-person to remote to in-person classes				No practice—what does this mean for anticipated athletic scholarships?			Not learning social skills
Children						No vaccine				Not learning social skills
Toddlers and Babies						Highly susceptible				

For the lead of his article "New Leash on Life: Group Finds Old Pets New Homes," Mike Householder described his observations from his visit to a unique animal rescue facility. The story described the circumstances and successful placement of older pets into new homes:

> A 15-year-old cat. A 14-year-old dog with a mouthful of bad teeth, a wart on his head and a kidney infection. Even a 17-year-old parakeet named Bubba.
>
> Tyson's Place Animal Rescue helps old pets find new homes.

(The Associated Press)

Jill Bannink-Albrect pets one of the cats in the Tyson's Place Animal Rescue shelter she founded in Holland, Michigan. By visiting the shelter and observing, reporter Mike Householder was able to provide compelling descriptions of the staff and the animals.

12.2.2 Interviews and Quotes

Interviews give the writer an understanding of a situation from several points of view. They interview more people than are included in the story because some interviews help with context or background information.

Quotes support narrative. Journalists might write several paragraphs of narrative, followed by a sentence or two of a source's quote to explain an idea or emotion, then some description and more quotes or narrative. Stories are not transcripts of interviews with quotes strung together. Journalists write the story and choose supporting quotes. The examples throughout this chapter show how professionals integrated narration and dialogue quotes.

12.2.3 Dialogue

Feature stories need dialogue. Journalists use quotes to show temperament, personality, plot, events, time, customs or continuity. They are careful to select only the best, most revealing quotes, and use them sparingly. For example, a former running back for the San Diego Chargers, LaDainian Tomlinson, was inducted into the Pro Football Hall of Fame. In his long-form narrative story, Associated Press journalist Barry Wilner included two short paragraphs from Tomlinson's induction speech about "Team America" to show why he received standing ovations from the audience during his passionate talk about Americans working together:

> "Football is a microcosm of America," Tomlinson said. "All races, religions and creeds, living, playing, competing side by side. When you're part of a team, you understand your teammates—their strengths and weaknesses—and work together toward the same goal, to win a championship.
>
> "Let's not choose [in America] to be against one another. Let's choose to be for one another. . . . I pray we dedicate ourselves to being the best team we can be, working and living together, representing the highest ideals of mankind. Leading the way for all nations to follow."

(The Associated Press)

LaDainian Tomlinson speaks during the ceremony at which he was enshrined in the Pro Football Hall of Fame in Canton, Ohio.

Journalists use dialogue for impact to support the narrative, which weaves the story together. Wilner wrote the following narrative to lead his story: "As he so often did in the field, LaDainian Tomlinson stole the show." Narrative introduces, summarizes, arranges, creates flow and transitions and links one idea to the next. Narratives are often unobtrusive and subtle, helping to guide the flow of the story. An analogy is to compare a narrative to a tree trunk and branches whereas the dialogue or quotations are like the leaves. Tree trunks and branches grow leaves, but not vice versa.

While gathering the information for feature stories, journalists consult several sources, perhaps a half-dozen or more, to obtain a well-rounded account. They gather two or three times as much information as they can use in the story, then discard all but the most telling details. Gathering a lot of information is essential to helping the reporter understand more about the issue or event.

After finishing a feature, journalists will edit and rewrite the narrative sometimes several times. They will also angle the feature for a particular audience, publication or news program, emphasizing the story's relevance and importance to it.

12.2.4 Data and Examples

Journalists look up records and include data and examples to support general statements. Statistics verify a story's message. Examples help readers understand a situation. For instance, a feature sidebar story that names local street intersections with the highest number of car collisions might accompany a hard news story on a recent accident or protesters advocating for better traffic signs where accidents happen regularly. The story would include the number of accidents for each intersection, examples and short descriptions of recent accidents and interviews with survivors, authorities, advocates and nearby residents. Journalists would personally visit and observe the intersections to describe what makes them dangerous.

12.3 Parts of Feature Stories

Journalists employ creativity in writing human-interest stories. They break away from hard news formulas. Skilled writers use different techniques for the lead, body and ending, depending on the type of feature. Great feature stories capture people's attention and carry them along like a flowing river. Before they know it, they have reached the end.

12.3.1 The Lead of a Feature Story

The only requirement for the lead of a feature story is that it interests people, making them want to stay with the story to learn more. The story can start with either a summary lead or a type of alternative lead (described in Chapters 7 and 8, respectively).

John Carlisle began his story on a lighthouse that is collapsing into Lake Michigan with the following:

> Not if, but when.
>
> Someday soon, a forgotten old lighthouse will crumble into Lake Michigan. And, along with it, the hopes of the man who spent half his lifetime trying to save it.
>
> After a century of abandonment, after seasons of water and ice tearing at its base, the Waugoshance Lighthouse will be swallowed by the lake. The only mystery is when.
>
> "It's going pretty quick now," said Chris West, the 45-year-old founder of the Waugoshance Lighthouse Preservation Society. "We, by no means, can see the future on how long it will last, but if what's happened over the past two years continues to happen, it doesn't have long for this world."
>
> *(Detroit Free Press)*

In another example, one cannot help but admire the flowing prose in the lead of "Nation Marks Lives Lost and Hopeful Signs of Healing," a story written to commemorate Sept. 11. The anniversary narrative by Robert McFadden and his colleagues appeared in The New York Times:

> Once more the leaden bells tolled in mourning, loved ones recited the names of the dead at ground zero, and a wounded but resilient America paused yesterday to remember the calamitous day when terrorist explosions rumbled like summer thunder and people fell from the sky.
>
> *(The New York Times)*

This lead rises to the solemn occasion it represents. It is an emotional, heavy and poetic lead that embodies great sorrow and history. The wording transports readers to another time and place and helps their imagination to hear the explosions and see people falling. It causes them to pause and reflect, which is the intended effect. Not all stories can carry this type of lead. Yet, no matter what kind writers choose for a feature story, they try to make it as unique as possible. Cliché leads, questions, figures of speech and shockers generally sound trite and should be used sparingly.

12.3.2 The Body of a Feature Story

Like the lead, the body of a feature story takes many forms. The inverted-pyramid style may be appropriate for some features and chronological order for others. Regardless of the form or style chosen, every feature is coherent. All the facts fit together smoothly and logically. Transitions, which are usually brief, guide the audience from one segment of the story to the next and clearly reveal the relationship between those segments. They might ask a question, announce shifts in time or place or link ideas by repeating key words or phrases.

Journalists write concisely and never waste their audience's time. Features emphasize lively details—the action—and they provide an occasional change of pace. Journalist James L. Edwards III varied his sentence length to emphasize the tension felt by a local golfer in an important game:

Nathan Clark knew the pressure was on.

By the time the former Mason High School and Michigan State golfer . . .

The lead was only seven words. The 45-word sentence that made up the second paragraph established the golfer's connection to the community and identified the tournament and his main competitor.

The 35 words in the third paragraph, composed of two sentences of 19 and 16 words, described Clark's competitor. The third graph was followed by:

And Clark knew he would have to refrain from any serious missteps to have a chance.

He did just that.

(Lansing [Michigan] State Journal)

The next paragraph described who won the tournament (40 words), followed by a narrative about the tournament and quotes from the winner.

Successful feature writers use elements such as characterization, setting, plot and subplot, conflict, time, dialogue and narrative. They outline their stories and plan the beginning, middle and end. They reveal the character of the people they write about with quotations and descriptions of mannerisms, body language, voice, appearance, dress, age, preferences, prejudices, use of personal space and a host of other traits.

The setting reveals the subject's character and provides context for the audience to understand this person. Geography and family may influence physical and mental traits, determine life span and impact ways of earning a living. Journalists tell where a subject grew up, what the person's surroundings are now and how these factors contribute to who they are. Such touches of description sprinkled throughout a story show what the subject is like.

Some plots describe obstacles that lie between people and their goals. The resolution of conflict presents the theme of many human-interest stories. The main variations are the challenges experienced between humans and nature, humans and their inner self, and humans and humans. As journalists ask people about events in their lives, plots naturally emerge. Often a subplot materializes, a secondary line of action that runs counterpoint or in tandem to the main action and either helps

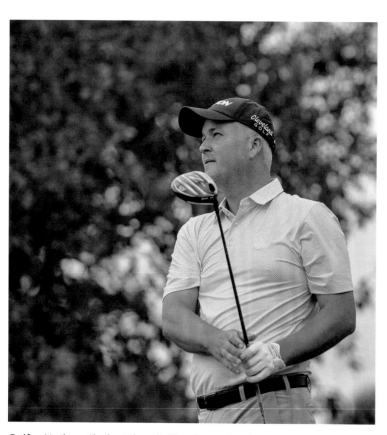

Golfer Nathan Clark at the All-City Championship.

or hinders the person's progress. If journalists listen and identify plot and subplot elements as the subject tells the story, a natural order appears.

Time is handled in a variety of ways. To organize some types of features, journalists use a dramatic episode in the present as an opener, then flash back to the beginning of the story and bring it forward in chronological order. Reporters can foreshadow the future or build in a series of flashbacks arranged in the order of occurrence.

THE MORNING CALL

Being young and transgender

Bethlehem teens seek treatment in Philadelphia after finding few resources in the Lehigh Valley.

BY SAM KENNEDY
OF THE MORNING CALL

This story shares the experience of Sebastian Montiel and Sasha Rivera—two transgender teenagers. The article includes a sidebar with a glossary of terms and ends with resources for transgender youths.

12.3.3 The Ending of a Feature Story

A feature has a satisfying conclusion, perhaps an anecdote, quote, key word or phrase repeated in some surprising or meaningful way.

Journalists avoid ending a feature story with a summary. These endings are too likely to state the obvious or be repetitious, flat or boring. For example, a story about children on an unusual field trip would not end with a summary sentence such as "And they all had a good time."

Some endings come back around to the beginning. A story titled, "New Leash on Life: Group Finds Old Pets New Homes," was used as an example earlier in this chapter of a journalist applying his observation skills to write his lead (see Sec. 12.2.1). The body of the story describes Tyson's Place Animal Rescue and uses Bosco, the "14-year-old rat terrier with the lousy choppers" to show how the shelter cares for the health of animals. Then the story ends with a quote that lets readers know the older dog is now in a good home:

> Eventually, Jen Wilson and her husband, Frank, came forward for Bosco, giving him a new home in Grand Rapids, where the now-15-year-old is rarely seen without his little tail wagging behind him.
>
> "We adore this dog. We love him," Jen Wilson said. "I started it with: 'Let's just give this dog a loving home throughout the last of his life, love him through his golden years and not get too attached.'
>
> "Well, that definitely didn't happen."

12.4 Types of Feature Stories

Feature stories come in a wide variety. The following sections describe a few of the most common types. One type of story is not more desirable than another; they are all different.

12.4.1 Profiles or Personality Features

Profiles describe interesting people—individuals who may have overcome a disability, had a unique hobby, pursued an unusual career or experienced an amazing adventure. Profiles reveal the person's character. They make audiences feel as if they know the person. Profiles do more than list achievements or dates, minutiae that no one remembers anyway.

To gather the necessary information, writers observe their subjects at work; visit them at home; and interview their friends, relatives and business associates. Completed profiles describe and quote the subjects. The best profiles are so revealing that readers, listeners and viewers feel as though they have actually talked to the person. Here's a shortened version of John Carlisle's profile of former Pfc. Orlando Padilla, as he honored his former colleagues on Veterans Day. It is titled, "On Veterans Day, One Vet Offers His Own Silent Salute."

His legs were tired. His arm grew numb. And still he stood.

It was Veterans Day, and former Pfc. Orlando Padilla was alone on the grassy plot of Ferndale's Memorial Mall, arm raised in salute toward the direction of the monuments to local veterans. He'd been standing as rigid as a statue for hours now. His Army uniform was utterly crisp, his ribbons and medals were pinned perfectly straight, his salute was stiff, his expression was stoic.

"It's for my brother and sister veterans that I served with, all those who weren't lucky enough like me to make it home," said the 63-year-old, speaking reluctantly, trying not to break his salute or his serious expression. "And, what's going on in the world, the political climate. But today is not about me."

Ferndale's war memorial was built 101 years ago to commemorate the War to End All Wars, and it grew larger with each monument to every war that followed. Padilla came here earlier in the morning for the city's annual Veterans Day flag raising and walked back to his house, two blocks away, but then was compelled to return by himself, to show his respect in his own, spur-of-the-moment way. It was the first time he'd ever done this. He didn't announce that he'd be there, didn't explain himself to passers-by.

Padilla served in the infantry in Germany, at the height of the Cold War, patrolling the border between West Germany and East Germany for several years in the 1970s.

"I've done a few careers since I got out of the Army, but those years in the Army are the most important years of my life. I could die today and be happy that I served and be honored that I served and be fulfilled that I served. It's the proudest thing I've ever done in my life, and I could die knowing I did something for my country."

His father was a veteran, too. World War II. He died a few months ago. It played a part, he said, in his inspiration to be here.

The hours ticked by. The sun passed in an arc before him, and the trees cast long shadows across the names of the dead on the monuments. At one point, a firefighter from the fire station across the street saw him frozen on the lawn and quietly laid a bottle of water for him near his feet.

Padilla didn't flinch. His face remained a mixture of sadness, intensity and resolve. And, he pledged to stay as long as he could in lone, silent gesture.

"Until my arm falls off," he said. "It's getting there."

(Detroit Free Press)

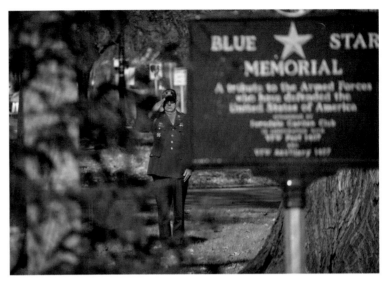

Army veteran Pfc. Orlando Padilla, 63, salutes the war memorial at Ferndale's Memorial Mall. Padilla remained in this position for several hours in recognition of the "brothers and sisters" he served with who did not return.

12.4.2 Historical Features

Historical features commemorate important events, such as the Boston Tea Party, the Civil War or the Great Depression. The 100th anniversary of the beginning of World War I and the commemoration of the attack on Pearl Harbor, precipitating the United States' entry into WWII, inspire a number of historical features about events and people. Stories on 9/11 memorialize the tragedy every year.

Current events can inspire historical features. The COVID-19 pandemic prompted feature stories about prior pandemics and comparisons to today, such as the number of deaths and methods to combat infectious diseases. If a tornado, flood or earthquake strikes the city, news organizations will likely produce stories about earlier disasters.

Tracing the histories of buildings, homes and meaningful events in the area, such as an Underground Railroad route, are also fodder for feature stories. Historical feature stories might describe famous landmarks, pioneers and philosophies; improvements in educational, entertainment, medical and transportation facilities; and changes in an area's ethnic composition, housing patterns, food, industries, growth, religions and wealth.

Perhaps in observance of #BlackLivesMatter and during Black History Month, Matt Miller of the Lansing State Journal researched and wrote a story commemorating the 25th anniversary of a sit-in by Black students at Michigan State University.

The first students arrived at Michigan State University's Administration Building at 4:31 p.m. Dozens more came in behind them. They brought books and blankets and waited in near silence for almost an hour.

Chronological order to describe events.

Unusual (news element) draws in audience, who doesn't know what is happening yet.

Jeffrey Robinson, head of the campus NAACP chapter and son of a prominent Detroit minister, broke it.

Contrast.

"The Administration building is supposed to close at 5:30 p.m.," he said, "but we're going to stay."

Direct quote to support prior sentence.

Audience now knows this is a flashback.

Explanation for the event.

Direct quote to support prior sentence.

Flash forward to the present. (Great to have found original subject!)

It was 1989, the 9th of May, a Tuesday, the culmination of discontent. No single incident sparked the protest. Over the winter, Black students had first asked and then demanded that the university do more to address racism on campus and the academic success of Black students. They felt they'd been brushed off, that the people in power weren't listening.

"There was this yearning, this desire for us to make a statement and have that statement heard and responded to by the administration," said Robinson, who is now the principal of Paul Robeson Malcolm X Academy in Detroit.

The full story continues with descriptions of the peaceful protest, sit-ins at other universities, interviews with those same students who are now alumni and the sentiment of Black students today. Visual communication components include a timeline of events that led to the demonstration and photos of the sit-in and rallies that occurred for eight days.

12.4.3 Seasonal and Holiday Features

Editors and news directors often assign feature stories about seasons and holidays: Christmas, Easter, Hanukkah, Ramadan, Chinese New Year, Valentine's Day, Independence Day and Martin Luther King Jr. Day, for instance. Journalists find new angles to make them interesting. Some writers focus on how celebrations differ globally while others delve into the history of the holiday. The week preceding Thanksgiving, one news outlet ran a story with lists and descriptions of classic movies that focused on the holiday and were now streaming. Another story was on holiday foods and hazards that were harmful to pets. It included an interview with the president of the American Veterinary Media Association and discussed holiday traditions that should be kept away from dogs and cats: turkey skin and chocolate; mistletoe, poinsettias, pine and other seasonal plants; decorations and electric lights; wrapping paper; and even a lot of guests can cause social anxiety for pets.

Lyndsay C. Green of the Detroit Free Press wrote her holiday story in first person and included her observations to draw in her readers. She used present tense and description for readers to feel as if they were with her. Excerpts of "$100 Chocolate Easter Egg is a Mouthwatering Work of Art" appear below.

Around me, pastry chefs are rolling dough into spirals of chubby croissants and plump rolls. I sidestep between racks of croissants layered with thin slivers of almonds. It's Good Friday and I'm on an Easter egg hunt for the kind of chocolate eggs that [Executive Chef Matt] Knio has been crafting since he started the business more than a decade ago.

"In the main area, there's flour and gluten in the air," Knio says as he holds the door for me to enter a new room led by an all-female crew.

The rich aroma of chocolate hits me seconds after I cross the threshold.

"This is where we make pastries and chocolate, so it's a completely different temperature and environment," he says.

In a far back corner, past the lemon tarts and across the way from the bright pistachio macarons dotted with plump raspberries are the Easter eggs. Of the 400 chocolate eggs that Knio crafted by hand, these seven eggs are the last of them.

Knio's chocolate Easter eggs are like works of art. Sprayed in cocoa butter and cocoa powder, I could be convinced the chocolate eggs are inedible and rather decorative domes cloaked in brown suede.

The process, he says, can take two full days to complete, and prices range between $30 and $100, depending on the size and detail.

"The thing about the giant egg is that it's so hard to put them together. Any sudden move and you'll crack it," he says, adding that he cracked his first egg this season. "It's stressful, but I get this happiness once it's done."

At 3 p.m. on Easter Sunday, the largest of the eggs, which are on display at stores in Detroit and Birmingham, will become a source of entertainment for diners. Some standing at around 3 feet tall, ornamented with hundreds of handcrafted chocolate leaves, the eggs will dual as chocolate piñatas as children are encouraged to crack the eggs to reveal their truffle-filled interiors.

"Cannelle [pastries] is my toy store," Knio says. It's like, you feed our people whatever they want to eat, but this is what feeds me."

(Detroit Free Press)

Green tucked in other information, including her observations of the different pastry work areas; chefs' preparations; comparisons, descriptions and ingredients of some of the eggs; shipping destinations; and themes in years past, such as caramel or truffles. The story ends with the bakery's website, in case readers are motivated to find out more information.

12.4.4 Explanatory Features

Explanatory features (also called "local situation" or "interpretive" features or "sidebars") often are the result of other news stories or accompany them. In these, journalists provide more detailed descriptions or explanations of organizations, activities, trends or ideas in the news.

Explanatory features might localize national events or personalize an issue or event. After news stories describe the federal health care reform law, an explanatory feature might highlight how it will affect people of different ages or individuals from different socioeconomic levels or with diverse health issues. An editor might couple a story about a family that won a lottery with a feature on how others who won are doing today or how they spent their winnings.

The announcement of a special exhibit on old Detroit families was the occasion for the following feature. Phoebe Wall Howard's story intertwines the history of one family to that of the city and begins with this lead:

At age 15, Julia Brunell sat on blanket-covered crates of whiskey as she drove alone on the streets of Detroit, making pickups for the speakeasy her parents ran near the riverfront. The bootleggers figured few would suspect a teen girl smuggler in 1930.

But Prohibition didn't stop Julia's mother and father. They had purchased 289 St. Aubin between Franklin and Woodbridge streets in 1905 to run a grocery store and eventually a blind pig with the help of their daughter.

The ban on making or selling alcohol in the U.S. dragged from 1920 to 1933. Still, people wanted it. And a lot of those people were sailors coming in on ships.

"This was the docks area, where the foundries were, a tough part of town," said Joel Stone, senior curator at the Detroit Historical Society. "Julia would go to various stills and pick up product. We hear about the Purple Gang and rum running but very seldom see the faces behind that."

(Detroit Free Press)

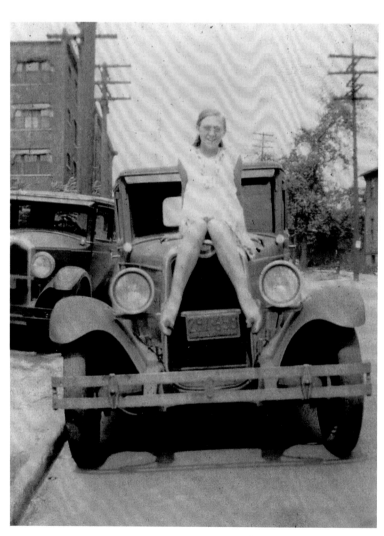

Julia Brunell sits on the hood of the 1928 Chevrolet she drove as a teenager to pick up liquor for her parents' speakeasy during Prohibition.

The story continues with how legendary businesses got started (in this case, a well-known tavern), pictures of families and short descriptions of the other exhibits.

12.4.5 Occupation or Hobby Features

Collectors and crafts enthusiasts often make good subjects for feature stories because they are passionately involved and often eccentric, quotable and entertaining. Strange or trendy hobbies and interests, such as urban exploration (of old, abandoned buildings), planking, escapology and taphophilia (a love of funerals, graves and cemeteries) also make good topics because they tend to involve colorful characters and unusual experiences.

Journalists might prepare feature stories about occupations that are dangerous (mining) or hobbies that are highly specialized (rock climbing). Or they could report on a job many people think is boring (being a server at a restaurant) and turn it into something exciting (meeting celebrities while working on the job). The following lead begins a story that honors the long legacy of a hospital worker.

Jane Parry has walked the halls of Sparrow Hospital for more than five decades.

Pushing a cart loaded with cleaning supplies, Parry, 69, an environmental services technician, has been a constant in the hospital's patient, emergency and operating rooms since she started working there at age 17.

Her nearly 52-year tenure is a rarity at Sparrow Hospital, where only one other current caregiver has been on the job as long as Parry, said hospital spokesman John Foren. She is tied for third place for all-time length of service at Sparrow Hospital, he said.

Parry has cleaned up in the aftermath of tragedy and triumph. She's witnessed the grief, struggle and recovery of countless patients and their loved ones and she worked in Sparrow's intensive care unit throughout the COVID-19 pandemic.

(Lansing [Michigan] State Journal)

The story continues with colleagues' quotes describing Parry and narrative on her challenges and achievements. Parry was also interviewed.

12.4.6 Behind-the-Scenes Features

Behind-the-scenes features convey a sense of immediacy, allowing the audience to see, feel, taste, touch, smell and understand the "backstage" work that goes into an event. Journalists look for people who perform jobs that are out of the public eye but essential to many citizens. They interview sources, visit them on location and use the source's own words to tell the story. They also include details they observe, such as atmosphere, working conditions, physical appearance of people and their workspace, specialized terms and conversations between workers.

A story about a dairy farm and the milking process became more exciting when readers were enticed by a headline to "Meet Ellie," the matriarch cow of the farm. R.J. Wolcott of the Lansing, Michigan, State Journal wrote a 19-paragraph profile about Ellie, describing her age ("The 11-and-a-half-year-old Holstein is two years older than the next eldest cow on the farm"), personality ("not a troublemaker") and appearance to readers ("Her dark-colored eyes shined bright as she hung her head below a nearby guard rail"). As readers followed Ellie through her day, they also learned about the inner workings of a dairy farm and the milking process. "Ellie contributed 28 pounds of milk during her time at the milking parlor . . . The 15-minute process involves . . . Over her lifetime, Ellie has given more than 240,000 pounds of milk, which becomes . . . Once the milking is done, . . ." Readers also learn interesting tidbits about the calves, the bulls, the naming process and when they could visit the farm.

12.4.7 Participatory Features

Participatory features give another kind of inside view, this time through the senses of a journalist who is actually experiencing an event or situation. Reporters might immerse themselves totally into the world of a police officer on patrol or a chimney sweep on the job. They arrange such experiences with the person they are shadowing, making it clear that they are journalists and will write a story about the experience that will appear in the media.

Whereas news stories are usually written in the third person, with the journalist as a neutral observer or outsider, feature stories can be written in the first person, addressing audience members directly. A participatory, first-person example is the "$100 Chocolate Easter Egg" story shown earlier in Section 12.4.3 on seasonal and holiday features.

12.4.8 Adventure Features

Adventure features describe unusual and exciting experiences—perhaps the story of someone who fought in a war, survived an airplane crash, climbed a mountain, sailed around the world or experienced another country. Many writers begin with the action, the story's most interesting and dramatic moments, and use quotations and descriptions.

12.4.9 How-to-Do-It Features

This type of feature tells audiences how to accomplish a psychological or physical task, such as communicating better with roommates or keeping emotions in check at the office. Stories might focus on strengthening a marriage or overcoming shyness. They can explain how to recognize voter intimidation, find a tattooist, check for signs of breast cancer, choose an insurance company, tie a tie, use silverware properly, seek out mentors for teens or adapt best practices for remote learning.

Journalists interview experts and get tips from people who have done what their stories describe. In addition, good reporters try to observe or participate in the procedure. For instance, they might watch a pet masseuse or tattooist to better understand the topic.

Journalists divide the task into simple, clear, easy-to-follow steps. They tell the public what materials the procedure requires and what it will cost in money and time. They often include a chart or a bulleted list of tips.

12.4.10 Other Types of Feature Stories

Successful journalists find the human interest on all reporting beats and topics—politics, medicine, sports, business, technology, education, medical and science.

Reporters find individuals affected by the status quo or by change. They look for emotion or inspiration within a story. Narratives may portray typical conditions or unique aberrations to common systems, but they all include a human element. Journalists gather facts from documents, experts and individuals affected by a situation to give context to a story and to present it on a personal level. They might talk to family and friends of individuals who are subjects for the story. They use quotes, allowing subjects to tell about their experiences and feelings. Journalists go to the scene of the story—a person's home or a place of business, for example. They observe the details found in the physical surroundings and in people's mannerisms and body language. Other elements such as smell, sounds, taste or texture make the story more interesting and realistic, drawing the reader into the narrative.

Guest Columnist

Writing About Celebrities Without Getting Starstruck

BY KURT KRUG

I fell into entertainment writing and reporting when I was working for a small weekly newspaper in Dearborn, Michigan, as a general assignment reporter covering various beats, primarily education and police. I was also assigned to write about concerts and plays. One of my first celebrity interviews was with the late Grammy-nominated singer Eddie Money when he came to town. I found it a welcome change from covering school board meetings and grisly murders. I also found that I had a knack for it and enjoyed doing it, given that I subscribed to Entertainment Weekly (the premier source for entertainment news).

That was fortuitous for me because, at the time, the Ritz Carlton hotel in Dearborn was the venue where many actors would have press junkets when in the area to promote their latest movies. It was there I interviewed Oscar nominee John Travolta (for "Pulp Fiction"), Oscar winner Joaquin Phoenix (for "The Joker"), Oscar winner Kevin Costner ("Dances with Wolves"), Emmy winner Tim Allen ("Home Improvement"), Emmy nominee Elizabeth Mitchell ("Lost"), Golden Globe nominee Dennis Quaid ("Far from Heaven"), Anna Faris ("Mom"), Robert Patrick ("Terminator 2: Judgment Day") and Rob Schneider ("Saturday Night Live"). As a film aficionado, I don't care about celebrity gossip (who's dating whom, who's cheating on whom, who's divorcing whom)—that doesn't interest me. What interests me is hearing about the filmmaking process and how they choose their roles.

When I was in graduate school, I paid for some of my tuition through freelancing. I felt I hit the big time when I got to interview actress Kristen Bell about her series "Veronica Mars." Not only was I a fan of the show, I wrote it for The Detroit News, a major daily newspaper. Since I was familiar with the series, that made for a much more in-depth, productive interview.

As the years went on, I continued freelancing for many media outlets, including USA Today, Reuters, Detroit Free Press, The Ann Arbor News, The Oakland Press, The Seattle Times, The Dallas Morning News and numerous others.

I've also gotten to interview Oscar winner J.K. Simmons ("Whiplash"), Oscar winner Kevin Kline ("A Fish Called Wanda"), Oscar winner Rita Moreno ("West Side Story"), Oscar nominee Sigourney Weaver ("Aliens"), Juliet Landau ("Angel"), James Marsters ("Buffy the Vampire Slayer"), Amy Acker ("Person of Interest"), Neve Campbell ("Scream"), Lacey Chabert ("Mean Girls"), Denis O'Hare ("True Blood") and the list goes on.

In the case of Neve Campbell, I was one of very few journalists in Michigan—if not the only journalist—to interview her about "Scream 4," which was filmed in Michigan. This came about because I sent my interview request six months in advance, knowing that many journalists (from Michigan and beyond) would want to interview her when "Scream 4" debuted.

If I can offer any advice when interviewing celebrities, it's the same advice I offer to all of my journalism students:

1. Don't get starstruck, which is easy to do. Think of the celebrity interview as any other you would have with a city official, an education professional or a private citizen. Some will be difficult and even rude, but that comes with the territory in this profession.

2. Do your homework. In most cases, you'll most likely only have 10-15 minutes to conduct an interview—especially with the bigger names (which will most likely be at a round table with other journalists or on the phone)—so you have to make every question count. Why are you interviewing them? If it's about their latest movie or TV show, be sure you see it beforehand.

3. Don't stray too far from the topic. Make your questions stand out. A lot of times when celebrities are promoting something, they've had the same questions thrown at them several times per day for weeks. It's inevitable you'll ask the same questions as other journalists. Ask a question they normally won't get pertaining to the topic at hand (don't play "gotcha" games because this is a features story, not hard news).

4. Be prompt, professional and polite. State which media outlet you're writing for and what your deadline is, and list your availability (be sure to

include your time zone to stave off any confusion if they're calling in from the West Coast or outside the United States). Include links to your recent or best articles to establish your credibility and your bona fides. Always err on the side of caution and plain, good manners. For example, ask them if it's OK to call them by their first name once you start the interview.

5. Be persistent. If you don't get an answer from an actor's publicist, keep at it. Keep knocking on doors until you get an answer. Stubborn persistence is powerful (however, you must toe that fine line between persistence and annoyance, which is a skill that you will develop over time through trial and error). It may not be the answer you want to hear,

but you'll finally get an answer and can move on from there.

6. Don't be afraid to be told "no." It's not the first time you'll hear that word in this line of work, nor will it be the last. You have nothing to lose. I make a lot of my interview requests expecting the answer to be "no" from the outset. I expected that to be the case with Kristen Bell and it wasn't. Look what happened: I interviewed her several times. I've been told "no" more than I've been told "yes" and have done OK.

Kurt Krug is a freelance entertainment writer with more than 20 years of experience in journalism and public relations. He works full-time in public relations while freelancing and teaching journalism classes on feature writing.

The Reporter's Guide to Features

1. Select a topic likely to interest a large number of readers.

2. "Human interest" means focusing on someone's experiences to which readers can relate.

3. Identify a major news story or event and explore spin-offs that connect to it.

4. Profiles or personality features reveal the character of the person who is the subject.

5. Historical features may be pegged to anniversaries, describe famous leaders or landmarks or illuminate trends.

6. Adventure features describe what happened to people who had unusual experiences, such as climbing a mountain or surviving a plane crash.

7. Seasonal features are tied to holidays, annual events or changes in the weather.

8. Explanatory features might illuminate new scientific discoveries or describe how people are coping with the aftermath of a disaster.

9. How-to-do-it features tell readers or viewers how to make something, accomplish some goal or solve a problem.

10. Hobby or occupation features describe what people with unusual hobbies or in interesting jobs do.

11. Behind-the-scenes features take readers or viewers backstage, describing what is involved in making a public event happen.

12. Participatory features often involve the journalists in the actions they are describing.

13. Feature stories are more likely to use alternative leads—ones that describe a scene or tell an anecdote—than they are to use a summary lead.

14. Quotes and dialogue support the narrative.

15. The ending of a feature story does not summarize the story, but it should use some scene, quotation or anecdote that brings it to a conclusion. Often the ending hearkens back to the lead.

Review Exercises

1. GENERATING IDEAS WITH GRIDS

1. The following grid lists universal needs for all people. To generate story ideas, fill in the blanks and then identify three different types of sources to interview. (Identifying three students is still one type of source—students. You might want to interview more than one source for each type.)

UNIVERSAL NEEDS GRID

	Food	Shelter	Love	Health	Education	Self-Esteem
Babies	Breast milk and formulas		Parental instincts	Premature births		Importance of smiles
Children	Socializing; the use of candy as a reward	Homeless numbers		Soft drinks and teeth	Watching TV	
Students	Fast food	Dorms vs. apartments	Leaving for college	Free medical clinics	Home-schooling	Peer pressure
Young Adults	Obesity		Suicides after breakups	STDs		
Adults	Meal kit delivery services			Insurance fees		Unemployment
Parents	Restaurant costs	Housing costs		Sleep and being a new parent	Incomes	In the workplace
Elderly	Ordering online: grocery store deliveries	Marriage		Social Security		Stereotyping

2. Prepare a version of a students' universal needs chart, using the example in the chapter and in Exercise 1 as guides. Write some universal needs across the top of the chart (e.g., finances, technology, food, time, health) and list different facets of college down the left side (e.g., classes, dorms, apartments).

3. What are some current fun events or concerns in your hometown (e.g., county fair, festivals, finances, embezzling, street conditions, court cases)? Create a grid that includes the problems across the top and those affected by them down the left side. Fill the grid with story ideas.

4. States' worries differ. List issues in your state across the top of the grid (for example, gender identification, voting laws, gun control, state fairs and industry). List those who might be affected down the left side. Or list the 50 states and find out how each one deals with the same concern. Fill the grid with story ideas.

5. List across the top of the grid some current national issues (e.g., mass shootings, the #MeToo movement, media literacy, military spending, Civil War monuments, health care, illegal immigrants, Social Security and foreign aid). List ethnicities, cultures, religions and genders down the left side.

As you fill in the grid spaces on how different groups might be affected, you might also make comparisons.

6. Identify some global discussions (e.g., Ukraine, climate change, agriculture and food, population, tourism, violence, drugs) across the top of the grid and various countries down the left side. Your intersection spaces might produce story ideas on how these global issues affect various countries.

7. You can also downsize the topics in a grid. For example, if a local university experiences a dramatic decrease in enrollment, how do the different areas associated with the decline (e.g., student population, housing, university employees, state funding and reputation) affect the university (e.g., budget, jobs, dorms, classrooms and cafeterias) or the community (e.g., businesses such as apartment owners, grocery stores and health clinics)?

8. Make up your own topics for a grid, such as parks, vacations, cruises, pets, etc.

2. FINDING IDEAS AND SELECTING A TOPIC

1. Politicians on the campaign trail make promises to their constituents. They espouse a particular political platform that makes up their beliefs and goals for when they are elected. Compare an elected official's platform goals to actual accomplishments and use the results to create a story idea. Elected officials may range from student body president to the mayor to the governor to the president.

2. Al Tompkins of The Poynter Institute offers 50 classic story ideas that can trigger other interesting topics: https://www.poynter.org/news/holiday-bonus-50-stories-you-can-do. Choose three ideas that interest you most and explain why.

3. Delve into the Census Bureau website to ignite your imagination on story ideas. Its "special topics" areas and its "press releases" site offer history and statistics on many subjects. Compare national and your state's stats with those of your local community. Click on the Newsroom menu to find Facts for Features and Stats for Stories: http://www.census.gov/.

4. Explore posts on social media, such as Twitter, Facebook, TikTok and blogs. What topics are people posting? What seems to be uppermost on their minds?

5. Find a list of the top 10 Google searches for the day or week. Create a story idea for three of the items on the list.

6. Listen and observe to find a feature topic. Ride a campus or city bus to the end of the line; sit in the student union or in a cafeteria. Based on what you see and hear, make a list of potential feature topics.

7. Survey students to get a story idea. Stand in the lobby of the student union or administration building or other popular places on campus and ask students about their major concerns. For instance, they might be troubled by financial aid, NFL players being arrested for domestic abuse, climate change, problems at their dorm, dating or student government. Qualify or narrow your questions to get informative responses.

8. Pair up with another student. Write for 10 minutes, completely free and uncensored, about one or more of the following topics: my pet peeves; things I am curious about; favorite places in my hometown; my biggest problem in school. Read each other's papers and discuss how you could conduct research and interviews to make a story from an idea one of you generated.

9. With your partner, list college experiences, such as advice to first-year students, what you wish you'd known when you first came to college, good experiences, medical facilities, how to find a job, and living arrangements. Which ones would generate the most interest for a school newspaper? How would you conduct research and whom would you interview? What type of research is needed for context?

10. Walk to class from your apartment or dormitory and observe your surroundings. Make a list of 10 potential story ideas, such as scooter, mini bikes and skateboard safety; students who talk or text

on their phone while crossing the street; or places to eat on campus.

11. People in every region, city and school have experienced interesting events. Some students get ideas for stories by reading newspapers that publish "On This Date in History" columns, by interviewing the historians of clubs or by visiting the community or state historical society. A good feature writer will learn more about those events, perhaps by consulting historical documents or by interviewing people who witnessed or participated in them.

12. Scan city government websites, chamber of commerce websites or news websites for community hobby club meetings and activities, church and school events and speeches on unusual topics. Develop a story idea based on your findings.

13. Ask other people what they do to relax or to break from their routine. Develop a story idea based on your findings.

14. Look for the human interest in stories of promotions, new businesses, the local economy and even the election of club officers. Find a human-interest angle by highlighting one person or aspect of local commerce. Consider, for example, fad businesses such as singing messengers and diaper delivery services; online dating sites; shopping services that respond to new needs in society; and old, established firms, perhaps focusing on the personality of a founder or dynamic leader.

15. Think about health and medical story ideas. Everyone is interested in mental, emotional and physical health stories, and subjects abound: the cost of being sick, new treatments for illnesses, pregnancy, child-rearing, andropause and menopause, death and the grief process, steroid use, sports and concussions, support groups, workshops for patients with a chronic disease, volunteer programs, new medical equipment and ethical issues surrounding medical advances. You can gather facts from medical experts, people with a particular condition, relatives and friends. Use the latest published research or go to the local hospital to discover any recent services.

3. IDEAS FOR CAMPUS FEATURES

Here are 20 ideas for feature stories that you can write about your campus. Interview some students affected by the issues as well as experts. You need to identify the purpose of the story to write it well.

1. Identify college trends happening nationally. Make a local comparison, using the people and data from your campus.

2. Tuition is increasing nationally because state support and enrollments are declining. Are there other reasons? What is the situation on your campus? How are students paying for their college education?

3. More campuses offer classes online and hybrid courses. How do students compare these educational experiences to campus classes?

4. Do more students today than 10 years ago work to support themselves? What are the numbers of students who work full or part time? Do they work on campus or elsewhere? How hard is it to find a job on campus?

5. Is the number of international students increasing on your campus? Compare your local statistics to national levels. Why do international students choose to attend undergraduate or graduate programs in the United States? Does international enrollment affect domestic acceptances?

6. What does your campus do to assimilate international students into the student body? Are international students comfortable on campus while pursuing a degree from your campus and in your city?

7. Some research says that reading a printed textbook and handwriting notes on paper (compared to using a computer to read a digital textbook and take notes in class) is better for learning and retention of information. What does the data indicate, and what do students and faculty think?

8. Most students do not get the amount of sleep they need. What is the average number of sleep hours for students on your campus, and how does this affect them?

9. The number and types of stressors that affect students have increased since the start of the pandemic. Are there different types of stress

associated with undergraduate, master's, doctoral, international or domestically diverse students?

10. Many campus counseling centers are overwhelmed, and students often wait several weeks for their first appointment. What are the most common reasons that students visit these facilities, and how are the counseling centers responding to student needs?

11. Does your campus have a university ombudsman? If so, what are the most frequent problems they hear?

12. Many colleges and universities have study-abroad programs, where faculty members take students to another country to study a topic for credit in a particular class. What are the most popular programs? Why are they so popular? Are there programs in warring countries, and, if so, what safety provisions are made? You should get some quotes from students who have participated in these programs.

13. Plagiarism and fabrication seem to be increasing on campuses nationally. What is the situation on your campus? Compare it to national figures. What are the most common reasons to plagiarize or make up information and what are the punishments for cheating?

14. Write about a first responder. Interview other students, friends, relatives and colleagues so you have enough information for a well-rounded portrait of the person.

15. Find a campus club that helps people, such as Alcoholics Anonymous or Gamblers Anonymous. Interview club members about their problem and how it affects their lives and how the club helps.

16. What reasons do your faculty members hear most often from students who miss classes, assignments and tests or simply do poorly in a class?

17. Write about the problems and perceptions of students with physical challenges. Are all buildings accessible? You might look specifically at the challenges of students who are blind or use wheelchairs.

18. Write a historical feature that describes your college's establishment and early years.

19. What, if any, are the advantages to being an athlete (or an honors student) at your institution? Do athletes meet the same entrance and graduation requirements as other students? Do they have special courses or degree plans, tutors, housing, food or financial aid?

20. How many students are in the National Guard on your campus? Are their studies interrupted because they are needed elsewhere during the academic year?

4. INFORMATION FOR FEATURES

Write a feature story based on the following set of information regarding missing people. Assume the data is correct. Check names in the City Directory. Revise writing errors and stereotypes. Avoid copying and pasting phrases into your story as they might need revising.

You won't believe the numbers involved. They're astonishingly high. Its typical of the situation in each and every one of the nations 50 states. Last year alone in just your one state alone a total number of 57,152 men, women, and children were reported at one time or another to be "missing." A total of 48,384 of the missing individuals sooner or later reappeared or were found or otherwise recovered. But nearly 9,000 remain missing, and that seems to be a typical number for a years total annual figures for your one state. Some of the missing people each year are kids—assumingly runaways.

Others are people with Alzheimers—supposedly old people who wander some distance away from their homes. There are deadbeat dads, too. There are people trying to run away from their debts. There are always young men and women running away with lovers with whom they are deeply and idealistically, and perhaps unrealistically, in love. And there are each year a few, but very few, bona fide crime victims: people apparently kidnapped or robbed or murdered, with their bodies hidden, perhaps burned or buried or tossed into some deep body of water somewhere and thus hidden.

Police estimate that the true crime victims total no more than 75 in number and perhaps as few as 40 or 50. Sgt. Manual Cortez of your citys police dept. said a woman may disappear, and everyone—friends, co-workers, relatives, everyone—swears that she was a totally reliable person and happy and stable, so everyone believes she's a victim of foul play. 5 years later she may call her parents to say she's now happily married and has three kids, a new job, and a new name, and ran off 5 years ago because she was in love with someone her parents didn't like, or didn't like pressures at home or work or just wanted to try someplace new, or hated a boyfriend or her husband at the time who, unknown to all others, perhaps drank or beat her or abused her both physically and mentally.

"I've worked around missing persons for the past 10 years, and it's rare to find someone after more than a year," Cortez said. "We find a lot of people disappear because they've got troubles, want to leave them behind and start over again. A lot of people think about it, and some do more than think about it. Normally its more men than women, except among juveniles. Among juveniles, runaway girls outnumber boys 3 to 1. Kids, particularly those 11 to 17, flee in droves." Another authority, Psychology Prof. Allen Christopher, says, "Most adults will stick around and handle their problems, but a lot of kids think its easier to run away. Or they just don't think. They see some place on social media, and it looks good, so they try to go there." Nationwide, 450,700 youngsters were reported to have fled their homes and juvenile facilities and all sorts of other places they were supposed to be living last year and another 127,100 were "thrown away," meaning their parents or guardians or whoever in the world was caring for them would not let them come back, according to statistics compiled by the U.S. Justice Dept.

Three-fourths of the missing persons in your state last year were runaway juveniles. Nearly 6,500 have not yet been found or located.

Sabrina Diez, a 14 yr. old, is an example, now residing at 1987 Holcrofte Ave. in your city. "My parents got divorced" she told you after you promised not to use her last name. "I hated my stepfather. He's a jerk. So, uh, I met this guy on Snapchat—'cause you only have to be 13 to use it—who was moving to New York, and sent him a picture of me. We talked and then met. He didn't want to take me, said I was too young, but I, uh, got him to change his mind. So, uh, like I was there two years, then got caught shoplifting and prostituting and the cops somehow they came up with my real name and my mom came and got me. She's separated from the jerk, so it's better now, just the two of us, and so we can, uh, talk and stuff."

Another example is Jason Abare, who is a 31 year old man currently residing in your county jail on charges of nonsupport. At the time of his divorce from his wife, Anne, of 9 years, he was ordered to pay alimony and child support for his four kids, a total of $940 a month. Anne currently resides at 855 Tichnor Way. "I wasn't going to give her a penny," he said. He left the state. "It was easy, real easy," he told you during a jailhouse interview today. "I'm in construction, a carpenter, and good, so I can pick up a job almost anywhere and kinda drifted around. If I liked where I was I'd stay a couple months, even a year. Other times I just stayed a week or two until I got my first payday then skipped town. I figured no one could ever find me that way. I got caught last month, charged with drunken driving and didn't have a drivers license anymore so they checked my prints and found out who I really was. Then they searched social media and found my old Facebook postings and returned me here. Bad luck, that's what it was, just bad luck."

13 WRITING FOR BROADCAST NEWS

At the time of writing this chapter, America is facing a deluge of seemingly intractable problems. A pandemic has left more than a million Americans dead, mass shootings and racially motivated attacks are on the rise, economic problems beset the world and in the U.S., a former president is being investigated for his role in an attack on the U.S. Capitol, trust in government and many institutions of democracy—including news organizations—is at an all-time low and a war half a world away threatens the security of Europe.

People want regular updates on these events because their standard of living is declining through runaway inflation, they may fear doing ordinary things they are used to because of the threat of gun violence or because the war in Europe could explode into a nuclear conflagration. During the day they check their news apps, listen to news on the radio or podcasts or read their RSS (really simple syndication) news feeds while working on their computer. When they get home from school or work they often pick up the remote to watch the news, either from their local station or a 24-hour news network.

Convergence of content creation has led print media to produce online video and podcasts, while television and radio news organizations are posting written news on their websites. In spite of convergence, radio, TV and podcast news informs audiences in ways different from print media. Text-based news—sometimes referred to as long-form journalism—provides detailed information structured to be read, using the eyes. It requires reporters to "paint pictures with words" and readers to interpret and visualize what they are reading. Broadcast news is sometimes referred to as short-form journalism. Audio news is written for the listener's ears, hearing only spoken words and environmental sounds that are combined to create a story. Video news is for viewers tuning in with their eyes and ears. Unlike print or audio consumers, TV viewers do not have to draw on their imaginations because they see exactly what happens as the journalist covers the event. Reporters convey important information with aural and visual elements, creating stories in real time (live) or delayed broadcast, satellite or cable, websites or social media.

This chapter introduces ways to think about broadcast news style and focuses on the basics of broadcast news writing. "Broadcast" is used here because it is a generally accepted term for news written for radio, TV or podcasts, although more precise terms might be "audio news" and "video news."

President Joe Biden speaks with reporters after he returns to the White House from Wilmington, Delaware, on Marine One.

13.1 The Broadcast News Story

Although writing styles vary among media, all choose similar news stories. Also, all value clear, concise writing and good news judgment. The best audio and visual stories typically resemble the best stories for print. They involve the audience. Compelling themes and writing draw people into a story, encouraging them to connect to the issue.

Like print reporters, broadcast journalists identify a newsworthy angle, or central point, for a story and then thoroughly research the issues and events to tell the story accurately. They home in on the central point, conduct background research on their sources, ask important questions and employ good interviewing skills to obtain interesting quotes because this part of the process is recorded.

All reporters write well and spell correctly so their work is easy to understand. Broadcast copy must be error-free so announcers can read it easily. It must be written smoothly because audiences have only one chance to hear it, unless the story is published online. And it must be written well because sometimes the transcript of the story appears online.

Whereas print journalists think about the readability of their story, broadcast reporters also consider how audiences hear or see the story. Print journalists write more formally, obeying general grammar rules and guidelines. Broadcast journalists must follow the same grammatical conventions, but try to write in a more conversational style and tone. Other differences between print and broadcast center on the structure and style of stories. The following is an example of how the same event is presented in each form. For a list of the differences between them, see Table 13.1.

Yamiche Alcindor is the moderator of Washington Week on PBS. She has covered the White House for PBS and The New York Times. She also is a political contributor at NBC News and MSNBC.

TABLE 13.1 DIFFERENCES BETWEEN THE ESCAPED CONVICT BROADCAST AND PRINT STORIES

Broadcast	Print
The lead focuses on one fact.	The lead is a summary of who, what, where, when and why.
The next sentence answers why.	The bridge answers how from an authority.
Verbs are in present tense.	Verbs are in past tense.
Attribution begins sentences (who said what).	Attribution follows statement (what, said who).
Listeners cannot hear quote marks.	Direct quotes signal authority.

Broadcast News Copy	Print News Copy
Escaped Convict	Escaped Convict
Shannon Ha	Shannon Ha
11-15-18	11-15-18
Police are looking for an Austin woman this afternoon.	A woman from Austin escaped Tuesday from the Travis County Courthouse after being convicted of assault and battery charges from last May.
Maria Lopez fled the Travis County Courthouse moments after being convicted of assault and battery.	Maria Lopez hit a guard after her trial ended at 3 p.m. and ran out of the courthouse, according to Darnel Rodriguez, a county assistant prosecutor.
Assistant prosecutor Darnel Rodriguez says Lopez hit a guard, and ran for freedom at three o'clock.	"We consider Lopez to be armed and dangerous," said Sheriff Lyle McNeil.
The woman is 28 years old and was wearing jeans, a white short-sleeved shirt and red tennis shoes.	Lopez, 28, was last seen wearing jeans, a white short-sleeved shirt and red tennis shoes.
Sheriff Lyle McNeil says Lopez is armed and dangerous.	###
###	

13.2 Leads

As the previous example shows, the lead of a broadcast story is shorter than that of a print story. When read aloud, print leads are longer and can be more difficult to follow, which frustrates listeners. Broadcast leads give one or two important facts and ease the audience into the rest of the story.

The best leads capture attention by connecting the news to audiences' lives. People care more about stories that they perceive to be relevant to them. For example, a story about severe weather in another part of the country may pique listeners' interest for a moment, but they may not continue to follow the story because the severe weather has not affected them. However, a good lead may tie the events to a larger problem that listeners realize could eventually affect them.

Consider the following two leads regarding an outbreak of severe weather. The first lead tells listeners what happened. The second lead sheds light on why it may have happened. The second lead also includes the body of the story:

> Thousands are without power and assessing damages to homes and businesses after a string of severe storms ripped through the South.

> ###

> Climate change is being blamed for a rash of severe storms across the country that have spawned destructive tornadoes and flooding rains.

> Forty tornadoes were reported over the weekend as strong thunderstorms spread a destructive path across the South from Texas to Georgia.

> The National Weather Service says some of the tornadoes had winds that topped 250 miles per hour.

> While property damage was extensive, officials reported that no one died in the severe weather. Emergency officials across the South are crediting severe weather early warning systems for giving people adequate time to seek shelter from the storms.

> ###

Although the lead focuses on one or two points, it also withholds much important information until later because people usually do not hear the first two or three words of a story. They mentally tune in after they hear or see something that interests them.

Broadcast journalists rewrite leads quickly throughout the day to update audiences waiting to hear the latest news about an ongoing story. When broadcast stories are rewritten, they focus on a new angle to update or localize the story.

Four common types of leads are the hard, soft, throwaway and umbrella. Each is written to intrigue and interest listeners or viewers and provides a transition to the rest of the story.

13.2.1 The Hard Lead

Hard leads give important information immediately. Some audience members want to hear the most meaningful details first. However, some broadcasters believe the significant facts are gone before audiences realize they need to "tune in" to what is being said. Here is an example of a hard lead, followed by the remainder of the story:

> A Russian missile strike on a mall in Ukraine [yoo-KRAYN] this afternoon killed at least 18 people and wounded many more.

> Ukrainian [yoo-KRAY-nee-uhn] officials said that more than one-thousand people were believed in the mall in Kremenchuk [CREM-en-chuck] when the attack occurred.

During news coverage of the House investigation into the Jan. 6, 2021, attack on the U.S. Capitol, CNN periodically switched from the hearings to a panel of experts who discussed the importance of the testimony being offered by witnesses. Bob Woodward and Carl Bernstein, who investigated and reported on the Watergate break-in and cover-up orchestrated by the Nixon administration in the 1970s, provided their analysis during CNN's coverage of the hearings.

One missile made a direct hit on the mall, and a second missile struck another building nearby.

Ukrainian [yoo-KRAY-nee-uhn] President Volodymyr Zelenskyy [vol-ODD-dimmer zia-LEN-skee] says investigators from Kiev [KAY-yev] are digging through the site looking for evidence.

Russian officials deny that their military is targeting the civilian population in Ukraine [yoo-KRAYN].

Notice that this copy contains the pronunciation of certain words. Including this information makes it easier for the announcer to read them and avoids mistakes.

13.2.2 The Soft Lead

The soft lead tells a broadcast audience that something important is coming up and invites them to continue with the story. Soft leads, like soft news stories, feature some information before getting to the hard news. This lead usually reveals why the upcoming information is important or how it affects people:

Drivers may be getting a bit of a break from the eye-popping gas prices that have been hitting their wallets hard lately.

The story continues:

The Biden administration is considering suspending the federal gas tax to give motorists some relief from record-setting gas prices. Gas is nearing six dollars a gallon in some parts of the nation.

###

13.2.3 The Throwaway Lead

The throwaway lead intrigues listeners or viewers and makes them focus on the story. The second sentence begins the real lead. A story would make sense without the throwaway—but, without it, the story might not attract attention:

It's 95 degrees outside. Do we really want to think about a warm winter coat?

Retailers are previewing fall and winter clothing lineups several weeks earlier than last year. Men's fall and winter fashions are being featured in several shows in the metropolitan area during July.

Retailers say they are hoping consumers will start shopping for their fall wardrobes before inflation pushes prices higher.

Shoppers can expect clothing prices to be ten to 15 percent higher than last year. Retailers believe inflation could push prices even higher by this fall.

13.2.4 The Umbrella Lead

The umbrella lead summarizes or ties together two or more loosely related news stories before delving into each separately. In other words, it describes the relationship between the stories:

The bitter cold snap outside is thought to be the cause of two separate deaths in the city this morning.

Here is the rest of the story:

Police say an 82-year-old woman who apparently fell on the ice outside of her home in Bunker Hill Township died of hypothermia this morning.

Alva Saint Clare slipped on her sidewalk sometime during the night, broke her hip and froze as temperatures dipped in the single digits.

About three hours later and a few miles away, neighbors found Joshua Johnson frozen to death in his truck in his driveway.

Police are unsure why Johnson, who was 57 years old, was sleeping in the vehicle on a night when temperatures dropped below zero.

13.3 The Body of a Story

The inverted-pyramid story structure discussed in Chapter 9 works well for news written for print or web, but it is not effective for broadcast writing. For the broadcast reporter, there is only so much information a listener can comprehend. Broadcast news stories need to capture the attention of the listener quickly and give major details in a brief span of time—sometimes as little as 30 to 60 seconds.

The body of broadcast news stories usually follows one of two patterns—pyramid or wineglass—depending on the story being reported. Broadcast hard news stories follow the pyramid formula, in which the one or two most important facts come first, followed by more information (Figure 13.1). The lead does not tell the whole story. And, because stories and newscasts are timed before they are aired, journalists can write a complete story, using as many facts as needed, without fearing that the ending sentence or paragraph will be edited out at the last moment.

Soft news stories follow more of a wineglass structure (Figure 13.2). The single most important or emotional information is placed toward the top of the story to catch the audience's attention. It is followed by several pieces of information

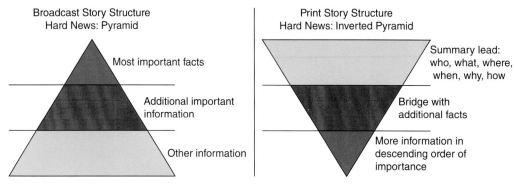

Broadcast Story Structure
Hard News: Pyramid

Most important facts

Additional important
information

Other information

Print Story Structure
Hard News: Inverted Pyramid

Summary lead:
who, what, where,
when, why, how

Bridge with
additional facts

More information in
descending order of
importance

FIGURE 13.1 Structures for Broadcast and Print News

MOST IMPORTANT/
EMOTIONAL
INFORMATION

IMPORTANT
DETAILS (FROM
EXPERT SOURCES)

MEMORABLE
ENDING

FIGURE 13.2 The Wineglass
Story Structure

important to understanding the issue or event, usually in the form of expert sources. The story then closes with a single memorable ending or summary, sometimes a lesson learned from the main subject.

Overall, broadcast stories keep to the point with shorter sentences and fewer facts than those used in print stories. Every sentence of a story is important because when someone leaves it, he or she is usually leaving the newscast and not just the story. Also, listeners and viewers generally cannot digest a lot of information all at once and cannot review it, so broadcast stories are short. Stories are tight, with every word tied to the central point. Although the most important information comes early, what follows is important, too.

Whatever the structure, the facts of any broadcast story are usually presented in one of two ways: descending order of importance or chronological order with a narrative format. For descending order, the broadcast journalist figures out the most significant piece of information, which normally goes in the story's lead. Then the journalist decides what else the audience wants or needs to know; this information makes up the body of the story. Although a story may contain several pieces of information, their order tends to be dictated by the facts given in the lead. If the lead reports that a man attacked his ex-wife and her husband, as the next example does, people will want to know who the victims are and where, how and why they were attacked. They also will want to know about the suspect and what police are doing about the case:

> Police are looking for a man who posed as a salesperson this afternoon and used a hammer to attack a Roseville couple.
>
> Janna and Dylan Banner are in stable condition at Community Hospital after Marten Keller repeatedly hit the couple and forced his way into their home.
>
> By the time police responded to a neighbor's 9-1-1 call, Keller had already fled in his car, a 2015 black Honda Civic. Janna Banner had a restraining order on Keller, who is her ex-husband.
>
> Keller is six feet tall, and was last seen wearing a light blue suit.

###

In the chronological broadcast news story, the climax—the most significant part—is the lead. Then, the journalist relates the details in the order of their occurrence, not the order in which he or she learned each fact:

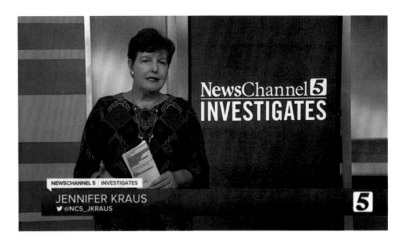

> A Roseville couple was hospitalized this afternoon after being repeatedly attacked by the woman's ex-husband.
>
> Authorities say Marten Keller knocked on the Banners' door at noon, posing as an evangelist.
>
> When Dylan Banner tried to shut his door, Keller became violent, repeatedly hitting Banner with a hammer while forcing his way into the house.
>
> Keller then attacked Janna Banner when she tried to help her husband.
>
> Keller had disappeared in a 2015 black Honda Civic by the time neighbors called police, who arrived about five minutes later.
>
> An ambulance took the Banners to Community Hospital where they are in stable condition.
>
> Police are looking for Keller, who is six feet tall and was wearing a light blue suit at the time of the attack.

Jennifer Kraus is weekend morning anchor at NewsChannel 5 in Nashville, Tennessee, and a member of its investigative team. She joined NewsChannel 5 as a general assignment reporter after working at stations in Alabama, Illinois and California. She has received numerous awards for her work, including regional Emmy Awards, Tennessee Associated Press awards, National Headliner Awards, National Press Club awards and a national Edward R. Murrow Award for investigative reporting.

Sometimes a broadcast story structure might mimic one used by print journalists, especially for longer broadcast stories and podcasts. In Chapter 9, you were introduced to the focus style of storytelling.

The focus story draws on a person or persons who are involved in the story as an example of a larger issue or problem that may affect millions of people. The focus lead begins with anecdotal information about the person and their involvement in the story. The lead is followed by a nut graph that explains the broader scope of the story before branching out into more detail. The story includes a conclusion that may refer back to the person who was highlighted in the lead. Broadcast writers can use a similar format if there is ample time for a longer story on the news broadcast. An example would be a story about parents struggling to protect their children who are not eligible for COVID-19 vaccines from being exposed. Opening shots could be an interview of a parent and then a switch to interviews with medical professionals and government officials before wrapping up the story with comments from the parent who opened the story.

13.4 Updating Broadcast News Stories

Many radio and television stations have several newscasts throughout the day. Different news stories replace old ones. In addition, stations keep the public updated on developments to older stories. Thus, the same story may be a topic throughout the day, but freshened with new angles, additional interviews or more recent information. The lead sentence and body of the story never stay exactly the same in successive newscasts. Here are three updated leads for the story on the Banners:

1. A Roseville man accused of attacking his ex-wife and her husband has been arrested in Houston (Or, Police have arrested a Roseville man. . . .)

2. Police say a man who attacked his ex-wife and her husband was trying to regain custody of his son.

3. A woman and her husband are out of the hospital this afternoon after her ex-husband attacked them with a hammer.

13.5 Guidelines for Copy Preparation

The format and aesthetics of broadcast news copy are important. Too many editing marks can distract an announcer and, consequently, detract from the story. If an announcer gets confused, the audience surely will be.

13.5.1 Formatting Copy

Many instructors require their students to submit printed copy of their stories. And announcers often practice with printed news copy. Television announcers usually read the final version from a teleprompter but might have printed stories or stories on an electronic tablet nearby for emergencies. Radio announcers use printed stories, monitors or tablets to read the news. The tablets have software that allows announcers to add hand-drawn symbols to personalize the copy, which can remind them to slow down their tempo, emphasize certain words or group certain words together in a phrase.

Broadcast news copy preparation may differ from station to station, but it is similar to print in many ways, such as including the slug in the top left corner and double-spacing the lines of the story for readability or for adding copy-editing symbols. Copy can be in all uppercase or all lowercase letters. Sentences and paragraphs begin and end on the same page so audiences do not hear the ruffling of pages, which might obscure the announcer's words in the middle of a story. Sometimes an announcer discovers that a page is missing or out of order. If sentences and paragraphs are kept together on one page, the story will sound coherent; the announcer will not scramble for something to say while he or she looks for the rest of the sentence or story. Using a symbol (###) at the end lets the announcer know that the story is finished.

13.5.2 Editing Copy

Broadcast reporters never use newspaper copy-editing symbols because they are too difficult for an announcer to interpret quickly while reading on air. To edit a word, simply black it out and rewrite it in the space above it. If the copy requires a lot of editing, type a new copy. The fewer editing marks, the fewer times an announcer hesitates or stumbles while reading.

13.5.3 Timing Copy

Margins are often set at 60, with an average of 10 words to a line. Depending on how fast one reads, three lines of copy take about 10 seconds. For most announcers, nine lines of copy are about 30 seconds and 18 full lines equal one minute of reading time. The timing of the story in seconds (for example, ":30") and the number of lines are written in the top right corner of the copy page. Some journalists prefer to note only the number of lines. And some announcers circle the timing, as well as the slug and end mark, to indicate that that it is not to be read on air.

13.5.4 Reviewing Copy

A journalist or announcer reads all copy aloud to become familiar with what has been prepared for the newscast. If the reader stumbles, the story must be revised. While reading each story, the announcer confirms that his or her reading time matches the average number of lines per minute. One reason announcers use printed copy is so they can make notes to personalize their reading style. The announcer marks the copy for word emphases or difficult pronunciations, for example.

13.5.5 Story Length

The time allotted for the story usually indicates story importance. Broadcast stories can run from 10 seconds in a radio newscast or audio podcast to five minutes for a TV or video story. If the story lacks visual or aural interest, it should run less than a minute. If the story warrants special attention, it could run from one to three minutes. If the story rambles, however, journalists eliminate details that detract from its focus. The type of news outlet—commercial or public—can also affect the story length.

13.5.6 Story Script

Journalists write their scripts after they have reviewed their audio and video bites captured in the field or from any syndicated news clips. Journalists use natural sound and visuals gathered at the scene so listeners can experience the story. The strength of broadcast stories is that they can trigger senses that cannot be experienced through written words.

Effective broadcast writing matches words to pictures and sounds. Journalists avoid repeating what the audience member already is hearing or seeing on the screen.

Television scripts also require captions, such as the names and titles of the people being interviewed. This information usually appears on screen and must be spelled correctly on the script.

Three examples of broadcast news scripts appear in the "From the News" box that follows. These are actual news stories in their original formats. Scott Pohl, a 25-year radio news veteran of WKAR, an NPR affiliate, wrote the first two stories. Robert Gould, who has been in the TV news business for about 20 years, wrote the third.

FROM THE NEWS

Examples of News Readers

1. EXAMPLE OF A RADIO NEWS READER
The announcer reads this story directly from news copy. It has no other sound.

QURAN BURNING UPDATE
DATE
POHL

East Lansing police say a person surrendered today in connection with the recent desecration of a copy of the Quran [ker AN] at the Islamic Center.

A 10-thousand-dollar reward was recently offered for tips on the case, but none of the money was paid out. Police say the individual is cooperating with investigators, and they have determined it was an isolated incident.

Officials expect to conclude their investigation early next week, and the case will then be sent to the Ingham County Prosecutor.

The burned Quran [ker AN] was found Saturday at the entrance to the Islamic [is LAM ic] Center of East Lansing.

###

2. EXAMPLE OF A RADIO NEWS READER WITH SOUND ON TAPE
This reader contains a sound bite. The SOT (sound on tape) from an interview is labeled and timed "(SOT: 0:14)."

STATE OF THE CITY
DATE
POHL

Lansing Mayor Virg Bernero [burr NARROW] will deliver his annual State of the City address tonight.

Mayor Bernero [burr NARROW] isn't expected to talk about the city of Lansing's looming 15-million-dollar budget deficit, as many people had hoped. He will wait to discuss the city budget at a press conference next week, instead.

Mayoral representative Randy Hannon says Bernero [burr NARROW] will talk about recent progress in the face of economic challenges, and the prospects for the year ahead.

(SOT: 0:14) "Things like GM's upcoming investment in the Lansing Grand River plant to create 600 new jobs, the long-awaited opening of the Accident Fund's new headquarters on our riverfront and the fact that the Lansing region is leading the state's economic recovery."

The speech will be delivered from the former Knapp's [NAP's] department store building downtown. The Eyde [EYE-d] Company is working on a 30-million-dollar plan to renovate the building.

This will be Bernero's [burr NARROW's] sixth State of the City address. It's set to begin at 7 p-m. The speech will be televised by W-I-L-X-T-V.

###

3. EXAMPLE OF TV NEWS VOICE-OVER WITH SOT
In this story, the viewer sees and hears the anchor read the introduction, then hears the anchor's voice over a visual (voice-over, VO), then hears and sees event participant Janie Mitchell talking about her experience (SOT) with a total running time of 12 seconds (TRT:12). The camera goes back to the anchor reading the ending of the story (tagline). The time of each tape is noted within the story.

MASON NEW ART MUSEUM
DATE
GOULD

Anchor Intro/lead:
AFTER 2-YEARS AND 16-MILLION-DOLLARS LATER, ART LOVERS ACROSS THE AREA FINALLY CAN CELEBRATE THE OPENING OF THE NEW MASON ART MUSEUM.
Take VO: (:25)
MAYOR JONAS CARTER AND THE MUSEUM'S CHIEF DONOR, ALANA LEE, CUT THE RIBBON THIS MORNING . . . THE FIRST VISITORS THEN GOT A V-I-P TOUR OF THE NEW FACILITY.

(continued)

HIGHLIGHTS OF THE MUSEUM INCLUDE 20TH CENTURY PAINTINGS, INTERACTIVE EXHIBITS AND A SCULPTURE GALLERY.

THOSE ON THE TOUR SAY THE NEW MUSEUM IS A CROWN JEWEL FOR THE CITY.

Take SOT: (Janie Mitchell-TRT:12)

This place is amazing. We loved every bit of it and our kids were fascinated with the interactive exhibits. This is a great thing for the area. We can't wait to come back and really explore it further.

Anchor Tag:

MUSEUM OFFICIALS EXPECT HUGE CROWDS THIS WEEKEND. THEY SUGGEST YOU ARRIVE EARLY SO THAT YOU HAVE A CHANCE TO SEE THE MANY EXHIBITS. THE NEW MUSEUM WILL BE OPEN BOTH SATURDAY AND SUNDAY, FROM 9 A-M to 7 P-M.

###

13.5.7 Using Audio

Planning to record audio requires several decisions: whom to record; where to record; what natural, or environmental, sound is needed; and what music, if any, is appropriate to use. Once journalists have decided what recording to include in a story, they have more choices to make: where to insert the audio clip into the story and how long it should be. The story could include brief statements—sometimes called sound bites—from someone explaining, emphasizing or dramatizing a point. Or the audio could be a long interview that tells almost the entire story.

The New York Times produces "The Daily," a 20-minute podcast that focuses on a single story per episode. It features audio clips from interviews and discussions between the host and other journalists. Through this format, audiences gain a better perspective of a news story and also feel a more personal connection to the journalists by hearing their voices. Many news organizations produce podcasts to enhance digital multimedia packages and give audiences an additional way to understand and connect with a story.

In addition to being an important form and element of news stories and podcasts, audio may also accompany news photo slideshows. As a series of pictures is displayed, the audio recording—or VO (voice-over)—of an announcer or narrator explaining the images can be heard. Sometimes, natural sound accompanies the slideshow.

13.5.8 Using Video

Journalists have the same considerations for video as for audio: It is used as a tool to better explain or illustrate a story. In planning for video in a story,

Ira Glass narrates and produces "This American Life," a long-running radio and podcast documentary series that was also on Showtime.

journalists decide if it will be a short clip of a source or subject, a several-minute analysis highlighting several people or VO analysis of a scene from b-roll video. "B-roll" is video of a person or place that supplements the main story. Many news documentaries use multiple long interviews interspersed as narratives over video scenes or photographs and music to give viewers a sense of place.

For a short TV news story or video podcast on a property tax increase, for example, reporters consider whom to record. Government officials would explain why they think the increase is needed and how the additional revenue will be spent. Business leaders and local residents would respond about how the proposed tax increase affects their businesses and personal income. B-roll might add context to the video story. It could be a city council meeting in which the proposal is debated or images of the community affected by an increase, such as storefronts in a downtown area or homes in a local subdivision. The reporter also may include video of the places that are to benefit from the increased tax revenue, such as local schools or road construction. (For more on using audio and visual elements, see Chapter 14.)

13.6 Sources for Broadcast News

Broadcast journalists get their news from the same sources print or online journalists use. However, instead of writing down what a source has said, broadcast reporters record the interviews for portions to be played on the air. This change in voice—the use of sound bites—enables the audience to feel close to the people involved in the news and to hear their exact words. Although personal interviews are best, broadcasters sometimes record telephone interviews with the source's permission. Common sources for broadcast news include news services or news feeds, people, newspapers, news releases from public relations agencies and internet resources, all of which are attributed.

13.6.1 News Services

News services, such as The Associated Press and Reuters, have written, audio and video stories on their websites for subscribing stations to use. "News feeds" is the term for audio or video stories that journalists can integrate into their newscasts. At designated times of the day, forthcoming story topics and lengths are listed by the news service, and the news feeds are transmitted to subscribing stations. Journalists can record any stories they want, then simply add the opening and closing.

13.6.2 Newspapers, Online News and Broadcast News Sources

Reporters scan local newspapers, broadcast competitors or other news outlets for news of important events to make sure their station has covered them. They can report on these events by focusing on different angles. On the rare occasions that journalists use information from their competition, they rewrite the story in broadcast style for newscasts and credit the source. The also acknowledge that the story was first reported by the competitor.

13.6.3 Public Relations News Releases

Public relations practitioners who represent governments and businesses flood news organizations with print and video news releases announcing events or happenings (see Chapter 19). Journalists can also go online to press release sites such as prnewswire.com. News releases are quite helpful on slow news days. Reporters look to them for ideas or additional information about changes within the community, updates on local companies or to localize a story happening elsewhere. Ideally, the release is regarded as a news tip, to be followed up with research and interviews that incorporate opposing viewpoints. Rarely are news releases objective; they always favor the PR company's client.

13.6.4 People

Many good news tips come from people who contact the station about an event that has just happened or is about to happen. Some stations encourage tips by advertising a telephone number to call or text or an email address. Some television stations and web news sites invite people to submit newsworthy videos. If someone captures cell phone video of a tornado or a fire or some other event, the station or website might include that in its report. Following up on tips with in-depth questions and research can uncover more sources and interesting stories. In addition, interviewing people about one subject can lead to tips and ideas on other subjects.

13.6.5 Broadcast Interviews

Interviewing for broadcast requires reporters to behave differently from those who interview for print because the audio or video footage is recording all sounds.

Broadcast journalists minimize their movements so that the microphone does not pick up unnecessary and distracting noise. They also respond nonverbally—with nods—to their subjects during the interview so that their voices will not be recorded. Facial expressions in an interview should be minimal because they can be misinterpreted as agreement with everything the source is saying. Nods should indicate that the source's words are being heard.

Journalists select sound bites that convey the heart of the story. Reporters ask open-ended questions to encourage discussion during an interview. Then, they write a script around the chosen sound bites that best represent the issue or event. Most sound bites are six to 20 seconds long. The text of the script lets the audience know that a sound bite is coming up, but it does not repeat what the subject will say on tape.

"Person on the street" interviews are often used to gauge public sentiment about a topic in the news or to gather information from witnesses at the scene of a news event. Digital technology has made newsgathering for broadcast much easier than in the past and allows broadcast reporters to gather, edit and post stories to the web or social media.

13.7 Writing the Broadcast Story

Broadcast journalists adhere to a combination of Associated Press (AP) general rules and a broadcast presentation style. Many networks and stations have their own style guides. The procedures given in the following sections point out the major differences between AP and broadcast writing styles but are by no means exhaustive. (Appendix B has a summary of AP style rules for both print and broadcast copy.)

No matter what style they use, broadcast journalists think in terms of time because newscasts fit into a standard time frame. Newscasts begin and end on the minute, considering introductions and closings, commercials or public service announcements and transitions from story to story. Thus, journalists must add the time for all their stories to make sure it fits the allotted time. In terms of presentation, they write for both the audience and the announcer.

13.7.1 Writing for the Audience

Broadcasters structure stories for audiences who multitask. They might be driving a car while listening to the radio or a podcast or eating dinner while watching TV. Thus, as emphasized throughout this chapter and book, a news story must capture and retain audience members' attention throughout their day and in concert with their habits.

Here are some general guidelines for broadcast news writing:

- **Adopt a conversational, informal and relaxed style.** Write the way you would talk to a friend. Sometimes this style includes using contractions, incomplete sentences and first- and second-person pronouns (e.g., I, me, us, we, you) to establish a rapport with listeners. Yet, one should keep the conversation more formal and respectful rather than too casual.
- **Write short, declarative sentences that are to the point and limited to one idea.** People cannot listen to a long sentence and always associate the end with the beginning. Sentences in broadcast style often have fewer than 15 words, and none should have more than 25 words. They are simple sentences in the active voice, keeping the subject, verb and object together—and in that order. Long sentences should be divided into shorter ones, as in this example:

  A park, or some people might call it a farm or facility, is being planned by several developers, who they themselves are not farmers but plan to rent acreage to others, will be ready on the east side with irrigation and other necessities that would make it one of the largest places to grow marijuana plants, sometimes termed "weed" or older folks called it "marijane" and they are still a controversy for our city.

  The following revision is clearer:

  A proposed two-hundred-acre medical marijuana park on the east of town will be the second-largest in the country.

- **Use present-tense verbs to emphasize recentness.** People turn to radio and TV news for quick updates to breaking stories. Examples include "says," not "said"; "is searching," not "searched." If the present tense does not work, try the present-perfect tense:

Two scientists have found a potential cure for hepatitis C.

- **If past tense is used, include the time element immediately after the main verb** to tell listeners how recent the information is:

Senator Deb Schmidt announced this morning that she will not run for public office again.

- **Use round numbers.** It is difficult for someone to remember the exact figure of 2,898. It is easier to remember "almost three-thousand."
- **Give numbers meaning.** What does it mean to a resident that "the school board approved a 64-million-dollar bond proposal to taxpayers"? Sound overwhelming? Saying that the additional tax to pay for the bonds will amount to "about 140 dollars a year for a person with a 100-thousand-dollar house." That gives listeners and viewers a personal context and clearer understanding.
- **Shorten long titles.** Long titles can be confusing and use up most of the time allotted to a story. Use one- to two-word titles. For example, "Andrea Dove is a lottery advocate with the North American Association of State and Provincial Lotteries" could be shortened to "lottery advocate Andrea Dove."
- **Never put a name first in a story.** People might miss it. Also, the individual's name is usually less important than the actual focus of the story. Delay the name until the story has captured the audience's attention, or at least until the second sentence of the script:

The uncle of the two missing boys says he is praying for their safe return. The last time Charles Hastings saw his two nephews was near the family's lake cabin this morning.

- **Omit a person's middle initial**, unless it is commonly recognized as part of that person's name. Broadcast writing uses a conversational style, and speakers rarely refer to others by their initials in conversation.
- **Place the description, age or identification before a person's name.** Newspaper style, with description often placed after the name, is not conversational:

Meredith Hinojosa [eenoh HO sah], 13, a Friendswood Middle School student, has won the national championship spelling bee.

In broadcast style, the sentence would be revised to

A Friendswood youth is being celebrated this afternoon in Washington, D-C.

- **Leave out ages and addresses if they are unimportant to the story.** However, writers might need to include general information to differentiate people with similar names, especially in stories reporting arrests or allegations of criminal conduct.
- **Place the attribution before what is said.** The broadcast formula "who said what" is the opposite of newspaper style "what, said who." Journalists

prepare the audience for the quotation or paraphrase coming next, to allow them to concentrate on what is being said:

> County Circuit Judge Horacio Diddi [hor RAY shee oh DEE dee] says that his colleague engaged in disruptive behavior while presiding over cases last week.

- **Avoid direct quotes.** People cannot hear quotation marks, so broadcast journalists paraphrase what someone said. If a direct quote is necessary, use special language to make it clear, as in these examples:

> And quoting directly here, ". . .
>
> As she put it, ". . .
>
> In his own words, ". . .

- **Avoid homonyms.** Words that sound alike but have different meanings and spellings can confuse listeners. ("The gambler cashed/cached his chips before going to his room.") Audience members might miss the rest of the story if they spend time wrestling with a confusing sentence.
- **Avoid too many pronouns.** Pronouns can make it difficult to figure out who is doing what. In this example, listeners might have trouble figuring out who rescued whom:

> Rasheeda Longman and Sung-Mi Lee were in the canoe when it tipped over. She is credited for saving her friend, who doesn't know how to swim.

- **Use descriptive language, but sparingly.** Some words help a listener to better visualize an event (e.g., "hurled" instead of "threw"). However, too much description can take away from the rest of the story. The audio or video that accompanies stories can provide the description.

13.7.2 Writing for Your Announcer

Broadcast copy is "announcer-friendly." At some stations, the writer is the announcer, but at many others, writers and announcers are different people. Therefore, a broadcast journalist writes stories that can be delivered aloud by someone else.

Here are common writing tips broadcast writers use to make announcing easier:

- **Add phonetic spelling.** To mispronounce a name on the air is a journalistic sin. Announcers often need the name of a place or person spelled out phonetically, directly after the word. The Voice of America has a pronunciation guide online for words that are in the national and international news.

> Juanita Diaz [Wha-NEE-ta DEE-ahz] has placed first in the Rifle Association's annual sharpshooters contest.

Sometimes, the same spelling is pronounced differently in different regions of the United States. Thus, "Charlotte" can be [SHAR-lot] in North Carolina or [shar-LOT] in Michigan.

- **Hyphenate words that go together in a group.** Announcers will then avoid taking a breath between these words, saying them as a group:

  A 15-year-old boy from Arkansas has won the national fishing contest.

  The 18-52 volume of "Uncle Tom's Cabin" is a first edition.

- **Spell out numbers one through eleven.** Spell out eleven because it might be confused with two letter l's. For example, an announcer might pause when reading "11 llamas" instead of "eleven llamas."

- **Use a combination of numerals and words for large numbers and generalize.** An example is "40-thousand." Also, the numeral 6,500 is written as six-thousand-500 or as 65-hundred. Announcers might stumble at the numeral "$10,110,011," but can glide along more easily when reading (and rounding) "about ten-million-dollars."

- **Use words instead of abbreviations.** Spell out rather than abbreviate titles, state names, months of the year, measurements and other words so that an announcer can easily recognize and pronounce them without guessing their meaning. The following are examples:

  Saint or Street, not St.

  Association, not Assn.

  miles-per-hour, not m.p.h.

- **Spell out figures, signs and symbols.** And never use a period for a decimal. Try to round numbers or use fractions instead of decimals, as shown here:

  70-percent, not 70%

  500-dollars, not $500

  three-and-a half-million or three-point-five-million, not 3.5 million

- **Hyphenate some numbers and some abbreviations on second reference.** Hyphens let an announcer know that the letters are to be read individually, not as a word:

  C-N-N News

  Triple-A Insurance

  Acronyms, such as Navy SEAL and OSHA [OH shuh], are written without hyphens because they are pronounced the way they are spelled.

- **Use hyphens for numbers to be read individually.** Numbers in phone numbers and addresses are usually read individually.

  That telephone number is 5-2-7-0-0-6-6.

  His apartment number is 21-85.

- **Avoid alliterations or tongue twisters.** These word combinations might trip up an announcer. Also avoid words in a series that have several snaking "S" sounds or popping "Ps." They don't translate well into a microphone, which magnifies these sounds.

- **Limit punctuation because it functions as a brake.** Use only periods, commas and ellipses. While reading the script, a comma denotes a slight pause, a period represents a little longer pause and an ellipsis (. . .) means that the announcer should take a much longer pause. However, in print, an ellipsis means that there is an omission of words. All other punctuation is unnecessary in broadcast because the audience cannot see it.
- **Never split a word between lines, or a sentence or a paragraph between pages of copy.** The announcer needs to read smoothly and not have to look for extended endings on other pages. Furthermore, the story will sound less confusing if a thought (paragraph) is completed even though the rest of the story happens to be on another page that might be missing.

13.8 Being a Broadcast Journalist

To many students, broadcast journalism looks glamorous. It is fun, but it requires hard work. For example, radio and TV stations have several daily newscasts. News outlets produce several podcasts daily. And public radio stations, such as NPR affiliates, host news talk shows and news documentaries and schedule longer news programs with more stories than do commercial radio stations. Many local and national radio and television news channels, such as MSNBC, Al Jazeera and Fox Business Network, run news stories 24 hours a day on cable and satellite and feature live stream and news podcasts.

Broadcast reporters obtain news tips from various sources, call people to verify information or interview and record sources at the scene, analyze what was recorded, write the news, read it aloud, personalize the copy and edit it for broadcast and again for online. Reporters have several daily deadlines, so they learn to connect to sources quickly while covering the issue accurately, efficiently and ethically. Radio and television require reporters to be physically at the location to cover the story, rather than gathering information via phone. Those who can become proficient at conveying the heart of a story in a few words should do well in this area of journalism. With enough practice, writing stories quickly and well can become a habit.

The Reporter's Guide to Broadcast News Writing Style

1. Write in a conversational style for the listener.

2. Make your copy announcer-friendly for quick, easy reading.

3. Use the present tense.

4. Construct simple sentences in subject-verb-object order.

5. Focus on one important news element when framing your story.

6. Do not start a story with a person's name or important information; capture your listener's attention first and save important information for when the listener has mentally tuned in.

7. Use numbers sparingly, round them and give them meaning.

8. Write out titles, numbers and symbols.

9. Keep sentences short, about 15 words or fewer. Details are added through the use of audio and visuals.

10. Place a person's title before his or her name. Attribute before what is said (who says what).

Review Exercises

1. IDENTIFYING BROADCAST STYLE

The following are correctly written broadcast leads. Explain how they differ stylistically from leads written for digital and print newspapers. Think about time, verb tense, titles, personal identification, amount of information and a conversational mode.

1. Another actress has stepped forward to accuse Hollywood producer Harvey Weinstein [WINE stine] of sexual harassment. Lena Headley [LEE na HEAD ly], the star of H-B-O's television show called Game of Thrones, tweeted today about her encounter with Weinstein [WINE stine] when she met him at the Venice [VEN iss] Film Festival a few years ago.

2. People are in shock over the Las Vegas shooter who killed almost 60 people and left 500 wounded.

3. Brace yourself for another scorcher. Temperatures are expected to hit 95-degrees today, the hottest it has been on this day in history since 19-0-7.

4. There's a new sheriff in town. Wanda Clarke has won the city's election for mayor with one-thousand votes over incumbent Asa Mullingsworth.

5. A Northwest University football player has been charged today with driving with a suspended license. This is the seventh driving violation for running back Stephen Marshal, and could mean up to one year in jail if convicted.

6. A Harrisburg woman was killed at about 8:30 this morning when her pickup truck hit a curb and struck a utility pole on Seagull Street.

7. A seven-year-old girl is credited with saving a man's life near Tulsa, Oklahoma.

8. A city council member wants to put an end to motorists' text messaging while driving within the city limits.

9. Good news for many workers. Minimum wage is expected to increase eight-percent in five months. Minimum-wage workers currently earn seven-dollars an hour.

10. The U-S has begun extradition procedures against the political leader of an Islamic militant group.

11. Prosecutors want more time to build a case against a city official accused of illegal trading.

12. After encountering barriers to raising money to pay for a new stadium, officials say construction finally is expected to begin next year.

13. Medicare officials say that a new auditing system will hold insurers more accountable.

14. About 40 members of the Texas Air National Guard returned to Dallas today after serving a year in Kuwait [Koo WAIT].

15. Government offices are closed in honor of Columbus Day.

2. IDENTIFYING DIFFERENT BROADCAST LEADS

The following broadcast leads (the first sentence) and the subsequent paragraphs are written correctly. Identify the style of each lead: hard, soft, throwaway or umbrella.

1. You hear a ring, and reach for your cell phone to find out that it actually is not ringing.

   Stanford University researchers are calling this state of panic . . . "ringxiety." Researcher David Hill says people feel as though the phone is another limb of their body. The cell phone has become people's connection to their friends, family and colleagues. The ring of the phone acts as a reassuring mechanism to let them know that they are not isolated from other people.

2. A Friendswood teenager is the center of attention today at the governor's mansion.

   Sixteen-year-old Gordon Elliott has received the state's Good Citizenship Award for saving two children from drowning in Grand River last fall.

3. Smoke still fills the air over western Colorado.

   A wildfire that injured 30 firefighters and threatened homes has already burned 12-thousand acres. High temperatures and strong winds make the job harder for the 15-hundred firefighters who continue working around the clock.

4. Police are looking into the possibility of a connection among 20 recent dognappings in the area. Parson's Animal Shelter Director John Ertos says he has received 12 inquiries about lost dogs since yesterday. Most of these dogs were in fenced-in back yards or on leashes.

   In nearby Colleyville, police officer Annie Bearclaw says the station has logged eight calls reporting missing dogs within two days.

5. The chair of the House Ways and Means Committee says she wants to abolish our current tax structure.

   Texas Republican Rachael Morgan set that as her goal today as she opened hearings on our tax system.

6. You can be 25-thousand-dollars richer if you tip police with information that helps solve a homicide case.

   Metropolitan Police Chief Stone Willow says that people who provide information that leads to a conviction stand to receive ten-thousand-dollars more than they did last year.

7. More than 165 passengers are safe, after a seven-47 jetliner made an emergency landing at the Minneapolis Metro Airport today.

   Airport director Jean Richards says shortly after takeoff, a door blew open in the luggage compartment. The plane then dumped its fuel and returned to the airport.

8. When faced with the choice of paper or plastic, environmentally conscious grocery shoppers should choose neither.

   It is more environmentally beneficial to instead purchase reusable quality bags or carts to take with you to the grocery store according to the Washington Post. Plastic bags are not biodegradable, and paper cannot degrade because of a lack of water and light available at most landfills.

9. The use of lethal injection in death penalty cases has been put on hold in Missouri and Delaware.

   Critics claim that the method is unconstitutional and inhumane because it causes unnecessary pain.

10. Even the South is no escape from cold weather this week.

    According to the National Weather Service, temperatures in parts of Arizona will reach an icy 20 degrees over the next two days.

3. BROADCAST STYLE AND FORMAT

The following are groups of facts, written for hard news text stories. Turn these stories into radio readers, using correct broadcast style and story format. Time each one for 30 seconds. Remember to use phonetic spelling when necessary, use a conversational tone, spell out large numbers and correct any errors. Think about putting the attribution first and shortening the description of someone's title.

Your instructor might ask you to use the same group of facts to write one or more of the following: radio stories with an SOT, TV stories that include a VO or TV stories with SOT.

1. Hundreds of thousands of people in cities across the country marched in protest as new details emerged about George Floyd's death. The marches were peaceful for the most part, but some demonstrations turned violent. Reports of vandalism and looting flooded police departments in a number of locations. Officials in Seattle and Minneapolis-St. Paul said some demonstrators have been arrested for breaking windows of local businesses and setting fires. Floyd died last week when police officers pinned him to the ground while making an arrest. Officials in your state are pushing for legislation that would punish people who engage in violent activity during a demonstration. Critics of the proposed legislation say the law is vague and overly broad. They say that people engaged in peaceful protest or innocently in the same area when a demonstration turned violent could face criminal charges and stiff penalties under the law. Representatives of the ACLU say the legislation would curtail rights under the First Amendment.

2. A St. Peter's Catholic High School student in your city who police said had a handgun in his locker is being treated at a psychiatric hospital and could face charges in juvenile court when he is released. Sherlock County sheriff's deputies were called to the school Oct. 13th, after a student told the principal that the boy had a gun in his locker. The school went on lockdown for about an hour. The boy was taken into custody, and his parents were called, officials said. Sherlock County Prosecutor Meredith McDougall said that her office is waiting for results of psychiatric tests and for the boy to be released from the hospital. She did not know when that might happen. McDougall would not say if she has decided to bring charges against the boy.

3. In an update to No. 2, apparently the gun was loaded with two bullets. According to a note in the boy's locker, one bullet was intended for his girlfriend and the other for himself. It is unclear as to whether the boy told a friend about the gun or whether the friend saw the gun in the locker.

4. In another update to No. 2, Sherlock County Prosecutor Meredith McDougall said that they boy might be tried as an adult because the evidence looks as if it could be premeditated murder.

5. A woman was mortally wounded when a car struck her as she was crossing Main St. yesterday. Apparently, Estrella Sanchez, who was 60, slipped and fell on some ice in the intersection of Main and Mountain Streets, according to police reports, as she was on her way to a church rummage sale at the First Presbyterian Church of your city. Due to the icy conditions of the weather, the car lost control as it rounded the corner at too high of a speed, according to a passenger in the car, the driver's sister, named Tina Concorde, who was not injured and neither was the driver. and it could not stop. There were no other passengers. The car was a 2002 black Honda Civic that the driver Eric LaFey had just bought secondhand. The victim was pronounced dead on arrival at St. Mercy Hospital.

6. Shabazz Daas, 19, of the 400 block of Turnball St., was charged Friday in your city with 11 felonies and 5 misdemeanors in connection with a series of home burglaries this month, mostly in the Beauregard neighborhood. From Sept. 9–17th, Daas, sometimes with others, broke into or attempted to break into 7 homes in the 1200 block of Elm St., the 1200 block of James Ave., the 2600 block of Downhill Lanes, the 4200 block of Johnson Blvd., the 1600 block of Quaker St., and the 300 block of McDonald Avenue, according to police. Daas admitted to police he stole electronics and guns and some other items, and sold some of them. He is on probation for burglary and has a prior conviction for robbery, according to court documents.

4. STORY IDEAS AND FORMAT

1. Choose several stories—one hard news, one soft news or feature—from today's newspaper (online or print) to rewrite in broadcast style as a radio news reader (all text format). Time each one for 30 seconds. Remember to use phonetic spelling when necessary, use a conversational tone and spell out large numbers. Think about putting the attribution first and shortening the description of someone's title.

2. Pretend that you are at the scene, covering the story you wrote in No. 1. Rewrite and format the radio story as if you were including a short sound bite.

3. Imagine that you are at the scene, covering the story you wrote in No. 1. Rewrite and format a TV news story, using a short video clip.

4. Choose a hard news story from today's newspaper (online or print). Rewrite it as two radio stories, the first story with facts appearing in chronological order and the second one with facts in order of descending importance.

5. Practice using broadcast style and radio reader format by rewriting the exercises for leads and stories in Chapters 7, 8 and 9.

VISUAL JOURNALISM

mages convey information. From the cave drawings at Lascaux, France, to the paintings of the Battle of Waterloo to photographs of the Great Depression, the Vietnam War and the Jan. 6, 2021, assault on the U.S. Capitol in Washington, D.C., audiences find compelling and dramatic images in newspapers and magazines and on television, websites and social media. While drawing and painting were the means of conveying visual messages for centuries, the development of photography, motion pictures and television introduced a sense of realism that the earlier formats lacked—with a painting, for example, an artist can make the subject more appealing or dramatic than it actually is. Paintings also require an artistic talent many individuals do not possess, so photography became the art form of the masses.

> "There is one thing the photograph must contain, the humanity of the moment."
>
> —Robert Frank, photographer and documentary filmmaker

Today, the internet and social media host millions of images taken by professional photographers and videographers with years of training and experience as well as by ordinary people with little or no training. In addition, these media are able to capture events as they happen and transmit that information quickly to an audience, making it an ideal tool for news organizations.

14.1 The Roots of Visual Journalism

Written communication has always been a visual medium. In ancient times, information was passed by word of mouth. People described or performed scenes that represented an event, but it was hard to maintain the accuracy of the message because the story changed with each retelling. As writing systems were invented, stories were carved into clay, stone or wood tablets. With the development

French inventor Louis Daguerre is credited as the father of modern photography with his creation of the daguerreotype.

of writing on paper by the Chinese and Egyptians, information became truly transportable and permanent. The Chinese began experimenting with printing ink on paper in the ninth century by carving an entire page backward in a block of wood, applying ink and then pressing a piece of paper onto the block. The Koreans began experimenting with movable type in the 13th century, although much of what was published was for nobility or religious purposes and was not widely distributed. In the 15th century, Johannes Gutenberg perfected his printing press and movable type to print a Bible that would be widely distributed throughout Europe. Gutenberg created a revolution that allowed information to be accurately reproduced and made available to a wider audience. The introduction of images—hand-drawn engravings at first, then photographs—made print media visual.

Frenchman Louis Daguerre is credited as the father of modern photography for his invention of the daguerreotype, the first commercially viable photographic system, in 1839. While its novelty made it spectacularly successful, other technological advances in the science of "picture-taking" soon overshadowed it, such as those by George Eastman, the founder of Kodak, bringing the world of photography and visual communication to the masses in the late 19th century. Photographers such as Matthew Brady and Alexander Gardner, whose images of the American Civil War in the 1860s brought the reality of war to the attention of Americans, helped transform photography from a scientific curiosity to a tool for visual journalism.

Initially, engravers had to make copies of photographs to print them on paper, which sometimes altered or eliminated details from the original. When the half-tone process was developed in the late 1870s, newspapers and magazines were able to reproduce photos more easily and thus included more with their stories. However, it was not until the early decades of the 20th century that modern photojournalism, the telling of stories with pictures, was born.

A number of people were involved in the development of photojournalism. Erich Salomon, who worked for the German pictorial magazine Berliner Illustrirte Zeitung, was in the vanguard of the field when, in 1928, he began taking candid photographs of world leaders. Eight years later, Henry Luce purchased Life magazine, a humor and general interest publication, and turned it into a newsweekly with a focus on photojournalism. Henri Cartier-Bresson, a French photographer whose emphasis on "street photography" led him to be credited as the father of modern photojournalism, shot numerous assignments for Life. From the 1930s through the 1960s, it and other magazines, such as Look, created the "window on the world" that served audiences until the widespread adoption of television assumed that role.

A photo used on the cover of Life magazine shot by Henri Cartier-Bresson, and a photo of Cartier-Bresson himself.

As photography developed, inventors strove to use the new medium to produce "moving pictures." Thomas Edison invented the first motion picture camera in 1891, which was improved upon by the French brothers Auguste and Louis Lumière. When the modern motion picture industry was born in 1895, audiences flocked to storefront "movie houses" to watch moving images of everyday life, some that lasted only several minutes. The debut of director D.W. Griffith's "Birth of a Nation" in 1915 ushered in the modern era of film in America. This feature-length silent film, which was three hours and 10 minutes long, introduced new filmmaking techniques, such as panoramic long shots and panning camera shots, and included an orchestral musical score to be played simultaneously. The sound era of film began in 1927 with the release of "The Jazz Singer," a film that featured actor Al Jolson singing to the audience. Two years later, the talking picture, or "talkie," had taken over the movie industry.

The concept of transmitting moving pictures, or television, was established in the 1870s. Like many ideas, it took decades and inventors in several countries to develop the required technology. In 1888, Heinrich Hertz, a German physicist, discovered radio waves; 11 years later, Italian inventor Guglielmo Marconi, who based his pioneering work on long-distance radio transmission on Hertz's findings, was sending radio signals nearly 10 miles over open water. By 1901, he was sending signals across the Atlantic Ocean.

Marconi's radio could send only coded signals, but improvements led to the transmission of voices and music. Other inventors explored the possibility of sending and receiving images on the same radio waves that carried sound. The first transmission—using a still image of letters of the alphabet—occurred in 1909. It was not until 1926 that Scottish inventor John Baird, using an electromechanical device, successfully demonstrated the first transmission of a moving image: a human face. The picture was very crude compared to today's standards, but it had a tremendous impact on the distribution of images.

In 1936, the British Broadcasting Corporation (BBC) began transmitting the first public television service from London. The company originally used Baird's electromechanical system, but it was soon replaced by an all-electronic system employing a cathode ray tube, which would become the dominant means of transmitting and receiving television signals until the digital age. The concept of this technology was established in 1908, but it was not successfully employed until the late 1920s and early 1930s. American inventor Philo Farnsworth was instrumental in developing an all-electronic television system. The system he helped develop began regularly scheduled broadcasts to the public in 1939, when the National Broadcasting Company (NBC) transmitted the opening of the New York World's Fair. Many people attending the fair were seeing television for the first time,

Scottish television pioneer John Logie Baird, seen here, invented the original television model. It includes a rapidly revolving disc with lenses that the object being recorded reflects through; a slotted disc that also spins quickly and breaks the light down further; and a light-sensitive cell that receives many flashes consisting of minute squares of the image and generates electrical impulses transmitted to the receiving apparatus.

In the first news event covered by television, David Sarnoff, founder of RCA, dedicates the company's pavilion at the 1939 World's Fair.

and it was not long before the new technology began spreading throughout the country. By the late 1950s, television had become the major means by which Americans received news and entertainment.

Technologically, film—a flexible, permanent material for capturing images for photography and television—was the prevailing medium used by journalists from the late 1880s until the digital revolution of the 1990s. The invention of videotape in the 1950s made capturing and editing images for television much easier than working with film clips during newscasts. Attempts to develop digital imagery began in the mid-1970s, but it was not until the 1990s that the process of digitizing and storing images became commercially viable. By the beginning of the 21st century, digital had supplanted film as the preferred means of capturing and distributing images to audiences.

14.2 Visual Journalism Today

With the introduction of the personal computer, followed by software applications for word processing, publication design, photography and video, the ability to create visual content for the media exploded. What artists, page designers and production people once did by hand could now be done on a computer in less time and with fewer people. Electronic pagination allowed newspapers and magazines to design pages and send them directly to production, eliminating several steps in the process. Digital production made it easier to create and incorporate elements such as pictures, illustrations and infographics on the pages, making them even more visual.

The digital revolution hit photography as advances in the quality of digital cameras began to rival film. News organizations adopted digital cameras because images could be captured, edited and put into production faster and more cheaply than processing film and making prints. Digital photography also eliminated the need for expensive and environmentally harmful chemical processing facilities. And when the internet arrived, it opened a visual platform that became a showcase for photography and video. Now, five hours of video is loaded onto YouTube every second and more than five billion videos are viewed every day. Over 350 million photos are added to Facebook every day. More than 50 billion

Shannon Stapleton of Reuters took this photo of protesters storming into the U.S. Capitol on Jan. 6, 2021, during clashes with police in a rally against the certification vote by Congress to officially declare Joe Biden's win in the 2020 U.S. presidential election.

photographs have been uploaded to Instagram since its launch in 2010, which is equivalent to 1,074 photographs every second.

The internet and social media play an increasingly important role in the dissemination of visual content, including news. Recall from Chapter 1 that more and more Americans get at least some of their news online. In today's world of digital journalism, visual elements are easy to record and distribute and have become integral to every story package (see Figure 14.1 for an example). Increasingly, people are getting their news and information from digital sources, and much of the content they access includes photography and video.

14.3 Ethics of Visual Journalism

As the digital age of photography and video began to evolve, it opened a Pandora's box of ethical concerns. A major issue for media analysts is the manipulation of digital imagery. Media organizations have been embarrassed when photo editors or photojournalists changed images. AdWeek magazine featured a photograph of actress Kerry Washington that had been manipulated in Photoshop to change the bone structure of her face and the color of her skin. Actress and singer Zendaya posted on social media side-by-side images of the real photo and the manipulated one that Modeliste magazine published, showing how photo editors had slimmed her torso and hips and altered her skin tone. In one of the historically more infamous examples, Time magazine digitally altered the police mug shot of O.J. Simpson to make him look blacker after he had been accused of killing Nicole Brown Simpson and Ron Goldman. Unfortunately for Time, Newsweek magazine ran the same photo—not manipulated—on its cover the same week. Audiences could compare the two images side by side on newsstands across America.

Whether they use film or digital, photojournalists have always had the ability to manipulate photographs and video. They can distort the scene by choosing whom and what to photograph and how to compose the shot. They can alter the image through cropping and other production processes. These changes can influence the message presented. Although it often takes a trained eye to see what has been manipulated, the willful elimination or digital alteration of elements in a photograph or video crosses an ethical line that has cost photojournalists their jobs and news organizations their credibility. When it comes to news, what readers and viewers see must reflect reality. The National Press Photographers

Tonga more powerful than atomic bomb
The volcanic eruption in Tonga was hundreds of times more powerful than Hiroshima atomic bomb, NASA says

1 Befor eruption: *Hunga Tonga-Hunga Ha'apai*—two pre-existing islands joined into single landmass in 2015 eruption

Caldera

500m
1,640ft

2 After eruption: Eruption of Jan 15 was so powerful that all new land has gone, along with "large chunks" of two older islands

HUNGA HA'APAI

HUNGA TONGA

PACIFIC OCEAN

New Zealand

Elevation (m)

0   25   50   72   >100

Hiroshima nuclear bomb
15 kilotons

15Kt

Mount St. Helens eruption, 1980
24 megatons

24Mt

Tonga's eruption unleashed energy equivalent to up to 30 megatons (30 million tonnes of TNT)

30Mt

Krakatoa eruption, 1883
200Mt

1 Kiloton = 1,000 tonnes   *1 megaton = 1,000,000 tonnes*

FIGURE 14.1 Compelling infographics are now important tools for delivering news.

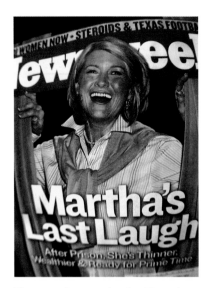

Newsweek magazine had its ethical judgment questioned when it ran this digitally manipulated cover photograph of Martha Stewart.

 HOT TIP

National Press Photographers Association's Code of Ethics

Visual journalists and those who manage visual news productions must uphold the following standards in their daily work:

1. Be accurate and comprehensive in the representation of subjects.

2. Resist being manipulated by staged photo opportunities.

3. Be complete and provide context when photographing or recording subjects. Avoid stereotyping individuals and groups. Recognize and work to avoid presenting one's own biases in the work.

4. Treat all subjects with respect and dignity. Give special consideration to vulnerable subjects and

Association (NPPA), a professional organization for photojournalists, states: "Accuracy in our work and integrity in our relationships with the public we serve are essential qualities for all photojournalists."

The question is, "What can and cannot be changed?" Editing images to improve quality is permissible. For example, editors and ethicists accept correcting exposure problems and cropping to eliminate unwanted background elements or emphasizing the subject. If a photographer wants to remove "red eye" in a head-and-shoulder image, it is easy to do in a software program such as Adobe Photoshop. Such improvements, however, do not alter the message or the reality of the scene recorded. In some cases, photographers may take multiple shots of a scene at different exposures, then combine them to get the best exposure possible. Again, the reality of the scene has not been altered. The photographer is trying only to provide the sharpest and best-exposed image. If something intrudes on the edge of the photograph—such as a pole, sign or other distracting element—the photographer can crop it out without affecting the reality of the image.

Changing the content of an image crosses the ethical boundary. However, there are times that, for artistic or illustrative reasons, a page designer or photo editor needs to manipulate an image. Doing so is unethical only if the public is not informed that the photo has been altered. Publications should label composite images so people know and understand that what they are seeing does not represent reality. In a well-known example, Newsweek ran a cover photo of Martha Stewart upon her release from prison, looking thinner and younger than usual; the magazine had put her head on a model's body and digitally altered her face. Officials at Newsweek responded to criticism by saying that the photo was never meant to represent reality and was only an illustration of what Stewart might look like when she was released. Editors had put a small credit line on the contents page, indicating that the photograph was a fake, but the image looked real; therefore, people could mistake it for an actual photograph of Stewart. The disclaimer should have been placed where readers could see it easily. Intentional or not, falsifying reality is unethical and undermines the media's credibility.

14.4 The Digital News Package

Beginning reporters need multiple skills to gather information in a variety of ways for dissemination on a variety of platforms. Creating news packages for digital media goes beyond writing and editing a story. Journalists working with digital media must be comfortable with not only the written word but also with creating other elements that enrich the web news environment—photography, video and audio.

Remember that visual elements should add value to the story, not merely repeat information that is already there. The images should create a richer story that will draw people to the website and keep them coming back.

14.4.1 Capturing Photographs

The web is changing the role played by photographs in journalism, sometimes making them seem less important than videos. Part of the reason perhaps lies in the nature of website design and how pictures are viewed online. While photographs have a central role in the design of a newspaper page, they may not be the main element of a website. The photos may be small and require readers to click on them to enlarge—or even see—them. However, photography on the web remains a powerful tool that can attract readers and help tell a story. The key is learning how to incorporate photos in the story and then planning what and how many are needed.

Photographs can dramatize or emphasize specific parts of a story, or they can tell the entire story. Life magazine was famous for its photo stories that featured numerous images surrounded by brief explanatory text. Newspapers occasionally run photo stories; however, they have less space to devote to photographs than Life did. Newspapers might normally include one to three photos with a story in a print edition, if warranted. Stories of historic importance, such as the Jan. 6, 2021, assault on the U.S. Capitol in Washington, D.C., by supporters of former president Donald Trump, would use numerous photographs to help tell the story.

Websites have unlimited space compared to print newspapers and unlimited time compared to television news programs. News websites can include numerous photographs with a story. The images do not have to be laid out on a page as they would be in the print edition, but could be "stacked" one behind another—the reader simply clicks on the series to "flip" through them. Thumbnail images can also be lined up beside or below the story or under the main photograph, and the reader can click on and view them in a larger format. Finally, a series of photographs can be arranged in a slideshow accompanied by narration and music and hyperlinked to the story. The reader can click on the link to see the images appear automatically in a timed sequence and hear the narrator tell the story.

An important aspect to remember when shooting digital photos for print or online use is the resolution, or the number of pixels, in the image. Photographs displayed on a website have 72 pixels per inch (ppi) to match the calibration of computer monitors. Saving an image at a higher resolution makes the file larger, which means longer download times for readers. Even with today's high-speed internet connections, the reader will "turn the electronic page" and move to another area of the website or to another site if a large file takes too long to download.

While photographs for websites display at 72 ppi, those printed in newspapers or magazines need higher resolution to appear sharp and clear when printed. Newspapers normally require resolutions of around 200 ppi because of the lower quality of newsprint. Magazines usually require 300 ppi because of the high-quality, coated paper used in printing, which allows the pictures to "pop" off the page.

When planning to shoot photos, one of the first things to consider is where the photographs will be used—online only, print only or both. Digital cameras can be set to shoot in small, medium or large image quality, which basically corresponds to the ppi of an image and the amount of space it takes up on a memory card. Photographers can pack more images on a memory card by shooting in the small format, which is suitable for pictures that will appear only online. Because reproduction quality is limited, the camera controls should be set to medium or large for photos that will appear in print. In these formats, the resolution will be

compassion to victims of crime or tragedy. Intrude on private moments of grief only when the public has an overriding and justifiable need to see.

5. While photographing subjects do not intentionally contribute to, alter, or seek to alter or influence events.

6. Editing should maintain the integrity of the photographic images' content and context. Do not manipulate images or add or alter sound in any way that can mislead viewers or misrepresent subjects.

7. Do not pay sources or subjects or reward them materially for information or participation.

8. Do not accept gifts, favors or compensation from those who might seek to influence coverage.

9. Do not intentionally sabotage the efforts of other journalists.

Ideally, visual journalists should:

1. Strive to ensure that the public's business is conducted in public. Defend the rights of access for all journalists.

2. Think proactively, as a student of psychology, sociology, politics and art, to develop a unique vision and presentation. Work with a voracious appetite for current events and contemporary visual media.

3. Strive for total and unrestricted access to subjects, recommend alternatives to shallow or rushed opportunities, seek a diversity of viewpoints and work to show unpopular or unnoticed points of view.

4. Avoid political, civic and business involvements or other employment that

compromise or give the appearance of compromising one's own journalistic independence.

5. Strive to be unobtrusive and humble in dealing with subjects.

6. Respect the integrity of the photographic moment.

7. Strive by example and influence to maintain the spirit and high standards expressed in this code. When confronted with situations in which the proper action is not clear, seek the counsel of those who exhibit the highest standards of the profession. Visual journalists should continuously study their craft and the ethics that guide it.

Source: https://nppa.org/code-ethics

high enough for the photos to print on paper. Journalists can then "shrink" the images with compression software or change the resolution for use on a website.

To get the best results when shooting photographs, keep the following points in mind:

Focus: Most digital cameras feature automatic focusing (autofocus) to ensure the subject appears clear and sharp. However, if the photographer points the lens at the wrong spot, such as just to the side of the subject, the camera may focus on the background instead. When taking photos of a person against a busy background, focus on his or her face.

Steady the camera: Keep the camera as still as possible; any movement can blur the image.

Move around: Instead of shooting the photo straight on, look for a different angle or viewpoint. Shooting from a slight angle is better than shooting from straight on because it creates depth. Shooting from a high or low viewpoint adds drama to a photo.

Take tight shots: Close-ups and medium shots usually tell the story best. Panoramic shots set a scene and can complement medium shots when publishing more than one photograph.

Shoot action: Static photographs are boring. Good photographs capture action at its peak. Whether shooting a sports event or a speaker at a presentation, take pictures of people in motion.

Avoid mergers and intrusions: Look at the subject carefully to make sure nothing is protruding into the photo or out of the subject's head or body that interferes with the image. A signpost or tree branch that appears to jut out of a person's head can create an unwanted merger with sometimes comical results.

Digital photographs can be downloaded to a computer and edited with software such as Adobe Photoshop, Corel AfterShot Pro, Apple's iPhoto or free online editing programs such as PicMonkey, Picasa, Pixlr, Nik Collection or SumoPaint, which offer basic and advanced photo editing tools. Here are some basic steps for this process:

Do not edit the original photo: Always edit a copy of the photograph rather than the original. Save the original image in case you need to use it again.

Neither photo is a successful visual element: the one on the left is out of focus, and the one on the right contains a merger (the plant seems to be growing out of the sleeping woman's head).

Crop the photo: Cropping a photo simply means cutting out unwanted background. This step can make a photo more dramatic and improve its composition. However, a photo should not be cropped so tight that it alters the meaning.

Size the image: Depending on the resolution at which the photo was taken, it will probably be too large to put online or in print. For online use, it can be resized as a small, low-resolution image. For publication in a magazine or newspaper, it will have to be a large, high-resolution image. The physical size of the photo is determined by the amount of space provided on the website, measured in pixels, or on the page, measured in picas or inches.

Set the resolution and file type: The resolution should be set while the image is being resized. Photos for display on websites are usually saved as JPEGs (Joint Photographic Experts Group), which allows the files to be smaller and thus load faster on a website. Photos that will be published on paper are usually saved as TIFFs (Tagged Image File Format), which are much larger files. Because JPEG is a compression format, photographs lose a bit of quality each time you edit and save them. If you are going to publish the image online and in print, save a copy of the original file as a TIFF and edit it instead of working from a JPEG. You can always change the resolution to 72 ppi and save it as a JPEG later.

Adjust exposure: Photo editing software provides tools to improve the image quality of a photograph by altering the brightness and contrast, both generally and for specific areas. You will need to adjust the exposure if you plan to use the image both online and in print. What seems normally exposed on a computer monitor may look very dark when printed because the reproduction process applies ink on paper rather than appearing on a brightly backlit computer display. An image that is to be printed often needs to be lightened as much as 20 percent to 30 percent for it to be properly exposed in a newspaper or magazine.

14.4.2 Capturing Video

Many reporters, from small to large news organizations, carry compact, handheld digital video recorders to capture images to be viewed on a computer monitor or a mobile device. Or, they use the camera on their smartphones, which have improved immensely in quality since they were first developed. National Public Radio (NPR) has developed a major presence in digital media with its website, which includes written stories and commentaries, blogs, video stories, photographs and numerous audio segments. NPR is a radio network, but its website shows the depth and richness digital media offer audiences.

With the advent of digital video technology, anyone—with patience and practice—can create digital video. Gone are the days of using small but bulky 8 mm or 16 mm film cameras to make grainy home movies that took time and effort to produce and edit and required a projector and screen to view. Many of the current recorders have overcome these limitations with standard or high-definition digital recording that is captured on internal hard drives or storage devices, such as compact flashes or SD cards, and downloaded to and edited on a computer. One has only to look at the growth of YouTube to see the impact that video has had in regard to digital media.

But reporters must decide how to use video and how much to use with the story. Digital journalists typically shoot much more video than they will need. There are three possible approaches to video story content: breaking-news, highlight and full documentary-style. Each one varies in content, time and presentation. There is no rule for how long a video segment in a web story package should run—it often depends on the subject and length of the story and the quality of the video available.

14.4.2.1 BREAKING-NEWS VIDEO

Breaking news is difficult to plan for because reporters do not know in advance what the story will be. They have to react to the situation as it develops, but they can have an idea of what video they need to shoot. For example, if they are covering a fire that is still burning, they will shoot the scene, capturing images of the burning building and the firefighters working to extinguish the blaze. This material will serve as background video, or b-roll. The story's main footage will be video reactions of witnesses and fire officials. Breaking-news video that accompanies a story may be from two to three minutes long.

14.4.2.2 HIGHLIGHT VIDEO

Highlight videos are short clips—sometimes no more than 15 or 20 seconds—that can be used to explain complex elements or emphasize dramatic moments of a story. Sometimes, only one person is interviewed in the video; other times, several people may offer comments. The clips can be assembled into a video story of one to three minutes long.

Many reporters use a highlight video in the same way as a breaking-news one, interspersing short segments of action with comments from sources. These short clips accompany the written story to dramatize the action and place the audience at the scene. One of the differences between the two forms is that reporters have time to plan for the highlight video. They can determine what footage they want to shoot and who may be the best source to capture on video.

Dr. Anthony Fauci, the director of the National Institute of Allergy and Infectious Diseases, explains the need to increase testing for COVID-19 as a tool for controlling the pandemic during a television interview on the White House lawn.

14.4.2.3 DOCUMENTARY-STYLE VIDEO

This type of video content is the longest of the three, often five or more minutes in length. The New York Times published a 40-minute, 32-second video going inside the Jan. 6, 2021, protest and riot that led to the storming of the U.S. Capitol. The Times' Visual Investigations team worked for months to compile videos from multiple sources and present a comprehensive view of the events. Some of the videos had been shot by rioters themselves; others came from the body-cams of police officers or footage shot by journalists. The videos allowed Times journalists to identify and follow key players through the events of the day. The documentary-style video is the most complex of video story formats and needs the most planning to be successful.

14.4.3 Creating Good Video

The key to creating good video for the web is to plan the shots around the story you are writing. Reporters usually have an idea of what video clips they need to capture, whether it is just a short series of comments from the person being interviewed interspersed with action and scenic shots or a longer documentary-style piece. However, even when journalists plan for the video they need, they must be flexible enough to change their plans as the facts demand. Part of that is thinking through the series of shots, which has to be logical, smoothly flowing and dynamic.

Static videos—such as those where the camera remains stationary and the scene never leaves the action or the subject's face—are boring, even if action takes place during an interview. Good videos combine a variety of shots: close-ups, or tight shots; medium shots; and distant, or wide-angle shots. A tight shot of the subject becoming emotional is more dramatic than a medium shot. Yet if there is action, a medium shot is needed so the viewer can make sense of the scene. A wide-angle shot places the scene in context. Changes from shot to shot, called jump-cuts, take practice to make the transitions smooth. Video editing software, such as Apple's iMovie and Final Cut Pro or Adobe Premiere, provide tools to make jump-cuts that flow seamlessly from one scene to the next.

Going from one shot to the next requires planning and practice. Nearly every digital video recorder has a zoom function that allows the videographer to go from one shot to another without having to move. Yet zooming in and out can create problems with focus as well as with the appearance of the video. The same problems arise with panning, or following the action with the camera. When recording a video story, it is best to stop recording, adjust the video recorder for the next shot and continue from shot to shot until done. Use the zoom function as sparingly as possible. The different shots can be pieced together during editing.

With longer video interviews, reporters sometimes become a part of the video by recording themselves or their voices as they ask questions. In this case, journalists should work from a script and rehearse the questions to avoid stumbling over them during the interview. Of course, the reporter needs flexibility to follow the interview where it leads, but having prepared questions ensures things will flow smoothly. Long pauses during an interview that is being recorded can lead to awkward jump-cuts.

While brief highlight videos may need only titles, credits and an introduction, longer videos may also need voice-overs, or narration, to introduce new segments or new subjects being interviewed, as well as background music. Adding voiceovers to a video can be done in the editing process and is usually best accomplished by first writing a script, as described in Chapter 13. Reporters often rehearse the script and warm up their throats by reading a few lines before they begin recording the narration. When reading, they try to talk in a normal, conversational tone that is not rushed or overly dramatic. Pace is important in narration, as is inflection. The former should not be so fast that the narrator runs out of breath, and the latter—the rhythm or pattern of speech—should not be monotone or too up and down.

14.4.4 Capturing Audio

Just as technology has simplified the process of recording video, so has it simplified gathering, editing and distributing audio. The New York Times and other news organizations sometimes include short audio clips on their websites to dramatize, emphasize or explain something in a story. Sometimes the full story or column is recorded on audio so the audience can either read it or listen to it.

Reporters may record entire interviews and then edit the audio for the parts that will make a good presentation. Or they may prepare a series of questions to ask a source specifically for the audio clip. They may also want to add narration to put the clip into context, along with environmental, or natural, sound. To ensure variation in natural sound, they should record 10- to 15-second segments from different places and times; doing so also provides options during editing. If a reporter is interviewing a contractor at a construction site, for example, he or she may gather several seconds of machinery and other construction noise to play in the background during a voice-over. The narration may include an introduction at the beginning of the clip and the questions posed to the source before his or her responses.

An audio clip that accompanies an online story may not need any context beyond the accompanying text and visual elements. But if the clip is for downloading, the narrator will have to provide the story's background in an introduction. Also, if the audio story includes the voice of more than one person, the narrator will have to identify each speaker. Audio stories can be any length, whether they accompany the story on the news organization's website or are posted as podcasts.

Interviews can be recorded face-to-face or over the telephone. As stated in Chapter 11, location is one of the most important considerations for in-person interviews. In the preceding example, the reporter would need to find a quiet place to conduct the interview and gather natural sound later. Background construction noise could drown out the speaker or force him or her to shout over the noise. If the noise ends, the person may still be shouting a response. An office or home is a good location, but avoid restaurants, coffee shops or anywhere with a lot of crowd or background noise.

If the audio is going to be used for a lengthy podcast, reporters usually prepare the subject. As with a written interview, they tell the person what the story will be about, how long the interview will last and where and when the podcast will be available. Journalists sometimes send questions to sources prior to the interview so that they have an opportunity to prepare answers. This practice helps when interviewing sources about complex topics. Sometimes reporters do not start recording at the start of the interview but talk to the subject to help relax him or her before turning on the recorder and beginning the real interview. The key to successful podcast interviews is to keep the tone conversational and natural sounding as though the listener is in the room with you.

When a reporter finishes recording material for a story, the editing process begins. Most digital audio recording devices can be connected to a computer with a USB cable and the audio files then downloaded for editing. A number of free software programs, such as Audacity, are available for both PCs and Macintosh computers.

Most of these programs offer time-track marks so that interview quotes can be flagged at minute/second marks and can be easily found when compiling the final audio story.

BuzzFeed employees use software to edit video and audio stories for the website.

The first step in editing is to cut poor or unnecessary segments. Remove long pauses in which there is no sound, the "ums" and "ahs" that sources sometimes utter, verbal gaffes and any small talk at the start or end of the interview. People sometimes do not realize they are still being recorded at the end of the interview and say something inappropriate or irrelevant.

Next, voice-overs, music clips and natural sound can be added. Anyone adding music to an interview should be sure to have permission to do so from the copyright holder.

Several techniques can be used to flow from one audio segment to another, such as fades and segues. There are also a number of helpful guides and online resources that offer detailed assistance in editing audio effectively for podcasting and audio highlights.

14.5 Required Technology

Reporters writing for the web need a wider array of tools than those who write only for print. Nevertheless, most of the technology is easy to learn and available at a reasonable cost. Even journalists new to digital media can create video and audio segments using a medium-priced video recorder and Apple's iMovie or Adobe's Premiere Elements digital video editing software. However, mastering the skills takes time, patience and practice.

14.5.1 Digital Video Recorder

More and more still photo cameras are able to shoot video clips. For shooting longer, more involved video stories and highlights, however, it is best to use a digital video recorder. Professional video cameras and recorders used for television and documentary films cost thousands of dollars, but amateur standard and high-definition digital video recorders cost from around $200 to $1,200 and take good quality video for display on a website or mobile device.

14.5.2 Digital Camera

While smartphones are becoming more popular for point-and-shoot photographs and will perform adequately in an emergency, professional photographers still favor the image quality of a standard digital still photo camera. There are hundreds to choose from at varying levels of complexity, quality and cost. Inexpensive point-and-shoot digital cameras have limited zoom range, flash power and ability to capture high-speed action, which makes such cameras less than ideal. The full-function point-and-shoot looks similar to digital single-lens reflex (DSLR) cameras but is a bit more compact. The difference is that the former has a fixed lens while the latter has an interchangeable lens system so that different focal length lenses, such as normal or telephoto, can be used. Cameras can range in price from $250 to $600 for a full-function point-and-shoot and from $600 to several thousand for a DSLR.

Many beginning photographers often question whether an 18-megapixel camera is better than a 10- or 12-megapixel in terms of image quality. "Megapixel" refers more to the file and print size than it does to overall sharpness of the image. The sharpness is controlled more by the photographer, the quality of the lens and the type and quality of sensor the digital camera uses to capture the image. A three-megapixel camera will produce an excellent 5×7-inch image at 300 ppi and a good quality 8×10-inch image at 200 ppi. A 12-megapixel camera will produce an excellent 10×15-inch print at 300 ppi and a good quality 14×21-inch image at 200 ppi. The questions to ask are: How big does the image need to be? Where will it be displayed? The answers will determine the size of the file.

14.5.3 Digital Audio Recorder

Miniature digital audio recorders can capture high-quality stereo sound at a very affordable price. Key things to consider when buying this device are recording quality, ease of use, battery life, computer compatibility for transferring files and external inputs for headphones and a microphone. Good digital audio recorders range from $100 to $200. High-quality recorders can cost as much as $500.

The Reporter's Guide to Visual Journalism

PHOTOGRAPHS

1. Create a list of photo opportunities for the story.

2. If posting online, decide how photos will be displayed on the website—as a series of photos or an audio slideshow.

3. Select image quality—small, medium or large—at which you want to capture images.

4. Make sure the subject is in focus.

5. Keep the camera steady.

6. Look for the best angle or viewpoint to shoot photos.

7. Take tight shots to dramatize and emphasize the subject.

8. Shoot action as often as possible to make photos more interesting.

9. Avoid background mergers.

10. Crop and size the photo when editing.

11. Set resolution at 72 ppi for the web and adjust the exposure when editing.

VIDEO

1. Determine how much video you want to or can use for the story.

2. Shoot close-up, medium and wide-angle shots.

3. Limit panning and zooming to prevent blurring video.

4. Edit the video to remove poor quality scenes; piece together different segments of video to tell the story.

5. Add voice-overs during editing to explain a scene or introduce a new source.

AUDIO

1. Decide whether you will use just clips of an audio interview or the entire interview as an audio story.

2. Decide whether the interview will be face-to-face or over the telephone; be sure to inform a source on the telephone that he or she is being recorded.

3. When interviewing face-to-face, pick a quiet spot for the interview to avoid intrusive background noise.

4. Record natural sound to use for background in the audio clip or story.

 # Review Exercises

1. PHOTOJOURNALISM PROJECT

Select a photo or photos of a news event, controversial issue or feature story (e.g., the aftermath of a natural disaster, a fire or accident, or a demonstration) from a newspaper, news magazine or news website. Choose an image that depicts the event or controversy, not a mug shot of someone involved. Analyze the photo(s) you selected by answering the following questions:

● What do you see?
● What story is the photographer trying to tell?

- What message is he or she sending? Is the photograph conveying it successfully? Why or why not?
- Does it dramatize, emphasize or help summarize the story? Give details to explain your answer.

- Why do you think the photographer chose that particular scene to capture and explain the story? Why do you think the photo editor and editor selected the photo or photos for publication?

2. VIDEO JOURNALISM PROJECT

Select a video embedded in a news story or one that stands alone. As with Exercise 1, choose something connected to a news event, a controversial issue or a feature story. Analyze the video by applying the questions from the previous exercise.

APPLYING THE SKILLS OF JOURNALISM

SPEECHES AND MEETINGS

The world witnessed in 2022 the beginning of something it had not seen in 77 years: a land war in Europe. On Feb. 24, Russian troops and tanks rolled into Ukraine from Russia in the east and Belarus in the north. Bombs, artillery shells and rockets turned Ukrainian cities into rubble and killed hundreds of people. Many Ukrainians fled the country. The Russian military is large and well-equipped; many feared the much smaller Ukrainian army would quickly collapse. But Ukraine's soldiers and citizens showed more skill and determination than had been expected, while the Russian military proved surprisingly inept. Ukraine also had the support of the United States and the countries that form the North Atlantic Treaty Organization, an alliance formed in the wake of World War II to thwart the expansion of the Soviet Union. Although the NATO countries had provided some military equipment to Ukraine, the country's president, Volodymyr Zelenskyy, knew he would need more and more powerful weapons. Less than a month into the war, Zelenskyy delivered emotional speeches to NATO member countries pleading for more aid. One of those speeches was a video address delivered to the U.S. Congress on March 16.

Covering speeches is a staple of journalism. What knowledgeable and important people say about current events is news, and journalists make that information available to members of the public who may not be able to attend the speech or listen to or read all of it. The reporter's job is to present in concise and clear form

> "I know from logic and from observation and from experience that the more powerless you are as a group, gender or ideology, the more you should defend your freedom of speech."
>
> —*Nadine Strossen, American lawyer and civil libertarian*

HOT TIP

Spelling the Ukrainian President's Name

Attentive news readers have probably noticed that the last name of the Ukrainian president is spelled differently by different news organizations.

Some spell his name "Zelensky." The New York Times, The Washington Post and CNN all have adopted this spelling.

Other news organizations, including The Associated Press, Fox News and MSNBC spell his name "Zelenskyy."

There are other spellings that show up in news reports. The British-based wire service Reuters and the Guardian newspaper spell it "Zelenskiy."

The differences arise over how the name should be transliterated from Cyrillic.

The Associated Press has adopted "Zelenskyy" as the preferred spelling at least in part because that is how the Ukrainian president spells it, and he sees that spelling as more consistent with Ukrainian linguistic traditions.

Because AP style has been adopted for this textbook, we will use "Zelenskyy" except when the name appears in a quotation from another source. Then the spelling will be that of the original source.

the essence of the speaker's message and some sense of what those who attended the event experienced.

Equally important, and equally common as assignments, are the meetings of local governments or of civic groups concerned about public issues. The actions taken at these meetings often directly affect how people in a community live.

Reporters assigned to cover speeches or meetings usually write at least two kinds of stories: an advance story and a follow story. The former alerts people to a soon-to-happen event, and the latter describes that event for those who were unable to attend it. Reporters may also write reaction stories and news analyses if the speech or meeting results in unusually important news. Reaction stories report the thoughts, opinions and sentiments of those who witnessed or were affected by the speech or meeting. Analysis stories may explore the implications of the speech or meeting for such things as political relations, economic conditions or social relations.

15.1 Advance Stories

News organizations usually publish advance stories the day a speech or meeting is announced or shortly thereafter. As a reminder to their audiences, they may publish a second advance story a day or two before the event. For an important speech or meeting, the initial announcement is often followed by additional advance stories about the purpose, participants and location of the event and about opportunities to attend.

For events of unusual importance, news organizations may run several advance stories. Zelenskyy had arranged speaking opportunities in several NATO countries shortly after the Russian invasion. He knew his country would need substantial military assistance from western countries. Addresses Zelenskyy had already made to the European Union Parliament, the British Parliament and to congressional leaders gave reporters a preview of what he was likely to say to Congress. Also, reporters and the public were aware of how the combat in Ukraine was developing and what the needs of the Ukrainian army were. The Associated Press published an advance story noting that Zelenskyy was asking western countries to provide more jet fighters to counter attacks from Russian planes. The aid he would be seeking from Congress would be in addition to the $13.6 billion the United States had already sent. The Arkansas Democrat-Gazette expanded on the AP report by noting that Zelenskyy's addresses to the European and British parliaments had a strong emotional effect on their members. The Daily News of New York called Zelenskyy charismatic and inspiring and said he had emerged as "an unexpected global hero." The Washington Post advance story speculated that Zelenskyy's speech could increase the political pressure on President Joe Biden to do more to support Ukraine. Some Republicans in Congress, The Post noted, were chiding Biden for not working a deal that would provide jets to Ukraine. Writing for Congressional Quarterly's Roll Call, Walter Shapiro compared Zelenskyy's speech to Congress to the one British Prime Minister Winston Churchill delivered in December 1941, just days after the Japanese attack on Pearl Harbor brought the United States into World War II.

The leads for advance stories should emphasize what is important and unusual, not just the fact that someone has scheduled a speech or meeting. Often, leads mention celebrities who will be involved or the topics that will be discussed. The rest of the story, sometimes no more than two or three paragraphs, might elaborate on the speaker or the topic or the most important items on the meeting's agenda. The date, time and location of the event should also be included. The story should mention whether there is a charge for attending or whether the event is open to the general public. Some news organizations will not publish advance stories about closed events. Only members of Congress could attend the viewing of the video of Zelenskyy's speech in the Capitol auditorium, but the address was also live streamed to the general public.

Ukrainian President Volodymyr Zelenskyy tells members of Congress Ukraine needs more military and humanitarian aid to defend itself from an ongoing Russian invasion.

Because of time limitations, broadcasters usually carry advance stories for only the most important speeches and meetings. Newspapers run more advance stories but, to save space, may publish them in roundups or digests (often called "Community Calendars") that list all the newsworthy events for the coming week.

15.2 Covering the Speech or Meeting

Speeches and meetings quickly become routine assignments for most reporters. Covering them effectively, however, requires perfecting some basic reporting skills: advance preparation, sound news judgment, accuracy, an ear for interesting quotations and an eye for compelling details.

Journalists may cover speeches about topics they are unfamiliar with or meetings about complicated issues. Meetings of some government agencies can be particularly confusing. In larger communities, a city council might vote on issues without discussing them at its regular meeting because all the discussion occurred earlier in committee meetings. Unless reporters are familiar with the committee action, they might misunderstand the full council's decision or fail to recognize newsworthy developments.

Preparation helps reporters cover speeches and meetings. Journalists usually try to learn as much as possible about the participants and issues before a speech or meeting. As a first step, they might go online or visit their news organization's library and research the topic, the speaker or the group. A reporter preparing to cover Zelenskyy's speech, for example, might review what he had said in his earlier speeches, study the military situation in Ukraine and talk to members of Congress about what they expected him to say.

Reporters who cover meetings should learn all the participants' names beforehand to identify the people who are speaking or making decisions. To understand everything that is said, they should also learn as much as possible about every item on the agenda. Journalists can get agendas before many meetings and research the issues that will be discussed.

In some cases, an agenda provides more than just a list of topics. It may be a small packet with supporting information on each item coming before the board or council. For instance, if a school board is considering a pay increase for substitute teachers, the agenda packet might include the superintendent's rationale for the increase, projections of its impact on the budget and comparisons with the pay substitutes earn in nearby districts. Even if the published agenda lists only the topics to be considered, additional documents and information presented to board and council members are public records under most state laws, and reporters can get copies simply by asking and paying for them.

Sometimes, unexpected or confusing issues arise during a meeting. Journalists prepare for those situations by arranging to see the leading participants to ask follow-up questions after a meeting adjourns.

Reporters who cover speeches often try to talk to a speaker so they can clarify issues or get additional information. Groups that sponsor speeches will sometimes accommodate journalists by scheduling press conferences with speakers before or after the speech. If no formal press conference is arranged, they may ask to see speakers for a few minutes immediately after their appearances. Reporters also like to get advance copies of speeches when possible. Instead of having to take notes, they can follow the printed text and simply record any departures from the prepared remarks.

15.3 Follow Stories

Published after a speech or meeting, follow stories report on the event in detail. Therefore, they are longer than advance stories and harder to write.

Like any story, a speech or meeting story needs a central point. But the fragmented nature of most meetings and some speeches complicates identifying that point. An expert on economic development might deliver a speech on the obstacles rural areas face in attracting new businesses and the resources for overcoming them. Should the central point be the obstacles or the resources? Or should it cover both and, therefore, be vague and difficult to understand? In a single meeting, a school board might adopt a set of achievement standards for district pupils, announce a major expansion of the district's soccer facilities and hear a report on why construction of a new high school has been delayed. All are important but unrelated issues. How can a writer work all three into a single coherent news story?

A reporter's decision on a central point depends on his or her news judgment about what is most important and interesting to the audience. As a result, journalists may differ in their approaches to a complicated story. For example, different news organizations emphasized different themes from Volodymy Zelenzkyy's speech to Congress. For several news organizations, the central point was Zelenskyy's effort to tie Ukraine's crisis to those experienced by the United States after the bombing of Pearl Harbor and the terrorist attacks of 9/11. The New York Times lead said:

> President Volodymyr Zelensky of Ukraine invoked the memory of America's darkest days on Wednesday as he pleaded for more military aid to combat Russia's "inhumane destruction" of his country,

directly challenging President Biden and members of Congress to help by showing a wrenching video of the carnage in Ukraine's cities.

The story specifically mentioned Pearl Harbor and 9/11 in the second paragraph. The New York Daily News mentioned those two events in the lead paragraph and described the video Zelenskyy showed as "grisly." The Washington Post's lead emphasized Zelenskyy's plea for more military aid and his call for "the world's preeminent superpower to do more to prevent his nation's destruction." The Post, too, mentioned the references to Pearl Harbor and 9/11 in the second paragraph.

Other news reports focused more directly on the aid Zelenskyy requested. The Los Angeles Times said the Ukrainian president requested financial support, more weapons and the creation of a no-fly zone over Ukraine to halt Russian bombing. The Associated Press, while mentioning the invocation of the attacks on American soil, focused on the plea for assistance and reported that President Biden had responded by agreeing to send more anti-aircraft and anti-armor weapons and drones. Politico described Zelenskyy's aid requests as both specific and potentially difficult. The story quoted one U.S. lawmaker as saying that a plea for the creation of a no-fly zone would lead to a direct military confrontation between the United States and Russia and World War III. The story also noted that providing more fighter jets to Ukraine also raised risks of escalating the war to involve more countries and, possibly, weapons of mass destruction. CNN's online coverage included the full text of Zelenskyy's speech with annotations. Among other things, the annotations noted the Biden administration's opposition to establishing a no-fly zone and to providing fighter jets, but Zelenskyy's request for more advanced air-defense missiles was more appealing to western countries.

Reporters who cover speeches remain alert for colorful details that will enliven their stories, add humor or humanize the people and ideas they are writing about. One detail that appeared in many of the stories about Zelenskyy's speech was the impact of a video he showed near the end. The video showed bombs and rockets hitting government buildings and apartment houses, bodies lying in streets, bodies being buried in mass graves and children hugging fathers about to leave to fight. The stories reported that members of Congress could be seen wiping away tears after watching the video. The Washington Post quoted Sen. Richard Blumental of Connecticut as saying of the legislators' reaction to the video, "Not a muscle moved, not a voice—just absolutely riveting." The New York Daily News noted that House Speaker Nancy Pelosi had introduced Zelenskyy by saying, "Slava Ukraini," which translates as "Glory to Ukraine." Stories also noted Zelenskyy delivered most of the speech in Ukrainian with a translator delivering the English version, but near the end, Zelenskyy switched to speaking in English. "I see no sense in life if it cannot stop the deaths," he said. And addressing President Biden he added: "You are the leader of the nation, of your great nation. I wish you to be the leader of the world. Being the leader of the world means to be the leader of peace."

Most stories included some reaction to the speech, mostly from members of Congress. The Los Angeles Times quoted Sen. Ben Sasse of Nebraska as saying: "Zelenskyy has the courage of his convictions. The question he asked the Congress and the United States government is, will we have the courage of ours?" Sen. Lindsey Graham of South Carolina told The Washington Post that while he

Ukrainian President Volodymyr Zelenskyy (fourth from right) meets with several U.S. officials, including Secretary of State Antony Blinken and Defense Secretary Lloyd Austin in Kyiv, Ukraine. Such meetings cover many topics, but news stories must identify the one that is most newsworthy for their leads. The stories must also include other topics that might be of interest to the public.

appreciated Ukraine's needs, he also feared that providing everything it wanted risked a direct confrontation between NATO and Russia.

Some news organizations prepared one or more separate reaction stories. WKYC-TV in Cleveland summarized in an online story the reactions of Ohio lawmakers. Sen. Sherrod Brown, a Democrat, told the station Ukraine needed more resources to fight the Russians and he was committed to making sure that the country had the military tools it needed. Sen. Rob Portman, a Republican, agreed Ukraine needed more lethal weapons, and he lauded Zelenskyy's courage. The story included either comments from Ohio members of the House of Representatives or screenshots of comments they posted on Twitter. The Hartford Courant reported that Connecticut Sen. Chris Murphy promised continuing support for Ukraine. The Atlanta Journal-Constitution also reported on the reactions of members of the Georgia congressional delegation. Most, like Sen. Raphael Warnock, expressed pride in the support the United States was extending to Ukraine. Rep. Marjorie Taylor Greene, however, said the only role the U.S. should play was helping to broker a peace between Russia and Ukraine. The Buffalo, New York, News reported that while senators and representatives from New York applauded Zelenskyy's speech and wanted to help Ukraine, they were opposed to the idea of a no-fly zone.

Some news organizations published follow-up stories that analyzed Zelenskyy's speech and the choices facing the United States. An analysis by Zach Beauchamp for Vox.com said the interests of the United States and Ukraine converge on the desire to defeat the Russian invasion, but the fact Russia and the United States control 90 percent of the world's nuclear weapons argued for avoiding a direct confrontation between the two. The support the U.S. could give Ukraine without provoking such a confrontation would be additional economic sanctions on Russia and its leaders and more weapons, like drones and anti-tank and anti-aircraft missiles. CQ Roll Call published John T. Bennett's analysis of the domestic political situation surrounding the Ukraine war. Polls showed that most Americans supported the measures the Biden administration was taking in support of Ukraine, but they also showed majorities wanted to avoid direct confrontation with Russia, such as using NATO fighter planes to enforce a no-fly zone over Ukraine. Ironically, while Americans told pollsters they supported the specific actions the Biden administration was taking, a plurality disapproved of Biden's handling of the crisis.

15.3.1 Organizing Speech or Meeting Stories

Reporters usually must select one idea or issue from a speech or meeting as the central point for the story. If an event involves several important topics, they generally focus on the most newsworthy in the lead and summarize the others in the next two or three paragraphs. Journalists then develop each topic in detail, starting with the most important. If the opening paragraphs mention only one topic, the audience will think the story discusses nothing else if other topics are not mentioned early in the story. If the topic in the lead fails to interest people, they may stop paying attention.

Some beginners report events in the order in which they occurred, as if the sequence were somehow important to the audience. Meeting agendas rarely reflect the importance of the topics discussed. Major issues may be taken up early or late, but readers, viewers or listeners should not have to endure descriptions of minor actions before learning about important ones. Although speeches usually have a more logical order, speakers tend to put their most important points at the middle or end.

Reporters write most follow stories in the inverted-pyramid style, presenting information in the order of its importance (see Chapter 9). They can move statements around; for example, they may begin with a statement made at the end of a one-hour speech or meeting, then shift to a topic discussed midway through the event. If topics brought up early are unimportant, reporters may not mention them at all. Although statements may be reported out of chronological order, they should never be taken out of context. Reporters should make sure they are not misunderstanding what a speaker said or conflating unrelated ideas.

When writing a follow story, journalists should never simply report that a speaker or group "discussed" or "considered" another topic, even if it is a minor one. If a topic is important enough to mention, give the audience meaningful information about it. As specifically as possible, summarize the discussion or action. The original sentence in the following example is vague; the second sentence is more specific:

> Finally, Commissioner Cycler expressed concern about the Senior Citizens Center on Eisenhower Drive.

> **Revised:** Finally, Commissioner Cycler said several people have called her to complain that the staff at the Senior Citizens Center on Eisenhower Drive is arrogant and unhelpful.

Another factor to keep in mind when organizing speech or meeting stories is attribution. When a writer fails to vary the location of the attribution, the story can seem dull and repetitious. If reporters see the following pattern or something like it in their finished stories, they need to rewrite:

- City Manager Faith An-Pong began by discussing the problems that recycling is creating for the city.
- Next, An-Pong said . . .
- Turning to a third topic, An-Pong said . . .
- She then went on to add that . . .
- Continuing, An-Pong said . . .
- In conclusion, she added . . .

15.3.2 Writing Effective Leads

Inexperienced reporters often err by writing overly broad leads that contain no news. These leads may say that a speaker "discussed" a topic or "voiced an opinion" or that a group "considered" or "dealt with" an issue. Consider the following examples:

> The president of the Chamber of Commerce discussed the dangers of higher taxes in a speech Tuesday night.

> The City Council considered the problems of billboards and panhandlers in an eight-hour meeting Monday.

Both are examples of label leads, and neither contains any news. (See Chapter 7.) The advance stories for these events would already have included the topic of the chamber president's speech and the agenda for the city council meeting. The news is what was said or done about these issues, as these revised leads illustrate:

> If the city continues to raise property taxes, major businesses will leave town, throwing thousands of people out of work, the president of the Chamber of Commerce warned Tuesday night.

> The City Council voted to ban most billboards and to restrict panhandling to about two dozen zones downtown during a meeting that lasted eight hours Monday.

Usually, leads for follow stories emphasize the most newsworthy information to emerge from a speech or meeting. Often that is the speaker's main point or the most important action taken or issue discussed at a meeting. Sometimes, other aspects are more newsworthy:

> **Follow Story Lead (Emphasis on Main Point):** UNITED NATIONS — Dozens of world leaders touted their efforts to reduce greenhouse gas emissions at the United Nations Climate Action Summit on Monday, but they were largely upstaged by youth activists angry at officials for not doing enough to prevent a catastrophic heating of the planet.
>
> The summit failed to produce new commitments from the world's largest countries to cut carbon pollution. As it got underway, 16-year-old Swedish activist Greta Thunberg delivered a blunt and emotional speech excoriating leaders for their "empty words" and insufficient steps to drive down emissions while temperatures continue to rise.
>
> (*Los Angeles Times*)

Although Greta Thunberg has become well known for her climate-change activism, she lacks the celebrity status of others who have been advocating for stronger action to reduce carbon emissions and halt global warming. Prominent politicians, like Al Gore, or movie stars, like Leonardo DiCaprio, have much higher name recognition and would be named in the lead. Thus, the substance of the message is more important and more meaningful than the fact the message is coming from Greta Thunberg. At other times, who said something is more important than what was said:

> **Follow Story Lead (Emphasis on Speaker):** Justice Clarence Thomas on Friday expressed dismay at the recent leak of a draft Supreme Court opinion that would strike down Roe v. Wade, comparing it to "an infidelity" and saying it has changed the culture of the nation's highest court.

The comments from the 73-year-old justice were delivered at an "Old Parkland Conference" event sponsored by the right-leaning American Enterprise Institute in Dallas. The remarks echoed those he had made earlier this month in Atlanta, when he said government institutions shouldn't be "bullied" into delivering what some see as the preferred outcome.

(CNN)

The leak of a draft opinion in the case of Dobbs v. Jackson Women's Health Organization, a decision that held women have no constitutional right to obtain an abortion, shocked many and drew wide condemnation. Legal authorities on both sides of the abortion issue said the leak violated long-standing Supreme Court traditions of decorum and secrecy surrounding unannounced decisions. Many wondered if the leak marked some shift in relations among the nine justices. When the longest-serving of those nine justices essentially confirms the cultural change, it is newsworthy.

Sometimes, the most important news is made not in the speech or the meeting but in reaction to it:

> **Follow Story Lead (Emphasis on Reaction):** BERKELEY, Calif. —A speech by the divisive right-wing writer Milo Yiannopoulos at the University of California, Berkeley, was canceled on Wednesday night after demonstrators set fires and threw objects at buildings to protest his appearance.

(The New York Times)

Audiences usually respond politely to speakers, even if they disagree with the views expressed. A completely different response faced Milo Yiannopoulos, then an editor at Breitbart News. Yiannopoulos, whom the Berkeley College Republicans had invited to speak, had been banned from Twitter for inciting trolls to attack actor-comedian Leslie Jones. He is also famous for his denunciations of political correctness, which have sometimes devolved into racially charged attacks. Opponents' response to his speech was notable not only for its violence but also for the criticism it evoked. Many conservatives cited the incident as an example of left-wing censorship.

Yet another approach to the follow story uses a lead that might be an anecdote from the speech, a description that sets a scene or a bit of dialogue from a meeting to introduce a nut graph that states the central point:

> **Follow Story Lead (Anecdotal):** When President Barack Obama visits his home in Chicago, he often peruses a stack of newspapers from before the 2008 election. Obama says he likes to look at what he said during the campaign and compare it with what he has accomplished in office.

Police carry a man into a building during a protest over a scheduled speech by Milo Yiannopoulos at the University of California, Berkeley.

FROM THE NEWS

Speech Story

Here's a speech story that illustrates how a description of a dramatic part of the speech can make an effective lead.

Internet Brings Pornography to Children, Researcher Says

"I sit down as a 14-year-old and type in a few words and let the mouse roam where the mouse will roam," said Edward Donnerstein as he started to demonstrate what's available on the internet.

And roam the mouse did.

Donnerstein, a professor of communication and dean of the division of social science at the University of California at Santa Barbara, typed the words "free porn" into the computer search engine he was using. The program responded with a list of dozens of websites offering pornographic images.

Donnerstein clicked on a few of the links as his audience of university students and faculty watched, and he brought to the screen still and moving pictures of naked women and men, vaginas, erect penises and couples having intercourse. And then he moved on to the rough stuff.

From sites that specialized in bondage and sadomasochism, Donnerstein opened photographs of women tied up and tortured. One image showed a naked woman with what appeared to be cigarette burns covering her breasts, belly and thighs.

"That's a 14-year-old not being asked age, not paying a cent and getting some pretty violent things," Donnerstein said.

Sex, violence, hate-group messages, bomb-building instructions and promotions for tobacco and alcohol are just some of the culturally nonconformist messages children have access to over the internet, Donnerstein said Monday during a lecture on children and the internet at the student union. And the most frequently mentioned solutions to the problem—government regulation, blocking software, ratings systems and safe sites for children—have weaknesses. The lecture was part of a lecture series on media and children sponsored by the university's Family Research and Policy Initiative.

Some parents may decide the best solution is to keep children off the internet altogether, but Donnerstein said that was wrong.

"The solution is not to pull the plug. In fact, it's just the opposite," he said. Children need to be online to access valuable educational information, Donnerstein said, adding that he cannot imagine writing a scholarly paper without using the web. And internet access is likely to become more important, he said, as people conduct online more and more of their daily business, from trading stocks to seeking medical advice.

Children have embraced the internet, Donnerstein said, but parents have little knowledge or understanding of what their children are doing.

Of children between 9 and 17, Donnerstein said, 79 percent say they are online daily and prefer using their computers to television or the telephone. And 44 percent of those children say they have found X-rated material; 25 percent say they have seen hate-group sites; and 14 percent have seen bomb-building instructions.

By comparison, parents are ignorant of computers, the internet and what their children are doing with them, he said. The internet is the first mass medium, Donnerstein said, where children and parents are at opposite ends in terms of their use and knowledge of

Speech Story *(continued)*

the medium. Most parents, he said, don't know what sites their children visit, don't have rules for using the internet and haven't installed blocking software, even if they own it, because it's too complicated for them.

Every new medium—movies, radio, television—has raised concerns among parents about how it will affect children, but the internet is different, Donnerstein said. The sex and violence in the movies and on television, even cable, are benign compared to what is on the internet, he said.

"The internet is whatever you want. Things that have no other media correlation are available," Donnerstein said. Also, the interactive nature of the internet may heighten any arousal the user experiences. Theoretically, he said, the effects of the internet may be much stronger than those of older media.

Parents are justified in worrying about what effects exposure to internet sex and violence may have on their children, he said, but the most frequently mentioned solutions have shortcomings.

Government regulation won't work, he said, in part because of the First Amendment, which allows government to prohibit only messages that meet the stringent legal definition for obscenity or that are child pornography. Even if the First Amendment allowed greater regulation of the internet, it would not stop access to sex and violence. Many of the most salacious sites, Donnerstein said, are based overseas, beyond the reach of U.S. law.

Ratings systems suffer a similar defect. They rely on the content providers to rate content as to its level of sex and violence, Donnerstein said. The systems are voluntary and would not bind content providers from other countries.

Parents can buy computer programs that block access to certain websites. But Donnerstein said studies of these programs show that sometimes they fail to block pornographic sites. Other times, he said, they may block access to valuable information, such as sites that deal with breast cancer or AIDS.

Websites specifically designed for children can provide a safe environment. National Geographic Kids, Kidsreads and How Stuff Works are examples of sites that allow children to see educational materials but not pornography, violence and hate. Such sites are not likely to satisfy older children, he said.

The best approach, Donnerstein said, may be for parents to learn more about the internet and what their children are doing with it. Parents can teach their children "critical viewing," he said, in which the children and parents view websites together and discuss what they see.

Children are aware of computer technologies and will make use of them, Donnerstein said; parents need to teach children how to use those technologies productively and safely.

"Lord knows I've made mistakes in this job," Obama said in a speech Monday at the presentation of the Toner Prize for political reporting, "and there are areas where I've fallen short, but something I'm really proud of is the fact that, if you go back and see what I said in 2007 and you see what I did, they match up."

A major reason the two match up, Obama said, is the work of political journalists like the late Robin Toner of The New York Times, for whom the prize is named. Knowing that journalists were recording what he said and would challenge him if he promised too much forced him to check his facts and be realistic, the president said.

The task of holding politicians to account and checking their statements and promises is even more important now, Obama said, in a presidential campaign that seems untethered to fact and reasoned analysis.

Quotations can hook readers with a colorful phrase, but they rarely make good summary leads. As a rule, writers should use a quotation in the lead only if it accurately and succinctly states the most newsworthy point of the meeting or speech. In practice, few quotations will satisfy that standard. Quotations can be effectively used in anecdotal or delayed leads, which offer an opportunity to grab an audience with a bit of narrative or description but must clearly lead into and support the nut graph.

15.3.3 Writing Transitions

Transitions shift a story from one idea to another. A good transition will connect the ideas and arouse the audience's interest in the topic being introduced.

Transitions should be brief. The repetition of a key word, phrase or idea can serve as a transition to a related topic or can shift the story to a new time or place. If the new topic is markedly different, a transitional sentence or question might be necessary. The transition should not, however, simply report that a speaker or group "turned to another topic." Instead, it should function as a secondary lead, summarizing the new topic by giving its most interesting and important details. In the next examples, a weak transition is rewritten to include specific information:

The board also considered two other topics.

Revised: The board also considered—and rejected—proposals to increase students' health and athletic fees.

Hunt then discussed the problem of auto insurance.

Revised: Hunt then warned that the cost of auto insurance rose 9.6 percent last year and is expected to rise 12 percent this year.

15.4 Write for Your Audience

Reporters should write with their audience in mind, clarifying issues so that people can understand how events will affect them and their neighborhood, city or state. Sometimes journalists forget this rule and try to please the people they are writing about instead of the people they are writing for. One news report of a city council meeting began by saying three employees received awards for their 25 years of service. Placing the awards in the lead probably pleased the city officials, but few people would care. The public was likely to have a greater interest in a topic presented later: plans for the city government to help people with low incomes buy their own homes.

Reporters also need to clarify jargon, especially the bureaucratic language used at government meetings, so that readers, viewers and listeners can understand the stories. A story reported that a county commission had imposed "stricter signage requirements" for adult bookstores, theaters and clubs. Instead of repeating such jargon, journalists should give specific details. In this case, the commissioners limited the size and location of outdoor signs advertising adult entertainment businesses.

15.4.1 Check Facts

Reporters have an obligation to go beyond what is said or done at the speech or meeting to check facts, find opposing points of view and get additional information and comments. People say things in speeches that may not be true or may be largely opinion. And because a speech represents the views of only the speaker, a journalist who does nothing more than report the speaker's words may be presenting a one-sided and inaccurate view of a topic.

Two websites devoted to checking the factual claims of officials, politicians and opinion leaders are PolitiFact.com and FactCheck.org. Politicians are an endless source of misinformation. Rep. Marjorie Taylor Greene of Georgia tweeted a photo that appeared to show the suspected killer of seven people in a mass shooting in Highland Park, Illinois, sitting in a cell. Greene said it was evidence the suspect had a dark past and added:

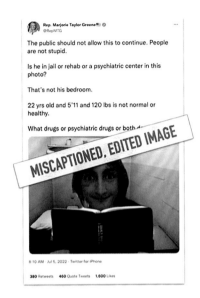

Rep. Marjorie Taylor Greene's tweet about the suspected Highland Park, Illinois, shooter as it appeared on the PolitiFact website. The original tweet has been deleted from Greene's Twitter feed.

> Until we are willing to rip open the ugly truth about the dark and destructive path these young men are on that lead them to mass shootings, then they will continue. No matter how many gun control laws are passed. Even with no guns at all, evil will find a way until it's fixed.

PolitiFact investigated the tweet and found that the image was faked and rated the tweet false. The suspect in the shooting had never been in jail or detained in any rehabilitation or psychiatric unit.

Mike Gibbons, a candidate for the Republican nomination for U.S. senator from Ohio, said during a candidate debate that 5 million more votes for president were cast in 2020 than there were registered voters. The claim has been promoted by several people questioning the validity of the 2020 election. It is also false. PolitiFact reported that 168,308,000 Americans are registered to vote in the 50 states and the District of Columbia. The total number of votes cast in the presidential race in 2020 was 154,628,000, which is more than 14 million less than the number of registered voters. Neither the total number of registered voters nor the total of votes cast is exact because both come from responses to surveys conducted by the U.S. Census Bureau. Nevertheless, the difference is substantial enough that PolitiFact could rate Gibbons' claim false.

Websites like PolitiFact and FactCheck help reporters spot and correct errors in speeches and other public comments because often politicians repeat the distortions spoken by others. Checking facts about state or local issues may require journalists to invest some of their own time in research. Still, much of the information for checking facts is already on the websites of state and local governments. The web has made the process of holding politicians and public officials accountable much easier than it was decades ago.

PolitiFact's Truth-O-Meter includes the following rankings of political claims: true, mostly true, half true, mostly false, false and pants on fire.

Reporters must be especially diligent about double-checking personal attacks in order to avoid libel suits. If a speaker makes a defamatory personal attack at a speech or meeting that is not an official government proceeding, the person who is attacked may sue both the speaker and any news organizations that report the statement. The fact that news organizations accurately quoted a speaker is not a defense. Even if a personal attack is not defamatory or is made in an official government meeting—and therefore cannot be the basis for a libel suit—the journalist still has an ethical obligation to check facts, get opposing points of view and give people who have been attacked a chance to respond.

15.4.2 Add Color

15.4.2.1 REPORT WHAT YOU HEAR

Quotations, direct and indirect, help the writer describe debates that occur in a public meeting. The public needs to know why certain actions were taken or why elected representatives voted a certain way. Simply recording votes and actions will not give citizens the information they need to make informed judgments. They also need to know the competing points of view.

School board meetings usually focus on budgets, taxes, staffing, bonds and buildings—all important but rarely exciting. But some issues produce strong emotional responses from parents, students and the public. In the wake of the school shooting at an elementary school in Uvalde, Texas, that left 19 children and two teachers dead, school safety became a major concern. At a Uvalde board meeting that lasted more than three hours, parents and students demanded the firing of the school superintendent, threatened to keep their children out of school until security was improved and criticized school board members. Here's how the Texas Tribune began its report of the meeting:

Parents, citizens and law enforcement officers attend a meeting of the Uvalde, Texas, School Board following the murders of 19 students and two teachers at the Robb Elementary School. Many attending the meeting angrily demanded the school superintendent's resignation.

UVALDE — Tina Quintanilla-Taylor's 8-year-old daughter joined an army of angry adults in this town of 15,000 people Monday night and stood at a microphone, looking up to school district officials who sat behind tables draped in maroon cloth on a high school auditorium stage.

The young girl wore the same sundress that she wore to Robb Elementary on May 24, when an 18-year-old gunman massacred 19 students and two teachers.

"Most of those kids were my friends, and that's not good," Quintanilla-Taylor's daughter told school board members and Superintendent Hal Harrell. "And I don't wanna go to your guys' school if you don't have protection."

(Texas Tribune)

School curriculum dealing with race and sex can also arouse passions. In Virginia Beach, Virginia, a member of the local school board questioned the use of six books, including "Good Trouble: Lessons from the Civil Rights Playbook" by Christopher Noxon, "Beyond Magenta: Transgender Teens Speak Out" by Susan Kuklin and "The Bluest Eye" by Toni Morrison. Board member Victoria Manning said those books and four others had sexual content that included assaults on children and oral sex. The discussion at the board meeting was described this way by WAVY-TV of Portsmouth, Virginia:

> Some of the passages are so graphic, the school board wouldn't allow them to be read aloud at a meeting.
>
> "Yet that book is being used in curriculum for our high school students and it's approved," Manning said, referring to Toni Morrison's "The Bluest Eye."
>
> Virginia Beach high school student Giana Lathan spoke in those same meetings in favor of keeping the books on shelves and in curriculum.
>
> "This is real world stuff. This happens to people all the time," Lathan said. "It's better if [students] are exposed to this in a classroom, where they can have open discussions with other peers and teachers and adults around them."
>
> Another student, Ure Emejuru points out there are plenty more books with graphic content that Manning did not ask to be pulled from schools.
>
> "'1984' or Shakespeare or parts of the Bible have examples of sexual actions," Emejuru said. "I think the fact that it's mainly LGBTQ+ books and books by POC [people of color] authors is very deliberate."
>
> *(WAVY-TV, Portsmouth, Virginia)*

The statements by and exchanges between the participants in these meetings give readers a sense of the atmosphere and emotion involved in these issues. Readers can start to visualize the meeting and sense the significance of the issues for the people involved.

15.4.2.2 DESCRIBE WHAT YOU SEE

Vivid descriptions of participants, audiences and settings add drama to speech and meeting stories. The descriptions can appear anywhere. The following example shows how vivid description can enliven a meeting story:

> A public hearing on an ordinance that would limit the number of animals allowed in homes drew a standing-room-only crowd to a County Commission meeting Thursday.
>
> Some of the spectators wore T-shirts inscribed with pictures of their pets, primarily cats and dogs.

The Reporter's Guide to Reporting Speeches and Meetings

ADVANCE STORIES

1. Report what speech or meeting will happen, when and where it will happen and who will be involved.

2. Keep advance stories short—normally three or four paragraphs.

COVERING THE SPEECH OR MEETING

1. Get background information on the group or speaker, including a copy of the agenda or the speech, if it's available.

2. Learn the names of all participants.

3. Find out if there will be an opportunity to interview the speaker or the participants before or after the event.

4. Arrive early and find a seat where you can see and hear as much as possible.

5. Introduce yourself to the speaker or the participants in the meeting if they do not know you.

6. Take detailed notes, making sure you record colorful quotations, information about the setting of the event and the responses of the participants and observers.

7. Identify and seek responses from people who may be affected by what happens or who may have views or interests different from those expressed at the speech or meeting.

FOLLOW STORIES

1. Identify the issue or decision that is most likely to interest your audience and make that your central point. If other important issues or decisions arose in the speech or meeting, be sure to mention them early.

2. Focus the lead on specific actions or statements to keep it from being overly broad.

3. Organize the story in inverted-pyramid fashion, not according to the order in which statements were made or topics considered.

4. Vary the location of the attribution in direct and indirect quotations so that the story does not become monotonous.

5. Provide transitions from one topic to another.

6. Avoid generalities and eliminate or explain jargon or technical terms.

7. Check controversial facts and give any person or group who has been attacked in the speech or meeting an opportunity to respond.

8. Include color in speech and meeting stories by providing direct quotations and descriptions of speakers, participants, settings and audience responses.

 # Review Exercises

1. EVALUATING SPEECH AND MEETING LEADS

Critically evaluate the following speech and meeting story leads, giving each a grade from A to F. Then discuss the leads with your instructor and classmates.

1. The County Commission voted unanimously Tuesday against raising the county tourism tax by one cent to pay for a new baseball stadium.

2. A spokesperson for Citizens Against Crime warned parents Wednesday night about violent crime and its impact on families in the city.

3. By a vote of 5-4, the City Council rejected on Monday night a proposal to build an apartment complex near Reed Road and State Road 419.

4. A heated debate took place at the City Council meeting Thursday night over the need for police dogs.

5. Fifty percent of the drug abusers entering treatment centers go back to using drugs within a year, Mimi Sota told an audience here Monday.

6. In a speech Monday, reporter Samuel Swaugger talked to journalism students about his past as a journalist and his experiences with the two largest newspapers in the state.

7. During a speech to the American Legion last night, former Marine Lt. Col. Oliver North discussed his work in the Reagan White House.

8. County commissioners heard testimony from more than 20 people Tuesday morning on plans to license and regulate snowmobiles.

9. The County Commission reviewed a resolution Wednesday to create a committee that will identify conservation and recreation lands within the county.

10. Blasting opponents of the plan, Mayor Sabrina Datoli last night defended a proposal to establish a police review board.

11. Traveling by airplane has never been more dangerous, Ramon Madea charged in a fiery speech Sunday night.

12. The City Council voted unanimously Monday to change the zoning along three streets from residential to commercial.

13. The business before the School Board flowed smoothly Tuesday night as the board proceeded through the agenda.

14. The county commissioners continued to struggle with the issue of protecting the water quality in Butler Lake at their meeting Monday. They eventually denied a petition to build a new boat ramp on the lake.

15. The County Commission unanimously passed an ordinance that makes it illegal for anyone to possess an open container of alcohol in a vehicle. A previous law made it illegal to drive while drunk, but legal to drink while driving.

2. WRITING ADVANCE AND FOLLOW STORIES

Write separate advance and follow stories about each of the following speeches. Because the speeches are reprinted verbatim, you may quote them directly. Correct the stories' grammatical and spelling errors, including all possessives. You may want to discuss with classmates the problem of handling speakers' errors in grammar and syntax and statements that seem sexist.

1. Americans' Work

INFORMATION FOR ADVANCE STORY

Leslee D'Ausilio will speak this forthcoming Saturday night to the Chamber of Commerce at the organizations annual meeting. The affair will start with an open bar at 6:30, dinner at 7:30, and the speech to begin promptly at 8:30 p.m., all in the spacious Grand Ballroom of the Downtown Hilton Hotel. Cost for the dinner and speech: $39.00 for members and their guests, $49.00 for nonmembers.

Tickets are conveniently available at the Chamber of Commerce office until Noon Saturday. The speaker, a famous celebrity and frequent TV guest commentator, is the author of 3 best-selling books, all about American workers, their jobs, their characteristics, their problems. She received her B.A. and M.A. from the University of Wisconsin in Madison Wisconsin where for both degrees she majored in Sociology, and Ph.D. from Harvard where she majored in Management with a speciality in Labor Relations. She currently teaches at Harvard, serves as a consultant for the UAW-CIO, and was Assistant Secretary of Labor in the Clinton administration. Her announced topic will be "Today's Workers, Workweeks, and Productivity."

SPEECH FOR FOLLOW STORY

Today, the U.S. ranks Number One in the world in productivity per worker. That has both advantages and disadvantages for workers, their families, and employers.

On the upside, American families are enjoying more prosperity, but not due solely to rising wages. More family members are working, especially among Black and Hispanic families. During the last 10 years, the average middle-class familys income rose 9.2 percent after inflation, but the typical familys wage-earners had to spend 6.8 percent more time at work to reap it. Without increased earnings from wives, the average middle-class familys income would have risen only 3.6 percent. The share of married women working full-time rose from 41 to 46 percent. Plus, the average workers workweek has risen from about 38 hours for full-time workers to slightly more than 41 hours a week. Executives, on average, work 47 hours a week.

On the downside, workers complain they're working harder and that they're having difficulty balancing their jobs and personal lives. American workers seemed to be squeezed during both booms and busts. In expansions, companies keep giving their workers more work, and in recessions companies downsize. Then, with fewer employees, those that remain have to work longer and harder to get everything done. So its not surprising that American workers are sometimes frustrated. Forty-one percent feel they do not have enough time to accomplish all their tasks each day.

Its a complex issue, and there're also other culprits. One is technology. More than ever before, technological advances keep people tethered to their office by cell phone and computer. Think about it! It doesn't matter where you go: to a movie, a nice restaurant, or even a golf course or your church. People carry telephones everywhere and, while some calls are social, many are business.

There's also the American psyche and culture. Much of the increase in time spent at work is voluntary. Workers want to earn more and to move up economically. They're eager to make a good impression: to impress their boss and co-workers. Also, work is important to them, sometimes the most important thing in their lives. Many are ambitious, even obsessed, with getting ahead. Increasingly, then, some Americans work even on holidays and are forgoing vacations and time with their families and friends.

During the past decade, Americans added nearly a full week to their work year, working on average 1,978 hours last year. That's up 36 hours almost a full week from ten years ago. That means Americans who are employed spent nearly 49 weeks a year on the job. As a result, they worked longer than all other industrial nations last year. Americans work 100 more hours (2 weeks per year) than Japanese workers. They work 250 hours (about 6 weeks) more per year than British workers, and 500 hours (12 weeks) more per year than German workers.

Why? Among the reasons for the differences are the fact that Europeans typically take 4 to 6 weeks of vacation each year while Americans take only 2 to 3 weeks. Also, while American employers offer or require lots of overtime, the French government has reduced that countrys official workweek to 35 hours. That's because the unemployment rate in France is high, and the government wants to pressure companies to hire more workers.

Clearly, all these trends, whether good or bad, have contributed to our countrys outstanding economic performance, which translates into more income for employees and more profits for employers. So, no one can deny that Americans are working harder, and I don't like that, but I don't see the situation as all bad. Our economy is booming. There are good jobs for most workers, and incomes are going up along with our productivity.

2. College Athletics
INFORMATION FOR ADVANCE STORY

Erik Nieves, your schools Athletic Director for the past twenty-four years, has previously announced his retirement, effective at the end of next month. Before then, he's planning a farewell speech and today he told you it will be "a candid discussion about some serious problems in athletics, primarily college athletics." Its all free this coming Saturday night at the annual meeting of members of your schools Athletic Boosters Club. The speech is being held in the beautiful Grand Ballroom of your Student Union with only Booster Club members and their guests invited. Each member of the club donates $500 or more annually to your schools Athletic Foundation. Bronze Key Club members donate $1000 or more, Silver Key Club members $5000 or more, and Gold Key Club members $10,000 or more. There's an open bar at 6:30, dinner at 7:30, and the speech at 9:00 p.m., with good fellowship for all. "Its my farewell address to the club," Nieves said. (Press kits will be available, with free seating available to the press. No radio or TV tapings or broadcasts of any type will be permitted, all such rights being exclusively retained by the Athletic Boosters Club.)

SPEECH FOR FOLLOW STORY:

As I look around this room, I see many familiar faces: good people, generous people who've been friends and supporters for as long as I've been here. Now, all of you know I'm retiring at the end of next month. I'm 64, and its time. What you don't know is that I've decided to devote the time I have left to increasing public awareness of a serious problem for our athletes and athletic programs. I'll continue with that effort after I retire. What I'm going to say isn't going to be popular, but its something I feel I have to say, something eating my heart out. The fact is, its no longer fun to play college football; its become a fatiguing grind. Its a full-time job, a year-around job, and that's true of every college football program across the country.

The insanity has to stop. Coaches demand more, colleges demand more. Alumni demand more, so college football has turned into a 12-month-a-year job that never ends. We've got fall games and winter workouts. There's spring practice, and there're summer conditioning drills. So our players work and work and work during the season. Then, when the season ends, they work even more. They push harder and stay longer, and it doesn't matter what time of the day or what month of the year.

You've got wonderful young players some still teenagers literally working themselves to death, dying so you can have a winning season. Eleven college football players died in the past 12 months year, and its a tragedy we have to stop.

Heatstroke is a part of the problem, especially during those damned summer drills. Heatstroke can cause your body temperature to soar to 108 degrees, cause a heart attack, and induce a coma. On college teams its hard to help people 50 to 100 pounds sometimes even 150 pounds above the ideal weight for their height. With people who are so overweight, often deliberately, you're going to have problems. We tell our players on a hot day he should drink 16 to 20 ounces of fluid and then continue to drink every 15 minutes whether he's thirsty or not. You can't depend on your thirst mechanism. The center of the brain doesn't click on and tell you that you're thirsty until a long time after all your fluids are gone. If you're a coach, whether in high school or college, and your kids aren't getting water every 15 or 20 minutes, you shouldn't be coaching.

Actually, heat stroke is one of the easier problems we deal with. Some of our players have pre-existing conditions we don't know about. We require players to have physical exams before letting them play. Still, right here in our state, we had a freshman die after a series of early-morning agility drills. He was just 19, 6 feet

4, and 230 pounds, with no history of heart problems. When he reported to campus doctors detected no heart abnormalities during his physical exam. That non-detection is no surprise. Many cardiologists say arrhythmia can be difficult to find.

Cardiac arrhythmia is an irregular heartbeat. The heartbeat is not constantly out of kilter, so the problem is not likely to be detected even in an athlete undergoing a yearly physical. But at some point under exertion, the heart is pushed beyond its limits, and there's no way of knowing when or why it will happen. There are a number of causes for this problem, including defects in the heart structure. People are born with these defects but often show no outward signs of the problems. Including high school teams and all sports, about 100 to 200 young athletes die each year from the condition.

Now, some of this is the coaches fault and some the fans fault. Coaches work their players too hard. They work themselves too hard. And players give every last drop of their time, energy and effort. They sacrifice way too much for far too little. They have tremendous pride and ambition, and they all want to be drafted into the professionals, so they push themselves through heat and pain.

To solve the problems, our coaches at every level need more sports medicine knowledge. We don't have a system of coaching certification in this country. In other countries, especially Europe, you have to have expertise and take courses and pass tests. In this country I could be an accountant who never took a course in first aid, and so long as I can win football games, it doesn't matter.

Other things are just common sense. If you're a coach, you take your team out at 7:00 in the morning or 5:00 or 6:00 in the evening. On hot days, you don't work outside at noon. Somehow, we also have to cut back on off-season drills. They take way too much of our athletes time, so an awful lot of these young men never graduate. There's just no time left for their studies.

We also need better physicals. That will cost several hundred dollars for every player every year but should be a priority, and schools can afford it.

Plus, fans put way too much pressure on their coaches, forcing coaches to put more pressure on their players. You see it in every game, high school, college, and professional. You see coaches send too many injured players back into games before they're ready.

We've also got fans who like to brag their teams linemen average 250 or 300 pounds. That's not healthy for young men to gain an extra 50 or 100 pounds. I'd rather have fans brag about how many of our athletes graduate. To get this awful pressure off coaches, give them tenure just like you give faculty members. No coach should be fired after just one or two losing seasons.

Now all this isn't going to happen soon, and it can't happen at just one or two schools. It has to be a national effort. Football is a game. Enjoy the game whether your team wins or loses. A few more victories aren't worth risking a players life.

3. The Police and the Press

INFORMATION FOR ADVANCE STORY

Barry Kopperud is scheduled to speak to the local chapter of the Society of Professional Journalists Monday of next week. The club meets for dinner the second Monday of every month at the Blackhawk Hotel. Both the dinner and the speech are open to the public.

The dinners are $28.50 per person. Those wishing to hear the speech only may attend free. The evening begins with a social hour and cash bar at 6 p.m. Dinner starts at 6:30 p.m., and Kopperuds speech will begin at 7:30 p.m. Anyone wishing to attend the dinner must make reservations in advance by calling LeeAnn Verkler at the university.

Kopperud is the chief of police, and he will speak about issues regarding press coverage of crime and the police.

SPEECH FOR FOLLOW STORY

Good evening, ladies and gentlemen. I've met most of you before. A couple of you I've seen just within the last hour. I'm glad we have this opportunity to talk under conditions that are more pleasant than when we usually meet.

The police beat is among the most active beats for any reporter. I've noticed that a good share of the content of the news broadcasts and the newspaper comes from the police.

This heavy reliance by the media on the police probably accounts for a situation police and news people have observed in many towns and cities. There is a symbiotic, co-dependent, love-hate relationship between cops and reporters that develops about everywhere.

Obviously, reporters rely on the police to provide information about some of the most important and dramatic events of the day. But police need reporters to get out information on the things they want to promote. Police understand that people read and watch news stories about crime. One of the first places people turn to when they get their daily paper is the police blotter. Although the police department has had generally good relations with the press, there are some common problems—points of friction, you might call them—that arise from time to time. One of these points of friction involves the release of information through unofficial channels.

The police department has lots of information, some of it secret that it doesn't want released to the public. A classic example is information relevant to a homicide, such as autopsy information and details about the scene of the crime. Why do we want to keep this information secret? Because doing so helps us investigate the crime. A few years ago we had a homicide in which a man was bludgeoned to death with a tire iron. The killer then doused the body with gasoline and tried to set it afire. The body was in a wooded area and not discovered for several weeks. We got a lot of tips about that murder. We also had a couple of people show up trying to confess. Because we withheld the details about the crime scene and cause of death, we were able to distinguish the real culprit from the cranks and the real sources from the phony ones. Because the details were never published in the media, we could trace leads back to the one person with firsthand knowledge—a person who is now serving a life sentence. But those details are exactly the kind of thing reporters most want.

One of the banes of my existence is that there are people in the police department who like to release that kind of information. Maybe these leaks are intentional—from disgruntled officers—or maybe the leaks are unintentional, where an officer tells a friend who tells a reporter. Either way, reporters will call us back asking for confirmation of these leaks, but the police department will never confirm or deny anything.

That brings me to some ethical questions. Both police and reporters deal with ethical issues. Sometimes we err and release information that we shouldn't. Sometimes we wonder why you folks in the media publish what you do. I just want to share with you some recent incidents that raise ethical issues and ask you to consider them.

A few weeks ago, a police dog bit its handler's daughter. The dog was retired from service but had been living with its handler. As a result of the incident the girl needed stitches. Somehow a TV reporter got onto the story and wanted to do an on-camera interview with someone from the department. We refused. The reporter suggested it was because the story would embarrass the department or suggest irresponsibility or create problems with the city council. But none of those was correct. We refused because the dog had been put down, and the little girl didn't know that. She was fond of the dog, and the dog had meant a lot to her. Her mom and dad asked that the story not be released, and we agreed.

In another recent case, we had an accidental death of a graduate student in a university dorm. The man had suffocated to death, and the newspaper reported—correctly—that he had died while practicing auto-erotic asphyxiation. I read that article and thought, "How crass!" Imagine how that must have made that students mother and father feel. I'd like to think that reporters would take that kind of thing into account before they publish a story. Sometimes the feelings of the family outweigh the publics need to know.

The case that for me presented the most searing ethical problem was the Wendy Ray case. You all remember that Wendy was a university student who was abducted from just outside her parents apartment one night, repeatedly raped, tortured and then murdered.

For weeks she was just missing, and no one knew where she was. We got our first break in the case when we arrested a couple of men for burglarizing an electronics store. After we had charged them, Donald Hendricks, the assistant county attorney, called and said one of them, Scott Reed, wanted to cut a deal: He'd tell us about Wendys murder if we promised not to seek the death penalty for him. Reed told us where to find Wendys body.

At this point, I went to Bill and Liz Ray, Wendys parents, and told them we had remains and believed them to be Wendys, pending a dental match. I also told them that we knew a lot more about how she had died and that I would tell them as much as they wanted to know when they wanted to know it. They understood that I meant there were grisly details about Wendys death. A few hours later, we had a positive dental match, but before I could get back to Wendy's parents, one of the radio stations had aired a news story with all the gory details. I can't tell you how devastated the Rays were. I think it was not a good way for the family to learn those details.

I guess the moral of these stories is a simple one: People really are affected by news stories. I hope reporters have enough humanity not to get caught up in the competitive practices of the business and realize how they may hurt others. I understand some people may reach different decisions about how to handle these ethical issues. I have no problem with someone who disagrees with me. I have a real problem, however, with reporters who won't consider other points of view.

3. SUMMARIZING SPEECHES

1. U.S. Withdrawal from the Paris Agreement on Climate Change

Using the background information and the official transcript provided, write a story summarizing President Trump's announcement that the United States would withdraw from the Paris Agreement on climate change.

BACKGROUND ON THE PARIS AGREEMENT

The Paris Agreement was negotiated in December 2015 within the United Nations Framework Convention on Climate Change (UNFCCC). It was signed by 195 countries and ratified by 148. Only Syria and Nicaragua did not sign the agreement.

The agreement's goal is first to hold the increase "in the global average temperature to well below 2 degrees C above pre-industrial levels and to pursue efforts to limit the temperature increase to 1.5 degrees C above pre-industrial levels." Temperatures in the first half of 2016 were already about 1.3 degrees C above 1880 levels, when records first were kept. The agreement also calls on signatories to do the following:

- increase "the ability to adapt to the adverse impacts of climate change and foster climate resilience and low greenhouse gas emissions development, in a manner that does not threaten food production"
- make "finance flows consistent with a pathway towards low greenhouse gas emissions and climate-resilient development"
- aim to reach "global peaking of greenhouse gas emissions as soon as possible"

Under the agreement, each country determines the steps it will take to mitigate climate change. Countries are urged to be ambitious in their goals, and they are supposed to report them every five years to the UNFCCC secretariat. Each new set of goals should be more ambitious than the previous set. Nothing compels any country to abide by its own targets or achieve them by a specific date, although the UNFCCC will report on how much success countries have had in meeting their objectives. This practice has been called a "name and shame" or a "name and encourage" system of enforcement. The agreement also calls for a Global Stocktake in 2018, to assess how much countries have accomplished toward achieving their nationally determined contributions to carbon-emission reduction. That will be followed by further evaluations every five years, the first being in 2023.

The participating developed countries said they would contribute $100 billion to finance initiatives to mitigate climate change by 2020 and spend an additional $100 billion a year. In 2016, the Obama administration issued a grant of $500 million to the Green Climate Fund, the first of the $3 billion it had committed to financing the agreement. By June 2017, the fund had received $10 billion, mostly from developed countries, but some from developing countries such as Mexico, Indonesia and Vietnam.

A country may withdraw from the agreement three years after it goes into effect in that country, with a one-year waiting period until the departure becomes effective. Therefore, the earliest the United States can fully withdraw from the agreement is November 4, 2020.

PRESIDENT TRUMP'S SPEECH

White House Rose Garden, 3:32 p.m. Eastern Time

THE PRESIDENT: Thank you very much. (Applause.) Thank you. I would like to begin by addressing the terrorist attack in Manila. We're closely monitoring the situation, and I will continue to give updates if anything happens during this period of time. But it is really very sad as to what's going on throughout the world with terror. Our thoughts and our prayers are with all of those affected.

Before we discuss the Paris Accord, I'd like to begin with an update on our tremendous—absolutely tremendous—economic progress since Election Day on November 8th. The economy is starting to come back, and very, very rapidly. We've added $3.3 trillion in stock market value to our economy, and more than a million private sector jobs.

I have just returned from a trip overseas where we concluded nearly $350 billion of military and economic development for the United States, creating hundreds of thousands of jobs. It was a very, very successful trip, believe me. (Applause.) Thank you. Thank you.

In my meetings at the G7, we have taken historic steps to demand fair and reciprocal trade that gives Americans a level playing field against other nations. We're also working very hard for peace in the Middle East, and perhaps even peace between the Israelis and the Palestinians. Our attacks on terrorism are greatly stepped up—and you see that, you see it all over—from the previous administration, including getting many other countries to make major contributions to the fight against terror. Big, big contributions are being made by countries that weren't doing so much in the form of contribution.

One by one, we are keeping the promises I made to the American people during my campaign for President whether it's cutting job-killing regulations; appointing and confirming a tremendous Supreme Court justice; putting in place tough new ethics rules; achieving a record reduction in illegal immigration on our southern border; or bringing jobs, plants, and factories back into the United States at numbers which no one until this point thought even possible. And believe me, we've just begun. The fruits of our labor will be seen very shortly even more so.

On these issues and so many more, we're following through on our commitments. And I don't want anything to get in our way. I am fighting every day for the great people of this country. Therefore, in order to fulfill my solemn duty to protect America and its citizens, the United States will withdraw from the Paris Climate Accord—(applause)—thank you, thank you—but begin negotiations to reenter either the Paris Accord or a really entirely new transaction on terms that are fair to the United States, its businesses, its workers, its people, its taxpayers. So we're getting out. But we will start to negotiate, and we will see if we can make a deal that's fair. And if we can, that's great. And if we can't, that's fine. (Applause.)

As President, I can put no other consideration before the wellbeing of American citizens. The Paris Climate Accord is simply the latest example of Washington entering into an agreement that disadvantages the

United States to the exclusive benefit of other countries, leaving American workers—who I love—and taxpayers to absorb the cost in terms of lost jobs, lower wages, shuttered factories, and vastly diminished economic production.

Thus, as of today, the United States will cease all implementation of the non-binding Paris Accord and the draconian financial and economic burdens the agreement imposes on our country. This includes ending the implementation of the nationally determined contribution and, very importantly, the Green Climate Fund which is costing the United States a vast fortune.

Compliance with the terms of the Paris Accord and the onerous energy restrictions it has placed on the United States could cost America as much as 2.7 million lost jobs by 2025 according to the National Economic Research Associates. This includes 440,000 fewer manufacturing jobs—not what we need—believe me, this is not what we need—including automobile jobs, and the further decimation of vital American industries on which countless communities rely. They rely for so much, and we would be giving them so little.

According to this same study, by 2040, compliance with the commitments put into place by the previous administration would cut production for the following sectors: paper down 12 percent; cement down 23 percent; iron and steel down 38 percent; coal—and I happen to love the coal miners—down 86 percent; natural gas down 31 percent. The cost to the economy at this time would be close to $3 trillion in lost GDP and 6.5 million industrial jobs, while households would have $7,000 less income and, in many cases, much worse than that.

Not only does this deal subject our citizens to harsh economic restrictions, it fails to live up to our environmental ideals. As someone who cares deeply about the environment, which I do, I cannot in good conscience support a deal that punishes the United States—which is what it does—the world's leader in environmental protection, while imposing no meaningful obligations on the world's leading polluters.

For example, under the agreement, China will be able to increase these emissions by a staggering number of years—13. They can do whatever they want for 13 years. Not us. India makes its participation contingent on receiving billions and billions and billions of dollars in foreign aid from developed countries. There are many other examples. But the bottom line is that

the Paris Accord is very unfair, at the highest level, to the United States.

Further, while the current agreement effectively blocks the development of clean coal in America—which it does, and the mines are starting to open up. We're having a big opening in two weeks. Pennsylvania, Ohio, West Virginia, so many places. A big opening of a brand-new mine. It's unheard of. For many, many years, that hasn't happened. They asked me if I'd go. I'm going to try.

China will be allowed to build hundreds of additional coal plants. So we can't build the plants, but they can, according to this agreement. India will be allowed to double its coal production by 2020. Think of it: India can double their coal production. We're supposed to get rid of ours. Even Europe is allowed to continue construction of coal plants.

In short, the agreement doesn't eliminate coal jobs, it just transfers those jobs out of America and the United States, and ships them to foreign countries.

This agreement is less about the climate and more about other countries gaining a financial advantage over the United States. The rest of the world applauded when we signed the Paris Agreement—they went wild; they were so happy—for the simple reason that it put our country, the United States of America, which we all love, at a very, very big economic disadvantage. A cynic would say the obvious reason for economic competitors and their wish to see us remain in the agreement is so that we continue to suffer this self-inflicted major economic wound. We would find it very hard to compete with other countries from other parts of the world.

We have among the most abundant energy reserves on the planet, sufficient to lift millions of America's poorest workers out of poverty. Yet, under this agreement, we are effectively putting these reserves under lock and key, taking away the great wealth of our nation—it's great wealth, it's phenomenal wealth; not so long ago, we had no idea we had such wealth—and leaving millions and millions of families trapped in poverty and joblessness.

The agreement is a massive redistribution of United States wealth to other countries. At 1 percent growth, renewable sources of energy can meet some of our domestic demand, but at 3 or 4 percent growth, which I expect, we need all forms of available American energy, or our country—(applause)—will be at grave risk of brownouts and blackouts, our businesses will come to a halt in many cases, and the American family will suffer the consequences in the form of lost jobs and a very diminished quality of life.

Even if the Paris Agreement were implemented in full, with total compliance from all nations, it is estimated it would only produce a two-tenths of one degree—think of that; this much—Celsius reduction in global temperature by the year 2100. Tiny, tiny amount. In fact, 14 days of carbon emissions from China alone would wipe out the gains from America— and this is an incredible statistic—would totally wipe out the gains from America's expected reductions in the year 2030, after we have had to spend billions and billions of dollars, lost jobs, closed factories, and suffered much higher energy costs for our businesses and for our homes.

As the Wall Street Journal wrote this morning: "The reality is that withdrawing is in America's economic interest and won't matter much to the climate." The United States, under the Trump administration, will continue to be the cleanest and most environmentally friendly country on Earth. We'll be the cleanest. We're going to have the cleanest air. We're going to have the cleanest water. We will be environmentally friendly, but we're not going to put our businesses out of work and we're not going to lose our jobs. We're going to grow; we're going to grow rapidly. (Applause.)

And I think you just read—it just came out minutes ago, the small business report—small businesses as of just now are booming, hiring people. One of the best reports they've seen in many years.

I'm willing to immediately work with Democratic leaders to either negotiate our way back into Paris, under the terms that are fair to the United States and its workers, or to negotiate a new deal that protects our country and its taxpayers. (Applause.)

So if the obstructionists want to get together with me, let's make them non-obstructionists. We will all sit down, and we will get back into the deal. And we'll make it good, and we won't be closing up our factories, and we won't be losing our jobs. And we'll sit down with the Democrats and all of the people that represent either the Paris Accord or something that we can do that's much better than the Paris Accord. And I think the people of our country will be thrilled, and I think then the people of the world will be thrilled. But until we do that, we're out of the agreement.

I will work to ensure that America remains the world's leader on environmental issues, but under a framework that is fair and where the burdens and responsibilities are equally shared among the many nations all around the world.

No responsible leader can put the workers—and the people—of their country at this debilitating and tremendous disadvantage. The fact that the Paris deal hamstrings the United States, while empowering some of the world's top polluting countries, should dispel any doubt as to the real reason why foreign lobbyists wish to keep our magnificent country tied up and bound down by this agreement: It's to give their country an economic edge over the United States. That's not going to happen while I'm President. I'm sorry. (Applause.)

My job as President is to do everything within my power to give America a level playing field and to create the economic, regulatory and tax structures that make America the most prosperous and productive country on Earth, and with the highest standard of living and the highest standard of environmental protection.

Our tax bill is moving along in Congress, and I believe it's doing very well. I think a lot of people will be very pleasantly surprised. The Republicans are working very, very hard. We'd love to have support from the Democrats, but we may have to go it alone. But it's going very well.

The Paris Agreement handicaps the United States economy in order to win praise from the very foreign capitals and global activists that have long sought to gain wealth at our country's expense. They don't put America first. I do, and I always will. (Applause.)

The same nations asking us to stay in the agreement are the countries that have collectively cost America trillions of dollars through tough trade practices and, in many cases, lax contributions to our critical military alliance. You see what's happening. It's pretty obvious to those that want to keep an open mind.

At what point does America get demeaned? At what point do they start laughing at us as a country? We want fair treatment for its citizens, and we want fair treatment for our taxpayers. We don't want other leaders and other countries laughing at us anymore. And they won't be. They won't be.

I was elected to represent the citizens of Pittsburgh, not Paris. (Applause.) I promised I would exit or renegotiate any deal which fails to serve America's interests. Many trade deals will soon be under renegotiation. Very rarely do we have a deal that works for this country, but they'll soon be under renegotiation. The process has begun from day one. But now we're down to business.

Beyond the severe energy restrictions inflicted by the Paris Accord, it includes yet another scheme to redistribute wealth out of the United States through the so-called Green Climate Fund—nice name—which calls for developed countries to send $100 billion to developing countries all on top of America's existing and massive foreign aid payments. So we're going to be paying billions and billions and billions of dollars, and we're already way ahead of anybody else. Many of the other countries haven't spent anything, and many of them will never pay one dime.

The Green Fund would likely obligate the United States to commit potentially tens of billions of dollars of which the United States has already handed over $1 billion—nobody else is even close; most of them haven't even paid anything—including funds raided out of America's budget for the war against terrorism. That's where they came. Believe me, they didn't come from me. They came just before I came into office. Not good. And not good the way they took the money.

In 2015, the United Nation's departing top climate officials reportedly described the $100 billion per year as "peanuts," and stated that "the $100 billion is the tail that wags the dog." In 2015, the Green Climate Fund's executive director reportedly stated that estimated funding needed would increase to $450 billion per year after 2020. And nobody even knows where the money is going to. Nobody has been able to say, where is it going to?

Of course, the world's top polluters have no affirmative obligations under the Green Fund, which we terminated. America is $20 trillion in debt. Cash-strapped cities cannot hire enough police officers or fix vital infrastructure. Millions of our citizens are out of work. And yet, under the Paris Accord, billions of dollars that ought to be invested right here in America will be sent to the very countries that have taken our factories and our jobs away from us. So think of that.

There are serious legal and constitutional issues as well. Foreign leaders in Europe, Asia, and across the world should not have more to say with respect to the U.S. economy than our own citizens and their elected representatives. Thus, our withdrawal from the agreement represents a reassertion of America's sovereignty. (Applause.) Our Constitution is unique among all the nations of the world, and it is my highest obligation and greatest honor to protect it. And I will.

Staying in the agreement could also pose serious obstacles for the United States as we begin the process of unlocking the restrictions on America's abundant energy reserves, which we have started very strongly. It would once have been unthinkable that an international agreement could prevent the United States from conducting its own domestic economic affairs, but this is the new reality we face if we do not leave the agreement or if we do not negotiate a far better deal.

The risks grow as historically these agreements only tend to become more and more ambitious over time. In other words, the Paris framework is a starting point—as bad as it is—not an end point. And exiting the agreement protects the United States from future intrusions on the United States' sovereignty and massive future legal liability. Believe me, we have massive legal liability if we stay in.

As President, I have one obligation, and that obligation is to the American people. The Paris Accord would undermine our economy, hamstring our workers, weaken our sovereignty, impose unacceptable legal risks, and put us at a permanent disadvantage to the other countries of the world. It is time to exit the Paris Accord—(applause)—and time to pursue a new deal that protects the environment, our companies, our citizens, and our country.

It is time to put Youngstown, Ohio, Detroit, Michigan, and Pittsburgh, Pennsylvania—along with many, many other locations within our great country—before Paris, France. It is time to make America great again. (Applause.) Thank you. Thank you. Thank you very much.

2. School Board Meeting

Assume that your school board held its monthly meeting at 7:30 p.m. yesterday. Write a news story that summarizes the comments and decisions made at this meeting. Correct all errors.

The school board opened its meeting by honoring seven retiring teachers: Shirley Dawsun, Carmen Foucault, Nina Paynich, Kenneth Satava, Nancy Lee Scott, Lonnie McEwen, and Harley Sawyer. Paynich worked as a teacher 44 years, longer than any of the others. Each teacher was given a framed "Certificate of Appreciation" and a good round of applause.

The school board then turned to the budget for next year. The budget totals $618.7 million, up 5 percent from this year. It includes $9.3 million for a new elementary school to be built on West Madison Ave. It will be completed and opened in two years. The budget also includes a 4.5 percent raise for teachers and a 6 percent raise for administrators. Also, the salary of the superintendent of schools was raised by $10,000, to $137,000 a year. The vote was unanimous: 9-0.

The school board then discussed the topic of remedial summer classes. Board member Umberto Vacante proposed eliminating them to save an estimated $2.1 million. "They're just too expensive, especially when you consider we serve only about 900 students each summer. A lot of them are students who flunked their regular classes. Often, if they attend the summer classes, they don't have to repeat a grade. If we're going to spend that kind of money, I think we should use it to help and reward our most talented students. They're the ones we ignore. We could offer special programs for them." Supt. Greg Hubbard responded, "Some of these summer students have learning disabilities and emotional problems, and they really need the help. This would hurt them terribly. Without it, they might never graduate." The board then voted 7-2 to keep the classes one more year, but to ask its staff for a study of the matter.

During a one-hour hearing that followed, about 100 people, many loud and angry, debated the issue of creationism vs. evolution. "We've seen your biology books," said parent Claire Sawyer. "I don't want my children using them. They never mention the theory of creationism." Another parent, Harley Euon of 410 East Third Street, responded: "Evolution isn't a theory. Its proven fact. Creationism is a religious idea, not even a scientific theory. People here are trying to force schools to teach our children their religion." A third parent, Roy E. Cross of 101 Charow Lane, agreed, adding: "People can teach creationism in their homes and churches. Its not the schools job." After listening to the debate, the board voted 6-3 to continue using the present textbooks, but to encourage parents to discuss the matter with their children and to provide in their individual homes the religious training they deem most appropriate for their families.

Finally, last on its agenda, the board unanimously adopted a resolution praising the school systems ADDITIONS: adult volunteers who contribute their spare time to help and assist their neighborhood schools. Last year, Supt. Greg Hubbard reported, there was a total of 897 ADDITIONS, and they put in a total of 38,288 hours of volunteer time.

3. City Council Meeting

Assume that your city council held a meeting at 8 p.m. yesterday. Write a news story that summarizes the comments and decisions made at this meeting. Correct all errors.

BACKGROUND

For 10 years, the First United Methodist Church at 680 Garland Avenue has provided a shelter for the homeless, allowing them to sleep in the basement of its fellowship hall every night and feeding them both breakfast and dinner. The church can house 180 people each night and relies on a staff of more than 200 volunteers. In recent years, they've been overwhelmed, and the church, by itself, is unable to continue to afford to shoulder the entire burden. It has asked for help: for donations and for more room, especially in winter, for the homeless to sleep. Civic leaders have formed the Coalition for the Homeless, Inc., a nonprofit organization, and hope to build a new shelter. The coalition has asked the city to donate a site, valued at $500,000. Coalition leaders said they will then raise the $1.5 million needed to construct the shelter. The coalition leaders say they will also operate the shelter, relying on volunteers; a small, full-time professional staff; and donations from concerned citizens.

FIRST SPEAKER

Ida Levine, president of the Coalition for the Homeless, Inc.:
"As you, uh, know, what we're trying to do here is raise $1.5 million to build the shelter. We're approaching everyone that might be able to help and, so far, have collected about $200,000 and have pledges of another $318,000, and thats just the beginning, in two months. So we're certain that if you provide the land, we'll be able to, uh, come up with all the money for this thing. The site we have in mind is the old fire station on

Garland Avenue. The building is so old that its worthless, and we'd tear it down, but its an ideal location for our purposes."

SECOND SPEAKER

Lt. Luis Rafelson:
"I'm here officially, representing the police department, to say that we're all for this. It costs the taxpayers about $350,000 a year to arrest homeless people for violating city ordinances like trespassing on private property and sleeping at night in parks and such. During the average month last year we arrested 300 homeless people, sometimes more. It takes about 2 hours to arrest a person and do all the booking and paperwork, while taking five minutes to transport them to a shelter. So you're wasting police time, time we could be spending on more important things. So if the city spends $500,000 on this deal, it'll save that much in a year, maybe more."

THIRD SPEAKER

Banker Irvin Porej:
"The people who stay in shelters are just like you and me. The difference is that we have a place to go. They're good people for the most part, just down on their luck. This would provide a temporary shelter for them, help them get back on their feet. Until now, we've had churches doing this, and the Salvation Army has a shelter, too, but we should put an end to the church shelters. Its not fair to them because the churches are burdened by a problem that everyone should be helping with, and the problem is getting too big for them to handle."

FOURTH SPEAKER

Council member Sandra Bandolf:
"We have to address this problem. It's not going to go away. And with this solution, it really won't cost the city anything. No one's asking us for money or anything, only for a piece of land that's been lying unused for years."

FIFTH SPEAKER

Council member William Belmonte:
"I suppose I'm going to be the only one who votes against this. Why should taxpayers suddenly start paying for this, people who work hard for their money and are struggling these days to support their families? And what happens if the coalition doesn't raise all the money it needs for the shelter, what happens then? What happens if they breach the agreement? Then we'll be left holding the bag, expected to pay for this damn thing and to support it for years. That'll add a whole new bureaucracy to the city, and where'll the money come from then?"

SIXTH SPEAKER

Trina Guzman, president of the Downtown Merchants' Assn.:
"The members of my association are strongly opposed to this. We agree that the city needs a shelter, that we have an obligation to help the people who are really homeless and needy, but not on Garland Avenue. That's just a block from downtown, and we've been having trouble with these people for years. Some of them need help, have all sorts of problems like alcoholism and mental illness that no one here's talking about. Remember too that these people aren't allowed to stay in the shelters during the day. Theoretically, they're supposed to go out and work, or at least look for work. What some of them do is hang around Main Street, panhandling and annoying people and using our parking lots and alleys for toilets. We've got customers who tell us they won't come downtown any more because they're afraid of being approached and asked for money and being mugged or something. Let's feed these people and help them, but put them out somewhere where they can't hurt anyone."

OUTCOME

The council voted 6-1 to donate the land. Belmonte cast the single vote against the proposal.

BRIGHTS, FOLLOW-UPS, ROUNDUPS, SIDEBARS AND OBITUARIES

Tell new reporters to write a speech or a meeting story and they will immediately understand what is required. However, those who have never worked in a newsroom might scratch their heads when asked to write a bright, follow-up, roundup, sidebar or obituary. Yet all are common assignments for beginning reporters.

16.1 Brights

Brights are short, humorous stories that often have surprise endings. Some are written in the inverted-pyramid style: After a summary lead, the story reports the remaining details in descending order of importance. Others have unexpected or bizarre twists, and reporters might try to surprise the audience by withholding them until the story's final paragraphs. Brights that have surprise endings are called "suspended-interest stories." These stories often begin with facts likely to interest people and end with facts that are the most newsworthy or put the rest of the story in a new and surprising light.

Here are two versions of the same story. The first uses a summary lead that puts the unusual facts of the story at the beginning. The second also uses a summary lead, but it withholds the most unusual facts until the end, giving the story an unusual and amusing twist.

Version 1	Version 2
Two armed men robbed the owner of a local pizzeria at gun point Tuesday night and took off with a bag full of dough—pizza dough, Police Chief Barry Kopperud said Wednesday morning.	Police arrested two men shortly before midnight Tuesday on suspicion of robbing the manager of a local pizza parlor at gun point.
Two men have been arrested in connection with the crime: Frederick C. Taylor, 25, of 4828 N. Vine St. and Grady Smith, 22, of 8213 Peach St.	The two in custody are Frederick C. Taylor, 25, of 4828 N. Vine St. and Grady Smith, 22, of 8213 Peach St.
	Police Chief Barry Kopperud told reporters Wednesday morning that two masked men confronted Y.Y. Cho,

The robbers, both of whom wore masks, confronted Y.Y. Cho, the manager of Giovanni's Pizza Parlor on North Wisconsin Avenue, as he was leaving the store, shortly after 11:30 p.m.

One of the robbers pointed a gun at Cho and demanded that he give them the bag he was carrying. Cho did so, and the robbers fled, Kopperud told reporters at his daily briefing. Cho told police he thought the robbers must have believed the bag contained the night's receipts, but all it held was five pounds of pizza dough he was taking to the Giovanni's parlor on Hazel Street.

Kopperud said Cho immediately called police and gave a description of the car the robbers used to escape. The car was spotted by Larry Chevez, a police detective who was on patrol in the vicinity, about 11:45 p.m. Chevez saw a bag in the back seat of the car, which turned out to contain pizza dough.

"If Mr. Cho had not had the presence of mind to call the police immediately and to get a description of the car, the robbers might not have been caught," Kopperud said.

Taylor and Smith were formally charged with armed robbery at an arraignment Wednesday afternoon.

the manager of Giovanni's Pizza Parlor on North Wisconsin Avenue, a little before 11:30 p.m. They demanded that Cho give them the bag he was carrying. He did so and the pair of robbers fled.

Cho immediately called the police department, Kopperud said, and gave a description of the car the robbers were using.

"If Mr. Cho had not had the presence of mind to call the police immediately and to get a description of the car, the robbers might not have been caught," Kopperud said.

The description of the vehicle was relayed to officers on patrol. Detective Larry Chevez saw a vehicle matching Cho's description and pulled it over at 11:45. Chevez saw a bag in the back seat of the car similar to the bag that had been taken from Cho.

When police opened the bag, it was found to contain exactly what Cho said had been stolen from him: five pounds of pizza dough. Cho had been taking the dough to the Giovanni's Pizza Parlor on Hazel Street. He told police the robbers must have thought the bag contained the evening's receipts.

Taylor and Smith were formally charged with armed robbery at an arraignment Wednesday afternoon.

Editors and news directors search for unusual and often humorous stories and display the best ones prominently in their newspapers and news broadcasts. Brights entertain people, arouse their emotions and provide relief from the seriousness of the world's problems. The Associated Press, as part of its newswire service, provides a category of news stories called "AP Oddities." When a man in a small town in Japan was accidently wired more than $360,000 in COVID-19 relief funds earmarked for low-income households, he refused to return the money in his bank account. Instead, he gambled the money away over 10 days on online gambling sites. Media organizations around the world picked up the story because of its unusualness.

When media in Los Angeles carried a story about a man who ran out on his blind dates, leaving them with the restaurant bills, it was picked up around the country. Thefts are common, and no one wants to be the victim of a crime, but the unusual nature of this incident—and the relatively minor harm it caused—made the story precisely the kind that editors and producers like to cover.

An American soldier pets Paris, a military working dog, during a security patrol in Farah province, Afghanistan. The relationship between people and animals is a common subject for brights.

The "serial dine-and-dasher" story illustrates another aspect of brights: Reporters must be careful not to make fun of the ill fortune others experience. One account quoted a victim who said the thief left her with a $163 bill at a pricey steakhouse, where he ordered "a ton of food." Another journalist noted that the alleged perpetrator had a minor criminal record. The story might have its lighter side, but reporters knew it had to be told tastefully and with respect for the victims' feelings.

Animals are a favorite topic for brights. Since the 1940s, the presentation of a National Thanksgiving Turkey to the U.S. president has been part of the holiday celebration. And every year, news organizations carry brief humorous stories about the turkeys, which are pardoned from winding up as dinner the next day. Other animal stories can bring a tear to a person's eye and generate a big reaction. Steve Hartman of CBS News told the story of Dexter, a dog who walks like a human. Dexter, a Brittany Spaniel belonging to Kentee Pasek, lost his right front leg and injured his left in an accident when he was a puppy. For a time, he used a wheelchair to get around, but one day he managed to climb the front steps of his owner's home in Ouray, Colorado, on his hind legs. Now, Ouray residents often see Pasek on the town streets accompanied by Dexter. The dog has built a social media following, not just because of his unusual skill but because he has inspired humans to overcome the obstacles they face, Hartman reported.

Some brights draw their humor from the stupid things even smart people might do. One example is the arrest of an 18-year-old for drunken driving. New York City police officers handcuffed him and put him in their squad car; he climbed into the front seat and took the vehicle on a 13-mile joyride.

16.2 Follow-Ups

Major news events rarely begin and end in a single day—reporters will often say that such stories have "legs," running each day as new developments occur. News organizations prepare a fresh article or package each time a new development arises. These stories are known as follow-ups, or "second-day" or "developing" stories. Coverage of trials, legislative sessions, political campaigns or flights to the moon might appear in the media every day for weeks. Major events, like the devastating fires that have swept California and the Southwest U.S. in recent years or the investigations into the Jan. 6, 2021, attack on the U.S. Capitol that attempted to interrupt the transfer of power from former President Donald Trump to President-elect Joe Biden, remain top news stories for weeks or months. Follow-up stories for such events might describe efforts to rescue or treat victims, government actions to help individuals and businesses, disruptions to the national or local economy and increased security or regulation to prevent similar events in the future. Although the follow-up is tied to a past event, its lead always emphasizes the latest developments. Follow-ups might summarize previous events, but that information is presented as concisely as possible and placed later in the story.

Ukraine became a part of the Soviet Union in 1922 when Soviet troops took control of the region. After the collapse of the Soviet Union, Ukraine declared its independence. In February 2022, Russian armed forces invaded Ukraine. The fact that Russia had invaded a neighboring sovereign nation without justification became a major news story. Russian propaganda claimed that the invasion was necessary to rid the country of the "Nazi" government that had been elected and the prospect that Ukraine would be admitted to NATO as other former Soviet republics had been.

Coverage of the build-up to war began weeks before the actual invasion as American news organizations began to report on U.S. government sources who were warning about Russian President Vladimir Putin's plans to take over the country. When the invasion began, news organizations had resources in Ukraine ready to report on the first major conflict in Europe since World War II. For weeks after the invasion began, The New York Times and other media carried multiple stories daily about the conflict, how the nations of the world were responding, the effects on the civilian population and alleged war crimes, the effects on the American and global economies, the impact on the international order and how the conflict might be resolved. Each story emphasized the day's newest and most important developments, and, because the conflict was so significant, new developments abounded:

February 24
SLOVYANSK, Ukraine — The Russian military plunged into Ukraine by land, sea and air on Thursday, killing more than 100 Ukrainian soldiers and civilians, and ominously touching off a pitched battle at the highly radioactive area around the Chernobyl nuclear reactor that melted down in 1986.

February 25
MEDYKA, Poland — Terrified by Russian bombs and missiles landing near their towns and villages, and rumors that Russian tanks would soon arrive, thousands of Ukrainians crossed into eastern Poland on Friday as a mass exodus from Ukraine gathered pace.

March 5
LONDON — The day after Russian tanks and troops poured across the Ukrainian border on Feb. 24, NATO leaders received a deeply frightening message. The alliance's secretary general, Jens Stoltenberg, opened an emergency video summit by warning that President Vladimir V. Putin had "shattered peace in Europe" and that from now on, he would openly contest the continent's security order.

March 16
WASHINGTON — President Biden said on Wednesday that the United States would send $800 million in additional military assistance to

This photo by Maksim Levin for Reuters shows Ukrainian soldiers next to a destroyed armored vehicle, which they said belonged to Russian forces, near Kharkiv, in eastern Ukraine. War photos in American media often show the aftermath of battles but rarely show bodies of soldiers.

Ukraine, shortly after the country's president, Volodymyr Zelensky, delivered an impassioned virtual address to Congress in which he appealed for more help in staving off Russia's invasion.

March 25

WASHINGTON — Russian mercenaries with combat experience in Syria and Libya are gearing up to assume an increasingly active role in a phase of the war in Ukraine that Moscow now says is its top priority: fighting in the country's east.

April 6

WASHINGTON — The United States and its allies, seeking to punish Russia for the killings of Ukrainian civilians, moved on Wednesday to impose full sanctions against Russia's largest financial institutions and to block access to U.S.-held financial assets for family members and close associates of President Vladimir V. Putin of Russia.

The Russian invasion of Ukraine and its effect on the U.S., European and global economies would continue well beyond when the conflict ended as news organizations explored the ramifications of the war on global peace and security. Even with stories of less scope and significance than a major conflict in Europe, each new event prompts a follow-up, and each follow-up recapitulates earlier stories.

Sometimes viewers and readers grow weary of the repetition and believe the news media do it only to sensationalize stories. People who were unhappy with the amount of coverage given to the defamation trials of Johnny Depp and Amber Heard often expressed such views. Yet news organizations cover trials, wars and disasters so intensely because large numbers of readers, viewers and listeners are interested.

Follow-ups have become more common as news organizations devote resources to making sure important stories are followed to their conclusions. Media critics sometimes complain that journalists, like firefighters, race from one major story to the next, devoting most of their attention to momentary crises. These critics claim that, as one crisis subsides, reporters move on to a newer one. The older crisis often disappears from the news before all the questions have been answered. To address this complaint, news organizations regularly return to important stories and report on what has happened since they dropped out of the headlines.

16.3 Roundups

To save space or time, news organizations summarize several different but related events in roundup stories. For instance, instead of publishing separate stories about each traffic death that occurs in a given weekend, newspapers and broadcast stations often summarize several fatal crashes in a single story. News organizations often report all the weekend crimes, fires, drownings, graduation ceremonies or football games in roundup stories.

Another type of roundup deals with a single event but incorporates facts from several sources. Reporters might interview half a dozen people to obtain more information about a single topic, to verify the accuracy of facts they have obtained elsewhere or to obtain new perspectives. For example, if a city's mayor resigns unexpectedly, reporters might ask her why she resigned, what she plans to do after she leaves office, what she considers her major accomplishments and what problems will confront her successor. They might then ask other city officials to comment on the mayor's performance and resignation, ask the city clerk how the next mayor will be selected, and interview leading contenders for the job. All this information could be included in a single roundup story.

The lead for a roundup emphasizes the most important or unique developments and ties all the facts together by stressing their common denominator, as in the following example from the Associated Press reporting on efforts by a city in Colorado to pass gun laws:

> BOULDER, Colo. (AP) — Boulder passed a package of gun control laws on Tuesday, including a ban on the sale and possession of assault weapons similar to one that was overturned shortly before 10 people were killed in a shooting at a supermarket.

The story included details on the legal ruling that overturned the original ban and how state lawmakers passed legislation allowing cities in Colorado to pass ordinances to control guns in their jurisdictions. The story then provided details on what the new package of gun control laws specifically included.

After the lead, roundups usually organize facts and quotations by topic, starting with the most newsworthy accident, crime, fire or drowning and moving on to the second, third and fourth most important. Some beginning reporters make the mistake of organizing their material by source. For example, they might start a crime roundup with all the information they got from the police chief and then all the information they got from the prosecuting attorney. Stories organized in this way are disjointed and repetitious. Each source is likely to mention the same events, and comments about a particular event will be scattered throughout the story.

16.4 Sidebars

Sidebars are separate news stories that describe developments related to a major event. Sometimes news organizations use sidebars to break long, complicated stories into shorter, more easily understood ones. They also use sidebars to report information of secondary importance to the main story. Sidebars may give readers additional information from a different source or perspective, provide background on the main topic or further explain its importance or offer more descriptive details of a scene. Sidebars also can be used to highlight the human side of a news story. A story about a fire at a housing complex might focus on the loss of life, amount of damage and the difficulty firefighters may have had in putting out the blaze, but a sidebar would focus on some of the people and the effect that losing their homes and belongings had on them.

Several news podcasts present brief coverage of the most important events of the day. For example, NPR News Now produces five-minute episodes; the podcast is updated hourly and highlights breaking news.

In addition to the main story about parents whose children were victims of the shooting at an elementary school in Uvalde, Texas, testifying before Congress, The San Antonio Express-News of June 9, 2022, ran a front-page sidebar on the funeral for one of the children who died in the shooting.

A month after a deadly shooting at a grocery store in a predominately Black neighborhood in Buffalo, New York, area residents gathered outside the store in one of dozens of March for Our Lives events held nationwide. The Buffalo News covered the local march, interviewing several participants and summarizing details of the previous month's shooting. The News published a sidebar to the story that highlighted the remarks of three Buffalo residents—including two men whose mother was killed in the grocery store shooting—who spoke at the Washington, D.C., March for Our Lives the same day.

The day after strong storms that spawned small tornadoes hit the Kansas City metropolitan area, The Kansas City Star published a story about the cleanup efforts, talking with a number of residents who lost power or whose homes were damaged about their experiences during the storms. A sidebar provided readers with more information on the storms themselves, much of it from the National Weather Service, and discussed why many residents had little warning of the storms' arrival.

News organizations often use sidebars to report on local angles to national stories. When a draft U.S. Supreme Court opinion in a Mississippi case—which would overturn previous rulings that legalized abortion in all 50 states—was leaked, stories about the opinion often were accompanied by sidebars that highlighted local impacts of such a decision. The Mercury News of San Jose was one of many California news organizations that published stories about state leaders' announcing legislation aimed at incorporating abortion rights into California's constitution. Like other news organizations in Missouri, the St. Louis Post-Dispatch wrote a story about that state's "trigger law," passed in 2019, that provides multiple ways for state officials to quickly implement an abortion ban if the Supreme Court no longer recognized abortion as a constitutional right.

Generally briefer than the main story it supplements, a sidebar usually is published adjacent to the main story in a newspaper or immediately follows it on a newscast. If a sidebar runs on a different page or later in the newscast, the editor or producer will tell the audience where or when it will appear. Because some people may read or view only the sidebar and not the main story, the sidebar usually provides a brief summary of the main topic, even when they appear together. On news organizations' websites, sidebars may be linked to the main story either with a separate link at the end of the main story or an embedded hyperlink in the main story itself.

16.5 Obituaries

Obituaries—descriptions of people's lives and notices of their deaths—traditionally have been among the most popular features of newspapers. Relatives scrutinize obituaries, townspeople inspect them and others who have moved away peruse them on their hometown paper's website.

Newspapers used to have reporters write an obituary for every local resident who died. They also carried obituaries for out-of-town celebrities and prominent political figures. Some smaller news organizations may still follow this practice, but it is largely a thing of the past at medium to large ones. Now it is more common that the funeral home or the family writes the obituary, in which case the latter pays for its publication. If a person is unusually famous, newspapers will publish a feature obituary written by a staff reporter and publish it at no charge. Charging for obits gives everyone the opportunity to have an obit in the newspaper. In addition, when family members write obits, the printed record is precisely as they want. A criticism of paid obituaries, however, is that newspapers lose their ability to check them for accuracy and completeness.

Many news outlets reported on this honest obituary—the posting on the funeral home's website went viral and crashed the site.

In a recent front-page feature, headlined "Haze the Dead! More Obit Writers Tell It Like It Was—Warts and All," The Wall Street Journal reported that family members increasingly offer "frank, humorous assessments of the departed." Citing several examples, the piece noted: "Most obituaries remain more solemn, but funeral directors have noted an increase in those that are a bit playful—tributes acknowledging that people tend to be mixed bags and that few are candidates for sainthood. Obituaries published by U.S. newspapers or websites over the past few years describe deceased relatives as 'cantankerous,' 'grouchy,' 'demanding old fart,' 'sore loser' and 'pain in the butt.'"

Obituary databases have become a popular part of online newspapers. Some publications, such as the Richmond (Virginia) Times-Dispatch, offer death notices, archives, a search engine and notices by email. Visitors can also write in a "guest book" for friends and family.

Newspapers publish three types of death reports: death or funeral notices, biographical obituaries and feature obituaries. Death or funeral notices are prepared by the funeral home and placed in the newspaper for a fee. In a short paragraph, they include only basic information—name, age, city of residence, date of death and funeral home. Some might include cause of death, the deceased's profession and time and place of the funeral.

Biographical obituaries include more details about the person, such as lists of accomplishments and survivors. The central point of the biographical obituary is the life of the deceased and what made it unusual or interesting. Well-written obituaries capture people's personalities and convey their unique attributes and experiences. Increasingly, these reports are written by either family members or funeral directors and, like death notices, run in newspapers for a fee. Regardless of who writes them, biographical obituaries appear on a page set aside for this type of notice.

Feature obituaries are full stories on the news pages and cover noteworthy individuals whose names are familiar to most readers. These stories cover events in the person's life and the circumstances surrounding his or her death. The feature obituary is much like the biographical obituary but is usually longer and more detailed.

16.5.1 Writing the Biographical Obituary

In some respects, a biographical obituary resembles a feature profile—it describes a person's life and work. Thus, reporters write obituaries as they would news stories about living people. Although journalists might be reluctant to question grieving relatives and friends, they soon discover most family members are willing to talk about the deceased.

A biographical obituary usually contains the following information, in the same approximate order:

1. Identification (full name, age, address).
2. Unique, outstanding or major attribute.
3. Time and place of death.
4. Cause or circumstance of death.
5. Major accomplishments.
6. Chronology of early life (place and date of birth, moves, education).
7. Place and date of marriage.
8. Occupation and employment history.
9. Honors, awards and offices held.
10. Additional interests and accomplishments.
11. Memberships in churches, clubs and other civic groups.
12. Military service.
13. Surviving relatives (spouse, children, grandchildren, etc.).
14. Religious services (location, officiating clergy, pallbearers).
15. Other burial and funeral arrangements.

Funeral directors give newspapers much of this information. Some have the families fill out forms provided by the newspapers and immediately deliver the completed forms to the papers. Just before their daily deadlines, reporters may call the funeral homes to be certain they have not missed any obituaries. Journalists gather more facts about people who have died by going to their newspaper's library and reading previous stories published about them or by calling family, friends and business associates. Most people cooperate with reporters; they accept the requests for information as part of the routine that occurs at the time of death. Also, people want their friends' and relatives' obituaries to be accurate, thorough and well written.

After journalists have gathered the details they need, they begin the obituary by establishing the central point: the unique, most important or most interesting aspect of the person's life or some outstanding fact about that person, such as a major accomplishment. The lead also includes the person's name and identification.

In the following examples, the original leads contain dull, routine facts: the people's ages, addresses and causes of death. These facts make dull leads. The revisions contain more specific and interesting facts about the people who died and their accomplishments. Other good leads might describe a person's goals, hobbies, philosophy or personality.

> Arizona D. Markham of North 13th Street died when a car hit her while she was jogging two miles from her home Saturday. She was 42.

> **Revised:** Arizona D. Markham, who never missed a trip in 23 years to gamble at the Kentucky Derby, died Saturday at the age of 42.

> Michael J. Jacobs, 68, of Eastwood, died Wednesday at his home surrounded by family and friends.

> **Revised:** Michael J. Jacobs, an award-winning fisherman and avid sportsman who was 68 years old, died Wednesday.

An obituary's second and third paragraphs should immediately develop the central point stated in the lead. For example, if the lead reports the deceased was an electrician who also won ballroom dancing contests, these paragraphs should describe that person's work and hobby.

Inexperienced journalists mistakenly shift too quickly to chronological order and, in their second paragraph, report the earliest and least interesting details of the person's life: dates of birth, graduation from high school or marriage. Instead, if time and space are available, reporters should include anecdotes about the person's life and recollections of friends and relatives, as well as other biographical highlights.

Some newspapers try to report the cause of every death because it is often newsworthy information. Others do not because that information is difficult to obtain. Family members and funeral directors might be reluctant to announce a cause of death. Some causes, such as suicide or drug overdose, have social stigmas attached to them. In such cases, news organizations may report the death, including the cause, in a short story separate from the obituary, carefully attributing the cause of death to some authority, usually the coroner.

After describing the deceased person's life, the obituary lists survivors. Usually, the list includes only the immediate family, beginning with the name of

Midwest Medical Examiner's Office
14341 Rhinestone Street NW, Ramsey, MN 55303
Phone: 763-323-6400 • Fax: 763-323-6479

A. Quinn Strobl M.D. Chief Medical Examiner

Anne Bracey M.D. • Michael Madsen M.D.

Press Release

As of June 2, 2016, the Midwest Medical Examiner's Office has completed its death investigation of Prince Rogers Nelson. The Midwest Medical Examiner's Office hereby releases all public data relating to this death investigation as specifically defined in Minnesota Statute, Section 13.83, subd. 2. This public data includes the manner and cause of death. Under Minnesota law, all other medical examiner data is considered private or nonpublic data. The Medical Examiner's Office is unable to make any further comments about its death investigation of Prince Nelson.

The Carver County Sheriff's Office continues its investigation.

MIDWEST MEDICAL EXAMINER'S OFFICE
14341 Rhinestone St NW, Ramsey, MN 55303

Release of Public Data MN Statute 13.83 Subd 2

Deceased: Prince Rogers Nelson   DOB: 06/07/1958   DOD: 04/21/2016

Address: 7801 Audubon Road   Age: 57   Sex: Male

City: Chanhassen   State: MN   Zip: 55317   Name of spouse: NA

Marital status: ☐ Never married ☒ Divorced ☐ Widowed ☐ Married ☐ Separated

Occupation: Artist   Business: Music

Citizenship: U.S.A.   Race: Black/African American   Served in armed forces of United States: No

Decedent's place of birth: Minneapolis, MN

Father's name: John L. Nelson   Birth name: —   Birthplace: unk

Mother's name: Mattie D. Nelson   Birth name: Shaw   Birthplace: unk

Type of disposition: Cremation   Date of burial: unk

Burial place name & location: unk

Funeral home: Cremation Society of Minnesota   Funeral director: Kevin J. Waterston

Place of death: Residence   Hospital: na

Date of injury: unknown   Place of injury: Residence

Death at work? No   Address of injury: Residence

How injury occurred: The decedent self-administered fentanyl

Height: 63 inches   Weight: 112   Hair color: Black   Eye color: Brown   Complexion: Light   Build: Petite

Identifying marks: na

Scars & amputations: Scar, left hip; scar, right lower leg

Description of decedent's clothing: black cap, black shirt, grey undershirt, black pants, black boxer briefs, black socks

Autopsy performed: Yes

MANNER: ☐ Natural ☒ Accident ☐ Homicide ☐ Suicide ☐ Undetermined

Cause: 1: Fentanyl toxicity
2: na
3: na
4: na

Other significant conditions: na

Signed by Medical Examiner's Office: _____

‡ A. Quinn Strobl, MD, Medical Examiner _____ Anne H. Bracey, MD, Assistant ME _____ Michael S. Madsen, MD, Assistant ME

Documents such as this press release regarding Prince's death can provide information for an obituary.

Stu Rasmussen, 73, First Openly
Transgender Mayor in America, Dies

The mayor, who served two terms in Silverton, Ore., defied many
conventions, gender being just one of them.

Stu Rasmussen in 2009. In addition to holding several elected offices, he was a Mr. Fix-It for neighbors and ran the town's only first-run
movie theater. Lisa Kereszi

 By Clay Risen

Dec. 3, 2021

Stu Rasmussen, who in 2008 became what is believed to be the first
openly transgender mayor in America, died on Nov. 17 at his home
in Silverton, Ore., where he had served in various elected offices
for the better part of 30 years. Mr. Rasmussen, who identified as a
woman but typically used masculine pronouns, was 73.

His wife, Victoria Sage, said the cause was prostate cancer.

The feature obituary focuses on Rasmussen's life in politics and his
groundbreaking transition while living in a small town. The obit includes quotes from townspeople who knew him as well as local city
officials who served with him. The story also includes highlights of his
home life, educational background and political philosophy.

the person's spouse and followed by the names
of parents, brothers and sisters, and children.
Other survivors—more distant relatives and
nonrelatives—may be included if they played an
important role in the person's life.

Normally, the times and places for the religious services and burial appear near the end
of an obituary. The information should be as
specific as possible so that mourners will know
when they can call on the person's family, and
when and where they can attend the funeral and
burial.

16.5.2 Writing the Feature Obituary

Obituaries for national or local celebrities emphasize different types of information from
that in obituaries for other people. Newspapers
almost always report the cause of death when
a celebrity dies. Politicians, athletes and enter-
tainers have lived their lives before the public,
and the public usually wants to know what
caused their death. When the celebrity's family
tries to withhold this detail—for instance, when
the celebrity dies of a drug overdose—reporters
will work to uncover it.

Because few readers are likely to know a
national celebrity personally or to attend the
funeral and burial, the obituary might not mention those services. For local celebrities, such information might be omitted if the family wants
only close friends and relatives at the service.
Instead, the obituary will emphasize the celebrity's personality and accomplishments.
Sometimes, journalists repeat what the person had said on earlier occasions to
show his or her character. Sometimes the person's personality will come through
in quotes from family and friends.

Here are the first two paragraphs from The New York Times' obituary for
Micki Grant, a groundbreaking Broadway composer:

> Micki Grant, who in the early 1970s became the first woman to write
> the book, music and lyrics of a Broadway musical, "Don't Bother Me,
> I Can't Cope," a soulful, spirited exploration of Black life, died on
> Saturday in Manhattan. She was 92.
>
> Her death, at Mount Sinai Morningside Hospital, was announced by
> Joan Allen, a family spokeswoman.

While listing the accomplishments of her career as an actress, composer, playwright and musician, the feature obituary explored her creative activities that

began at the age of 14 when she first began writing music and years later her winning a Grammy for best musical theater album. The obituary also discussed the influence she had on Black musical theater and her roles as a Black actress on daytime television in the 1960s and early 1970s when few minority actors were present in many daytime dramas.

Obituaries for celebrities report both the good and the bad about the person's life. Obituaries for Washington Post publisher Katharine Meyer Graham reported on the obstacles she overcame in her personal life as she built one of the world's most important media companies. Newsweek said, "Katharine Meyer grew up in a kind of chilly grandeur. She was surrounded by governesses and private tutors, but once had to make an appointment to see her mother. Agnes Meyer was a self-dramatist who fed her own ego by trampling on her daughter's." The Orlando Sentinel reported that her father invited her husband, Philip, to become The Post's publisher at 31 and later gave him the newspaper. "Eugene Meyer also arranged for him to hold more stock in the company than his daughter because, he explained to her, 'no man should be in the position of working for his wife.'" U.S. News & World Report reported, "Manic-depressive illness turned Phil into an erratic, abusive husband who played upon his wife's insecurities. Taunting her before friends with the nickname 'Porky,' he briefly abandoned her for another woman."

The Reporter's Guide to Writing Brights, Follow-Ups, Roundups, Sidebars and Obituaries

BRIGHTS

1. Choose either an inverted-pyramid style or a suspended-interest style for the story.

2. If you use a suspended-interest approach, write a lead that will intrigue readers without revealing the story's bizarre or amusing twist.

FOLLOW-UPS

1. Write a follow-up each time something newsworthy develops in a continuing story.

2. Stress the new developments in the lead and body of the story.

3. Summarize the important background and earlier developments.

ROUNDUPS

1. Emphasize the most important or unique incident or development in the lead.

2. Explain in the lead what is common to all the incidents reported in the roundup.

3. Organize facts and quotations by topic, not by source.

SIDEBARS

1. Focus the lead on background, color, mood or some other aspect of the story not emphasized in the lead to the main story.

2. Summarize the news event described in the main story.

OBITUARIES

1. Gather basic information about the individual's life: name, age, occupation, area of residence, activities (hobbies and organizational memberships), honors and awards, survivors and funeral arrangements.

2. Find the unique trait or ability of the individual that makes him or her stand out from all other individuals and that can be expanded into another paragraph or two.

3. Paint a picture of this person, using character traits and personality and, perhaps, physical characteristics.

4. Gather quotes from family and friends. Quote something the deceased had said, if it reflects his or her personality.

5. Consider the good and not-so-good. No one is perfect, and it is often people's quirks that make them human or give them character.

6. Add some historical context to give readers a better feel for what it was like to grow up or live as this person did.

7. Remember that the obituary is about a life, not a death.

 # Review Exercises

1. BRIGHTS

Use the following information to write brights. Write some with a summary lead and others with a surprise ending. Correct all errors of spelling, punctuation, grammar and style.

1. Little Red Corvette

Police in your city made an arrest Thursday evening after a chase that involved a sports car and several city, county and state police vehicles. Officer Kevin Barlow was on routine patrol about 6:15 p.m. in the evening when he observed a bright red 2022 Chevrolet Corvette that he believed was being operated recklessly. The car was speeding and weaving through traffic, passing other vehicles on the right-hand side while travelling in the 3000 block of Oakland Boulevard. Oakland Boulevard is a wide four-lane thoroughfare that is divided by a four-foot grass median strip with concrete berms. The speed limit for that stretch of road is 45 miles per hour. As Barlow began to follow the vehicle, he clocked speeds of 55 to 65 miles per hour. The way the vehicle was being driven, Barlow thought it might be a stolen vehicle. Barlow switched on his patrol vehicle's flashing warning lights to signal the driver of the Corvette to pull over. The driver of the Corvette ignored the lights and continued on Oakland Boulevard toward the city limits. Police Chief Barry Kopperud said Barlow requested back up and continued to follow the vehicle. He pulled up beside the vehicle thinking the driver could not see his flashing lights and activated his siren. The vehicle slowed slightly, but did not pull over and stop. Barlow said he could not see who was operating the sportscar because the windows were darkly tinted. Officer Barlow, who lives at 3363 Andover Drive, continued to follow the vehicle as it crossed the city limits. Barlow requested assistance from the state police as the vehicle left the city. Within minutes, two state police vehicles joined in the chase along with another patrol car with Officer Barlow's department and a county sheriff's deputy. The five police vehicles continued following the Corvette for nearly two miles when the sheriffs deputys vehicle sped ahead of the Corvette to warn other vehicles to get out of the way. Officer Barlow contacted his supervisor for permission to attempt a precision immobilization technique, or PIT. The PIT is a maneuver that involves a police vehicle pulling alongside a target vehicle it is chasing and tapping the rear quarter panel with its front fender. Nudging the fleeing target vehicle in the side causes the rear wheels to lose traction and the vehicle to spin out of control. Other police vehicles then surround the target vehicle to prevent it from fleeing the scene. Kopperud told reporters later that Barlow got permission from his supervisor to attempt a PIT to stop the vehicle, which police had been following for almost ten miles. Just as Barlow was about to position his vehicle to perform the PIT, the Corvettes right turn signal began to flash and the car slowly rolled to a stop. Police

officers in the other vehicles who had been assisting in the chase blocked the car in with their vehicles and exited them with their guns drawn. Barlow ordered the driver to get out of the car. The door opened slowly and an elderly woman stepped out of the car and stood with her hands up. Barlow said extremely loud music was coming from inside the car. Police identified the driver as Betsy Aaron. Aaron is 86 years old and a retired accountant. She had her own accounting firm for nearly 40 years before she sold it. She lives at 410 Hillcrest Street Apartment 302. As an accountant, she had also done tax returns—some of her clients were members of the city's police force, including Police Chief Barry Kopperrud. Officers performed a sobriety test on Aaron, but it was negative. Aaron told police that all her life she had never been in trouble, had never even gotten a traffic ticket, had always been "a good girl." She told Barlow that when she put her "bucket list" together a year ago, she decided that one of the things she wanted to do was spend a night in jail. Police charged Aaron with speeding, reckless driving, failure to stop and fleeing and eluding a police officer. Barlow handcuffed Aaron and placed her in the back of his patrol vehicle. She was taken to the county jail to await her arraignment. The Corvette was towed from the scene and impounded by police.

2. Misdirected Love

Joseph R. DeLoy told the judge today that he's in love. DeLoy, 26, said he loves a 29-year-old woman, Patty McFerren. DeLoy met McFerren while they were both shopping at a supermarket in the city. DeLoy asked McFerren for a date. McFerren refused. "But she was wonderful, and I could tell she really liked me, so I called her," DeLoy said. In fact, DeLoy tried to call McFerren more than 200 times, sometimes in the middle of the night. However, it wasn't really her number that he called. By mistake, he got the wrong number and called Patrick McFerren instead. The two McFerrens are unrelated and do not know each other. Patrick informed DeLoy that he was dialing the wrong number. DeLoy said he didn't believe him and continued to call. "I was hoping that she'd answer," DeLoy said in court today. Patrick began screening his calls and finally called the police, who told DeLoy to stop making the calls, but no charges were filed against him. The calls continued, so Patrick sued, accusing DeLoy of intentional infliction of emotional distress and invasion of privacy. The calls were a costly mistake for DeLoy. In court today, DeLoys attorney explained that his client was acting "on his heart and hormones, not his head." A jury of 5 men and 7 women decided that his calls were worth $25 each—for a total of $5,000. The jury ordered DeLoy to pay that sum—$5,000—to Patrick. "I'm satisfied," Patrick said.

3. Underage Driver

Charles Todd Snyder was charged with drunk driving following a traffic accident in your city one week ago. He was also charged with driving without a drivers license in his possession. He was scheduled to appear in court at 9 a.m. this morning. He failed to appear in court. As a consequence, Judge Edward Kocembra ordered police to go to Snyders home and to haul Snyder into court. Police went to the address Snyder had given officers at the time of the accident: 711 Broadway Avenue. The police returned to the court at approximately 10:15 a.m. and appeared before Judge Kosembra with Snyder. Snyder was in his mothers arms. He is a 13-month-old child, and his mother insisted that he drinks only milk and that the only vehicle he ever drives is a stroller. So the judge apologized for the inconvenience and told the officers to give Snyder and his mother a ride back to their home. Snyder, apparently frightened by the unfamiliar surroundings and people, cried. Police said that whoever was stopped had falsely given the arresting officers Snyders name and address when he signed the drunken driving ticket and the ticket for driving without a drivers license in his possession. They told the judge that they have no idea who that person might be.

4. Truck Theft

There was a motor vehicle theft which occurred in the city at some time in the middle of last night. The vehicle was taken from a building located at 7720 Avonwood Dr. The building was unlocked at the time, and 12 occupants sleeping in an upstairs room said they heard nothing unusual. They were all in bed by midnight and the first got up at 6 a.m., discovering the theft at that time. Police describe the missing vehicle as a bright canary-yellow fire truck, marked with the name of the city fire department. The custom-made truck cost a total of $192,000 and was delivered to the city just three months ago. Firemen said it had a full tank of gas, about 50 gallons. However, it gets only 1.5 miles to the gallon. It contained enough clothing and equipment for six firemen, a dozen oxygen tanks, 1,000 feet of hose, four ladders (each up to 60 feet tall) plus miscellaneous other equipment. The people sleeping upstairs were all firemen and the building was a fire station. The firemen suspect that someone opened the stations main door, then either pushed or towed the truck silently outside and started its engine some distance away from the building. It is the first time in its history that the city fire department has reported that one of its trucks has been stolen. It was not insured. The keys are always left in the truck to reduce the response time when firemen receive a call for help.

5. Uninvited Guest

Sunni McGrath is a custodian at Washington Elementary School. McGrath is being praised for her quick thinking when a situation arose Tuesday morning at the school. Sunni lives at 109 Nineteenth Street, in your city. McGrath is 52 years old. Sunni has worked at Washington Elementary School for twenty-five years and has been a familiar face for the school children who populate the elementary schools classrooms and hallways. She often takes the time to care for student projects when the students are away from the classroom. Tina Alvarez teaches fifth grade at Washington Elementary School. Her class has taken on a project this school year of raising two pet rabbits. The children named the rabbits Bambi and Thumper. The two rabbits are now six months old and weigh more than twelve pounds each. McGrath stops in on weekends to make sure that Bambi and Thumper have food and water available. Alvarez created the project of raising the rabbits to teach the students about responsibility for caring for others and provide them with an understanding of nature and the natural world. The rabbits are kept in cages overnight and on weekends, but allowed to freely roam the classroom during the school day. The children are responsible for feeding and caring for the rabbits as well as studying their habits. The students feed the rabbits pellet rabbit food and hay along with vegetables such as carrots, cucumbers, kale, asparagus and celery, and fruit such as bananas, apples, strawberries and raspberries. McGrath came to school on Wednesday of this week before the children arrived and, as she always does, went to Alvarez's classroom to check on Bambi and Thumper. She propped the classroom door open, and saw that the bottle of water that the children use to fill the rabbits water bottles was empty. She took the bottle to fill it with spring water that she keeps in a refrigerator in her office in the maintenance supply room. When she returned to the classroom with the full jug of water, something caught her attention out of the corner of her eye. The bag of rabbit pellet food the students kept on a shelf near the cages had tipped over and an animal was partway in the bag. She realized that it was not Bambi or Thumper, who were still in their cages. When the animal backed out of the bag of rabbit food, it looked directly at McGrath. It was a skunk. McGrath quickly turned and left the classroom and shut the door behind her. She then called the police department and officers told her to contact the city's animal control officer to determine

what to do with the uninvited quest in the classroom. When students arrived at the school for classes, they were taken to the schools cafeteria while animal control officers trapped and removed the skunk from Alverezs classroom. School officials think the skunk got into the classroom when McGrath left to fill the water jug and did not close the door behind her, but they do not know how the animal got into the school building. Milan Scott, a biology teacher at Kennedy High School, said that skunks have a keen sense of smell and will eat anything, especially in the winter when their preferred sources of food are not available. He said that skunks do not fully hibernate in the winter. He said skunks are very opportunistic and will raid garbage cans and any food left out in the open. School officials advised Alvarez and her students to keep the bags of rabbit food and vegetables and fruits in sealed containers from now on.

2. FOLLOW-UPS

Write a story summarizing the initial set of facts and then the lead for a follow-up about the later developments. Your instructor might ask you to write a complete news story about each day's developments. Correct all errors.

Yesterday

Two boys were playing in Nichols Lake in Lakeside Park in your town. They were wading along the shore of the lake at about 12 noon at a point where the bottom drops off steeply. The two boys were Randy Stockdale, age 9, son of George and Lillian Stockdale, 472 Bolling Dr., and Edward McGorwan, age 10, son of Karen McGorwann, 4320 Elsie Drive, Apt. Six. Edward waded too far from shore, lost his footing and was unable to get back to shore. He and Randy started to yell for help. A man whose name has not been released by police heard their screams and ran to the lake to help. James Kirkman, a cab driver who was taking his lunch break in the park, heard the screams, too. He radioed his dispatcher who called 911. Kirk-man said later that the unidentified man waded out as far as he could and tried to reach out to Edward, but the boy had drifted too far from shore. "When the boy went under and didn't come back up for air, this guy dove under to find him. But he didn't come back up, either," Kirkman said. Police Officers Kevin Barlow and Eddie

Linn arrived on the scene at 12:18. Barlow immediately stripped to his shorts and started diving into the lake to find the victims. After several dives, he came back up with Edward McGorwan, who was unconscious. Linn tried to resuscitate the boy, but he was still unconscious when he was taken by ambulance to the Regional Medical Center. Barlow continued to search for the unidentified man for another 20 minutes until Dorothy Heslin, a scuba diver who assists the police on a volunteer basis, arrived. She pulled him from the water about 1:15 p.m. Wayne Svendson, a paramedic, tried to resuscitate the man. Svendson said the water was unusually cold and hypothermia had set it, which was indicated by the fact the mans skin had started to turn blue. The man was taken to the Regional Medical Center. Dr. Catrina Lowrie, a physician at the Medical Center, said the man was pronounced dead when he arrived. She also said that Edward McGorwan was in critical condition. Officer Barlow also was treated at Regional Medical Center for minor shock caused by the long period of time he spent in the water looking for the victims. He was released that afternoon.

Today

This morning, the police department released the name of the man who died trying to save Edward McGorwann from Nichols Lake. His name is

William McDowell and he is an unemployed house-painter. He was 30 years old and he had lived at 1429 Highland Dr. Police Chief Barry Koperud said, "McDowell risked his life without hesitation to try to save someone in trouble. He was a real hero." Also this morning, Dr. Lowrie at the Regional Medical Center announced that Edward McGorwann had died. "He spent the night on a respirator, but his condition did not improve. This morning, at his mothers request, we took Edward off the respirator. He died less than half an hour later." McDowells sister lives in your town. Her name is Janice Carson and she lives at 2197 Marcel Av. She said her brother had dropped out of Colonial High School one year before graduating and joined the navy. He spent six years in the navy, and after he left he held a succession of jobs, including electronics technician, cook, construction worker and painter. She said he always enjoyed his jobs but was too restless to stay at one for more than a couple of years. "I guess some people would call him a drifter, but to me he was a free spirit. He loved people but he didn't want to be tied down with a house and a mortgage and all of that. There were only two things he never learned how to do. He couldn't hold a job for more than two years and he could never say no to anyone who needed help," she said with tears in her eyes.

3. ROUNDUPS—MULTIPLE EVENTS

Write a single news story that summarizes all three things described that occurred at a city council meeting in your city Tuesday afternoon. Correct all errors.

Event 1

City council members heard a report from Director of the City Health Department Dr. Cathleen Graham. Dr. Graham voiced concerns about the rise in COVID-19 cases reported by physicians and healthcare facilities throughout the city. She told city council members that there has been a sixty percent increase in the number of reported cases and a fifty percent increase in the number of hospitalizations over the last month and believes city health officials should be authorized to take action. Mayor Sabrina Datoli asked Parker if she had any suggestions as to what actions health officials want to take. City Councilor Roger Lo asked if the figures that Graham cited could be trusted and if health officials were just panicking needlessly. He said that residents were tired of restrictions after nearly two years dealing with the pandemic. Graham said that at the very least, the city should require masks indoors, especially in areas where crowds may gather. Catrina Lowrie, a pulmonary doctor at Regional Medical Center, told the council that by taking action now, healthcare workers would be able to stay ahead of the disease and not be overwhelmed as they had been when the pandemic first broke out. Lowrie said that an ordinance requiring masks and limiting the number of people in closed environments such as restaurants and theaters would help control any outbreaks.

Councilmember William Belmonte made a motion to require masks indoors in all public and private businesses. Councilor Luis Ramirez seconded the motion. Datolli asked Graham to keep council updated if the numbers increased or decreased so the council could revisit the health departments request in the future. Councilmembers voted to approve the mask ordinance. The vote was six to one. Councilor Lo voted against the ordinance.

Event 2

City councilmembers had a discussion that sometimes was heated. They are at a loss of what to do with a 2.2 acre lot on Central Boulevard in the city. The lot is overgrown with weeds and has become an eyesore. The plot of land is zoned low-density residential. Randall Whitlock is vice president of Wagnor Development Corporation. Wagnor Development Corporation has been in business for more than 50 years and has developed many areas in the city from high-rise luxury condominiums to single family homes. Wagnor is working with George Valesquez, architect and owner of Valesquez Design Group on a solution. However, Whitlock said he would need a variance to the current zoning for the plan to work. Tom Onn, director of the city housing authority, is in favor of the plan and requested the approval of the variance. The variance being requested is to change the zoning from low-density residential to medium-density residential. Under the current zoning, only four houses would be able to be built on the 2.2-acre lot. Whitlock said he would have to charge more than $1.5 million dollars for each house in order to make a low-density residential plan work because of the cost of the property. His company wants to build a five story low-rise condominium and several small duplex houses on the property. This would allow for more affordable housing on the lot and provide affordable housing for up to 20 families. James and Margaret Ungarient live at 7314 Byron Avenue. Byron Avenue is a block west of the proposed building site. The Ungarients are attorneys who own The Law Office, a prestigious law firm in your city. They live in an upscale housing area on Byron Avenue where homes cost from $750,000 to $1,000,000. They do not want the city to approve the variance because they say it will have a negative impact on the value of their home and the homes of their neighbors. They claimed that a higher density housing development in the neighborhood would "ghettoize" the neighborhood and lead to crime, drugs and other problems. Onn said that the city does not have enough affordable housing for middle income families and the Central Boulevard location is close to schools and shopping areas. Mayor Sabrina Datolli said the city is doing all it can to provide affordable housing for its low and middle income residents, but there is only so much the city can do. The council voted against approving the rezoning plan by a vote of five to two. Councilor Sandra Gandolf and Councilor Luis Ramirez voted to approve the rezoning request.

Event 3

Mayor Sabrina Datolli has promised to combat rising crime rates in the city. While violent crimes such as murder and sexual assaults have declined, there has been a major increase in reports of robberies, burglaries, drug offenses and vandalism throughout the city. Several city council members have demanded action from the mayor to increase law enforcement resources in parts of the city that have seen the biggest jump in crime. Datoli announced that preliminary budget

projections for the city are positive, but that there will be no significant increase in the budget for the police department. City Council President Luis Ramirez told Datolli in budget negotiations that the city needs to increase spending for other departments and in other areas of the city that have seen major budget cuts over the past 5 years. Ramirez said that the budget cuts had placed a burden on educational institutions, youth programs and social support agencies that have restricted their ability to deliver needed and necessary programs. He believes that a lack of support for those programs is one of the reasons for the increase in crime rates. Datolli was seeking an increase of six million dollars for the police departments budget that will allow the department to hire more officers, purchase more patrol vehicles, modernize its aging computer system and develop a new anti-gun unit. The police budget currently is running the city just over thirty-five million dollars a year. Ramirez says cuts to support programs over the past five years has amounted to three times what the mayor is requesting in the police departments new budget. Councilor Joseph Tucshak said the city needed to address rising crime rates as quickly as possible and supports the mayors request for more money for the department. Tuscak told his fellow councilors that once crime rates are reduced that money can be restored to the support programs that had their budgets cut the past five years. Police Chief Barry Kopperud said the department needs the increase in the budget, especially for the new anti-gun unit he is proposing. "We're fighting a losing battle against all the guns on our citys streets," Kopperud said. The council voted six to one to table discussion on the budget discussion until more data on crime rates can be gathered and additional information on budget requests from Gary Hubbard, superintendent of city schools, and Emil Plambeck, superintendent of the City Park Commission, can be presented to the council. Hubbard and Plambeck have been requesting funds to support more afterschool programs and community programs using the city's parks.

4. SIDEBARS

Use the following information to write two separate stories, first a news story reporting the Senate's action and then a sidebar based on the interview with the sheriff. Correct all errors.

Main Story

The state Senate today approved a bill overwhelmingly. The bill has already been approved by the house and now goes to the Governor, who has indicated that she will sign it. The bill was passed almost unanimously by angry lawmakers who want inmates housed in jails throughout the state to help pay the costs of their room and board. There were only 2 votes against the measure in the senate and none against it in the house. The bill will go into effect next January 1st. It will require persons housed in a jail within the state to reveal their incomes and, if they can afford it, to pay the entire cost of their room and board behind bars, or whatever share of the cost they can reasonably afford. The bill requires the State Department of Offender Rehabilitation to draw up guidelines on how prisoners will disclose their finances and how much they will be required to pay. The department will consider a number of relevant variables, such as whether a prisoner must support a family and devote all his or her income to that family. The idea for the bill arose a number of months ago when lawmakers touring a state prison were told that some inmates received Government benefits (mostly Social Security and veterans' benefits). The lawmakers were told that some of the prisoners opened bank accounts in the prisons and that the money they received piled up so they had thousands of dollars accumulated in the accounts when they were released. A subsequent survey requested by legislative leaders found 19,000 inmates in the state and that, of that total, 356 received government payments of some type. The same survey found that the inmates had a total of $8.1 million in inmate accounts at state prisons. Prison officials cautioned that the prisoners may have more money deposited in banks outside the prison system and that it would be difficult to locate those accounts. To enforce the new bill, lawmakers stipulated that prisoners who refuse to disclose their finances cannot be released early on parole. Officials have not yet determined how much each prisoner will be charged. Lawmakers also noted that some inmates may have other assets, such as farms, homes, automobiles, and stocks and bonds, and that those prisoners can also be expected to help defray their prison expenses.

Sidebar

Gus DiCesare is the county sheriff. He has held that position for 11 years. To retain the position, he must run for re-election every four years. As sheriff, DiCesare is in charge of the county jail, which has a capacity of 120 inmates, mostly men but also a few women. Criminals sentenced to terms of less than one year in prison usually are sentenced to the county facility rather than to a state prison. Despite its capacity of 120 persons, the county jail usually holds 140 to 150 persons—20 or 30 more than its rated capacity. When interviewed today about the legislatures approval of the bill in question, DiCesare said: "Hey, I think its a great idea. Some of these prisoners got more money than I'll ever have. When we pick them up, they're driving fancy cars, living in big homes and carrying a thick wad of money. Not most of them, but there're always a few in here, mostly drug dealers. We sentence them to jail as punishment, but it punishes honest taxpayers who pay to keep them in here—pay for this building, their food, clothes, jailers and all the rest. A couple of years ago, we calculated that it cost about $75 to keep one prisoner here one day. Hell, if they can afford it, prisoners should help pay for it all; that could be part of their punishment. I'll bet our costs are up to nearly $110 a day apiece now, and they're still rising. It'd help me too. I've got a damned hard problem trying to run this place on the budget the county gives me. With a little more money, I could improve the food, come up with more recreational facilities and maybe even try to rehabilitate a few prisoners—bring in some teachers and counselors and that type of thing. Now, all I really do is keep them locked behind bars all day, and that's not going to rehabilitate anyone."

5. WRITING OBITUARIES

Using the information provided, write an obituary for each individual described. Correct all errors.

1. Obituary Notice Form: Terrence C. Austin

   Full Name of Deceased Terrence C. Austin
   Age 81
   Address 418 Cottage Hill Rd.
   Date and Cause of Death Died late last Sunday of cancer of the throat

   Place of Death Mercy Hospital
   Time and Date of Funeral 4 p.m. Friday afternoon so his entire family have time to travel here for the funeral.
   Place of Funeral St. Mark African Methodist Episcopal church
   Place of Burial All Saints Cemetery with a reception afterwards at the family home.

Officiating Cleric The Rev. James J. Burnes

Place of Birth Chicago

Places and Length of Residences Mr. Austin moved here as an infant with his family and lived in the city all his entire life except three years service in the marines during the Korean War.

Occupation Retired. Former chef at Deacosta's Restaurant

Did Deceased Ever Hold Public Office (When and What)? None

Name, Address of Surviving Spouse Wife Anna Austin, 418 Cottage Hill Rd.

Maiden Name (if Married Woman)

Marriage, When and to Whom Married to his widow the former Anna L. Davis 56 years

Names, Addresses of Surviving Children Three sons. Walter J. Austin and Terrence L. Austin both of Atlanta. Also James K. Austin of Chicago. Two daughters who live locally, Heather Kocembra of 388 31st St. and Betty Sawyer of 2032 Turf Way Apt. 512.

Names, Addresses of Surviving Brothers and Sisters Brothers Edward John Austin of Chicago and Robert Wesley Austin of Montreal in Canada.

Number of Grandchildren (Great, etc.) 14 grandchildren, 27 great grandchildren and 2 great great grandchildren.

Names, Addresses of Parents (if Living) Mother Lulu T. Austin died 10 years ago and his father Frank died 27 years ago.

Other Information Mr. Austin was a retired chef for Deacosta's Restaurant for more than 25 years. He was also a member of the New Day Singers male chorus and a member of St. Mark African Methodist Episcopal church. After retiring from the restaurant he and his wife catered for weddings and other social gatherings. He learned to cook as a child from his mother, and was further trained as a cook in the Marines but then was moved to rifleman, winning two purple hearts and a bronze star during service in Korea. After returning home he got a job in a restaurant kitchen and learned more via on-the-job training. In recent years he never tired of playing with his grandchildren and great grandchildren. He said he missed spending as much time with his own children as he wanted since he often went to work at 11 a.m. or 12 noon and didn't get back home until after midnight.

Reporter's Additional Notes—Interviews with Friends, Relatives and Coworkers:

His wife said, "He worked hard cooking all week at work and then relaxed by cooking at home, but he refused to do the dishes which was fine with us. Until he retired his job didn't often allow him to be with the family for the holidays. Those were the times he worked 12 hours a day preparing other people's feasts. Since he retired he just loved singing at church. But he smoked those damn Camels, 2 or more packs a day, and that's what killed him, caused his cancer. I wanted him to stop but he was hooked, really hooked on 'em ever since Korea."

His son Walter said, "Dad loved to cook, and he loved working with people. During the holidays and family gatherings he'd cook up a storm. As soon as we stepped in the door we'd smell the hams, turkeys, greens, and baked pies. He liked Deacosta's because they let him use his imagination to create new dishes and they gave him a big bonus every Christmas. He always went right out and spent every penny of it on toys for us kids and things for the house and Mom, which made Christmas a really happy time for our family."

Peggy Deacosta said, "His specialty was creating dishes filled with edible colors and designs using fresh fruits and vegetables. Plus desserts, he made the best desserts in town."

2. Obituary Notice Form: Anne "Kitty" Capiello

Full Name of Deceased Anne "Kitty" Capiello

Age Twenty

Address 8210 University Boulevard, Apartment 311

Date and Cause of Death Police say apparent suicide via overdose of prescription drugs

Place of Death Corpse found at 7:40 a.m. this morning on a bench in Riverside Park.

Time and Date of Funeral Not yet scheduled. Body awaiting autopsy. Coroners report on cause of death is due in a few days.

Place of Funeral University Chapel

Place of Burial Body to be cremated/no burial

Officiating Cleric Campus ministry/The Reverend and Professor Mildred Berg

Place of Birth Mercy Hospital in this city

Places and Length of Residences A life-long resident of the city.

Occupation College student currently in her 2nd year of study, major in pre-med.

Did Deceased Ever Hold Public Office (When and What)? no

Name, Address of Surviving Spouse Parents said she was committed to her boyfriend, Jorge Alberto Coto. The two shared a college apartment.

Maiden Name (if Married Woman)

Marriage, When and to Whom Never married

Names, Addresses of Surviving Children Gave up her only child for adoption 3 years ago, a baby girl.

Names, Addresses of Surviving Brothers and Sisters A brother, Burt, age 17, and a younger sister, Amy, age 15, both still living with their mother and stepfather.

Number of Grandchildren (Great, etc.) None

Names, Addresses of Parents (if Living) Mother Sara Knoechel and stepfather Alvin Knoechel; father and stepmother Otto and Sandra Capiello.

Other Information An honors student at Kennedy high school in this city and on the deans list at your college with a 3.92 GPA (only 1 B and all her other grades As) during her first completed semesters of college. The winner of several scholarships. Enrolled in your colleges Honors Program. Not a member of a sorority or any church. Secretary of the Pre-Med Club. To help pay her college expenses she worked part time, twenty hrs. a week, as a clerk in the Student Health Center.

Reporter's Additional Notes—Interviews with Friends, Relatives and Coworkers:

Friend Thomas Alvarez said, "She was a top student, got As in everything. She was very giving, caring, and I think that's why she wanted a career in medicine. She was a smart, beautiful person, but never very secure. She'd do anything for you and never ask anything in return."

Sue DaRoza, another friend, said, "At first she wanted to major in engineering, then switched to premed, but wasn't always certain if she wanted to be a nurse or a doctor. She loved kids and wanted to help them, kids with special needs. I think she really wanted to be a doctor, but her family couldn't afford to send her to med school, and she didn't want to be a burden."

Friend Patricia Richards said, "Ann was very serious, very competitive, always pushing herself, trying to do better, to be Number One. We've been friends since elementary school. She was 14 when her parents got divorced, and that really hurt her. I'd gone through the same thing and we were always talking about it, trying to understand it. She wanted to marry Jorge but he said he wanted to wait until they finished college, and then they started having problems a couple months ago, and she caught him with someone else. They'd been going together since high school, and it was hard, so hard for her."

6. WRITING THE FEATURE OBIT

News organizations often write feature obituaries about prominent people—celebrities, athletes, political officials as well as well-known people in a local community. Feature obits of prominent people not only announce their deaths, but also highlight their lives, citing what made them prominent and how they became that way. Such stories require research. As prominent people age, many news organizations will begin to compile information about them and store the background material so it is readily available. Select a prominent person—a national celebrity or local person. Conduct research on the person to gather background information about them—when and where they were born, where they went to school and the degrees they earned. What did they do in their life to make themselves prominent and how and what did they accomplish? Sometimes, the person is prominent for all the wrong reasons. When President Richard Nixon died, his feature obituary was a contradiction in terms of his notoriety. While his obituary highlighted his many accomplishments, it also highlighted his involvement in the Watergate break-in and cover-up, which led to his resignation from the presidency. Collect as much information as you can and then begin to craft a feature obituary with the information you have gathered. The only thing you will not have for the story is a day and time of death.

PUBLIC AFFAIRS REPORTING

17

T he answer to the climate-change crisis is blowing in the wind, advocates of wind turbines say. The United States has more than 66,000 wind turbines in 41 states generating more than 8 percent of the country's total electricity. And the industry has been growing by more than 3,000 turbines a year. Growing with equal rapidity is opposition to the turbines.

In Lincoln County, South Dakota, plans to build a wind farm roused broad opposition from residents. The residents persuaded local officials to prevent the installation of a 150-unit wind farm. The company that wanted to build it circulated a petition to have the issue put on the ballot, but the measure was overwhelmingly defeated. One 30-year resident of the county told the Associated Press the only people who voted for the wind farm were those who expected to get money from leases to build the turbines on their land.

In Massachusetts, a company called Cape Wind sought to build an offshore wind farm near Cape Cod. Such projects are common in Europe, but local opponents stopped the project. Wealthy and politically influential residents of the Cape Cod area, including the late Sen. Edward Kennedy, opposed the project. They said an offshore wind farm would mar their view of the ocean, obstruct historical sites and clog waterways used by humpback and pilot whales. After a 16-year political and legal battle, Cape Wind abandoned the project. The Biden administration, however, has recently approved the construction of 2,000 offshore turbines near Martha's Vineyard, Massachusetts.

More than 100 city, county and state governments have enacted laws restricting, delaying or prohibiting the construction of renewable energy projects. Often they use zoning regulations to restrict where wind turbines can be built, such as requiring large spaces between the turbines and any property owned by people not leasing land to the wind farm operator.

Opponents use a variety of arguments against wind turbines. They claim the turbines are noisy, may reduce property values, are unsightly and endanger other

> "Democracy is not a state. It is an act, and each generation must do its part to help build what we called the Beloved Community, a nation and world society at peace with itself."
>
> —*John Lewis, U.S. politician and civil rights leader*

Donald Trump was a hero in 2012 to these Scots who protested the construction of wind farms off the Scottish coast. Trump opposed the windmills because they were to be built near his golf resort in Scotland. Elsewhere, the construction of wind farms on land and off shore has provoked protests and counterprotests.

 HOT TIP

Qualities of a Public Affairs Reporter

- **Be diligent.** Public affairs reporters must follow a regular pattern of checking sources.

- **Know the sources.** Public affairs reporters must know how to use both people and documents to find information quickly.

- **Be accurate.** Reporters must understand and describe the details of complicated issues correctly.

- **Write clear explanations.** Reporters must explain issues and decisions clearly to readers, listeners or viewers. Unless reporters explain governmental actions clearly, citizens will not understand how their lives and interests may be affected.

wildlife, especially birds. The opponents sometimes have the support of organizations affiliated with or supported by the fossil-fuel industry.

The fight over wind farms illustrates the importance of public affairs journalism at the local, state and federal levels. At the local level, reporters may be covering county commission or city council meetings at which residents and activists on all sides of an issue may be pressuring elected officials to decide in their favor. At the state and federal levels, the political pressure may be applied in ways that are less public, through one-on-one lobbying of legislators and campaign donations. But it is also at those levels that experts in energy production, economics and environmental issues present the most thorough and accurate information.

Climate change affects the entire planet, but many important decisions will be made at the local level. The elected and appointed officials and the public to whom they are accountable need the best information possible. Heated public hearings on building and regulating wind farms and other energy-producing facilities make for interesting news stories. The color and human interest generated by intense arguments must be reported, but the reporting must also include reliable information. For instance, a study by researchers at the Lawrence Berkeley National Laboratory found that only 16 percent of people living within five miles of wind farms noticed any noise from the turbines. Information like this helps place fears about excessive noise in a clearer context.

The work of the reporters at small town newspapers and broadcasters and large, international news organizations provides citizens and public officials with facts and insights they need to understand their world and to make good decisions. While news serves people in many ways, reporting on public affairs is the core function of the news business. Much public affairs reporting focuses on government at the local, state and federal levels. But, as the conflicts over wind farms illustrates, public affairs reporting is about more than government. It's also about such issues as the environment, the economy and public health.

17.1 Local Government

A series of three winter storms swept across much of the United States over 10 days in February 2021. The storms dropped sleet, ice and snow on several states, including some, like Texas, Oklahoma and Louisiana, that are unaccustomed to such weather. The state that experienced the greatest hardship was Texas. The storm brought the lowest temperatures Texas had experienced in 72 years—as low as minus 2 in Dallas on Feb. 16. Those sub-zero temperatures played havoc with the Texas power grid. Nationwide, the storms knocked out power for more than 10 million people, more than 4 million of them in Texas. The power outages disrupted a wide range of public services and killed at least 210 people. Some estimated more than 700 died.

Because of the loss of power, water service was disrupted in many cities. Pipes and water heaters burst causing substantial damage to homes. Some people in San Antonio were so desperate for water they were collecting it in trash cans from the city's River Walk, according to MySA.com. BBC news reported that 12 million Texans were ordered to boil their drinking water, and many others had no water service at all. The Texas Tribune reported that many grocery stores were closed and the ones that were open had sold out their supplies of bread, milk, eggs and other basic foods. With no electricity and no natural gas service, many struggled to stay warm. Some died from the cold; others died from carbon monoxide poisoning from using grills, vehicles or generators to heat their homes without proper ventilation. In Houston, one family sat in their running car in the garage to

Snow surrounds the Texas State Capitol Building in Austin in February 2021. A massive snow storm and freezing temperatures shut down much of the Texas power grid, leaving millions of homes without heat or power for days.

keep warm. The mother and her daughter died; the father and the son were hospitalized with carbon monoxide poisoning, The New York Times reported.

Adding to the anguish Texans experienced was the discovery that some private companies had profited from the disaster. According to Reuters, companies that supply natural gas or run pipelines and banks that trade commodities gained billions of dollars in profits. One pipeline company, Energy Transfer, apparently made $2.4 billion in additional profits from the storm.

Much of the money was made because Texas agencies that regulate companies that generate and sell electricity and gas allowed prices to spike. The wholesale price of natural gas had been about $3 per million British thermal units prior to the freeze. At its height, the price soared to $1,192.86 per million Btu. Some Texas customers got gas bills in the thousands of dollars for that period.

Why did Texans suffer more in this storm than residents of other states? A report by the Federal Energy Regulatory Commission concluded Texas companies had failed to winterize their generators. There had been other years when extreme cold had caused problems. After similar events in 1989 and 2011, Texas companies were admonished to invest in winterizing their equipment but doing so was voluntary. Since the freeze, Texas news organizations have published hundreds of stories about the storm's effects and what local and state government was doing to prevent a similar disaster. Months afterward, reporters were continuing to follow the story. For example, the Texas Tribune reported that state senators were dismayed to learn that a law they had passed to require energy producers to weatherize their facilities contained a major loophole: If a company does not voluntarily declare itself part of the state's critical infrastructure, it does not have to comply with the weatherization mandate.

The task of dealing with roads, bridges, water and sewer service, police and fire protection falls to state and local governments. These, and many other services, are vital to the health, safety and prosperity of communities. Watching how well these governments handle their responsibilities, how they manage the tax money entrusted to them is a central task for news organizations.

17.1.1 City and County Governments

City governments provide residents with a wide range of services: police and fire protection, sewage treatment, water, street construction and maintenance and parks and recreation services. Some cities also include trash pickup and disposal, public transportation and electricity or natural gas. Others operate hospitals or control the local school system. They also adopt ordinances regulating such things as local speed limits, zoning and the use of outdoor signs by businesses.

County governments usually have more limited powers. They collect taxes levied by all governments in the county. They may assess the value of all property and hear appeals from citizens who believe those assessments are too high. County governments are repositories for records of births, deaths, marriages, real estate transactions and motor vehicle registrations. They also supervise elections and handle voter registration in many states.

17.1.1.1 LOCAL BUDGETS AND TAXES

Reporters covering city or county government write about such issues as the awarding of contracts for construction or major equipment purchases, the creation of fire protection districts, the progress of urban redevelopment projects and the regulation of adult movie theaters. An important annual story is the budget, which determines how much money a local government will have to collect from taxpayers and how it will spend that money for the coming year. It is the blueprint by which a local government works.

City budgets are set by the council or commission, county budgets by the commissioners. Usually, department heads or officeholders submit budget requests for the coming year. The council or commission reviews the requests and makes the changes it considers prudent. Some states have statutory limits on spending increases; others have been forcing local governments to roll back taxes and spending. Such restrictions force the council or commission to make difficult budget choices.

To help meet budgetary needs, local governments get some money from federal and state governments, sales taxes, local income taxes, user fees and other miscellaneous sources. But taxes on personal and real property provide the bulk of local revenue in most communities (see Figure 17.1). Personal property includes such things as automobiles, boats, stocks and bonds. Real property is land and buildings.

The annual budget is a news story in itself, but it can also be the starting point for other important and interesting stories about local government. For instance, how much is the city or county spending on fire protection? Is the spending concentrated in certain neighborhoods? Martin Stolz, a reporter for the Cleveland Plain Dealer, wanted to know whether Cleveland and Cuyahoga County had more fire stations than it needed. Stolz's colleague Thomas Gaumer used mapping software to show the locations of all 103 fire stations and to draw a one-mile radius circle around each. The resulting map showed some areas where fire stations were densely clustered and other parts that appeared to have gaps.

Calculating a city's property tax levy

	$19,000,000	Projected spending
−	$8,000,000	Income from other sources
=	$11,000,000	Amount from property taxes
÷	$875,000,000	Assessed valuation of city
=	.01257	Tax rate
X	100	
=	1.257 cents	Tax per $1 assessed value of taxable property

Explaining the tax levy

	$119,000	Median home value Assume it is assessed at 100 percent of market value.
X	.01257	Tax rate
=	$1,495.83	Property taxes due on median-priced home

FIGURE 17.1 Property Tax

17.1.1.2 CITY AND COUNTY SOURCES

Covering city hall or the county courthouse requires establishing a routine for visiting the various offices and departments and taking the time to get to know each officeholder or department chief. Reporters also should cultivate contacts among office workers, such as assistants, staff members and secretaries. Department staff can steer journalists to information for a story and help them find important documents.

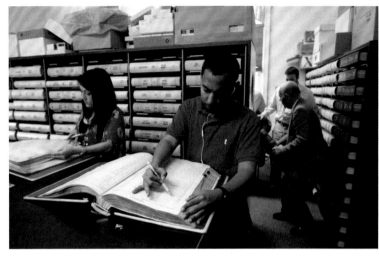

Ahren Menard (left) and Adam Batist check mineral rights records at the Fairfield, Illinois, county clerk's office.

Some local officials fear press coverage or want to control information released to the press. When they do talk, they often speak in jargon and technical terms: "ad valorem taxes," "capital outlays," "percolation ponds," "rapid infiltration basins," "secured and unsecured debts," "tax-increment financing" and "tangible personal property." If a legal or technical word is essential to a story, the reporter should define it. Otherwise, those terms should be replaced with simpler and more familiar ones.

City hall and county courthouse reporters also need to be familiar with public records. Not every document held by government is a public record, but a wide range of information is available in city halls and county courthouses (see Table 17.1 for a list of examples). Jonathan Austin, the editor and publisher of the Yancey County News, a weekly published from 2011 to 2014 in Burnsville, North Carolina, was curious about the pawn shop business. The state requires pawn shop owners to record each transaction and keeps the information at county courthouses, where it is available to law enforcement officers. Austin's inspection of some of these records revealed that a person with the same name as a sheriff's deputy—Tom Farmer—had pawned guns. Austin then used the state open records law to get a copy of the inventory list of firearms owned by the sheriff's office. The serial numbers on some of those weapons matched the numbers on the pawned ones. Farmer was eventually charged with a felony but pleaded guilty to a misdemeanor and was placed on probation.

For generations, local governments kept their records on paper. Now those records are stored on computers. This transfer has created both problems and opportunities for reporters. Most states consider records public whether they are in electronic or paper form. However, states differ on whether journalists and citizens are able to get copies of records in electronic form. The difference is important because reporters can analyze data that are available in electronic form in ways that would be impossible with paper documents.

17.1.2 School Districts

More local tax money flows into public schools than into any other area of government, and parents want to know the schools their children attend are effective and safe. For these reasons, public interest in news about schools is high, but digging out stories requires patience and time from reporters.

TABLE 17.1   LOCAL GOVERNMENT DOCUMENTS

City or County

Purchase orders (paid and not paid) show what products or services were obtained from what vendors at what prices.

Payroll records tell not only how much each employee was paid but also deductions, time records, sick leave, vacations and other absences.

Expense records may show which public officials are traveling, where they are going and how much they are spending.

Telephone records, including cell phone records, for top officials may show who is trying to influence government decisions.

Bids and bid specifications are the government agency's description of what it wants to buy or build and are sent to all contractors or vendors that might want to submit bids.

Contracts between a government and vendors for goods or services can show who is getting paid, how much and for what. Sometimes government agencies can award contracts without taking bids, but the contracts should always be public.

Licenses are issued by cities for various kinds of businesses (liquor stores and food markets), occupations (private detectives and security guards), pets and many other things.

Inspection reports from fire departments, building inspectors and health inspectors can reveal information about fire, safety and health dangers.

Zoning records include maps, reports, petitions and case files pertaining to planning and zoning actions and are usually public.

Campaign contributions and financial statements show where city officials got the money they needed to run for office and how they spent it. In some states, officials also must disclose the sources of their income and where they have their money invested.

Resumes tell where public officials were educated, where they have worked in the past and what they've done.

County Only

Tax-assessment records reveal the owner, legal description and assessed value of the land and buildings for each piece of property in a community. The records usually are cross-indexed so they can be accessed in a number of ways.

Motor vehicle registration records show who owns what vehicles, their value and the taxes paid on them. In some states, counties keep tax records on motor vehicles; in others, the state keeps all motor vehicle and driver's license records. Much of this information is no longer public because of a law Congress passed to protect privacy.

Deeds indicate who owns a piece of property, who sold it and when the transaction occurred. These are usually found in the register of deeds office.

One measure of a school system's effectiveness is its graduation rate, so Minnesota Public Radio (MPR) looked at the numbers in its state, how those rates varied for different ethnic groups and how they compared with those of other states. The results were disappointing. Overall, about 82 percent of Minnesota public school students graduate in four years, which is close to the national average. But that figure hides some dramatic ethnic disparities. For Native Americans, Asian-Americans, Blacks and Hispanics, graduation rates in Minnesota are at or near the worst in the United States. Black students had a graduation rate of

62 percent, the third lowest among states, and the rate for Hispanics was 63.2 percent, the worst in the country.

Many factors affect graduation rates, including whether students are native English speakers and whether they are poor. Minnesota has higher levels of immigrant students and poor students than many other states. But MPR found another factor that helped explain the schools' poor performance: state spending for non-classroom student support. Reporters working on the story learned that the key predictors for graduation are attendance, behavior and course performance—the ABCs of high school graduation—and that counselors, social workers and other support staff are best able to track these measures and help students at risk of failing.

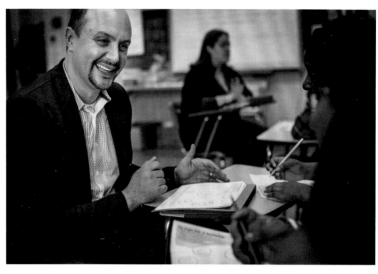

Jon Zentner, a construction lawyer, volunteers as a graduation coach with AchieveMpls at Minneapolis' Henry High School. The program helps students stay on top of their schoolwork and graduate on time, as well as gain confidence and develop life skills.

MPR reported that Minnesota had been spending about as much as most other states on these services until the early 2000s, when then-Gov. Tim Pawlenty campaigned for reducing such spending as an austerity measure. Local school districts got the message and complied. Now the state spends about 2.6 percent of its education money on non-classroom support, or less than half of the national average of 5.5 percent.

MPR's reporting on this issue is the kind of journalism that can help the public evaluate the performance of an essential area of local government.

Many news organizations prepare report cards for local school districts. Journalists have discovered that they must do more than simply report scores on standardized tests and compare the results from different schools and districts. Test scores vary depending on such things as the percentages of pupils who have one or more parents with a college degree, who qualify for free or reduced-price lunches, who enter or leave school during the year and who speak a native language other than English. Accumulating data for a school report card and analyzing it correctly can take months, but the work can pay off in a story or series that many people will read, listen to or watch.

17.1.2.1 SCHOOL SOURCES AND DOCUMENTS

Education reporters should remember that the sources who are highest placed and most often quoted could have the least knowledge of what is happening in classrooms. Boards of education often concentrate on financial and administrative matters and pay less attention to curriculum issues. The superintendent of schools has day-to-day authority to direct the district and carry out policies set by the board. Superintendents generally deal willingly with reporters, but their contact with classrooms might be limited. In large districts, a number of assistant superintendents and program administrators report to the superintendent. They may have information about specific areas such as elementary education, art education, nutrition and foreign-language instruction. Principals and teachers know the most about what is happening in classrooms, yet they may be among

The Booster Redux

Pittsburg High School. 1978 E. 4th Street Pittsburg, KS 66762 Vol. 98, Issue 2 www.boosterredux.com

Friday, March 31, 2017

DISTRICT HIRES NEW PRINCIPAL

Background called into question after discrepancies arise

THE BOOSTER REDUX STAFF
🐦 @PHSStudentPub

Following the hiring of incoming Pittsburg High School (PHS) principal Dr. Amy Robertson on March 6, discrepancies arose between Robertson's personal accounts of her education and information provided by education institutions she said she attended. The discrepancies cast doubt on the accreditation of a university she said she attended and the degrees she listed.

Robertson said she currently works as the CEO of an education consulting firm known as Atticus I S Consultants in Dubai, and has resided there for over 20 years.

According to a Pittsburg Community Schools press release on Thursday, Robertson "gained leadership and management ex

Robertson said she will arrive in the US in April and is eager for the new experience. "I'm excited about the opportunity," Robertson said. "I could easily stay [in Dubai] for another 10 years working in schools as a principal here, but I want to come home. I want to be in the US, and I want to be a part of a community. Pittsburg is the right community to put down roots in."

The Booster Redux staff typically introduces each new administrator at PHS with a news story. During the interview process with Robertson, the Booster staff found inconsistencies in Robertson's credentials. The staff presented these concerns to Pittsburg Community School superintendent Destry

After the conference call interview, the staff conducted further research online and by phone interview to confirm her credentials. These are the findings.
EDUCATIONAL BACKGROUND
Robertson said in the conference call interview she earned a Master's degree in Comparative Literature and a Ph.D. in English from Corllins University.

Corllins, however, has been under fire in the national media for its lack of legitimacy. Furthermore, the Better Business Bureau's website said, "This business is not BBB accredited." The posting online in 2010 also stated, "The true physical address of Corllins University is unknown."

By researching Amy Robertson's background, student reporters of The Booster Redux exposed inconsistencies in the principal's claims.

the least accessible sources. Some of the best sources could be next door—or at the next desk. Neighbors, friends and colleagues who have school-age children could have a wealth of ideas or anecdotes for fleshing out stories.

School districts keep records on many of the things that happen in their buildings and the people who work in them (see Table 17.2). Reporters can put those records to good use. Students at Pittsburg High School in Pittsburg, Kansas, did just that when they investigated the background of Amy Robertson, who had just been selected as the school's new principal. While working on a profile of Robertson, they quickly discovered that some of the experiences and education she claimed on her résumé did not check out. For example, she claimed she had earned a bachelor of fine arts degree from the University of Tulsa, but the student journalists found the university does not award such a degree. Robertson also said she had a master's and a doctoral degree from Corllins University. Although Corllins has a website, it

TABLE 17.2 EXAMPLES OF SCHOOL RECORDS OPEN TO THE PUBLIC

Laws and policies should be a starting point for any story about or investigation of a school. Until reporters know how a school or a program is supposed to run, they cannot evaluate how well it is running.

Budget and financial records show the district's priorities, and a comparison of budgets over several years can show how those priorities have shifted.

Bills and warrants show how a district actually spent its money.

Federal grant documents reveal what administrators said the money would be used for. Reporters can compare those proposals with vouchers showing how the money was actually spent.

Salary information for administrators and teachers is public record in most states. What constitutes a person's salary may vary—some states, like North Carolina, exclude bonuses and benefits. Mississippi holds that a public employee's net salary is closed, and Florida closes payroll deduction records. Many states, such as Hawaii, make only salary ranges or salary scales available. In still other states, disclosure of salary information may be subject to a balancing of the public's interest in disclosure against the employee's interest in privacy.

Employment contracts for school superintendents and principals are public record in many states. The contracts reveal what perks the administrator is getting in addition to a salary—travel expenses, automobile allowances and club memberships are some possibilities.

Accreditation reports, state audits and other assessment records can indicate how well a school district is performing. For accreditation, schools prepare a self-study report. A visiting team uses the self-study to guide its on-site investigation of the school and then issues a final report. Schools also prepare a variety of reports for state education officials, covering curriculum, personnel, students and district finances. The reports, which might include recommendations for upgrading school facilities, curriculum or personnel, can give reporters criteria for evaluating school performance over time.

Food service records may contain analyses of menus and receipts and expenditures for school lunch programs.

Transportation records may include inspection reports and service records on buses and reports of crashes, even minor ones.

lists no physical address, and the university has been the subject of a number of consumer complaints.

A few days after the students ran their story in The Booster Redux, the school's newspaper, Robertson resigned from the $93,000-a-year job. Destry Brown, the Pittsburg superintendent of schools, praised the students' work. "I believe strongly in our kids' questioning things and not believing things just because an adult told them," he said to The New York Times.

Many school records, however, are closed to the public. Educational documents on specific students are closed by state and federal laws. Directory information on a student—name, age, address, major areas of study and height and weight (for athletes)—is usually available unless he or she objects to its release. Personnel records for district employees and supervisors may be confidential, depending on the law of the state.

Journalists cannot rely on records alone, however, to inform the public about schools and the education system. They have to observe what happens in classrooms. Schools are semipublic places, but administrators try to control access to school buildings to protect students and prevent disruptions. Reporters who want to cover classroom activities should arrange their visits in advance with the teacher and the principal and possibly with the superintendent as well.

17.2 Crime and Accidents

The first assignment many newspaper reporters have is the police beat. Beginning television or radio journalists might have more varied assignments, but covering crimes and car accidents will be a major part of their jobs as well.

Not all police reporters are beginners; some have covered the beat for many years. Nevertheless, it is an excellent training ground. Police reporters quickly learn their community, both geographically and sociologically. They develop their sense for what is newsworthy and their appreciation for accuracy. They also develop sources who will serve them for many years, no matter what beats they cover.

The work of police reporters varies with the size and type of community they cover. In a small community, even a minor theft might be newsworthy. In big cities, where two or three homicides a day are common, only the most bloody, most unusual crimes receive detailed coverage. Police reporters also cover the activities of the department, including community service projects, promotions, retirements and internal investigations. They might cover traffic accidents, but usually only the most noteworthy ones.

A lot of the information for these stories is available at police headquarters or the precinct stations. Thus, reporters might be able to write their stories without ever leaving headquarters or the newsroom. But experienced journalists know that they must go to the scenes of crimes and accidents to be able to report on them vividly.

17.2.1 Keeping Police Reports in Perspective

If the only information about the arrest of George Floyd that ever became public was the statement released by the Minneapolis Police Department, his death would have passed unnoticed.

The evening of Floyd's death, the police released the following statement under the headline, "Man Dies After Medical Incident During Police Interaction":

> May 25, 2020 (MINNEAPOLIS) On Monday evening, shortly after 8:00 pm, officers from the Minneapolis Police Department responded to the 3700 block of Chicago Avenue South on a report of a forgery in progress. Officers were advised that the suspect was sitting on top of a blue car and appeared to be under the influence.
>
> Two officers arrived and located the suspect, a male believed to be in his 40s, in his car. He was ordered to step from his car. After he got out, he physically resisted officers. Officers were able to get the suspect into handcuffs and noted he appeared to be suffering medical distress. Officers called for an ambulance. He was transported to Hennepin County Medical Center by ambulance where he died a short time later.
>
> At no time were weapons of any type used by anyone involved in this incident.

The press release gives the impression Floyd died of a heart attack, a stroke or a drug overdose. No one would think a police officer had drawn a gun and pointed it at Floyd's head. Only because a witness, 17-year-old Darnella Frazier, recorded video of it on her cell phone and because the city released police bodycam video days later did the world learn the truth. Frazier's video showed that one of the officers, Derek Chauvin, had knelt on Floyd with his knee pressed into Floyd's neck for nine minutes and 29 seconds. The official autopsy report classified Floyd's death by asphyxiation a homicide.

The deceptively low-key description of Floyd's death is part of a pattern of law enforcement whitewashing the conduct of officers. In 2019, Ronald Greene, a barber and Black male, died in an encounter with Louisiana State Patrol officers near the city of Monroe. The initial police report said Greene had died on impact when his car slammed into a tree after a high-speed chase. Two years later, the Associated Press obtained 46 minutes of bodycam video that told a very different story. Greene had pulled over after the chase and when approached by police, raised his hands and said, "OK, OK, I'm sorry." Officers stunned Greene while he was sitting in his SUV. He managed to get out of his SUV, then officers wrestled him to the ground. Once he was on the ground, officers put him in a choke hold, punched his face repeatedly and called him a "stupid motherfucker." After Greene had been beaten repeatedly, handcuffed and shackled, he was left face down on the ground, moaning while officers used sanitary wipes to clean his blood from their hands. Greene was dead when he finally arrived at a hospital. The emergency room physician to examine him first doubted the troopers' story that Greene had died in an

People view a memorial for George Floyd in Minneapolis, Minnesota. A subsequent investigation led to criminal homicide charges against the four police officers who arrested Floyd. One of the four, Derek Chauvin, was eventually convicted of second-degree murder.

accident. "Does not add up," the doctor wrote on his report. In spite of that, the coroner classified Greene's death as accidental. A state grand jury indicted the five state troopers involved on charges of negligent homicide, malfeasance in office and obstruction of justice.

The Floyd and Greene cases illustrate a problem with police reporting: the excessive reliance of reporters on the accounts they receive from law enforcement officers and the documents they prepare. The problem has existed for as long as there have been police and news reporters. But the popularity of cell phones with the capability of recording video and audio along with the growing use of body-cams by police departments have made the problem apparent. What police say happened sometimes contradicts what really happened. The discrepancies may be intentional in some instances, like the Floyd and Greene cases, where police may have used unnecessary force and caused grave injury or death. In other instances, the discrepancies may arise from negligence or misunderstanding. In either case, reporters should not assume the police version of events is entirely accurate. Instead, they should use police reports to identify possible witnesses who can provide their own descriptions of the events and then use them to crosscheck what the police are saying.

The frequency of police killings suggests news media need to pay attention. One killing that deserved—and received—close scrutiny from the media is that of Breonna Taylor, an emergency medical technician in Louisville, Kentucky. Police were investigating Jamarcus Glover and another man who were suspected of selling drugs out of a house far from where Taylor lived with her boyfriend. A judge, however, had signed a search warrant allowing police to search Taylor's apartment. At one time, she had been Glover's girlfriend, but she had broken off the relationship. Police thought Glover might have stored drugs at Taylor's apartment. In fact, Taylor had no involvement in Glover's drug dealings, which Glover later confirmed.

What happened when police arrived at Taylor's apartment shortly after midnight is in dispute. Police said they knocked and announced who they were. Taylor's boyfriend, Kenneth Walker, said they were awakened by loud pounding on the door. He denies that the police identified themselves and said he feared Glover was at the door. When the police knocked in the door with a battering ram, Walker fired a gun and wounded one of the officers. The police returned fire. Taylor was hit five times and died. Police found no drugs in Taylor's apartment.

These and other incidents have led reporters and social scientists to ask questions: Has police violence against minority members increased? Are police more likely to harm or kill Black people than white? Is the apparent surge in the use of lethal force against minorities just an illusion created by the media attention?

Police use deadly force more frequently than many realize. From 2013 through 2019, the U.S. averaged 1,097 instances of police killing people each year—about three each day. And a private organization, Mapping Police Violence, says the data are incomplete because police departments often fail to provide the information. The organization calculates that on the basis of deaths per one million population, Blacks are three times more likely to be killed by police than whites. The Blacks who are killed are also more likely than the whites to be unarmed.

Different studies have reached different conclusions, however. Roland G. Fryer Jr., a Harvard economist, looked at 10 years of data on police arrests and use of force from 10 major cities. He found that although police are more likely to stop and arrest and to use non-lethal force against Black people, there was little difference in the rates at which police shot Black and white suspects. But ProPublica looked at two years of federal data on 1,217 fatal shootings by police and concluded that Black males between 15 and 19 years were killed at a rate of 31.17 per million while whites of the same age were killed at a rate of only 1.47 per million.

The studies used different methodologies, which partly explains the different results. The major obstacle to figuring out exactly what is happening, however, is a lack of systematically collected data. The FBI collects data on justifiable homicides by police, but that count relies on information voluntarily provided by local law enforcement agencies, and experts believe it greatly understates the number of shootings. The FBI does not ask for data on how often police shoot civilians, on shootings that are not justifiable or on police-involved shootings by the race of the victim.

Partly in response to the news coverage, the U.S. Department of Justice will start collecting data on all "arrest-related" deaths, whether by shooting, physical force, Tasers or certain vehicular collisions. Until more reliable data are available, reporters and news organizations should refrain from drawing any conclusions about trends in police-involved shootings unless they have conducted a systematic and thorough investigation of their own.

17.2.2 Police-Reporter Relations

Reporters and law enforcement officers often are leery of one another, which sometimes deters thorough reporting. Journalists must work to overcome the suspicion and distrust of the police because they need information from officers to write their stories. The first step to gaining officers' confidence is to spend as many hours as possible at police headquarters and precinct stations. Reporters should chat with officers about their work and their professional concerns. They also should try to get permission to ride along in patrol cars. Those who do will see how officers spend their time and will learn what their lives are like. The best way journalists build trust with the police is to prove their professionalism by reporting on police matters accurately and thoroughly and by treating sources fairly.

How well police officers cooperate with reporters depends on the public records laws of each state and on the traditions and culture of each community. In some communities, either the police department has a policy of openness and cooperation with news reporters or state open records laws compel disclosure of much information. Elsewhere, police routinely may withhold as much information as possible, particularly where open records laws are weak or ambiguous. Most states allow police to withhold investigative records. Some states permit

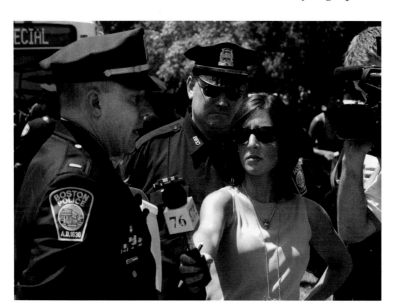

A reporter interviews a Boston police officer. To have a successful professional relationship, each party must gain the other's trust.

the withholding of almost any kind of investigative record, even if it is not part of a criminal investigation. Others say police can withhold only the records of active criminal investigations; once the investigation is complete or a prosecution has ended, the records become public.

Even if a police department's public information officer provides information readily, reporters still need to talk to the officers who investigated the crime or accidents. Reporters need details to make their stories complete. Public information officers, who rarely visit crime scenes, cannot furnish those specifics. Only the officers who were present know the information a reporter needs.

Reporters find the information they need when they develop good work habits. This means following a regular pattern for checking sources, such as police reports, jail records, the medical examiner's office and the department's public information officer. Other helpful sources journalists should cultivate are police union leaders, prosecutors, defense attorneys and bail bond agents.

17.2.3 Key Police Documents

Along with human sources, public documents enable reporters to put together stories that inform citizens and public officials about how their law enforcement agencies operate. Journalists should learn how to use the following records, available from police departments, courts and other agencies:

- The police blotter is a record of all calls for assistance received by the police. It usually tells where and when an event occurred and, possibly, whether someone was arrested and charged. The blotter best serves as a lead to other sources.
- Incident reports give a more complete description of events, including the nature of the crime, its location and time; the name of the victim; what property was stolen or damaged; and the name of the investigating officer. Other information might be available, depending on the law of the state. Some states withhold information about witnesses and victims; others suppress the investigating officer's narrative of the crime.
- Affidavits for arrest and search warrants can provide detailed information about investigations and help reporters understand what police are doing and why. Officers usually must get a warrant from a magistrate before they can arrest a suspect or legally search private property. They get warrants by filing affidavits—identifying the suspect they want to arrest or the place they want to search and the items they are searching for—with a court. The affidavits also provide more details about the suspects and their alleged crimes than police might be willing to divulge directly to reporters. Affidavits and warrants usually become public records once the arrest or search is complete; they and related documents can be found in district or circuit court files, not at the police station.
- Jail booking records indicate when a person was taken into custody and when that person was released.
- Autopsy reports are completed by coroners in cases involving violent or unexplained deaths. These documents describe the cause and manner of death. The cause of death is the medical reason the person died, such as gunshot wound to the heart or poisoning. The manner of death refers to the

circumstances under which the person died: accident, suicide or homicide. Some states withhold autopsy reports from the public.

- Medical examiner's reports may be separate from the autopsy, and they often include information about the crime scene, witnesses and next of kin that might not be in the police incident report.
- Arrest reports describe a person who has been arrested and the offense, name the officers involved, list the witnesses and, eventually, give the outcome of the case.
- Criminal history records disclose a person's previous arrests and convictions. The information is public in some states; others limit access to it. Disclosing that suspects have a criminal record can turn public opinion against them and make it harder for them to receive a fair trial. Journalists should use such information carefully and only after weighing the risks and benefits.
- Police misconduct investigation records reveal how a department has handled allegations that officers have broken the law or violated department regulations. In some states, these documents are confidential personnel records; other states open them to the public.
- Accident reports describe motor vehicle accidents and identify the time and place of the accident, the drivers involved, the passengers, the injuries and the property damages. The reports usually describe how the accident occurred as reconstructed by the investigating officer.

One example of using public documents is a series by Leila Atassi and Rachel Dissell, reporters at the Cleveland Plain Dealer. When Cleveland police tried to serve an arrest warrant on Anthony Sowell, they discovered 11 bodies hidden or buried in his home and backyard. This finding led to another revelation: In an earlier incident, a woman had reported being attacked by Sowell, but police had not considered her story credible. The two journalists decided to examine how police in the city and other Cuyahoga County communities handled sexual assault reports.

Atassi and Dissell, who described their work in the IRE Journal, began their investigation by collecting data on sexual assaults in Cuyahoga County. They compiled police reports, prosecutors' reviews of cases and court dispositions. From that data, the journalists learned that police often improperly cleared sexual assault cases. National standards and Cleveland Police Department policies required identifying suspects, but police failed to do so in 52 instances. They also discovered that many reports of sexual assaults were misclassified as "miscellaneous" or "departmental information." And they learned that the police had failed to record which rape kits had been tested for DNA and which had not. Atassi and Dissell's stories led to the institution of a countywide standard for handling sexual assault cases.

Police departments also keep records on how they spend money, and reporters can use them to examine police performance. A story for The

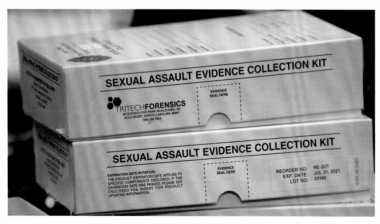

A sexual assault evidence collection kit.

Chicago Reporter by Jonah Newman examined 655 misconduct lawsuits filed against the Chicago Police Department between 2012 and 2015. While half of the cases were won by the city or dismissed, the other half resulted in jury awards or settlement payments to the plaintiffs. These cases cost the city $215 million plus another $53 million paid to outside law firms. The cost of the awards and settlements exceeded the city's budget for such expenses by about $50 million a year. The city borrowed money to pay for the lawsuits, increasing its already high debt load. Newman also found that the police department was not using the cases to identify and correct police practices that led to the lawsuits, a practice common in many other U.S. cities.

Approximately a year after the Sandy Hook tragedy, victims' relatives gave a press conference about the formation of MySandyHookFamily .org, a website that allows the families to honor their loved ones.

17.2.4 Respecting Victims

Because crime stories arouse strong emotional responses, they tempt news organizations to over-report them. The intensive coverage can distort the public's understanding of the accused, interfere with the work of police and the courts and traumatize the victims and their relatives. The killing of 20 children and six adults at the Sandy Hook Elementary School in Newtown, Connecticut, was a major news story that deserved extensive coverage. But as the people of Newtown faced the one-year anniversary of the killings, they feared the arrival of a wave of reporters, television cameras and satellite trucks. Citizens pleaded with reporters to stay away: "Give us some space. Give us the opportunity to recover together as a community," Patricia Llodra, the Newtown first selectman, told the Bergen (New Jersey) Record. Many news organizations complied with the town's request: CNN, NBC and CBS all kept their camera crews away. But others, including The Associated Press, argued they had an obligation to inform the public about how Newtown was coping. They sent reporters but promised to be respectful of the community's wishes.

17.2.5 Writing the Crime or Accident Story

Most crime stories have summary leads that identify the central point immediately. Usually, that point is the aspect of the crime that makes it newsworthy—deaths, money taken or some unusual or ironic twist to an incident. The stories should describe the specific crimes involved, not just the legal charges, which often fail to reveal exactly what happened. Moreover, because they are expressed in general terms, the same legal charges could be repeated in thousands of stories:

●   Three people arrested in a church parking lot Sunday morning were
                 siphoning gasoline from a car
    charged with ∧~~petty larceny~~.

As instructed in Chapter 3, never report a suspect's race or religion unless it is clearly relevant to the story. In the past (and sometimes even today) journalists mentioned the race only of suspects and criminals who were minorities. Race is relevant, however, in the description of a suspect who is at large.

If police have identified suspects in a crime, reporters must be careful not to imply that they committed the offense. Until someone has been tried and convicted or pleaded guilty, that person should be presumed innocent. To avoid implying guilt, news organizations say a suspect has been "arrested in connection with" a crime instead of "arrested for" one. Police or prosecutors may allege the suspect robbed a store, beat up a witness or murdered someone, but the story should make it clear that those are accusations from law enforcement officers, not facts.

Reporters should strive to include the following information in crime stories or in follow-up stories as the details become available:

- Any deaths or injuries. When they occur, they are often the most important facts and should appear early in the story.
- The nature and value of any property stolen or damaged.
- As complete an identification of the suspect as possible: full name (including middle initial), age, address and occupation. Complete identification prevents the audience from confusing the suspect with someone else with a similar name, which can lead to libel suits.
- Identification of victims and witnesses. To protect them, some news organizations will not publish their addresses. News organizations also routinely withhold the names of victims of sex crimes.
- Whether weapons were used in the commission of the crime and, if so, what types.
- The exact charges filed against the suspect.
- A narrative of the crime and arrest of the suspect.

Accident stories resemble crime stories in many of their elements. The central point of an accident story usually is deaths or injuries, property damage or unusual circumstances. The body of the story may include the recollections of the people involved in the accident or of other witnesses and the observations of the investigating officer. If people were injured in the accident and taken to hospitals, journalists try to get reports on their conditions.

Reporters covering accidents should avoid saying that one party or another was responsible. If police officers state in an accident report that one driver's conduct led to the car crash or issue a ticket to a driver, the information should be included in the story. But such statements should be treated as allegations by the police and not assumed to be fact. The people involved in the incident may have a different view, and the differences may have to be resolved in court. The Associated Press says that although "accident" is an appropriate word to use for automobile collisions or wrecks, when negligence is allleged on the part of one party or another, use "car crash" instead. "Accident" is sometimes taken as exonerating the person involved.

17.2.5.1 WORDS AND PHRASES TO AVOID

Never say a crime was committed by an "unidentified" person. Criminals rarely announce their identities, and most crimes are never solved. Thus, most criminals are never "identified." Similarly, if police do not know a criminal's identity, the story cannot report that the police are looking for "a suspect." Police have a suspect only if they have good reason to believe a particular person committed the crime.

Reporters also should avoid using the phrase "person of interest." Terms like "suspect," "target" and "material witness" have specific legal meanings; "person of interest" does not. Law enforcement agents sometimes use the phrase as a synonym for "suspect." When used that way, it encourages audiences to think of people as guilty long before they have been formally accused of a crime, let alone convicted by a jury.

Finally, journalists do not say that a person "received" injuries (see Figure 17.2). People "receive" gifts but normally "suffer" injuries.

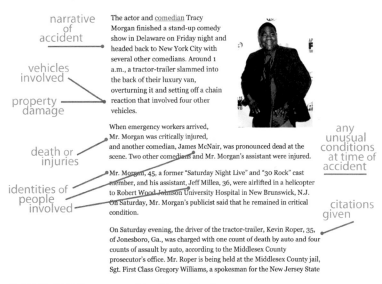

FIGURE 17.2 Elements of Accident Stories
This article includes the important details of the accident.

17.3 Courts

Most crimes are local matters. The perpetrators and the victims often are members of the same community, and the effects of crime are felt most intensely by that community. The trials usually are local matters. The most noteworthy crimes, usually homicides, may be covered by local or regional news organizations. Others may receive little or no news coverage. Occasionally, however, a crime attracts national and even international attention. The trial of Derek Chauvin in connection with the murder of George Floyd is an example.

Chauvin and three other Minneapolis police officers arrested Floyd on suspicion that he had used a counterfeit $20 bill to buy a pack of cigarettes in a convenience store. The officers said Floyd resisted arrest. They restrained him by putting him face down on the street. Chauvin kept his knee on the back of Floyd's neck for more than nine minutes. Floyd died of asphyxiation, which the coroner called a homicide. Chauvin was charged with murder in the second degree.

Chauvin's trial, which began nearly 10 months after Floyd's death, was closely watched for many reasons. Floyd's death was one of many in which Black men had died in confrontations with police or in police custody. Only rarely were police officers prosecuted in connection with these deaths and even rarer still were convictions. Floyd's death had ignited nationwide protests of police conduct, and in some instances, those protests were violent and destructive. The public wanted to know whether this case would result in a conviction.

Dramatic moments filled the trial. One of the early witnesses was Daniella Frazier who was 17 when she watched and videoed the killing of George Floyd. At times in tears, she testified that Floyd seemed to realize he was going to die. "It seemed like he knew it was over for him," Frazier said, according to The New York Times. "He was terrified. He was suffering. This was a cry for help, definitely." Several police officers testified that Chauvin's actions in restraining Floyd exceeded what was necessary and were contrary to police training and policy. Notably, Medaria Arrondondo, the Minneapolis police chief, testified that continuing to kneel on Floyd's neck as Chauvin did "in no way, shape or form" reflected police policy, training or values. Dr. Martin J. Tobin, a pulmonologist from the Chicago area, analyzed the video of the arrest and concluded Floyd died of a lack of oxygen. The way the police officers were holding Floyd's arm behind his back and pressing him into the street deprived him of much of his ability to breathe. "So, basically, on the left side of his lung, it was almost like a surgical pneumonectomy. It was almost to the effect that a surgeon had gone in and removed the lung," Tobin said.

After hearing this testimony and much more, the jurors needed only 10 hours to reach a verdict. They found Chauvin guilty of all the charges brought against him: second-degree murder, third-degree murder and second-degree manslaughter.

Two of the three officers who were with Chauvin pleaded guilty to aiding and abetting manslaughter. The third was convicted of that offense in a separate trial. All four officers were also convicted in federal court of depriving Floyd of his civil rights.

The trial of Derek Chauvin was both important and sensational. But focusing on such trials, as news organizations often do, can cause Americans to hold misconceptions about law and the courts. People might think criminal prosecutions depend heavily on scientific evidence, such as DNA tests. In fact, police and prosecutors on tight budgets often skimp on laboratory tests and rely on confessions to build their cases. People also might think criminal cases always result in trials that last weeks or even months, but most criminal cases are settled by plea bargains and never go to trial. When there is a trial, it usually lasts less than a week. Newsworthy cases might make people think lawyers engage in courtroom theatrics and make inflammatory statements to reporters. Generally, attorneys behave courteously toward one another and are restrained in what they say to the media. Some have a policy of never talking to reporters.

Even if most trials lack ballyhoo, they still can make interesting and important news stories. Crimes disrupt the community and challenge its moral order. The nation was shocked when a young white supremacist, Dylann Roof, killed nine Blacks during a church prayer service in Charleston, South Carolina. Readers, viewers and listeners want to know that people like Roof who commit crimes are arrested, prosecuted and punished. As U.S. Chief Justice Warren Burger noted, the ability to see how the justice system handles crime has a cathartic effect on the public.

Citizens also want to know that law enforcement officers, prosecutors, defense attorneys and judges are doing their jobs. In most instances, the justice system works well, but a number of innocent people have gone to prison. Reporters who cover the courts must remain vigilant and skeptical of what police, prosecutors and judges do. In 1986, Christine Morton was found bludgeoned to death in her bedroom in the Austin, Texas, area home she shared with her husband and 3-year-old son. Police almost immediately suspected Christine's husband, Michael. During the trial, his defense attorneys suspected the prosecutor, Ken Anderson, was withholding evidence, but Anderson assured the court he had given the defense team all the materials it was entitled to examine. Morton, who maintained his innocence throughout, was convicted and sentenced to life in prison. Eventually, he won the right to have DNA tests performed on evidence in the case; the results showed that he had not committed the murder. By the time he was freed, he had spent almost 25 years in prison.

Michael Morton speaks to the media during the 2013 case that determined if prosecutorial misconduct led to his wrongful conviction.

As they fought for DNA tests, Morton's attorneys also sought and obtained information from the prosecutor's files. Those records showed Anderson had withheld important evidence that might have convinced Morton's jury he was innocent. The concealed evidence included these facts: The Mortons' son had been in the house at the time of the murder and said the killer had not been his father; neighbors said a man had parked a green van near the Mortons' house on the day of the murder; and someone had tried to use Christine Morton's credit card, which had been stolen, at a store in San Antonio.

The Morton case inspired the Texas Legislature to pass a law expanding the right of criminal defendants to access evidence in prosecutors' files. Anderson, who had become a district judge by the time Morton was released, was prosecuted for failing to disclose evidence. He resigned his judgeship and reached a deal in which he agreed to serve nine days in jail and surrender his law license. In the meantime, Mark Alan Norwood, whose DNA linked him to the murder, was convicted of the crime.

Since 1989 more than 3,000 people, some of them sentenced to death, have been exonerated, often by DNA evidence, of the crimes for which they had been convicted. But DNA is irrelevant or unavailable in many cases; thus, the number of wrongful convictions might be quite large. A study supervised by a University of Michigan law professor concluded that more than 28,000 people may have been wrongfully convicted over a 15-year period. Reporters are not detectives or crime scene investigators, but they can keep their minds open about the evidence compiled by police and prosecutors and be willing to listen to defendants as well as victims.

17.3.1 General Information About the Court System

Criminal cases begin when the state charges someone with violating a criminal statute. Courts also hear civil cases, in which one individual sues another in matters such as divorce, contracts, personal injury and antitrust. Civil cases rarely attract as much press as criminal cases, but they may change more lives.

For example, news organizations paid close attention to the arrest and prosecution of Justin Bieber on charges that he had been racing his yellow Lamborghini on the streets of Miami Beach while under the influence of alcohol, marijuana and prescription drugs. In contrast, a lawsuit brought by a coalition of doctors, researchers and patients against a company that had discovered and patented genes associated with higher rates of hereditary breast and ovarian cancer received a good deal less news coverage. The latter case, however, resulted in a U.S. Supreme Court decision that naturally occurring genes cannot be patented, a ruling that may lower the cost of genetic testing but also discourage companies from investing in some genetic research. Either consequence may affect millions of people more directly than the outcome of Bieber's prosecution.

Court systems vary from state to state, but the general outlines are similar. Like the federal system, most have trial courts in which cases are initially heard, intermediate appellate courts and a highest appellate court.

The steps in a criminal court case resemble those for civil cases, but there are distinctions that might affect news coverage. Also, court procedures may differ from one state to another or between federal and state courts. Reporters who cover courts regularly should spend some time with local judges, prosecutors and defense attorneys to learn the state procedures. Bar and press associations in many states have collaborated to produce handbooks for journalists. These handbooks can be valuable resources as reporters follow court cases, both criminal and civil. The following sections summarize some of the major phases in criminal and civil cases and issues they present for news coverage.

17.3.2 Criminal Cases

17.3.2.1 PRETRIAL STAGES

Court action in a criminal case usually begins when a complaint is filed against the defendant. This stage happens at the initial appearance when the defendant is brought before a judge in a magistrate or county court and informed of the charges. Misdemeanors can be settled at this level. If the case is a felony, the judge sets bail and a date for a preliminary hearing.

The purpose of the preliminary hearing is to persuade a judge that the state has enough evidence against the defendant to merit a full trial. The judge can decide to free defendants or have them bound over for trial. Preliminary hearings usually are open to the press and public. About half the states use preliminary hearings in place of grand jury action. State use of grand juries is often limited to investigating public corruption or some similar task. In the federal system, however, people can be tried for felonies only if they have been indicted by a grand jury. If a grand jury finds probable cause to believe a defendant committed a crime, it will vote a bill of indictment, or a "true bill." Grand juries also may issue presentments, which give the results of their investigations.

Grand jury proceedings are closed to the press and public, but reporters can sit outside grand jury rooms and watch who goes in to testify. Witnesses are free to discuss their testimony with reporters, but grand jurors and attorneys are sworn to secrecy. Anyone who violates that oath risks being charged with contempt of court. Journalists who publish stories based on grand jury leaks may be subpoenaed to testify about their sources; if they refuse, they may be held in contempt.

Once defendants have been charged, either by a grand jury indictment or by a document called an "information" filed by a prosecutor, they are arraigned in the trial court. They enter their pleas, and trial dates are set. Because defendants have a constitutional right to a speedy trial, the proceedings usually begin within two or three months of the arrest. Before the trial begins, each side must disclose to the other all witnesses and exhibits. At any time, the defense and the prosecution may reach a plea agreement, which usually requires the defendant to plead guilty to a lesser charge or to some of the charges if others are dropped.

As reporters cover these pretrial steps, they must remind themselves and their readers, viewers and listeners that people who are charged with crimes are not always guilty.

17.3.2.2 TRIAL

The trial begins with the selection of the jurors (except in a bench trial, which is heard by the judge alone). Prospective jurors are asked whether they have a connection to the case or any of the people involved. Any who does can be dismissed. Attorneys for each side also have a limited number of opportunities to dismiss prospective jurors without giving a reason. Lawyers use these peremptory challenges to exclude prospective jurors who they believe will view their clients unfavorably.

Jury selection, like the rest of the trial, is almost always open to the public and the press, although the court may protect the jurors' identities in highly publicized cases. The prospective jurors may be referred to by number rather than by name. In this way, overly eager reporters and people with opinions about the case cannot speak to a juror by telephone or in person.

Courts always hear testimony in public, unless some overriding interest justifies closing the courtroom. Such an interest might be protecting a child from the emotional trauma of testifying in public about a sexual assault. Documents introduced as evidence become court records and also are open to the public. Here, too, the court might limit access in certain cases. For example, the court may prohibit public access to or copying of photographs, audiotapes or videotapes containing salacious or gory material.

The central point of a story about court proceedings should emphasize the most important testimony or ruling of the day. Mistakenly, beginners often emphasize a witness's identity or topic of testimony instead of what was said. Leads usually do not say whether a witness testified for the state or defense; that can be reported later in the story. The news—the witness's most telling remarks—is more important.

The trial ends when the jury delivers its verdict. Jurors deliberate in private, but journalists try to talk to them after the trial to find out what evidence and arguments they found most persuasive and how they evaluated the witnesses, attorneys and defendant. Occasionally judges try to protect jurors either by reminding them they have no obligation to speak to reporters or by ordering reporters not to approach them. The latter approach may violate the First Amendment unless the judge has a powerful reason for protecting jurors in a particular case.

17.3.2.3 POST-TRIAL

If the trial ends in an acquittal, the reporter will want to interview the defendant, defense attorney, prosecutor, jurors and witnesses for a post-trial wrap-up. If the defendant is convicted, the next major step is sentencing. Congress and state legislatures have restricted judges' discretion in imposing sentences. Nevertheless, judges still can impose sentences within broad ranges.

Convicts usually undergo a series of examinations by psychologists and penologists to determine the appropriate sentence. These officials' recommendations are contained in pre-sentence evaluations. The severity of the sentence depends partly on these reports and partly on such factors as mitigating or aggravating circumstances associated with the crime.

Prosecutors cannot appeal an acquittal, but defendants always have the right to appeal a conviction. To succeed on appeal, defendants must show that the trial court made some grave error of law that warrants reversing the conviction and ordering a new trial. Although appeals rarely succeed, the process can go on for years, particularly in cases involving a death sentence. It might also take a case through several state and federal courts.

17.3.3 Civil Cases

17.3.3.1 PRETRIAL

A civil case begins when one party files a complaint in court against another party. The person filing the complaint is the plaintiff, and the other party is the defendant. The complaint, which is a public document, states the factual and legal basis for the lawsuit and tells the court the plaintiff's desired remedy. Usually, plaintiffs want money to compensate for injuries, lost wages, lost property or misfortunes arising from the defendant's conduct. However, plaintiffs might seek a court order prohibiting the defendant from doing something or requiring the defendant to do something. Such orders are called "equitable relief." Plaintiffs ask for both kinds of remedies in some cases.

Reporters should be skeptical of the money demanded in lawsuits. Plaintiffs can demand any amount they want, even though it might be obviously exorbitant. To attract news coverage, some lawyers encourage clients to demand millions of dollars as compensation for minor injuries. The plaintiffs normally settle for much less. News stories, therefore, generally should not emphasize the amount demanded. Dominion Voting Systems asked for $1.5 billion in damages in its libel suit against Fox News or allegations of rigging the 2020 presidential election, but it settled for about half that amount, still an extraordinarily large sum.

The complaint presents only the plaintiffs' charges; defendants are likely to deny them, and a judge or jury may decide (months or even years later) that they are unfounded. Thus, a news story should indicate clearly that the charges are the plaintiffs' allegations, not accepted facts. For example:

- ~~Because of the accident,~~ Samuelson ∧ will require medical care for the rest of his life. *'s lawsuit says he*

Defendants who cannot persuade the court to dismiss the complaint must file answers, which set forth their version of the facts and interpretation of the law. Like complaints, the defendant's answers are public records. Whenever possible, the news story should include this response to the charges. If it is not in the case file, reporters should interview the defendant or his or her attorney. The following example and revision illustrate the inclusion of a defendant's response. They also illustrate the need to condense, simplify and attribute the claims in a plaintiff's lawsuit. Consider the following example; the second version is more concise than the first.

> He was caused to slip, trip and fall as a direct result of the negligence and carelessness of the store because of a liquid on the ground. This fall injured his neck, head, body, limbs and nervous system and caused him to be unable to lead a normal life and to lose his normal wages for a prolonged period of time.
>
> **Revised:** The suit charges that he slipped and fell on a wet sidewalk outside the store, dislocating his shoulder and tearing several ligaments.
>
> The store's manager responded, "He was running to get out of the rain and slipped and fell on the wet pavement."

As the case goes forward, both sides engage in the discovery process, during which they take sworn statements from witnesses and the opposing parties. They seek documents and other evidence from each other. The discovery process happens outside of court, and the press and public have no right of access to it. Exchanged information remains confidential unless it is filed with the court. Even then, the side producing the information can ask that the court seal material that is highly personal or that might disclose trade or business secrets.

In some jurisdictions, the practice of sealing the records in court cases has become almost routine. However, doing so deprives the public and even government agencies of information about problems and about how the courts function. The Boston Globe won a Pulitzer Prize for its stories about Catholic priests sexually abusing children in the city, but it was able to report fully on the problem only after persuading courts to unseal documents in scores of lawsuits. Some states have tried to limit the sealing of court records, either through legislation or through changes in court rules.

17.3.3.2 TRIAL

A civil trial proceeds much as a criminal one, and it is usually open to the press and public. The trial may be heard by a judge, who decides the case alone, or by a jury. Some states use juries that have fewer than 12 members to hear civil cases.

A civil trial, like a criminal one, can end at any time if the two sides reach an agreement. In fact, civil proceedings are more likely to conclude in this manner. Judges encourage settlements, preferably before the trial. The parties to the case usually keep secret the terms of any agreement. Sometimes a settlement must have court approval and thus may become public record.

17.3.3.3 POST-TRIAL

If the parties do not reach a settlement, the trial ends with the verdict. If the result is a large damage award to the plaintiff, the defendant may ask the judge to reduce it, often arguing that the award was the product of emotion rather than reason on the part of the jury. Judges sometimes grant such motions.

Losing parties—either defendants or plaintiffs—also may ask the judge to set aside the jury's verdict and render one in their favor (called a judgment as a matter of law) or ask for a new trial. Neither request is granted frequently. More commonly, the losing party appeals the verdict to a higher court. Again, the loser must argue that the trial court committed a legal error serious enough to warrant a reversal of the verdict or a new trial. Appeals rarely succeed.

17.4 Environment

The proper focus of public affairs reporting is any issue that touches on the well-being of people in the community, the country and the world. No issue fits this definition better than the environment. Toxic chemicals, air pollution and climate change all constitute threats to the lives and prosperity of people who consume news. They also carry implications for politics and the economy.

Global climate change brought about by the release into the atmosphere of carbon dioxide, methane and other gases causing the warming of the planet represents a major threat. Scientists agree almost unanimously that these gases—called greenhouse gases because they trap the heat from the sun—have caused average global temperatures to rise by more than 1 degree Celsius since the beginning of the industrial age. The rate of warming is increasing and could exceed 1.5 degrees Celsius (2.7 degrees Fahrenheit) unless governments around the world take drastic and sustained action.

At the global level, news about climate change involves international diplomacy and the competing interests of countries large and small. The countries that have contributed the most to the levels of greenhouse gases are the United States, Great Britain, France, Germany and other European countries. China, by becoming a major industrial power, is the largest emitter of such gases. But the costs of climate change are borne by small countries that contribute little to the problem. They want money from the more prosperous countries to help them deal with the impacts of climate change. Many countries are trying to switch their economies from reliance on fossil fuels—oil, coal and natural gas—to renewable sources like wind and solar power. They face resistance, however, from the wealthy and highly influential companies that extract, distribute and sell fossil fuels.

Some of the effects of climate change are distant and make news only when scientists report them or journalists make a special effort to travel to a remote island or continent. An example is the news that ice in one part of the Arctic Ocean had become more vulnerable to the warming climate. The Wandel Sea, which is just north of Greenland, has been thick with sea ice. In 2020, however, scientists on a research expedition found the ice covering had become thin, and many areas were completely free of ice. Natural variability of the winds in the region explain some of the change, but Melinda Webster, a researcher from the University of Alaska Fairbanks, said the warming climate will make the thinning of the Arctic ice more common.

Other effects of climate change are closer to home. The Texas freeze of 2021 is one example. Another is the triple-digit heat wave that blanketed much of the Pacific Northwest in June and July 2021. Such high temperatures are uncommon in the Northwest, and many people were unprepared for the heat that lasted several weeks. Oregon reported 116 deaths attributable to the heat. Other affected states also reported deaths. A team of scientists from several nations conducted computer simulations and concluded the heat wave would not have happened without global warming. Before humans started burning fossil fuels in massive amounts, such a heat wave might have happened once in 1,000 years, the study said. But now, it might happen every five to 10 years.

The heat wave contributed to massive wildfires in California, Oregon, Washington and other western states. Although the wildfires were concentrated in the West, the health effects were felt across the United States. Three-fourths of the deaths and emergency room admissions related to smoke inhalation were in states east of the Rocky Mountains. Research published in GeoHealth, a publication of the

Flames consume trees during the Dixie Fire in Genesee, California. The Dixie Fire consumed almost 1 million acres and destroyed several small towns. It was the second largest wildfire in California history and one of dozens in the western United States in the summer of 2021.

American Geophysical Union, found that the long-term exposure to smoke caused 6,300 additional deaths. Only 1,700 were in western states; the rest were in more populous states farther east.

Reporters can find stories about climate change and its effects on the local level, too. As heat waves like that of 2021 become more common, demand for air-conditioning will increase in cities like Denver, Portland and Seattle, places where people have considered it unnecessary. Air-conditioning more homes will increase energy demand, however, and may aggravate the climate problems. Some communities are looking to encourage residents to replace central air-conditioning with heat pumps, which are more energy efficient. Heat pumps can cool a home in the summer and heat it in the winter. They can replace natural gas furnaces for most heating needs, thus reducing the demand for fossil fuels. Heat pumps are more expensive than traditional air conditioners, so some communities are experimenting with subsidizing the purchase of heat pumps.

Climate change has also affected a long-standing American tradition: summer camp. The New York Times reported that summer camps across the country were forced to change their practices because of heat, algae blooms in lakes, proliferations of ticks and bans on outdoor burning. Hot days are an accepted part of the summer-camp experience, but climate change has meant warmer nights, too. Some camps have started installing air-conditioning in the bunk houses. They have also had to remodel their facilities to handle more extreme weather events such as flooding, snowstorms, microburst storms and derechos (widespread long-lived windstorms that produce strong, straight-line winds). Camps in fire-prone regions have had to evacuate campers because of wildfires. The threat of fire in dry, hot areas means some camps have abandoned traditional campfires for flashlight campfires. The flashlights cut the risk of wildfires, but they don't help with making s'mores.

The Chicago Theatre had closed in mid-March 2020 because of the COVID-19 pandemic, along with almost everything else in American life. Nearly one billion people were confined to their homes worldwide by that time. In every country, people struggled to adapt to life during the shutdown.

17.5 Public Health

In late 2019, authorities in China were reporting severe illnesses and deaths from a new coronavirus. The virus, later designated COVID-19 because it was discovered in 2019, quickly spread to the rest of the world. By early spring 2020, public life in many countries, including the United States, came to a standstill. The virus had proved to be highly contagious and potentially lethal. Some people who survived COVID experienced days of agony during which they struggled to breathe. By the end of 2020, more than 2 million had died of COVID worldwide, more than 355,000 of them Americans.

The COVID-19 pandemic proves that accurate information about threats to public health can save lives. Unfortunately, accurate information has had to battle misinformation. The Kaiser Family Foundation, an organization that tracks public health issues, discovered in a survey that 78 percent of Americans believed or were unsure about at least one of eight false statements about COVID. Nearly two-thirds believed at least four of the false statements. The false statement that was most widely believed was that the U.S. government was exaggerating the number of people who died of COVID. Other false statements that were widely believed were that pregnant women should not receive vaccines against the disease, that the government was hiding deaths caused by the vaccines, that the vaccines caused infertility, and that the vaccines gave COVID-19 to those who receive them.

The news sources respondents said they trusted most correlated with the degree to which they believed the falsehoods. People who said their trusted sources of information were Fox News, One America News or Newsmax were much more likely to believe the falsehoods about COVID than people who listed network news, National Public Radio or CNN as a trusted news source.

While some news organizations have published falsehoods about the pandemic and the COVID vaccines, either intentionally or negligently, part of the problem has been inconsistent advice from the government. When the virus first appeared in the United States, authorities believed it was spread by contact with surfaces as much as or more than by air. People were advised to sanitize furniture and goods regularly. Health officials said it was probably unnecessary for people to wear masks. Later, the advice changed. Sanitizing surfaces was downplayed, and masks became mandatory. Then, when vaccines became available, most scientists and doctors said two shots of the Moderna or Pfizer vaccines and one of the Johnson & Johnson vaccine would be sufficient. But only a few months later, the Centers for Disease Control and Prevention said booster shots were necessary for all.

The changing advice reflected the fact scientists are continuing to learn about COVID-19. As the virus spread and as people became sick, sometimes with unexpected symptoms, scientists discovered more about how it worked and what steps might protect people. For scientists, this process of discovery is routine, but the changing advice confused the public.

One criticism of the way the COVID-19 pandemic has been covered is that U.S. news reports have been too negative. A study of pandemic coverage by three university scholars found media coverage in the U.S. much more negative than coverage in the United Kingdom. One example of the negative nature of the coverage is how news organizations reported the surge in cases following the release of vaccines. The stories emphasized the number of new cases and the fact that some people who had received the vaccine became infected. The stories gave less attention to the fact people who had received the vaccine were much less likely to require hospitalization or to die than people who had not been vaccinated. Dr. Ashish Jha of the Brown University School of Public Health told a New York Times reporter, "I don't actually care about infections. I care about hospitalizations and deaths and long-term complications." By that standard, the vaccines have been spectacularly effective. An unnamed official in the Biden administration told a CNN reporter that the news coverage, with the emphasis on infections, was hardening resistance to vaccinations.

Some of the suspicion about the vaccines may arise from the lack of knowledge about how the vaccines were developed and how they work. Major news organizations have paid little attention to these more technical topics. Two of the vaccines, those from Pfizer and Moderna, employ a relatively new technology using messenger ribonucleic acid—mRNA. These vaccines were developed within months of the discovery of COVID-19, and because of the rapidity of their release, some may fear the vaccines were not adequately tested. They also misunderstand how the vaccines work. According to the Centers for Disease Control and Prevention, the mRNA vaccines enter muscle cells at the injection site and instruct the cells to produce a harmless spike protein on their surfaces like the spike found on the surface of the virus. The body's immune system recognizes the cells with the spike protein as an invader and produces antibodies to fight them. This teaches the immune system how to fight off the COVID-19 virus if it enters the body.

The mRNA technology is relatively new, but it is something scientists have been researching for decades. Scientists discovered mRNA in the early 1960s. By the mid-1970s, scientists recognized it could be used for delivering vaccines for a variety of illnesses. The problem with putting that to practical use was the vulnerability of synthetic RNA to the body's immune defenses. Scientists overcame that problem by slightly modifying the mRNA to evade the defense. That development came shortly before 2005 and spawned the start-up of companies seeking to put the technology to use. Thus, although mRNA vaccines were novel when introduced in late 2020 and early 2021, they were the product of decades of research and testing.

Reporting on public health issues requires journalists to develop sources in science and medicine. A problem for some of these potential sources is the fear that the information they have will be misunderstood, sensationalized or distorted. It helps if reporters have some science background, preferably in biology or chemistry, enabling them to understand what their sources are saying and ask intelligent questions. Some science reporters also will do something reporters on other beats, particularly political ones, are reluctant to do: They let scientists review the stories or parts of the stories before they are published. The reporter may send a scientist a copy of a story in which that person is quoted or may read back to the source the parts of the story attributed to that person. Because of the highly technical nature of the information and the need for scrupulous accuracy, editors often agree to this arrangement.

Guest Columnist

Developing Sources on the Police Beat

BY ANDREW J. NELSON

The police beat is the most fascinating beat in any news organization. It has it all: Jealousy. Death. Drama. Political shenanigans. Reporters who have never spent at least part of their careers covering public safety are missing out.

Sourcing the police beat is much like sourcing any other beat. You figure out who the key people are, and you get to know them. And you don't just do that on deadline. You seek people out well before you need something from them.

Let's assume you have just been hired as a cops reporter. What do you do?

First of all, talk to your predecessor. With any luck, he or she is still working for your organization. Ask that person to tell you who the key people are. If your predecessor has moved to a different news organization and is unreachable, you may have to figure it out for yourself.

Once you figure out who the key people are, go out and meet them—lunch, coffee, a sit-down in their office.

Generally, the first people you need to get to know will be the police chief and his or her principal deputies. Plus the precinct commanders if the city is big enough. It goes without saying if your department has a dedicated information officer, you need to get to know that person, too. But he or she certainly should not be your only source—more on that in a moment.

If you work for a larger publication and begin, as many do, as the night cops reporter, getting to know the chief may not be as important as getting to know the night duty commander, the night patrol director or the night supervisor of detectives. All communities and news organizations are a bit different.

When you meet your top sources, show an interest in them and their work. Share a bit of yourself that won't be objectionable to the person you are trying to turn into a source.

Be genuine. Don't try to be something you are not or mislead someone about what your goals are. By the same token, you should legitimately be curious about the person who is your source and their work. If you are not, you are probably on the wrong beat. If you are not curious about anything at all, you shouldn't be in journalism.

Some police officers will be suspicious about any overtures on your part. The best thing to do is to tell yourself, and them, that we are going to be seeing a lot of each other and it is in our best interest and that of the public for us to get to know each other a little.

Do not give anyone the false impression that you are their department's public relations agent. You aren't.

In your stories, try to speak to the police officer who caught the mugger or solved the homicide. Often departments prefer you speak to a senior officer or the public information officer, and sometimes you are going to have to settle for that. But it is much better to speak to the street cop directly. The information is usually more accurate, it leads to more dramatic stories and it helps police officers who do good things get their due.

When dealing with police, be punctual. Police culture tends to emphasize punctuality.

But it is not enough to get the police to like and respect you. With them you are getting only one side of the story. Sourcing only the cops is like sourcing only one side of a political race.

Every police department has its critics. Get to know them. They could be:

- A criminal justice professor at a local university.
- A criminal defense attorney.
- A civil rights organization.

Other people you should try to source:

- Retired officers.
- Low-level officers and detectives, even if you have to agree never to quote them by name.

Good practices to perform upon assuming the cops reporter role:

- Ask for a tour of the police station, the jail, places like that.
- Go on a ride-along. Get a feel for what it's like to be on patrol.
- Visit the early shift briefings (sometimes called "lineup") and introduce yourself to the police.

All this could take several months, and it is a never-ending process. But you really have to kick it into gear your first few months on the job.

Andrew J. Nelson is freelance writer and former reporter for the Omaha (Nebraska) World-Herald.

Guest Columnist

Journalists Deliver the Information the Public Needs

BY DON STACOM

Fire damages a major factory, and suddenly a lot of jobs are on the line. Everyone is wondering whether the owners will rebuild.

Health inspectors accuse a tattoo parlor of using filthy equipment. Are the charges true, or just a way to shut down an unpopular business?

In the middle of the year, the community college reports it's running out of money and needs an emergency tuition increase next semester. Students, parents and faculty are all asking the same thing: What went wrong?

Situations like those come up every day in small farm towns, big cities and every type of community in between. Those situations are at the heart of journalism. People want somebody to tell them what's going on, somebody to make sense of events in this ever-more-complex world.

That somebody is usually a professional journalist.

Even as the journalism industry undergoes crises of finance and identity, the market for professionally reported news is still extraordinary. Perhaps "citizen journalism" will someday live up to its hype, but for now, the heavy lifting in the news field is still being performed by professionals.

Whether on the air, in print or online, the professionals carry the responsibility of finding out what's going on— and then telling everyone else. So often now, forums and workshops about the future of journalism can't get past debates about platforms and delivery modes, and seem to forget the very basics of why people bother listening to, reading or viewing the news. The core reason is the *information*—and that's where traditional journalists still do work that nobody else does.

Who else will phone the mayor to ask why local roads are still rutted with potholes even after last spring's big tax increase? Who else gets to press the detective commander for answers about the wave of armed holdups downtown? Who else will use freedom of information laws to get copies of the high school's phone bills and then scrutinize them to see whether teachers are making long personal calls on the taxpayers' bill? Who else confronts the executive at a plant closing, asking about the company's guarantee just a year ago that it wasn't going anywhere?

On a day-to-day basis, that work simply isn't done by anyone else. Take away the journalists, and nobody will ask the questions, spot the patterns or challenge the spin doctors. It's a wildly imperfect profession that often falls short of "good" and never reaches "perfect," but it remains one of the few fields where an individual stands a good chance of making a difference in the community.

Don Stacom is a reporter for The Hartford Courant in Connecticut.

The Reporter's Guide to Public Affairs Reporting

LOCAL GOVERNMENT

1. Learn how your local governments are organized, what their powers and limitations are and how the various governmental units interact.

2. Study the budgets of local government units, and learn how governments raise their money.

3. Develop a routine for visiting the local government offices on your beat, and become familiar with the people who work in those offices.

4. Learn what public records are kept in each office and how to use them.

5. Go beyond covering school board meetings; visit schools and talk to principals, teachers, parents and students.

CRIMES AND ACCIDENTS

1. Spend time at the police station and talk to officers; try to learn their concerns.

2. Get as much information as possible from the investigating officers, witnesses, victims and suspects.

3. Check out all police reports and allegations as thoroughly as possible.

4. Learn what records are available at the police station and what information they do and do not contain.

5. When writing crime stories, avoid implying that a suspect is guilty.

6. Avoid referring to a suspect's race or religion unless it is clearly relevant to the story.

COURTS

1. Remember that the state files criminal charges against people suspected of violating criminal laws, whereas civil cases are usually between private parties.

2. Learn how state courts are organized, what the various courts are called and what kinds of cases they hear.

3. Learn how court records are kept and how to find the records on any particular case.

4. Do not imply that a defendant in a criminal case is guilty; only the judge or jury can make that decision.

5. Be skeptical of allegations and damage claims that appear in civil complaints; they present only one side of the story.

6. Be alert to the possibility that a plea bargain or a settlement will end a case before or during a trial.

ENVIRONMENT

1. Identify the state and federal agencies that deal with environmental issues and learn how they are organized.

2. Identify nongovernmental sources who can discuss environmental issues. These may include sources in business, agriculture and education.

3. Some environmental problems are global in nature, but they may have effects on local businesses and activities. Be alert to the local implications.

PUBLIC HEALTH

1. Avoid being excessively negative in describing public health problems.

2. Provide readers and viewers with accurate information about how they can protect themselves from health threats.

3. Include information that will help readers and viewers understand the nature of the health threats and how medicines, vaccines and other medical treatments can help them.

4. Develop sources in science and medicine and read bulletins and other information from authoritative sources, such as the U.S. Centers for Disease Control and Prevention.

 # Review Exercises

Many of the documents available to a public affairs reporter—lawsuits and police reports, for example—provide all the information needed for minor stories. Examples of such documents are reprinted in the following exercises. Write a news story about each document. Unless the instructions say otherwise, assume that the police reports have been prepared by officers who investigated incidents in your community, and that all other legal documents have been filed in your city hall, county courthouse or federal building.

Most of the exercises use genuine copies of actual government documents. Even the most unusual police reports are based on actual cases.

1. 911 EMERGENCY: A CHILD'S HEROISM

Laura Burke, the 6-year-old daughter of Lynn and Randy Burke of 412 Wilson Avenue, placed the following call to a 911 dispatcher in your city today. Police arrested a neighbor, Andrew Caspinwall of 416 Wilson Avenue, and charged him with raping Mrs. Burke. Bail has been set at $250,000, and Caspinwall, 24, is being held in the county jail.

DISPATCHER: 911 emergency. Hello?

GIRL: My mommy needs help.

DISPATCHER: What's wrong?

GIRL: Somebody's hurting my mommy.

DISPATCHER: Where do you live?

GIRL: At home with my mommy and daddy.

DISPATCHER: No, uh, that's not what I mean. Can you tell me where your house is, your address?

GIRL: Wilson Avenue.

DISPATCHER: Do you know the address, the number?

GIRL: Hurry. My mommy's crying.

DISPATCHER: No, honey, do you know your address?

GIRL, CRYING: I gotta think. It's, uh, it's, uh, 4 something, I'm not sure. 412. 412.

DISPATCHER: OK. I'll send help.

GIRL, CRYING: Hurry.

DISPATCHER: What's your name?

GIRL: Laura. Laura Anne Burke.

DISPATCHER: Can you tell me what's wrong, who's hurting your mother?

GIRL: A man. He came in the back door and hit my mommy.

DISPATCHER: Where are you now?

GIRL: Upstairs.

DISPATCHER: Does the man know you're there?

GIRL: No. I'm hiding.

DISPATCHER: Where are you hiding?

GIRL: In my mommy and daddy's room. Under the bed.

DISPATCHER: Can you lock the door?

GIRL: I don't know. Maybe.

DISPATCHER: Don't hang up. Just put the phone down and go lock the door. Then come back, talk to me some more.

GIRL: My mommy. What'll happen to my mommy?

DISPATCHER: We've got three police cars coming. They'll be there in a minute. Now go lock the door, and don't let anyone in until I tell you. OK?

GIRL: I guess so.

DISPATCHER: Hello? Hello? Laura, are you there?

GIRL: I locked the door.

DISPATCHER: How old are you, Laura?

GIRL: Six.

DISPATCHER: You're doing a good job, Laura. You have to be brave now to help your mommy. Tell me, is the man armed?

GIRL: What's that mean?

DISPATCHER: Does he have a gun?

GIRL: No. A knife.

DISPATCHER: OK, a knife. Is the man still there, Laura?

GIRL, SOBBING: I don't know. I'm afraid. Will he hurt me, too?

DISPATCHER: No one will hurt you, Laura. Be brave. The police are outside now. They'll be coming into your house. You may hear some noise, but that's OK. Stay in the bedroom, and don't let anyone in, OK?

GIRL: OK.

DISPATCHER: Your daddy's coming, too. We've found your daddy.

GIRL: Soon?

DISPATCHER: The police say they're in your house. They're helping your mommy now. They've found your mommy, and they're going to take her to a doctor, a hospital.

GIRL: The man?

DISPATCHER: He's been caught, arrested. It's OK. It's safe to go downstairs now. There are people there to help you. They want to talk to you, Laura. Can you unlock your door and go downstairs? Laura? Hello? Are you there? Laura? Hello? Laura?

2. COMPLAINT REPORT

SHERIFF'S OFFICE

COMPLAINT REPORT

ZONE __1__ UNIT __5, 3, 9, & 14__   CASE NO. __K51-1020C__

GRID __One__   PAGE __One__ OF __One__   OTHER AGCY CASE NO. __None__

MESSAGE NUMBER __31847P__   DATE __Today__ (MONTH / DAY / YR)

TIME RECEIVED __01:22__   TIME DISPATCHED __01:22__   TIME ARRIVED __01:30__   TIME IN-SERVICE __03:12__   WEATHER __NA__

NATURE OF CASE __Armed Robbery__   CHANGED TO _____   F.S.S. ____ FEL. ____ MISD. ____

LOCATION OF OCCURRENCE (INCL. NAME OF BUSINESS/SCHOOL) __Jiffy Foods, 4010 Holbrook Dr.__

VICTIM __Terry DaRoza__ (LAST) (FIRST) (MIDDLE)   AGE __34__ R/S ___ DOB MO. ___ DAY ___ YR ___

HOME ADDRESS __410 University Boulevard #80__   PHONE __823-4771__

CITY __Yes/Local__   STATE _____   ZIP _____

BUSINESS ADDRESS __4010 Holbrook Dr.__   PHONE __823-0333__

CITY __Yes/local__   STATE _____   ZIP _____

REPORTER ☐ WITNESS ☐ __See below__   PHONE _____

CITY _____   STATE _____   ZIP _____

PROPERTY MISSING/STOLEN			EST. VALUES	
QUAN	ITEM	DESCRIPTION - SERIAL NO. - MFG NO. - ETC	STOLEN	RECOVERED
		Cash register contained approx $80 but nothing was actually stolen		

■ MISSING ■ SUSPECT ■ ARRESTED ■ WITNESS ■ OTHER

NAME __Suspect #1: Keel, Timothy__ (LAST) (FIRST) (MIDDLE)   AGE __19__ R/S ___ DOB MO. ___ DAY ___ YR ___

ADDRESS __1413 Griese Dr.__   PHONE __823-3411__

CITY __Yes/local__   STATE _____   ZIP _____

BUSINESS OR SCHOOL ADDRESS __Plaza Barber Shop   2140 West Av.__

HEIGHT __5' 4"__ WEIGHT __120__ HAIR __Black__ EYES __Black__ COMPLEXION __Pocked__ OCCUPATION __Barber__

CLOTHING, ETC.. __Blue plaid shirt, tan pants, dark blue jacket, Braves baseball cap__

VEHICLE INVOLVED

☒ USED   ☐ STOLEN   ☒ TOWED   ☐ DAMAGED   ☐ BURGLARIZED   ☐ WRECKER   ☐ OTHER _____

YEAR __'94__ MAKE __Toyota__ MODEL __Celica__ BODY STYLE __2-door__ COLOR __Brown__ DECAL _____

LICENSE TAG NO. _____   STATE _____   YEAR EXPIRES _____   I.D. OR VIN NO. _____

REMARKS _____

ENTERED FCIC/NCIC ☐ YES ☐ NO   BOLO ☐ YES ☐ NO   MESSAGE NO. _____

NARRATIVE __The complainant is currently employed full-time as a clerk at Jiffy Foods, a convenience store open 24 hrs. DaRoza states 2 men entered said premises approx. 01:15 today. DaRoza was cleaning a popcorn machine when the 2 asked to use the toilet. DaRoza walked behind the counter to get the key and was followed by Keel who then pulled a knife. DaRoza was recently injured in a construction job, with one leg still in a cast, and uses a cane. DaRoza adds he swung the cane as hard as he could into the arrestee's face, hitting him repeatedly. Paramedics say Keel's nose and jaw and other facial bones are broken. Suspect #1 fell to the floor and suspect #2 then tried grabbing the cane from DaRoza, who proceeded to turn it on him. While suspect #2 fled, DaRoza got help from an entering customer, Stuart Adler, 1847 Oakland Boulevard, who helped tie suspect #1 with their belts until we arrived. Keel is charged with armed robbery and resisting a merchant. DaRoza said he was not injured. He is 6' 4" tall and weighs about 260 pds and works at the store while__

DISPOSITION: __recuperating from injuries received in a construction job accident.__

FURTHER POLICE ACTION TAKEN   ☐ YES ☒ NO   REFERRED TO __Robbery Division__

__S. Cullinan__   __D. Aneja__

REPORTING OFFICER'S NAME (PRINT)   I.D. NO. (INITIAL)   APPROVED BY

3. TRAFFIC ACCIDENT REPORT NO. 1

An explanation of the numerical codes used in the following report can be found on the companion website. You may assume you obtained the additional information provided from interviews with the identified sources. Passages in quotation marks may be used as direct quotations. Check all names and addresses by using the City Directory.

Additional Information: Statements

Ruth Herwarthe, witness: "The car seemed to come over the hill just this side of 44th Street and for a moment it seemed to be airborne. Then when it hit ground, that's when it seemed to go out of control. In a flash it was over the curb and then it hit my tree so hard I thought it was going to knock it over. Two of the kids in the car were hurt pretty bad. I think the girl hit the windshield with her head. Her face was all bloody and she wasn't moving. One of the boys was hurt bad enough he couldn't walk. The other boy—I don't know if he was the driver—seemed just fine."

Barry Kopperud, police chief: "Nicole Ping was in the back seat and was not wearing a seat belt. The force of the impact propelled her into the windshield, which she struck headfirst. She was not responsive at the scene of the accident and was taken to Sacred Heart Hospital at 3:45 p.m. She was pronounced dead about an hour later. The driver, Anthony Gould, was also taken to the hospital. I understand he's been released but did receive serious injuries. Gould wasn't wearing a seat belt or shoulder harness, but his airbag did deploy. The third person in the car was Kevin Shadgott. He was the only person wearing a seat belt. Gould had his license revoked two months ago after two previous incidents of negligent and reckless driving. Neither of those incidents resulted in injuries, but one did involve his losing control of the vehicle, leaving the roadway and striking a mailbox."

Additional Information About Nicole Ping

Nicole Ping was a sophomore at Colonial High School. Sara Shepard, the daughter of Frank and Helen Shepard and a close friend of Nicole's said, "I just started screaming when I heard Nicole had died. I can't believe she's gone. We both loved music and science and math. We helped each other and cared for each other. Now she won't be there anymore."

Jeanette Weinstein, a teacher at Colonial, said Nicole was a 4.0 student and was especially strong in mathematics. "She was so bright that there was no topic she could not master. She was just one of the best," Weinstein said.

Louis Ping, Nicole's father, said, "For Nicole's mother and me, the light of our lives has just gone out. The shock and emptiness are beyond words right now. I don't understand what has happened or why it has happened. I just know that life will never be the same."

4. TRAFFIC ACCIDENT REPORT NO. 2

An explanation of the numerical codes used in the following report can be found on the companion website. You may assume you obtained the additional information provided from interviews with the identified sources. Passages in quotation marks may be used as direct quotations. Check all names and addresses by using the City Directory.

Additional Information about Michelle Sessions

Dr. Stephanie R. Jamison: physician and surgeon at Sacred Heart Hospital: "Michelle Sessions apparently suffered a broken neck in the accident. It appeared she struck the pavement headfirst. She may have hit at an angle that caused her neck to break, although a more precise determination will depend on the autopsy. She was dead when she arrived at the hospital. This is a particularly sad event for all who work at Sacred Heart because of her husband's long association with this facility. We all share his grief."

STATE TRAFFIC ACCIDENT REPORT FORM

TIME & LOCATION

DATE OF ACCIDENT: MO: May	DAY: 14	YEAR: 2016	DAY OF WEEK: Thursday	TIME OF DAY: 3:25 p.m.

COUNTY: Langford CITY OR TOWN: This city ACCIDENT REPORT NUMBER: 16-00376

ROAD ON WHICH ACCIDENT OCCURRED: Baltimore Av. EXIT RAMP ☐ ENTRANCE E ☐ AT INTERSECTIN WITH: ___ INFLUENCED BY INTERSECTION: ___

IF ACCIDENT WAS OUTSIDE CITY, INDICATE DISTANCE FROM NEAREST CITY OR TOWN: ___ ☐ FEET ☐ MILES ☐N ☐S ☐E ☐W OF: ___

IF NOT AT INTERSECTION, ACCIDENT WAS: 25 ☒ FEET ☐ MILES ☐N ☐S ☐E ☒W OF: 45th Street

DO NOT WRITE IN ABOVE SPACE

TYPE MOTOR VEHICLE ACCIDENT

| OVERTURNING | PARKED MV | RAILWAY TRAIN | MV IN TRANSPORT | OTHER NONCOLLISION | MV IN OTHER ROADWAY |
| ANIMAL | PEDESTRIAN | PEDAL CYCLIST | FIXED OBJECT X | OTHER OBJECT | HIT AND RUN | NONCONTACT |

VEHICLE 1

TOTAL NO. VEHICLES INVOLVED

| YEAR 2013 | MAKE Chrysler | TYPE sedan | LICENSE PLATE 357 AJK | STATE This | YEAR 2016 | VIN 1C96KD248DW268946 |

AREAS OF VEHICLE DAMAGE 01 | DAMAGE ESTIMATE 5 | AMOUNT (approx.) $17,000 | SAFETY EQUIPMENT 05 | VEHICLE REMOVED BY: Trendway Towing

NAME OF INSURANCE CO. Consolidated Insurance of No. Am. POLICY NUMBER KYS-3479-6600021

OWNER: Savila & Darlene Gould ADDRESS 4178 N. 11th Av. CITY and STATE/Zip Code This city

DRIVER: Anthony K. Gould ADDRESS 4178 N. 11th Av. CITY and STATE/Zip Code This city

| OCCUPATION student | Driver's License Type N/A | DRIVER'S LICENSE NUMBER none | STATE This | DOB 05/02/99 | RACE C | SEX M | Safety E. 05 | Eject. 01 | Injury 02 |

OCCUPANTS Front Right Kevin Shadgott	8471 Chestnut Dr.	AGE 17	RACE C	SEX M	Safety E. 05	Eject. 01	Injury 05
Rear Left							
Rear Right Nicole Ping	348 Conroy Rd.	AGE 16	RACE C	SEX F	Safety E. 01	Eject. 01	Injury 01

VEHICLE 2

| YEAR | MAKE | TYPE | LICENSE PLATE | STATE | YEAR | VIN |

AREAS OF VEHICLE DAMAGE | DAMAGE ESTIMATE | AMOUNT (approx.) | SAFETY EQUIPMENT | VEHICLE REMOVED BY:

NAME OF INSURANCE CO. POLICY NUMBER

OWNER ADDRESS CITY and STATE/Zip Code

DRIVER ADDRESS CITY and STATE/Zip Code

| OCCUPATION | Driver's License Type | DRIVER'S LICENSE NUMBER | STATE | DOB | RACE | SEX | Safety E. | Eject. | Injury |

OCCUPANTS Front Right		AGE	RACE	SEX	Safety E.	Eject.	Injury
Rear Left		AGE	RACE	SEX			
Rear Right		AGE	RACE	SEX			

PROPERTY DAMAGE—Other than vehicles: tree, mailbox AMOUNT $650 OWNER–Name Ruth Herwarthe ADDRESS 4410 Baltimore Av CITY This city

INVESTIGATOR: Ofc. Julius Tiller Julius Tiller BADGE NO. 468 DEPARTMENT Middletown P.D. DATE OF REPORT 5/14/16

DIAGRAM WHAT HAPPENED - (Number each vehicle and show direction by arrows)

INDICATE NORTH WITH ARROW

← To 44th St.   ← —— Baltimore —— →   To 45th St →

V1   V1   V1 ⊗   V1   N

≡ = gouges
● = utility pole
⊗ = mail box
⊕ = tree

Driveway

4410 Baltimore Av

POINT OF IMPACT

V1	V2	
☐	☐	Front
☐	☐	Right front
☐	☐	Left front
☐	☐	Right side
☐	☐	Left side
☐	☐	Rear
☐	☐	Right rear
☐	☐	Left rear

DESCRIBE WHAT HAPPENED - (Refer to vehicles by number)

V1 was traveling eastbound on Baltimore at high rate of speech. After cresting a hill east of 44th V1 bottomed out. V1 then left the roadway striking the south curb of Baltimore before proceeding eastbound through yard of 4410 Baltimore, striking mailbox and tree. Witness Herwarth observed V1 eastbound on Baltimore accelerating rapidly, squealing its tires and revving its engine before V1 lost control and left roadway.

WHAT VEHICLES WERE DOING BEFORE ACCIDENT

VEHICLE No. 1 was traveling ☐ ☐ ☒ ☐ On Baltimore Av. at 70 MPH
VEHICLE No. 2 was traveling ☐ ☐ ☐ ☐ On at MPH
N S E W

Vehicle 1 2		Vehicle 1 2		Vehicle 1 2		Vehicle 1 2	
☒ ☐	Going straight ahead	☐ ☐	Making right turn	☐ ☐	Slowing or stopping	☐ ☐	Starting from parked position
☐ ☐	Overtaking	☐ ☐	Making left turn	☐ ☐	Changing lanes	☐ ☐	Stopped or parked
						☐ ☐	Other (Explain above)

WHAT PEDESTRIAN WAS DOING BEFORE ACCIDENT

PEDESTRIAN was going ☐ ☐ ☐ ☐ Along
N S E W ☐ Across or into ___ From ___ to ___ Color of Clothing ☐ Light ☐ Dark

☐ Crossing at intersection ☐ Stepped into path of vehicle ☐ Getting on or off Vehicle ☐ Playing in roadway
☐ Crossing not at intersection ☐ Standing in roadway ☐ Hitching on Vehicle ☐ Other roadway
☐ Walking in roadway - with traffic ☐ Standing in safety zone ☐ Pushing or working on Vehicle ☐ Not in roadway
☐ Walking in roadway - against traffic ☐ Lying or sitting on roadway ☐ Other working in roadway ☐ Other (explain above)

DRIVERS AND VEHICLES

		VEHICLE 1	VEHICLE 2
PHYSICAL EFFECTS (Drivers)		01	
VEHICLE DEFECTS		01	
CONTRIBUTING CIRCUMSTANCES		04	09
			e

ACCIDENT Characteristics

LIGHTING CONDITION	01	ROAD DEFECTS	01	TRAFFICWAY CHARACTER	02	CLASS OF TRAFFICWAYS	01
WEATHER	01	TRAFFIC CONTROL	01	TRAFFICWAY LANES	02	TYPE TRAFFICWAY	01
ROAD SURFACE	02	TRAFFIC LOCATION	03	VISION OBSCURED	01		

WITNESSES other than occupants NAME Ruth Herwarth ADDRESS 4410 Baltimore Av City and State/ZIP Code This city

FIRST AID GIVEN BY Bryan Best ☐ Doctor or nurse ☒ Cert. First Aider ☐ Cert. First Aider (Police) ☐ Other (Explain)

CHEMICAL TEST: TEST RESULTS: Neg. Driver No. 1 ☒ ☐ Driver No. 2 ☐ ☐

INJURED TAKE TO Sacred Heart Hosp BY ☒ Priv. Ambulance ☐ Other (Explain) ☐ Gov't Ambulance

ARREST NAME Anthony K. Gould CHARGE manslaughter Citation No. AO-16-17355
NAME CHARGE Citation No.

PHOTOGRAPHS TAKEN ☒ Yes ☐ No

DATE AND TIME NOTIFIED OF ACCIDENT May 14, 2016 | TIME ARRIVED AT SCENE 3:34 p.m. | WAS INVESTIGATION MADE AT SCENE yes | IS INVESTIGATION COMPLETE yes

STATE TRAFFIC ACCIDENT REPORT FORM

TIME & LOCATION

DATE OF ACCIDENT:	MO: Jan.	DAY: 24	YEAR: 2022	DAY OF WEEK: Saturday	TIME OF DAY: 10:55a.m.

COUNTY: Langford	CITY OR TOWN: This city	ACCIDENT REPORT NUMBER: 22-00057

ROAD ON WHICH ACCIDENT OCCURRED: Bell Av.	EXIT RAMP ☐ ENTRANCE ☐	☐ AT INTERSECTIN WITH: University Av. ☐ INFLUENCED BY INTERSECTION:

IF ACCIDENT WAS OUTSIDE CITY, INDICATE DISTANCE FROM NEAREST CITY OR TOWN: _____ ☐ FEET ☐ MILES ☐ ☐ ☐ ☐ N S E W OF: _____

IF NOT AT INTERSECTION, ACCIDENT WAS: _____ ☐ FEET ☐ MILES ☐ ☐ ☐ ☐ N S E W OF: _____

DO NOT WRITE IN ABOVE SPACE

TYPE MOTOR VEHICLE ACCIDENT	OVERTURNING	PARKED MV	RAILWAY TRAIN	MV IN TRANSPORT	OTHER NONCOLLISION X	MV IN OTHER ROADWAY
	ANIMAL	PEDESTRIAN	PEDAL CYCLIST	FIXED OBJECT	OTHER OBJECT	HIT AND RUN	NONCONTACT

VEHICLE 1

TOTAL NO. VEHICLES INVOLVED 2

YEAR 2019	MAKE Buick	TYPE Riviera	LICENSE PLATE DAJDGE	STATE This	YEAR 2022	VIN 1GZHE17X7OR414785

AREAS OF VEHICLE DAMAGE 08						DAMAGE ESTIMATE 2	AMOUNT (approx.) $950	SAFETY EQUIP-MENT 06	VEHICLE REMOVED BY: Trendway Towing

NAME OF INSURANCE CO. Consolidated Insurance of No.	POLICY NUMBER SVD-7892-4538915

OWNER (Type or print full name) Bryce R. Levine	ADDRESS 8521 Shady Glenn Dr.	CITY and STATE/Zip Code This city

DRIVER (Exactly as on driver's license) Bryce R. Levine	ADDRESS 8521 Shady Glen Dr.	CITY and STATE/Zip Code This city

OCCUPATION retired	Driver's License Type n/a	DRIVER'S LICENSE NUMBER BJ90031-D	STATE This	DOB (mo/day/yr) 12/17/36	RACE C	SEX M	Safety E. 06	Eject. 01	Injury 05

OCCUPANTS n/a	Name	ADDRESS	AGE	RACE	SEX	Safety E.	Eject.	Injury
Front Right			AGE	RACE	SEX	Safety E.	Eject.	Injury
Rear Left			AGE	RACE	SEX	Safety E.	Eject.	Injury
Rear Right								

VEHICLE 2

YEAR 2012	MAKE Honda	TYPE Motorcycle	LICENSE PLATE 971 VVI	STATE This	YEAR 2022	VIN JM2GP57891Y22789

AREAS OF VEHICLE DAMAGE 03			DAMAGE ESTIMATE 4	AMOUNT (approx.) $1,750	SAFETY EQUIP-MENT 10	VEHICLE REMOVED BY: Trendway Towing

NAME OF INSURANCE CO. Western Mutual Ins. Corp.	POLICY NUMBER 65-NZJR-66847

OWNER (Type or print full name) Jeffrey D. & Michelle A. Sessions	ADDRESS 9303 Vale Dr.	CITY and STATE/Zip Code This city

DRIVER (Exactly as on driver's license) Michelle A. Sessions	ADDRESS 9303 Vale Dr.	CITY and STATE/Zip Code This city

OCCUPATION n/a	Driver's License Type n/a	DRIVER'S LICENSE NUMBER HT88651-R	STATE This	DOB (mo/day/yr) 05/11/1992	RACE N	SEX F	Safety E. 10	Eject. 03	Injury 01

OCCUPANTS n/a	Name	ADDRESS	AGE	RACE	SEX	Safety E.	Eject.	Injury
Front Right			AGE	RACE	SEX	Safety E.	Eject.	Injury
Rear Left			AGE	RACE	SEX	Safety E.	Eject.	Injury
Rear Right								

PROPERTY DAMAGE-Other than vehicles n/a	AMOUNT	OWNER-Name	ADDRESS-Number and Street	CITY and STATE/Zip Code

INVESTIGATOR-Name and rank (Signature) Ofc. Allison Biagi	BADGE NO. 722	DEPARTMENT This city P.D.	DATE OF REPORT 01/24/2022

DIAGRAM WHAT HAPPENED–(Number each vehicle and show direction by arrows)

INDICATE NORTH WITH ARROW

POINT OF IMPACT		
V1	V2	
☐	☐	Front
☐	☐	Right front
☒	☐	Left front
☐	☒	Right side
☐	☐	Left side
☐	☐	Rear
☐	☐	Right rear
☐	☐	Left rear

DESCRIBE WHAT HAPPENED–(Refer to vehicles by number)

D1 was westbound on Bell Av., which is one-way. D1 started to turn left from the center lane onto University Av., which is one-way southbound. D2 was in left lane and continuing westbound. D1 driver said he did not see D2 until he struck it. D2 driver was knocked off cycle hit pavement. Witness said D2 driver appeared to hit the pavement head first. D2 driver was unresponsive at the scene of accident.

WHAT VEHICLES WERE DOING BEFORE ACCIDENT

VEHICLE No. 1 was traveling ☐ ☐ ☐ ☒ On Bell Av. at 15 MPH

VEHICLE No. 2 was traveling ☐ ☐ ☐ ☒ On Bell Av. at 30 MPH

N S E W

	Vehicle 1 2		Vehicle 1 2		Vehicle 1 2		Vehicle 1 2	
	☐ ☒	Going straight ahead	☐ ☐	Making right turn	☐ ☐	Slowing or stopping	☐ ☐	Starting from parked position
	☐ ☐	Overtaking	☒ ☐	Making left turn	☐ ☐	Changing lanes	☐ ☐	Stopped or parked
							☐ ☐	Other (Explain above)

WHAT PEDESTRIAN WAS DOING BEFORE ACCIDENT

PEDESTRIAN was going ☐ ☐ ☐ ☐   ☐ Along

N S E W   ☐ Across or into ___ From ___ to ___

Name of street, highway, etc.   N.E. corner to S.E. corner, etc.

Color of Clothing ☐ Light ☐ Dark

☐ Crossing at intersection   ☐ Stepped into path of vehicle   ☐ Getting on or off Vehicle   ☐ Playing in roadway
☐ Crossing not at intersection   ☐ Standing in roadway   ☐ Hitching on Vehicle   ☐ Other roadway
☐ Walking in roadway–with traffic   ☐ Standing in safety zone   ☐ Pushing or working on Vehicle   ☐ Not in roadway
☐ Walking in roadway–against traffic   ☐ Lying or sitting on roadway   ☐ Other working in roadway   ☐ Other (explain above)

DRIVERS AND VEHICLES

	VEHICLE 1	VEHICLE 2
PHYSICAL DEFFECTS (Drivers)	01	01
VEHICLE DEFECTS	01	01
CONTRIBUTING CIRCUM-STABCES	06	

ACCIDENT Characteristics	LIGHTING CONDITION	01	ROAD DEFECTS	01	TRAFFICWAY CHARACTER	01	CLASS OF TRAFFICWAYS	02
	WEATHER	06	TRAFFIC CONTROL	02	TRAFFICWAY LANES	03	TYPE TRAFFICWAY	04
	ROAD SURFACE	02	TRAFFIC LOCATION	02	VISION OBSCURED	01		

WITNESSES other than occupants

NAME Dianna Grant   ADDRESS–Number and street 810 Village Lane   City and State/ZIP Code This city

FIRST AID GIVEN BY Allison Biagi   ☐ Doctor or nurse   ☐ Cert. First Aider   ☒ Cert. First Aider (Police)   ☐ Other (Explain)

CHEMICAL TEST: TEST RESULTS:

Driver No. 1 ☐ ☐ ___
Driver No. 2 ☐ ☐ ___

INJURED TAKE TO: Sacred Heart Hospital   BY   ☐ Priv. Ambulance   ☐ Other (Explain)   ☒ Gov't Ambulance

ARREST

NAME Bryce R. Levine   CHARGE careless driving   Citation No. 22-722-0016

PHOTOGRAPHS TAKEN ☒ ☐ Yes No

NAME   CHARGE   Citation No.

DATE AND TIME NOTIFIED OF ACCIDENT 01/24/22 10:59 a.m.   TIME ARRIVED AT SCENE 11:10 a.m.   WAS INVSTIGATION MADE AT SCENE (If not, where) yes   IS INVESTIGATION COMPETE (If not, why) yes

5. INJURY REPORTS

For this exercise, your instructor might ask that you
write about only one of the reports.

Submitting Agency	Police Dept.

Description of Victim	Sex	Descent	Age	Height
	M	Hispanic	20	6'

Weight	Hair	Eyes	Build	Complexion
160	Brown	Brown	M	Clear

Identifying Marks and Characteristics

None visible at scene

Clothing & Jewelry Worn

Restaurant uniform of tan pants
& shirt & cap

Victim's Name (last - first - middle)	Comp. No.
Alvarez, Thomas J.	87B-1241-GL

Location of Occurrence	Dist.	Type
Tom's Pizza	4	

Date & Time Occurred	Date & Time Reported to P.D.
11 PM yesterday night	11:07 PM yesterday night

Type of Premises (loc. of victim)	Cause of Injury (instr. or means)
Carry-out pizza restaurant	Pistol

Reason (Acc.-ill health, etc.)	Extent of Injury (Minor or Serious)
Robbery/shooting	Fatal

Remove To (address)	Removed By
County morgue	Coroners office

Investigative Division or Unit Notified & Person(s) Contacted
Homicide

INJURY REPORT   UCR

CODE	R - Person Reporting	D - Person Discovering	W - Witness				
	Victim's Occupation	Resident Address City	Res. Phone	x	Bus. Phone	x
	College student/part-time worker	854 Maury Rd., Apt. 11B	823-8892		823-5455	
W/R	Name Anne Capiello	8210 University Blvd., #311	823 4117		None	
W	Andrew Caspenwall	416 Wilson Avenue	823-4417		823-5455	

(1) Reconstruct the circumstances surrounding the injury. (2) Describe physical evidence, location found, & give disposition.

The deceased, a pizza clerk, was shot fatally at about 11pm in a failed robbery attempt. A lone gunman entered the premises and faked that he wanted a pizza. When asked what he wanted on it suspect #1 said "I really want all your money". The clerk appeared to reach beneath the counter and suspect #1 then shot him although we found no alarm or weapon the clerk might have reached for, but our suspect claims that's what triggered the shooting. The suspect then ran behind the counter and tried to open the register, even throwing it to the floor but didn't know how to open it and then emptied his gun into it, 5 or 6 shots. He proceeded to run outside to a waiting vehicle described by 2 eyewitnesses as an old Ford mustang white in color. It was driven by another white male, and a deliveryman arriving at this time chased the perpetrators vehicle. In the area of Pauley Park the perps fired several shots at deliveryman Caspenwall who was not hit. Said getaway vehicle attempted to make a left turn onto Parkvue Av. but was speeding too fast and flipped on its side. Suspect #1 William McDowell, 1429 Highland Dr., was found dazed inside but otherwise unhurt and was identified as the shooter. We are continuing to look for suspect #2. Witness #1 (Capiello) identified herself as the victims girlfriend. She was present when the shooting occurred, and the gunman may not have seen her as she was studying in a back corner of the kitchen. McDowell said he has no job and admits to having a crack problem and that he went in to rob the place for money. He's charged with murder.

If additional space is required use reverse side.

Supervisor Approving	Emp. No.	Interviewing Officer(s)	Emp. No.	Person Reporting Injury (signature)
Sgt. A. Wei		Detective J. Noonan		*Anne Capiello*

Submitting Agency	Police Dept.				Victim's Name (last - first - middle) Curtis, Derek Andrew		Comp. No. 87B-1336K

Description of Victim	Sex M	Descent AA	Age 8	Height 4' 1"

Weight 70	Hair Black	Eyes Black	Build Medium	Complexion Clear

Location of Occurrence
663 Harding Av.   Dist. 2   Type

Date & Time Occurred
About 4PM yesterday   Date & Time Reported to P.D. 6:52 PM

Type of Premises (loc. of victim)
Family home   Cause of Injury (instr. or means) Fall into freezer

Reason (Acc.-ill health, etc.)
Accident   Extent of Injury (Minor or Serious) Fatal

Remove To (address)
Mercy hospital   Removed By Paramedics

Identifying Marks and Characteristics

Chipped front tooth.

Small scar on lower left leg.

Clothing & Jewelry Worn

T-shirt, bluejeans,

white sneakers.

Investigative Division or Unit Notified & Person(s) Contacted

None. No further action required

INJURY REPORT   UCR

CODE   R - Person Reporting   D - Person Discovering   W - Witness

	Victim's Occupation / Name	Residence Address	City	Res. Phone	x	Bus. Phone	x
	Child	663 Harding Av.	Yes	823-8019			
R	Sara Curtis	663 Harding Av.	Yes	823-8019		823-6400	
D	Danny Jones, grandfather	1152 Arlington	Yes	823-1097		823-4110	

(1) Reconstruct the circumstances surrounding the injury. (2) Describe physical evidence, location found, & give disposition.

The deceased was located in a box-type freezer in the garage area at his home. He

apparently fell in while trying to reach some popsicles. There was a small tool chest and

some other boxes piled in front of the freezer that he apparently used as steps. It now

appears that the deceased crawled high enough to open the lid and tumbled in. The lid

closed on him & latched. We were dispatched to the scene in answer to a call of a missing

child. The victims mother Sara Curtis said the boy disappeared at about 4pm after

returning from school. He'd asked for one of the popsicles and she said she told him to

eat some fruit instead. Neighbors aided in the search and at 8:30pm we instituted a full

scale search of the neighborhood using dogs, the dept. helicopter, and more than twenty

officers. The boy was recovered during a 3rd search of the premises by a grandfather at

11:10pm. Paramedics already on the scene said the boy, who was age 8, had no heartbeat and

a body temperature of only 70. Icicles had formed on his body and he apparently spent

approximately around 7 hours trapped inside the freezer. Hospital personnel said they

managed to get the boys heart beating and returned his body temperature to normal while on

life support but he never regained consciousness and died shortly after 1am today. When we

opened the lid and let it go it did fall back in place and latch itself each time. A box

of popsicles was open and its contents scattered over the bottom of the freezer, which was

only about 1/3 full of food.

If additional space is required use reverse side.

Supervisor Approving Sgt. T. Dow	Emp. No.	Interviewing Officer(s) M. Hennigen	Emp. No.	Person Reporting Injury (signature) Sara Curtis

602 - 07 - 23A   INJURY REPORT

6. FIRE/INCIDENT REPORTS

For this exercise, your instructor might ask that you write about only one of the reports.

FIRE/INCIDENT REPORT

Date of incident: _____Today_____ Time call received: _____01:34_____ Time of arrival on scene: _____01:38_____

Time of return to station: _____08:12_____ Total time at scene: _6 hr., 34 min._ Response time: _____4 min._____

Address of location: _____2048 Main Street_____ Type of premises: _____218 seat restaurant_____

Name of owner: _____Mr./Mrs. Michael Deacosti_____ Telephone: _____823-0666_____

Nature of call: _____ 911 _X_ Phone _____ Box _____ Police _____ Other _____ Alarms sounded: 1 ② 3 4 5

Units dispatched: _4_ Pumper _2_ Ladder _1_ Rescue _____ Chemical _X_ District Chief _____ Other

Injuries: _X_ Yes _____ No _____ Fatalities: _____ Yes _X_ No

Commanding officer's narrative: First call came by phone from a passing motorist at 01:34 today regarding a fire at Deacosti's Restaurant. The structure was already fully involved when the 1st units arrived on the scene with flames having broken through the roof and shooting some twenty to thirty ft. up into the air. Heavy black smoke was pouring from the structure and flames flaring out the front door. We got 4 men inside via a west side window and a second alarm was immediately sounded. Upon arrival the District Chief ordered everyone outside for safety reasons.

The original building is old, having been opened somewhere around 1940 and was a wooden structure, remodeled and expanded several times. Fire was between and behind the current walls and difficult to reach and extinguish. Two tower trucks and 4 pumpers with deck guns doused all the flames by approx. 02:30. Two pumpers remained at the scene until approx. 08:00 when power company and other crews began coming to the scene in case any flames were re-ignited. Fire apparently started in the back NE corner of the restaurant, in either the kitchen or possibly an adjacent office area, possibly due to electrical problems, after the 11:00 closing hour. Private investigators from the insurance company are helping in the inquiry and an electrical engineer will inspect the damages later today. This may be a slow investigation because of extensive damage to the building which was totally and completely destroyed. There were no sprinklers. If it was constructed or remodeled today current codes would require the restaurant to have a sprinkler system. It would have been a whole different story if there were sprinklers. Sprinklers possibly could have saved the building.

2 firefighters were injured. FF John Charlton was taken to Mercy Hospital for treatment of smoke inhalation and released this a.m. FF Al Moravchek received 2nd and 3rd degree burns to his face, hands, and neck and is reported to be in satisfactory condition at the same hospital where he remains, having suffered said injuries during an explosion within the kitchen area at about 02:08 that sent a ball of flames up into his overhead ladder. No estimate of damage is likely to be available for several days. The premises were insured for $1.2 million.

Alarm system on premises: _____ Yes _X_ No   Alarm system activated: _____ Yes _____ No

Sprinkler system on premises: _____ Yes _X_ No   Sprinkler system activated: _____ Yes _____ No

Premises insured: _X_ Yes _____ No   Insurer notified: _X_ Yes _____ No

Recommended followup:
_____ None _____ Arson Squad _X_ Fire Marshal _____ Inspection Division _____ Prevention Division

Commanding officer's name: _____Lieut. Ron Sheppard_____ Signature _____Ron Sheppard_____

FIRE/INCIDENT REPORT

Date of incident: ___Yesterday___ Time call received: ___16:48___ Time of arrival on scene: ___16:52___

Time of return to station: ___17:57___ Total time at scene: ___1 hr., 5 min.___ Response time: ___4 min.___

Address of location: ___West end of Liberty Av.___ Type of premises: ___Pond/undeveloped field___

Name of owner: ___Wagnor Development Corporation___ Telephone: ___823-3404___

Nature of call: _X_ 911 _X_ Phone ___ Box ___ Police ___ Other   Alarms sounded: (1) 2 3 4 5

Units dispatched: _1_ Pumper _1_ Ladder _2_ Rescue ___ Chemical _X_ District Chief ___ Other

Injuries: ___ Yes _X_ No   Fatalities: _X_ Yes ___ No

Commanding officer's narrative: The victim has been positively identified as a boy, age eleven, by the name of James Roger Lo, son of Joan and Roger Lo, home residence at 1993 Collins Av. The deceased was a student at Lincoln Elementary School. Witnesses at the scene said the deceased and 3 other neighborhood boys were digging a tunnel in the side of a hill overlooking a pond at the West end of Liberty Av. and it collapsed. One boy ran for help while the others began trying to dig him out. The one boy's mother dialed 911, then ran directly to the scene with neighbors. When we arrived about twenty adults from the neighborhood and passing motorists were at the scene, digging mostly with their hands and few shovels. We took over the work and got the boys head exposed about ten minutes into the rescue but before medics could begin resuscitation efforts another collapse occurred. Victim was freed at 17:24, taken to the Regional Medical Center, and pronounced dead there by doctors from an extensive lack of oxygen. The collapse occurred about 16:40.

Neighbors and witnesses at the scene were angry, expressing that they had told the property owner on numerous occasions and written him that the area was dangerous and that they needed a good fence around the entire pond area so none of the neighborhood children would drown in it, as it was apparently a popular play area for them. The survivors said they were building a fort and while the deceased was in it the walls caved in. When we arrived the boy had been buried about 12 minutes and completely covered. We found his body six feet from where the opening had been. It was basically a crawl-type cave, and getting the boy out was difficult because dirt (the sides and roof) kept collapsing back on us, and we had to be careful not to hit and further injure the victim without equipment. For that reason we were unable to use any heavy equipment. To expedite the rescue we tore sections from a fence at a residence at 8397 Liberty Av., using it as makeshift shoring in an effort to hold back the sand and dirt continuing to cave in on our men removing the interior dirt. The homeowner should be contacted as they may file a claim or have to be compensated for fence repairs.

Alarm system on premises: _NA_ Yes ___ No   Alarm system activated: ___ Yes ___ No

Sprinkler system on premises: _NA_ Yes ___ No   Sprinkler system activated: ___ Yes ___ No

Premises insured: ___ Yes ___ No   Insurer notified: ___ Yes ___ No
        Unknown

Recommended followup:
___ None ___ Arson Squad ___ Fire Marshal ___ Inspection Division ___ Prevention Division
Notify City Attorney of fence and Zoning Board of possible hazard for children

Commanding officer's name: ___Lt. Steven Chenn___ Signature ___Steven Chenn___

7. COURT DOCUMENTS

In the Circuit Court of

The 9th Judicial Circuit

in and for (your) County

Division: Civil

THADDEUS DOWDELL   **Case No.: 1-78-1440**

and LAURA DOWDELL,

individually and as next friends

and parents of JAMES

DOWDELL, a minor,   *Plaintiffs,*

vs.

MARVIN FERRELL,

GREG HUBBARD

and (YOUR CITY'S)

SCHOOL DISTRICT,   *Defendants.*

COMPLAINT

COME NOW the Plaintiffs, THADDEUS DOWDELL and LAURA DOWDELL, individually and as next friends and parents of JAMES DOWDELL, a minor, by and through their undersigned counsel, and sue the Defendants, MARVIN FERRELL, GREG HUBBARD, AND (YOUR CITY'S) SCHOOL DISTRICT, jointly and severally, for damages and allege:

1. That this is an action for damages of $500,000, exclusive of interest, costs and further demands.

2. That at all times material to this cause, JAMES DOWDELL was and is the minor son of THADDEUS DOWDELL and LAURA DOWDELL, residing together with them in a family relationship as residents of this county.

3. That at all times material to this cause, the Defendant MARVIN FERRELL held and now holds the position of Principal of Kennedy High School, and that the Defendant GREG HUBBARD held and now holds the position of School Superintendent.

4. That the minor JAMES DOWDELL is and has been a student in Kennedy High School for the past three years and has been told that he will graduate from that school on or about the First Day of next June.

5. That the minor, JAMES DOWDELL, of this date, can barely read or do simple arithmetic and obviously has not learned enough to be graduated from high school or to function successfully in a society as complex as ours.

6. That the problem is not the fault of the minor JAMES DOWDELL, who, according to tests administered by guidance counselors at the high school, enjoys a normal IQ of 94.

7. That the failure of the minor JAMES DOWDELL to master the skills expected of high school students is the fault of the Defendants, MARVIN FERRELL, GREG HUBBARD, and (YOUR CITY'S) SCHOOL DISTRICT, that said defendants failed to employ competent teachers, to maintain discipline, to provide remedial help and to provide an atmosphere in which learning might take place.

WHEREFORE, the Plaintiffs, THADDEUS DOWDELL and LAURA DOWDELL, individually and as next friends and parents of JAMES DOWDELL, a minor, sue the Defendants MARVIN FERRELL, GREG HUBBARD and (YOUR CITY'S) SCHOOL DISTRICT, jointly and severally, for compensatory damages in the amount of $500,000, exclusive of interest and costs.

FURTHER, the Plaintiffs demand that the minor JAMES DOWDELL be retained in Kennedy High School until he masters the skills expected of a high school graduate.

FURTHER, the Plaintiffs demand trial by jury of all issues triable as of right by a jury.
PILOTO and HERNDON, Attorneys
1048 Westmore Drive
Attorneys for Plaintiffs
BY: <u>Kenneth T. Piloto</u>
KENNETH T. PILOTO

8. HOUSE BILL 371

Assume that the vote on the bill reprinted here and the subsequent Senate debate both happened today. You may quote the senators' remarks directly. Assume also that your state's House of Representatives has already passed the bill by a vote of 101 to 23. In the text of the bill, the crossed-out passages will be deleted from the current law, and underlined passages will be added to it.

H.B. 371

An Act relating to crimes and offenses.

Section 1. Section 28-105, Revised Statutes, is amended to read:

28-105. (1) For purposes of the Criminal Code and any statute passed by the Legislature after the date of passage of the code, felonies are divided into eight classes which are distinguished from one another by the following penalties which are authorized upon conviction:

Class I felony	Death
Class IA felony	Life imprisonment
Class IB felony	Maximum—life imprisonment
	~~Minimum—ten years imprisonment~~
	<u>Minimum—twenty years imprisonment</u>
Class IC felony	Maximum—fifty years imprisonment
	Mandatory minimum—five years imprisonment
Class ID felony	Maximum—fifty years imprisonment
	Mandatory minimum—three years imprisonment
Class II felony	Maximum—fifty years imprisonment
	Minimum—one year imprisonment
Class III felony	Maximum—twenty years imprisonment
	Minimum—one year imprisonment
Class IV felony	Maximum—five years imprisonment
	Minimum—none

(2) <u>A person convicted of a felony for which a mandatory minimum sentence is prescribed shall not be eligible for probation.</u>

Section 2. Section 28-1205, Revised Statutes, is amended to read:

28-1205 (1) Any person who uses a firearm, a knife, brass or iron knuckles, or any other deadly weapon to commit any felony which may be prosecuted in a court of this state, or ~~any person~~ who unlawfully possesses a firearm, a knife, brass or iron knuckles, or any other deadly weapon during the commission of any felony which may be prosecuted in a court of this state commits the offense of using ~~firearms~~ <u>a deadly weapon</u> to commit a felony.

(2) <u>(a)</u> Use of ~~firearms~~ <u>a deadly weapon other than a firearm</u> to commit a felony is a Class III felony<u>.</u>

<u>(b) Use of a deadly weapon which is a firearm to commit a felony is a Class II felony.</u>

Section 3. Section 28-1206, Revised Statutes, is amended to read:

28-1206. (1) Any person who possesses any firearm ~~with a barrel less than eighteen inches in length~~ or brass or iron knuckles who has previously been convicted of a felony or who is a fugitive from justice commits the offense of possession of ~~firearms~~ <u>a deadly weapon</u> by a felon or a fugitive from justice.

(2) <u>(a)</u> Possession of ~~firearms~~ <u>a deadly weapon other than a firearm</u> by a <u>felon or a</u> fugitive from justice ~~or a felon~~ is a Class IV felony.

<u>(b) Possession of a deadly weapon which is a firearm by a felon or a fugitive from justice is a Class III felony.</u>

Section 4. Section 29-2221, Revised Statutes, is amended to read:

29-2221. (1) Whoever has been twice convicted of a crime, sentenced, and committed to prison, in this or any other state or by the United States or once in this state and once at least in any other state or by the United States, for terms of not less than one year each shall, upon conviction of a felony committed in this state, be deemed a habitual criminal and shall be punished by imprisonment in a Department of Correctional Services adult correctional facility for a ~~term of not less than ten nor~~ <u>mandatory minimum term of ten years and a maximum term of not</u> more than sixty years, except that:

(2) If the felony committed is manslaughter, armed robbery, rape, arson or kidnapping, as those terms are defined in the Criminal Code, or vehicular homicide while under the influence of alcohol, and at least one

of the habitual criminal's prior felony convictions was for such a violation or a violation of a similar statute in another state or in the United States, the mandatory minimum term shall be twenty-five years and the maximum term not more than sixty years.

Section 5. Section 29-2262, Revised Statutes, is amended to read:

29-2262. (1) When a court sentences an offender to probation, it shall attach such reasonable conditions as it deems necessary or likely to insure that the offender will lead a law-abiding life. No offender shall be sentenced to probation if he or she is deemed to be a habitual criminal pursuant to section 29-2221.

Section 6. Section 29-2525, Revised Statutes, is amended to read:

29-2525. (1) In cases where the punishment is capital, no notice of appeal shall be required and within the time prescribed by section 25-1931 for the commencement of appeals, the clerk of the district court in which the conviction was had shall notify the court reporter who shall prepare a bill of exceptions as in other cases. The Clerk of the Supreme Court shall, upon receipt of the transcript, docket the case. The Supreme Court shall expedite the rendering of its opinion on any appeal, giving the matter priority over civil and non-capital matters.

Section 7. The following shall be added to the Criminal Code of the Revised Statutes:

(1) A person commits the offense of assault on an officer using a motor vehicle if he or she intentionally and knowingly causes bodily injury to a peace officer or employee of the Department of Correctional Services (a) by using a motor vehicle to run over or to strike such officer or employee or (b) by using a motor vehicle to collide with such officer's or employee's motor vehicle, while such officer or employee is engaged in the performance of his or her duties.

(2) Assault on an officer using a motor vehicle shall be a Class IV felony.

Excerpts of Final Debate in the Senate

Sen. Dan Twoshoes, D-Henderson: "If a farmer finds a weasel in his henhouse, he shoots it. I wish we could do the same with some of the two-legged weasels. But at least we can lock them up and keep them away from decent people. That's what this bill will do. It increases the prison sentence for criminals who use deadly weapons—especially guns—in the commission of crimes and it increases the penalties on felons and fugitives who possess deadly weapons. This bill will keep criminals off our streets by preventing judges from placing criminals on probation when this legislature has imposed a mandatory minimum sentence. And most importantly, this bill sets a mandatory minimum sentence for habitual criminals who commit serious crimes."

Sen. Sally Ong, R-Wakarusa: "I agree with Sen. Twoshoes that we need to keep habitual criminals off our streets, and if it were not for one provision, I could support this bill. I speak of the inclusion of vehicular homicide while under the influence of alcohol as one of those offenses requiring a 25-year mandatory minimum sentence. I understand the pain felt by those who lose a loved one in an accident caused by a drunken driver. That's how my brother died five years ago. But the people who drive while drunk need help, not a 25-year prison sentence."

Sen. John Percy, D-(Your city), and chairman of the Judiciary Committee: "I want to address Sen. Ong's concerns about the vehicular homicide provision. The Judiciary Committee debated this provision extensively, and we heard testimony from many people in law enforcement and social work. It was clear to us that a person who abuses alcohol and then drives an automobile is aware that she or he is behaving recklessly. If a habitual criminal engages in such reckless behavior and causes a fatal injury, then that should be treated as an extremely serious crime."

Sen. William Antonucci, R-(Your city): "We're fooling ourselves if we think that this bill will have any impact on crime in this state. Criminals don't think they'll be caught when they rob or kill, so increasing the penalties mean nothing to them. What we'll be doing is wasting money warehousing criminals for years and years. The more people we jam into our prisons, the more we are going to have to pay to operate the prisons—even if we let the prisons become pigsties. We would do better to hire more police, prosecutors and judges. We will deter more crime by increasing the chances that crooks will be caught and prosecuted than by increasing the sentences for the few who now are prosecuted."

After debate, the Senate voted 40-12 in favor of the bill. The bill now goes to the governor, Laura Riley, who must sign it before it can become law. Her press secretary says the governor supports the bill and intends to sign it.

INTRODUCTION TO INVESTIGATIVE REPORTING

18

U.S. news organizations function as watchdogs for the country. Investigative reporting has been a part of American journalism almost since the beginning of the modern newspaper industry in the 1830s. Holding government and corporate officials accountable for their actions has been the hallmark of investigative reporting, and many stories have led to major changes in laws and regulations for the benefit of citizens. Names such as Ida M. Tarbell, Nellie Bly, Lincoln Steffens, Ida B. Wells, Edward R. Murrow, Carl Bernstein and Bob Woodward became synonymous with investigative reporting.

> "At the core of investigative journalism is exactly the same thing that drives a page-turning thriller: telling a great story."
>
> —*Hank Phillippi Ryan, investigative reporter and writer*

The roots of investigative reporting can be found in both fiction and nonfiction. For instance, Upton Sinclair's "The Jungle," a novel that exposed Chicago's meatpacking industry, spurred passage of the Pure Food and Drug Act of 1906. "Silent Spring," Rachel Carson's nonfiction account of pesticide misuse, helped launch the modern environmental movement. Sinclair and Carson are just two of many writers who pursued stories of political or social injustice.

Newspapers have a long tradition of investigating scandals in and out of government. In the 1870s, stories in The New York Times detailed how William M. Tweed—a politician who controlled New York City's Democratic political machine—bilked millions of dollars from taxpayers. It is estimated that he and his associates stole more than $200 million (in 1870 dollars and approximately $4.5 billion in today's dollars) to run his illegal political patronage operation. The newspaper's pursuit of Tweed ended when he was arrested and sentenced to jail.

In the early 1970s, Bob Woodward and Carl Bernstein of The Washington Post investigated a burglary of the Democratic National Committee headquarters, located in the Watergate office complex in Washington, D.C. Their investigation uncovered efforts by the Committee for the Re-Election of the President to sabotage the Democratic Party's presidential campaign, which led to the discovery

"The Jungle" recounts Upton Sinclair's experience working incognito in the meatpacking plants of the Chicago stockyards.

that then-President Richard Nixon had sanctioned attempts to cover up the secret program of "dirty tricks" and the involvement of administration officials in the break-in. The Watergate stories eventually hastened the resignation of Nixon, the first American president to ever step down.

Today, newspapers, television investigative documentaries, websites, blogs and social media all illuminate malfeasance and corruption by politicians, government officials, as well as public and private corporations. Online news organizations especially have played a pivotal role in the depth and breadth of investigative reporting in the 21st century. From an investigative piece by ProPublica that explored how school shutdowns and remote learning during the COVID-19 pandemic slowed learning by low-income and disadvantaged children, to a three-part series by Reveal that exposed the questionable working conditions at retail giant Amazon and its drive for domination, online investigative reporting has broken some major news stories.

Investigative reporting is a form of hard news. As defined in Chapter 2—and as the previous examples show—this type of news includes timely coverage of topics involving government meetings or actions, politics, crime, fires, accidents, speeches, labor disputes and other matters that affect public welfare. Invesitigative stories dig deeply into issues that have major implications for the community a news organization serves. In this chapter, we will discuss the elements of investigative reporting and the ethical problems that arise.

18.1 What Is Investigative Reporting?

News reporting can be reactive or proactive. For example, something happens—a natural disaster (such as an earthquake), a plane crash, political upheaval or war—and news organizations react to it, providing coverage in newspapers and on websites, social media, radio and television. They publish stories about the who, what, when, where, why and how. In some cases, they investigate the how and why of the event more deeply to help people make sense of the circumstances or issues involved.

For example, when the first cases of COVID-19 were reported in China, news organizations covered the emergence of the disease as it spread into a global pandemic. Stories of infection rates, deaths, strains on hospitals and health systems and developments of vaccines flooded airwaves, newspapers, online news sites and social media. As the pandemic progressed, however, investigative reporters began to expose problems in nursing homes that saw high death rates among elderly patients in their care as well as the role of politicians and some government officials in spreading false or misleading information about the disease.

News organizations followed a similar pattern of reactive reporting during the Jan. 6, 2021, assault on the U.S. Capitol by supporters of President Donald Trump who were attempting to stop the certification of President-elect Joe Biden as the 46th president of the United States. Reporters covered the events as they unfolded that day, but then investigative reporters began exploring the causes of the assault and those responsible for it—including those who financed and supported it.

An investigative story is not always tied to an event. Reporters get tips, hear rumors or observe things that raise questions and launch the search for answers.

In such cases, journalists are being proactive in their approach to the story. Whether it is government or corporate corruption, faulty products, unsafe workplaces, shoddy construction or medical, environmental or social issues, reporters often take weeks, months or years to gather information and write the stories. Investigative reports frequently require exhaustive research because the consequences of being wrong can be damaging. The reputations of news organizations, reporters and the people they write about can be ruined if the information in the story is not accurate and verified. Inaccuracies can also lead to libel suits.

Because of the work involved, an investigative report cannot follow the usual daily deadlines of other news stories. A news organization also must commit resources for the story to be successful. And while it is not always popular, investigative reporting is often supported by the public when it is done well and reveals something that can have a major impact on people's lives now and in the future. The Boston Globe's investigation into sexual abuse in the Roman Catholic Church prompted several official investigations and ended in the prosecution and conviction of some former priests for their actions. It also brought attention to a worldwide problem and encouraged victims to come forward with their stories. The investigative report by the Globe was the basis for the Academy Award-winning movie "Spotlight."

An important part of investigative journalism is the reporters themselves. While some claim that many investigative pieces are sensational accounts published or broadcast to hike ratings and circulation numbers, investigative reporters believe in the importance of what they do. They are concerned with seeking fairness and the truth and with helping those who lack the power to correct something that is wrong. Some journalists fail in their attempt to do investigative stories because their reporting is shallow and sometimes sensationalistic, but those with experience know that they need to spend many hours digging for information and chasing leads. They know that their stories must include everything an audience needs to know to make sense of the story and its impact.

18.2 Whom and What to Investigate

Just about any topic can be developed into an investigative story. While the supply of ideas may seem endless, investigative reporters know the limitations they face regarding available resources. Large news organizations have more resources than smaller ones and can often allow a journalist the time to conduct the extensive research needed to complete an investigative story. The New York Times was able to investigate in depth the extent of civilian casualties from U.S. bombing and drone attacks in Afghanistan and Syria and the effect of those casualties on the people of those countries. The Times won a Pulitzer Prize for international reporting and an award for investigative reporting from Investigative Reporters and Editors.

INVESTIGATION

THE AD BLOCK

With millions of dollars at stake, companies are blanketing Pennsylvania with ads about how to get a medical marijuana card. But if doctors do the same, they risk their license.

by ED MAHON
SPOTLIGHT PA
Illustration by LEISE HOOK for SPOTLIGHT PA

When Pennsylvania lawmakers legalized medical cannabis in 2016, they struck an unusual deal: Physicians can approve patients for the program but they are banned from advertising that power.

Lawmakers feared advertising would encourage thousands of patients to flood the same doctor's office solely seeking a medical marijuana card, or motivate physicians to excessively approve patients for profit.

Or, as one marijuana legalization advocate put it, lawmakers didn't want "pot doctors."

But six years later, that rule and the inconsistent enforcement that followed have given an advantage to largely unregulated certification businesses that stand to rake in millions of dollars each year courting Pennsylvania medical marijuana patients, a Spotlight PA investigation has found.

Those businesses typically offer to connect patients with partner physicians who can certify patients without actually advertising or identifying those physicians by name, a tactic that would be nearly impossible for an individual doctor or a private practice.

As a result, marijuana card companies promote themselves on the airwaves, run newspaper ads, offer discounts on sites like Groupon, and dominate Google searches for medical marijuana.

KEY POINTS

- Patients in Pennsylvania need approval from a physician before they can buy cannabis at dispensaries. Initial certifications can cost $125 to $225 and must be renewed annually.
- Most physicians don't participate in the state's medical cannabis program, but those that do can face harsh penalties if they advertise that they can certify patients.
- Companies that offer to connect patients to physicians for certifications do not face the same advertising restrictions and receive little to no oversight from state officials — gaps that give them an advantage.
- The Department of Health has issued roughly a dozen warning letters to physicians for alleged advertising violations, going so far as to threaten potential loss or suspension of a medical license.

This story by Ed Mahon about problems with the medical marijuana industry in Pennsylvania appeared in the online investigative website Spotlight PA. Spotlight PA is an independent, nonpartisan newsroom powered by The Philadelphia Inquirer in partnership with PennLive/The (Harrisburg, Pa.) Patriot-News, TribLIVE/Pittsburgh Tribune-Review and WITF Public Media.

The Madison County RECORD
"News Of The Week Since 1879"

The Madison County, Arkansas, Record, a weekly with 4,000 circulation, proved that even small news organizations can carry out investigations that have a major impact on their communities.

Reporters at smaller news organizations lack the numbers and the money to carry out such broad investigations, but they can still conduct investigative journalism. The Madison County, Arkansas, Record, a weekly newspaper with a circulation of about 4,000, investigated allegations that some members of the local junior high boys basketball team had sexually assaulted other team members. The investigation revealed that the local school board had tried to cover up the allegations, lessened recommended punishments for some of the youths accused in the assaults and violated state open-meeting laws. The paper's publisher, general manager and five staff members examined thousands of pages of documents and conducted many hours of interviews with people involved to uncover the story. Investigative efforts, like those of the Madison County Record, benefit the public and add to the prestige and credibility of the paper and journalism generally.

The same news values that apply to standard reporting—timeliness, impact, prominence, proximity, singularity, conflict—are relevant for investigative stories. However, impact is of utmost importance. If the story will affect a majority of people in the community, a news organization may be more inclined to provide the needed resources for an investigative piece. For example, a story that a building inspector has been taking bribes to ignore unsafe construction practices will have more impact than a story about construction defects in a single apartment house.

If you want to become an investigative reporter, look at your beat and determine where possible stories exist. Make notes at meetings about possible story ideas to pursue. Stay in touch with the community and follow up on tips and rumors. You never know when one will lead to a really good story.

18.3 Developing an Investigative Story

Investigative reporters Donald L. Barlett and James B. Steele (who were mentioned in Chapter 7) note that journalists who want to develop investigative pieces need to create a "documents state of mind." Like Barlett and Steele, beginning investigative reporters need to research their stories thoroughly, gathering documents and conducting interviews. All of this information needs to be organized, such as in a database or filed by organization and topic, to make the information easy to find and analyze as the story develops.

International Consortium of Investigative Journalists
INVESTIGATIONS · JOURNALISTS BLOG ABOUT   🔍 LEAK TO US   FOLLOW US

| ALL OUR INVESTIGATIONS

The Panama Papers: Exposing the Rogue Offshore Finance Industry
One year after launching the biggest investigation in journalism history, the global response to the Panama Papers continues.

Secrecy for Sale: Inside the Global Offshore Money Maze
Former top EU official among high profile names in a leak that reveals 175,000 offshore companies registered in the Bahamas.

Evicted and Abandoned: The World Bank's Broken Promise to the Poor
The World Bank regularly failed to follow rules for protecting millions of people by development.

Fatal Extraction: Australian Mining's Damaging Push Into Africa
Australia is a giant in African mining, but its vast, sometimes deadly footprint has never been examined—until now.

Swiss Leaks: Murky Cash Sheltered by Bank Secrecy
How one of the world's largest banks helped shelter millions in accounts linked to arms dealers, dictators and tax evaders.

Luxembourg Leaks: Global Companies' Secrets Exposed
New files obtained by ICIJ disclose secret structures sought by "Big 4" accounting global brand name companies.

Founded in 1997, the International Consortium of Investigative Journalists (ICIJ) consists of over 200 journalists in 70 countries working together on investigative stories. Examples of topics covered by the group include secret corporate tax structures, war contracts in Iraq and Afghanistan, the climate change lobby and tobacco smuggling.

The internet and online databases have made it easier for reporters to find documents and statistics. But reporters still must know what information they need for their stories. Then they have to analyze it to spot trends or discrepancies between what sources tell them and what documents or statistics indicate. Crowdsourcing, also discussed later in this chapter, can be an important tool in developing an investigative story. Reporters can reach out through social media, probing for information and leads. This method can also help reporters develop sources—both human and document—for an investigative piece.

18.3.1 The Story Idea

Ideas for investigative stories can come from many sources, but some are standard and developed by investigative journalists over many years.

18.3.1.1 TIPS AND RUMORS

Sometimes a tip can come from someone in the community who has observed something or a disgruntled employee who has insider information on his or her organization. In the case of the Madison County Record's investigation, it received tips from the parents of victims who had received Title IX notifications, documents required under a federal law on sexual discrimination, including sexual assault, in education. The parents wanted to make sure the school district did not cover up the problem.

Whatever the case, the reporter must verify the tipster's information to determine its credibility; doing so may mean digging into available documents or contacting some reliable sources. No investigative reporter should charge into a story without checking the information first.

18.3.1.2 TAPPING COLLEAGUES AND REGULAR SOURCES

Beat reporters cultivate sources to cover their beats efficiently. They know that anyone—from the mayor to the assistant financial officer to the maintenance worker—can be a source of information. At smaller news organizations, these journalists can develop story ideas from their sources. Investigative reporters at larger news organizations can also tap into the beat reporter's network of sources to generate ideas.

18.3.1.3 FOLLOWING UP ON BREAKING NEWS OR OTHER STORIES

Investigative reporters need to read a lot and watch and listen to television news programs. They must be able to analyze a story to identify missing information. General assignment and beat reporters often lack the time to follow up on a story; the investigative journalist may develop an idea that expands on the why or how of the event. Investigative reporters might read or hear something that piques their curiosity and leads to a story. Therefore, they need to stay connected with the community and the world beyond it.

18.3.1.4 USING BLOGS AND SOCIAL MEDIA

Staying connected in today's media landscape means being connected to online media. Investigative journalists should be consistent readers of blogs—both independent ones and those sponsored by news organizations—and should be

LOST MOTHERS

How We Collected Nearly 5,000 Stories of Maternal Harm

Asking if readers knew women who died or almost died in childbirth drew an outpouring that carries lessons for both traditional and engaged journalism.

by Adriana Gallardo, March 20, 2018, 11:28 a.m. EDT

LOST MOTHERS
Maternal Care and
Preventable Deaths

About a year ago, ProPublica and NPR launched Lost Mothers, a project investigating the dangers of pregnancy and childbirth in the U.S. We soon learned that the U.S. was one of the most dangerous countries in the developed world to give birth. About 700 to 900 women die each year from pregnancy- or childbirth-related complications. For each woman who dies, more than 70 nearly die.

We knew the statistics. Maternal advocacy organizations and other sources had provided names of some expectant and new mothers who had died, including Lauren Bloomstein, a neonatal nurse in New Jersey. But we still didn't have enough of the human stories we needed for this project. So we set out to find women and families willing to share intimate experiences. To do that, we published a request: Do you know someone who died or nearly died in childbirth? Help us investigate.

Choose an option
I almost died.
I know someone who died.
✓ I know someone who almost died.

The form was designed to capture three different case scenarios that would help us investigate maternal harm.

The form asked users about the type of maternal health complication that occurred, about follow-up care, and about lingering long-term consequences. Within a few days of publishing our maternal health questionnaire, we received about 2,500 responses. Today, we have almost 5,000. We've had submissions come in from all 50 states, Washington, D.C., and Puerto Rico. We have stories of maternal deaths dating as far back as 1920 and as recent as December 2017. The people who answered that request helped fuel much of the Lost Mothers project. And we're going to tell you how we did it.

ProPublica and NPR used crowdsourcing as a way to reach sources for a story about the dangers of childbirth and maternal health care. The crowdsourcing outreach garnered nearly 5,000 responses that provided a wealth of information for the investigative story.

connected to Facebook and Twitter, as well as other forms of social media. When US Airways pilot Chesley "Sully" Sullenberger safely performed an emergency landing on the Hudson River in 2009 after his plane hit a flock of geese, a witness tweeted about the incident well before mainstream media started reporting the story. Several other onlookers posted the first pictures of passengers evacuating the plane. An investigative reporter might follow up on that story with one on flight safety and how well prepared airline pilots are to deal with such emergencies.

As discussed later in the chapter, it is essential for today's reporters to use the internet and social media as idea-generating tools and a means to develop sources. The interactive capability of social media allows the investigative journalist to build a community of followers who can be sources as well as readers or viewers.

Reporters use Twitter to stay in touch with sources, editors and other reporters as well as to update people on news stories. Some journalists use social media or microblogs to verify information with sources and develop story ideas. The key is to build a network of sources and followers who can help reporters gather and disseminate information.

18.3.1.5 OBSERVATIONS

The community a person works and lives in can be a source of ideas, but he or she needs to know that community. Is it blue-collar with a lot of industry? Or is it white-collar with mostly technology or financial organizations and perhaps a major college or university? What stories can an investigative reporter generate from these areas? The simple question to ask is, "What isn't being covered or written about in the daily routine of news gathering?" Making a list of things that are not being covered in depth can lead to potential investigative stories.

In communities with many big industries, stories about labor unions, environmental issues, wages and benefits, tax deals for companies moving to the area or kickbacks and cronyism involving local officials can be investigated. A joint investigative report by The Kingstree (South Carolina) News and the Charleston Post and Courier newspapers found that a county official had given herself a $30,000 raise from a fund of federal money that was created to help child support enforcement efforts.

Possible story ideas for white-collar communities include medical facilities and health organizations, banking practices, savings and loans, insurance companies or educational institutions. Eric Lipton, a reporter for The New York Times, conducted a nine-month investigation into corporate lobbying of state attorneys general across the United States to get the state officials to drop cases or change policies. The Houston Chronicle investigated the failure of Texas health officials to prepare for and react to the COVID-19 pandemic when it first emerged in the state, allowing the virus to spread unchecked.

In some cases, investigative reporters turn their spotlights on the media industry itself. Nicholas Confessore of The New York Times investigated the career and power of former Fox News prime-time host Tucker Carlson in a three-part series that detailed cable news' biggest star and the danger he poses.

18.3.2 Resources

Once they develop a story idea and pitch it to their editor, investigative reporters must determine what resources are needed and accessible. Can reliable human sources be developed for the story? Are records or documents available? If the files are highly technical, are there expert sources who can help analyze and interpret them? Can the reporter or the news organization commit the time and money required to complete an investigative story successfully? Can one reporter handle the research and writing or does the size of the investigation require a team?

Knowing what resources are needed and available helps the news organization and the investigative reporter decide the scope of the story. Determining where and how to get documents and the possible cost to obtain them is part of that process. Are the documents available locally or online or will the journalists have to travel to another location to access them? If the documents are online, in what format are they? Are they PDFs or are they Excel spreadsheets? And does the news organization have the programs and trained users capable of working with the data?

18.3.3 Planning the Story

Planning is critical when working on an investigative piece. Once an idea has been identified, it is important to develop the central point of the story, which will help the writer maintain the focus of the piece throughout. Investigative stories are often longer than standard hard news stories and are sometimes broken into a multi-part series. The central point has to drive the story from beginning to end even if the story is published or broadcast over several days.

Creating a schematic like the story tree (see Chapter 7) can identify necessary sources and documents and establish a timeline for research and writing. The story tree also can help organize information as the investigation evolves. Interviews or other information from a source can be coded, dated and stored under the source's name or code name.

Initial research is part of the planning process and is as necessary as the in-depth research needed to complete the story. The reporter needs to understand everything he or she possibly can about the subject of the investigation, and initial research can provide that information. The material collected in this discovery phase of research can be filed and used later with the story if needed. If a journalist is investigating an individual, what is the person's personal and professional background? Is the information about the person complete and accurate? If a company or organization is the subject, what is its history? What is the organization's structure? Who owns and operates it, and are there any subsidiaries or connections to other companies? What is the organization's culture and reputation? Knowing as much as possible about the person or the organization at this stage can help guide the rest of the research and the story.

18.3.4 Gathering Documents

Exhaustive, in-depth research is vital to publishing a good investigative piece. And it is the first step in the process, before conducting extensive interviews with the human sources involved in the story.

Reporters and their editors do not want to waste time chasing a trail of documents that contribute nothing to the investigation. Some documents and records may be public; others, such as personal bank statements and medical records, are private information. Some may be held by local, state or federal government agencies and require the filing of a request under either a state open-records law or the federal Freedom of Information Act. Filing such requests can sometimes delay the research. Investigative reporters know when this step is necessary and how to file the request. They also know which government agencies store the various documents they will need—whether it is the clerk of courts, the election commission, the recorder of deeds or the county tax assessor. On the federal level, it might be the Securities and Exchange Commission or the Environmental Protection Agency.

Table 18.1 provides just a short list of the types of documents that can be accessed, depending on federal or state regulations. Note that there are two types of public records—operational and disclosure. Operational documents, which are readily available for public inspection, involve the expenditure of public (tax) money. Government agencies, school districts and other public offices must keep records showing how their spending provides services. Disclosure documents contain personal information about a citizen. They are completed when someone buys property, applies to practice law or medicine or licenses a dog. The information can be made public under certain conditions.

Public records can be in electronic form, too. Much of the routine paperwork and record-keeping of government at all levels is now done electronically. Communications between public officials or between officials and the public may be in electronic form as emails, text messages or direct messages. Most states and the federal government treat electronic and paper records as equally accessible to the public.

Investigative reporters must know and understand the public records laws of the state in which they work. They do not have to be lawyers, but they have to know the terminology used to access documents. Journalists first need to learn whether the information they want is held by a federal, state, or local government agency. In the case of federal groups, they will have to file a FOIA request to acquire documents or use the U.S. Government in the Sunshine Act to get access to meetings. If it's a state or local department, reporters must use the state's public records law or public meetings law.

The federal government and many states have tried to make it easier for citizens to get information. Often, you just have to ask or write a short letter requesting the material. But the laws have their complexities. Records available under federal law may not be available under some state laws, and state laws vary

TABLE 18.1 TYPES OF DOCUMENTS USED IN INVESTIGATIVE RESEARCH

Published Information
- Biographies: personal and professional information on government or corporate figures
- Stories in trade magazines: background information about a government or organization
- News releases: public relations efforts by government agencies or organizations
- Published scientific articles

Public Records

Operational Documents
- Minutes of meetings
- Budgets and budget negotiations
- Contracts
- Payrolls
- Elections

Disclosure Documents
- Licenses
- Lawsuits
- Inspection reports
- Political contributions
- Filings with the SEC

Private Papers
- Personal letters
- Bank statements
- School papers
- Medical records
- Legislative voting records
- Annual financial reports
- Emails, text messages, Twitter communications
- Audio and video recordings of public hearings
- Video surveillance recordings at government buildings

greatly as to what records and meetings are open to the public. The Reporters Committee for Freedom of the Press website (rcfp.org) contains details about the U.S. Freedom of Information Act, as well as the public records and meetings laws of all 50 states and the District of Columbia. The website can help reporters know what records and meetings are open under the relevant laws and how to go about requesting copies of documents.

18.3.5 Developing Sources

Researching documents can provide only so much information. Investigative reporters have to develop human sources to tell the entire story. When Woodward and Bernstein were investigating the Watergate scandal, they were aided by an inside source codenamed "Deep Throat." This source—who turned out to be W. Mark Felt, then associate director of the FBI—provided the journalists with invaluable information as they pursued the story that would ultimately bring down Nixon's administration. Shortly before his death in 2008, Felt revealed his identity, telling reporters that he became a source because he was upset that Nixon was trying to use the FBI as a political tool and to obstruct justice.

Government records are important for many investigative stories. Sometimes, government agencies refuse to release them. The Sun Herald in Biloxi, Mississippi, fought in court to obtain records of the state Department of Marine Resources. Eventually, state courts ruled the newspaper was entitled to the information. In this photo, the records are being delivered to the Harrison County Courthouse where reporters and the public were able to view them.

Determining a source's motivation for providing information to the press is sometimes difficult. Whistleblowers may have altruistic motives, such as a desire to correct an existing problem that they cannot correct within their organization. Some whistleblowers are less noble and provide information because they want to gain publicity or they have a grudge against an organization or officials in it. It is important that reporters try to determine a source's motives and verify the accuracy and credibility of the material provided before publishing their stories. They also must evaluate the reliability of the information. A source with firsthand knowledge of a situation or event is more useful than one who has only second- or third-hand details.

Reporters should place the person being investigated or who leads the organization under investigation at the top of their source list, but they must determine when and how to interview that person. Interviews will be most fruitful after the journalists have spoken with all other sources and reviewed all relevant documents. Remember, every effort must be made to allow those involved to tell their side of the story. Further, reporters cannot assume that the subject of the investigation will not talk to them.

Locating sources, especially those no longer involved with the agency, organization or company, can be a problem. Reporters can use the internet and online directories, printed telephone or city directories or workplace directories. As mentioned earlier, social networking is another means of locating sources.

18.4 The Investigative Interview

When sources have been identified, the difficult part—interviewing—begins. Interviewing sources for background information may be less challenging than confronting the subject of the investigation.

Unprepared reporters risk losing the source early in the interview. Therefore, as with gathering information and developing sources, investigative journalists need to know beforehand what they need from the source during the interview. That knowledge helps focus the interview and the questions. Investigative reporters have to be good interviewers, able to analyze a situation

Newspapers covered the testimony of a former Facebook employee who left the company and took thousands of documents that highlighted the company's business practices. Whistleblower Frances Haugen is shown here before testifying at a Senate subcommittee hearing in October 2021.

quickly and react accordingly. They should not be intimidated by threats if subjects become belligerent, especially if they feel threatened by the line of questioning.

When searching documents, reporters look for discrepancies in a person's biographic material or the company's history or financial records. They prepare questions about the inconsistencies and work them into the interview without sounding accusatory. They pose the questions as though they are trying to understand or clarify information. Journalists who ask, "Why did you lie on your résumé?" may find the source ending the interview unless they first explain they are attempting to clarify any discrepancies.

Some critics of investigative journalism cite reporters' desires to sensationalize a story with a "gotcha" or "ambush" interview. Critics contend that this practice is unethical because it puts sources on the spot and can make them appear guilty in the court of public opinion even before the facts are known. This device should be a last resort when all other attempts to contact a source have failed. Along with making every effort to seek an interview with sources, reporters should also give them adequate time to respond to allegations. Approaching sources a couple of days before a story will be published or broadcast may not give them enough time to gather information for a response. Good investigative stories are detailed and balanced, giving all sides the opportunity to address the issues.

Because an investigative story can take weeks or months to compile, reporters try to stay connected to sources and give them progress updates, especially sources who are whistleblowers and who need to prepare for any repercussions. In addition, keeping in touch with sources opens the door for them to provide additional or updated information as the story develops.

18.5 Writing the Investigative Story

When the research is complete and the interviews have been conducted, it is time to write the story. Although reporters may begin sketching out their stories or putting together an outline earlier, they should save the bulk of the writing until all the research and interviews are done. That way, they will not miss important information and will keep the story flowing rationally from beginning to end.

It is best to work from an outline to maintain a logical order to all the facts that will appear in the story. Some reporters lay out the story from the beginning of the research to the end, placing documents and interviews together in chronological order. They may not write the story in that sequence, but the chronology helps them organize massive amounts of information and spot trends or links between sources and documents.

Investigative stories often include a lot of facts and statistics. They can involve multiple sources and direction changes throughout the narrative. Keep in mind, however, that the audience wants to learn about people. The people involved in the story are often the most compelling part. Don't hide them under an avalanche of information. Connect the readers, viewers and listeners to the people in the story—the victims and the antagonists. Explain how the issue under investigation will affect people's lives. It will help to make the story more interesting.

As with any news story, the investigative reporter needs a powerful lead to open the story and grab the audience's attention. Some stories work best with a direct summary news lead or a shocking or ironic lead that piques the public's interest. Sometimes, investigative journalists will write their stories in the focus style. They will begin with a focus lead, or anecdotal narrative highlighting an individual involved, and use that person's experiences to introduce the piece before laying out the central point in a nut graph later in the story. Whichever lead is used, however, the writer should not oversell or hype the story. Good writing that tells a compelling story will attract people's attention and keep them involved.

The body of the investigative story should not get bogged down in long lists of statistics that bury the subjects of the story or confuse the audience. Make numbers come alive by interpreting them through examples.

When a Malaysian jetliner disappeared over the Indian Ocean in 2014, a story in USA Today said one of the search areas was 198,000 square miles in size but did not give a point of comparison. If the story had noted that the search site was bigger than the states of Oregon and Wyoming combined, readers would have had a sense of the searchers' difficult task.

To keep the audience's attention throughout the body of the story, keep the controversy at the forefront. Writers remember what piqued their interest or outraged them enough to pursue the story. That should be part of the central point. Investigative stories revolve around conflict, and conflict moves the story along.

Investigative reporters plan the ending of the story as well as the lead. Some will write the ending of the story first and use it to formulate the lead. The ending can provide the "aha" moment for the audience when the writer has tied up the various strings of the story. Whether reporters use a tieback to the lead or a dramatic conclusion to the story, knowing how it will end provides them with a basic blueprint of how to structure the rest of the story. The ending should leave the audience thinking about the story and pondering its implications, but the ending should not editorialize. Let people draw their own conclusions.

Investigative reporters also plan visual elements for their stories. Photographs, illustrations and infographics can explain complex statistical information more easily than a long narrative. Some information is best presented as text, but other details are more clearly presented visually. Graphics have to stand on their own and be appealing; however, they should not simply parrot information that is in the story.

Finally, when investigative reporters finish writing the story, they edit it carefully—not just for grammar or style errors, but also for weak areas or holes that need more detail for clarity and accuracy. The final editing process should include extensive fact-checking. Some writers will do line-by-line fact-checking before a story is published. Accuracy is key to investigative reporting. A story containing errors will lose credibility very quickly. As we pointed out earlier in the chapter, the reporter and his or her news organization will lose credibility as well and open themselves to possible legal action.

18.6 Using Technology in Investigative Reporting

18.6.1 Using Computers to Get Answers

Investigative reporters sometimes have to analyze thousands of documents to spot trends or find important information. Computer-assisted reporting has made the process much easier. For example, reporters rely heavily on the internet to gather information and to communicate with sources and other reporters.

An outgrowth of computer-assisted reporting is data-driven journalism, or simply data journalism. Data-driven journalism uses digital tools and collaborative efforts of news organizations to explore the massive amounts of information available today from a variety of sources. It combines journalism with other fields such as graphic design, computer science and statistics to tell detailed stories in visually interactive ways. The Pandora Papers investigation by International Consortium of Investigative Journalists (ICIJ), which uncovered the financial dealings of 35 current and former heads of state and more than 300 other public officials and politicians around the world, involved more than 600 journalists from 150 news organizations who collectively analyzed nearly 12 million documents leaked by 14 offshore providers.

Data-driven journalism has existed for decades, but sophisticated and powerful computers in news reporting made it possible for reporters to analyze large quantities of data. Reporters had to compile in digital form some of the data, but much of it already exists in electronic databases obtained from government agencies. These databases contain vast amounts of information, and analyzing them without computers would take months. Reporters who are skilled in working with spreadsheets and statistical tools can analyze data such as budgets, reports, surveys and polls quickly and thoroughly. (For more about data journalism see the guest column "How to Interview Data" at the end of Chapter 9.)

Where the virus is surging

| Deaths | **Cases** | Adj. for population | Totals | Since last week | Cumulative |

100,000 1 million 5 million
REPORTED CASES

The Washington Post used data from its own reporting and from the Center for Systems Science and Engineering at Johns Hopkins University to track COVID-19 cases and deaths around the world.

Databases are nothing new. A common example is a city directory—an alphabetical listing of people and businesses (see Appendix A). But because the data are in a paper format, analysis is challenging. For instance, it would be difficult to calculate what percentage of the people listed owned their homes instead of renting. Once the data are in electronic form, a database management program can quickly make that calculation.

Computer-assisted projects can compare databases from a variety of sources, but government and public record databases are often key sources. The Atlanta Journal-Constitution filed an open records request to access information about high school graduation rates in the state. The search and subsequent story found that state education officials were inflating the number of students graduating across the state and underreporting the number of dropouts by more than half.

Other news organizations have used computers and databases to report stories about agriculture, business, child welfare, crime, discrimination, education, the environment, health care, highway safety and the justice system, to name some general areas. The opportunities are endless. And the stories often attract readers, viewers and listeners.

With continuing advances in computer technology and its use by news organizations, even small papers are using data journalism methods to give their readers more in-depth information on issues. News editors and station managers require more such skills of the reporters they hire. Students who graduate with some basic computer skills in using spreadsheet software (such as Quattro Pro and Excel) and relational databases (such as FoxPro, Paradox, dBase and Access) will move to the front of the line in the job market. It also will be important for students to prove they can apply that knowledge to real stories. Journalists must learn to see the possibilities, develop story ideas and write stories that use these skills.

A computer-assisted reporter does not replace good old-fashioned reporting skills. Computers do not interview sources, and they are only as good as the information that goes into them. They are merely another tool used by reporters to provide information to the public.

18.6.2 Using Social Media

When social media first came to the attention of the public at the beginning of the 21st century, it was more a curiosity than a journalistic tool. People used it to connect with friends and family. Messages were mostly personal notes about, for example, a movie they had seen, a restaurant they liked or a vacation they took. Around 2007, however, journalists began to explore using social media to connect with their audience.

The explosion in the use of social media has changed the face of many news organizations, making them more interactive and more accessible to their audiences. It has also given news organizations more sources for information, more eyes to look for wrongdoing and more people to scan documents. Social media are thus making investigative journalists more efficient and more effective.

Investigative reporters using social media sites can build a community of readers who are familiar with their bylines. Journalists can tap into that community when seeking information or trying to identify sources. A simple tweet can expand into several queries from the network, even from people who may not regularly follow the reporter.

Building a social media community can take time, but it can be an effective tool in developing story ideas and gathering information. News organizations often tweet their followers to ask if they have information or know something about a topic. As the 50th anniversary of the New York World's Fair was nearing, The New York Times tweeted its readers to locate people who had participated in or attended the event. Investigative reporters can use the same technique.

A major element is knowing which stories will benefit from crowdsourcing and which will not. If secrecy is a priority, it may be best to conduct the investigation without using social media. But if the story is one that can benefit from public assistance in research—an investigation into an internet banking scam, for example—tapping into social media resources can locate people who may have relevant information. People affected by the scam could relate their personal experiences, thereby adding a human-interest element to the story.

18.6.3 Using Statistics

Much of the information that reporters gather is statistical. Statistics appear almost daily in news stories concerning budgets, taxes, census data, sports, politics, profits, dividends and annual reports. Other pieces based largely on statistics report rates of crime, productivity, energy consumption, unemployment and inflation. Journalists must learn to present statistics to the public in a form that is interesting and understandable.

Reporters who write stories based on statistics translate as many numbers as possible into words, which an audience can understand more easily. Writers also try to analyze the statistics, explaining their significance instead of simply reporting the numbers. Explaining the statistics requires looking for and emphasizing major trends, record highs and lows, the unusual and the unexpected.

Numbers by themselves lack context, and using percentages without a framework can be meaningless and misleading. Assume the FBI reported that in one year there were 143 murders in Washington, D.C., which has a population of approximately 600,000. If 215 murders were committed the following year, reporters could write that the murder rate had risen 50 percent. On the other hand, if a crime reporter in Green Bay, Wisconsin, used a percentage figure to report an increase in that city's murder rate, it would be mostly meaningless. Assume the same year Washington had 143 murders, Green Bay had only one. If there were two the next year, the increase would be 100 percent. Comparing percentages suggests that violence is increasing more rapidly in the latter city. Journalists need to explain the numbers with helpful comparisons.

Emphasizing the story's human interest is another way to explain statistics. The following example gives numbers only in a routine and dull series:

> The fire department's annual report states that last year it responded to the following numbers and types of calls: bomb threats, 60; electrical fires, 201; false alarms, 459; first aid, 1,783; mattress fires, 59; burned pots left on the stove, 78; rescues, 18; washdowns, usually of leaking gasoline at the scene of automobile accidents, 227; and water salvage, 46.

The revision includes a human element from a person who received first aid from the fire department. Another version could have examined the false alarms in greater detail. Did they come from a certain area of the city? Was anyone caught and prosecuted for setting off those false alarms? Where were the bomb threats? Was anyone injured?

> When Sarah Kindstrom needed help, the fire department responded. Kindstrom's heart attack last week was one of 5,024 calls the department answered last year. First aid requests were the most common, according to the department's annual report, which was released today.
>
> The five leading types of calls included, in order of frequency: first aid, 1,783; false alarms, 459; washdowns, usually of leaking gasoline at the scene of automobile accidents, 227; electrical fires, 201; and burned pots left on stoves, 78.
>
> Other types included: bomb threats, 60; mattress fires, 59; water salvage, 46; and rescues, 18.

Stories that rely too heavily on numbers can be deadly for an audience, who might perceive them as boring and hard to understand. The reporter's job is to make the numbers interesting so readers, listeners and viewers will stay with the story until the end. The unusual nature of statistical information and its impact on people are what make the story interesting.

Reporters describing election results include more than who won and the number of votes that each candidate received. They search for additional highlights: Did incumbents win or lose? Was any bloc of voters (such as ethnic groups, women or conservatives) decisively for one candidate or another? Were there noticeable differences in precincts or voting districts from previous elections? Did any candidates win by unusually large or small margins? Answering those kinds of questions can make election stories more interesting.

Journalists who include statistics in their stories try to present them as simply as possible. They avoid a series of paragraphs that contain nothing but statistics. Instead, they use transitions, explanations and narrative to break up strings of numbers and clarify the information. Reporters also avoid the temptation to editorialize about statistical information. Readers, listeners or viewers might not agree with a writer's characterization of a budget increase as "big" or "huge." Although one person might think a 2 percent increase in a $1 billion budget is small, another might think that adding $20 million to the budget is a great deal.

18.7 Ethical Issues in Investigative Reporting

Newly licensed physicians pledge to "first, do no harm" when they take the Hippocratic oath. By its very nature, investigative journalism seeks to "cure" a problem. Every story leads to consequences for the reporter, the news organization, the sources and the subject. Even when the story is accurate and complete, some people may feel that the media sensationalize a story. Sometimes—whether through careless reporting or unethical behavior—an investigative piece can harm the reporter, the news organization or the subject of the story. Therefore, journalists need to know, understand and be able to justify their actions and the consequences to their audience.

A famous example is ABC's exposé of the Food Lion grocery store chain's handling of meat, dairy and other products. The story prompted a major discussion on the ethical and legal issues of investigative reporting, especially the secret video recording of subjects on private property. Two ABC News producers got jobs at Food Lion stores in North Carolina and South Carolina. Their applications falsified information regarding their employment histories, educational backgrounds and references. They worked at the stores for only a couple of weeks and used hidden video cameras to record employees at the stores treating, wrapping and handling meat as well as discussing meat department practices. The resulting segment, which aired on "Primetime Live," alleged that Food Lion required employees to engage in unsafe and unhealthy or illegal practices. After the story aired, the chain closed a number of stores.

According to Reporters Committee for Freedom of the Press, Food Lion sued ABC in North Carolina's federal court. The lawsuit did not attack the content of the story but the means the network used to gather the information. The supermarket chain alleged fraud, breach of the duty of loyalty, trespass and unfair trade practices under North Carolina law. The jury found ABC liable and awarded Food Lion $1,400 in compensatory damages, $5.5 million in punitive damages for fraud and $2 in damages for breach of duty of loyalty and trespass. The court later reduced the punitive damages to $315,000.

Both parties appealed the judgment, and a federal appeals court later rejected the fraud claim, eliminating the punitive damages, but held the $2 award for trespass and breach of duty of loyalty. The court said the producers had a right to be in the store because they had been hired by Food Lion to work there. However, the company had never given them permission to record other employees in non-public areas of the store. The decision demonstrated that the First Amendment does not protect journalists who trespass or commit other torts to gather news.

The Food Lion case raised ethical issues as well. Critics of ABC's use of hidden cameras questioned the use of deceptive practices to gather information about a subject or an organization. Supporters of the network said that journalists are sometimes justified in using deceptive means to expose wrongdoing that can harm people.

Is deception ever justified? The earliest days of "yellow" journalism and "muckraking" saw competing newspapers and magazines send their reporters to investigate numerous government agencies and corporate entities to increase circulation. In the late 1880s, Elizabeth Jane Cochran, better known by her pen name Nellie Bly, became famous for investigating inhumane conditions at a women's insane asylum in New York by feigning insanity and having herself committed. After spending 10 days in the asylum, she was released at the request of her employer, Joseph Pulitzer's New York World. Bly's reporting led to reforms at the asylum and more funds to care for the mentally disabled. Some would say that Bly's deception was necessary to get the story.

In 1900, Ida Tarbell, who worked for McClure's Magazine, began working on an investigative report of the Standard Oil Co. Employing modern methods of investigative journalism, Tarbell gathered documents pertaining to the company's business practices from all over the country and began to analyze them.

She interviewed current and former executives and employees, government officials, executives at competing companies and legal experts. When the stories detailing the practices of Standard Oil and its founder, John D. Rockefeller, began to appear in McClure's in 1902, they galvanized public opinion and led to regulatory action that broke up Rockefeller's monopoly of the oil industry.

Many would say that Tarbell's hard work and attention to detail accomplished the same goal as the deception employed by Nellie Bly. Who is right? It often comes down to an ethical decision on the part of news organizations. Ethics deals with the gray areas that the law cannot answer—the areas between right and wrong. For some news organizations, deception can never be justified. For others, deception may be a last resort, employed when every attempt to document wrongdoing by traditional reporting has failed.

Investigative reporters are bound by the same ethical guidelines as beat and general assignment reporters. Chapter 6 discussed the Society of Professional Journalists' code of ethics. While SPJ has no power to its code, investigative reporters and their colleagues in the newsroom are bound by the organizational rules and policies of the news organization that employs them. It is best to raise possible ethical problems regarding investigative stories with senior editors and producers. Reporters should make sure their supervisors are aware of what they are doing to pursue the story.

Guest Columnist

Developing Investigative Story Ideas

BY PAULA LAVIGNE

When I'm trying to generate story ideas for television or for online, I have a few goals in mind. I want stories that reveal something new or make people think of something in a different way.

The key is to be counterintuitive. The reaction I'm going for is, "Huh, I didn't realize that," or "You've got to be kidding me."

I do a lot of work with data, because I have a background in computer-assisted reporting, and that kind of work lets you make connections and present findings that are unique and that get beyond anecdotal stories that don't really break the surface.

The story ESPN's "Outside the Lines" did in 2010 on sports stadium food safety is a good example. Local media had done plenty of stories about restaurants, concession stands and so forth that received bad ratings from health department inspectors. That wasn't new. But what we really wanted to do was see how bad it was across the board and to draw some comparisons. (People love rankings and ratings, whether it's a story for sports, business or lifestyles.)

We requested—using state and provincial public access laws—records of health department inspection reports for all stadium food outlets at professional sports stadiums and arenas in the United States and Canada. Compiling those results allowed us to say how much at risk people were overall and show which venues were the best and worst. Combing through the records also revealed some fascinating—and disgusting—examples, like this one, to punch up the story with sometimes gory and gross details:

> Mold in ice machines at six stands at Miller Park in Milwaukee. A cockroach crawling over a soda dispenser in a private club at Mellon Arena in Pittsburgh. Food service workers repeatedly ignoring orders to wash their hands at a stand at Detroit's Ford Field. ... At 30 of the venues (28 percent), more than half of the concession stands or restaurants had been cited for at least one "critical" or "major" health violation. Such violations pose a risk for foodborne illnesses that can make someone sick, or, in extreme cases, become fatal. —ESPN.com

Another key to generating good stories is to know a great idea when it comes across your desk, and that can take some research. "Outside the Lines" got a tip a few years ago from a viewer who had seen a story we did that broached the topic of gambling among college athletes. His message on our tip line was, in essence, if we thought that was bad, we should see the gambling around little league football in South Florida.

That tip actually prompted a series of stories that led to a criminal investigation and arrests for illegal gambling, and earned the network a number of awards, including a part in ESPN's first ever duPont Award from Columbia University in December 2013.

But when I first started looking into it, I wasn't sure whether it was even worth a phone call. (And the tip was anonymous.) I looked online and through some of our newswire services to see if any stories about this had been done before. I didn't find anything. That could have deterred me, but it actually made me more interested in this because I thought perhaps we were on to something new, a scandal that no one else had reported.

Through a series of phone calls to sources in South Florida—and finally tracking down the original tipster—we had a handle on what was going on. Then it was a matter of catching the behavior in action, which meant going to several games just to see what was going on.

Producer Greg Amante and I did a great deal of shoe-leather investigating before we actually started reporting the story—by which I mean putting interviews to tape, shooting footage and getting reactions.

I bring this up because I think it's important to realize the value of really exploring an idea, developing it and putting it in context before you start to compile it into a story. So much of the media environment today is knee-jerk reaction, in-and-out reporting of rumor or surface-level treatment of an incident. And when that happens, really good ideas don't get the treatment and the opportunity to blossom into the really great stories that they can become.

Paula Lavigne is a reporter for ESPN's enterprise unit. Her stories appear on "Outside the Lines," "SportsCenter" and ESPN.com.

The Reporter's Guide to Investigative Reporting

INVESTIGATIVE REPORTING

1. Use a variety of methods to develop story ideas.

2. Follow blogs, websites and social media to connect to readers.

3. Determine what resources are available to conduct an investigative story.

4. Use a story tree to determine the required sources and documents.

5. Know how and where to get pertinent documents for the story.

6. Prepare for the investigative interview by studying the issue, the organization or the source so you can ask knowledgeable questions.

7. When writing the story, keep the controversy and the people involved in the forefront.

8. Make the ending of the story as important as the lead.

9. Use social media to gather and verify information as well as reach out to readers.

10. Follow best practices, and be ethical in your reporting.

USING STATISTICS

1. Verify the accuracy of statistical information.

2. Make sure the story's central point reflects the most important or unusual aspects of the statistical information.

3. Present statistical information in a concise and understandable way.

4. Look for links between statistics that might make the story more interesting.

5. Do not editorialize about statistical information. Let the numbers speak for themselves, and let people make their own judgments.

 # Review Exercises

1. INVESTIGATIVE REPORTING

1. You hear a rumor that the recycling program at your college is not following state and local guidelines. A member of the college maintenance staff and a student who has worked with the maintenance department claim that, instead of recycling plastic, aluminum and other metals, glass and paper as required by law, your college allegedly has been carting recyclables to the local landfill. The staff member and student claim that the college administration is not recycling because it costs too much and would require the college to hire more staff to handle the recycling program. You decide to investigate their claims.

How would you approach the story? Where would you begin? What information would you need to gather? What sources—primary and secondary—would you pursue? Are there primary and secondary off-campus sources you would need to include in the story? What ethical boundaries would you have to consider? In previous chapters, you were introduced to concepts of digital and visual journalism. How would you employ those concepts in creating a web and social media package for this story? What visual elements, still photography or video, would you need to gather for the story?

2. A classmate approaches you because she knows that you work for the student media. She is on the field hockey team, and she tells you that the graduation rate for student-athletes at your college has dropped significantly in the past three years. Budget concerns at the institution

resulted in the elimination of all staff in the student-athlete support services office five years ago. What sources—primary and secondary—would you need for the story? What kinds of data would you need to gather to support the facts in the story?

As in Exercise 1, think of digital and visual journalistic elements that you would employ in creating a package for the web and social media.

What sources would you interview on video or for audio clips? What b-roll would you record? What still photography might you include? How could you use crowdsourcing through social media to gather information for this story? Finally, thinking ethically, what implications or consequences might arise for the college from the publication of the story? How do you defend your decision to pursue and publish the story?

19

JOURNALISM AND PUBLIC RELATIONS

Journalists and PR practitioners need each other. Journalists want to know what is happening in the different sectors of their community and PR practitioners work with journalists to get their stories about clients in the news.

Both journalists and public relations practitioners research and write nonfiction stories for the public. The journalist writes stories to provide an objective account of current events and issues. The PR practitioner writes news releases that promote a client, in the hopes of getting stories published in news media or circulated on social media. Their purpose is to get their message to audiences as a news story, which means thinking like a journalist.

The more newsworthy the news release story and the closer it is to journalistic style, the more likely it will appear in a news media outlet. Thus, PR practitioners usually have degrees in journalism or a public relations specialization. A survey of the Public Relations Society of America's members found that professionals consider a news reporting course more important than any PR course for PR majors. A journalism class teaches students such things as news judgment, news writing style, media audiences and the importance of deadlines. In addition, many companies hire former journalists to handle PR because they have writing skills essential to the job; they can also translate complicated information into clear, readable stories and understand journalists' definitions of news.

While PR practitioners need journalists to be interested in their stories, journalists need PR people for information and story ideas. The best PR practitioners know their client or organization well, locate information quickly for journalists and arrange interviews with experts and top executives. PR practitioners use these skills to build trust and a working relationship with reporters.

This chapter describes the PR practitioner's job, with a focus on writing news releases for the media and working with journalists. This type of PR is called media relations.

19.1 What Is PR?

Public relations is planned and continuous communication designed to promote an organization and its image, products or services to the public. Practitioners write news releases (also called press releases), create visual communication (photos and information graphics, for example), produce video news releases (VNRs) for broadcast and YouTube, orchestrate viral campaigns online, monitor social media, organize special events such as press conferences and celebrations, research markets and evaluate the success of publicity, all to improve their client's image.

The overall objective of this field is to promote the client and get its name, product or service into the news without paying for advertising. Some releases indirectly promote a client. Green Valley, a company that specializes in skin-care products with natural ingredients, published a news release stating that other companies' personal care items still use chemicals banned by the U.S. FDA. The release quoted the company's chief executive officer, thereby promoting Green Valley.

Practitioners might be generalists, doing it all. Or, they might specialize in a particular skill, such as writing or video production or design. Or, they might be an expert in a particular area of public relations, such as strategic communications, risk communication, crisis communication or speech writing for public officials.

Strategic communication is creating and developing a plan that effectively communicates a consistent message to particular audiences. The PR practitioner's goal might be for general audiences to know that their client has researched and developed new packaging for its products and is doing everything possible to be environmentally friendly. Or, the goal might be to promote excitement within a community when a client, such as Trader Joe's, is opening a new store in the area. The opposite of strategic communication is to churn out news releases and do lots of inefficient busywork without a specific goal and master plan in place, and without assessing if the plan worked.

Risk communication involves preventative planning for any potential problems that might occur and having an action plan if they do. For example, chemical companies need risk communication plans in case their products leak and affect a community. An action plan needed to be in place when Thailand's Star Petroleum Refining leaked 11,000 gallons of oil 12 miles from the shore, ruining beaches and plant and animal life. Automotive companies need to know how to react if their manufactured parts cause deaths or injuries and are recalled. Presidential candidates have a victory and a concession speech already prepared to cover either outcome.

Crisis communication is after-the-fact (i.e., when a problem has already occurred), when PR must smooth things over between their client and

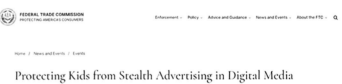

Protecting Kids from Stealth Advertising in Digital Media

Like many businesses and government agencies, the Federal Trade Commission puts its news releases online. This one announces an agency program on protecting children from online advertising that is disguised as noncommercial content.

Workers in protective gear try to remove oil from a popular beach near Bangkok, Thailand. The oil came from an offshore platform that leaked about 11,000 gallons of crude oil. This also created public-relations problems for the company that operates the facility.

the public. For example, Kentucky Fried Chicken needed PR help when it ran out of chicken supplies in many of its 900 restaurants. Rapper Travis Scott needed crisis communication experts when 10 people died of asphyxiation and hundreds were injured as fans stampeded the stage at his Astroworld concert in Houston. Scott has an image problem because he pled guilty to charges of reckless conduct for inciting crowds in the past, although it might not be the case this time. Being a sponsor of the Euro football tournament backfired for Coca-Cola when it lost $4 billion in the minutes after Portuguese soccer player Cristiano Ronaldo removed bottles of Coke from his press conference desk and and hyped water.

A form of public relations is also speech writing. Traci E. Carpenter was a speechwriter for former President Clinton and is now the communications manager and speechwriter for Google. She explained she spends hours with the speaker of her speeches in order to understand and write in that person's voice and style. A major distinction between political and corporate speech writing is that politicians are speaking to voters while corporate officers are speaking to customers and shareholders.

An important component of a PR practicioner's job is preparing for three types of interviews:

1. As a representative of their client, a PR person must be up-to-date on everything about that organization. Journalists often interview PR practitioners about the organization.

2. Practitioners must also prepare their client's CEO and other leaders to speak to the media for press conferences or in times of crisis.

3. To write news releases and stories about the client, the PR person must interview key people within the organization.

PR practitioners work in independent agencies with several clients or in a corporation's communications department, representing only that company. No matter where one works or the area of expertise, PR success depends on excellent writing, visual and interpersonal communication skills acceptable to the news media.

19.1.1 PR Agencies

Some practitioners work in a PR agency, representing companies or other organizations either throughout the year or for special events, such

News releases are a large part of public relations. Goodwill International Industries stores its releases on the company website to allow easy access for journalists and the public.

as a store opening, an anniversary celebration or an election campaign. Those in agencies handle several accounts simultaneously. Agencies may be as small as a one-person consultant contracted to write and edit a company's print and online communications, which could include news releases, newsletters, brochures, blogs, tweets, social media posts, RSS newswires, websites, webcasts and videos. Or an agency can be large, with many specialists in a global network of offices. International conglomerates usually hire agencies to handle their public relations needs in different countries and cultures.

VOTING MOVES CALIFORNIA

MIXTE COMMUNICATIONS, INC

2021 Winner for Community Engagement

Mixte Communications and the League of Women Voters of California (LWVC) collaborated on a digital campaign to motivate young adults to vote, with a specific focus on Black and Latinx communities. The campaign hinged on influencers creating compelling content, easy access to voting resources and a variety of content on Snapchat and TikTok to encourage civic engagement. The team developed a creative campaign and a hashtag (#VotingMovesCA) to track engagement; built a custom bilingual landing page sourced 16 TikTok influencers that represented target communities; and designed interactive filters for Snapchat.

19.1.2 Corporate, Nonprofit and Government PR

Mixte Communications was PRSA's 2021 Winner for Community Engagement. Mixte Communications and the League of Women Voters collaborated on a campaign to motivate young adults to vote, with a specific focus on Black and Latinx communities.

PR people may work within a for-profit company (Mattel Inc.), a nonprofit organization (Salvation Army), a government agency (U.S. Department of Agriculture) or for a celebrity (Beyoncé). In these settings, they communicate with two groups: an internal audience of officers and employees and an external audience of the general public or specific publics such as company partners, investors or consumers. Practitioners may handle internal or external communications, or both, depending on the size of the organization. In addition, they might specialize in a skill or specific area of PR such as strategic communications. For example, Brian O'Connor, vice president for brand and corporate communications for Princess Cruises, handles external communications that includes issues management, incident response and crisis communication, using media relations, public relations and social media. He also leads internal communications by sharing professional services and HR benefits with employees and communicating with staffers on shore and at sea.

19.1.2.1 INTERNAL COMMUNICATIONS

Practitioners handling internal communications work to keep a company's employees informed about the organization. They ensure that all staff, whether in the same building or in a remote branch office, think of themselves as part of the company.

For example, supervisors for Harley-Davidson in the Milwaukee, Wisconsin, headquarters want their employees, whether they work in a production plant in Missouri or stores in Singapore or England, to understand how they contribute to the company's success. The PR practitioner creates lines of communication between supervisors and employees to make the latter aware of their roles in, and contributions to, the company's operations. Through the company website, newsletter and annual report, the PR person informs staff of activities at headquarters, as well as at other plants or offices. They help employees understand changes in policies, government regulations or business practices that will affect them, such as the opening of a plant or the launching of a new health-care plan.

Some practitioners write features about employees and their role in the company. Others publish photographs and brief biographies of new employees in

TheQuartering (Humble Bean Merchant)
@TheQuartering   ...

I spend thousands a year on @Carhartt hoodies, jackets & winter gear. Today that ends. I guess I am looking for alternatives. Seriously, this is insane given their target market. I am done purchasing any of their stuff and giving them thousands in free advertising.

> Carhartt Associates,
>
> Many of you have asked how the recent Supreme Court decision on the OSHA mandate for large employers will impact our associates so we want to provide some clarity. The ruling does not change Carhartt's mandatory vaccination program, which went into effect on January 4th. As you know, we have extended the vaccination deadline for both RCV and Madisonville associates to February 15th. This date also remains in effect.
>
> We put workplace safety at the very top of our priority list and the Supreme Court's recent ruling doesn't impact that core value. We, and the medical community, continue to believe vaccines are necessary to ensure a safe working environment for every associate and even perhaps their households. While we appreciate that there may be differing views, workplace safety is an area where we and the union that represents our associates cannot compromise. An unvaccinated workforce is both a people and business risk that our company is unwilling to take.
>
> If you have additional questions please send them to covidquestions@carhartt.com and we will respond as quickly as possible.
>
> Thank you,
> Mark Valade

10:09 PM · Jan 17, 2022 · Twitter Web App

1,859 Retweets   **1,044** Quote Tweets   **8,763** Likes

HOT TIP

Skills for PR

Jan Thornburg has been senior communications manager for Sarasota, Florida, for more than 15 years. She spent an equal amount of time working in various parts of the country as a broadcast news reporter and anchor, which she says, well prepared her for her media relations job. She knows what stories attract reporters' attention and she can prepare her stories to fit right into the news media lineup. Thornburg offered the following advice for novices preparing for a career in media relations.

What Skills Do You Need?

- Obtain some media experience so that you can understand the kinds of stories

a company newsletter or news release. Still others stage company-wide competitions or host awards banquets for all personnel. They might do the following to promote employees who won awards: Interview and quote the chief executive officer praising the staff member and then write about it for a newsletter story, take photos of the CEO shaking hands with the award winner for a press release, or write a speech for the CEO to read at the awards banquet. In many ways, the PR staff coordinates the performances of others and the way they are perceived in the company and by the media.

PR practitioners realize that communications intended for employees do not always stay within the company. Memos can be leaked with unintended consequences. When clothing company Carhartt reinforced its COVID mandatory vaccination policy, a few employees circulated the internal memo on social media. The effect was that some consumers said they would boycott the brand, while others who had not heard before of Carhartt thanked the company and said they would buy its products.

19.1.2.2 EXTERNAL COMMUNICATIONS

PR practitioners promote a positive image of an organization by identifying different segments of the public and researching the best ways to reach them for messaging news. These publics may be investors, customers, business associates, suppliers, government officials, industry advocates, community activists or opinion leaders.

To influence opinions or project a positive image, most practitioners write news releases and feature stories to send to news outlets. Other tools include media press kits on the client's website that contain information such as a background on the organization, management and staff bios, news releases, noteworthy press coverage on the organization, visuals for journalists' use and contact information. Practitioners also set up speakers' bureaus; create special events; film news clips; write public service announcements; hold meetings; and design posters, brochures and pamphlets. They tweet and blog and search social media and news stories for mentions of their clients' names to assess if their promotion campaigns are successful.

19.2 Working with Journalists and News Media

Public relations practitioners use various news media to get information about their client to the public. They determine which media outlets will best serve their purposes. They also know the writing styles, deadlines and other procedures of each target medium. A news release has a better chance of being picked up by the media if it is newsworthy, well written and adheres to the organization's style guidelines. News releases are written in AP style. Releases for radio are written in broadcast style and in a format for the announcers to read easily over the air. Video news releases—VNRs—are produced so they can be inserted directly into a TV newscast.

To make their promotional efforts effective, practitioners also learn whom to contact. They identify the proper news departments and the people in charge before sending out a release. "Shotgunning" a release—sending it to multiple departments in a news organization—wastes time and money. For example, most editors will delete a press release about a promotion, but a business editor might report it in a weekly column or section devoted to the topic. Similarly, most editors would discard a release about a church's Christmas program or a synagogue's Hanukkah celebration, but a religion editor might mention it in a roundup about holiday activities. By sending news releases to the right editor, practitioners increase the likelihood the story will be used and decrease the chance of harming their reputations by wasting an editor's time.

Reporters might follow up on an idea presented in a news release, but interview their own sources, write their own stories and present their own angles. This still achieves the purpose of a news release to get client news into the media and help journalists stay informed about their community.

Some practitioners use a press release distribution service, such as PR Newswire and PRlog.com. On one hand, they might be expensive and unnecessary depending on the intended news coverage area. On the other hand, services might save practitioners a lot of time from researching news outlets and sending emails. Because most are automated, they might miss your target publications and spam others.

The most common types of press releases are advance releases that announce an upcoming event, releases that tell about the event after it happened, releases that are feature stories about discoveries and results. Practitioners are writing mostly about events; new businesses, hirings, products, services, partnerships; and awards.

19.2.1 Advance Stories

Chapter 15 in this textbook on speeches and meetings says journalists often write advance stories. They often originate from advance news releases. PR practitioners write announcements whenever their company or client sponsors an upcoming activity or event. Advance stories often use an agenda lead, telling news organizations or readers what the event is, where it will be, whom it is for and whether those who want to attend will have to pay or register.

The advance release may also include some background information explaining the event's importance or why the public should attend. For example, a movie theater might send a news release that it will mark the anniversary of the Battle of Dunkirk (May 26–June 4, 1940) by showing the movie "Dunkirk" and honoring a World War II veteran who lives in the community. Another news release might feature an opening of a new drive-in theater that offers entertainment to people who want to get out of the house but stay in the safety of their own cars during the pandemic.

journalists need, know how to pitch a story, respect their deadlines and speak media professionals' jargon.

- Be responsive. Respond quickly via email, text, direct message—communicate however the journalist does—and let them know you're working on their request and ask for their deadline.

- Always ask what the reporter needs, including subject matter, expert interviews, talking points, fact sheet, photos/headshots, deadlines.

- Be able to distill a complex story into a few sentences. (How would you tweet it?)

- Understand why "No Comment" is never the correct response.

- Write well.

- Listen well.

- Be flexible because sometimes the story you set up is dropped for breaking news; pitch the story another day.

- Be a good team player. Journalists and you need each other.

Words of Wisdom, Based on Experience

- Find a mentor in your field.

- Use LinkedIn as an excellent resource for professional connections and resources. (Follow hashtags such as #mediarelations, listen to podcasts.)

- Ask questions. There is no such thing as a dumb question.

- Don't think you can control the media—you can't. Develop strong, respectful working relationships with journalists.

- Never lie, mislead, speculate or bait and switch journalists. (Your reputation might not recover.)

"National Lampoon's Vacation" is shown at the Electric Dusk Drive-In in Glendale, California. Drive-in movies regained popularity during the COVID-19 pandemic. News releases informed movie fans of a safer entertainment option.

19.2.2 Event Stories

A PR person sometimes writes about an event as though it already had happened and the news media is reporting on it. For example, a release about the grand opening of a new hotel might include events surrounding the opening and quotes from the hotel owner and hotel guests—just as the practitioner hopes the occasion will go. This type of release serves two main purposes: It lets reporters know what will occur at the event, in case they want to cover it, and it helps the story get published quickly after the event.

Journalists rarely publish these releases verbatim. If the release is newsworthy, journalists attend and cover the event themselves. They verify the event occurred because nothing is more embarrassing than publishing a story only to find out later that the event did not happen.

Practitioners also give reporters copies of speeches before they are delivered. This practice enables reporters to quote the speakers accurately. Nonetheless, journalists attend the speeches because speakers may change some of their comments at the last moment.

19.2.3 Features

Practitioners often write feature stories as news releases, and some may interest a local audience while others might have national appeal (see Chapter 12). Feature releases deal with subjects as varied as health, science, personal finance, home repair and auto care. A well-written feature appears as an informative story rather than a publicity piece. It includes the client or organization as the sponsor of an event or quotes the person or company as an authority or source for the article.

For example, a news release about a local grocery store chain might feature that it is offering a free delivery service for a month during a particularly peak period of the pandemic. The story might describe something unique about the service, quote an executive as to why the store is offering this service and the people who might be helped. This release also promotes the store's image of being a good neighbor.

19.2.4 Discoveries and Results

Universities, hospitals, corporations and research institutions want the public to know about their discoveries and the results of their work. Such announcements highlight and enhance an organization's reputation and make people aware of new advances in science and technology.

A news release from a university might discuss their reseach on the effects of different coronavirus vaccines on children in different age groups. It would quote the scientist as to why this discovery is particularly important.

19.3 Tips for Effective News Releases

Journalists get their story ideas and information from myriad sources. In worldwide Cision media relations surveys, journalists consistently rank press releases and news announcements as their preferred type of content from PR practitioners. Yet, a lack of quality news releases causes most journalists to dismiss releases outright. Journalists use only press releases that are newsworthy and well written.

Karen Twigg-May, managing director of media relations for United Airlines, said one of the ways she gets stories published in the media is by following what is happening in the news and aligning her company's information with any trends. Media relations professionals should offer important information the public needs, have local angles and be timely. This section discusses components of successful news releases.

19.3.1 List a Contact and a Follow-Up Person

Reporters follow up interesting news releases to verify information or ask a question. Thus, an effective release lists the contact information (name, email address, telephone number) of someone at the organization—usually the PR person who wrote the release—who is familiar with the subject. In Figure 19.1, the contact person is the public information officer for the Michigan Department of Health and Human Services, the organization issuing the news release. The name and a link to the organization's website usually is included at the end of the release so that the journalist can research the organization and access its online media kit.

19.3.2 Send the Release on Time

Timing is important. A release received too close to a news deadline is less likely to be used because editors have little or no time to verify information or get answers to questions. One sent too early will likely be forgotten. The example notes, "For Immediate Release," because the free masks are being given away now. Releases describing an event may be embargoed, meaning the information should be published only after a specific day and time.

19.3.3 Include News Values

Successful releases are stories that journalists consider newsworthy and have an impact on the public. They have the news elements of timeliness, magnitude or impact, prominence, proximity, unusualness or conflict. For example, the state's health department news release announces the distribution of free KN95 masks for everyone in that state and locations to obtain the masks. What news elements does this press release include?

19.3.4 Use Journalism's Five W's

Write like a journalist. News releases answer the questions of who, what, where, when, why and how. The best releases are written in a journalistic style that makes them hard to distinguish from published news stories. The lead in Figure 19.1 is the following: "The state's Department of Health and Human Services is distributing 3.5 million free masks as part of the state's Mask Up, Mask Right campaign." It answers the who (Department of Health and Human Services),

The Parts of a Press Release

The organization's contact information: Complete mailing and web address of the organization sending the release should be here. Also provide the name, telephone number and email address of a contact person the journalist can reach in case of questions.

Release date: The release date tells when the information may be published. It might say, "For Immediate Release," or it might specify a date and time. News organizations have no legal obligation to adhere to release dates, but they usually do so as a matter of professional courtesy.

The headline: Summarizes the information. It is typed in capital letters. If it requires two lines, it is single-spaced.

The body: Almost all releases are one page. If it is longer, then "more" needs to be placed at the bottom of the first page and a slug with the page number is at the top of the second page.

Some news releases repeat the contact information here or give a short descriptor of the company, if it is not in the body of the story.

The closing: Type three number signs (###), or the word "end" or the number "30" within quotes or dashes.

Michigan Department of Health and Human Services
333 S. Grand Ave
P.O. Box 30195
Lansing, Michigan 48909
https://www.michigan.gov/coronavirus
Contact: Bob Wheaton, 517-241-2112

FOR IMMEDIATE RELEASE
January 4, 2021

IT'S EASIER FOR MICHIGANDERS TO 'MASK UP, MASK RIGHT' WITH FREE KN95 FACE COVERINGS TO PROTECT THEM FROM COVID-19

LANSING, MICH. The Michigan Department of Health and Human Services (MDHHS) is distributing 3.5 million free masks as part of the state's Mask Up, Mask Right campaign.

Free KN95 masks provided by MDHHS will be distributed by community organizations, including local MDHSS offices, health departments and Area Agency on Aging offices.

"We are urging Michiganders to Mask Up and Mask Right to protect themselves, their loved ones and their communities from COVID-19," said MDHHS Director Robert Gordon. "Wearing the right kind of mask is important. Today's distribution of effective masks will help more Michiganders limit the spread of COVID to save lives and get back to normal sooner."

Masking right includes wearing one of three options of masks that provide stronger protection: three-layered washable cloth face coverings, three-layered disposable masks or KN95 masks. It also includes wearing the mask correctly: having it secured over the nose and mouth and snugly fitting without gaps. KN95 masks are similar to but should not be confused with N95 masks that are intended for health care workers who are engaged as part of their work in higher-risk settings.

In addition to MDHHS offices, local health departments and Area Agency on Aging offices, the free masks are available from Community Action Agencies, and Programs of All-Inclusive Care for the Elderly (PACE). Some agencies will further distribute the masks to local partners such as homeless shelters.

Residents who need masks can pick one up from partner sites across the state. Find a distribution site at Michigan.gov/MaskUpMichigan or call the COVID-19 hotline at 888-535-6136.

Information around this outbreak is changing rapidly. The latest information is available at Michigan.gov/Coronavirus and CDC.gov/Coronavirus.

###

FIGURE 19.1 The Parts of a Press Release
This example shows the information that most press releases contain and the typical arrangement.

what (is distributing 3.5 million free masks), where (in that state), when ("is distributing" present tense means now) and how (by "community organizations" answered immediately in the bridge). The why is answered in both the heading and first quote after the bridge (to protect from COVID-19).

19.3.5 Write Well

Like journalists, PR writers synthesize sometimes difficult-to-understand information from different sources into something that is clear and useful to the public. A news release is written so readers with varying education levels can understand it. Language is concise and simple; grammar and spelling are perfect; sentences average about 20 words and are in active voice; and paragraphs are short and get to the point immediately, as in the KN95 mask news release example. Releases also include a quote from an authority or other source. This example quotes the director of the Department of Health and Human Services.

19.3.6 Localize Information

News releases often omit how the information affects people in a community. Too often, practitioners think of localization as only geographic, such as a particular town or community. Localizing also can mean reflecting a psychological closeness. The release from the state's health department about mask safety affects everyone. In addition, the news is for the people of that particular state and the release names local government agencies that will have masks available in almost every town.

19.3.7 Provide Visuals

Visuals, such as photographs or information graphics, catch the eye of readers, draw them into the story and illustrate major points. PR practitioners think about what visuals might be relevant to the news in a release. The release about free masks includes graphics for the recommended types of masks and on the correct way to wear a mask. Thinking visually can help practitioners get their releases accepted by editors. But don't overwhelm them with visuals. If the news release is digital, then an audio or video podcast, photos or animated graphic might help.

19.3.8 Provide Links

Effective releases have adequate details and links for reporters to get additional information on the topic addressed in the release. Links to the featured client's website might lead to background on the client, if journalists want to follow up. Links to statistical information or other related data may help answer reporters' questions. In our example, links are to the Department of Health and Human Services, affiliated organizations and other associated news releases.

19.4 From the Journalist's Perspective: Working with Press Releases

News media are besieged by individuals and organizations seeking free publicity. Metropolitan news organizations receive thousands of releases each week, and smaller ones receive hundreds. In a study of almost 2,000 journalists worldwide,

Wired Magazine fired blogger and author Jonah Lehrer as a result of press-release plagiarism, other plagiarism and recycling of his older work, among other issues. He also resigned from The New Yorker after it was discovered that he had fabricated quotes for one of his books. An investigator of Lehrer's work said he had a "reckless disregard for the truth."

media relations company Cision found that the journalists considered less than 25 percent of news releases relevant to the public.

Reporters handle news releases as they would any other type of story—and they follow up for verification. Their first task is to identify a central point. If there isn't one, they discard it. If a central point is there, they find the relevant information and scrap the rest. They also use the central point to identify what information is missing.

Some editors do not read all the news releases they receive. They throw away those they recognize as coming from sources that regularly submit trivial information. Editors also discard releases from companies outside of the area because they hold little interest to people in the community. In some instances, however, the release may be an idea for a local story.

Editors rarely use news releases as submitted—nor do they simply repackage a press release. They know the same releases are sent to many news organizations and they want their story to be different. Some editors use releases primarily as a source of ideas and assign reporters to confirm the accuracy of the information, interview people named in the release, gather more information and write a story. The published story should be very different from the one presented in the release.

When journalists use any information from a news release, they attribute it properly. For example, if they use a quote from a company representative from a news release, they reference the release to indicate that they did not personally interview the source—someone else did the work and the writing. Taking the credit for another's person's work is wrong, sloppy and lazy. In a Poynter Institute survey, a majority of journalists responded that it is acceptable to use passages from press releases, but only if the release is attributed.

19.5 The No. 1 Problem: Lack of Newsworthiness

Journalists prefer press releases that have news elements that satisfy their definitions of news. They look for topics that are new, local, interesting, unusual, relevant and important to their audience. They also look for information likely to affect hundreds or thousands of people. Action is more newsworthy than opinions, and a genuine or spontaneous event is more newsworthy than a contrived one.

19.5.1 Limited Interest

News organizations reject releases similar to the following because the topics interest few people—except, of course, members of the organizations they mention:

> Brown & Brown Motor Company announced the launch of their charitable giving initiative, Brown Motors 4 Charity. The president said that 100 percent of the employees agreed to donate a portion of their paycheck in May to a charity of their choice.

Employees' promotions and awards also interest few people outside of the company:

> Hotel New York announces the appointment of Julianna Santos as
> Senior Vice President of Retail. She is known for her good taste, and her
> vast business experience well prepares her for overseeing the growing
> number of affluent stores located within Hotel New York.

19.5.2 Contrived Events
Editors would discard the following news release because it announces a contrived event:

> The Red Cross has joined with the blood bank community in proclaiming January as National Volunteer Blood Donor Month and is urging everyone who is healthy to donate blood to help others.

This release states the obvious. Certainly, the Red Cross would urge "everyone who is healthy to donate blood to help others." Also, every month of the year is dedicated to dozens of causes. For example, May is Arthritis Month, National High Blood Pressure Month, National Foot Health Month, Better Speech and Hearing Month, National Tavern Month and American Bike Month.

19.5.3 Stating the Obvious
Public relations writers who lack journalism training often write releases that state the obvious:

> Today, the state fire marshal's office emphasized the importance of having working smoke detectors in homes and businesses as a way to save lives.

and

> Parents are worried more than ever about the amount of violence in our society.

These are not news. A fire marshal is expected to encourage the use of smoke detectors to save lives. That is a routine part of the official's job, not news. Similarly, violence has always been a problem; generations of parents have worried about it.

19.5.4 Buried News
Writers of news releases sometimes are more interested in pleasing their bosses than in satisfying the media and informing the public. They inappropriately begin their releases with the CEO's name. Or they might begin with the organization's name and information about the company before focusing on the news aspect of the release. The following is a poorly written news release:

> Rep. Wayne Smith, R-Mo., is leading the fight to push the Federal Trade Commission to combat predatory and exorbitant interest rates charged by the nation's banks and credit card companies.

> Smith is sponsoring legislation in Congress to cap interest rates that can reach as high as 24 percent on some credit cards. In addition, Smith says banks and credit card companies continue to send out credit card solicitation offers to people who already are weighed down by a mountain of debt.

"These solicitations go out to everyone, but young people and seniors are among the most affected by these practices because they can get into debt quickly and never get the balances paid off," Smith said. "The payments are so low on many of these cards that the only thing that gets paid if there is a balance due each month is the interest."

Smith said many people carry huge amounts of credit card debt because the high interest rates add so much to the balance each month.

A journalist might rewrite it this way:

Congress is considering legislation to lower the interest rates that banks and credit card companies charge consumers.

The legislation, sponsored by Rep. Wayne Smith, R-Mo., will seek to have the Federal Trade Commission investigate lending institutions accused of charging consumers exorbitant interest rates on their credit cards or practicing predatory soliciting to get consumers' business.

Other news releases are editorials that philosophize or praise a client rather than report information beneficial to the public. Journalists do not editorialize in a news story. Thus, a release submitted by a county's dairy association announcing National Dairy Milk Week and praising the flavor and health benefits of milk is unlikely to be used.

19.5.5 Wordiness

Many news releases bury the most important information among a lot of words:

The National Coalition on Television Violence (NCTV) has just released its most recent monitoring results of prime-time network programs. TV programs that try to portray violence as exciting and fun entertainment are positioned to lead the new Fall programs. Violence is portrayed at the rate of about seven violent acts per hour, with new programs taking three of the top four violent spots.

A journalist gets to the point of the news immediately:

Prime-time network programs contain about seven acts of violence every hour, and this fall's new programs are among the most violent, according to the National Coalition on Television Violence.

Quotes from authorities are important to include in news releases, but only if they have something to say. Otherwise, they can merely add to the wordiness of a release:

"Consequences of long-term usage of this chemical are very real, yet its functional purpose is questionable," stated Dr. Mi Na Park.

This quote is more informative:

"The chemical has limited benefits and unknown long-term effects," said Mi Na Park, a scientist with the U.S. Food and Drug Administration.

Deputy Editor of Audubon Magazine Jennifer Bogo said many news releases to the science magazine are sexist. They also don't check her name and assume she is a man. Releases can be offensive: "There is a press release in my spam box right now titled 'Rein in Your Girly Thoughts.'"

19.6 The No. 2 Problem: Lack of Objectivity

The purpose of public relations and news releases is to promote awareness about a client. Unfortunately, many have no news value and are similar to advertisements. They contain laudatory adverbs and adjectives, not facts.

19.6.1 Advertisements

The worst news releases are blatant advertisements, obviously written to help sell an image, product or service. Most journalists would reject the following news release for that reason.

> Nothing says romance like an intimate getaway to a beautiful sugar-white sand beach, an evening of dancing, champagne toasts, culinary delights and spectacular sunsets. With several love-themed packages, the Baycliff Sandy Beach Golf Resort & Spa—located on the beaches of Northwest Florida—is giving couples the opportunity to experience the ultimate romantic escape this February.

19.6.2 Laudatory Adjectives and Puffery

Journalists eliminate laudatory adjectives when rewriting news releases. Terms such as "world famous," the "best" or the "greatest" are subjective and difficult to verify. No news story—or release—should call a program "wonderful," "successful," "timely" or "informative." Similarly, nothing should be called "interesting" or "important." Everyone might not agree on how great something is. If a speaker is "famous," the public already will know the person and will not have to be told of the fame.

How many words of puffery can you identify in the press release below?

> Jason Taylor is a well-known expert and extremely talented speaker on the subject of handling conflict. His six-step program on conflict resolution has been touted as the best program ever to help ordinary people deal with the huge conflicts that can arise in their lives and rob them of the quality of life they so richly deserve.
>
> Taylor will be presenting a two-hour seminar about his program beginning at 7 p.m. Thursday, Sept. 9, in the Fellowship Hall of First Presbyterian Church, 1387 Downing Ave. The title of the program is "Managing Conflict in Your Life." It's free for everyone.

A journalist eliminates the laudatory adjectives and writes the facts:

> Jason Taylor, an expert in conflict resolution, will lead a seminar on resolving conflict, at 7 p.m. Sept. 9, in the Fellowship Hall of First Presbyterian Church, 1387 Downing Ave. The public is invited at no charge.

19.6.3 Empty Quotes

Generalities, platitudes, self-praise and gush often appear in direct quotations, but that never justifies its use. If a quotation lacks substance, journalists will discard it:

"We're very excited about the opening of the new store," said Betty McKinney, president. "The store represents a new direction for us and extends our commitment to provide customers with the highest quality products at the lowest possible prices."

These platitudes and generalities sound familiar because they are used so often. They are contrived and have lost meaning. For example, the following news releases, from different companies, use similar language to describe new employees. (Neither quote would be used. And, if the news release is about a new hire, then it would likely not make the news.)

We are fortunate to have a woman with Russell's reputation and background as a member of the team. Her knowledge and experience will be invaluable as we broaden our sales and marketing base.

and

We were impressed with Belmonte's accomplishments and his professionalism. We're extremely pleased with our good fortune in having him join us.

19.6.4 Bossing the Public

Instead of reporting news, some releases tell people to donate their time and money, buy new products, attend events or join organizations:

Tickets for the inspirational benefit concert are available to the public from the Performing Arts Center by calling 422-4896 or going on the website, for $15 each. Seating will not be reserved, so the public is urged to arrive early to hear this most important message on the subject of mental health care.

Journalists delete editorial comments or rewrite them in a more factual manner. For example, a reporter might summarize a story and, in the final paragraph, tell readers how they can respond, but not say that they should. Here is a revised version of the previous example:

Tickets for the benefit concert on mental health cost $15 and can be obtained at the Performing Arts Center by calling 422-4896 or going online to www.performingarts.org.

19.6.5 One-Sided Stories

Almost all news releases are biased to benefit the client, and the client's opinions sometimes are presented as fact. Thus, journalists investigate the other sides of the story that were left out—and they localize the story. They also check the facts in a release to avoid serious errors.

Checklist for Writing a News Release

Checklist for PR Practitioners

Does the News Release Provide the Proper Information?

1. A contact person, telephone number and email address?

2. Website and/or address of the client?

3. A release date? (Normally, news releases are written in advance of an event.)

4. Links to related information?

Is the News Release Written in Journalistic Style?

1. Is it newsworthy to a local audience and does it contain news elements?

2. Does it have a short headline summarizing the release?

3. Does the lead answer one or more of the 5 W's and H of the story or offer a narrative feature lead?

4. Does it have short, clear and concise paragraphs?

5. Does the text conform to AP style, especially in the handling of addresses, employee titles, dates and times?

6. Is puffery eliminated?

7. Is it contained to a page, if printed?

8. Are visuals considered?

Checklist for Journalists Handling News Releases

Does the News Release Have News Value?

1. What is the central point of the release?

2. Is the central point of the release newsworthy?

3. Does it involve an issue likely to interest many members of the local community or only a few, such as the members of the organization distributing the news release?

4. Does it involve a genuine rather than a contrived event, such as a proclamation, groundbreaking or ribbon cutting?

Does the News Release Need Rewriting?

1. Does the lead emphasize the news, or is it buried in a later paragraph?

2. Does it state the obvious?

3. Does it begin with an unnecessary name?

4. Does the story need to be localized?

5. Is the release clear and concise and easily readable?

6. Does the release contain only information necessary to support its central point?

7. Does the release contain clichés, jargon or generalities?

8. Whom does the news release benefit, the public or its source?

9. Is it objective, or does it include puffery, self-promotion or unsubstantiated claims?

10. Does the news release present only one side of a controversial issue? Most releases are not balanced, so the journalist has some work to do.

 # Review Exercises

1. DECIDING WHAT IS NEWS

Review some recent news releases at prnewswire.com/news-releases or einpresswire.com/all-press-releases or any news release service and complete the following tasks.

1. List five news releases that are well written for news media. Explain why you chose them.

2. List five releases that are terrible, and explain why.

3. List 10 story ideas that originated from the news releases you read and explain why they would make good stories. How can you localize the story? Some releases may give you more than one idea.

2. REVIEWING NEWS RELEASES

The following are actual news releases. For each one, identify the problems in regarding it as a news story. For each one, pretend to be the editor who received it. Ask yourself the following questions: Is the topic newsworthy, and why or why not? If so, then where can the writing be improved or rewritten for journalism standards?

LogiGear Corporation Expands Business and DX Offerings Through M&A—Jim Ellis appointed CEO of LogiGear Group Companies

NEWS PROVIDED BY
LogiGear Group
February 04, 2022, 22:36 GMT
SHARE THIS ARTICLE

Jim Ellis to head up LogiGear Group and helm efforts expanding business and digital transformation products and services made possible by recent acquisitions.

Digital Hearts Co. Ltd (TSX:3676)

SAN MATEO, CALIFORNIA, UNITED STATES, February 4, 2022 /EINPresswire.com/ — LogiGear, a leading provider of test automation and QA services, continues to expand and transform its business into an enterprise solutions services company through strategic M&A and new services offerings, beyond premium test automation and QA services. Jim Ellis assumes the role of CEO of LogiGear Group to focus on future expansion and integration of the growing group of companies, offering clients digital modernization and transformation services. Mr. Ellis brings to LogiGear several decades of entrepreneur experience including new business formation and enterprise value creation, accelerating growth and M&A. While the company pushes forward with its expansion plans, Hung Nguyen will continue to serve as Chairman/CEO of LogiGear Corporation.

> **"Through strategic M&A, we are expanding our offerings across all the major SaaS services to support all of our global customers."**
>
> — *Jim Ellis, CEO LogiGear Group*

"With the expansion into digital transformation services that include CRM/ERP specializations in SFDC, Oracle Cloud, JD Edwards EnterpriseOne and SAP implementation and customization, testing and long-term support, to modern Agile Software Customer Facing/Consumer Applications, the LogiGear Group is poised to support end-to-end projects throughout the Enterprise Services value stream." said Hung Nguyen, Chairman/CEO of LogiGear Corporation.

"We continue to offer our flagship test automation and QA services, along with adding a full range of enterprise level digital and business transformation services and products, to enable customers to accelerate development and deployment of new enterprise services and applications both internally and to the market. Through strategic M&A, we are expanding our offerings across all the major SaaS services to support all of our global customers." said Jim Ellis, CEO LogiGear Group.

As part of its expansion program over the last 12 months, LogiGear acquired MK Partners, a California-based SFDC consulting and implementation firm, TP&P Technologies, a Vietnam-based software development services company, and most recently, DWS, a UK based JDE/Oracle Test Automation Services Company.

Looking forward, LogiGear has more M&A on the horizon, as part of providing specialization across all major SaaS services, platforms, and technologies, specifically focusing on CRM and ERP, delivered on a global scale.

About Jim Ellis

Prior to his tenure at LogiGear, Jim Ellis has grown his career as a tech industry veteran, serving in engineering and management roles with Intel, and in the Salesforce Ecosystem, working for twelve years in the Vietnam/APAC region involved in M&A, tech start ups, business transformation, and setting up offshore software development centers and enabling cloud based services across the region.

He has been serving as Chief Revenue Officer at LogiGear and has been instrumental in transforming operations, aligning previously siloed business units, and delivering a reimagined organizational focus that has paved the way for the recent acquisitions and expanded LogiGear's services and offerings to their client-base, positioning LogiGear as a new lodestar in the Digital Transformation space.

He will now expand those efforts across LogiGear Group, aligning its constituent organizations and delivering 360-degree technological transformation potential and offerings to the clients and partners of TP&P Technology, DWS, and MK Partners.

About LogiGear Corporation

LogiGear is a leading provider of Software Testing Services, Test Automation Tools, Custom Software Development, and Enterprise Services and Solutions helping organizations improve operations and deliver better products while saving time and money. Since 1994, LogiGear has completed testing projects with hundreds of businesses, from early stage start-ups to Fortune 100 enterprises, across a wide range of industries and technologies. LogiGear continues to expand its global footprint through strategic M&A, providing a wider range of enterprise services to its clients.

For more information or interview requests:
Chris Stegall
LogiGear Group
+1 818-760-8285
email us here
Visit us on social media:
LinkedIn

Rep. Nancy Mace Shepherds Sweeping Ban on Mink Farming to Passage Citing Cruelty and Contagion Risks

NEWS PROVIDED BY
ANIMAL WELLNESS ACTION
February 05, 2022, 00:48 GMT
SHARE THIS ARTICLE

Legislation comes after hundreds of mink farms experience SARS-CoV-2 Outbreaks
CHARLESTON, SC, USA , February 4, 2022 /EINPresswire.com/ — Today, with passage of the America COMPETES Act, the U.S. House of Representatives included a provision to ban mink farming throughout the United States, signaling disapproval of an industry that harms and kills animals for their pelts, exports them to China for a sliver of elite consumers, and presents a threat of SARS-CoV-2 spillover to people in the homeland.

The amendment was led by U.S. Representatives Nancy Mace, R-S.C., Rosa DeLauro, D-Conn., and Peter DeFazio, D-Ore., and cosponsored by Reps. Jim Cooper, D-Tenn., Andy Levin, D-Mich., and Joe Neguse, D-Colo. It is a follow up to H.R. 4310, introduced by these same lawmakers and two dozen others from both parties, including Reps. Mike McCaul, R-Texas, Jan Schakowsky, D-Ill., Lance Gooden, R-Texas, and Vern Buchanan, R-Fla.

"One of the many lessons we learned at the beginning of the COVID-19 pandemic is the real danger of animal-to-human transmission of disease. In fact, If COVID-19 could design its perfect habitat for mutation and transmission, it would closely resemble a mink farm, where thousands of mink are kept in small, often unsanitary, overcrowded cages, for days on end," said Representative Mace. "Today, through working together on both sides of the aisle, we have the chance to end the abusive and inhumane mink farming practice that puts Americans' health at risk."

> **Today, through working together on both sides of the aisle, we have the chance to end the abusive and inhumane mink farming practice that puts Americans' health at risk."**
>
> — *Rep. Nancy Mace*

"We applaud Rep. Mace's tireless work for both animals and humans alike," said Marty Irby, executive director at Animal Wellness Action. "Nancy has very quickly emerged as the top Republican leader in Congress on animal protection issues, and I have never seen a new Member of Congress and their staff work harder to achieve the victories we're seeing in 2022."

"There's nothing good about keeping aggressive and solitary wild mink in cages on factory farms, killing them for a product nobody needs, and then shipping their exteriors to luxury consumers in China," said Wayne Pacelle, president of the Center for a Humane Economy. "The case against mink farming is clinched when one understands a new variant from one or more of these factory farms may disrupt our economy and put millions of Americans at risk."

The amendment was approved as part of a larger bloc of amendments, including a separate measure to crack down globally on live wildlife markets because of infectious diseases risks they also pose.

There have been approximately 6.1 million mink infected with SARS-CoV-2, with approximately 675,000 mink dying from the virus. This contrasts with perhaps just a few hundred COVID-19 infections among all other captive non-human animals, including big cats, domesticated dogs and cats, gorillas, and ferrets.

"This cage-confinement environment, where mink are crowded together by the thousands, maximizes chances for intraspecific aggression, viral infections, and mutations," observed Jim Keen, D.V.M., Ph.D., director of veterinary sciences for the Center for a Humane Economy and a former infectious disease specialist at the U.S. Department of Agriculture. "No amount of good animal husbandry can prevent this kind of aggression and the onset of disease among these captive, immune-compromised wild animals."

Mink farms have already spawned three variants—in Denmark, France, and the United States. As such, they are a proven source of multiple novel virus variants that may compromise human vaccine effectiveness or increase human virus virulence or transmissibility. Mink are a top candidate as the "missing link" between bats which most scientists believe to be the original source of COVID, and people according to the World Health Organization.

USDA reported 2.7 million pelts sold in 2019, and 1.4 million mink pelts sold in 2020. According to a review by Animal Wellness Action, there are just 60 farms operating in the U.S. There is no domestic market for mink, and it is an export-market commodity only, with 80 percent of pelts sold to China.

The amendment was supported by Animal Wellness Action, the Animal Wellness Foundation, Center for a Humane Economy, the Michelson Center for Public Policy, SPCA International and dozens of other organizations, from the Idaho Humane Society to the Iowa Federation of Humane Societies to the Oregon League of Conservation Voters.

Click here to see the video of Mace and Irby discussing the passage of this historical amendment in Congress.

Animal Wellness Action (AWA) is a Washington, D.C.-based 501(c)(4) organization with a mission of helping animals by promoting legal standards forbidding cruelty. We champion causes that alleviate the suffering of companion animals, farm animals, and wildlife. We advocate for policies to stop dogfighting and cockfighting and other forms of malicious cruelty and to confront factory farming and other systemic forms of animal exploitation. To prevent cruelty, we promote enacting good public policies, and we work to enforce those policies. To enact good laws, we must elect good lawmakers, and that's why we remind voters which candidates care about our issues and which ones don't. We believe helping animals helps us all.

The Animal Wellness Foundation (AWF) is a Los Angeles-based private charitable organization with a mission of helping animals by making veterinary care available to everyone with a pet, regardless of economic ability. We organize rescue efforts and medical services for dogs and cats in need and help homeless pets find a loving caregiver. We are advocates for getting veterinarians to the front lines of the animal welfare movement; promoting responsible pet ownership; and vaccinating animals against infectious diseases such as distemper. We also support policies that prevent animal cruelty and that alleviate suffering. We believe helping animals helps us all.

The Center for a Humane Economy (CHE) is a non-profit organization that focuses on influencing the conduct of corporations to forge a humane economic order. The first organization of its kind in the animal protection movement, the Center encourages businesses to honor their social responsibilities in a culture where consumers, investors, and other key stakeholders abhor cruelty and the degradation of the environment and embrace innovation as a means of eliminating both.

Marty Irby
Animal Wellness Action
+1 202-821-5686
email us here
Visit us on social media:
Facebook
Twitter

3. ELIMINATING PUFFERY

Rewrite the following sentences and paragraphs to make them more objective. Correct any errors of style, spelling and grammar. Also, decide if the content is a necessary news story for the public.

1. As a proponent of innovative hiring practices, the companys president has worked diligently to hire older workers, disabled workers and the homeless.

2. The outrageously funny british farce, RUN FOR YOUR WIFE!, will romp across the Lake Street Players stage may 25–27 and may 31-june 2. It will be a fun-filled evening for the whole entire family, with each hilarious performance starting promptly at 8 p.m. in the evening. Hurry to get tickets now before we run out!!

3. In a move that shows how decisive she can be, the chancellor of the state system of higher education today appointed a very, very highly qualified search committee comprised of 14 distinguished members of the academic community to find a replacement for retiring board of trustees president Harold Walters. The chancellor charged the committee with the task of finding a replacement who could match Walters magnificent dedication toward education in the state.

4. Oak Ridge Homes is proud to announce the opening of its newest and most spectacular subdivision—Oak Crest. These unparalleled luxury four- and five-bedroom homes with spectacular views of Paradise Valley offer some of the latest in-home conveniences newhome buyers will surely want in their new homes. Built on 1/4-acre lots and beginning at $350,000, the quality of these new luxury homes has to be seen to be believed. Open houses are being scheduled by six of the areas finest and most prestigious real estate firms that have been selected to list homes in the Oak Crest subdivision.

5. Emerson is dedicated and committed to his work as president of the board of directors and while serving in that capacity has

distinguished himself admirably as a proven leader. Other executives can't hold a candle to his unmatched drive to make Emerson Industries an unrivaled leader in precision manufacturing

processes. During Emersons visionary leadership, production and sales of the companys products have increased a spectacular 37 percent for the year so far.

4. EDITING AN ADVANCE NEWS RELEASE: WHAT'S IMPORTANT?

Exercises for writing advance news stories for speeches and meetings are in Chapter 15 and can be used here. Advance news stories can originate from advance news releases.

The following news release is much too long. Edit the release for publication by eliminating unnecessary information and correcting any errors in AP style and possessives.

Author to Share Grandfather's War Stories of WWII Unsung Heroes in "When the Beaches Trembled: The Incredible True Story of Stephen Ganzberger and the LCIs in World War II"

When the Beaches Trembled: The Incredible True Story of Stephen Ganzberger and the LCIs in World War II is a vivid narrative written by Zach S. Morris, grandson of Ganzberger, who spent more than ten years gathering interviews, maps, photos, and declassified military documents in order to share this untold story.

"We are very excited and honored to have Zach S. Morris speak with us," says Marialina Rodriguez, owner of The Booksellers bookstore. "This is a real treat to have such an amazing person visit us to discuss his outstanding chronicle of history."

The bookstore invited Morris to talk at a book signing at an apropos time. This week is the anniversary of the Japanese bombing of Pearl Harbor, which had happened on December 7, 1941. The plan was for his talk is to commemorate the anniversary.

Rodriguez says, "Morris will give an insightful discussion into how he researched his grandfather's service in WWII in addition to some insight as to his grandfather's heroic experiences."

When Stephen Ganzberger enlisted in the U.S. Navy at the outset of World War II, he never imagined what would await him and his shipmates in the Pacific Islands.

Stephen Ganzberger was stationed aboard the Navy's newly designed amphibious ships called Landing Craft Infantry (LCIs) that were small but capable of landing large numbers of troops and equipment directly onto enemy-held beaches during some

of the fiercest combat of the war. Designed with a flat bottom, LCIs were square-sterned and blunt-browed, drew only a few feet of water and could carry up to 200 men. As part of General Douglas MacArthur's South Pacific campaign, Ganzberger faced death from Japanese bombers, torpedoes and kamikaze attacks. All during the largest naval conflict in history.

In his book, Morris takes us chronologically through his grandfather's WWII journey as he earned seven battle stars aboard two LCIs, but also explains the story of the creation of the LCIs at the start of the war and the epic tale of LCI Flotilla Five as they fought valiantly through the South Pacific. The book was written as a tribute to the "Greatest Generation" and is filled with the deeply personal accounts of other veterans, including the late Congressman John D. Dingell Jr., a lifelong friend of Ganzberger.

Morris, an award-winning senior financial analyst and certified screenwriter, continues to share his extensive knowledge of WWII history by volunteering as editor-in-chief of *LST Scuttlebutt*, the quarterly magazine newsletter of the U.S. Landing Ship Tank (LST) Association—composed of Navy and Coast Guard veterans who served aboard LSTs in World War II, Korea, and Vietnam. Like LCIs, LSTs were another type of landing ship used to win the Second World War.

"I first became captivated by history from listening to my grandfather tell me war stories growing up, and from then on I was hooked," explains Morris. "While my original plan was to document all his WWII experiences over the course of several interviews spanning the summer of 2011, he passed away two days after our only interview, which set me on an entirely new journey that would lead to shocking discoveries and the creation of my book."

Morris will speak at the bookstore, situated at 2750 Parman Rd., at about 6:30 p.m.

When the Beaches Trembled: The Incredible True Story of Stephen Ganzberger and the LCIs in World War II is available in paperback at the bookstore for $19.99. For more information, please call the bookstore.

5. REWRITING NEWS RELEASES

The following is an actual news release. Your instructor might ask you to write only the lead or to rewrite the entire story.

AARP Calls for Nursing Homes to Require Booster Shots for Residents and Staff

JACKSON, Miss.— With a large number of seniors living in nursing homes and other assisted living facilities facing potential infection from the COVID-19 omicron variant, AARP Mississippi State Director, Kimberly L. Campbell, Esq., is calling for immediate action to get residents and staff vaccinated and boosted. Campbell says there were 67 confirmed COVID-19 cases among staff and 49 confirmed cases among residents in the first two weeks of January.

"The COVID-19 virus has demonstrated repeatedly that it is very dynamic," Campbell said. "AARP urges nursing homes to immediately prioritize boosters for both residents and staff. While still providing protection against severe illness and death, being fully vaccinated without a booster is no longer protecting nursing home residents from contracting COVID-19; the data are clear that a booster is necessary to remain protected. The rate of new infections in nursing home residents who have received a booster dose is more than 90 percent lower than the rate among residents who are not fully vaccinated, or who are vaccinated without an additional booster dose, according to CDC data for the week ending January 9."

Campbell says only about 13 percent of direct care staff at Mississippi nursing homes have received a booster.

"Families who have loved ones in nursing homes want to know that they are safe," Campbell said. "For those with a spouse, sibling, parent or other loved one in a nursing home, AARP has developed 10 key questions to ask facilities—including questions about booster shots—to help keep them safe and stay informed."

10 Questions to Ask if a Loved One Is in a Nursing Home

1. What is the status of COVID-19 vaccinations in the facility?
2. Is the facility screening and testing residents and staff for COVID-19 in line with government recommendations and regulations?
3. If COVID-19 is detected, is the facility ready to respond quickly to prevent further spread?
4. Has a positive case been identified at the facility in the past two weeks?
5. Is the facility managing visits in line with government regulations?
6. How is the facility helping residents stay connected with their loved ones virtually?
7. Does the facility have sufficient levels of personal protective equipment (PPE) — masks, face shields, hand sanitizer, gowns and gloves?
8. How is the facility communicating important COVID-19 information?
9. Is the nursing home currently at full staffing levels for nurses, aides and other workers?
10. Are healthy-living programs back up and running?

For more information, visit www.aarp.org/ms.

AARP is the nation's largest nonprofit, nonpartisan organization dedicated to empowering people 50 and older to choose how they live as they age. With a nationwide presence and nearly 38 million members, AARP strengthens communities and advocates for what matters most to families: health security, financial stability and personal fulfillment. AARP also produces the nation's largest circulation publications: AARP The Magazine and AARP Bulletin. To learn more, visit www.aarp.org, www.aarp.org/espanol or follow @AARP, @AARPenEspanol and @AARPadvocates, @AliadosAdelante on social media.

Contact: Your Name 55-989-5417 or 365-209-1495 (cell)

SOURCE AARP Mississippi

6. WRITING NEWS RELEASES

The following information is from actual news releases. Write a release from each set of details.

Remember to use AP style. Eliminate or keep as much information as you think is necessary to create an effective release and add phrases and transitions to make it acceptable to editors. List yourself as the contact person for each sponsor, decide on the release date and write a headline.

1. The following information is being released by your county's Board of Elections.

Anyone who wishes to vote in the upcoming municipal primary must be registered to vote.

The deadline to register to vote in the primary election is April 16 and all applications must be postmarked by that date.

Voter registration applications can be obtained by calling the Voter Registration Office at 555-1212 or by emailing a request to voter@county.gov.

The form cannot be submitted online. It must be downloaded, printed, completed and mailed to the County Voter Registration Office, 157 W. Washington St. (your city or town).

The registration forms are free of charge.

The application must indicate any change in name, address or party affiliation.

Absentee ballot applications also are available.

Absentee ballot applications are available for persons who will not be able to go to the polls because of absence from their municipality, illness or physical disability.

Absentee ballot applications are available by calling 555-1212.

Absentee ballot applications must be received by May 8.

All absentee ballots must be returned to the county courthouse by 5 p.m. May 11.

Excepting for absentee voters who have a disability, all absentee ballots must be delivered in person or through the United States Postal Service. Absentee ballots delivered by any other means for absentee voters who do not have a disability will not be accepted or counted by the County Board of Elections.

2. The following results were released by your state's Department of Health and Human Services.

A report was presented today at the American Diabetes Association's 67th Annual Scientific Sessions.

The report indicated that an eight-year partnership among the Centers for Disease Control and Prevention (CDC), your state's Department of Health and Human Services, your County

Human Services Department, and many facets of the community resulted in a significant change in behavior related to diabetes prevention and care, and reduced the expected rate of increase in the prevalence of Type 2 diabetes in your county.

Nearly 21 million Americans have diabetes, a group of serious diseases characterized by high blood glucose levels that result from defects in the body's ability to produce and/or use insulin. Diabetes can lead to severely debilitating or fatal complications, such as heart disease, blindness, kidney disease and amputations. It is the sixth leading cause of death in the U.S.

Type 2 diabetes involves insulin resistance—the body's inability to properly use its own insulin. It used to occur mainly in adults who were overweight and ages 40 and older. Now, as more children and adolescents in the United States become overweight and inactive, Type 2 diabetes is occurring more often in young people. African Americans, Hispanic/Latino Americans, American Indians and some other ethnic groups are at particularly high risk for Type 2 diabetes and its complications.

The prevention program is called Project DIRECT, which stands for Diabetes Interventions Reaching and Educating Communities Together.

"Project DIRECT has been a successful program of outreach, health promotion, and diabetes care, in which the community participated in developing the interventions from the outset," said Walter Ames, M.D., Ph.D., a Medical Epidemiologist at the CDC and Project Officer of Project DIRECT, in a recent interview. Dr. Ames added that the rate of increase in the prevalence of diabetes was markedly lower in the county compared to a comparable county, 80 miles away.

The program involved three key areas:

a. *Outreach*—A major media campaign was launched with talk show appearances, cooking segments on TV shows, and newspaper ads. Other events included outreach to educators and church leaders to encourage them to talk about diabetes prevention and diabetes screenings conducted in schools, churches and at civic and fraternal group meetings.

b. *Health Promotion*—A "Ready, Set, Walk" program trained lay exercise leaders who then promoted self-paced walking programs based in schools, churches, community centers, YMCAs, senior centers and other spaces where people naturally congregate, to encourage walking at least 30 minutes a day. School- and church-based nutrition programs worked with their cooks to help them reduce the fat content in lunches served at their facilities, and worked with officials to bring in health messages and professionals to help improve the health of members of their organizations, such as through cooking classes and health fairs on diabetes.

c. *Diabetes Care*—Workshops were held for physicians, nurses, physician assistants, nutritionists and health educators on the American Diabetes Association guidelines for management and diagnosis of diabetes with the goal of improving the quality of care of the disease. Workshops were given to people with diabetes on basic self-management to help them control their blood glucose and prevent complications.

Pre- and post-intervention surveys were conducted in each county six years ago and again last year using randomly selected samples of the population aged 18 to 75. The 2,311 pre- and 3,083 post-intervention participants were interviewed and had health examinations, including a fasting blood glucose test.

The prevalence of Type 2 diabetes in your county increased from 10.5 percent four years ago to 16.7 percent last year. The prevalence of Type 2 diabetes in the other county tested increased from 9.3 percent four years ago to 18.6 percent last year.

The American Diabetes Association is the nation's leading voluntary health organization supporting diabetes research, information and advocacy. Founded in 1940, the Association has offices in every region of the country, providing services to hundreds of communities. For more information, please call the American Diabetes Association at 1-800-555-1212 or visit http://www.diabetes.org. Information from both these sources is available in English and Spanish.

3. The following program is sponsored by your county's Women In Need (WIN) Victim Services.

Women In Need (WIN) is in need of help from members of communities across the county.

The prevention of any crime begins with awareness and the commitment and resolve to get involved.

The work of preventing sexual violence is a work that must become the commitment of everyone in every community in the county.

One in four girls and one in six boys will become the victim of sexual abuse before their 18th birthday. This kind of violence has a devastating effect on both its victims and their families.

This month is Sexual Assault Awareness Month and WIN Victim Services is encouraging the community to take action against this silent crime.

There are many ways to take action against sexual violence, but often sexual violence is a crime not often talked about openly. Campaigns against bullying and for respecting others can impact the amount of sexual violence occurring in communities throughout the county. Ways that can work to make a difference include:

a. Families should talk openly in regard to age-appropriate discussions about healthy sexuality and the importance of loving and respectful relationships.

b. Educators should be encouraged to teach non-violent conflict resolution skills and promote anti-bullying values.

c. Employers should be encouraged to enforce policies against sexual harassment.

d. Young people can learn to value everyone's uniqueness and begin to recognize positive relationships and reach out to at-risk peers. They can learn leadership skills and show respect, modeling these behaviors as positive ones to their peers.

e. Community groups can invite WIN into their meetings to learn how they can identify and support a victim of violence.

f. Creating change starts with each individual family. Parents can teach their children well when they teach them to respect others.

CITY DIRECTORY

Like other city directories, this directory lists only the names of adults (people 18 and older) who live in your community. The directory does not list children under the age of 18 or adults who live in other cities. Also, city directories (like telephone books) are published only once a year. Thus, they might not list people who moved to your community within the past year.

When information in the exercises conflicts with that in the City Directory, always assume that the information in this directory is correct. You will be expected to correct the fact errors in the exercises. If a name in an exercise is not listed in the directory, assume that the name is correctly spelled.

As you check the names of people involved in news stories, also check their addresses and occupations, as they might also be erroneous. Sources often make errors while supplying that information to police and other authorities. Also, the City Directory may provide information not in the exercise, information that may add to a story's newsworthiness. You will find, for example, that some of the people involved in stories are prominent government officials.

Finally, assume that the people listed as university professors teach at your school.

SECTION I: Directory of City Officials

Belmonte, William. Member, City Council
Brennan, Rosemary. Director, City Library
Cycler, Alice. Member, City Council
Datolli, Sabrina. Mayor
DeBecker, David. Member, School Board
Drolshagen, Todd. Director, Code Enforcement Board
Farci, Allen. City Attorney
Ferguson, Tony. City Treasurer
Gandolf, Sandra. Member, City Council
Graham, Cathleen, M.D. Director, City Health Department
Hernandez, Ramon. District Attorney
Hubbard, Gary. Superintendent of Schools
Kopperud, Barry. Police Chief
Lieber, Mimi. Member, School Board

477

Lo, Roger. Member, City Council
Lu, Judie. Member, School Board
Maceda, Diana. Member, School Board
Nemechek, Anna. Member, School Board
Nyad, Carole. Member, City Council
Nyez, Jose. Member, School Board
Onn, Tom. Director, City Housing Authority
Plambeck, Emil. Superintendent, City Park Commission
Ramirez, Luis. Member, City Council
Stoudnaur, Marlene, M.D. Medical Examiner
Sullivan, Tony. Fire Chief
Tribitt, Jane. Member, School Board
Tuschak, Joseph. Member, City Council
Vacante, Umberto. Member, School Board

SECTION II: Directory of County Officials

Alvarez, Harold. County Administrator
Chenn, Anne. Member, County Commission
Dawkins, Kerwin. Director, Public Works
Dawkins, Valerie. Member, County Commission
DiCesari, Gus. Sheriff
Ellis, Faith. Member, County Commission
Gardez, Jose. Member, County Commission
Grauman, Roland. Member, County Commission
Hedricks, Donald. Assistant County Attorney
Laybourne, Raymond. Member, County Commission
McNally, Ronald. County Attorney
Morsberger, Diedre. Supervisor of Elections
Shenuski, Anita. Member, County Commission
Sindelair, Vernon. County Treasurer
Smith, Ronald. County Clerk
Wehr, Helen. Assistant County Attorney

SECTION III: Judges

Municipal Court

Hall, Marci   Kocembra, Edward

Circuit Court

Johnson, Edwin	Ostreicher, Marlene
Kaeppler, JoAnn	Pfaff, Randall
Levine, Bryce R.	Picott, Marilyn
McGregor, Samuel	Stricklan, Julian

SECTION IV: Abbreviations

acct	accountant	agcy	agency	apt	apartment
admn	administration	agt	agent	archt	architect
adv	advertising	appr	apprentice	asmbl	assembler

assn	association	exec	executive	prof	professor
asst	assistant	facty	factory	pst	postal
athom	at home	fed	federal	pub	public
attnd	attendant	ff	firefighter	r	resident/roomer
atty	attorney	formn	foreman	rd	road
aud	auditor	gdnr	gardener	recpt	receptionist
av	avenue	govt	government	rel	relations
bd	board	h	homeowner	rep	representative
bkpr	bookkeeper	hairdrsr	hairdresser	repr	repairer
bldr	builder	hosp	hospital	rept	reporter
blvd	boulevard	hwy	highway	restr	restaurant
brklyr	bricklayer	inc	incorporated	retd	retired
bros	brothers	ins	insurance	Rev	reverend
capt	captain	insp	inspector	sav	savings
carp	carpenter	jr	junior	sch	school
cash	cashier	jtr	janitor	sec	secretary
cc	community college	jwlr	jeweler	secy	security
ch	church	la	lane	sen	senator
chem	chemist	lab	laborer	serv	service
chiro	chiropractor	librn	librarian	sgt	sergeant
cir	circle/circuit	lt	lieutenant	slsp	salesperson
clk	clerk	lwyr	lawyer	slsr	sales representative
clns	cleaners	mach	machinist	soc	social
co	company	mech	mechanic	sq	square
colm	council member	med	medical	sr	senior
com	commissioner	mfg	manufacturing	st	street
const	construction	mgr	manager	stat	station
cpl	corporal	min	minister	studt	student
crs	cruise consultant	mkt	market	supm	supermarket
ct	court	mstr	master	supt	superintendent
ctr	center	mtce	maintenance	supvr	supervisor
cty	county	muncp	municipal	tech	technician
custd	custodian	mus	musician	techr	teacher
dent	dental/dentist	nat	national	tel	telephone
dep	deputy	ofc	office	ter	terrace
dept	department	ofer	officer	treas	treasurer
det	detective	opr	operator	univ	university
dir	director	optn	optician	USA	U.S. Army
dispr	dispatcher	pcpl	principal	USAF	U.S. Air Force
dist	district	pers	personnel	USM	U.S. Marines
dr	drive/driver	pharm	pharmacist	USN	U.S. Navy
drgc	drug abuse counselor	photog	photographer	vet	veterinarian
econ	economist	phys	physician	vp	vice president
ele	elementary	pl	place	watr	waiter
electn	electrician	plmb	plumber	wdr	welder
emer	emergency	pntr	painter	wid	widow
emp	employee	po	post office	widr	widower
eng	engineer	polof	police officer	wkr	worker
est	estate	pres	president		

SECTION V: Sample Entries

Hurley	Carl J & Mary;	printer	Weisz Printing Co	& ofc sec	Roosevelt Ele Sch
1	2	3	4	5	6
h	140 Kings Point Dr	Hurley Ralph	studt	r	140 Kings Point Dr
7	8	9	10	11	12

1 = Family name

2 = Names of spouses in alphabetical order

3 = First listed spouse's occupation

4 = First spouse's employer

5 = Second listed spouse's occupation

6 = Second spouse's employer

7 = Homeowner

8 = Home address

9 = Name of roomer or renter 18 years of age or older

10 = Roomer/renter's occupation

11 = Resident or roomer

12 = Address

SECTION VI: Entries

Aaron Betsy retd r 410 Hillcrest St Apt 302

Abare Ann recpt Chavez Bros Chevrolet h 855 Tichnor Way

Abbondanzio Anthony & Deborah; brklyr Wagnor Bros & athom h 473 Geele Av

Abbondanzio Denise pub rel rep Haile Associates r 3218 Holbrook Av Apt 832

Acevede Esther & Louis; both retd h 8484 Highland Dr

Acevede Miguel atty h 812 Bell Av

Adams Jenna & Donald mgr Wendy's Old Fashion Hamburgers & pst wkr h 1943 Hope Ter

Adcock George & Lydia; mgr Blackhawk Hotel & soc wkr Catholic Social Services h 141 N Cortez Av

Adler Sandra & Stuard athom & min Ch of Christ r 1847 Oakland Blvd

Adles Dora & John; athom & rep Bach & Co h 1218 S 23rd St

Ahl Thomas C facty wkr Vallrath Plastics r 2634 6th St Apt 382

Ahrons Tommy managing editor The Daily Courier h 1097 Leeway Dr

Ahsonn Jeffrey R & Teresa; both retd h 49 Groveland Av

Albertson Wanda pers dir Vallrath Plastics h 529 Adirondack Av

Alicea Carlos city emp h 2930 Leisure Dr

Allen Christopher univ prof Pierce CC h 1810 Collins Av

Allen James D & Margie; mach opr Collins Industries & atty h 28 Rio Grande Rd

Allen Michael mech Allison Ford r 410 Hillcrest St Apt 82

Allersen Alice & Thomas; athom & acct Mercy Hosp h 418 Meridan Av

Allyn Christopher & Julie; dir Center for Arts & univ prof h 1504 Lincoln Dr

Alvarez Harold & Tina; cty administrator & techr Washington Ele Sch r 854 Maury Rd Apt 11B

Alvarez Jose cpl state hwy patrol h 1982 Elmwood Dr

Alvarez Thomas studt r 854 Maury Rd Apt 11B

Amanpor Effie & Elton; athom & technical writer Wirtz Electronics h 823 E Pierce Av

Ames Robert & Emily asst mgr University Bookstore & sec Cypress Av Med clinic h 2380 Wendover Av

Anchall Mildred dir Sunnyview Retirement Home r 2202 8th Av Apt 382

Andrews Ira auto mech Allison Ford h 561 Tichnor Way

Andrews Paula wid aud Blackhawk Hotel h 4030 New Orleans Av

Aneesa Ahmad univ prof h 1184 3rd Av

Aneja David & Tracy; sgt sheriff's dept & carp h 488 Tulip Dr

Ansell Herman clk Blackhawk Hotel r 2814 Ambassador Dr Apt 61

Antonucci William plmb Rittman Engineering Co r 107 Hillside Dr Apt B

Arico James K pntr Kalina Painting & Decorating r 9950 Turf Way Apt 703C

Austin Anna & Terrance C; chef & athom h 481 Cottage Hill Rd

Baille Maggy wdr Halstini Mfg h 810 N Ontario Av

Baliet Karen & Thomas; adv exec Bailet & Associates & pres Republican Bldrs h 1440 Walters Av

Ball James studt r 1012 Cortez Av Apt 870

Barber Herbert & Irene; vp Denny's Restr Group & athom h 2440 College Dr

Barlow Janet & Raymond; hairdrsr Lynn's Styling & dir United Way h 2868 Moor St

Barlow Janie & Wesley; r 977 4th St Apt 2

Barlow Kevin polof r 3363 Andover Dr

Barlow Robert A mech Allison Ford r 112 Hope Cir

Barsch Margaret & Michael; athom & sgt police dept h 2489 Hazel La

Barton Eileen owner/mgr Barton Sch of Dance h 1012 Treasure Dr

Basa Shannon optn r 6718 Fox Creek Dr Apt 1010

Baugh Marcia state consumer advocate h 350 Meridan Av

Bealle Denise univ prof h 1018 Cortez Av

Beasley Ralph pntr Kalina Painting & Decorating r 810 Howard St

Beaumont Edward & Hazel; pst wkr & athom h 7240 N Ontario Av

Beaumont Roger studt r 7240 N Ontario Av

Becker Maurine & Ricky; athom & publisher The Daily Courier h 1521 Cole Rd

Belcuor Christine & Paul; watrs Holiday House Restr & librn h 497 Fern Creek Dr

Belmonte Lucy & William; mus & city colm & archt Belmonte & Associates h 177 Andover Dr

Berg Mildred univ prof h 984 Elmwood Dr

Best Bryan para Sacred Heart Hosp r 4320 Michigan Av

Biagi Allison polof r 2634 6th St Apt 906B

Biegel Franklin custd Filko Furniture r 782 12th Av

Blackfoot Jason & Veronica Dawn; archt & atty h 2045 Wendover Av

Blake Amanda C & Carl P; nurse & electn r 3314 Santana Blvd

Blanchfield Elaine owner/mgr Elaine's Jewelry r 780 Cole Rd Apt 282

Bledsoe Edward & Rosalie; photog The Daily Courier & athom h 833 Meridan Av

Blohm Kevin cook North Point Inn r 5604 Woodland St

Bolanker Timothy studt r 854 Murray Rd Apt 107B

Boudinot Marilyn sec Westinghouse Corp r 4340 Virginia Av

Boyette Willis A jtr Barton Sch of Dance r 2121 Biarritz Dr

Boyssie Betty & Lee; bkpr Allstate Ins & polof h 1407 3rd Av

Brame Don city emp h 3402 Virginia Av

Brayton Wayne studt r 410 University Av Apt 279

Brennan Rosemary dir City Library h 1775 Nair Dr

Brooks Oliver & Sunni; univ prof & technical writer Halstini Mfg h 5402 Andover Dr

Brown Howard slsp Prudential Ins Co h 2745 Collins Av

Bulnes Karen atty sch board h 43 Princeton Pl

Burke Lynn & Randy; athom & capt USA h 412 Wilson Av

Burmeister Abraham & Esther; pres First Nat Bank & athom h 4439 Harding Av

Burmester Herman A & Sally; const wkr Rittman Eng Co & athom h 1412 S 23rd St

Burnes James J min St. Mark African Methodist Episcopal Church r 3155 Marcel Av

Burnes Todd polof r 1502 Matador Dr Apt 203

Burnes Tyrone min United Methodist Ch r 8430 Wilson Av

Butler Irene & Max; athom & courier First Nat Bank r 444 Jamestown Dr

Cain Fred & Irma; mus & athom r 427 Hidden La

Cantrell Michael pres/mgr Mr. Muscles r 410 South St

Capiello Ann studt r 8210 University Blvd Apt 311

Capiello Otto A & Sandra J; photog & wdr Rittman Industries h 47 Rio Grande Rd

Carey John priest St. John Vianney Catholic Ch r 2020 Oak Ridge Rd

Carey Myron univ prof h 641 N Highland Dr

Carigg Craig & Susan; min Allen Chapel AME Ch & athom h 453 Twisting Pine Cir

Carigg James R studt r 453 Twisting Pine Cir

Carson Frank & Janice; serv formn Allison Ford & athom h 2197 Marcel Av

Carter Deborah counselor Lovell Psychiatric Assn r 550 Oak Parkway Apt 821

Caruna Alyce min Howell Presbyterian Ch h 423 Charrow La

Carvel Reba techr Colonial Ele Sch r 1883 Hope Ter

Casio David & Gretta; atty & athom r 711 N 31st St Apt 220

Caspinwall Andrew r 416 Wilson Av

Caspinwall Nadine phys h 416 Wilson Av

Cessarini Maxine & Richard M; univ prof & phys r 4184 Cypress Av

Charton John city ff r 3158 Virginia Av

Cheesbro Marylin asst pub defender r 1010 Eastview Rd Apt 3

Cheng Beverly exec dir State Restr Assn h 643 Wymore Rd

Chenn Anne & Steven; city com & lt fire dept r 91 Melrose Av

Chevez Larry det police dept h 4747 Collins Rd

Chmielewski Albert nurse Mercy Hosp r 2814 Ambassador Dr Apt 82

Cho Jaclyn & Yung Yee techr Colonial High Sch mgr Giovanni's Pizza Parlor r 2032 Turf Way Apt 202

Christopher Alan univ prof h 4850 Elm Dr

Chuey Karen & William J; slsp Allison Ford & clk police dept r 5710 Michigan Av

Cisneroes Andrew & Lillian; min Redeemer Lutheran Ch & athom r 818 Bell Av

Claire Richard & Wanda; dir state Dept of Corrections & athom h 12142 Decatur Rd

Clauch Amy clk Annie's Auto Parts r 2418 Seasons Crt Apt B

Clayton Amy univ pres r 820 Twisting Pine Cir

Cohen Abraham & Estelle; asst dir computer serv city sch system & pub rel rep Evans Pub Rel Group r 1903 Conway Rd

Collin Ronald const wkr Wagnor Development Corp r 2814 Ambassador Dr Apt 47D

Colson Jonathan studt r 7240 N Ontario Av

Conaho Henry & Jeanne; supvr sales ERA Realty & pres Lake CC h 820 Hope Ter

Correia Bobby & Dawn; supvr Delta Airlines & athom h 9542 Holbrook Dr

Cortez Manuel & Nina; polof & bkpr North Point Inn r 1242 Alton Rd

Cosby Minnie agt Watson Realty r 487 Jamestown Dr

Coto Jorge Alberto studt r 8210 University Blvd Apt 311

Courhesne Adolph & Gloria; mech Fridley Volkswagen & athom h 1186 N Highland Av

Cowles Stephen jtr VFW Post 40 h 8217 Cypress Av

Cross Andrea & Lee; chiro & city acct h 2 Virginia Av

Cross Dina & Raymond; athom & pst wkr r 101 Charow La

Cruz Jena atty r 48 DeLaney Av

Cullinan Charles A & Susan; both sheriff's dep r 848 Rio Grande Rd

Curtis Sarah sr vp SunBank r 663 Harding Av

Cycler Alice & Richard; city colm & atty r 7842 Toucan Dr

Daigel Annette hairdrsr Anne's Beauty Salon r 431 E Central Blvd

DaRoza Sue & Terry; studt & clk Jiffy Food Store r 410 University Av Apt 80

Datolli Roger & Sabrina; retd & mayor r 845 Conway Rd

Dawkins Agnes & Kerwin; athom & dir cty Dept of PubWorks r 2203 Coble Dr

Dawkins Ronald & Valerie; bklyr & cty com r 1005 Stratmore Dr

Dawson Shirley wid techr Colonial Ele Sch h 492 Melrose Av

Deacosti Amy studt r 3254 Virginia Av

Deacosti Michael & Peggy; pres Deacosti's Restr & hostess h 3254 Virginia Av

Deboare Ann & Jack R; dir emp rel Rittmann Industries & mgr Lucky's Supm r 1415 Idaho Av

DeCastro Wilma teacher Kennedy High Sch h 3277 Pine Av

Dees Karen studt r 410 University Av Apt 52

DeLoy Joseph R phys r 280 Lancaster Rd Apt 110

Desaur Roland studt r 700 Classics St

DeVitini Brenda & Ronald; asst min Redeemer Lutheran Ch & mach Rittman Industries r 313 Coble Dr

DeWitt Tony studt r 2230 Cortez Av Apt 828

Deyo Ashley & Ralph; graphic designer & dent r 2814 Ambassador Dr Apt 7

DeZinno Marc & Nancy; asmbl Vallrath Industries & athom h 205 Rockingham Ct

Diaz Diane & Richard; author & nurse St. Nicholas Hosp h 1978 Holcroft Av

Diaz Enrique & Lisa; atty & pst wkr r 3224 Mt Semonar Av

Diaz Juanita watrs Pancake House r 408 Kasper Av Apt 322

DiCesari Gus & Henrietta; cty sheriff & athom h 980 Atlantic Av

Dillan Martha atty Westinghouse Corp h 702 S Kirkmann Av

DiLorrento Anthony univ prof h 666 Texas Av

Dolmovich Sandra M clk Dayton-Hudson h 714 N 23rd St

Dow Tammy sgt police dept r 2208 17th Av

Dowdell Laura & Thaddeus; clk & jwlr Dowdell Jewelry h 620 Lexon Av

Doyle Cynthia & Wayne; techr Colonial Ele Sch & pres National Homebuilders Assn h 428 Wilson Av

Drolshagen Illse & Todd; athom & dir City Code Enforcement Board h 2406 Alabama Av

Dwyer Margaret studt r 2047 Princeton Av Apt 405

Dysart Tony & Wendy; athom & attnd Sunnyview Retirement Home r 724 Aloma Av Apt 24F

Edwards Traci psychiatrist h 3303 Lake Dr

Einhorn Doris & Robert; athom & univ phys h 8320 Meadowdale Rd

Eisen Priscilla phys r 1118 Bumby Av Apt 204

Ellam Dorothy R & Roger A; techr Madison Ele Sch & landscape contractor r 2481 Santana Blvd

Ellerbe Robert widr pres Ellerbe's Boats h 3213 Hidalgo Dr

Emory Jonathan & Lori eng & athom h 849 Groveland Av

Eulon Harley & Martha; jtr St. Nicholas Hosp & athom h 410 E 3rd St

Evans Mark & Trish W; cty soc wkr & owner/mgr Evans Pub Rel Group h 4232 Stewart Av

Evans Nikki & Timothy; loan ofer First Fed Sav & Loan & mgr Allstate Ins r 806 Apple La

Fairbairn Sean owner Advance Investments h 5235 Robinhood Dr

Farci Allen widr atty h 818 Texas Av

Favata Celia J wid h 9930 Bumby Av

Ferguson Marcia & Tony; vet & city treas h 96 West Av

Ferrell Fannie & Melvin; atty & pcpl Kennedy High Sch h 2384 West Av

Firmett Rene J serv stat attnd Bert's Shell Stat r 4474 Colyer Rd

Flavel Vernon J dir Becker Express h 827 Pigeon Rd

Forlenza Henry custd Kmart r 4620 Alabama Av Apt 22

Forsythe Scott cpl sheriff's dept h 1414 S 14th Av

Foucault Carmen wid techr Aloma Ele Sch h 1452 Penham Av

Foucault James studt r 1452 Penham Av

Fowler Barbara K & Fritz; polof & owner Fowler Allstate h 88 Eastbrook Av

Fowler Joel studt r 2006 Hillcrest St

Frank Lucas cpl State Patrol r 854 Murray Rd Apt 220A

Franklin Allen sgt USA r 840 Apollo Dr Apt 322

Friedmann Leo asst dist atty r 2814 Ambassador Dr Apt C2

Fusner Charles tech h Peachtree Dr

Gable Frances & Jay; athom & truck dr Becker Express h 1701 Woodcrest Dr

Gandolf Sandra wid city colm h 8 Hillcrest Av

Gant Diana univ prof h 810 Village La

Gardepe Ellen serv mgr Derek Chevrolet h 210 Lake Dr

Garland Charlotte & Chester; athom & city health insp h 2008 N 21st St

Garner Cheryl & David; athom & emp City Recreation Dept r 2814 Ambassador Dr Apt 88

Gianangeli David gdnr r 48 Stempel Apt 53D

Giangelli Marlene P pres Pestfree Inc h 214 Lake Dr

Gill Todd watr Fred's Steakhouse r 410 University Av Apt 279

Goetz Beryl dent & writer h 1010 McLeod Rd

Golay Evelyn & Thomas; cash & ownr/mgr Tom's Liquors h 1203 Texas Av

Goree Linda exec dir city Girl Scout Council r 2202 8th Av Apt 302

Gould Darlene & Savilla; athom & slsp Anchor Realty Co h 4178 N 11th Av

Graham Cathleen & Ross R; dir City Health Dept & phys h 710 Harding Av

Grauman Roland & Tina; cty com & asst supt for pub education r 3417 Charnow La

Grauman Alice & Samuel; athom & min First Covenant Ch r 610 Eisen Av

Green Joey atty h 604 Michigan Av

Greenhouse Irwin & Trina; administrator Mercy Hosp & athom h 9575 Holbrook Dr

Griffin Marlene det police dept h 3130 Joyce Dr

Guarino Anne chiro r 4100 Conway Rd Apt 611

Guarino Gerhard chiro h 1813 Texas Av

Guarino Tony A techr Colonial High Sch h 6139 Eastland Dr

Guarino Belva retd r 84 Lakeland Av

Guerin Anita & Ronald E; athom & city ff r 1045 Eastvue Rd

Guitterman Daniel bartender Jim's Lounge r 550 Oak Park Way Apt 7

Gulas Gail & William J; studt & phys h 3405 Virginia Av

Guyer Joseph & Rita; artist & athom h 4043 S 28th St

Guzmann Trina mgr Sports Unlimited r 2032 Turf Way Apt 230

Haile Jeffrey polof r 2634 6th St Apt 847

Hall Marci muncp ct judge h 34 Magee Ct

Halso Beverly & Jeff; pres Haslo Pub Rel & vet r 879 Tichnor Way

Hamill Margaret studt r 811 N Cortez Av

Hamill Kimberly mgr Albertson's supm h 811 N Cortez Av

Hammar Margaret J secy ofer Macy's Dept Store h 1181 6th St

Hana Edward & Jena; min Unity Ch of Christianity & athom h 134 Eisen Av

Hana Kyle cust Unity Ch of Christianity r 134 Eisen Av

Hanson Lydia atty r 880 6th St

Hanson Myron widr retd h 880 6th St

Harmon Rhonda watrs Red Lobster r 816 Westwinds Dr Apt 8

Harnish Cheryl & David; supvr sales Cargell Corp & state sen h 288 Hillcrest St

Harris Jerry R & Jewel; asst mger House of Pancakes & athom h 2245 Broadway Av

Haselfe Jennifer & Richard; athom & pres Haselfe Development Corp h 554 Beloit Av

Haserott Mildred wid ticket agt Greyhound Lines r 411 Wisconsin Av

Haskell Thomas widr lt fire dept h 2482 Elmwood Dr

Hattaway Willie widr retd r 411 Wisconsin Av

Hedricks Donald asst city atty r 4320 Elsie Dr Apt 884

Hermann Andrew J & Jennifer; acct & teller First Nat Bank h 1888 Hope Ter

Hernandez Ramon dist atty h 84 Lake Cir

Herndon Joyce atty h 310 Mill Av

Herrin Raymond W univ prof h 410 Park Av

Herwarthe Gregory L & Ruth; pres Knight Realty & asst mgr Harrington & Co Investments h 4410 Baltimore Av

Heslinn Dorothy L mgr Mr. Grocer r 8197 Locke Av

Heslinn Allison & Burt; clk Kmart & slsr Prudential Bache h 8197 Locke Av

Higginbotham Gladdies Anne mgr Secy Fed Bank h 1886 Hope Ter

Hilten Randall J & Virginia; lt fire dept & athom h 915 Baxter Dr

Hoequist Thomas owner/pres The Jewelry Shoppe h 2418 Collins Av

Hoffmann Vivian wid clk Quik Shoppe h 711 Meadow Creek Dr

Hoffsinger Nora wid retd r 411 Wisconsin Av

Holland George & Tanaka; dr Greyhound Lines & athom h 4368 Normandy Dr

Holland Maryanne adv exec Wilson Associates h 947 Greenbrier Dr

Holland Keith studt r 410 University Av Apt 11

Holman Evelyn & Leonard; athom & phys h 4366 Normandy Dr

Holten Liz owner Holten Doughnuts h 9512 Forest Grove

Holtzclaw Norma J wid slsp ERA Realty h 739 West Av

Horan Roger sheriff's dep r 118 Hillside Dr Apt C3

Howard Sarah polof h 812 Bell Av

Howe Lynn studt r 410 University Av Apt 318

Howland Ruth & Terry; owner Blackhawk Hotel & secy ofer Memorial Hospital h 1808 Gladsen Blvd

Hubbard Gary & Peggy; supt of city schs & athom h 384 Hilcrest St

Hyde Marie & Roger; asst supt of city schs & slsp Ross Chevrolet h 1381 Lakeview Dr

Iacobi Neil atty r 6214 Maldren Av

InnisAlvin & Sarah; lt police dept & athom h 1305 Atlantic Blvd

Jabil Stephen dr Becker Express r 800 Crestbrook Loop Apt 314

Jacbos Martha mgr Mom's Donuts r 1889 32nd St

Jaco Milan & Robyn; dir Blood Bank & athom h 2202 S 8th St

Jacobs Bill & Carol; sgt police dept & dispr Yellow Cab h 2481 Lakeside La

James Edwin cour Pinkerton Security Ser r 1010 Eastview Rd Apt 12

Jamison Peter J & Stephanie R; phys & phys/surg Sacred Heart Hosp h 6004 Beech St

Janviere Jeanne techr Colonial Ele Sch r 1883 Hope Ter

Jeffreys Michael dir Humane Society h 2781 Collins Av

Jimenez Edwin C mgr Quik Shoppe r 3611 31st St

Joanakatt Cathy asst dir We Care h 2442 Collins Av

Johnson Edwin & Susan; cir ct judge & athom h 148 West Av

Johnson Marc const wkr r 2643 Pioneer Rd

Johnson Karen asst supt of city schs h 2344 S 11th St

Johnson Mary bkpr Vallrath Plastics h 6181 Collins Rd

Jones Danny & Margaret; min Metro Life Ch & athom h 1152 Darlington Av

Jones Lucinda & Samuel; athom & lt USM h 4851 Edmee Cir

Jones James dr City Cab Co r 977 4th St. Apt 10

Jones Robyn & Sean; med tech Mercy Hosp & capt USN h 4216 Winford Cir

Kaeppler JoAnn cir ct judge h 2192 West Av

Kaeppler Lori & Ronald; athom & sgt USM h 9540 Holbrook Dr

Kalani Andrew mgr Kalani Bros Bakery h 2481 Kaley Way

Kalani Charles pres Kalani Bros Bakery h 2481 Kaley Way

Kasandra Kelli retd r 9847 Eastbrook La

Kasparov Linda univ dietitian r 9103 Lake St

Keegan Patrick Jr fed atty h 505 Walnut Dr

Keel Sally & Timothy; asmbl Cargell Corp & barber Plaza Barber Shop h 1413 Griesi Dr

Kehole Marvin mtce wkr Cargell Corp r 182 W Broadway Av

Kernan Russell mach Vallrath Industries r 168 Lake St

Kindstrom Sarah watrs Steak & Ale h 4828 N Vine St

Kirkmann James dr Yellow Cab r 816 Westwinds Dr Apt 202

Knapp Erik A cook Frisch's Restr r 2314 N 11th St

Knoechel Alvin & Sara; plmb & slsr The Daily Courier h 1112 E Lisa La

Kocembra Edward & Heather; muncp ct judge & athom h 388 31st St

Koche Ellen Jane atty Neighborhood Law Ofc h 4214 Azalea Ct

Kopez Frank & Lisa; city mech & athom h 1067 Eastland Av

Kopp Suzanne wid retd r 4200 S 11th St Quality Trailer Ct

Kopperud Barry widr chief of police h 458 Kaley Way

Kostyn Elizabeth & Ralph E; athom & asst supt for ele education city schs h 284 Erie Av

Krueger Melody & William; athom & pres Aladdin Paints h 48 Michigan Av

Kubic Marilyn & Ralph; both techrs North High Sch h 1452 N 3rd St

Kunze Lauren & Robert; athom & mach Vallrath Industries r 94 Jamestown Dr Apt 318

LaCette Cecil serv stat attnd r 2814 Ambassador Dr Apt 61

Lasiter Harriet & James; athom & techr Roosevelt Ele Sch h 374 Walnut Dr

Layous Michael E studt r 212 N Wisconsin Av

LeClair George cir ct judge h 501 Mont Clair Blvd

Lee Fred owner/cook Kona Village h 1181 24th St

Leforge Ted dent h 537 Peterson Pl

Leidigh Floyd & Rose; const wkr Rittman Engineering Co. & athom h 1812 Dickins Av

Levine Ida mgr Mr. Waterbeds r 8521 Shady Glen Dr

Levine Bryce & Trina; cir ct judge & athom h 8521 Shady Glen Dr

Lewis Jacquelin & Jonnie; watrs Holiday House & insptr Vallrath Industries h 1840 Maldren Av

Linn Eddy & Marie; sgt police dept & athom h 6287 Airport Blvd

Linn Ronald studt r 6287 Airport Blvd

Lo Joan & Roger; athom & city colm h 1993 Collins Av

Logass Jeffrey econ Larco Corp h 81 Venetian Way

Lowdes Enrico & Sandra; dir Regional Medical Ctr & athom h 77 Maldren Av

Lowrie Cynthia studt r 118 Hillside Dr Apt 74

Lowrie Catrina phys Regional Medical Ctr r 118 Hillside Dr Apt 74

Lozando Marie clinical dir Mercy Hosp r 234 E Markham Dr Apt 4

Lucas Frank cpl hwy patrol h 2417 Country Club Dr

Lydin Charles R mgr LaCorte Printing Co h 888 Melrose Av

Macbos Martha dir of nursing Mercy Hosp h 1889 32nd St

Macco Alan mus r 503 29th St

Madea Ramon exec dir Bon Voyage Travel Agcy r 118 Hillside Dr Apt 606

Mahew Arthur mgr Fische's Bowling Alley h 1918 Pacific Rd

Majorce Albert & Monica; archt & athom h 2882 Ambassador Dr

Marcheese Harvey O & Joyce; min & organist Faith Baptist Ch h 1481 Cole Rd

Mariston Saundra watrs Freddy's Inn h 822 Kentucky Av

Matros Margo univ prof r 410 University Av Apt 818

McCartney Mildred wrk Holten Doughnuts h 1212 Alexandrea St

McCauley Melvin & Veronica; truck dr Becker Express & athom h 540 Osceola Blvd

McDonald Herbert J & Rosalie; owner/mgr Tastee Popcorn & athom h 1842 Hazel La

McDowell William pntr r 1429 Highland Dr

McEwen Lonnie & Victoria; techr Washington Jr High Sch & athom h 1024 Nancy Cir

McFarland Charlotte nursing supvr Sand Lake Hosp h 1090 Timberline Trail

McFerren Patrick J widr U.S. postmaster h 1227 Baldwin Dr

McFerren Patti const wkr Rittmann Engineering Co r 816 Westwinds Dr Apt 3

McGorwann Karen cc prof r 4320 Elsie Dr Apt 6

McGowen Bill & Rosalind; const wkr Rittmann Engineering Co & maid Hyatt Hotel h 4842 S Conway Rd

McGowin William sheriff's dep h 4224 N 21st St

McGrath Sunni jtr Washington Ele Sch h 109 19th St

McGregor Carol & Samuel; mgr trainee Albertson's Supm & cir ct judge h 1501 Southwest Ct

McIntry Eugene & Irene; pres McIntry Realty & athom h 2552 Post Road

Meir Sharon pers dir Vallrath Industries r 810 Kalani St Apt 2

Mejian Colette pcpl Risser Ele Sch h 415 Ivanhoe Blvd

Merrit Jacob & June; eng WTMC-TV & athom h 301 Wymore Rd

Meserole Alexander & Teresa; owner Deerfield Country Club Restaurant & adv slsr The Daily Courier h 5293 Mandar Dr

Meyer Robert & Sonia; sgt USAF & credit mgr Sears h 811 Moor St

Miehee Margaret & Richard; athom & asst U.S. postmaster h 1190 Euclid Av

Millan Timothy cook Grande Hotel r 1112 Huron Av

Miller Sharon optn LensCrafters h 2827 Norwell Av

Minh Stephen retd r 410 Hillcrest St Apt 842

Morales Renata techr Washington Ele Sch h 1987 Holcrofte Av

Moravchek Albert & Dorothy; city ff & clk police dept h 4187 N 14th St

Moronesi Donna slsr Adler Real Estate h 623 N 5th St

Morrell Cathy & Wayne; athom & mgr Bon Voyage Travel Agency h 382 Arlington Cir

Morsberger Diedre city supvr elections h 898 Hemlock Dr

Muldaur Eddy studt r 660 S Conway Rd

Murhana Thomas lab Cargell Corp r 40 W Hillier Av

Murphy Joseph & Kathleen; dir research Collins Industries & athom h 114 Conway Rd

Murray Blair & Patricia; mgr Beneficial Finance & athom h 1748 N 3rd St

Murray Harold & Marty; atty & curriculum resource techr h 1801 Hillcrest St

Neely Myron A det police dept h 1048 Jennings Rd

Nego Alan polof r 1840 Wymore Rd Apt 10

Nemnich Harland & Helen; electr & retd h 1331 Mt Vernon Blvd

Nicholls Cheryl fed emp h 1287 Belgard Av

Nieves Erik & Krystal univ athletic dir & hairdrsr h 2894 Ambassador Dr

Noffsinger Nora wid retd r 411 Wisconsin Av

Noonan Jack widr det police dept h 5928 Jody Way

Nouse Sharon pilot Aerial Promotions Inc r 4740 Valley View La

Novogreski Harry R & Melba; mach Keller Plastics & athom h 2891 Morris Av

Nunez Carolynn & Roger; athom & eng Kelle-Baldwin Corp h 2820 Norwell Av

Nunziata Carmen h 1410 1st Av

Nyad Carol city colm h 850 Sutter Loop

Nyer Diana studt r 550 Oak Park Way Apt 264

Nyer JoAnne sec Washington Ele Sch r 550 Oak Park Way Apt 264

O'Hara Allison city sec r 4729 Texas Av

Oldaker George polof r 2117 Wisconsin Av Apt 488

Oldaker Thomas polof r 2117 Wisconsin Av Apt 488

Oliver Franklin R & Jeanette; exec Gill Assoc Inc Pub Rel & athom h 1121 Elm Blvd

Onn Esther & Tom C; athom & dir City Housing Authority h 3869 Jefferson Av

Ortiz Lynn & Randy; athom & brklyr HomeRite Builders r 816 Westwinds Dr Apt 78

Ortson Martha & Thomas J; athom & vp Secy First Bank h 810 N 14th St

Ostreicher Marlene wid cir ct judge h 449 Ferncreek Cir

Paddock Cynthia & Thomas C; credit mgr Belks Dept Store & mach Cargell Corp h 1736 Hinkley Rd

Palomino Molly & Ralph R; athom & vp Genesco Inc h 374 Douglas Rd

Parkinson Marie studt r 857 Murray Rd Apt 204A

Patterson Michelle electn r 1012 Cortez Av Apt 915

Patzell Bruce & MaryAnne; carp & athom h 915 Bishop Dr

Patzell Larry studt r 915 Bishop Dr

Paynick Nina & Stanley; techr Washington Ele Sch & owner Paynick's Carpets h 901 2nd St

Peerson Marc univ prof h 4851 Edmee Cir

Perakiss Ethel & Michael; athom & atty h 876 Collins Av

Percy John atty h 1037 2nd St

Perez Jason const wkr Wagoner Development Corp r 2414 Skan Ct

Perez Joseph & Vicki; city emp & lt police dept h 2414 Skan Ct

Petchski Pearl asst cash Morrison's Cafeteria r 411 Wisconsin Av

Peters Frederick & Rene C; pharm Kmart & pres Humane Society h 484 Sugar Ridge Ct

Peterson Sara wid h 1671 Drexel Av

Pfaff Randall cir ct judge h 2134 Oak Ridge Rd

Phillips Teresa M clk The Jewelry Shoppe r 800 Crestbrook Loop Apt 228

Picardo Marie nurse r 510 Concord St Apt 48

Picott James & Katherine; slsp Allison Ford & dent asst h 640 Lake Dr

Picott Marilyn cir ct judge h 901 2nd St

Piloto Claire & Kenneth T; interior decorator & atty Piloto & Herndon h 1472 Bayview Rd

Pinccus Jennifer atty Piloto & Herndon r 2021 Dyan Way Unit 2

Pinckney Samuel & Terest; retd & athom h 976 Grand Av

Pinero Jim Timmons dvlpr Pinero Developers h 2411 Windsong Dr

Ping Dorothy & Louis; athom & plumb Lou's Plumbing h 348 Conroy Rd

Plambeck Dolly & Emil; athom & supt City Park Com h 6391 Norris Av

Porej Irvin vp for loans First Fed Sav & Loan h 112 Anzio St

Povacz Julius city paramedic r 210 E King Av Apt 4

Proppes Richard E asst mgr Safeway Supm h 1012 2nd St

Pryor Lynne R const wkr Rittmann Engineering Co r 2634 6th St Apt 45

Rafelsin Louis lt police dept h 934 Old Tree Rd

Ramirez Harriet & Luis; dent asst & city colm h 982 Euclid Av

Randolph James const wkr Rittmann Engineering Co r 654 Harrison St

Ray Elizabeth & William David; both retd r 550 Oak Park Way Apt 157

Reeves Charlton E & Polly; state health ofer & athom h 658 Lennox Av

Reimer Maurice & Mildred; acct & athom h 2529 Barbados Av

Richards Patricia r 42 Tusca Trail

Richardson Inez & Thomas E; athom & polof h 5421 Jennings Rd

Richbourg Bud & Kathleen; owner/ mgr Buddy's Lounge & athom h 1014 Turkey Hollow

Richter Robyn Anne retd h 42 Tusca Trail

Riggs Gladies Ann wid retd r 1080 Harvard Rd Apt 4

Rivera Hector phys Medi-First Clinic r 800 Crestbrook Loop Apt 38

Rivera Maxwell tech h 11 Calico Crt

Robbitzsch John W psychiatrist h 1014 Bear Creek Cir

Roehl Cecil & Esther; polof & athom h 1228 Euclid Av

Romaine Gerri & Nickolas H; athom & wdr h 2876 Post Av

Romansaik Michael const wkr Wagnor Development Corp r 118 Hillside Dr Apt 8

Rudnike Harold & Martha; athom & sales mgr Vallrath Industries h 4825 N Vine St

Rue Alexander studt r 8420 University Blvd Apt 218

Rueben James & Elizabeth state sen & atty h 12494 Hillcrest Rd

Ruffenbach Laura univ prof h 6741 Waxwing La

Ruiz George & Lila; polof & athom h 263 9th St

Ruiz Guillermo & Harriet; asst city med examiner & dir pub affairs Regional Med Ctr h 4718 Bell Av

Rybinski Kim owner Kim's Pets r 2634 6th St Apt 710

Salcido Martha & Tony; athom & city ff h 10 Exeter Ct

Saleeby Claire & John; athom & lt colonel USA h 626 N 3rd St

Saleeby Henry widr retd r 84 Sunnyvale Rd

Saleeby Olivida & Wesley; both retd h 1916 Elizabeth La

Salvatore Hector R & Juanita M; atty & athom h 1716 Forest Ridge Rd

Sanchez Gumersinda hairdrsr Lillian's Beauty Salon h 173 Burgasse Rd

Satava Kenneth widr techr Kennedy High Sch h 2204 Marcel Av

Saterwaitte Benjamin widr retd h 307 E King Blvd

Sawyer Betty & Harley; athom & techr Kennedy High Sch r 2032 Turf Way Apt 512

Sawyer Claire min Christian Redeemer Ch h 7400 Southland Blvd

Schifini Destiny vp SunBank h 3620 Timber Ter

Schipper Michele studt r 4100 Conway Rd Apt 814

Schweitzer Ralph city building insp r 816 Westwinds Dr Apt 160

Scott Kerry & Nancy; slsp Kohlerware & athom h 4189 Hazel St

Scott Milan & Nancy; techr Kennedy High Sch & techr Wilson Ele Sch h 20 Magee Ct

Sessions Jeffrey D & Michelle A; emer rm phys/dir emer sers Sacred Heart Hosp & athom h 9303 Vale Dr

Shadgott Carol & Frank D; athom & phys h 8472 Chestnut Dr

Sharp Lynita L clk Jiffy Foods r 5836 Bolling Dr

Shattuck Christina & Dennis A; mgr Perkins Restr & emp city garage h 532 3rd St

Shearer Ethel cocktail watrs Melody Lounge r 408 Kasper Av Apt 718

Shenuski Anita & Frederic; cty com & dis mger IRS h 1230 Embree Cir

Shepard Frank & Helen; techr & rept The Daily Courier h 107 Eastbrook Av

Shepard Linn Marie studt r 854 Murray Rd Apt 107B

Sheppard Ronald lt fire dept r 2024 Vincent Rd Apt 1020

Shisenauntt Arthur & Lillian; secy consultant & pharm Walgreen h 1243 Washington Av

Shoemaker JoAnn techr Colonial High Sch r 6139 Eastland Dr

Silverbach Daniel G & Jill; polof & athom h 3166 Wayne Av

Simmons Karen dist dir Greenpeace r 708 E Lisa La

Simmons Rachel & Wayne; athom & slsp Prudential Ins h 708 E Lisa La

Sindelair Elaine & Vernon; athom & cty treas h 4164 Mandar Dr

Skinner Dorothy & Roger; clk typist Lawson Bros & polof h 2080 Washington Av

Skurow Melvin widr carp h 4138 Hennessy Ct

Slater Carolyn & David; athom & chiro h 8443 Turkey Hollow

Smith Grady r 8213 Peach St

Smith Linda M & Ronald; studt & city clk h 1814 N 3rd St

Smitkins Marlene & Myron; athom & mach Kohlarware h 417 Huron Av

Smythe Asa A & Carol; city emp & athom h 4280 Timber Trail

Smythe Terry bartender Bayside Bar & Grill r 4280 Timber Trail

Snow Dale & Terri; athom & nurse Mercy Hosp h 4381 Hazel St

Snowdin Elizabeth clk state employment ofc h 952 Kasper Av

Snyder Christina dir pub rel Mercy Hosp h 711 Broadway Av

Sodergreen Karl & Lillian; phys & athom h 788 Timber Trail

Sota Mimi dir Drug Abuse Unit Mercy Hosp h 655 Brickell Dr

Stevens Julie Ann mus h 624 N 3rd St

Stockdale George & Lillian; capt USM & athom h 472 Bolling Dr

Stoudnaur John & Marlene; mgr Rexall Drugs & city med examiner h 1350 41st St

Stovall Iris wid mgr Quikke Clns h 7204 Southland Blvd

Straitten Karen & Walter; athom & city building insptr r 4450 Richmond Rd

Stricklan Julian cir ct judge h 4268 Wayne Av

Sulenti Allen D studt r 800 Crestbrook Loop Apt 1010

Sullivan Tony widr fire chief h 863 Benchwood Ct

Svec Wallace A mech Allison Ford r 4320 Elsie Dr Apt 1

Svendson Lillian & Wayne; athom & city paramedic h 814 Washington Av

Swaugger Charlotte & Samuel; cc prof & rept The Daily Courier h 4987 Huron Dr

Sweers Daniel & Karen; fed emp & det police dept h 108 Eastbrook Av

Tai Wendy housekeeper Hilton Hotel r 84 Chestnut Dr

Talbertsen Sarah A artist h 3214 Riverview Dr

Taylor Frederic C r 4828 N Vine St

Taylor Marsha L mgr McDonald's h 2012 Lincoln Av

Temple Roger polof r 2032 Turf Way Apt 818

Thistell Dirk & Mildred R; eng Rittmann Industries & counselor Roosevel High Sch h 528 Kennedy Blvd

Thomas Joseph techr Kennedy High Sch r 2848 Santa Av Apt 2

Thompsen Yvonne studt r 1012 University Av Apt 812

Tifton Albert & Marsha; capt fire dept & athom r 2814 Ambassador Dr Apt 417

Tijoriwalli Cathy owner Cathy's Sandwiches r 1320 Embree Cir

Tiller Ida & Julius; athom & polof h 539 Sheridan Blvd

Tilman Marion & Randall C; athom & city health insptr h 818 N 41st St

Tontenote Eldred L & Lisa; mech Ace AutoBody & athom r 2634 6th St Apt 17

Totmann Gloria & Marvin; dent asst & secy guard Brinks h 1818 4th St

Tribitt Jane mgr Colonial Apts r 1040 Colonial Way Apt 101

Tuschak Arlene & Joseph; master electn & city colm h 2094 Byron Av

Ungarient James R & Margaret; both attys The Law Office h 7314 Byron Av

Uosis Bobbie & Michael; both retd h 4772 E Harrison Av

Vacante Mary & Umberto; athom & technical writer Lockheed Martin h 3202 Joyce St

Vacanti Carlos & Carol; polof & athom h 4910 Magee Ct

Valderama Lynn dir secy JC Penney h 1020 Lincoln Av

Valesquez George & Paula; archt/ owner Valesquez Design Group & atty univ bd of trustees h 5405 Conway Rd

Van Atti Joseph & Trina; city ff & athom h 960 Stratmore Dr

Van Den Shuck Margaret pub serv rep Allstate Ins h 7663 Robinhood Dr

VanPelt Audrey W & James; min First United Methodist Ch & serv mgr Lane Toyota h 420 N Wilkes Rd

Vasquez Guillermo & Miranda; dir State Dept of Corrections & athom h 2801 Norwell Av

Veit Helel Lynn min First Covenant Ch h 184 Nelson Av

Verdugo Maureen pcpl Kennedy High Sch r 816 Westwinds Dr Apt 482

Verkler LeeAnn univ prof r 800 Crestbrook Loop Apt 10A

Vernell Cathy S dr Yellow Cab r 1010 Vermont Av

Vorholt Andrew A owner/mgr Hallmark Cards h 10 E Lake Rd

Wagnor Kristine & Timothy Sr; athom & owner/mgr Tim's Coffee Shop h 418 N Wilkes Rd

Ward Frances & Jon H; athom & sgt/ recruiter USA r 3113 DeLaney Av

Ward Lonnie D mtce wkr Colonial Apts r 2814 Ambassador Dr Apt 22

Warniky Clara & Wayne; mgr Hertz Rent A Car & polof h 428 N Wilkes Rd

Washington Bruce R atty David Casio & Associates r 1104 Esplada Av Apt 19

Waundry James R & Lisa; mgr 2-Hour Clns & athom h 5310 Stratmore Dr

Weber Nancy techr Washington Ele Sch h 44 E Princeton St

Wehr Helen asst cty atty h 1298 Vermont Av

Wei Albert sgt police dept h 964 Jody Way

Wei Constance P & Donald S; state rep & atty h 206 N Wabash Av

Weinstein Jeanette techr Colonial High Sch h 6139 Eastland Dr

Weiskoph Herman asst min John Calvin Presbyterian Ch h 4817 Twin Lakes Blvd

Wentilla Lorrie & Reid R; athom & pres Keele-Baldwin Corp h 640 Clayton Av

West Billy L asst min John Calvin Presbyterian Ch h 452 Central Blvd

Whidden Bonnie sec cty fair h 2913 Oak La

White Katherine mgr Blackhawk Hotel h 4218 Bell Av

Whitlock Randall vp Wagnor Development Corp h 504 Sutter Loop

Wiess Robert A wkr Belks Moving & Storage r 2032 Turf Way Apt 338

Wilke Alan & Tracie; state dir National Federation of Independent Business & techr North Mid Sch h 818 Woodland Dr

Wilke James & Laura; sgt police dept & sheriff's dep h 2420 Highland Av

Willging Judy & Jurgen; athom & owner/mgr Choice Video Rentals h 2204 S 8th St

Willging Marty & Tessie; dir YMCA & athom h 1808 Gadsden Blvd

Williams Jon R tech K107 Radio r 814 Harding Av

Williams Patricia J retd h 1338 Biarritz Dr

Williams Phyllis nurse Lovell Psychiatric Assn r 1220 Jasper Av Apt 56

Williams Thomas & Mary Lee emp Parson's Funeral Home & athom h 2338 Vermont Av

Wong Phyllis & Steven I; mgr Sears & athom h 441 S 28th St

Woods Amy dir State Federation of Independent Businesses h 640 Sherwood Dr

Wymann Barbara & Paul; athom & mech Layne Toyota h 2020 Lorry La

Yamer Frank studt r 118 Hillside Dr Apt 1020

Yapenco Nancy & Thomas; athom & writer h 4941 Pine St

Younge Rachel techr Kennedy High Sch r 3361 Bolling Dr

Zarrinfair Lois retd r 411 Wisconsin Av

Zerwinn Sarah h 2021 Dyan Way

Zito Allen & Linda; archt Zito Associates & marketing dir Blood Bank h 818 Jamestown Dr

Zito Nancy & Robert; athom & pharm Kmart h 328 Winford Cir

Zozulla Wesley polof h 5219 Ranch Rd

Zumbaddo Carlos mgr cty fair h 1902 White Av

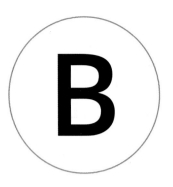

B SUMMARY OF AP STYLE

This appendix, based on the Associated Press Stylebook and Briefing on Media Law, summarizes some of the most commonly used rules in The Associated Press Stylebook and Briefing on Media Law. Section and subsection numbers have been added. Most newspapers in the United States—both dailies and weeklies—follow the rules recommended here.

Complete copies of The Associated Press Stylebook and Briefing on Media Law can be ordered from most bookstores.

SECTION 1: ABBREVIATIONS

1.1 **COMPANY.** The words *company, companies, corporation, incorporated, limited* and *brothers* (*Co., Cos., Corp., Inc., Ltd.* or *Bros.*) should be abbreviated and capitalized when used after the name of a corporate entity. *The board hired him to run Ford Motor Co.* Do not use commas before any of these abbreviations. When the words are used by themselves, do not capitalize or abbreviate: *He joined the company last summer.*

FOR BROADCAST: Use informal constructions (*Ford, GM, Apple, McDonald's*) rather than formal company names whenever possible. *Apple urged iPhone users to update the operating system on their phones to improve security.* When using a company's formal name, do not abbreviate *company* or other words that are part of the name and use commas before *limited* and *incorporated* (*Texas Instruments, Incorporated, . . .*).

1.2 **DEGREES.** Avoid abbreviations for academic degrees in most cases. Instead, use a phrase that identifies the person's degree and academic specialty: *Jane Austin, who has a doctorate in sociology, spoke at the conference.* Because it indicates possession, use an apostrophe in *bachelor's degree, master's degree (or a master's),* or *doctor's degree.* When identifying many individuals by degree on first reference, use abbreviations such as *B.A., M.A., LL.D.* and *Ph.D.* because the preferred form would make the sentence cumbersome.

1.3 DO NOT ABBREVIATE. The words *assistant, association, attorney, building, district, government, president, professor, superintendent* or the days of the week should not be abbreviated in news stories, nor should the ampersand (&) be used in place of *and*.

1.4 INITIALS. Some organizations and government agencies, such as *CIA, FBI, NASA, NBC, YMCA*, are so familiar to readers that they may be identified by their initials on first reference. Use the full names of less familiar organizations or agencies on first reference. If the initials would be recognizable to most readers, they may be used on second reference. Generally, do not use periods with initials unless a more specific rule requires them.

FOR BROADCAST: Unless the organization is well known to the public, avoid using initials to refer to organizations. Use hyphens to separate letters that should be read individually (*F-B-I, C-I-A*). Do not put hyphens between letters of initials that are read as a word (*NASA*).

1.5 JUNIOR/SENIOR. *Junior* and *senior* should be abbreviated and capitalized after someone's name: *Martin Luther King Jr.* (omit the comma).

FOR BROADCAST: Spell out *junior* or *senior: Martin Luther King Junior* (no comma).

1.6 MPG/MPH. The abbreviation *mph* (miles per hour) is acceptable on all references. The abbreviation *mpg* (miles per gallon) is acceptable when paired with a number (*36 mpg*), but it should be spelled out in other contexts. (*For a large car, this one delivers many miles per gallon.*) Neither abbreviation uses periods.

FOR BROADCAST: Do not abbreviate either. Use *miles-per-hour* or *miles-an-hour* or *miles-per-gallon*. Hyphenate the phrases.

1.7 STATES. Spell out the names of states when used in the body of a story whether they stand alone or follow the name of a city or county. Place commas before and after the state name unless it is the last word in the sentence. *The flight originated in Wichita, Kansas, and landed in Columbus, Ohio.* The following 30 city names may be used without the name of the state:

Atlanta	Houston	Philadelphia
Baltimore	Indianapolis	Phoenix
Boston	Las Vegas	Pittsburgh
Chicago	Los Angeles	St. Louis
Cincinnati	Miami	Salt Lake City
Cleveland	Milwaukee	San Antonio
Dallas	Minneapolis	San Diego
Denver	New Orleans	San Francisco
Detroit	New York	Seattle
Honolulu	Oklahoma City	Washington

Use state names with all other city names on first reference.

State names should be abbreviated only when they are used in datelines, tabular matter and short forms for a public official's party affiliation: *Sen. Alex Padilla, D-Calif.* Use the following abbreviations for states: *Ala., Ariz., Ark., Calif., Colo., Conn., Del., Fla., Ga., Ill., Ind., Kan., Ky., La., Md., Mass., Mich., Minn., Miss., Mo., Mont., Neb., Nev., N.H., N.J., N.M., N.Y., N.C., N.D., Okla., Ore., Pa., R.I., S.C., S.D., Tenn., Vt., Va., Wash., W.Va., Wis.* and *Wyo.* Eight state names are never abbreviated: *Alaska, Hawaii, Idaho, Iowa, Maine, Ohio, Texas* and *Utah.* Do not use U.S. Postal Service abbreviations for states, such as *PA, CA, NY,* etc.

FOR BROADCAST: Do not abbreviate state names in the body of a story or a dateline. Always put a comma between the names of the city and the state and after the name of the state unless it is the last word in the sentence.

1.8 **TITLES.** The following titles should be abbreviated when used before a full name both inside and outside direct quotations: *Dr., Gov., Lt. Gov., Rep., the Rev., Sen.* and military titles such as *Pfc., Cpl., Sgt., 1st Lt., Capt., Maj., Lt. Col., Col., Gen., Cmdr.* and *Adm.* These titles are capitalized when abbreviated before a full name, but lowercase and spelled out when standing alone: *Gen. Adam Smith . . ., The general . . .* On second reference, use only the last name: *Smith said . . .* These rules also apply to military-style titles for firefighters or police officers. Do not use courtesy titles—*Mr., Mrs., Ms.*—except in direct quotations or when necessary to distinguish between two people with the same last name, such as a married couple.

FOR BROADCAST: Abbreviate *Mr., Mrs., Ms.* and *Dr.* when used before a name. Spell out all other titles.

1.9 **U.N./U.S.** *U.N.* and *U.S.* are acceptable as a noun or adjective for *United Nations* and *United States,* respectively (no space between initials). Omit the periods when used in headlines (*UN, US*).

FOR BROADCAST: *U-N* is acceptable in all references for *United Nations* and may be used as either a noun or an adjective. Spell out *United States* as a noun. Use *U-S* as an adjective before a noun.

SECTION 2: ADDRESSES

2.1 **ADDRESSES.** Always use figures for an address number, including numbers less than 10: *321 W. Main St.; 8 Strawberry Circle.*

FOR BROADCAST: Use addresses only when they are specifically relevant to the story. Spell out *one* through *eleven.* Use numerals for *12* and higher. Hyphenate numbers read as two-digit groups: *17-43 Willow Avenue.*

2.2 **DIRECTIONS.** Compass points used to indicate directional ends of a street or quadrants of a city in a numbered address should be abbreviated: *671 W. King St.; 38 S. 42nd St.; 600 33rd St. NW.* Use periods after the abbreviations for compass points (*300 E. 12th St.*) but omit the periods for quadrants (*7582 Michigan Ave. SE*) unless local custom uses them. If the address number is omitted, spell out both the compass point and street: *West King Street; 33rd Street Northwest.*

FOR BROADCAST: Spell out directional terms: *Six-71 West King Street; 600 33rd Street Northwest.*

2.3 STREETS. Spell out and capitalize *First* through *Ninth* when used as street names; use figures with two letters for *10th* and above: *101 Eighth Ave.; 2055 21st St.* Abbreviate *Ave., Blvd.* and *St.* only when used with a numbered address: *1600 Pennsylvania Ave.* Spell out and capitalize *Avenue, Boulevard* and *Street* when part of a formal street name without a number: *Pennsylvania Avenue.* Always spell out words such as *alley, circle, drive, road, terrace,* etc., with or without a numbered address.

FOR BROADCAST: Use words for streets named *First* through *Eleventh.* Use numerals for streets *12th* or higher. Spell out all terms for streets—such as *avenue, boulevard, circle, road, street, terrace*—in all contexts.

SECTION 3: CAPITALIZATION

In general, avoid unnecessary capitals. Use a capital letter only if it is required by one of the principles listed here or in the full AP Stylebook.

3.1 ACADEMIC DEPARTMENTS. Use lowercase when mentioning an academic department, except for words that are proper nouns or adjectives: *the department of sociology, the sociology department, the department of English, the English department.*

3.2 AWARDS/EVENTS/HOLIDAYS/WARS. Capitalize awards (*Medal of Honor, Pulitzer Prize*), historic events (*Treaty of Versailles*), periods (*the Middle Ages, the Great Depression, Prohibition*), holidays (*Christmas Eve, Mother's Day*) and wars (*the Civil War, World War II*).

3.3 BIBLE/GOD. Capitalize *Bible* (no quotation marks) to refer to the Old and New Testaments. Capitalize related terms, such as *the Gospels, the Scriptures.* Lowercase *bible* when used in a nonreligious context (*This recipe book is my bible.*) Capitalize *God* to refer to any monotheistic deity. Lowercase pronouns referring to the deity (such as *he, his, thee*). The preferred spelling for the Muslim holy book is *Quran.*

3.4 BRAND NAMES. Capitalize brand names: *Coca-Cola, Cadillac, Samsung, Nike.* Lowercase generic terms: *soda; a car, athletic shoes.* Use brand names only if they are essential to a story. Do not use brand names when a generic name should be used: Use *bandage* and not *Band-Aid* when referring to coverings for cuts and abrasions.

3.5 BUILDINGS/ROOMS. Capitalize the proper names of buildings, including the word *building* if it is an integral part of the proper name: *the Chrysler Building.* Do not abbreviate *building.* Capitalize the names of specially designated rooms: *Blue Room, Oval Office.* Use figures for room numbers and capitalize *room* when used with a figure: *Room 2, Room 211.*

FOR BROADCAST: Capitalize *room* and spell out numbers below 12. Capitalize numbers that are spelled out: *Room Eight, Room 213.*

3.6 **CAPITOL.** Capitalize *U.S. Capitol* and *the Capitol* when referring to the building in Washington, D.C., or to the capitol of a specific state.

3.7 **CONGRESS.** Capitalize *U.S. Congress* and *Congress* when referring to the U.S. Senate and House of Representatives. Lowercase when used as a synonym for *convention.* Lowercase *congressional* unless it is part of a proper name: *congressional salaries, the Congressional Research Service.*

3.8 **CONSTITUTION.** References to the *U.S. Constitution* should be capitalized with or without the *U.S.* as a modifier. Lowercase *constitutional* in all uses. Also capitalize *Bill of Rights* and *First Amendment* (and all other amendments to the Constitution). Use numerals for amendments after the Ninth: *The 13th Amendment abolished slavery.* Lowercase clauses within the Constitution or an amendment: *The court said Congress had exceeded its authority under the commerce clause.* When referring to the constitutions of states or other countries, capitalize only when used with the name of the state or country: *French Constitution, Montana Constitution.*

FOR BROADCAST: *U-S Constitution.*

3.9 **DIRECTIONS/REGIONS.** When indicating a compass direction, lowercase *north, south, northeast,* etc.; capitalize when used as nouns or adjectives to designate geographical regions, including widely known sections of states or cities: *the South, the Northwest, the Atlantic Coast states, Sun Belt, Midwest. She moved west,* but *She moved to the West Coast. The thunderstorm is heading southeast. The North was victorious. She has a Southern accent. He grew up on the East Side of New York City. The earthquake shook Southern California.*

3.10 **DO NOT CAPITALIZE.** The following generally are not capitalized, unless part of a formal name: *administration, government, presidential, presidency, priest,* seasons of the year (*summer, fall, winter, spring*), and years in school (*freshman, sophomore, junior, senior*). Terms like *first lady* and *first gentleman* are not official titles and should not be capitalized even when used with a name (*first lady Melania Trump*). Lowercase the common-noun elements of all names in plural uses: the *Democratic and Republican parties, King and Queen streets, lakes Michigan and Superior.*

3.11 **EARTH.** Generally lowercase *earth;* capitalize when used as the proper name of the planet: *The satellite fell to Earth. She has an earthy quality about her.*

3.12 **GOVERNMENT.** The full names of government agencies should be capitalized: *U.S. Department of Defense, Defense Department,*

Texas Department of Public Safety, Public Safety Department.
Capitalize *city, county, state* and *federal* when part of a formal
name: *Cook County, Federal Housing Administration.* Also capitalize *city council, county commission, city hall, police department,*
legislature, assembly and all other names for governmental agencies when part of a proper name: *Chicago City Council, New York*
Police Department. Retain capitalization if the reference is to a specific city council, legislature, police department, etc., but the context does not require the specific name: *The City Council met last*
night. Generally, lowercase elsewhere: The *council approved the or-*
dinance. Do not capitalize *state, city, county, town, village* or similar words when they are used as adjectives to identify a jurisdiction:
the state Department of Roads, the county Sheriff's Department, the
city of Chicago.

FOR BROADCAST: Always refer to governmental bodies by the
name that is most familiar to the audience. Capitalize full proper
names, and hyphenate *U-S* when that's part of the name. *U-S Defense*
Department.

3.13 **HIGHWAYS.** Use numerals even for highways numbered 1 through
9. Capitalize *highway* or *route* for highways identified by number. Use
U.S., interstate, state or a state name to differentiate highways: *U.S.*
Highway 6, U.S. Route 30, U.S. 36, Pennsylvania 533, Pennsylvania
Route 533, state Route 533, Route 533, Interstate Highway 81,
Interstate 81. On second reference only for Interstate: *I-81.* When a
letter is appended to a number, capitalize it but do not use a hyphen:
Route 1A.

FOR BROADCAST: Spell out highway numbers *one* through *eleven*;
use numerals for larger numbers: *U-S Highway One, state Route 34.*
Hyphenate appended letters to show they are read separately: *Route*
One-A.

3.14 **MILITARY.** Capitalize names of the U.S. armed forces: *the U.S.*
Army, the Navy, Marine regulations. Use lowercase for the forces of
other nations: *the French army.*

FOR BROADCAST: *U-S Navy.*

3.15 **NATIONALITIES/RACE.** Racial and national identifications should
be used only when necessary to the story. It may be appropriate in stories about significant events: *Ketanji Brown Jackson is the first Black*
woman to be a U.S. Supreme Court justice. Race is also relevant in
stories about missing people or suspects in crimes where detailed descriptions can help members of the public find or identify individuals.
The descriptions should consist of more than just a race or nationality.
Reporting on demonstrations or protests involving issues of race or
civil rights also are occasions when racial idenifications may be appropriate. In other instances, race or nationality should be used only when
it is clearly relevant to the story.

Capitalize the proper names of nationalities and tribes: *Korean, Iranian, Sioux, Rohingya*. Capitalize, but do not hyphenate, terms for people of dual heritage, such as *Arab American, African American*.

Capitalize *Black* as an adjective in a racial, cultural or ethnic sense: *Black people, Black churches, Black culture*. Do not capitalize *white, mulatto* or other similar terms. Use *Negro* and *colored* only in the names of organizations: *United Negro College Fund, National Association for the Advancement of Colored People*. Do not use *Black* or *white* as a singular or plural noun to refer to an individual or group of people.

Use *Asian*, not *Oriental*, to refer to people from East Asian nations.

Native American or *American Indian* are acceptable terms for indigenous people of the United States of two or more different tribal affiliations. Otherwise, use the specific tribal identification: *He is a citizen of the Cherokee Nation; She is a member of the Lakota Sioux*.

The terms *Latino* and *Latina* are capitalized and are acceptable as adjectives for people who are from or whose ancestors are from Spanish-speaking countries. *Latino* is used for males (plural *Latinos*) and *Latina* for females (*Latinas*). *Latinos* is appropriate for a group that includes both males and females. Some prefer the gender-neutral *Latinx*, which may be used if the individual requests it and should be followed by a short explanation: *Martinez prefers the term Latinx*. *Hispanic* is also acceptable for people from Spanish-speaking lands. The choice of terms should follow the preference of the person being described.

Do not use *brown* as an adjective in a racial, ethnic or cultural sense except in a direct quotation. Do not use *BIPOC (Black, indigenous and people of color), POC* or *BAME (Black, Asian and minority ethnic)* except in direct quotations. The phrase *people of color* is acceptable as a broad reference to multiple races other than white, but be aware that some find the phrase objectionable or overly inclusive. Do not use *person of color* to refer to an individual.

Consult the full AP Stylebook section on race-related coverage for additional guidance on the proper forms for reporting on race, nationality and ethnicity.

3.16 PLURALS. To form the plural of a number, add *s* (no apostrophe): *1920s*. To form the plural of a single letter, add *'s*. To form the plural of multiple letters, add only *s: Mind your p's and q's. He learned his ABCs*.

3.17 POLITICAL PARTIES. Both the name of a political party and the word *party* should be capitalized: *the Republican Party*. Also capitalize *Communist, Conservative, Democratic, Socialist*, etc., when they refer to a specific party or to individuals who are members of it. Lowercase when they refer to a political philosophy. Do not capitalize *tea party* unless it is part of an organizational name: *The candidate* *said she generally supported the tea party movement. The candidate welcomed the support of the Tea Party Express.* After an officeholder's name, use this short form, set off by commas, to identify the person's home state and party: *D-Minn., R-Ore., Sen. Marco Rubio, R-Fla., said.* . . . Note that no period is used after the letter identifying the official's political party.

FOR BROADCAST: Use party affiliation only when it is relevant to the story. Do not abbreviate the name of the party or state: *Kentucky Republican Senator Mitch McConnell; Governor Gavin Newsom, a California Democrat, said.* . . .

3.18 **PROPER NOUNS.** Proper nouns that constitute the unique identification of a specific person, place or thing should be capitalized: *Michelle, Philadelphia, the Mississippi River.* Lowercase common nouns when they stand alone in subsequent references: *the party, the river, the city.*

3.19 **SATAN.** Capitalize *Satan* but lowercase *devil* and *satanic.*

3.20 **TITLES.** Capitalize formal titles when used immediately before a name: *Mayor, Chairman, former President George W. Bush.* Lowercase formal titles used after a name, alone or in constructions that set them off from a name by commas. Use lowercase at all times for terms that are job descriptions rather than formal titles: *movie star George Clooney; peanut farmer Jimmy Carter; Darrell E. Issa, a representative from California,* . . . Do not capitalize or abbreviate *professor* when used before a name.

SECTION 4: NUMERALS

4.1 **GENERAL RULE:** Whole numbers below 10 are spelled out but use figures for 10 and above. Exceptions: Figures are used for all ages, betting odds, dates, dimensions, percentages, speeds, times and weights. Spell out a number at the beginning of a sentence, except for a calendar year: *Twenty-five students joined the club. 2008 saw the economy collapse.* Avoid beginning a sentence with a large number or a calendar year: WRONG: *Three thousand thirty-three people attended the conference.* BETTER: *More than 3,000 people attended the conference. The economy collapsed in 2008.* For ordinal numbers, spell out *first* through *ninth,* and use figures and *-st, -nd, -rd* or *-th* for larger numbers: *31st, 75th.*

FOR BROADCAST: Spell out *one* through *eleven.* Use numerals for 12 through 999. For numbers above 999, use words or combinations of numerals and words, such as *thousands, millions, billions, trillions,* but use commas to separate hundreds from thousands, thousands from millions, etc. Use hyphens to combine numerals and the words *hundred* or *thousand: Nearly two-thousand students attended the lecture. Authorities estimated the fire damage at 250-thousand dollars. More than 85-thousand, 500 people attended the game.*

Hyphens are not needed with the words *million, billion* or *trillion: The satellite will travel eight (m) million miles. The state has a 300 (b) billion dollar budget.*

Use the same rules for ordinals. Spell out *first* through *eleventh*. Use numerals and *-st, -nd, -rd* or *-th* for larger numbers: *12th; 21st; 32nd; 43rd; 77th.*

4.2   AGES. Use figures for all ages. Hyphenate ages expressed as adjectives before a noun or as substitutes for a noun: *a 7-year-old girl, the 7-year-old,* but *the girl is 7 years old. The boy, 5, has a sister, 10. The man is in his 50s* (no apostrophe).

FOR BROADCAST: Follow the general rule of spelling out numbers less than 12: *the five-year-old girl, The suspect is 36 years old.* Do not follow a person's name with the age set off with commas. WRONG: *Smith, 26, has two children.* BETTER: *Smith is 26. He has two children.*

4.3   CENTS. Use numerals for amounts less than a dollar and spell out the word *cents* and lowercase: *2 cents, 12 cents.* Use the *$* sign and decimal system for larger amounts: *$2.01.*

FOR BROADCAST: Always spell out *cents.* Spell out amounts less than 12: *five cents; 25 cents.*

4.4   DECADES/CENTURY. Use Arabic figures to indicate decades of history. Use an apostrophe to indicate numbers that are left out; show the plural by adding the letter *s: the 1920s, the '20s, the Roaring '20s, the mid-1920s.* Lowercase *century* and spell out numbers less than 10: *the first century, the 21st century.*

FOR BROADCAST: Spell out centuries under 12th and lowercase *century: eleventh century, 19th century.* Use figures to indicate decades. Place an apostrophe after the figures but before the *s.* For the late 20th and early 21st centuries, use only the decade: *the 60's.* For earlier centuries, use the century as well as the decade number: *the 1890's; the 1770's.*

4.5   DOLLARS. Lowercase *dollars.* Use figures and the *$* sign in all except casual references or amounts without a figure: *The dinner cost $19.75. Dollars are flowing overseas.* For amounts of more than $1 million, use the *$* sign and numerals up to two decimal places: *He is worth $5.85 million. He proposed a $500 billion budget. The national debt exceeds $31 trillion.* For foreign currencies, use lowercase and spell out the name of the currency after the amount: *5 euros; 24 pounds.*

FOR BROADCAST: Always spell out *dollars,* and never use the *$* sign. Use words for amounts less than 12: *five dollars; 500-thousand dollars.* Use commas to separate units: *five dollars, ten cents; 135-thousand, 312 dollars.* For large amounts, round and use a *more than* or *almost* construction: *more than five (m) million dollars.* Avoid decimal constructions for amounts in the millions or billions: *three (b) billion, 200 (m) million dollars;* NOT *three-point-two (b) billion dollars.* Make references to monetary amounts as informal as possible: *two and a-half dollars.* Explain large amounts in terms people can understand, such as ratios or per-capita amounts.

4.6 **ELECTION RETURNS/VOTE TABULATIONS.** Separate vote totals with the word *to* (not a hyphen) for reporting results with 1,000 or more votes: *Hillary Clinton won the popular vote from Donald Trump 65,853,516 to 62,984,825.* For results that involve fewer than 1,000 votes on each side, use a hyphen: *Trump defeated Clinton in the electoral vote 304-227; The Senate voted 61-39 to pass the bill.* Spell out numbers below 10 in other phrases related to voting: *the five-vote majority.*

FOR BROADCAST: Use numbers sparingly, and use percentages rather than raw totals: *Clinton received 48 percent of the popular vote to 46 percent for Trump.* Always try to simplify.

4.7 **FRACTIONS.** Amounts less than one should be spelled out, using hyphens between the words: *one-third, three-fifths, nine-sixteenths.* For precise amounts larger than one, convert to decimals whenever practical: *4.25, 6.5.*

FOR BROADCAST: Spell out, using hyphens between units: *four and a-half; two-thirds.* Simplify fractions where possible: *quarter of a dollar.* Spell out decimal amounts and the word *point.* Use *oh* in place of *zero: four-point-two; point-oh-eight.* Use decimal values only when directly relevant to the story. Convert to fractions when possible.

4.8 **MEASUREMENTS/DIMENSIONS.** Use figures and spell out *inches, feet, yards,* etc. Hyphenate adjectival forms before nouns: *the 5-foot-6-inch man, the 9-by-12-foot rug.* Do not hyphenate in other constructions: *He is 5 feet 6 inches tall; The rug is 9 feet by 12 feet.*

FOR BROADCAST: Spell out numbers less than 12. Use commas to separate units of measure. Hyphenate adjectival forms: *He is five feet, six inches tall; The five-foot-six man. . . .*

4.9 **MILLION/BILLION/TRILLION.** Use numerals followed by *million, billion* or *trillion: The deficit dropped to $500 billion last year.* Do not go beyond two decimals: *8.62 million people, $3.75 billion.* Decimals are preferred where practical: *1.5 million,* not *1 1/2 million.* Do not drop the word *million* or *billion* in the first figure of a range: *She is worth from $6 million to $8 million,* not *$6 to $8 million,* unless you really mean $6.

FOR BROADCAST: For *million, billion* and *trillion* put the first letter in parentheses before the word. This helps avoid typographical errors: *15 (b) billion dollars, five (m) million miles.*

4.10 **NUMBER.** Use *No.* as the abbreviation for *number* in conjunction with a figure to indicate position or rank: *No. 1 team, No. 3 choice.*

FOR BROADCAST: Do not abbreviate *number: the Number 1 draft choice.*

4.11 ODDS. Betting odds should be expressed in figures and hyphenated: *The odds were 2-1. He won despite 3-2 odds against him.*

FOR BROADCAST: Use figures, hyphens and the word *to: 3-to-2 odds; the odds were 3-to-2.* Spell out the numbers when a sentence starts with odds: *Three-to-two were the odds on success.*

4.12 PERCENTAGES. Use figures and the percent sign (%) with no space between them: *3%, 4.75%.* For amounts less than 1%, put a zero before the decimal point: *The state raised gas taxes 0.8%.* Spell out numerals and *percent* in casual uses: *You're a hundred percent correct.* Avoid starting a sentence with a percentage, but if it is necessary, spell out both the number and *percent.* Use *percentage*, and not *percent*, in constructions without a numeral. *Only a small percentage of the faculty lack doctoral degrees.*

Use singular verbs after a construction in which the percentage stands alone or where it is followed by a singular noun in an "of" construction: *A score of 60% qualifies for a C grade. At least 80% of the congregation donates weekly.* Use a plural verb after a percentage if it is followed by a plural noun in an "of" construction. *At least 80% of the congregants donate weekly.*

For ranges, the following forms are acceptable: *5%-7%; 23% to 28%; between 50% and 60%.*

FOR BROADCAST: Spell out *percent* and numbers less than 12: *eleven percent; seven and a-half percent.* Repeat percent with each figure unless the sentence is too cumbersome.

4.13 POLITICAL DISTRICTS: Use numerals: *1st Ward, Precinct 34, 10th Congressional District.*

FOR BROADCAST: Spell out numerals below 12: *First Ward, Tenth Congressional District.*

4.14 PROPORTIONS: Use figures for all proportions: *6 parts per million.*

FOR BROADCAST: Spell out numerals below 12: *six parts per million.*

4.15 RATIOS. Ratios should use numerals and hyphens: *The 2-1 ratio.* If the numbers follow the word *ratio*, use *to* and hyphens: *The ratio was 2-to-1, a ratio of 2-to-1.*

FOR BROADCAST: Spell out numerals below 12 and separate them with hyphens and the word *to. It was a 50-to-one ratio.* Use *ratio* or *margin* where there might be confusion between a ratio and an actual figure.

4.16 SCORES. Use figures for all scores. Put a hyphen between the winning and losing team totals: *The Phillies defeated the Cardinals 6-4. The Patriots scored a 21-7 victory over the Broncos. The golfer had a 5 on the last hole but finished with a 2-under-par score.*

FOR BROADCAST: Use figures only (an exception to the general rule on numerals), and use the word *to* with hyphens: *The Giants beat the*

Dodgers 2-to-1, or *The final score was San Francisco 2, Los Angeles 1.*
When reporting only one team's score, however, spell out amounts less
than 12: *The Orioles scored seven runs in the eighth inning to beat the
Twins.*

4.17 TEMPERATURES. Use figures for all temperatures except *zero* and
spell out *degrees: The high Monday was 10 degrees.* Use a word, not a
minus sign, to indicate temperatures below zero: *minus 10 degrees.*

FOR BROADCAST: Spell out numbers less than 12. *The overnight
low was minus five degrees.*

4.18 WEIGHTS. Use figures for all weights. *The baby weighs 9 pounds,
13 ounces.*

FOR BROADCAST: Spell out numbers below 12: *The baby weighs
nine pounds, 13 ounces.*

SECTION 5: PUNCTUATION

5.1 COMMA

5.1.1 AGE. Use commas before and after a person's age when it follows the name: *Barack Obama, 47, was sworn in as president of
the United States.*

FOR BROADCAST: Put ages and hometowns in separate sentences rather than setting them off with commas. *The university
has named Regina McCarthy dean of the College of Fine Arts.
She is 52 years old and comes from Madison, Wisconsin.*

5.1.2 CITY-STATE. Use commas before and after the name of or abbreviation for a state when it follows the name of a city or county,
unless the state name or abbreviation ends the sentence: *Thomp-
son lived in Little Rock, Arkansas, for 20 years before he moved
to Loraine, Ohio.* Use parentheses if the state name is inserted in
a proper name: *the Charlotte (North Carolina) Observer.*

5.1.3 CONJUNCTIONS. When clauses that could stand as independent sentences are joined by a conjunction (*and, or, for, nor, but,
so, yet*), place a comma before the conjunction: *Congress must
approve the emergency funding, or the federal government will
have to shut down. Childhood obesity is becoming more common,
and doctors are seeing more patients with diabetes.*

5.1.4 HOMETOWN. Put commas before and after a person's hometown when it follows the name: *Sgt. Roger Walker, Houston, and
Pvt. Wanda Lu, San Francisco, were the two soldiers killed in the
attack.* The better practice, however, is to use an "of" construction, which eliminates the need for commas: *Sgt. Roger Walker
of Houston and Pvt. Wanda Lu of San Francisco were the two
soldiers killed in the attack.*

5.1.5 QUOTATION. When the attribution precedes a single sentence
of direct quotation, put a comma after the attribution: *Gingrich*

said, *"I am tired of the elite media's protecting Barack Obama by attacking Republicans."* Never put a comma at the beginning of a partial direct quotation or an indirect quotation: *Gingrich said he was tired of "the elite media's protecting Barack Obama." Gingrich said the elite media were protecting Barack Obama.* If the attribution concludes a sentence of direct quotation, change the period at the end of the quotation to a comma and put the period after the attribution. *"I am tired of the elite media's protecting Barack Obama by attacking Republicans," Gingrich said.* Remember that periods and commas always go inside closing quotation marks. *"Because of the budget crisis," the governor said, "the state will have to cut spending on the university."*

FOR BROADCAST: Use paraphrases or tape in broadcast stories rather than direct quotations. If a direct quotation is necessary for a story, punctuate it as it would be for print, but introduce it with a phrase that makes clear to listeners that the words are those of the source, not the reporter. *In the words of football coach Paul Brown, "A winner never whines."*

5.1.6 **SERIES.** Separate elements in a series with commas. Do not, however, put a comma before a conjunction: *His favorite teams are the Red Sox, the Braves and the Cardinals. She said she would vote for Richards, Noto or Ashton.*

5.2 COLON

5.2.1 **LISTS.** Colons frequently are used to introduce lists, tabulations or texts that follow a full sentence: *The candidate named three national leaders he hoped to emulate: Thomas Jefferson, Abraham Lincoln and Franklin D. Roosevelt.*

5.2.2 **QUOTATIONS.** Place a colon at the end of attribution that precedes a direct quotation of two or more sentences. *Obama said: "Change will not come if we wait for some other person or some other time. We are the ones we've been waiting for. We are the change that we seek."* Colons should also be used at the end of paragraphs that introduce a paragraph of direct quotation.

5.3 DASH. Use dashes before and after material inserted in a sentence that abruptly changes the thought: *The mayor agreed to the tax hike—one of the largest in the city's history—as necessary to balance the budget.* Dashes are also used to set off a series in the middle of a sentence: *The most valuable players on the team—Gordon, Hosmer and Perez—stayed healthy all season.*

5.4 ELLIPSIS. Use an ellipsis (. . .) to indicate an omission of one or more words from a direct quotation or text: *"Their pitcher . . . just dominated our batters," Wilson said.* Do not use an ellipsis at the beginning or end of a direct quotation.

5.5 EXCLAMATION POINT. The exclamation point (!) ends a sentence that expresses a high degree of emotion, surprise or incredulity. *"What a horrible fate!" she exclaimed.* Note that the exclamation point replaces the comma when attribution follows the quotation. Do not use exclamation points for sentences that express mild emotion.

5.6 HYPHEN. The hyphen (-) joins words that form compound modifiers before a noun: *full-time employee, man-eating shark, fashion-conscious actor, well-known attorney.* Do not hyphenate when the modifiers follow the noun: *The employee works full time.* If a phrase that would be hyphenated before a noun follows some form of the verb *to be*, hyphenate it: *The employee is full-time.* Hyphens are also used with some prefixes and suffixes.

5.7 PERIOD. Use periods at the end of declarative sentences, mild imperatives, indirect questions and rhetorical questions that are more suggestions than questions: *The council voted to raise police salaries. Kline asked why Main Street had not been repaved. Why don't we take a vote.*

5.8 POSSESSIVES. See Appendix C for the rules for forming possessives.

5.9 QUESTION MARK. Place question marks (?) at the end of sentences that ask direct questions. *Who scored the winning touchdown? "What time is the meeting?" he asked.* Note that the question mark replaces the comma when attribution follows the question.

5.10 QUOTATION MARKS. See Chapter 10 for guidelines on the use and placement of quotation marks.

5.11 SEMICOLON

   5.11.1 SERIES. Semicolons separate elements in a series when at least one of the elements contains internal punctuation: *Stewart sent the plans to Allied Industries in Overland Park, Kansas; Panhandle Technologies in Pensacola, Florida; and Western Electronics in Bakersfield, California.* In such sentences, the semicolon is used before the conjunction that introduces the final element in the series.

   5.11.2 INDEPENDENT CLAUSES. Use semicolons to join closely related independent clauses with or without a conjunctive adverb (*however, therefore, moreover, nevertheless*) between them: *The House passed the bill; however, the president said he would veto it. The truck swerved sharply; it hit the bridge railing.*

5.12 IN GENERAL FOR BROADCAST COPY. The rules for punctuating broadcast copy are generally the same as those for punctuating print copy. But the broadcast writer should keep in mind that the purpose of punctuation is to make it easier for another person to read the story.

SECTION 6: PREFERRED SPELLINGS

aboveboard (one word)
adviser
advisory
afterward (not afterwards)
all right (never alright)

amok
ashtray
ax (not axe)
babysit, babysat, babysitting,
   babysitter

backward (not backwards)

bellwether

bloodbath

brand-new (adjective)

cellphone

changeable

changeover

check-in (as a noun or adjective); check in (as a verb)

checkout (as a noun or adjective); check out (as a verb)

crowdfunding, crowdsourcing

damage (for destruction); damages (for a court award)

database, data center

daylong, dayslong

daytime

dissociate (not "disassociate")

doughnut

e-book

email

e-reader

farmworker

flood plain

floodwaters

forward (not forwards)

freelancer (noun); freelance (verb and adjective)

front line (noun); front-line (adjective)

glamour (noun); glamorous (adjective)

goodbye

goodwill

gray (not grey for the color); greyhound (for the breed of dogs)

hemorrhage (use "bleed" or "bleeding" in most cases)

homepage

judgment

kidnap, kidnapped, kidnapping, kidnapper

know-how

lawsuit

life-size

life span

lifestyle

lifetime

likable (not likeable)

livable

login, logon, logoff (nouns), log in (verb)

memorandum, memorandums

menswear (not *men's wear*)

nationwide (also "citywide," "statewide" and "worldwide")

news writing

nighttime

offline, online

overall

percent, percentage (one word)

pipeline

policymaker

politicking

pothole

prime time (noun), prime-time (adjective)

protester

questionnaire

Quran (not "Koran")

recur, recurred, recurring (not *reoccur*)

referable

sacrilegious

salable

semitrailer or semitractor-trailer (not *semi-tractor trailer*)

sizable

sport utility vehicle

straitjacket

successor

supersede

teen, teenager (noun), teenage (adjective) (Do not use "teen-aged.")

theater (except when "theatre" is part of a proper name)

throwaway (noun and adjective)

timeout (one word)

total, totaled, totaling

travel, traveled, traveling, traveler

T-shirt (always capitalize the first "t")

underway (always one word)

upward (not *upwards*)

U-turn (noun and adjective)

vacuum

vice president (no hyphen)

web/World Wide Web

webpage, website

web address, web browser

whiskey

whistleblower

whitewash (noun, verb and adjective)

Preferred spellings for broadcast copy:

Teen, teen-ager, teen-age

SECTION 7: TIME

7.1 HOURS AND MINUTES. Use numerals and *a.m.* or *p.m.* for all clock times, except *noon* and *midnight*. Separate hours and minutes with a colon: *1:27 p.m., 8:30 a.m.* If the time is on the hour, do not use a colon and zeros: *2 p.m., 7 a.m.* The following expressions are redundant and should not be used: *12 midnight, 9 a.m. this morning, 8:30 p.m. tomorrow night.* When using both time and day, put the hour before the day: *2 p.m. Wednesday.* Use lowercase letters and periods for *a.m.* and *p.m.*

Use clock time whenever it helps the reader better understand the event or sequence described in the story. Sometimes words or phrases such as *dawn* or *late afternoon* are more effective.

FOR BROADCAST: Use numerals for clock times, except for *noon* and *midnight*. As in print style, separate hours and minutes with a colon, but use a hyphen, rather than periods with *a-m* and *p-m: 8:30 p-m, 10:17 a-m.* An exact time of day rarely is necessary for a broadcast story. Use it only if is important to the story. Otherwise, use phrases like *shortly before dawn, early evening, midafternoon.* For some stories it is necessary to specify a time zone, such as when a story occurs in one time zone but may interest or affect people in other time zones. Capitalize the full names of time zones and the short forms as well: *Eastern Standard Time, Mountain Daylight Time, Central time, Pacific time.* Use capitals and hyphens for abbreviations of time zones: *E-S-T; M-D-T.*

7.2 DAYS. For an event that occurred or will occur within seven days of the day of publication, use the day of the week: *The City Council will decide on the budget at Tuesday's meeting.* Do not use *today, yesterday, tomorrow, tonight* or similar words except in direct quotations or in phrases that do not refer to a specific date: *Economic challenges today are greater than those of the 1970s.* Phrases like *last Thursday* or *next Monday* are redundant. Just use the day of the week and omit words like *last* or *next.*

FOR BROADCAST: The words *today, this morning, tonight, yesterday* and *tomorrow* may be used in broadcast copy. When referring to days within seven days of the broadcast, use the day of the week. Do not use redundant constructions like *next Wednesday* or *last Saturday*; the tense of the verb conveys that information. *The mayor spoke Tuesday. The mayor will speak Tuesday.*

7.3 DATES. If the story refers to something that happened or will happen more than seven days before or after the day of publication, use the month and day: *Voters will not go to the polls until Nov. 3.* Never add *-st, -nd, -rd* or *-th* to a date in Arabic numerals in print copy. Use month, date and year for dates outside the current calendar year. *The Allied invasion of France in World War II was on June 6, 1944.*

FOR BROADCAST: The dates first through eleventh should be spelled out and capitalized: *The deadline for filing for the City Council race is March First.* For dates above eleventh, use numerals with *-st, -nd, -rd* or *-th: Income tax returns must be postmarked no later than April 15th.*

7.4 **MONTHS.** The names of months are always capitalized. Never abbreviate the name of a month when it stands alone or with just a year: *The Iraq War began in March 2003 and ended in December 2011.* If a specific date is used with the name of a month, use the following abbreviations: *Jan., Feb., Aug., Sept., Oct., Nov.* and *Dec. Valentine's Day is Feb. 14.* Do not abbreviate *March, April, May, June* or *July*, even when used with a specific date. *The company's fiscal year ends June 30.* When using only month and year, no comma is necessary. *September 2001 was filled with sadness.* When a specific date is used with the month and year, use commas before and after the year: *Sept. 11, 2001, was the date of the terrorist attacks.*

FOR BROADCAST: Never abbreviate the names of months.

SECTION 8: TITLES

8.1 **GENERAL RULE.** Only formal titles that immediately precede a name should be capitalized. The title should be abbreviated if it is one of those listed in rule 1.8: *Gov. John Kasich.* Abbreviate only those titles that have accepted abbreviations. Spell out and lowercase titles when used as appositives or when the name is an appositive for the title: *John Kasich, the governor, will sign the bill. The governor, John Kasich, will sign the bill.* Titles that follow a name or that are used alone should be lowercase and spelled out. *John Kasich, governor of Ohio, delivered the keynote address. The proposal won the support of the senator from New Mexico.* Do not use a person's title on second reference: *Sen. Shelby Watson denied the allegation. Watson insisted he had been unaware of his aide's activities.* Titles that are abbreviated when used before a name should be abbreviated when used before a name in direct quotations: *"Gov. Thatcher's tax-cut plan will deprive schools of the money they need," the superintendent said.*

FOR BROADCAST: Formal titles should be capitalized when used immediately before a name, but long titles should be avoided or condensed where possible: *Defense Secretary Leon Panetta*, instead of *Secretary of Defense Leon Panetta.* If a title cannot be easily shortened, place it in a separate sentence: *Wanda Cummings said the university's plan would help students graduate on time. Cummings is the associate vice chancellor for academic affairs.*

8.2 **BOY/GIRL.** These terms are acceptable for people younger than 18. For people 18 or older, use *man* or *woman*. Referring to a Black male of any age as *boy* may be regarded as demeaning in light of the history of using that term to refer to Black men. Use a specific age, if possible (*a 12-year-old Black male*), or use phrases such as *Black youths, Black teen* or *Black child.*

8.3 **COMPOSITIONS.** Capitalize the main words of titles, including any initial articles and any prepositions or conjunctions of four or more letters. Put the title in quotation marks. These rules apply to titles of books, operas, plays, albums, songs, movies, radio and television programs, lectures, speeches and works of art: *He enjoyed "Raiders of the Lost Ark" and all its sequels. Barack Obama wrote "Dreams From My Father." The exhibition will include Vincent van Gogh's "Starry Night."* Never underline or italicize composition titles. Do not put quotation marks around the names of reference works, such as dictionaries, encyclopedias and atlases; computer software; computer games; or sculptures.

8.4 COURTESY TITLES. Do not use the courtesy titles *Miss, Mr., Mrs.* or *Ms.* on any reference. On first reference, identify people by first name, middle initial and last name. On subsequent references, use the last name only. A person's marital status should not be mentioned unless it is clearly pertinent to the story. Use courtesy titles only if they are part of a direct quotation or after first reference for a woman who specifically asks to be identified as *Mrs. Johnson* or *Ms. Johnson.*

The first reference to a couple should use both first names: *Barack and Michelle Obama.* Use first names and last names on subsequent references if it is necessary to distinguish two people with the same last name, such as wife and husband or brothers and sisters.

FOR BROADCAST: Generally, do not use courtesy titles. Use first and last name on first reference and last name alone on subsequent references. Do not use courtesy titles on subsequent references unless they are necessary to distinguish two or more people with the same last name. Readability should be the guide.

8.5 INITIALS. Middle initials help identify individuals and distinguish people with similar names: *George H.W. Bush, George W. Bush.* In general, use middle initials to help identify specific individuals. Middle initials are most important in stories reporting when people are accused of crime or casualty lists from accidents or disasters. Initials should not be used with the names of people who are widely known by first and last name only: *LeBron James, Jennifer Lawrence.*

For a person who uses only initials instead of a first name, use periods and no space between the initials: *R.W. Mahoney.* Unless it is the individual's preference or the first name cannot be determined, do not use a single initial alone: *R. Mahoney.*

FOR BROADCAST: Use middle initials only when it is essential to distinguishing a person (as in a casualty list or a report of a crime) or is the way the person is usually identified. In all other circumstances, omit initials. If a person is known by his or her initials, use both first and middle, not just the first: *A.Q. Khan,* not *A. Khan.*

8.6 LEGISLATIVE TITLES. The preferred form for members of the U.S. House of Representatives is *Rep.* or *Reps.* when the title immediately precedes the name: *Rep. Jeb Hensarling, R-Texas, said he would confer with his caucus.* The words *congressman* and *congresswoman* may be used in subsequent references in place of the person's name. *The congresswoman emphasized her opposition to the proposal. Congressman* and *congresswoman* should be capitalized and used before a name only in direct quotations. Never use *congressperson.* For members of the U.S. Senate, use *Sen.* or *Sens.* immediately before the name on first reference. On subsequent reference, *senator* may be used in place of the name. Use *U.S.* or *state* before *Rep.* or *Sen.* as necessary to avoid confusion. Spell out *senator* or *representative* in all other uses. Other legislative titles, such as *assemblyman, assemblywoman, delegate, city councilor, commissioner,* etc., should never be abbreviated but should be capitalized when immediately before a name. Organizational titles, such as *speaker, majority leader, minority leader, majority whip, chairman, chairwoman,* etc., should be capitalized before a name, but they should never be abbreviated. Legislative titles should not be used before a name on second reference unless it is in a direct quotation.

FOR BROADCAST: Always spell out legislative titles, including organizational titles. Capitalize the title if it immediately precedes a name. Members of the U.S. House of Representatives may be referred to as *congressman, congresswoman* or *representative.* On second reference, do not use the title. Do not use party affiliation unless it is relevant to the story, and in such cases spell out the name of the party and the legislator's home state: *Senator Joni Ernst; Congressman Adam Schiff; Republican Senator John Cornyn of Texas.*

8.7 **MAGAZINES.** Titles should be capitalized but should not be in quotation marks. Capitalize the word *magazine* only if it is part of the title: *Rolling Stone magazine; HomeCare Magazine.*

8.8 **NEWSPAPERS.** Capitalize the names of newspapers. Do not place the names in quotation marks or underline them. If the publication includes *the* as part of the newspaper's name, it should be capitalized: *The New York Times; the Los Angeles Times.* If the name of the state is necessary to identify where the newspaper is published but is not included in the formal name, insert it in parentheses after the name of the city: *The Kansas City (Missouri) Star.*

FOR BROADCAST: If the location where a newspaper is published is not clear from its title, insert the name in the copy: *The Oregonian published the results of its investigation Sunday. The Portland newspaper said the accident could have been avoided.*

8.9 **REFERENCE WORKS.** The titles of reference works such as dictionaries, almanacs, encyclopedias, gazetteers, handbooks, school yearbooks, etc., should be capitalized. Do not use quotation marks, italics or underlining: *Black's Law Dictionary, the Encyclopedia Britannica, the Hammond World Atlas, the World Almanac.* The same rule applies to the Bible.

8.10 **RELIGIOUS TITLES.** Capitalize religious titles used before a name on first reference: *Bishop, Archbishop, Cardinal, Pope, Sister.* When coming before a name, *Reverend* should be abbreviated and should always follow the word *the: the Rev. Joseph Grey, the Most Rev. Joseph Grey, the Very Rev. Joseph Grey.* On subsequent references, omit all titles.

FOR BROADCAST: Never abbreviate *Reverend: the Reverend Joseph Grey.*

RULES FOR FORMING POSSESSIVES

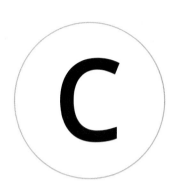

1. For common or proper nouns, whether singular or plural, that do not already end in the letter *s*, add an apostrophe and *s* to form the possessive. For example:

SINGULAR	man	child	Johnson	Microsoft
SINGULAR POSSESSIVE	man's	child's	Johnson's	Microsoft's
PLURAL	men	children	alumni	
PLURAL POSSESSIVE	men's	children's	alumni's	

2. If the word is a singular common noun that already ends in the letter *s*, add an apostrophe and *s* to form the possessive, unless the next word also begins with an *s*.

   the hostess's request   the hostess' seat
   the witness's answer   the witness' story

3. If the word is a singular common or proper noun that ends in a letter other than *s* but has an *s* sound (such as *ce*, *z* and *x*), add an apostrophe and an *s*.

   the fox's den
   Butz's policies
   Marx's theories
   the prince's life

4. Singular proper nouns that end in *s* add only an apostrophe:

   Descartes' philosophy
   Hercules' labors
   Socrates' execution
   Tennessee Williams' plays

5. Plural common and proper nouns ending in *s* add only an apostrophe:

   the churches' association
   the girls' toys
   the horses' food
   the Smiths' car
   the Williamses' children
   the Carolinas' coastline

507

6. If a term is hyphenated, make only the last word possessive:

SINGULAR	mother-in-law	She is my mother-in-law.
SINGULAR POSSESSIVE	mother-in-law's	It is my mother-in-law's car.
PLURAL	mothers-in-law	The program featured mothers-in-law.
PLURAL POSSESSIVE	mothers-in-law's	The mothers-in-law's cars were damaged by vandals.

7. If an object is jointly possessed by two or more people or entities, make only the last noun possessive:

   Mary and Fred's entry won a prize.
   Acme Co. and Smith Corp.'s joint business is profitable.
   My mother and father's home was destroyed by fire.

8. If the objects are not jointly owned—if they are separate objects owned or possessed by different people—make both nouns possessive:

   Mary's and Fred's entries won prizes.
   The Smiths' and the Browns' luggage was lost.

9. Some special expressions that do not end in *s* but have an *s* sound use only an apostrophe: *for appearance' sake; for conscience' sake.* In other expressions, use *'s: the appearance's cost.*

10. Indefinite pronouns such as *everyone* follow the same rules. However, personal pronouns have special forms that never use an apostrophe. The possessive forms of personal pronouns include such words as *his, hers, mine, ours, theirs, whose* and *yours.*

11. Do not add an apostrophe to descriptive phrases ending in *s: citizens band radio; teachers college.* The phrase is descriptive rather than possessive if *for* or *by* rather than *of* would be appropriate in a longer form of the phrase: *a radio band for citizens; a college for teachers.* An *'s* is required, however, when the term in the descriptive phrase is a plural that does not end in an *s: women's clinic; people's government.*

12. Generally, avoid making inanimate objects possessives. Instead, try to rewrite the passage, either dropping the possessive or converting the passage to an *of* phrase:

    AWKWARD: the table's leg
    BETTER: the table leg OR the leg of the table
    AWKWARD: the book's chapter
    BETTER: the book chapter OR the chapter of the book

13. When mentioning the name of an organization, group or geographical location, always use the common or preferred and official spelling. Some names use the possessive case, such as *Actors' Equity Association,* but others, such as *Pikes Peak,* do not.

14. The word *it's,* spelled with an apostrophe, is a contraction of *it is.* The possessive form, *its,* does not contain an apostrophe:

    WRONG: Its higher than I thought.
    RIGHT: It's higher than I thought OR It is higher than I thought.
    WRONG: It's height scares me.
    RIGHT: Its height scares me.

CREDITS

INDEX